Electronics for
Scientists and Engineers

PRENTICE-HALL ELECTRICAL ENGINEERING SERIES*

William L. Everitt, *Editor*

*This title is also in the Prentice-Hall International Series in Electrical Engineering. Prentice-Hall, Inc.; Prentice-Hall International., Inc., United Kingdom and Eire; Prentice-Hall of Canada, Ltd., Canada.

ELECTRONICS

R. Ralph Benedict

Professor of Electrical Engineering
University of Wisconsin

FOR SCIENTISTS AND ENGINEERS

Prentice-Hall, Inc., Englewood Cliffs, New Jersey

ELECTRONICS FOR
SCIENTISTS AND ENGINEERS
R. Ralph Benedict

© 1967 by Prentice-Hall, Inc.
Englewood Cliffs, New Jersey

Library of Congress Catalog Card Number:
67-11761

Current printing (last digit):
10 9 8 7 6 5 4

PRENTICE-HALL INTERNATIONAL, INC., *London*
PRENTICE-HALL OF AUSTRALIA, PTY. LTD., *Sydney*
PRENTICE-HALL OF CANADA, LTD., *Toronto*
PRENTICE-HALL OF INDIA PRIVATE LTD., *New Delhi*
PRENTICE-HALL OF JAPAN, LTD., *Tokyo*

Printed in the United States of America

Preface

This book is intended for the reader who needs a broad, yet fairly thorough, treatment of the principles of electronics which are basic to electronic instrumentation, measurement, data processing, and automatic control. The needs of the nonspecialist who uses electronic devices, instruments, and control systems in development and research work have also been kept in mind. Considerable guidance concerning the choice of subject matter and the level of the treatment has come from the work of an interdepartmental effort that has continued for a number of years at the University of Wisconsin on a course which has the objective of introducing seniors and graduate students to the principles basic to electronic methods of measurement and instrumentation.

A grounding in electricity and magnetism, elementary circuit analysis, and college mathematics is assumed, but little or no prior knowledge of electronics is required. The level is suitable for use in courses for advanced undergraduates or beginning graduate students in science or engineering. The book should also be useful for self-study for people who feel a need for a better understanding of the principles basic to electronic instrumentation and control.

Owing to the vast expansion of the electronic field, including that arising from the advent of semiconductor devices and circuits, and to the extensive applications of electronics in instrumentation and control systems, an electronics book obviously cannot cover the details of the whole field of devices, circuits, and applications, even in this limited area of interest. Since the trend in most laboratories is toward the plan of purchasing commercial transducers, amplifiers, instruments, and the like, it becomes increasingly important to be able to judge the suitability of a component from its specifications and to determine whether its input and/or output characteristics are suited to the rest of the system; rather than to design and build the components themselves.

This book includes brief descriptions of the more important devices, emphasizes the fundamental principles of electronics, and presents the principles of selected electronic instruments and measurement and control systems. While qualitative descriptions are not neglected, the quantitative approach is emphasized. The details of many derivations, however, have

vii

been omitted in the interest of saving space. The compromise that has been made between breadth of coverage and depth of treatment is such that the reader should gain sufficient knowledge of principles and of technique to be able, with the aid of some reference to more specialized works, to design and assemble or develop electronic systems for his special needs.

This book provides more material than is needed for a course of 40 to 50 lectures, so some selection of topics must be made for a course of that length. The concepts that are basic to the objectives outlined earlier are presented in Chapters 3 through 14 and in Chapters 16 and 17. Some portions of these chapters, however, can be omitted or given cursory attention in order to save time for other topics. The choice of portions to be studied in a cursory manner depends on personal opinion, but the following are suggested: the portion of Chapter 6 that uses the T-equivalent circuits, sections 7-12 through 7-14, and all of Chapters 8, 10, and 11. In this way some attention can be given to portions of Chapters 15, and 18 through 21.

In the author's opinion actual laboratory experience with electronic apparatus is essential to an understanding of the subject. A suggested list of topics for a sequence of 14 experiments follows: familiarization with test instruments and the cathode-ray oscillograph; gain and phase tests on passive networks; characteristic curves of triode, tetrode, and pentode portrayed on the cathode-ray oscilloscope; design and test of a grounded-cathode triode amplifier; common-emitter transistor amplifier; common-collector amplifier; a transistorized voltage-regulated dc power supply; a pentode RC-coupled amplifier with and without feedback; tests on transistor phase shift and thyratron relaxation oscillator circuits; two-stage transistor differential amplifier; analog computer; diode logic circuits; and waveshaping and multivibrators, and demonstrations of electronic instruments such as counters and X-Y recorders.

The writer acknowledges his debt to the authors of review articles and reference books too numerous to mention specifically. Selected references are included at the end of most chapters to indicate sources of specialized information or for supplementary reading.

It is a pleasure to acknowledge the helpful suggestions of a number of colleagues, including John L. Asmuth, John B. Miller, Arthur T. Tiedemann, Elmer H. Scheibe and Allan K. Scidmore, who read individual chapters. I am indebted to my son, Thomas R. Benedict, of the Cornell Aeronautical Laboratory, for the major portion of Chapter 21. A number of valuable suggestions made by a pre-publication reviewer have been incorporated into the book. The author must take the responsibility for the shortcomings or errors that remain. He would, of course, be glad to have these called to his attention.

R. Ralph Benedict
Madison, Wisconsin

Contents

1
Review of Elementary Circuit Theory   *1*

2
Responses of Electric Circuits   *19*

3

Thermionic and Semiconductor Diodes 56

4

Vacuum Tubes as Circuit Elements 78

5

Physical Principles of Semiconductor Devices *111*

6

Small-Signal Analysis of Transistor Amplifiers *133*

10

Gaseous Diodes and Triodes *250*

11

Rectifier Circuits, Filters and dc Power Supplies *263*

12

Oscillator and Inverter Circuits 288

13

Modulation, Demodulation, and Related Topics 312

14

dc Amplifiers and the Analog Computer 337

21

Data Acquisition, Transmission, Recording, and Processing; Telemetry 555

A

Physical Constants, Abbreviations for Units, and Multiplying Factors 595

B

Selected Device Data and Characteristics 597

C

Transformations among the Circuit Parameters *608*

D

Outline of the Fourier Analysis of Periodic Functions, with an Application to Electric Circuit Calculations *610*

E

Transmission Lines; Delay Lines *614*

1

Review of
Elementary Circuit Theory

1-1
Introduction

To a degree the science of electronics can be divided into the study of electronic devices and the study of electronic circuits. In this book the emphasis will be on the functioning of the electronic circuits basic to a wide range of applications in instrumentation, data processing, and control. Because our aim is to give as quantitative a treatment as space will allow, we wish to make maximum use of the basic techniques of electric circuit analysis. Chapters 1 and 2 are devoted to an outline of these techniques and principles. The presentation will be brief, with a mimimum of proofs.

Let us identify some of the electric circuit functions in a typical electronic measurement system, such as a thermocouple temperature indicator. The temperature at the thermocouple develops a voltage, called the *signal*. The signal voltage may be matched against a *reference* voltage, and the difference may be *amplified* in order to perform a self-adjustment function on the reference voltage and also to operate an indicator, or mechanical pointer. In this and in other more complex systems, the interest is in the *electrical signals*, the *signal transmission* through the electronic circuits, and the conversion of the information contained in the signal into a form useful to a human observer. In such systems the power level is often so low that the power efficiency is unimportant. On the other hand, in some control systems the output power may be so high that high efficiency is an economic necessity.

1

1-2
Electrical quantities

The reader will recall that electric *charge* is defined in terms of the Coulomb electrostatic forces in an electric field. In the mks system, the unit charge is the coulomb, which is equivalent to the magnitude of charge of 6.25×10^{18} electrons.

Electric *current* is defined as the time rate of passage of charge across a given area, such as the cross section of a wire, and can be expressed as

$$i = \frac{dq}{dt} \qquad (1\text{-}1)$$

where i is the instantaneous current in amperes, dq is the charge in coulombs crossing in time dt in seconds.

Electric *potential*, *potential rise* or *drop*, or *voltage rise* or *drop* are all defined in terms of the *work* done by or against the electrostatic forces that act on a unit charge as it is moved between two points in a field or in a circuit. Let us define the *voltage drop* (or potential drop) from a to b as the algebraic value of the work done by the *electrostatic field* in moving a *positive* unit charge from a to b; thus

$$e_{ab} = \frac{dW_{ab}}{dq} \qquad (1\text{-}2)$$

Here e_{ab} is in volts, if dW_{ab} is in joules and dq is in coulombs. Since voltage drop is algebraic, it can have either a positive or a negative value. The potential *rise* from a to b is the negative of the voltage drop from a to b. With reference to electronic circuits it is often convenient to discuss the *potentials* of individual points in the network. In this context the *potential* of a point means the voltage drop from that point to a reference point, which is usually the so-called *ground* (metal shield box or chassis) of the system.

If the voltage drop from a to b is e_{ab} and a current i traverses this portion of the circuit in the direction a to b, then the electrical power absorbed is

$$p = \frac{dW}{dt} = e_{ab}i \qquad (1\text{-}3)$$

Here p is the instantaneous power in watts. The power is also algebraic, and a negative value of power means that electrical power is developed, i.e., this region is an electric generator or source.

Tremendous ranges of numerical values are encountered in electronic work, not only in the electrical quantities, but also in values of time, frequency, power, etc. For this reason the standard prefixes for various positive and negative powers of ten are often employed to indicate the multiple or submultiple of the unit in question. The most common are the following:

10^{6}	mega	10^{-3}	milli	10^{-9}	nano
10^{3}	kilo	10^{-6}	micro	10^{-12}	pico

Abbreviations for the prefixes used in connection with the units are M or Meg for mega, k for kilo, m for milli, μ for micro, and p for pico.

1-3
Constant and variable voltages
and currents

A wide variety of time variations of voltage and current occur in electronic circuits, particularly in the modern circuits that carry pulses and various wave forms. A few types are illustrated in Fig. 1-1, including the unidirectional or *direct voltage* in (a), the *pulsating direct* voltage in (b), the *unidirectional transient* voltage in (c), the *harmonic* voltage in (d), the *oscillating transient* voltage in (e), and the *step* voltage in (f).

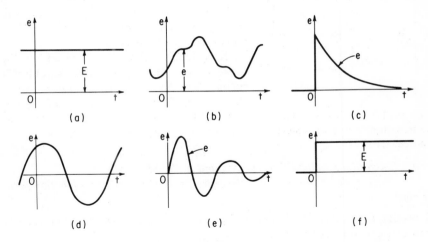

FIGURE 1-1   Constant and variable voltages.

In the interest of simplicity the illustrations of networks in Chapter 1 are limited to those containing only voltage and current sources and resistors, though the principles discussed have a much wider range of application, as will become evident in Chapter 2. When capacitors and inductors are present in the circuit, it is necessary to consider the time rate of change of the current or of the voltage. But with only resistors present, we have the relation $e = Ri$, and if i is some function of the time t, say $i(t)$, then e will be a function of the same form. In the following, therefore, we use the symbols e and i and think of these as identical functions of t of whatever form.

In Chapter 2 we shall treat the behavior of circuits carrying transient current and steady-state alternating currents. In the following discussion, if steady direct currents and voltages are involved, e and i may be replaced by E and I to indicate this fact.

1-4
Voltage and current sources; Kirchhoff's laws

An *ideal* voltage source delivers the specified voltage e at the terminals of the device (Fig. 1-2a) regardless of the size of the current drawn from the source. *Actual* or *real* voltage sources generally have an internal voltage drop such that the terminal voltage drops as the current increases. Usually this is a nearly linear effect; therefore the circuit in Fig. 1-2b, comprising an ideal voltage source and an internal source resistance R_s, will serve as an *equivalent circuit* or *model* to represent the actual device.

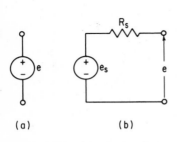

(a)   (b)

FIGURE 1-2   (a) Ideal voltage source and (b) real voltage source.

Kirchhoff's voltage law, based on the conservation of energy, and Kirchhoff's current law, based on the conservation of charge, are basic to the study of electric circuits. They may be stated as follows as applied to instantaneous values:

   1. *The algebraic sum of all the voltage drops taken in a specified direction around a closed path is zero.*

   2. *The algebraic sum of all of the currents directed toward a junction point is zero.*

Consider Fig. 1-3a, which shows a portion of a network. The voltage law can be expressed as follows:

$$e_{ab} + e_{bc} + e_{cd} + e_{da} = 0 \tag{1-4}$$

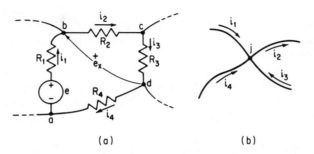

(a)   (b)

FIGURE 1-3   Portions of networks illustrating Kirchhoff's laws.

Note that the order of the double subscripts indicates the positive sense of the voltage drop. Using Ohm's law, Eq. (1-4) yields

$$-e + R_1 i_1 + R_2 i_2 + R_3 i_3 + R_4 i_4 = 0 \qquad (1-5)$$

In this example the voltage drops are taken in the clockwise direction around the closed loop. In general, the current arrows encountered in going around a loop will not always be in the same direction. A general rule is that the Ri term is positive if the voltage drop is desired in the current arrow direction but is negative for the counter-arrow direction.

The junctions, as at a, b, c, and d are called *nodes*. A portion of the network between two nodes is called a *branch*. Thus i_1, i_2, i_3, and i_4 are the *branch* currents.

Sometimes a voltage between two nonadjacent nodes, such as e_x in Fig. 1-3a, is of interest. In this case Kirchhoff's voltage law can be written

$$-e + R_1 i_1 + e_x + R_4 i_4 = 0 \qquad (1-6)$$

That is to say, the circuit can be "closed" through the imaginary path from b to d via e_x. The algebraic polarity for a symbol such as e_x must be indicated in the circuit diagram by some convention. Two conventions are shown in Fig. 1-3a, namely, the arrowhead on the arrow from d to b and the + sign on e_x. Either is sufficient to indicate that e_x is the voltage drop *from b to d*.

Figure 1-3b illustrates the application of the current law. At the junction j we write

$$i_1 - i_2 + i_3 + i_4 = 0 \qquad (1-7)$$

At this junction three arrows are directed toward the junction and one away.

Consider next the voltage source E_s and R_s in Fig. 1-4a. If a load R_L is connected at the terminals, the load voltage E will be related to the load current I by the equation

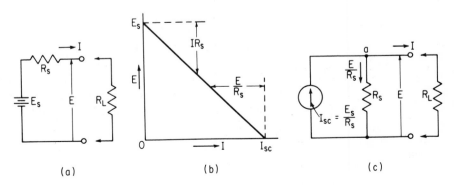

(a)   (b)   (c)

FIGURE 1-4   (a) Voltage source, (b) *E-I* relation, and (c) current source.

$$E = E_s - R_s I \qquad (1\text{-}8)$$

This straight-line relation is shown in Fig. 1-4b. When $R_L \longrightarrow 0$, the current reaches the short-circuit value I_{sc} and the terminal voltage is zero.

Suppose that we think of the load current I as the dependent variable. The same straight-line relation can be expressed in the form (divide (1-8) through by R_s and rearrange)

$$I = I_{sc} - \frac{E}{R_s} \qquad (1\text{-}9)$$

The equivalent circuit in Fig. 1-4c. which contains the *constant current* source I_{sc}, corresponds to Eq.(1-9), since (1-9) expresses the current law at junction a. Therefore Fig. 1-4a and Fig. 1-4c show equivalent representations of a particular source, as far as external E-I variations are concerned. The constant current source is important for two reasons: (a) its use sometimes simplifies the solution of a network problem, and (b) some electronic devices, such as transistors and pentodes, deliver a nearly constant current, and the constant-current representation is more appropriate.

1-5
Resistances in series and parallel

Let a number of resistances $R_1, R_2, \cdots, R_n$ be connected in series. They all carry the same current. Let R_{eq} be the equivalent resistance that will replace the group of series-connected resistors. Direct application of Kirchhoff's voltage law will show that

$$R_{eq} = R_1 + R_2 + \cdots R_n \qquad (1\text{-}10)$$

Further, the voltage drop across each unit is proportional to its resistance, so we may write

$$\frac{e_1}{e_t} = \frac{R_1}{R_{eq}} \qquad (1\text{-}11)$$

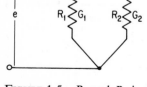

FIGURE 1-5 R_1 and R_2 in parallel.

This gives the drop e_1 across R_1 in terms of the total drop e_t and the total resistance R_{eq}.

The voltage divider action of two resistors R_1 and R_2 connected in series and attached to a source of E volts is an important application of series-connected resistors. Suppose that we want the voltage E_2 across R_2. Then Eq. (1-11) will yield

$$E_2 = \frac{R_2}{R_1 + R_2} E \qquad (1\text{-}11a)$$

This equation is known as the *voltage divider formula*.

Consider two resistors connected in parallel (Fig. 1-5). Let us find the equivalent resistance of the combination. We seek $R_{eq} = e/i$. But $i = i_1 + i_2$. Also $i_1 = e/R_1$ and $i_2 = e/R_2$. Therefore

$$R_{eq} = \frac{e}{i} = \frac{e}{\dfrac{e}{R_1} + \dfrac{e}{R_2}} = \frac{1}{\dfrac{1}{R_1} + \dfrac{1}{R_2}} \qquad (1\text{-}12)$$

or

$$R_{eq} = [R_1 \| R_2] = \frac{R_1 R_2}{R_1 + R_2} \qquad (1\text{-}13)$$

Here the symbol $[R_1 \| R_2]$ for the parallel resistance is introduced for future reference.

If conductance G, the reciprocal of resistance, is used, we obtain the simpler expression

$$G_{eq} = G_1 + G_2 \qquad (1\text{-}14)$$

To discuss the division of current, let us consider the ratio of i_1 to the total current i. Using conductances, this ratio is

$$\frac{i_1}{i} = \frac{G_1}{G_{eq}} \qquad (1\text{-}15)$$

Similar relations hold for three or more resistors in parallel. For example, the equivalent conductance equals the sum of all the conductances of the parallel paths.

1-6
Network analysis

After all the series and parallel groups of resistances have been replaced by their equivalent resistances, a multiloop circuit with one of more voltage sources often remains. The usual problem is to solve for the currents in the network. This can be done by the application of Kirchhoff's laws, but great care is needed to set up a correct set of independent equations and solve them. We shall discuss the simpler "planar" networks, which can be spread out on a plane without having any wires crossing other branches.

a. The branch current method

In this method each branch is labeled with a current symbol and an arrow. The current law is then applied at the junctions, and all except one junction are used to get independent equations. The voltage law will give as many independent equations as there are loops. In writing the voltage equations each additional equation must include at least one new branch, and when the last equation has been written, all the branches must have been traversed at least once. The resulting sets of current and voltage equations are solved for the unknown currents.

When defining (labeling) the current symbol for a particular branch, the choice of the arrow direction is entirely arbitrary. Of course, in a branch in which the positive direction of the actual current can be predicted by inspection, it is logical to choose the arrow direction for the current symbol to agree with the known current direction. In general, however, the direction of the current in one or more branches is not immediately obvious, so the arrow for the current symbol is chosen arbitrarily. When the circuit equations are solved for the values of these current symbols, some may be positive and some negative. A negative value means that the actual current is in the counter-arrow direction.

b. The Maxwell mesh current method

The setting up of the equations is simplified and systematized by a scheme of J. C. Maxwell. A fictitious *loop* or *mesh* current is assigned to each closed loop of the network in a clockwise sense, as shown in the example in Fig. 1-6. The branches common to two loops therefore carry two mesh currents simultaneously. Thus the middle branch in Fig. 1-6 carries a total current of

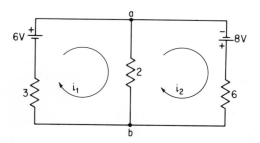

FIGURE 1-6   Network with mesh currents.

$(i_1 - i_2)$ in the direction *a* to *b*. Note that the mesh currents automatically satisfy Kirchhoff's current law. The potential law is applied to each loop in turn, and all currents must be considered. In the example we find for the left-hand loop

$$-6 + (3 + 2)i_1 - 2i_2 = 0 \qquad (1\text{-}16)$$

and for the right-hand loop

$$-8 + (6 + 2)i_2 - 2i_1 = 0 \qquad (1\text{-}17)$$

Writing these equations in standard form, we find

$$5i_1 - 2i_2 = 6$$
$$-2i_1 + 8i_2 = 8 \qquad (1\text{-}18)$$

Solving, we find $i_1 = \frac{16}{9}$ A (amperes) and $i_2 = \frac{13}{9}$ A. Thus the current in the middle branch is $\frac{16}{9} - \frac{13}{9}$, or $+\frac{1}{3}$ A from a to b.

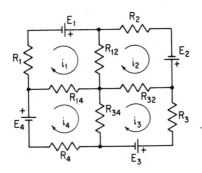

FIGURE 1-7   Four-loop network.

Consider the four-loop network in Fig. 1-7. It can be seen that the voltage equations can be written as follows, using the loops numbered 1, 2, 3, and 4 in sequence,

$$R_{11}i_1 - R_{12}i_2 + 0 - R_{14}i_4 = E_1$$
$$-R_{12}i_1 + R_{22}i_2 - R_{32}i_3 + 0 = E_2$$
$$0 - R_{32}i_2 + R_{33}i_3 - R_{34}i_4 = -E_3 \qquad (1\text{-}19)$$
$$-R_{14}i_1 + 0 - R_{34}i_3 + R_{44}i_4 = E_4$$

where $R_{11} = R_1 + R_{12} + R_{14}$ (the sum of all of the R's bounding loop 1) and R_{22}, etc. are defined similarly. The simultaneous equations (1-19) can be solved for the currents (a) by the method of substitution and elimination, or (b) by the use of determinants.

The reader will notice a definite pattern for the signs of the terms on the left side of Eq. (1-19). Thus the terms involving R_{11}, R_{22}, etc. are positive, and all the rest are negative. This result stems from choosing all the mesh currents to be positive in the clockwise sense. This choice is advantageous as an aid in checking the signs but is not essential. For example, one of the current arrows in Fig. 1-7 could be reversed, and an independent set of equations similar to (1-19) could be written. The writing of such a set of equations could well be undertaken as an exercise.

c. Nodal analysis method

This method, like the mesh current method, also systematizes the setting up of a set of independent equations. However, the unknowns are potentials rather than currents, and the current law is used at the nodes to get the set of equations. To illustrate the method, we take the example network in Fig.

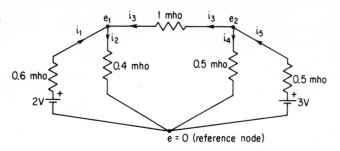

FIGURE 1-8   Three node network.

1-8. One of the nodes is chosen as the reference node, and its potential is taken to be zero. The other nodes are assigned voltage symbols, such as e_1 and e_2 in the figure, and are considered as positive potentials with respect to the reference node. Then the current law is applied at all nodes except the reference node. In this example current symbols are added to aid the discussion, but these are not needed. The algebra is simplified by the use of conductances. The current law gives, at e_1, $i_1 - i_2 + i_3 = 0$, and at e_2, $-i_3 - i_4 + i_5 = 0$. But $i_1 = 0.6 (2 - e_1)$, $i_2 = 0.4e_1$, $i_3 = 1.0(e_2 - e_1)$, etc. Therefore,

$$0.6(2 - e_1) - 0.4e_1 + 1.0(e_2 - e_1) = 0 \quad \text{at node } e_1 \qquad (1\text{-}20)$$

$$-1.0(e_2 - e_1) - 0.5e_2 + 0.5(3 - e_2) = 0 \quad \text{at node } e_2 \qquad (1\text{-}21)$$

Simplifying,

$$2e_1 - e_2 = 1.2 \qquad (1\text{-}22)$$

$$-e_1 + 2e_2 = 1.5 \qquad (1\text{-}23)$$

Solving, we find $e_1 = 1.3$ V and $e_2 = 1.4$ V. The currents can now readily be calculated.

If desired, the branches containing a voltage source and a resistance can be converted into a current source shunted by a resistance. This will leave the number of nodes the same; therefore the same number of simultaneous equations will be needed as before.

In this example there are three loops, so that three equations would be needed in the mesh current method. Whenever the total number of nodes is equal to, or less than, the number of loops, fewer equations using the nodal analysis will be required.

1-7

The Wheatstone bridge circuit

In the most common application of this network (Fig. 1-9), one of the resistors is unknown and the remaining three are adjustable precision resistors. These are adjusted until the voltage drop from node a to node b is zero, so the cur-

rent indicator reads zero. Under this
condition the voltage drop across R_2
must equal that across R_4, i.e., $e_a = e_b$.
If we express the voltages e_a and e_b by
means of the voltage divider formula,
Eq. (1-11a), we can write

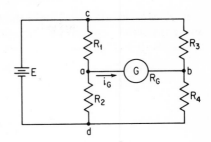

FIGURE 1-9   Wheatstone bridge
circuit.

$$\frac{R_2}{R_1 + R_2}E = \frac{R_4}{R_3 + R_4}E \quad (1\text{-}24)$$

If we cancel the E's and invert the
equation, we get

$$\frac{R_1 + R_2}{R_2} = \frac{R_3 + R_4}{R_4} \quad (1\text{-}25)$$

Algebraic manipulation leads to the following form:

$$\frac{R_1}{R_2} = \frac{R_3}{R_4} \quad (1\text{-}26)$$

which gives the condition for balance. Usually three of the R's are known;
therefore the fourth can be calculated.

The problem sometimes arises: How large is the current i_G for a specified
unbalance of the bridge? This question could be answered by application of
the methods of analysis already presented, but it can be answered more
expeditiously by an application of Thévenin's theorem, to be discussed
presently.

1-8
The π to T (delta to star)
transformation

Networks of the π or T form, as shown in Fig. 1-10, occur frequently in electronic circuits. We shall present here the relations between the constants of

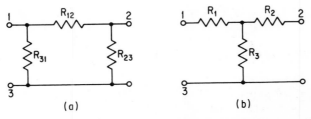

(a)   (b)

FIGURE 1-10   (a) π (or delta) network. (b) T (or star) network.

the two networks that will make the two equivalent as far as external voltages and currents are concerned. First we write the transformation formulas for the equivalent-T parameters in terms of the others

$$R_1 = \frac{R_{31}R_{12}}{R_{12} + R_{23} + R_{31}}$$

$$R_2 = \frac{R_{12}R_{23}}{R_{12} + R_{23} + R_{31}} \qquad (1\text{-}27)$$

$$R_3 = \frac{R_{23}R_{31}}{R_{12} + R_{23} + R_{31}}$$

The symmetry of these relations is striking. In each case the numerator involves the product of the two π resistors that branch off from the terminal concerned, e.g., $R_{31} R_{12}$ in the case of R_1.

When solved the other way around, the transformations are

$$R_{12} = \frac{R_1 R_2 + R_2 R_3 + R_3 R_1}{R_3}$$

$$R_{23} = \frac{R_1 R_2 + R_2 R_3 + R_3 R_1}{R_1} \qquad (1\text{-}28)$$

$$R_{31} = \frac{R_1 R_2 + R_2 R_3 + R_3 R_1}{R_2}$$

As a mnemonic device we note that the resistance in the denominator on the right side has the subscript that is *not* present on the resistance on the left side.

These transformations can sometimes be applied to a part of a network to facilitate its solution. Figure 1-11 shows such a network. Suppose that we replace the portion in the dotted rectangle by its equivalent π circuit.

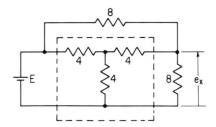

FIGURE 1-11   Bridged-T network.

Then the resulting circuit is a series-parallel arrangement, though the original was a three-loop network.

1-9
Network theorems

a. Superposition theorem

In any linear system the *effects* are linearly related to the *causes*, so the separate effects of a number of causes may be added (*superimposed*) to get the total effect. When it is applied to a network, we may say that a particular current (or voltage) is the algebraic sum of the currents (or voltages) that would be produced by each of the sources acting alone. This means that a particular branch current, for example, can be calculated as the sum of the currents in this branch caused by the sources taken one at a time. While one voltage source is being considered the other voltage sources are removed (short-circuited, or replaced by their internal resistance), and the ideal current sources are also removed (open-circuited).

b. Thévenin's and Norton's theorems

Thévenin's theorem is an important aid in solving electronic circuit problems and is also basic to useful ways of considering circuit behavior. It has to do with the current-voltage relation at a selected pair of terminals of a network at which an external branch (or any other two-terminal network) is attached. In effect, the theorem states that a complex network containing a number of sources and resistances can be replaced, as far as the two specified terminals are concerned, by a single equivalent source consisting of a voltage and a series (Thévenin) resistance. The source voltage is the voltage that would be measured at the two terminals when the external circuit is open. The Thévenin resistance is the resistance that would be measured at the two terminals with the internal sources removed (ideal voltage sources short-circuited, ideal current sources open-circuited).

Thévenin's theorem can be better understood after applying it to the example network in Fig. 1-12a. We set ourselves the problem of calculating the current i_L when resistor R_L is connected across terminals a-b. First think of terminals a-b as open. The effective (Thévenin) voltage is the voltage e_t which appears across a-b. This voltage can be calculated to be

$$e_t = \left(\frac{e_1}{R_1} + i_1\right)\frac{R_1 R_2}{R_1 + R_2} \qquad (1\text{-}29)$$

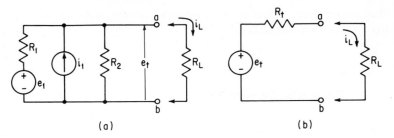

FIGURE 1-12   Illustrating Thévenin's theorem.

The Thévenin resistance R_t is that from a to b with e_1 short-circuited and i_1 open and thus consists of R_1 and R_2 in parallel

$$R_t = \frac{R_1 R_2}{R_1 + R_2} \tag{1-30}$$

The network to the left of terminals a and b can now be replaced by e_t and R_t in series, as shown in Fig. 1-12b. Thus i_L has the value $e_t/(R_t + R_L)$.

A common application of Thévenin's theorem is to obtain an equivalent circuit for a source and voltage divider. The circuit and its Thévenin equivalent are shown in Fig. 1-13.

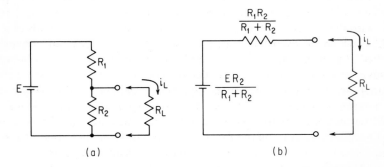

FIGURE 1-13   Thévenin's theorem applied to a voltage divider.

Let us now return to the problem of calculating the current i_G in an unbalanced Wheatstone bridge (Fig. 1-9). One approach is to think of R_1 and R_2 as one voltage divider and R_3 and R_4 as another. The voltage dividers can be replaced with respect to terminals a-d and b-d by the Thévenin equivalent sources. Finally, the resistance of the indicator R_G is connected

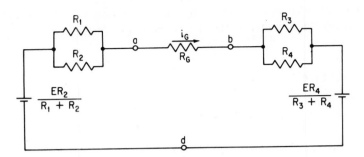

FIGURE 1-14   Thévenin equivalent of Wheatstone bridge circuit.

from a to b, as shown in Fig. 1-14. This is a series-parallel circuit, so i_G can be obtained easily.

If we replace the e_t and R_t of Thévenin's theorem by an equivalent current generator (constant current generator e_t/R_t in parallel with R_t), we have *Norton's equivalent circuit.*

In the examples a single resistor was connected across the terminals of the Thévenin equivalent circuit. However, the theorem is not restricted to this situation; in fact a network containing sources and resistors can be connected to the specified terminals.

c. Maximum power transfer theorem

At low power levels it is often desirable to obtain a maximum power output from a given network. Consider the network in Fig. 1-12a with R_L connected. If R_L is varied, for what value of R_L is the power going to R_L a maximum? Thévenin's theorem is helpful here because we need only consider the simpler equivalent circuit in Fig. 1-12b. A simple derivation will show that the maximum power is obtained when R_L is made equal to R_t. This is said to be the *matched* condition, i.e., the load resistance R_L matches the Thévenin resistance of the network. The corresponding maximum power is

$$P_{\max} = \frac{e_t^2}{4R_t} \quad \text{for } R_L = R_t \tag{1-31}$$

As R_L varies on each side of the matched condition, the power delivered to R_L varies as shown in the following table:

R_L/R_t	0.1	0.2	0.5	0.8	1.2	1.5	2.0
$P/P_{\max}$	0.33	0.55	0.89	0.99	0.99	0.96	0.89

We see that the function has a fairly broad maximum, and a considerable *mismatch* can be tolerated without serious loss of power.

REFERENCES

See the references at the end of Chapter 2.

EXERCISES

1-1 Develop a formula for the equivalent resistance of three resistors R_1, R_2, and R_3 connected in parallel.

1-2 A voltmeter is connected to the terminals of a battery, and an external load draws current through an ammeter. When the current is 2.0 A, the voltmeter reads 5.8 V, and at 5.0 A, the voltage is 5.5 V. (a) Find the open-circuit voltage and the internal resistance of the battery. (b) Find the elements of an equivalent current source. *Note:* The meters do not affect the circuit.

1-3 Moving-coil dc voltmeters have an ohm-per-volt rating, for example, a 1000 ohm-per-volt instrument has a resistance of 100,000 Ω on a 100-V full-scale range. Consider a series circuit comprising an ideal 100-V source and two 20,000 Ω resistors. A voltmeter is connected across one of the resistors. What voltmeter readings will result in each case if the voltmeter has a rating and full-scale range of (a) 1000 Ω/V and 50 V, (b) 100 Ω/V and 200 V, and (c) 5000 Ω/V and 50 V?

1-4 (a) A battery has an open-circuit voltage of 10 V and an internal resistance of 2 Ω. Represent this battery by means of two equivalent circuits and label the values of the circuit elements. (b) Show that these two equivalent circuits yield the same results for the terminal voltage and the load current if a load resistor of 18 Ω is placed across the battery.

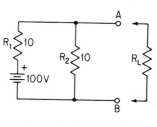

FIGURE 1-15

1-5 (a) Find the Thévenin equivalent source for the circuit to the left of terminals AB in Fig. 1-15. (b) Suppose that load resistor R_L is connected to terminals A and B, and R_L is varied from zero to infinity. What must be the power ratings of resistors R_1 and R_2 so as not to be overheated by the worst loading condition?

1-6 The bridge circuit of Fig. 1-9 has the following parameters: $E = 20$, $R_1 = 2$, $R_2 = 3$, $R_3 = 4$, and $R_4 = 4$, all in ohms. Find the equivalent Thévenin source with respect to terminals ab.

1-7 Find the current delivered by the 2-V battery in Fig. 1-16 by (a) the Maxwell

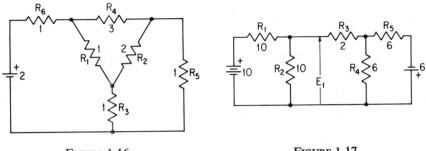

FIGURE 1-16   FIGURE 1-17

mesh current method, and (b) by a method which uses the T to π (or π to T) transformation.

1-8 Consider the network in Fig. 1-17. Solve for the voltage E_1 (a) by using superposition, (b) by using nodal analysis, and (c) by reducing the network to a simpler network by applying Thévenin's theorem. *Suggestion:* Use the theorem twice to replace the sources and adjacent resistors by equivalent sources.

1-9 Solve for E_1 and E_2 in Fig. 1-18.

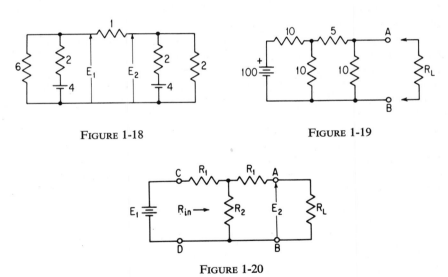

FIGURE 1-18   FIGURE 1-19

FIGURE 1-20

1-10 (a) What value of R_L placed across AB in Fig. 1-19 will absorb maximum power? (b) What is the value of this maximum power?

1-11 Figure 1-20 shows a network comprising the T arrangement of resistors R_1 and R_2 that is intended to reduce voltage E_2 to a known fraction of E_1. This network, called an *attenuator*, is also designed to have $R_{in} = R_L$, so that insertion of the attenuator into the circuit will not change the loading of the source. Let

$E_2 = \alpha E_1$, where α is the per unit attenuation. Show that R_1 and R_2 should be chosen to have the values

$$R_1 = \frac{1-\alpha}{1+\alpha}R_L \quad \text{and} \quad R_2 = \frac{2\alpha}{1-\alpha^2}R_L$$

in order to satisfy the stated requirements.

1-12 Calculate the voltage e_x in Fig. 1-11 for a value of E of 10 V. *Suggestion:* Use the T to π transformation to facilitate the solution.

2

Responses
of Electric Circuits

2-1
The basic circuit equations

Reference was made in Chapter 1 to the wide variety of voltage and current wave forms in electronic circuits, such as direct voltage, step voltage, and decaying exponential and alternating harmonic voltages. In this chapter we are concerned particularly with the response of circuits containing resistors, capacitors, and inductors to variable voltages and currents. Owing to the extent of this subject we must be content to give outlines of (a) the general mathematical basis of circuit behavior, (b) the responses of elementary circuits to a step voltage and to steady-state alternating voltage, and (c) the theory of four-terminal networks.

The reader will recall that capacitance C is defined as the constant of proportionality between the charge and the potential difference of a capacitor

$$q = Ce \qquad (2\text{-}1)$$

With q measured in coulombs and e in volts, C is in farads. Therefore, if q and e are functions of the time, the current passing through the capacitor is given by

$$i = \frac{dq}{dt} = C\frac{de}{dt} \qquad (2\text{-}2)$$

19

An expression for the voltage of the capacitor in terms of the current is obtained by integrating Eq. (2-2)

$$e = \frac{1}{C} \int i\,dt \qquad (2\text{-}3)$$

The use of the indefinite integral in Eq. (2-3) implies that an integration constant will be added when the integral is evaluated.

We limit our discussion of inductors to those which have a linear relation between magnetic flux and exciting current. Then the voltage drop e in the same direction as the current i is given by

$$e = L\frac{di}{dt} \qquad (2\text{-}4)$$

The self-inductance L is measured in henrys in the mks unit system.

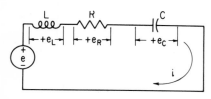

FIGURE 2-1   Series circuit of L, R, and C.

Kirchhoff's laws applied to the instantaneous voltages and currents of the network yield the equations that govern the network response. Consider first the series RLC circuit in Fig. 2-1. Let us assume that the source voltage e is some as yet unspecified function of the time. Kirchhoff's voltage law applies; therefore

$$-e + e_L + e_R + e_C = 0 \qquad (2\text{-}5)$$

We transpose the first term and replace the others in terms of the current to obtain

$$L\frac{di}{dt} + Ri + \frac{1}{C}\int i\,dt = e \qquad (2\text{-}6)$$

This can be converted to a differential equation by differentiating each term with respect to time

$$L\frac{d^2 i}{dt^2} + R\frac{di}{dt} + \frac{i}{C} = \frac{de}{dt} \qquad (2\text{-}7)$$

Thus, the current in the circuit is governed by a second-order, linear differential equation having constant coefficients.

An alternative problem is that of finding the variation of the capacitor voltage. For this purpose Eq.(2-6) should be expressed in terms of the capacitor charge q; thus,

$$L\frac{d^2 q}{dt^2} + R\frac{dq}{dt} + \frac{q}{C} = e \qquad (2\text{-}8)$$

After solving for q, we can find e_c, the capacitor voltage, by means of $e_c = q/C$.

In general the problem of finding the response to a specified form of impressed voltage reduces to the problem of solving a linear differential equation. We shall outline some solutions in the following articles, by using the so-called classical method of solution.

2-2
Response of LR and RC series circuits

a. Response to a step voltage

Let a series LR circuit be switched on to a constant voltage E at zero time, as shown in Fig. 2-2a. Kirchhoff's voltage law gives the following equation, which holds for $t \geqslant 0$,

$$L\frac{di}{dt} + Ri = E \tag{2-9}$$

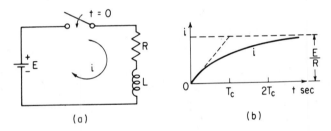

(a)   (b)

FIGURE 2-2   Response of LR circuit to dc emf.

In common with other linear differential equations, this equation has a solution that consists of the sum of the *particular integral* and the *complementary function*. Letting i_p be the particular integral and i_c the complementary function, we can write

$$i = i_p + i_c \tag{2-10}$$

The value of i_c is obtained as the solution of the differential equation with the right side set equal to zero (the *homogeneous* equation)

$$L\frac{di_c}{dt} + Ri_c = 0 \tag{2-11}$$

The homogeneous equation is always satisfied by an exponential function of the form

$$i_c = A \exp \lambda t = Ae^{\lambda t} \tag{2-12}$$

Substitution of (2-12) into (2-11) yields

$$L\lambda A \exp \lambda t + RA \exp \lambda t = 0 \tag{2-13}$$

The common factor $A \exp \lambda t$ can be factored out; therefore, $L\lambda + R = 0$, or $\lambda = -R/L$. Use this value in (2-12) to obtain

$$i_c = A \exp\left(-\frac{R}{L}t\right) \tag{2-14}$$

Here A is an integration constant yet to be determined. We remark that i_c is also called the *transient* part of the solution because it vanishes as the time t becomes very large.

The particular integral corresponds to the *steady-state* current caused by the driving voltage E. This has the value $i_p = E/R$. The actual current, therefore, is given by

$$i = \frac{E}{R} + A \exp\left(-\frac{R}{L}t\right) \tag{2-15}$$

The constant A is found from the known initial conditions. At $t = 0$ the current is zero, since the current cannot "jump" in an inductive circuit. Putting $i = 0$ in Eq. (2-15) at $t = 0$ shows that $A = -E/R$. The complete solution then is

$$i = \frac{E}{R} - \frac{E}{R} \exp\left(-\frac{R}{L}t\right) \tag{2-16}$$

This is a rising function having an exponentially decaying negative component as shown in Fig. 2-2b. Of particular interest is the value of time that reduces the exponential factor to $\exp(-1)$, or 0.368. This value of time, called the *time constant* of the circuit, is given by

$$T_c = \frac{L}{R} \tag{2-17}$$

The time constant may be defined as the time during which *all but* 0.368 of the *total change* has taken place.

Let us discuss a slightly modified problem. Assume that a resistor is added across the open switch in Fig. 2-2a and that a steady current flows in the circuit. Then at $t = 0$, the switch is closed, thereby short-circuiting the added resistance. The steps in the solution of this problem would be the same as before down to and including Eq. (2-15). The only difference arises in the determination of the value of the constant A. This would be carried out much as before, except that the current i has a value at $t = 0$

Next consider the series RC circuit in Fig. 2-3. Suppose that the voltage (and charge) of the capacitor is initially zero. Let the switch move to contact 1 at $t = 0$. The differential equation in terms of the charge q is

$$R\frac{dq}{dt} + \frac{q}{C} = E \tag{2-18}$$

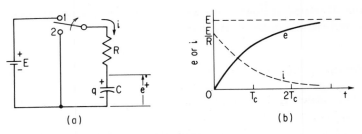

FIGURE 2-3   Response of RC circuit to dc emf.

In the steady state, dq/dt is zero, so the particular integral is $q_p = CE$. The complementary function is the solution of

$$\frac{dq_c}{dt} + \frac{q_c}{RC} = 0 \qquad (2\text{-}19)$$

which is,

$$q_c = A \exp\left(-\frac{t}{RC}\right) \qquad (2\text{-}20)$$

Therefore,

$$q = q_p + q_c = CE + A \exp\left(-\frac{t}{RC}\right) \qquad (2\text{-}21)$$

At $t = 0$, $q = 0$; therefore, $A = -CE$, and (2-21) yields

$$q = CE - CE \exp\left(-\frac{t}{RC}\right) \qquad (2\text{-}22)$$

Whence we obtain the capacitor voltage

$$e = E - E \exp\left(-\frac{t}{RC}\right) \qquad (2\text{-}23)$$

This shows that e varies on a rising curve which has the time constant

$$T_c = RC \qquad (2\text{-}24)$$

With R expressed in ohms and C in farads, T_c will be in seconds.

To find the equation for the current in the circuit, we differentiate (2-22) and obtain

$$i = \frac{E}{R} \exp\left(-\frac{t}{RC}\right) \qquad (2\text{-}25)$$

This is a decaying exponential having a time constant of RC seconds.

The reader can show that if the capacitor is allowed to become fully charged with the switch on contact 1 and then the switch is moved to contact 2 the capacitor voltage will decay according to

$$e = E \exp\left(-\frac{t}{RC}\right) \qquad (2\text{-}26)$$

and the discharge current pulse will have the same form as given by Eq. (2-25), but the direction is reversed.

b. *Response of RC circuit to a voltage pulse*

Let the switch in Fig. 2-3a move to position 1 at time $t = 0$, and T seconds later return to position 2. In effect a rectangular voltage pulse of magnitude E and duration T (Fig. 2-4a) is impressed on the RC circuit.

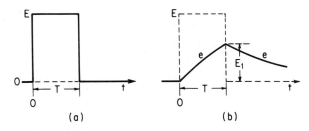

(a)   (b)

FIGURE 2-4   (a) A voltage pulse. (b) Showing the response of the capacitor voltage.

The first portion of the response of the capacitor voltage is the same as was calculated for the step voltage, e.g.,

$$e = E - E \exp\left(-\frac{t}{RC}\right) \quad \text{for } 0 < t < T \tag{2-23}$$

but now the equation holds only for times between 0 and T.

At time T the capacitor has reached the voltage E_1 and has a corresponding stored charge. The ensuing voltage variation is governed by the differential equation

$$R\frac{dq}{dt} + \frac{q}{C} = 0 \tag{2-27}$$

and we know the solution to be

$$q = A_1 \exp\left(-\frac{t}{RC}\right) \tag{2-28}$$

To evaluate the constant A_1, we use the known values at instant T, namely,

$$q = CE_1 \quad \text{at} \quad t = T \tag{2-29}$$

Inserting these values in (2-28) we find

$$CE_1 = A_1 \exp\left(-\frac{T}{RC}\right) \tag{2-30}$$

or

$$A_1 = \frac{CE_1}{\exp\left(-\dfrac{T}{RC}\right)} = CE_1 \exp\left(\frac{T}{RC}\right) \tag{2-31}$$

Consequently, using this value in (2-28), we have

$$q = CE_1 \exp\left(\frac{T}{RC}\right) \exp\left(-\frac{t}{RC}\right) \tag{2-32}$$

which may be written

$$q = CE_1 \exp\left(-\frac{t-T}{RC}\right) \tag{2-33}$$

In terms of the capacitor voltage $e = q/C$, Eq. (2-34) yields

$$e = E_1 \exp\left(-\frac{t-T}{RC}\right) \quad \text{for } t > T \tag{2-34}$$

We can interpret Eq. (2-34) as the discharging voltage transient of a capacitor that was initially charged to the voltage E_1. The quantity $t - T$ gives the elapsed time from the start of the discharge.

Further analysis of the pulse response of RC circuits will be found in Chapter 16.

2-3
Response of LR circuit to an alternating voltage source

Exponential functions can aid us in the solution when the driving voltage is an alternating harmonic function. First recall the Euler formula for the expansion of the exponential function of the pure imaginary variable $j\theta$.

$$\exp(\pm j\theta) = \cos \theta \pm j \sin \theta \tag{2-35}$$

But we wish to deal with the harmonic function of angular frequency ω and phase ϕ, so we write

$$\exp j(\omega t + \phi) = \cos(\omega t + \phi) + j \sin(\omega t + \phi) \tag{2-36}$$

If we wish to consider the response to a source voltage $E \cos(\omega t + \phi)$, we can just as well use the *real part* of the function $E \exp j(\omega t + \phi)$, which is written $\text{Re}[E \exp j(\omega t + \phi)]$. Though this appears to be more cumbersome than using trigonometric functions, we shall find that the use of the exponential functions facilitates the solution for the particular integral. Using this form the differential equation for the series LR circuit with a harmonic emf is

$$L\frac{di}{dt} + Ri = \text{Re}[E \exp j(\omega t + \phi)] \tag{2-37}$$

The complementary function is known, so we seek the particular integral. Let i_p have the form $\mathrm{Re}\,[B \exp j(\omega t + \phi)]$, in which B is a constant to be determined and which may be complex. Upon substituting this form in (2-37) we find

$$\mathrm{Re}\,[LBj\omega \exp j(\omega t + \phi) + RB \exp j(\omega t + \phi)] = \mathrm{Re}\,[E \exp j(\omega t + \phi)] \tag{2-38}$$

or

$$\mathrm{Re}\,[B(R + j\omega L) \exp j(\omega t + \phi)] = \mathrm{Re}\,[E \exp j(\omega t + \phi)] \tag{2-39}$$

This equation is satisfied if

$$B = \frac{E}{R + j\omega L} \tag{2-40}$$

Therefore,

$$i_p = \mathrm{Re}\left[\frac{E}{R + j\omega L} \exp j(\omega t + \phi)\right] \tag{2-41}$$

Before evaluating the right side of (2-41) consider the quantity $R + j\omega L$ as sketched in the complex plane in Fig. 2-5. We define

$$\mathbf{Z} = R + j\omega L \tag{2-42}$$

as the complex *impedance*. Let Z denote $|\mathbf{Z}|$. Then $R = Z \cos\theta$, and $\omega L = Z \sin\theta$, where $\theta = \tan^{-1} \omega L/R$. Recalling Eq. (2-35), we can express $\mathbf{Z}$ in exponential form

$$\mathbf{Z} = Z(\cos\theta + j\sin\theta) = Z \exp j\theta \tag{2-43}$$

We can use this form to convert (2-41) as follows:

$$i_p = \mathrm{Re}\left[\frac{E \exp j(\omega t + \phi)}{Z \exp j\theta}\right] = \mathrm{Re}\left[\frac{E}{Z} \exp j(\omega t + \phi - \theta)\right] \tag{2-44}$$

Using Euler's formula, we obtain the trigonometric form

$$i_p = \frac{E}{Z} \cos(\omega t + \phi - \theta) \tag{2-45}$$

where

$$Z = \sqrt{R^2 + (\omega L)^2} \quad \text{and} \quad \theta = \tan^{-1} \frac{\omega L}{R}$$

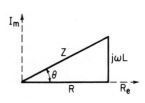

FIGURE 2-5   Diagram of complex impedance.

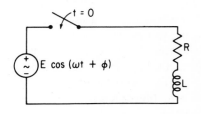

FIGURE 2-6   *LR* circuit with ac emf.

The total current is the sum $i_c + i_p$

$$i = A \exp\left(-\frac{R}{L}t\right) + \frac{E}{Z}\cos(\omega t + \phi - \theta) \qquad (2\text{-}46)$$

The integration constant A depends on the instant at which the voltage is impressed on the circuit and the value of current, if any, at this instant. We let $i = 0$ at the instant of closing the circuit, namely, at $t = 0$, as in Fig. 2-6. Using this initial condition in Eq. (2-46) gives the value of A

$$A = -\frac{E}{Z}\cos(\phi - \theta) \qquad (2\text{-}47)$$

Therefore the current is given by

$$i = -\frac{E}{Z}\cos(\phi - \theta)\exp\left(-\frac{R}{L}t\right) + \frac{E}{Z}\cos(\omega t + \phi - \theta) \qquad (2\text{-}48)$$

The first term, the transient term, decays exponentially with a time constant of L/R. Its amplitude depends on E, Z, ϕ, and θ. The ratio E/Z gives the peak value of the *steady-state* current, while the angle θ is its *angle of lag* behind the impressed voltage. The angle ϕ can be called the *switching angle*, since it determines the phase of the impressed voltage at $t = 0$. When $\cos(\phi - \theta) = -1$, the transient term has its maximum amplitude. A typical variation of the total current is shown in Fig. 2-7. This is sketched for the condition of maximum amplitude of the transient term and for approximately $\theta = 80°$, and $\phi = -100°$.

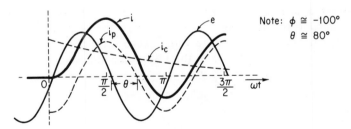

FIGURE 2-7   Response of LR circuit to harmonic voltage.

2-4
Techniques for use with steady-state alternating currents and voltages

Often only the steady-state response of a network or system is needed. Then the transient terms are of no interest, so our attention is directed to the particular integral of the system differential equation. The foregoing article demonstrated the utility of the exponential functions of a pure imaginary quantity in the solution for the particular integral. Furthermore, the concept of a complex impedance was introduced in the same solution. In the following discussion these ideas will be extended and the concept of a *phasor* quantity will be introduced after a review of some aspects of harmonic functions.

a. Peak and root-mean-square values

For purposes of illustration we use a steady-state current, which has a frequency f, given by

$$i = I_m \cos 2\pi f(t + t_0) \tag{2-49}$$

Here I_m is the amplitude, or *peak value* of the current. We next replace $2\pi f$ by ω, called the *angular frequency*, and replace $2\pi f t_0$ by ϕ, called the *phase angle;* then ,

$$i = I_m \cos(\omega t + \phi) \tag{2-50}$$

The period T of the harmonic function is the reciprocal of the frequency, i.e., $T = 1/f$. If the cosine curve is shifted by $\pi/2$ radians, it becomes a sine curve; thus

$$i = I_m \cos\left(\omega t + \phi \pm \frac{\pi}{2}\right) = \mp I_m \sin(\omega t + \phi) \tag{2-51a}$$

A phase change of π radians (180°) inverts the curve, or changes the sign

$$i = I_m \cos(\omega t + \phi \pm \pi) = -I_m \cos(\omega t + \phi) \tag{2-51b}$$

The *root-mean-square* or *effective* value of a voltage or current is defined to equal the constant (or dc) value that would cause the same amount of heat to be dissipated in a resistor as the actual wave form. For example, if the current is expressed by (2-50), then the instantaneous power is

$$p = Ri^2 = RI_m^2 \cos^2(\omega t + \phi) \tag{2-52}$$

If p is averaged over a complete cycle (or an integral number of cycles), the average power P is found to be

$$P = \tfrac{1}{2}RI_m^2 \tag{2-53}$$

But a direct current I_d would produce a power of $I_d^2 R$. Let I represent the *root-mean-square* (rms) value. Then, on the basis of equal heating effectiveness, $I^2 R = I_m^2 R/2$, or

$$I = \frac{I_m}{\sqrt{2}} \tag{2-54}$$

Other wave forms will, of course, have a different ratio of rms to peak value of the wave.

A general formula for the rms value of a periodic current of period T is the following:

$$I_{rms} = \sqrt{\frac{1}{T}\int_0^T i^2\, dt} \tag{2-55}$$

It will aid the memory to observe that the formula takes the *root* of the *mean* of the current *squared*. An analogous formula gives the rms value of a periodic voltage wave.

Suppose that a section of a circuit (for example, a series-connected R and L) is traversed by a current $i = I_m \cos \omega t$ and that the voltage drop in the direction of $+i$ is given by $e = E_m \cos(\omega t + \theta)$. The instantaneous power absorbed is $p = ei$. When the instantaneous power is averaged over a period, the result is

$$P = EI \cos \theta \qquad (2\text{-}56)$$

Note that E and I are rms values. The factor $\cos \theta$ is called the *power factor*. If $\theta = \pm 90°$, no net power is absorbed. This condition obtains for an ideal capacitor or inductor. Note also that if $90° < \theta < 270°$, the power is negative, i.e., the circuit is a *source* of electrical power.

b. Phasors, phasor representation and manipulation

In the foregoing section we made use of the real part of an exponential function to express a trigonometric function, in the form

$$e = E_m \cos(\omega t + \phi_1) = \text{Re}\,[E_m \exp j(\omega t + \phi_1)] \qquad (2\text{-}57)$$

The quantity in square brackets can be interpreted geometrically as a line of length E_m which rotates in the counterclockwise sense with the angular frequency ω. This is the so-called *rotating phasor* illustrated in Fig. 2-8. We note that the instantaneous value of the projection of the rotating phasor on the real axis is interpreted as the cosine function.

We wish to discuss the use of phasors for simplifying the addition and subtraction of harmonic functions. However, we first change the concept of the phasor in two respects. Since we deal more often with rms values than peak values, we let the length of the phasor represent the *rms value*. We want the phasor to convey information about the *magnitude* and the *phase* of a harmonic function. For this purpose the phasor rotation is unnecessary. Therefore, we consider the phasor as fixed in the complex plane, but fixed at a definite phase angle with respect to a specified reference angle. To be sure, we can revert to the rotating phasor concept if we need to find the instantaneous value at a particular value of ωt, or if we wish to trace out the harmonic waves.

An example will be helpful. Suppose that we wish to add two voltages,

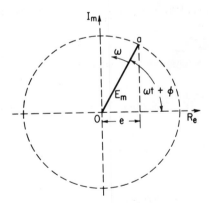

FIGURE 2-8   A rotating phasor.

$e_1 = E_{1m} \cos(\omega t + \phi_1)$ and $e_2 = E_{2m} \cos(\omega t + \phi_2)$. Letting $e_3 = e_1 + e_2$, we want to find

$$e_3 = E_{1m} \cos(\omega t + \phi_1) + E_{2m} \cos(\omega t + \phi_2) \qquad (2\text{-}58)$$

This addition can be done by means of trigonometric identities, and the sum is a function of the same frequency with different amplitude and phase. To

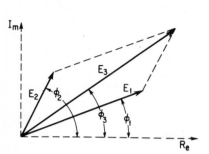

use the phasor technique we think of the rms values laid out in the complex plane (Fig. 2-9) *with reference to* the Re axis. That is, the stationary phasors are laid out where the rotating phasor would have been at $\omega t = 0$. It can be shown† that if the phasors $\mathbf{E}_1$ and $\mathbf{E}_2$ are added by the rules of vector addition, the resultant phasor $\mathbf{E}_3$ gives the correct magnitude and phase of the sum. Note that the symbols for the phasors are printed in boldface type

FIGURE 2-9   Stationary phasors.

to indicate that they are complex quantities. The same symbol in italic type is the magnitude of the quantity.

The techniques of complex algebra are convenient to use for adding or subtracting phasors. In the foregoing example of the addition of two voltages let

$$\mathbf{E}_1 = a + jb \quad \text{and} \quad \mathbf{E}_2 = c + jd \qquad (2\text{-}59)$$

where $a = E_1 \cos\phi_1$, $b = E_1 \sin\phi_1$, etc., Then

$$\mathbf{E}_3 = \mathbf{E}_1 + \mathbf{E}_2 = (a + c) + j(b + d) \qquad (2\text{-}60)$$

Thus, the magnitude and phase angle of the sum are

$$E_3 = |\mathbf{E}_3| = \sqrt{(a + c)^2 + (b + d)^2} \qquad (2\text{-}61)$$

and

$$\phi_3 = \tan^{-1} \frac{(b + d)}{(a + c)} \qquad (2\text{-}62)$$

Additional equivalent forms for expressing complex quantities that are applied to phasors are as follows:

$$\mathbf{E}_1 = E_1\underline{/\phi_1} = E_1 \exp j\phi_1 \qquad (2\text{-}63)$$

Here the reference direction is the Re axis.

Phasor manipulations involving multiplication and division and taking powers will also be needed. These follow the rules for complex numbers.

†See, for example, P. R. Clement and W. C. Johnson, *Electrical Engineering Science*, McGraw-Hill Book Company, New York, 1960, pp. 311 ff.

To illustrate these manipulations, we use the complex numbers **A** and **B** as follows:

$$\mathbf{A} = a + jb = \mathbf{A}\underline{/\phi_a} = \mathbf{A}\exp j\phi_a \qquad (2\text{-}64)$$

and

$$\mathbf{B} = c + jd = \mathbf{B}\underline{/\phi_b} = B\exp j\phi_b \qquad (2\text{-}65)$$

The product is most readily expressed in the polar or exponential forms; thus,

$$\mathbf{AB} = AB\underline{/(\phi_a + \phi_b)} = AB\exp j(\phi_a + \phi_b) \qquad (2\text{-}66)$$

We remark that this product is different from the products used in vector analysis. Next we calculate the ratio

$$\frac{\mathbf{A}}{\mathbf{B}} = \frac{A}{B}\underline{/(\phi_a - \phi_b)} = \frac{A}{B}\exp j(\phi_a - \phi_b) \qquad (2\text{-}67)$$

Furthermore,

$$\mathbf{A}^n = A^n\underline{/n\phi_a} = A^n\exp jn\phi_a \qquad (2\text{-}68)$$

Multiplication can also be done using the "$a + jb$" forms; thus

$$\mathbf{AB} = (a + jb)(c + jd) = ac + j(bc + ad) + j^2bd \qquad (2\text{-}69)$$

But $j^2 = -1$, so

$$\mathbf{AB} = (ac - bd) + j(bc + ad) \qquad (2\text{-}70)$$

To use these forms for division it is necessary to carry out the process known as *rationalization*. In this process the denominator and numerator are multiplied by the *conjugate* of the denominator. To demonstrate, we calculate **A/B**

$$\frac{\mathbf{A}}{\mathbf{B}} = \frac{a + jb}{c + jd} = \frac{(a + jb)(c - jd)}{(c + jd)(c - jd)} = \frac{(ac + bd) + j(bc - ad)}{c^2 + d^2} \qquad (2\text{-}71)$$

If desired, this can be written in the form $m + jn$. It is obvious that the manipulations in Eqs. (2-66) and (2-67) are to be preferred over those using the phasor components.

c. *Phasor relations of voltage to current; impedance; reactance*

The solution of the differential equation (2-37) in Sec. 2-3b led to the definition of impedance as a complex number, which in the case of R and L in series took the form $\mathbf{Z} = R + j\omega L$. A study of the steady-state term of current in Eq.(2-46) compared with the impressed alternating voltage in Eq. (2-37) will show that the (stationary) phasor current and impressed voltage are related by the equation

$$\mathbf{E} = \mathbf{ZI} = (R + j\omega L)\mathbf{I} \qquad (2\text{-}72)$$

This is a special case of the general equation

$$\mathbf{E} = \mathbf{ZI} \tag{2-73}$$

where $\mathbf{Z}$ is the *complex impedance* of the portion of the circuit concerned. Since the definitions of $\mathbf{E}$ and $\mathbf{I}$ go back to instantaneous voltage drop and current, it is important to have reference polarities for these phasors, as indicated in Fig. 2-10a. Then the phasor diagram in Fig. 2-10b, based on Eq. (2-73), has a precise meaning in relation to the actual circuit.

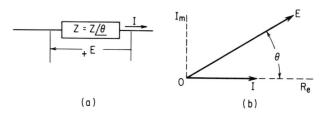

(a)   (b)

FIGURE 2-10   Phasor relations for an impedance $Z\underline{/\theta}$.

A summary of the phasor relations and the impedance values for ideal elements of R, L, and C is given in Table 2-1. The relation for the capacitor is in accord with Eq. (2-2). The phase relation of e to i is immediately obvious from the phasor diagram. For the inductor the voltage *leads* the current by 90°, or conversely, the current *lags* the voltage. For the capacitor the current *leads* the voltage.

Table 2-1   Phasor Relations and Impedance Values of Ideal Circuit Elements

	Resistor	*Inductor*	*Capacitor*
Phasor diagram:			
Phasor equation:	$\mathbf{E} = R\mathbf{I}$	$\mathbf{E} = j\omega L\mathbf{I}$	$\mathbf{E} = \dfrac{1}{j\omega C}\mathbf{I}$
Impedance of element:	$\mathbf{Z}_R = R$	$\mathbf{Z}_L = j\omega L$	$\mathbf{Z}_C = \dfrac{1}{j\omega C}$

The term *reactance* is used for the j part of the impedance $\mathbf{Z}$. Thus, inductive reactance X_L equals ωL, and capacitive reactance X_C equals $1/\omega C$.

The total voltage drop across a number of impedances connected in series is the sum of the individual voltages. Therefore, if $Z_1 \ldots, Z_n$ are connected in series, the total voltage is given by

$$\mathbf{E}_t = \mathbf{Z}_1 \mathbf{I} + \mathbf{Z}_2 \mathbf{I} + \cdots + \mathbf{Z}_n \mathbf{I} \qquad (2\text{-}74)$$

or

$$\mathbf{E}_t = \mathbf{I}(\mathbf{Z}_1 + \mathbf{Z}_2 + \cdots + \mathbf{Z}_n) \qquad (2\text{-}75)$$

A series circuit is shown in Fig. 2-11a, where Z_1 represents a coil of resistance R_1 and inductance L_1, and Z_2 consists of R_2 and C_2 in series. The total series impedance $\mathbf{Z}$ can be written as

$$\mathbf{Z} = \mathbf{Z}_1 + \mathbf{Z}_2 = R_1 + j\omega L_1 + R_2 - \frac{j}{\omega C_2} \qquad (2\text{-}76)$$

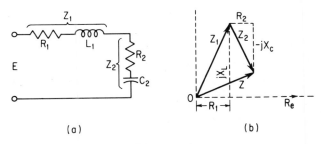

(a)   (b)

FIGURE 2-11   Series circuit and impedance diagram.

The addition of the complex impedances could take the form in Fig. 2-11b for a particular set of resistances and reactances. In this example the total impedance has a smaller magnitude than the separate impedances. This is an interesting aspect of the phenomenon of *series resonance*, which will be examined subsequently.

d. *Parallel circuits; admittance*

Consider the parallel connection of the three ideal circuit elements in Fig. 2-12a. Kirchhoff's current law yields

$$\mathbf{I} = \mathbf{I}_R + \mathbf{I}_c + \mathbf{I}_L \qquad (2\text{-}77)$$

The individual currents can be expressed in terms of the impressed voltage and the element impedances

$$\mathbf{I} = \frac{\mathbf{E}}{R} + \frac{\mathbf{E}}{j\omega L} + j\omega C \mathbf{E} \qquad (2\text{-}78)$$

A phasor diagram can be constructed (Fig. 2-12b) according to Eq. (2-78) to illustrate that $\mathbf{I}$ is the sum of the three current phasors. The figure shows that

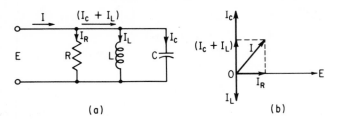

FIGURE 2-12   Parallel circuit of R, L, and C.

the inductive branch current partially cancels the capacitive branch current resulting in partial *parallel resonance*.

Just as conductance is defined as the reciprocal of resistance in a dc circuit, the reciprocal of impedance is termed *admittance*, symbolized by **Y**. Thus,

$$\mathbf{Y} = \frac{1}{\mathbf{Z}} = \frac{\mathbf{I}}{\mathbf{E}} \qquad (2\text{-}79)$$

The admittance at the terminals of the circuit in Fig. 2-12a is obtained from Eq. (2-78) by calculating $\mathbf{I}/\mathbf{E}$, to find

$$\mathbf{Y} = \frac{1}{R} + \frac{1}{j\omega L} + j\omega C \qquad (2\text{-}80)$$

Equation (2-80) illustrates the general rule that the total admittance **Y**, of a number of admittances $\mathbf{Y}_1$, $\mathbf{Y}_2$, ..., $\mathbf{Y}_n$ connected in *parallel* is given by

$$\mathbf{Y} = \mathbf{Y}_1 + \mathbf{Y}_2 + \cdots + \mathbf{Y}_n \qquad (2\text{-}81)$$

The circuit shown in Fig. 2-13 will serve to illustrate some points concerning the calculation of admittances. Based on Eq. (2-81), we write for the admittance of the whole circuit

$$\mathbf{Y} = \mathbf{Y}_1 + \mathbf{Y}_2 = \frac{1}{\mathbf{Z}_1} + \frac{1}{\mathbf{Z}_2} = \frac{1}{R_1 + j\omega L_1} + \frac{1}{R_2 - \dfrac{j}{\omega C_2}} \qquad (2\text{-}82)$$

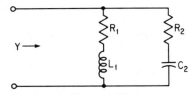

FIGURE 2-13   Parallel circuit.

In a numerical problem the most expeditious procedure is to use the polar forms for the first step in the calculation; thus,

$$\mathbf{Y} = \frac{1}{Z_1 \exp j\theta_1} + \frac{1}{Z_2 \exp j\theta_2} = \frac{1}{Z_1} \exp\left(-j\theta_1\right) + \frac{1}{Z_2} \exp\left(-j\theta_2\right) \qquad (2\text{-}83)$$

Here θ_1 and θ_2 are the power factor angles of the branch impedances. The polar forms would then be converted to the rectangular forms to perform the addition. A study of $\mathbf{Y}$ in terms of the circuit symbols can be made by rationalizing the two terms on the right of Eq. (2-82), with the result

$$\mathbf{Y} = \frac{R_1}{R_1^2 + \omega^2 L_1^2} + \frac{R_2}{R_2^2 + \dfrac{1}{\omega^2 C_2^2}} - j\left(\frac{\omega L_1}{R_1^2 + \omega^2 L_1^2} - \frac{\dfrac{1}{\omega C_2}}{R_2^2 + \dfrac{1}{\omega^2 C_2^2}}\right) \qquad (2\text{-}84)$$

It is convenient to have names and symbols for the real part and the j part of the admittance. By definition,

$$\mathbf{Y} = G + jB \qquad (2\text{-}85)$$

where G is the *conductance* and B the *susceptance*. As Eq. (2-84) shows, the conductance contributed by a series RL branch is a function of R, L, and ω, rather than simply $1/R$ as in dc circuits. The component susceptances are functions of the frequency and of the circuit constants. Equation (2-84) also shows that the susceptance contributed by the RL branch is negative and that the susceptance contributed by the RC branch is positive.

2-5
Circuit equations and network theorems applied to steady-state ac quantities

The foregoing section has shown how the use of phasors and complex impedances and admittances facilitates the analysis of the steady-state response of circuits to an ac driving voltage. It should be recognized that phasors and impedances are basically different, though both are expressed by complex numbers. A stationary phasor *represents* a sinusoidal function of the time but merely gives information about magnitude and phase. If the actual function of time is desired, we must go through the mental process of converting to a rotating phasor and taking the component on the real axis. Further, the length of the rotating phasor must represent the peak value of the function. Impedance and admittance are in the nature of complex operators which rotate and multiply one phasor to give another phasor.

The laws that were applied to dc circuits all apply when extended to phasors. These can be summarized as follows: Extended Ohm's law

$$\mathbf{E} = \mathbf{ZI} \qquad (2\text{-}86)$$

or

$$\mathbf{I} = \mathbf{YE} \qquad (2\text{-}87)$$

Extended Kirchhoff's laws

$$\text{currents into a junction:} \quad \Sigma\, \mathbf{I} = 0 \qquad (2\text{-}88)$$

$$\text{around any closed loop:} \quad \sum \mathbf{E} = 0 \qquad (2\text{-}89)$$

In these phasor equations the same care must be taken concerning directions and senses of $\mathbf{I}$ and $\mathbf{E}$ that was used with direct currents and voltages.

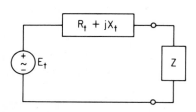

FIGURE 2-14 Thévenin equivalent source and load.

Most of the network theorems discussed earlier may be applied to phasor calculations without modification except for substituting $\mathbf{E}$, $\mathbf{I}$, and $\mathbf{Z}$ for E, I, and R; including (1) the superposition theorem, (2) Thévenin's and Norton's theorems, and (3) the π to T transformations. However, the *maximum power transfer* theorem requires additional consideration. We think in terms of the Thévenin equivalent circuit (Fig. 2-14), no matter how complex the actual network may be. The Thévenin impedance in general will consist of a real and a j part, i.e., $R_t + jX_t$. Let us think of the load as a series combination of resistance and reactance, i.e., $\mathbf{Z} = R + jX$. The total series impedance will be $\mathbf{Z}_{\text{tot}} = R_t + R + j(X_t + X)$. We wish to maximize the power I^2R. Let us first maximize I by varying X. To do this, we minimize $|Z_{\text{tot}}|$, which means that the j part should be zero; therefore $X = -X_t$. Then the maximization of I^2R is the same problem as in Sec. 1-9, and the result is $R = R_t$. Thus, the load impedance should be† the *conjugate* of the Thévenin impedance, or

$$\mathbf{Z} = R_t - jX_t \qquad (2\text{-}90)$$

Thus, a *matched load* is the conjugate of the Thévenin impedance.

2-6
Effect of frequency on Z and Y; resonance

Often a knowledge of the response of a circuit over a wide frequency range is needed. For example, the signal may have a variable frequency, or there may be an interfering voltage of a different frequency superimposed on the desired signal, and the interference should be suppressed.

A study of the impedance or admittance as a function of frequency will give a basis for prediction of the circuit response. We have seen that a resistance has no frequency effect, that the capacitive reactance is $1/\omega C$, and that the inductive reactance is ωL. These are, of course, for ideal elements. Real

†A rigorous proof gives the same result.

elements deviate from the ideal by a greater or lesser degree. A wire-wound resistor may have a slight inductance, or a capacitor may have an *equivalent* series resistance owing to its dielectric losses. Inductors all have resistance, and they may have enough capacitance between successive turns to have a noticeable effect at higher frequencies. We shall be concerned with ideal circuit elements in the following discussion.

Consider first the impedance of a series-connected resistance and inductance, $\mathbf{Z} = R + j\omega L$. We prefer to put the equation into a nondimensional form by dividing through by R and replacing R/L by the new parameter ω_0; thus,

$$\frac{\mathbf{Z}}{R} = 1 + j\frac{\omega L}{R} = 1 + j\frac{\omega}{\omega_0} \tag{2-91}$$

We remark that ω_0 is the reciprocal of the time constant of the circuit and that it has the same dimension as ω. When the frequency is varied, the complex quantity $\mathbf{Z}/R$ varies as shown in Fig. 2-15a. The locus of $\mathbf{Z}/R$ is the vertical

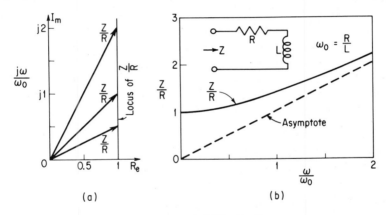

FIGURE 2-15　Frequency response of *RL* circuit.

line erected at the point $1 + j0$. We think of R as a constant, so the variation of $\mathbf{Z}/R$ shows how $\mathbf{Z}$ varies both in *magnitude* and *angle*. The reference frequency ω_0 is useful to indicate over what ranges of frequencies the reactive component of the impedance is important or unimportant. For example, when ω is small compared with ω_0, we may say that Z is little greater than R and that the angle of $\mathbf{Z}$ is small. A further comment on ω_0 is in order. Suppose that we impress a certain voltage E on the circuit and compare the power absorbed at $\omega = 0$ and at $\omega = \omega_0$. At $\omega = 0$ we have $P = E^2/R$. At $\omega = \omega_0$, $(\mathbf{Z}/R) = 1 + j1 = \sqrt{2}\,\exp j\pi/4$, and because the magnitude of the current is E/Z, or $E/\sqrt{2}\,R$, the power works out to be $E^2/2R$. This is just *one half* of the power at zero frequency, therefore ω_0 is often called the *half-power* angular frequency.

If only the *magnitude* of $\mathbf{Z}$ is of interest, the plot in Fig. 2-15b is useful. Here the relation is plotted against linear scales, but such curves are sometimes plotted on log-log scales to permit covering a wider range of frequency values.

The locus diagram and amplitude-frequency curve for $\mathbf{Z}/R$ for a series RC circuit is shown in Fig. 2-16. The diagrams are plotted to follow the relation

$$\frac{\mathbf{Z}}{R} = 1 - \frac{j}{\omega RC} = 1 - j\frac{\omega_0}{\omega} \tag{2-92}$$

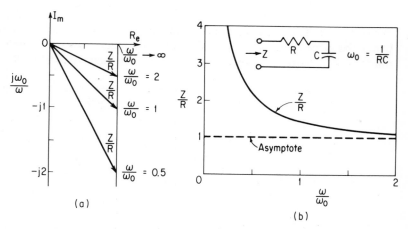

(a)   (b)

FIGURE 2-16   Frequency response of RC circuit.

where the half-power angular frequency has the value $\omega_0 = 1/RC$. In this circuit Z approaches infinity as ω approaches zero, and also Z approaches R as ω approaches infinity.

A series circuit of R, L, and C, similar to that in Fig. 2-11a, deserves further study. Its impedance is

$$\mathbf{Z} = R + j\left(\omega L - \frac{1}{\omega C}\right) \tag{2-93}$$

We introduce the parameters

$$\omega_0 = \frac{1}{\sqrt{LC}} \quad \text{and} \quad Q = \frac{\omega_0 L}{R} = \frac{1}{\omega_0 CR} \tag{2-94}$$

Then Eq. (2-93) can be expressed in the form

$$\frac{\mathbf{Z}}{R} = 1 + jQ\left(\frac{\omega}{\omega_0} - \frac{\omega_0}{\omega}\right) \tag{2-95}$$

If we need the magnitude only, then

$$\frac{Z}{R} = \left[1 + Q^2 \left(\frac{\omega}{\omega_0} - \frac{\omega_0}{\omega} \right)^2 \right]^{\frac{1}{2}} \qquad (2\text{-}96)$$

A comment on the parameter Q is in order. Suppose that the circuit consists of a coil having constants L and R in series with a capacitor C. Then Q is called the *quality factor* of the coil referred to the angular frequency ω_0. As we shall see, a low resistance (high Q) gives the circuit a desirable characteristic.

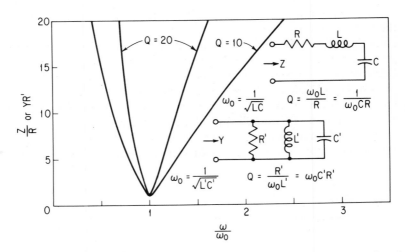

FIGURE 2-17   Illustration of resonance.

Two plots of Z/R as a function of ω/ω_0 are shown in Fig. 2-17 for different Q's. We notice, particularly for $Q = 20$, that the impedance rises rapidly on each side of the frequency ω_0. Therefore, with constant impressed voltage, the current would rise to a sharp maximum at $\omega = \omega_0$ and fall off on either side of this frequency. This phenomenon is known as *series resonance*, and ω_0 is the *resonant angular frequency*. At the resonant condition the inductive and capacitive reactances are equal and cancel each other's effects. Thus, $\omega_0 L = 1/\omega_0 C$, in accord with the definition of ω_0 in Eq. (2-94).

An analogous phenomenon occurs when R', L', and C', are connected in parallel as shown in Fig. 2-17. The admittance of the combination is

$$\mathbf{Y} = \frac{1}{R'} + j \left(\omega C' - \frac{1}{\omega L'} \right) \qquad (2\text{-}97)$$

Here we define

$$\omega_0 = \frac{1}{\sqrt{L'C'}} \quad \text{and} \quad Q = \frac{R'}{\omega_0 L'} = \omega_0 C' R' \qquad (2\text{-}98)$$

Then Eq. (2-97) yields

$$\mathbf{Y}R' = 1 + jQ\left(\frac{\omega}{\omega_0} - \frac{\omega_0}{\omega}\right) \tag{2-99}$$

The magnitude of $\mathbf{Y}R'$ is

$$YR' = \left[1 + Q^2\left(\frac{\omega}{\omega_0} - \frac{\omega_0}{\omega}\right)^2\right]^{\frac{1}{2}} \tag{2-100}$$

Comparison of Eq. (2-100) with Eq. (2-96) will show that the right sides are identical. Therefore, the curves in Fig. 2-17 also serve as curves of YR' versus ω/ω_0. If we recall that $\mathbf{I} = \mathbf{YE}$, we can see that the variation of the total current with constant impressed voltage as the frequency varies is the same as given by the curves in Fig. 2-17. The current is a *minimum* at $\omega = \omega_0$, i.e., at the condition of *parallel resonance*. This characteristic is useful if currents of one particular frequency are to be suppressed or filtered out, and currents of other frequencies are to be allowed to pass more or less undiminished. It is notable that R' should be high to have a high-Q circuit, in contrast to the relation for the series resonant circuit. This will be understandable if we consider that a smaller power is absorbed for a fixed voltage as R' is increased.

Similar parallel resonant effects are obtained when a capacitor and a lossy coil are placed in parallel, but the quantitative relations are different.

2-7
Equivalent circuits

In several examples we have obtained a total or combined impedance, called the *equivalent impedance*, for a group of series- or parallel-connected elements. This can be done for more complex circuits also. The equivalent impedance will, in general, be a function of the frequency, as indicated mathematically

$$\mathbf{Z}_{eq}(\omega) = R_{eq}(\omega) + jX_{eq}(\omega) \tag{2-101}$$

If the frequency is specified, then Eq. (2-101) can be used to specify a *series* connection of R and L, or of R and C, which at the *specified frequency* is equivalent to the more complex network.

As an example, consider a series circuit of $R = 10$ ohms, $L = 1$ henry, and $C = 2 \times 10^{-6}$ farad subjected to a voltage having $\omega = 1000$. Then Eq. (2-93) gives $\mathbf{Z}_{eq} = 10 + j(1000 - 500) = 10 + j500$. The equivalent resistance is $10\ \Omega$ and the equivalent inductance is 500/1000, or 0.5 H. However, if ω had been 100, then the equivalent circuit would have consisted of a resistor and capacitor in series.

A common task is to replace a series combination of two elements, such as R and L or R and C by an equivalent circuit consisting of (different) parallel-connected elements, say R' and L', R' and C'. This can be done by calculating $\mathbf{Y}_{eq} = 1/\mathbf{Z}_{eq}$ and deducing the required circuit elements.

A similar transformation consists in replacing a pair of parallel-connected elements by a pair of equivalent (at the specified frequency) series-connected elements. Formulas can be worked out for these transformations, if desired.

2-8
Mutual inductance; transformers

a. Mutual inductance

When two coils are placed so that the magnetic field of one coil penetrates the turns of a second coil, the two coils are said to be magnetically coupled. A changing current in one coil will induce a voltage in the second coil. If we exclude nonlinear magnetic materials from the field of the coils, we may express the relation between the induced voltage in coil 2 (Fig. 2-18a) and the changing current in coil 1 as follows:

$$e_2 = \pm M \frac{di_1}{dt} \tag{2-102}$$

where M is a constant called the *mutual inductance*. M has the same nature as self-inductance and is measured in henrys.

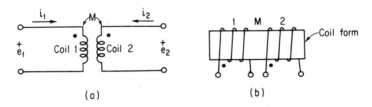

$$(a) \qquad\qquad\qquad (b)$$

FIGURE 2-18   (a) Two magnetically coupled coils. (b) Illustrating the dot convention.

Equation (2-102) is written with a $\pm$ sign to indicate that if M is always taken to be a positive number (sometimes M is treated as algebraic), then it is necessary to choose the proper sign for the induced voltage. The proper sign depends on (a) the choice of positive direction for i_1, (b) the positive sense for e_2, and (c) the relative directions of the two windings. One scheme for keeping account of the winding directions is illustrated in Fig. 2-18. A mark or dot is placed on one terminal of coil 1. Then a dot is placed on a terminal of coil 2 such that if positive current is sent into the two dot terminals, the magnetic fluxes linking the coils will reinforce each other. The coils are said to be *aiding*. If the coils are both wound on the same coil form (Fig. 2-18b), the wire leaving the dot terminals winds around the form in the same direction for both coils. With the dot terminals as marked in Fig. 2-18a, and with the senses for i_1 and e_2 as marked, the sign in Eq. (2-102) will be positive, i.e., $e_2 = +M(di_1/dt)$.

The *coefficient of coupling* k is defined by the following equation:

$$M = k\sqrt{L_1 L_2} \qquad (2\text{-}103)$$

where L_1 and L_2 are the self-inductances of the two coils. If the coils are so tightly coupled that all the flux from one coil also links the second coil, then k has the value unity, and in general k has a value between zero and unity.

The mutual inductance of two coils is the same regardless of which coil carries the varying current. Thus, in Fig. 2-18a we can also write $e_1 = M(di_2/dt)$ for the emf induced in coil 1 by the changing current in coil 2.

b. The transformer

Two magnetically coupled coils (Fig. 2-18a) constitute a transformer. The cores may be nonmagnetic, giving the so-called *air-core* transformer, or may consist of laminated steel sheets, powdered iron alloys, or the like. The linear theory is an approximation when applied to an iron-core transformer. Suppose a transformer is connected between a voltage source and a resistor as shown in Fig. 2-19a. Here R_1 and R_2 represent the resistances of the *primary* and *secondary* coils, respectively. Let us write the differential equations that govern this circuit. Using Kirchhoff's voltage law, first around the primary loop and then around the secondary, we find

$$-e + R_1 i_1 + L_1 \frac{di_1}{dt} - M \frac{di_2}{dt} = 0 \qquad (2\text{-}104)$$

$$(R + R_2)i_2 + L_2 \frac{di_2}{dt} - M \frac{di_1}{dt} = 0 \qquad (2\text{-}105)$$

If the voltage e were specified, we could solve this set of equations to find the resulting currents.

A somewhat different circuit is shown in Fig. 2-19b. Here a sine wave source $\mathbf{E}_s$ is connected to the transformer through an impedance $\mathbf{Z}_s$ and the load impedance is $\mathbf{Z}_L$. Let us investigate the steady-state condition using the phasor technique. Since we are interested in both $\mathbf{E}_s$ and the input voltage $\mathbf{E}_1$, we write two voltage equations for the primary circuit

$$-\mathbf{E}_s + (\mathbf{Z}_s + \mathbf{Z}_1)\mathbf{I}_1 - j\omega M \mathbf{I}_2 = 0 \qquad (2\text{-}106)$$

and

$$-\mathbf{E}_1 + \mathbf{Z}_1 \mathbf{I}_1 - j\omega M \mathbf{I}_2 = 0 \qquad (2\text{-}107)$$

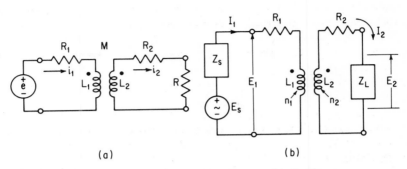

FIGURE 2-19   Circuits utilizing a transformer. (a) Resistance
load. (b) Sinusoidal source and impedance load.

For the secondary loop

$$(\mathbf{Z}_2 + \mathbf{Z}_L)\mathbf{I}_2 - j\omega M \mathbf{I}_1 = 0 \qquad (2\text{-}108)$$

Here $\mathbf{Z}_1 = R_1 + j\omega L_1$, and $\mathbf{Z}_2 = R_2 + j\omega L_2$. If we combine (2-107) and
(2-108) to eliminate $\mathbf{I}_2$, we can find the input impedance at the primary
terminals, with the result

$$\mathbf{Z}_{\text{in}} = \frac{\mathbf{E}_1}{\mathbf{I}_1} = \mathbf{Z}_1 + \frac{\omega^2 M^2}{\mathbf{Z}_2 + \mathbf{Z}_L} \qquad (2\text{-}109)$$

An expression for $\mathbf{I}_2$ in terms of $\mathbf{E}_s$ and the circuit constants can be found by
using Eqs. (2-106) and (2-108)

$$\mathbf{I}_2 = \frac{j\omega M \mathbf{E}_s}{(\mathbf{Z}_s + \mathbf{Z}_1)(\mathbf{Z}_2 + \mathbf{Z}_L) + \omega^2 M^2} \qquad (2\text{-}110)$$

The current ratio $\mathbf{I}_1/\mathbf{I}_2$ is obtained directly from Eq. (2-108)

$$\frac{\mathbf{I}_1}{\mathbf{I}_2} = \frac{\mathbf{Z}_2 + \mathbf{Z}_L}{j\omega M} \qquad (2\text{-}111)$$

To obtain the voltage ratio $\mathbf{E}_1/\mathbf{E}_2$, we first notice that $\mathbf{E}_2 = \mathbf{Z}_L \mathbf{I}_2$, then use
Eqs. (2-107) and (2-108) to find

$$\frac{\mathbf{E}_1}{\mathbf{E}_2} = \frac{(\mathbf{Z}_2 + \mathbf{Z}_L)\mathbf{Z}_1 + \omega^2 M^2}{j\omega M \mathbf{Z}_L} \qquad (2\text{-}112)$$

The foregoing exact formulas are required for calculations on air-core
transformers, but for iron-core transformers the so-called *ideal transformer*
theory, to be given next, is often sufficiently accurate.

c. The ideal transformer

Let the turns be n_1 and n_2 in coils 1 and 2. If we assume that the magnetic
flux in the iron core links both windings, then $L_1 = Cn_1^2$, $L_2 = Cn_2^2$, and
$M = Cn_1 n_2$, where C is a constant. Then we have unity coupling ($k = 1$),

and $M = \sqrt{L_1 L_2}$. Usually, R_1 and R_2 are relatively small, so we assume $R_1 = R_2 = 0$. Using these conditions on Eq. (2-112), we find

$$\frac{\mathbf{E}_1}{\mathbf{E}_2} \simeq \frac{-\omega^2 L_1 L_2 + \omega^2 M^2 + j\omega L_1 \mathbf{Z}_L}{j\omega M \mathbf{Z}_L} \tag{2-113}$$

But $M^2 = L_1 L_2$; therefore,

$$\frac{\mathbf{E}_1}{\mathbf{E}_2} \simeq \frac{L_1}{M} = \frac{Cn_1^2}{Cn_1 n_2} = \frac{n_1}{n_2} \tag{2-114}$$

which says that the terminal voltages are proportional to the turns. Furthermore, if $\mathbf{Z}_2 \gg \mathbf{Z}_L$, we can neglect $\mathbf{Z}_L$ in the numerator of Eq. (2-111); therefore,

$$\frac{\mathbf{I}_1}{\mathbf{I}_2} \simeq \frac{\mathbf{Z}_2}{j\omega M} = \frac{j\omega L_2}{j\omega M} = \frac{Cn_2^2}{Cn_1 n_2} = \frac{n_2}{n_1} \tag{2-115}$$

That is to say, the currents are in the inverse ratio of the numbers of turns.

Finally, we write the input impedance, Eq. (2-109), using a common denominator, and use the conditions for an ideal transformer; thus,

$$\mathbf{Z}_{\text{in}} = \frac{\mathbf{Z}_1(\mathbf{Z}_2 + \mathbf{Z}_L) + \omega^2 M^2}{\mathbf{Z}_2 + \mathbf{Z}_L} = \frac{j\omega L_1 \mathbf{Z}_L}{\mathbf{Z}_2 + \mathbf{Z}_L} \tag{2-116}$$

But we are assuming that $\mathbf{Z}_2 \gg \mathbf{Z}_L$; therefore, we neglect the $\mathbf{Z}_L$ in the denominator of (2-116),

$$\mathbf{Z}_{\text{in}} \simeq \frac{j\omega L_1 \mathbf{Z}_L}{j\omega L_2} = \frac{L_1}{L_2}\mathbf{Z}_L = \frac{n_1^2}{n_2^2}\mathbf{Z}_L \tag{2-117}$$

Thus, a load impedance of $\mathbf{Z}_L$ connected to the secondary terminals is transformed into an equivalent impedance, of value $(n_1^2/n_2^2)\mathbf{Z}_L$, at the input terminals.

Audiofrequency transformers for electronic circuits are often specified in terms of the impedance values on the two sides of the transformer. Thus, a transformer stated as an 8000/8-Ω transformer could satisfactorily transform an 8-Ω load into an 8000-Ω impedance at the primary terminals. From Eq. (2-117) we see that in this example $n_1^2/n_2^2 = 1000$, so the turn ratio would be $\sqrt{1000}$, or 31.6. To satisfy the assumptions for the ideal transformer it would be required that $\omega L_2 \gg 8$, $R_2 \ll 8$, and $R_1 \ll 8000\ \Omega$.

2-9

Attenuation and phase characteristics of simple two-terminal-pair networks; the decibel

The signals transmitted through devices such as amplifiers, attenuators, transformers, and the like are often steady sinusoidal voltages. The voltage may be amplified or attenuated, or the wave may suffer a phase shift. The frequency variations of the voltage attenuation and of the phase shift through such devices can be studied by means of equivalent circuits, so it will be worth-while to examine these variations for some elementary circuits. In each circuit we designate two terminals as the *input* termi-nals and two terminals as the *output* terminals. Such a circuit is called a *two-terminal-pair* net-work. The characteristics which are developed here will aid our study of amplifiers and of servomechanisms.

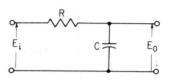

FIGURE 2-20 Low-pass filter circuit.

Consider first the series *RC* circuit in Fig. 2-20. A sinusoidal voltage $\mathbf{E}_i$ of frequency ω is impressed on the input terminals, and we are concerned with the output voltage $\mathbf{E}_o$ under the assumption that no additional elements are connected across the output terminals. The phasor methods of the foregoing articles may be used to calculate $\mathbf{E}_o/\mathbf{E}_i$, with the result

$$\mathbf{G}(j\omega) = \frac{\mathbf{E}_o}{\mathbf{E}_i} = \frac{1}{1 + j\omega RC} \qquad (2\text{-}118)$$

This equation also defines the complex *attenuation* (or *gain*) $\mathbf{G}(j\omega)$. If we replace RC by the parameter $1/\omega_1$, then

$$\mathbf{G}(j\omega) = \frac{1}{1 + j\dfrac{\omega}{\omega_1}} = M \exp j\theta \qquad (2\text{-}119)$$

Here the ratio is expressed in terms of the magnitude of the ratio M and the phase angle θ. Another name for the complex voltage ratio is the *voltage transfer function*.

Before examining the effect of frequency on the transfer function of a circuit we introduce the concept of a voltage ratio expressed in *decibels*. Basically, a *decibel* (dB) is a unit of measure for the ratio of two powers and is *defined* by the equation

$$dB = 10 \log_{10} \frac{P_2}{P_1} \qquad (2\text{-}120)$$

If P_1 is due to a voltage V_1 across a resistor R_1, and P_2 due to V_2 across R_2, then (2-120) becomes

$$dB = 10 \log_{10} \frac{V_2^2 R_1}{R_2 V_1^2} \qquad (2\text{-}121)$$

If we assume $R_1 = R_2$, then

$$dBv = 10 \log_{10} \left(\frac{V_2}{V_1}\right)^2 = 20 \log_{10} \frac{V_2}{V_1} \qquad (2\text{-}122)$$

It is customary to use Eq. (2-122) as the *definition* of the decibel measure of a voltage ratio, regardless of the value of the resistances across the two pairs of terminals.

When we are concerned with a wide range of frequencies, it is advantageous to plot the magnitude of $\mathbf{G}(j\omega)$ in decibels against the log of ω or the log of ω/ω_1. This then is actually a log-log plot. For the circuit in Fig. 2-20 we find the value of M from Eq. (2-119); thus,

$$M = \frac{1}{\left[1 + \left(\frac{\omega}{\omega_1}\right)^2\right]^{\frac{1}{2}}} \tag{2-123}$$

The log magnitude plot for this function is shown in Fig. 2-21. At low frequencies, such that $\omega \ll \omega_1$, we see from (2-123) that M approaches unity, and the decibel value approaches zero asymptotically. At high frequencies, where $\omega \gg \omega_1$, we can discard unity in the denominator of (2-123), so that M approaches $1/(\omega/\omega_1)$. Expressed in decibels, this leads to

$$\mathrm{dBv} = 20\log_{10}M \cong -20\log_{10}\frac{\omega}{\omega_1} \tag{2-124}$$

This equation shows that if ω/ω_1 increases by a factor of 10, then dBv changes by the amount -20 dB. The transfer function is said to be falling at the rate of 20 *decibels per decade* (of frequency ratio). Thus, the function approaches this slope asymptotically, as seen in Fig. 2-21.

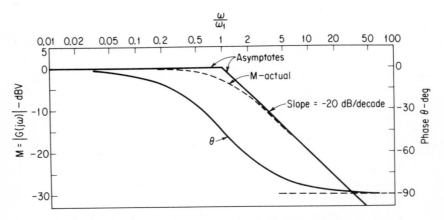

FIGURE 2-21   Attenuation and phase plots for low-pass filter.

When the two asymptotes are extended, we find that they intersect at $\omega = \omega_1$, i.e., at a frequency called the *corner frequency*, which therefore has the value

$$f_1 = \frac{\omega_1}{2\pi} = \frac{1}{2\pi RC} \tag{2-125}$$

The radian frequency ω_1 is the same as the *half-power angular frequency* for this circuit defined in Sec. 2-6.

The advantage of the frequency plot in Fig. 2-21 is that the straightline asymptotes may easily be located with only a knowledge of ω_1. For some purposes the attenuation values taken from the asymptotes may be accurate enough. In the neighborhood of the corner frequency more accurate values may be needed. Corrections to apply to the asymptotes can be calculated by means of Eq. (2-123), with the following results:

value of ω/ω_1	0.2	0.5	1	2	5
correction to asymptotic value of M (dBv)	-0.17	-0.97	-3.0	-0.97	-0.17

When the phase shift θ is calculated by Eq. (2-119) and plotted, we obtain the curve in Fig. 2-21. The phase shifts are negative, which means that $\mathbf{E}_o$ lags $\mathbf{E}_i$. For this reason the circuit is called a *lag* circuit in servomechanism practice. The circuit may also be regarded as a *low-pass filter*, since the higher frequencies are attenuated, while the lower frequencies are transmitted without attenuation.

If the series RC circuit is rearranged so that the output voltage is taken across the resistor, then the attenuation and phase characteristics shown in Fig. 2-22 are obtained. The voltage transfer function has the form

$$\mathbf{G}(j\omega) = \frac{R}{R + \dfrac{1}{j\omega C}} = \frac{j\omega RC}{1 + j\omega RC} \qquad (2\text{-}126)$$

We introduce ω_1 to replace $1/RC$ and obtain

$$\mathbf{G}(j\omega) = \frac{j\dfrac{\omega}{\omega_1}}{1 + j\dfrac{\omega}{\omega_1}} = M \exp j\theta \qquad (2\text{-}127)$$

As Fig. 2-22 shows, the low frequencies are attenuated; therefore, the circuit acts as a *high-pass filter*. Furthermore, the phase of the output voltage is

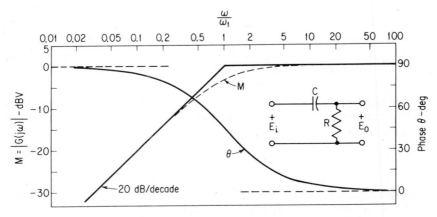

FIGURE 2-22   Attenuation and phase plots for high-pass filter.

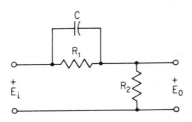

FIGURE 2-23   Phase lead circuit.

advanced relative to the input signal, so that the circuit may also be called a *phase lead* network.

The modified phase lead network shown in Fig. 2-23 finds application in some servo systems. The transfer function for this network can be put into the form

$$G(j\omega) = \left(\frac{R_2}{R_1 + R_2}\right)\left(\frac{1 + j\omega CR_1}{1 + \dfrac{j\omega CR_1 R_2}{R_1 + R_2}}\right) \tag{2-128}$$

We define the new parameters α and ω_1 as follows;

$$\alpha = \frac{R_2}{R_1 + R_2} \quad \text{and} \quad \omega_1 = \frac{1}{CR_1} \tag{2-129}$$

Then (2-128) may be written

$$G(j\omega) = \alpha\frac{1 + j\dfrac{\omega}{\omega_1}}{1 + j\dfrac{\alpha\omega}{\omega_1}} \tag{2-130}$$

A rapid method of plotting this function is obtained by an extension of the ideas developed for the RC series circuit. First we express the complex terms in (2-130) in polar form thus

$$G(j\omega) = \alpha\frac{M_1 \exp j\theta_1}{M_2 \exp j\theta_2} = \alpha\frac{M_1}{M_2} \exp j(\theta_1 - \theta_2) \tag{2-131}$$

Here α is real and independent of ω, but M_1 and M_2 are functions of ω. To express the magnitude of $G(j\omega)$ in decibels, we note that

$$\text{dBv} = 20 \log_{10} \alpha + 20 \log_{10} M_1 - 20 \log_{10} M_2 \tag{2-132}$$

That is to say, the magnitude in decibels of the right side of Eq. (2-130) can be obtained by adding (algebraically) the decibel value of each of the three component factors. Furthermore, Eq. (2-131) shows that the phase angle is the difference of the angles contributed by the complex factors.

A study of the complex factors in Eq. (2-130) will show that each factor can be analyzed by means of two asymptotes, one for low frequencies and one for high frequencies. The term in the numerator has a corner frequency of ω_1 and above this frequency has a rising asymptote that rises at the rate of 20 dB per decade. The term in the denominator has a corner frequency of ω_1/α. The total decibel value of the magnitude is found by adding the three decibel components at each frequency. The resultant curve obtained by this technique for a value of $\alpha = 0.2$ is shown in Fig. 2-24. At very low frequencies the attenuation is -14 dBv, since the voltage ratio is α, and $20 \log_{10} 0.2 =$

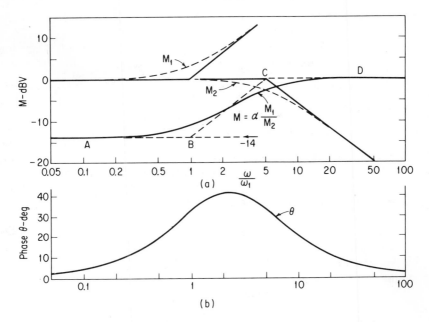

FIGURE 2-24   Attenuation and phase curves for phase lead circuit in Fig. 2-23, drawn for $\alpha = 0.2$.

—14. At high frequencies the voltage ratio approaches unity, or zero decibels. The linear approximation to this function is the broken straight-line curve *ABCD*.

The phase of the transfer function can likewise be obtained from the phase shifts of the component terms as indicated in Eq. (2-131). The resultant curve (Fig. 2-24) shows that the phase advance goes through a broad maximum in the region between the two corner frequencies.

2-10
Parameters and equivalent circuits for a linear, two-terminal-pair network

In electronic applications we are often concerned with the effect of inserting a two-terminal-pair network, an amplifier for example, between a signal source and a load. In this situation we can make use of the formal theory†

†E. A. Guillemin, *Communication Networks*, John Wiley & Sons, Inc., New York, 1935, vol. 2, pp. 132 ff.

for this type of network. This theory is particularly useful in dealing with circuits involving transistors.

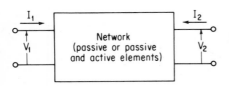

FIGURE 2-25 General two-terminal-pair network.

A generalized circuit is shown in Fig. 2-25 which defines the four variables, two currents and two voltages, to be used in the discussion. These are regarded as phasors representing sinusoidal quantities, though the resulting equations can be applied to instantaneous values if reactive elements are absent or negligible. We note that the current direction for I_2 is chosen toward the network so as to yield symmetrical equations.

Any pair of variables may be regarded as the *dependent* variables, and since the system is assumed to be *linear*, these variables can be related to the other variables by a pair of linear equations. Thus, there are six possible sets of equations, but we shall deal briefly with only the three more useful sets.

When V_1 and V_2 are taken as the dependent variables, the *z parameters* are the coefficients on the right sides, as in the following equations:

$$V_1 = z_i I_1 + z_r I_2 \qquad (2\text{-}133)$$

$$V_2 = z_f I_1 + z_o I_2 \qquad (2\text{-}134)$$

The z's can be interpreted in terms of measurements made on the network with either the input or output open-circuited. For example, if the output terminals are open-circuited so that $I_2 = 0$, then $z_i = V_1/I_1$. In general, then, the z's are complex quantities that have the dimensions of impedance.†

When I_1 and I_2 are taken as the dependent variables, then the network equations involve the *y parameters;* thus

$$I_1 = y_i V_1 + y_r V_2 \qquad (2\text{-}135)$$

$$I_2 = y_f V_1 + y_o V_2 \qquad (2\text{-}136)$$

The y parameters are called the *short-circuit* parameters. For example, if the output is short-circuited, then $y_i = I_1/V_1$ because $V_2 = 0$. Further, $y_r = I_1/V_2$ with $V_1 = 0$, and is a short-circuit transfer admittance.

Equivalent circuits can readily be devised that will conform to the basic equations, as shown in Fig. 2-26. These circuits include *current-controlled* ideal voltage generators as in Fig. 2-26a, or *voltage-controlled* ideal current generators (Fig. 2-26b). An alternative equivalent circuit involving the z

---

†In general circuit studies a different set of subscripts is used on the network parameters, as follows: $z_i = z_{11}, z_r = z_{12}, z_f = z_{21},$ and $z_o = z_{22}$. The letter subscripts have an advantage in electronic work in that i refers to *input*, r refers to a *reverse* transfer effect, f to a *forward* transfer effect, and o to *output*.

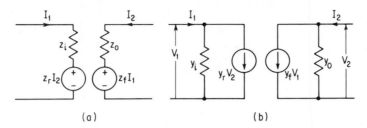

FIGURE 2-26 Equivalent circuits using (a) z parameters and (b) y parameters.

parameters is shown in Fig. 2-27. This circuit has the so-called *equivalent-T* form and involves only one generator. This form will be used in the low-frequency analysis of transistor circuits.

In *passive* networks, i.e., those containing only resistance, capacitance, inductance, and mutual inductance, the transfer impedances are equal $(\mathbf{z}_r = \mathbf{z}_f)$. As a result the generator voltage in Fig. 2-27 is zero for a passive network. In an *active* network, i.e., one which contains one or more controlled sources of energy at the signal frequency, generally,

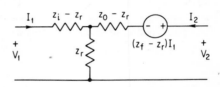

FIGURE 2-27 Equivalent-T circuit in terms of z parameters.

$\mathbf{z}_r \neq \mathbf{z}_f$, so the generator in Fig. 2-27 would represent the controlled source.

In transistor circuit analysis a third set of network equations has proved useful. In this set $\mathbf{V}_1$ and $\mathbf{I}_2$ are taken as the dependent variables. Thus, a mixed, or *hybrid*, set of equations is used

$$\mathbf{V}_1 = \mathbf{h}_i \mathbf{I}_1 + \mathbf{h}_r \mathbf{V}_2 \tag{2-137}$$

$$\mathbf{I}_2 = \mathbf{h}_f \mathbf{I}_1 + \mathbf{h}_o \mathbf{V}_2 \tag{2-138}$$

It may be worthwhile to define the h parameters in detail, as follows;

$$\mathbf{h}_i = \left(\frac{\mathbf{V}_1}{\mathbf{I}_1}\right)_{V_2=0} = \text{input impedance with short-circuited output} \tag{2-139}$$

$$\mathbf{h}_r = \left(\frac{\mathbf{V}_1}{\mathbf{V}_2}\right)_{I_1=0} = \text{reverse voltage ratio with open-circuited input} \tag{2-140}$$

$$\mathbf{h}_f = \left(\frac{\mathbf{I}_2}{\mathbf{I}_1}\right)_{V_2=0} = \text{forward current ratio with short-circuited output} \tag{2-141}$$

$$\mathbf{h}_o = \left(\frac{\mathbf{I}_2}{\mathbf{V}_2}\right)_{I_1=0} = \text{the output admittance with open-circuited input} \tag{2-142}$$

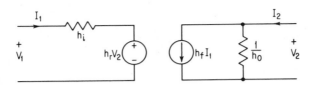

FIGURE 2-28   Equivalent circuit based on h parameters.

We see that $\mathbf{h}_i$ is an impedance, $\mathbf{h}_o$ an admittance, and that $\mathbf{h}_r$ and $\mathbf{h}_f$ are dimensionless ratios. An equivalent circuit that conforms to the basic equations is that in Fig. 2-28. When this circuit is applied to the study of a transistor, we shall find that the current generator provides the amplifying effect and the voltage generator represents a small inherent feedback in the device.

We now have three sets of parameters that can characterize a particular device or circuit. We expect that these parameters are dependent on one another, so that if one set is known, any of the others can be calculated, and this is indeed true. Relationships among the parameters are listed in Appendix C. These are useful, for example, when it is preferable to measure the parameters of one set but to use another in network calculations.

2-11
Network properties in terms of network parameters

Let us discuss a general two-terminal-pair network driven by a signal voltage $\mathbf{V}_s$ through a source impedance $\mathbf{Z}_s$ and terminated in a load impedance $\mathbf{Z}_L$ (Fig. 2-29). A typical example of such a system is a transistor amplifier. It is useful to derive formulas for such quantities as voltage and current ratios or gains and input and output impedances for this system in terms of the various parameters. We define the current gain $\mathbf{A}_i$ as $\mathbf{I}_2/\mathbf{I}_1$ and the voltage gain $\mathbf{A}_v$ as $\mathbf{V}_2/\mathbf{V}_1$. Also let $\mathbf{Z}_i$ denote the input impedance and $\mathbf{Z}_o$ the output (Thévenin) impedance.

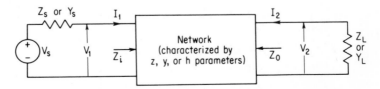

FIGURE 2-29   System comprising signal source, network, and load.

We shall list the formulas for these quantities (without proof) in terms of the parameters and certain determinants defined by

$$\Delta_z = \mathbf{z}_i\mathbf{z}_o - \mathbf{z}_r\mathbf{z}_f \quad \Delta_y = \mathbf{y}_i\mathbf{y}_o - \mathbf{y}_r\mathbf{y}_f \quad \Delta_h = \mathbf{h}_i\mathbf{h}_o - \mathbf{h}_r\mathbf{h}_f \qquad (2\text{-}143)$$

Then the impedances and gains may be written as follows:

$$\mathbf{Z}_i = \frac{\Delta_z + \mathbf{z}_i\mathbf{Z}_L}{\mathbf{z}_0 + \mathbf{Z}_L} = \frac{\mathbf{y}_o + \mathbf{Y}_L}{\Delta_y + \mathbf{y}_i\mathbf{Y}_L} = \frac{\Delta_h + \mathbf{h}_i\mathbf{Y}_L}{\mathbf{h}_o + \mathbf{Y}_L} \qquad (2\text{-}144)$$

$$\mathbf{Z}_o = \frac{\Delta_z + \mathbf{z}_o\mathbf{Z}_s}{\mathbf{z}_i + \mathbf{Z}_s} = \frac{\mathbf{y}_i + \mathbf{Y}_s}{\Delta_y + \mathbf{y}_o\mathbf{Y}_s} = \frac{\mathbf{h}_i + \mathbf{Z}_s}{\Delta_h + \mathbf{h}_o\mathbf{Z}_s} \qquad (2\text{-}145)$$

$$\mathbf{A}_i = \frac{-\mathbf{z}_f}{\mathbf{z}_0 + \mathbf{Z}_L} = \frac{\mathbf{y}_f\mathbf{Y}_L}{\Delta_y + \mathbf{y}_i\mathbf{Y}_L} = \frac{\mathbf{h}_f}{1 + \mathbf{h}_o\mathbf{Z}_L} \qquad (2\text{-}146)$$

$$\mathbf{A}_v = \frac{\mathbf{z}_o\mathbf{Z}_L}{\Delta_z + \mathbf{z}_i\mathbf{Z}_L} = \frac{-\mathbf{y}_f}{\mathbf{y}_o + \mathbf{Y}_L} = \frac{-\mathbf{h}_f}{\Delta_h + \mathbf{h}_i\mathbf{Y}_L} \qquad (2\text{-}147)$$

The choice of the kind of parameters to use in a particular situation depends on the type of circuit. The *h* parameters are more readily measured for transistors, and calculations on transistor circuits are often conveniently made using the hybrid parameters.

REFERENCES

2-1 J. A. Edminister, *Theory and Problems of Electric Circuits*, Schaum Publishing Co., New York, 1965.

2-2 A. E. Fitzgerald and D. E. Higginbotham, *Basic Electrical Engineering*, 2d ed., McGraw-Hill Book Company, New York, 1957, Chaps. 1–5, 7.

2-3 H. H. Skilling, *Electrical Engineering Circuits*, 2d ed., John Wiley & Sons, Inc., New York, 1965.

2-4 J. L. Studer, *Electronic Circuits and Instrumentation Systems*, John Wiley & Sons, Inc., New York, 1963, Chaps. 1–6.

EXERCISES

2-1 Express the following in polar $(A\underline{/\alpha})$ form: (a) $4 + j3$, (b) $-1 + j3$, and (c) $8 \exp j\pi/6$.

2-2 Express the following in rectangular $(x + jy)$ form: (a) $8 \exp j\pi/6$, (b) $5\underline{/53.1°}$, and (c) $5(\exp j\pi/4)\,(10\underline{/90°})$.

2-3 (a) Rationalize the quantity $1/(4 - j3)$ by multiplying numerator and denominator by the complex conjugate of $4 - j3$. (b) Rationalize the same quantity by converting the denominator to polar form, taking the reciprocal and then converting to rectangular form.

2-4 Reduce the quantity $(2 + j2)/(4 + j3)$ to the form $x + jy$ in part by the method of Prob. 2-3a or 2-3b. Which is the faster method?

2-5 Assume that the sinusoidal voltages e_1 and e_2 in Fig. 2-30 take on the pairs of values given in parts (a) and (b) below. Find e_3 and express it as a single sinusoidal quantity. *Suggestion*: Use the phasor method.
(a)　$e_1 = 10 \sin \omega t$, $e_2 = 5 \cos \omega t$.
(b)　$e_1 = 10 \cos (\omega t + 60°)$, $e_2 = 8 \cos (\omega t - 30°)$.

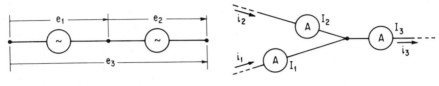

FIGURE 2-30　　　　　　　　　　　　　　　FIGURE 2-31

2-6 The currents i_1, i_2, and i_3 in Fig. 2-31 are harmonic waves of the same frequency. The ammeter readings are: $I_1 = 2.6$ A rms, $I_2 = 3.9$ A rms, and $I_3 = 5.3$ A rms. Taking i_1 as the reference for phase, what are the phase angles of i_2 and i_3? List all possibilities.

2-7 A phasor voltage expressed as $\mathbf{E} = 10 + j17.32$ V is impressed on a circuit and the resulting phasor current is $\mathbf{I} = 4 + j3$ A. These are rms values. Find (a) the average power delivered to the circuit, and (b) the complex circuit impedance.

2-8 A series circuit comprises $R = 80\ \Omega$, $L = 12$ mH, and $C = 0.5\ \mu$F. What is the impedance $\mathbf{Z}$ if $\omega = 2\pi f = 10^4$?

2-9 A servo motor has a control winding that has an impedance of $100 + j150\ \Omega$ at a frequency of 400 Hz. It is required that this winding be tuned by means of a shunt capacitor (see Fig. 2-32) so as to present a resistive load, without a reactive component, to an amplifier. (a) Find the value of C required. (b) What is the equivalent resistance of the combination?

2-10 Consider a series circuit comprising $R = 5\ \Omega$, $L = 0.1$ H, and $C = 10\ \mu$F. This circuit is energized by an ac source having a constant voltage but a variable radian frequency ω. As ω is varied, the current will vary as shown in Fig. 2-33

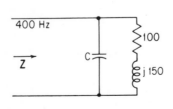

FIGURE 2-32

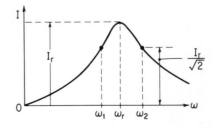

FIGURE 2-33

and will reach the maximum I_r at the resonant frequency ω_r. The radian frequencies ω_1 and ω_2 are defined to be the values for which $I = I_r/\sqrt{2}$. These are called the *half-power* frequencies. Calculate (a) ω_r, (b) ω_1, (c) ω_2, and (d) $\Delta\omega/\omega_r$ where $\Delta\omega = \omega_2 - \omega_1$. Optional: Show that $\Delta\omega/\omega_r = R/\omega_r L$.

2-11 The circuit in Fig. 2-34 is used to obtain a voltage E_x that is shifted in phase with respect to E_s. Assume that $\omega = 10^4$. Find the phase of E_x, with E_s as the reference, for values of R equal to (a) 1 $k\Omega$, (b) 10 $k\Omega$, and (c) 40 $k\Omega$. Also find the magnitude of E_x as a fraction of E_s.

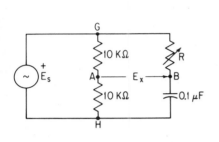

FIGURE 2-34   FIGURE 2-35   Compensated voltage
                            divider.

2-12 We require a low-pass filter that has a corner frequency of 10^4 rad/sec. (a) If the capacitor has a value of 0.1 μF, what value of R should be used? (b) What is the magnitude of the attenuation when $\omega = 10^6$ rad/s? Express in dBv and as a ratio.

2-13 Let the phase-lead network in Fig. 2-23 have the parameter values $R_1 = 10^4 \ \Omega$, $C = 0.1 \ \mu$F, and $R_2 = 10^3 \ \Omega$. (a) Sketch an approximate log-magnitude (in dB) versus log of angular frequency characteristic using the "corner frequency and asymptote" method. (b) Estimate the maximum angle of phase lead provided by this circuit.

2-14 An equivalent circuit of a compensated voltage divider is shown in Fig. 2-35. When this network is used at the input of a CR oscilloscope it reduces the loading on the circuit being tested and has other desirable attributes. In this application the $R_1 C_1$ combination is contained in a probe at the end of a shielded test cable, and R_2 and C_2 represent the input impedance of the CRO amplifier plus the effect of the cable capacitance. (a) Show that if $R_1 C_1 = R_2 C_2$, the voltage E_2 will be in phase with E_1 and that E_2/E_1 will be independent of the frequency of a harmonic test signal. (b) If $R_2 = 10^6 \ \Omega$ and $C_2 = 50$ pF, choose values for R_1 and C_1 to give $E_2/E_1 = 0.1$.

2-15 Verify the portions of (a) Eqs. (2-144), (b) (2-145), (c) (2-146), and (d) (2-147) expressed in terms of the h parameters. *Suggestion*: Insert the equivalent circuit based on the h parameters into Fig. 2-29 and solve the resulting network for the required ratios.

2-16 Repeat Exercise 2-15, except verify the z parameter formulas.

3

Thermionic and Semiconductor Diodes

3-1
Introduction

For the purposes of this book the term *electronics* means the area of study concerned with semiconductor devices and vacuum and gaseous tubes and with systems employing such devices, particularly those systems useful in the fields of measurement, control, and data processing. This field of applications is so broad that we must restrict ourselves to basic principles and to illustrative applications. Whereas most basic relations will be developed in detail, some will be presented without proof in the interest of economy of time and space. In the main, the treatment will be quantitative, but a qualitative study must suffice for some topics.

3-2
Devices and circuits

The study of an electronic device can be based on an investigation of the internal physical action of the device, or merely on the external characteristics that can be established in the laboratory. However, enough of the internal physical action should be understood so that the external characteristics become more meaningful and so that the limitations of the device are better appreciated.

In some applications we have a choice of several different devices which

56

may be used in the same circuit. In such situations we need study only one device in this circuit and point out what modifications in the analysis are required when a different device is used.

Our circuit studies will begin with circuits involving two element tubes and semiconductor diodes and then proceed to those using three-element and multielement devices. The basic electronic circuits, namely, amplifiers, oscillators, modulators, detectors, wave-shaping and data-processing circuits will be discussed next. Then some electronic systems which combine these basic circuits will be described. Thus we need to know how the basic circuits behave with different input signals and also with various loads.

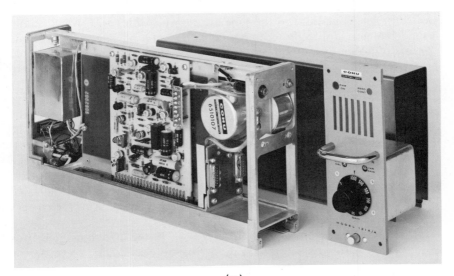

(a)

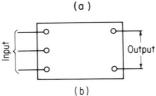

(b)

FIGURE 3-1 (a)   Differential amplifier (Courtesy of Cohu Electronics, Inc.). (b) Block diagram symbol.

When a complex electronic system is under study, it is advantageous to use a highly symbolic representation of the actual basic component circuits. For example, the differential amplifier shown in Fig. 3-1a will be represented in a diagram by the rectangle shown in Fig. 3-1b, with no indication of the internal circuit details. However, only after a study of representative electronic devices and the details of the basic electronic circuits can we safely analyze complex electronic systems by means of diagrams which utilize a *block diagram* representation such as in Fig. 3-1b.

3-3
The thermionic diode

The high-vacuum thermionic diode consists of a hot cathode and a cold anode or plate placed in a highly evacuated glass or metal tube. The function of the cathode is to give off electrons and that of the anode is to collect the electrons. The conditions in the tube are shown in Fig. 3-2a, which shows a diode connected directly to an anode battery of voltage E_b. The cathode consists of a thin metal tube heated by means of current-carrying insulated heater wires within the tube. The tube reaches a temperature high enough to give off a generous supply of electrons.

In Fig. 3-2a the anode battery serves to charge the anode with positive electrostatic charges. These tend to attract the negative electrons from the cathode. Consequently, the electrons stream through the vacuum to the anode, enter the anode, and then drift around the circuit in a clockwise direction under the influence of the anode battery. However, the conventional positive direction of currents is the direction in which positive charges tend to flow, so that the current $+I_b$ has a counterclockwise direction as indicated in Fig. 3-2a. For convenience we refer to the complete path of the current I_b as the *anode circuit* or *plate circuit*.

The plate current of the diode always flows in the direction shown, for if the anode battery is reversed (Fig. 3-2b), the electrostatic force on the

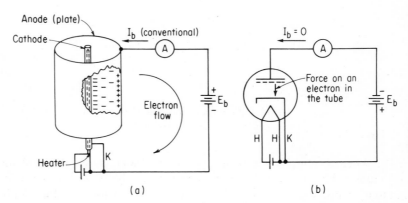

FIGURE 3-2   (a) Thermionic diode in test circuit. (b) No current flows with reversed anode battery.

electrons is reversed and no electrons can move through the tube. The tube acts as an insulator in one direction and as a conductor in the other. In terms of the analogous hydraulic circuit we may liken the diode to a check valve which allows a flow in one direction but not in the other. Thus it has the properties that permit the rectification of alternating current, i.e., the conversion of alternating current into direct current. One of the simplest, but also important, applications of both thermionic and semiconductor diodes is in rectifier circuits (see Chapter 12).

As the voltage impressed across a diode (E_b in Fig. 3-2a) varies, the current through the diode varies also, as shown by the curves in Fig. 3-3. These curves are called the *plate characteristic curves* of the tube. Over certain ranges of voltage the current depends to a large extent on the temperature of the cathode as indicated in the figure, and over other ranges the temperature has a

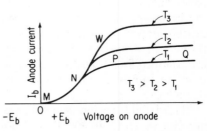

FIGURE 3-3   Diode characteristic curves. T = cathode temperature.

minor effect. Where the curve is nearly flat, as from P to Q, the current is said to be *saturated* or *temperature-limited*. Over the curving region, as from M to N for cathode temperature T_1, or from M to W for T_3, the current is controlled by the density of the electron cloud between the electrodes of the tube and is said to be *space-charge*-controlled. The nature of the control of the current by the effect of space charge is discussed in Sec. 3-5.

3-4
Electron emission; practical cathodes

Hot-cathode tubes are nearly always operated in the space-charge-controlled region of their characteristics. Therefore the cathode temperature must be kept high enough, and the cathode must have suitable properties to avoid danger of inadequate electron emission during the life of the tube.

Besides the temperature, the work required to remove an electron from the surface, called the *work function*, primarily determines the emission current. The Richardson-Dushman equation, which has a theoretical basis but is presented here as an empirical relation, describes the emission current

$$I_{\mathrm{Th}} = SAT^2 \exp \left(\frac{-E_W}{E_T} \right) \tag{3-1}$$

Here I_{Th} is the emission current, S is the area of the cathode, A is an empirical constant, T is the temperature in degrees Kelvin, E_W is the work function in electron volts,† and E_T is the equivalent of T in electron volts, that is, $E_T = T/11,600$.

Three kinds of cathode materials are in common use. The most common is the *oxide-coated* cathode, typically produced by coating a nickel sleeve or tube with a mixture of barium and strontium oxides. After undergoing suitable heat treatment and an activation process, this surface will emit copiously at 1000°K, which is a dull red heat. The common low-voltage electron tubes contain this type of cathode. In high-voltage-diode rectifier tubes the cathode may consist of a filament of pure tungsten wire. This requires an operating temperature of 2500°K and consequently a considerable heating power to maintain this temperature. The third kind of cathode is the thoriated-tungsten filament in which a thorium layer of one atom depth is developed on a tungsten base. This combination has a lower work function than pure tungsten and will emit satisfactorily at 2000°K, which is at a yellow-white heat.

Thoriated tungsten filaments are used in high-power tubes which operate at voltages up to 10,000 V, and pure tungsten is used in this range and at higher voltages.

A measure of the power needed to heat the cathode is the so-called *cathode efficiency*. This is the ratio of emission current to heating power, usually in milliamperes per watt. Though these values vary considerably, typical values are given in Table 3-1.‡

Table 3-1

Cathode	Constant A, A/cm² °K²	E_w, eV	Operating temp., °K	Cathode efficiency, mA/W
Oxide-coated	0.01–0.05	1.0–1.5	1000	270
Thoriated tungsten	3.0	2.62	2000	100
Tungsten	72	4.52	2500	6

As already stated, oxide-coated cathodes are often tubular and may have a circular or flat-sided oval cross section. The tube is heated by an internal resistance wire, which is insulated from the tube by a refractory material like magnesium oxide. Because this insulation will withstand up to 200 or 300 V, in some applications the *heater* may be at a different potential than the cathode. The construction described, which produces a separately

†The electron volt (eV) is a unit of energy equal to 1.6×10^{-19} joules(J). Thus an energy of W J becomes $W/1.6 \times 10^{-19}$ eV.

‡Data from Karl R. Spangenberg, *Fundamentals of Electron Devices*, McGraw-Hill Book Company, New York, 1957, pp. 140, 154.

heated *unipotential* cathode, has an important advantage over a filamentary cathode. This is due to the absence of the disturbing signal that is introduced when a filament is heated with alternating current.

3-5
Space-charge relations in the diode

When the current is space-charge-limited, we infer that the hot cathode is emitting more electrons than actually reach the anode but that the electrostatic repulsive action of the electrons in transit serves to control the current. The internal conditions for an ideal diode assumed to have parallel plate electrodes is shown in various states of conduction in Fig. 3-4. In each part

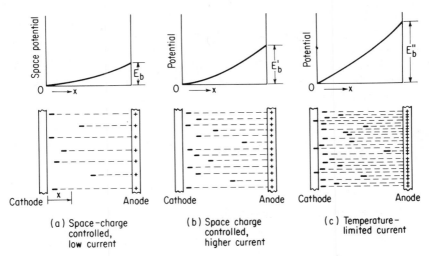

(a) Space-charge controlled, low current

(b) Space charge controlled, higher current

(c) Temperature-limited current

FIGURE 3-4   Conditions in the parallel plate diode.

of the figure the lower diagram shows the electrostatic charges on the electrodes and of the electrons in transit, and the upper part shows how the electrostatic potential (referred to the cathode as zero potential) varies for points between the electrodes. The concept of lines of force extending between charges of opposite sign is helpful here; hence, these have been drawn as dotted lines. In Fig. 3-4a the anode voltage is low, as shown by E_b, and the flow of electrons is small. In Fig. 3-4b the anode voltage has been increased to E'_b, with the result that there is a greater number of electrons between the electrodes at any instant. Furthermore, these electrons are moving more rapidly than in Fig. 3-4a because of the higher forces in the field. The combined effect of the greater numbers of electrons and their higher velocities increases the current.

The reader will observe that in both Fig. 3-4a and 3-4b the positive charges on the anode are exactly balanced by the electronic space charge. In the rather idealized situation pictured, the electric field strength (equal to the rate of change of potential with distance) at the cathode surface is zero and the electric force on the electrons emerging from the cathode will be zero. How, then, can there be any current? We recall that current density is equal to volume density of charge times the drift velocity. Since we assumed a very large available charge density of electrons at the cathode surface, an electric force approaching zero can still give rise to a finite current. In actuality, the situation is complicated by the fact that the electrons are emitted with a distribution of initial velocities. These have the effect of lowering the potential curve near the cathode and of causing a point of zero field strength slightly to the right of the cathode surface.

When the anode voltage is increased to the point where saturation begins, the conditions are as shown in Fig. 3-4c. Here a few lines of force end on electrostatic charges on the cathode, so that there is a field of force urging the electrons toward the anode at all points in the gap. A further increase of anode voltage will not increase the current appreciably but will increase the electron velocities and reduce the number present in the gap at any instant.

The following theoretical relation, called the Langmuir-Child law, holds for the space-charge-limited current under the assumption of zero initial electron velocities

$$I = 2.33 \times 10^{-6} \frac{A E_b^{3/2}}{d^2} \tag{3-2}$$

where A is the cathode area, d the gap, I the current in amperes, and E_b the anode voltage in volts. The units for A and d may be either meters or centimeters. The effect of the gap width is important when the tube voltage required to force a certain current through the tube is considered. For example, if the gap is made three times as large, it will require $9^{2/3}$, or 4.33, times the voltage for the same current. Therefore the anode-cathode spacing is made as small as the other requirements will allow.

3-6
The gas-filled thermionic diode

When an inert gas or mercury vapor is introduced at a pressure of about 1/1000th of an atmosphere into a thermionic diode, a profound change in the voltage-current characteristic results. The gas diode has a nearly

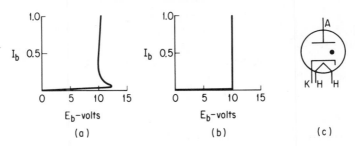

FIGURE 3-5   Characteristics and symbol for gas-filled diode.

constant voltage drop over its usual current range, as shown in Fig. 3-5a. Furthermore, no current is conducted with negative anode voltage within a certain maximum voltage range, so that the tube is a good rectifier. For purposes of circuit analysis, the tube characteristic can be approximated by the constant voltage characteristic shown in Fig. 3-5b. The circuit symbol (Fig. 3-5c) shows the dot added to indicate the presence of gas in the tube. Further details concerning the internal action of gas diodes are given in Chapter 10.

3-7
Conductors, semiconductors, and insulators

A number of semiconductor devices had been invented over the last half century by empirical methods. However, it was not until the electron theory of solids and particularly of crystals was well advanced that rapid development in the semiconductor field ensued. Following the original invention of the transistor[†] there has been, and continues to be, a rapid development of new devices. We begin a qualitative discussion of the nature of electrical conduction in semiconductors by referring to the definition of a semiconductor.

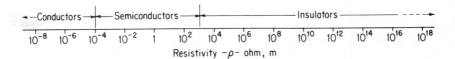

FIGURE 3-6   Resistivity of conductors, semiconductors, and insulators.

[†] J. Bardeen and W. H. Brattain, "The Transistor, a Semi-conductor Triode," *Phys. Rev.*, **74**, 230 (1948).

All solid materials can be classified in terms of electrical resistivity as illustrated in Fig. 3-6. Here the materials having resistivities ranging roughly from 10^{-4} to 10^{+3} ohm-meters at room temperature are classed as *semiconductors*, whereas *conductors* have resistivities below this range and *insulators* above this range.

3-8
Conduction processes in semiconductors

In *metallic* conductors the low resistivity is accounted for by the presence of swarms of electrons that are not tightly bound to any particular atom and therefore are relatively free to move under the influence of an externally applied electric field. In *insulators*, on the other hand, there are relatively few so-called *conduction* electrons, and most electrons are more or less bound to an atom, so they cannot normally take part in carrying current through the material. Theoretically, these bound electrons could become conduction electrons if their energy were raised sufficiently. However, the amount of added energy required is relatively large, so that the change from the bound state to the conduction state occurs infrequently at room temperature.

Semiconductors have an intermediate number of conduction electrons at room temperature. Furthermore, the amount of energy that must be added to a bound electron to convert it to a conduction electron is relatively small, so this transition may add to the conduction capability, for example, as the temperature is raised. In addition to conduction by conduction electrons, there is a process of conduction by the displacement of valence electrons into locations where valence electrons are missing. Consider the schematic diagram of a small group of the atoms in a crystal of a semiconductor

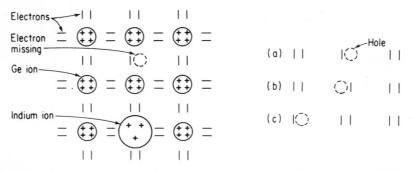

FIGURE 3-7   Hole formation in the germanium crystal.

FIGURE 3-8   Illustration of hole motion.

as in Fig. 3-7. This represents the germanium crystal and illustrates the four valence electrons per atom. A single impurity atom (larger circle) having a valence of 3 is present. The impurity atom would normally have three valence electrons, but in this crystal it is likely to have four adjacent valence electrons as shown. Consequently there is a valence electron missing at some other location, shown by the dotted circle. Next consider what happens when an external electric field is applied. One valence electron may shift under the force of the field and thus will fill the vacancy where an electron is missing. The motion can be visualized in an idealized form as in Fig. 3-8 where successive instants of time are depicted in parts (a), (b), and (c) of the figure. Here the electric field moves the electrons to the right, and the vacancy moves to the left. It is convenient to designate the vacancy as a *hole* and to refer to the motion of the hole almost as if it were a particle. Because the motion of the hole is occasioned by the motions of electrons to the right, the hole motion considered alone must be regarded as the motion of a *positively charged* particle of magnitude of the electronic charge. In certain types of semiconductors the hole motions predominate as the primary carriers of the current.

3-9
P-type and n-type semiconductors

We have seen how the addition of a small fraction of an impurity of valence 3 to germanium is able to provide a distribution of holes throughout the material. The impurity atom is called an *acceptor* because it accepts an extra electron from the crystal. This type of material is called a *p-type semiconductor*. Alternative schematic illustrations of the p-type material are shown in Fig. 3-9. The motion of the holes is the main cause of current flow in the p-type material. This motion may arise owing to the applied

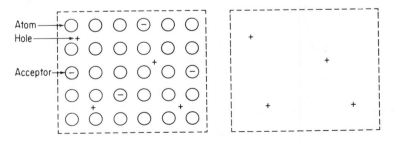

FIGURE 3-9   (a) Atoms, acceptor ions, and holes in p-type semiconductor. (b) Simplified picture.

electric field, or also to the *diffusion* of the holes from regions where the concentration of holes is high to regions where the concentration is lower.

The *p*-type material may also have some conduction electrons, owing either to the gain of energy of an electron from the thermal vibrations or to the entrance of conduction electrons at the boundary from the adjacent material.

When a small percentage of an impurity of valence 5 is added to germanium (or silicon), the impurity atoms in effect donate an electron that becomes a conduction electron. This type of impurity atom is called a *donor* atom. The conditions in a semiconductor containing a distribution of donors is shown in Fig. 3-10. This material is called an *n-type semiconductor* because conduction is primarily by electron motion.

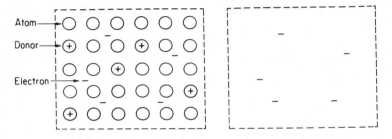

FIGURE 3-10   (a) Atoms, donor ions, and conduction electrons in *n*-type semiconductor. (b) Simplified picture.

It is also possible for the *n*-type material to contain a relatively small number of holes. These can be generated by thermal effects or can enter the material at the boundary. It is convenient to refer to the electrons in the *n*-type material as the *majority carriers* of current and the holes as the *minority carriers*. In the *p*-type material the holes are the majority carriers and the electrons are the minority carriers.

3-10
Energy band picture for crystalline semiconductors

From the foregoing discussion it is clear that the electrical behavior of semiconductors is determined primarily by the actions of the electrons and holes in the crystal. Just as the electron energy level diagram for an atom is a powerful aid to the understanding of the nature of an isolated atom, so also the modern electron energy band picture of solids is a great help in the study of semiconductor devices. Though the following outline of the energy band theory must be rather brief, it will serve as a basis for the understanding of semiconductor diodes and transistors.

When atoms are brought together in close proximity to form a crystal, their electrons interact so strongly that the allowed energy levels for electrons are no longer the same as those for the isolated atom. In effect the crowding together of the atoms causes a splitting of the original levels into multiple levels that differ slightly in energy. Another viewpoint regards the whole crystal as a gigantic molecule that must obey the quantum theory laws. This view would require that a given electron energy level (or state) of the isolated atom would break up into as many levels as there are atoms in the crystal. Since a cubic crystal of germanium 1 mm on an edge contains 4.4×10^{19} atoms, we can see that a tremendous number of levels occur in the crystal. These allowed, or available, levels are spread over a range of energies, and a particular group is called an *energy band.*

Just as in an isolated atom there may be an electron in the crystal which exists in a state that corresponds to a particular level. In this event the level is said to be *occupied.* However, there are higher levels that are available but not occupied. The quantum theory laws specify which energy levels are available and which are *forbidden.* As a result, certain ranges of energies may not ordinarily be "occupied" by electrons. Such a range is called a *forbidden band.*

In the study of semiconductors of the covalent crystal type the energy bands of interest are the highest, or *conduction* band, the adjacent *forbidden* band, and below that the *valence* band. Additional bands at lower energies are present but are disregarded here. The conduction band is partly filled at room temperature. Consequently these electrons can move freely through the crystal under an electric field, for they can occupy slightly different vacant levels, if necessary, in their motion. An energy band completely filled with electrons cannot contribute to the conduction, for if an electron is displaced, it only changes places with another electron and no net charge transfer occurs.

A schematic energy band picture for a semiconductor is shown in Fig. 3-11. At absolute zero the conduction band is vacant, but at room temperature (Fig. 3-11b) some electrons occupy states at the lower edge of the conduction band. These electrons formerly occupied states in the valence band which now remain empty. The empty levels correspond to *holes* in the crystal. The electrons are said to have been *excited* across the forbidden gap of energy ΔE. As the temperature is raised, additional electrons are excited across the gap, and so this picture accounts for the increase in conductivity with increase in temperature. In semiconductors the gap energy ΔE is about 1.0 eV or less.

A simplified energy band picture is shown in Fig. 3-12a for the room

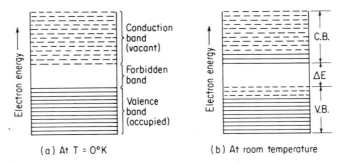

FIGURE 3-11   Occupied and vacant electron energy levels at two temperatures.

temperature condition. Here only two electrons and two holes are shown, though in an actual crystal the number of carriers would be immense indeed. Furthermore, the horizontal direction labeled the x direction is conceived to represent some line through the crystal. Slight energy variations along a line in the crystal have been smoothed out in the idealized picture shown. Now when we speak of an electron jumping from the valence band to the conduction band, we can associate this electron with a particular x position in the crystal, though of course, the vertical position in the energy band diagram has no relation to the actual location of the electron in space.

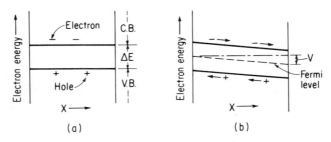

FIGURE 3-12   Energy level diagrams showing the effect of an added electric field.

When an x-directed electric field is applied on a crystal, the energy levels are affected as in Fig. 3-12b. Here the positively charged end of the crystal is at the right side. As a result the energy levels slope downward to the right, for an electron has less potential energy as it increases in electrical potential, owing to its negative charge. The electric field urges the electrons in the $+x$ direction and the holes in the $-x$ direction. However, they maintain their energy level relative to the edges of the forbidden gap, as pictured in Fig.

3-12b. The electrons go "downhill" in the field, and the holes "uphill." However, the actual motions, on the average, are directed in the $+x$ or $-x$ direction.

A certain energy level, called the *Fermi* level, is established in the quantum theory of metals and semiconductors in terms of the probability function for the occupancy of energy states. We shall be content to regard the Fermi level primarily as the reference level for electrical potentials as measured by the usual means at the surface of the crystal. In the intrinsic (pure) semiconductor whose energy band diagram is depicted in Fig. 3-12b the Fermi level lies midway between the edges of the conduction and valence bands. We notice that the distance labeled V equals the magnitude of the battery voltage applied to the two ends of the crystal.

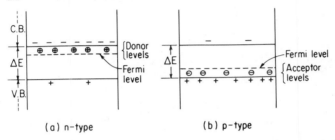

(a) n–type   (b) p–type

FIGURE 3-13   Energy level diagrams for *n*-type and *p*-type semiconductors.

Figure 3-13 shows the energy band diagram for the important impurity type semiconductors. The effect of the donors in the *n*-type material is to create some electron energy levels in the forbidden band which are close to the conduction band. At absolute zero temperature these levels are occupied by electrons, but at room temperature these electrons are displaced to levels in the conduction band. The donors remain as ions, thus these levels are symbolized by a plus sign when vacant. The Fermi level moves upward close to the donor level. The diagram for the *p*-type material (Fig. 3-13b) shows new levels near the edge of the valence band, called *acceptor* levels, and the lowered Fermi level. At room temperature the acceptor levels are filled by valence electrons, thereby creating holes in the valence band.

3-11
The semiconductor junction diode

An important type of rectifying junction results when a *p*-type semiconductor is formed as an extension of a section of *n*-type material, sometimes with a thin transition region between the two. Figure 3-14a shows such a junction

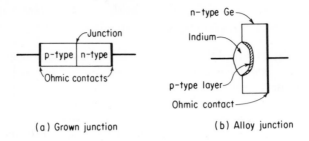

(a) Grown junction   (b) Alloy junction

FIGURE 3-14   Elementary *pn* junction diodes.

produced by the crystal-growing process in which a single crystal is grown from a seed crystal. This process consists in slowly pulling the seed crystal from a molten bath, for example, of germanium, whose temperature is close to the freezing point. If the bath contains donor atoms as an impurity, the crystal will also contain this impurity and will be an *n*-type crystal. However, if the bath contains both donor and acceptor types of impurity, the predominate impurity in the crystal will under some conditions depend on the rate of crystal growth. Thus a *pn* junction can be formed by growing the crystal at one rate for a time and then changing the rate to obtain the opposite type of material.

An alternative construction is illustrated in Fig. 3-14b. Here a small dot of indium is alloyed with a tiny wafer of *n*-type germanium. As a result a *p*-type layer is formed, so that a *pn* junction is produced. Larger junctions are produced in a thin sandwich type of construction with a larger area appropriate to the desired current capacity.

A careful study of the internal phenomena that account for the behavior of a *pn* junction diode is important, not only because diodes are valuable circuit elements, but also because the study will form a basis for our understanding of the related phenomena in a transistor. We picture the internal conditions in a *pn* junction in Fig. 3-15a for the short-circuit (zero bias) condition but show only the electrons and holes. However, the illustration cannot show the high concentration of electrons and holes, nor can it show the thermal motions of these particles. These thermal motions are important, for they cause electrons to tend to diffuse from the *n*-type material toward the *p*-type, where the electron concentration is low. Likewise, holes tend to diffuse from left to right across the junction. Under equilibrium conditions (no net current flow, no temperature differences) an inner potential energy barrier that tends to oppose the diffusion of both electrons and holes across the junction builds up. This barrier is a result of the removal of the charge carriers from a narrow region on each side of the junction, called the *depletion* region. Thus in the portion of the depletion region in the *n*-type material there is a deficit of electrons, and in the portion of the depletion region in the *p*-type material the hole density is reduced. As a result the donor and acceptor

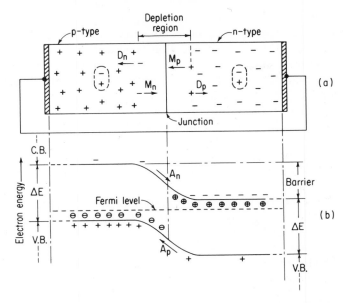

FIGURE 3-15 (a) pn junction with zero bias. (b) Energy level diagram. Key: − electron; + hole; ⊖ acceptor (ionized); ⊕ donor (ionized).

ions are no longer exactly neutralized by electrons or holes (as they are in the main body of the semiconductor) but produce layers of electrostatic charges. The forces caused by these charges produce the energy barrier.

What determines the height of the barrier? This question can only be answered after further study of the electron and hole motions. There will be some generation of holes and conduction electrons by thermal motions, as indicated by the dotted ovals in Fig. 3-15a. When this occurs in the n-type material the additional electrons have little effect when added to the large numbers already present, but the newly generated holes diffuse toward the junction and are swept "downhill" toward the p side. This action is indicated by the arrow M_p. Thermally generated electrons from the p side constitute the source of the electrons undergoing the motions labeled M_n. In an equilibrium condition there must be just as many electrons diffusing into the p side represented by D_n as are lost through the motions shown by M_n. Likewise the motions represented by D_p and M_p must, on the average, represent equal current flow, otherwise holes would be accumulating on one side or the other. The height of the barrier (and the width of the depletion region) adjusts itself so that the diffusion current and the current caused by thermally generated carriers just balance.

A study of the energy band picture of the pn junction (Fig. 3-15b) will clarify these ideas. Because the junction is short-circuited, the Fermi levels in the *p*-type and *n*-type materials must line up. Recalling the location of the Fermi levels in the impurity-type semiconductors (Fig. 3-13), it is reasonable to expect that the edges of the conduction band and the valence band will be skewed as shown. Thus an energy barrier is formed in the depletion region. Arrow A_n indicates the tendency of the electrons to move to lower levels or to go downhill in the barrier region, corresponding to the motion M_n in the upper part of the figure. As stated before, the forces urging the electrons toward the right are electrostatic in origin and arise from the space-charge effect of the donor and acceptor ions in this region. (Donor and acceptor ions are neutralized by electrons or holes in the parts of the crystal away from the depletion region.) Arrow A_p indicates that holes tend to move to higher levels and consequently tend to move to the left in the depletion region. Motions due to diffusion are opposite to the arrow A_n and A_p for electrons and holes respectively. As a result, the diffusion motions are hindered by the energy barrier, and under the short-circuit condition the flow of carriers by diffusion is small. The net current is of course zero.

Now consider the effect of a small *forward* bias voltage *V*, say 0.2 V, which raises the *p*-type material to a positive potential relative to the *n*-type. The result is to reduce the height of the energy barrier and to reduce the width of the depletion layer (Fig. 3-16a). The reduction in the barrier allows much larger numbers of electrons and holes to cross the barrier against the local fields, so that a large net current flows across the junction and around the circuit. At some distance from the junction the majority carriers carry

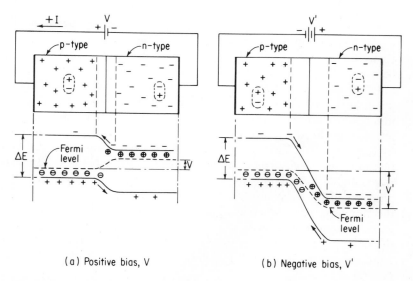

(a) Positive bias, V   (b) Negative bias, V'

FIGURE 3-16   The biased *pn* junction diode.

most of the current, but nearer to the depletion layer the minority carriers carry a portion of the current. For example, in the *n*-type material there will be an appreciable movement of holes to the right (not shown in Fig. 3-16a). The number of holes gradually diminishes toward the right, owing to *recombination*, a process in which an electron fills a hole, and thereby both are removed as carriers. A similar situation prevails in the *p* region, except that the number of electrons is diminishing toward the left.

With a *reverse* bias voltage the effects described in the foregoing paragraph operate to reduce the current. The energy barrier is increased and the depletion region becomes wider (Fig. 3-16b). The number of electrons and holes crossing the junction by diffusion is reduced markedly. However, the number of electrons and holes formed by thermal processes remains constant, and these carriers crossing the junction constitute the major portion of the current when the reverse voltage is over a few tenths of a volt.

3-12
Junction diode voltage-current relation

The phenomena described in the foregoing article give the physical basis for the complete voltage-current relation shown in Fig. 3-17a. The polarity conventions used are specified in Fig. 3-17b. The typical high current with

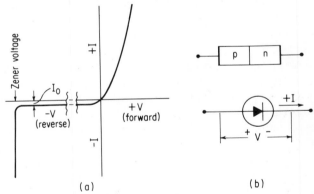

(a)   (b)

FIGURE 3-17   The *pn* junction diode: (a) characteristic and (b) symbol.

small forward voltage is shown, as well as the small current (exaggerated in the figure) with reverse voltage. This reverse current in an *ideal* diode approaches a limiting value I_o, called the *reverse saturation* current. When, however, the reverse voltage exceeds a certain value, called the *breakdown* or *Zener* voltage, the reverse current suddenly increases. This increase is caused by the rapid increase in the formation of electron-hole pairs by the action of the internal electric field in the region of the junction.

We have seen that an energy barrier develops in the unbiased pn junction and that an added bias voltage V in effect alters the barrier height by the value V. In general, in a situation where energetic particles diffuse over an energy barrier, the Boltzmann factor, of the form exp (W/kT), where W is the barrier height, governs the flow of the diffusing particles. It is not surprising, therefore, that a factor of the form exp (eV/kT) appears in the following theoretical expression for the diode current I as a function of the bias voltage V:

$$I = I_o\left[\exp \frac{eV}{kT} - 1\right] \qquad (3\text{-}3)$$

Here k is the Boltzmann constant, e is the *magnitude* of the electronic charge, and T is the absolute temperature.

First we interpret Eq. (3-3) for the forward direction, i.e., for positive values of V. We assume that the junction is at room temperature, $T = 300°K$, and therefore the value of kT/e is 0.026 V. Now if $V = 0.12$ V, the exponential term in Eq. (3-3) is 100 or more, so the quantity -1 can be neglected and (3-3) reduces to the approximate form, $I \cong I_o \exp (V/0.026)$. Thus the current rises as an exponential function of the voltage. However, Eq. (3-3) is based on the assumption that V is the change in the inner barrier height from the zero-bias condition. At high currents the effect of the ohmic voltage drop in the semiconductor material becomes important; therefore Eq. (3-3) is only approximate in this range if V is taken to be the terminal voltage.

The reverse saturation current I_o in an *ideal* diode equals the sum of (1) the electrons thermally generated in the p-type material that arrive at the depletion region and move across the junction, plus (2) the holes thermally generated in the n-type material that cross the junction in the opposite direction. In practical diodes there are also surface leakage effects which add to the reverse current. When V is more negative than -0.12 V and the diode is at $300°K$, the exponential quantity in (3-3) is negligible; therefore $I = -I_o$, provided that V is not too close to the breakdown voltage.

The reverse saturation current depends on the internal physics of the diode, i.e., on such factors as impurity concentrations, carrier diffusion, carrier lifetimes, and thermal generation of minority carriers. The higher forbidden gap energy in silicon compared with that in germanium leads to a value of I_o for silicon diodes that is of the order of 10^{-3} of that in comparable germanium diodes. As one result (see Eq. (3-3)), the forward voltage needed at a particular current for a Si diode is much higher than for a Ge diode (e.g., 0.7 V for Si versus 0.2 V for Ge rectifier diodes). Sample forward voltage curves for small junction diodes are shown in Fig. 3-18a.

The saturation current is highly temperature-dependent, principally owing to the effect of temperature on minority carrier concentration. Over

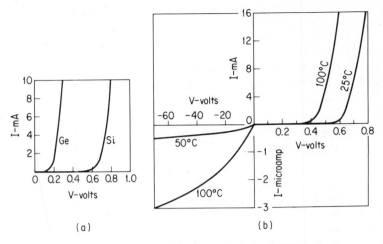

FIGURE 3-18   (a) *V-I* curves for *Ge* and *Si* junction diodes at room temperature. (b) Showing the effect of temperature on a *Si* diode *V-I* curve. Note change of current scale from *mA* for forward current to microamp for reverse current. Reverse current for 25°C is too small to be shown.

short temperature ranges I_o may be taken to be an exponential function of the temperature of the form

$$\frac{I_o(T)}{I_o(T_r)} = \exp \delta(T - T_r) \qquad (3\text{-}4)$$

where $I_o(T_r)$ is the current at the reference temperature T_r and the parameter δ depends on the type of diode. This temperature effect is very great, in fact in typical germanium diodes I_o *doubles* for a 10° C temperature rise, and in silicon diodes for a 9°C rise. Similar temperature-dependent leakage currents are encountered in transistors.

In practical diodes the value of the reverse voltage (as well as the temperature) has an effect on the reverse current, as shown in Fig. 3-18b. This voltage effect is mainly due to the surface leakage currents. The figure also shows the effect of temperature on the forward characteristic. The decrease in forward voltage, at a fixed current, is linearly related to the temperature change.

Semiconductor diodes are divided into two broad classes: *signal* diodes and *rectifier* diodes. Signal diodes are used in detector circuits and in logic and computer circuits. In these diodes the forward current and reverse voltage requirements are not high, say, 50 mA and 60 V, but small leakage current, low capacitance, and fast response times are essential. Early signal diodes depended on the rectifying action at the contact between a fine wire point and a chip of silicon or germanium, but most modern diodes contain small-area silicon *pn* junctions.

Rectifier-type diodes are nearly all silicon junction diodes, with the junction area dependent on the current rating required. The available sizes start from about 150 mA and range to several hundred amperes in a single rectifier cell. Reverse voltage ratings range from 50 V to 500 or 600 V, and for a few designs to 1000 or more V.

3-13
Diode ratings

Different kinds of diodes have slightly different types of ratings for maximum current and voltage. However, some generalizations can be made because all are adversely affected by overheating. A theoretical calculation of the heating effect is complicated by the variety of current wave forms encountered in different rectifier circuits and by the nonlinear current-voltage relations of the diodes. In gas diodes and semiconductor junction diodes the heating is approximately proportional to the average value of the current wave, so that they have a *maximum average current* rating. For junction diodes this rating decreases as the ambient temperature increases. Too high a *recurrent peak* current may damage a gas diode or a junction diode, so that this quantity is subject to a rated limitation. An additional rating is the *surge current* rating, which indicates how high an overload current the device can withstand for a specified short time without serious damage.

All devices may be damaged by an excessive reverse voltage, consequently they have a *peak reverse voltage* (PRV) rating.

A small silicon junction diode for example, has the following ratings. The peak reverse voltage is 500 V. The maximum average current at 50°C ambient temperature is 650 mA, the recurrent peak is 3.5 A, and the sine wave surge current allowed for one-half cycle is 15 A maximum. At an ambient temperature of 100° C the average current rating falls to 425 mA.

REFERENCES

See the references at the end of Chapter 4.

EXERCISES

3-1 A thermionic diode has an oxide-coated cathode with a work function of 1.0 eV and a constant A in Eq. (3-1) of 0.01 A/cm^2 °K^2. This diode has a thermionic emission capability of 100 mA when the cathode temperature is 1000°K. What is the thermionic emission current if the temperature drops to 950°K?

3-2 A high-vacuum thermionic diode has a thoriated tungsten filament wire 3 cm long and 0.7 mm in diameter. (a) What is the saturation emission at 2000°K? Neglect end effects. (b) Estimate the heating power needed for this filament at 2000°K.

3-3 An oxide-coated cathode that has a work function when new of 1.1 eV is operated at a temperature of 1000°K. Suppose that during a particular life test the cathode deteriorates so that the work function rises to 1.2 eV. What is the deteriorated emission current as a fraction of the original current?

3-4 Consider that a filamentary cathode loses heat energy by (1) radiation, (2) heat conduction at the supports, and (3) electron evaporation. How would the cathode efficiency of a short, fat filament compare with that of a long, thin filament made of the same material and operated at the same maximum temperature?

3-5 A space-charge-limited electron current flows between a plane cathode and a parallel-plane anode. The electrons are assumed to have zero initial velocities at the cathode but to be available in large numbers. (a) Sketch qualitative estimates of the curves of electric potential, electric field intensity, space charge density, and electron velocity versus the distance from the cathode. (b) Derive the mathematical relations for the variations in (a).

3-6 A thermionic diode has an indirectly heated tubular cathode with an outside diameter of 2 mm that is 15 mm long and a coaxial tubular anode with an inner diameter of 3.6 mm. Obtain an estimate of the anode voltage required to cause a space-charge-limited current of 20 mA by assuming that the formula based on parallel-plane geometry may be applied.

3-7 In impurity-type semiconductors at room temperature the resistivity is primarily dependent on the motion of majority carriers and can be expressed as $\rho = 1/(en\mu)$, where e is the electronic charge (1.6×10^{-19} coul), n is the number of majority carriers per unit volume, and μ is the mobility or the ratio of the carrier drift velocity to the field strength. Suppose that a sample of silicon contains 6×10^{24} donor atoms/m³ and that all of these are ionized at 300°K. If the mobility is 0.12 m/s per V/m, what is the resistivity of the sample?

3-8 What fraction of the silicon atoms in a piece of pure silicon would have to be replaced by donor impurity atoms to give an impurity concentration of 6×10^{24}/m³? The atomic weight of silicon is 28.08 g and its density is 2.33 g/cm³. The number of atoms in a gram-mole is 6.02×10^{23}.

3-9 A grown junction silicon diode has a square cross section of 1.5 by 1.5 mm and is 4 mm long. Its reverse saturation current at 300°K is 10^{-9} A. (a) Calculate the diode current for applied voltages of +0.2, +0.4, +0.6, −0.1, −0.2, and −0.6 Volts, if its temperature is 300°K. (b) If the resistivity of both sections of silicon is taken to be 10^{-2} Ω-m, what is the ohmic resistance of the diode? Comment on the effect of the ohmic resistance voltage drop on the validity of the calculated results in (a).

4

Vacuum Tubes as Circuit Elements

4-1
Electronic circuits

We shall study the circuits that use electronic devices to amplify signals, generate voltage wave forms or modify their shapes, and produce or detect modulated waves, and the like. All electronic devices exhibit nonlinear relations to a greater or lesser degree, as suggested by the sketches in Fig. 4-1. Sometimes the desired action of the circuit depends on the nonlinearity of the device, but often the device is operated over a limited range so that its response is essentially *linear*.

Circuits that contain *nonlinear* devices are more difficult to analyze mathematically than are those containing only linear elements, so that our treat-

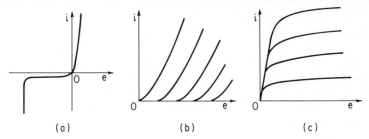

$$(a) \qquad\qquad (b) \qquad\qquad (c)$$

FIGURE 4-1   Characteristic curves for (a) semiconductor diode, (b) vacuum triode, and (c) transistor or pentode.

ment of the nonlinear cases will be limited to the graphical analysis of non-reactive circuits, to selected approximate solutions, and in some cases to only a qualitative analysis.

When the electronic device can be represented by an *equivalent linear circuit*, we can apply the techniques of linear circuit theory as outlined in Chapters 1 and 2, but with the added feature that we are dealing with *active* circuits. A *passive* circuit is one comprised of resistors, capacitors, inductors, transformers, and transmission lines. An *active* network is one comprised of passive elements plus one or more dependent sources of power at the signal frequency. For example, an amplifier has a local dc power source, the output of which is controlled so as to feed power at the signal frequency into the circuit and is therefore an example of an active network.

In this chapter the elementary diode circuit will be used to introduce concepts of nonlinear circuit analysis and also of the quasilinear analysis by means of a model based on incremental voltage and current. The concepts of dc resistance and dynamic (incremental) resistance will be introduced. An introduction to the internal action in a high-vacuum triode is followed by a graphical analysis of a triode amplifier. Then small-signal (linear) parameters and equivalent circuit models are developed for the triode. Here we shall need the controlled generator typical of an active network. The three basic triode amplifier circuits are analyzed by means of the equivalent circuits. Throughout the chapter we disregard the effects of the small capacitances between the electrodes of the tubes. This means that if the signals are sine waves, the frequency must be low enough so that these capacitances do not influence the circuit behavior.

4-2
Graphical analysis of a diode circuit

We choose the diode circuit in Fig. 4-2a to serve as an introductory example of a nonlinear circuit analysis. We wish to find the current in this circuit when the resistance R, the source voltage E_{bb}, and the tube characteristic, given as curve OQH in Fig. 4-2b, are known. Kirchhoff's voltage law tells us that

$$e = E_{bb} - Ri \qquad (4\text{-}1)$$

The diode voltage can be given in the functional form

$$e = f(i) \qquad (4\text{-}2)$$

where the functional relation is given by the known curve OQH. Now if the straight-line relation of Eq. (4-1) is drawn in Fig. 4-2b, it will intersect the voltage axis at E_{bb} and the current axis at the short-circuit current, $I_s = E_{bb}/R$. This line, which has a slope of $-1/R$, is known as a *resistance*

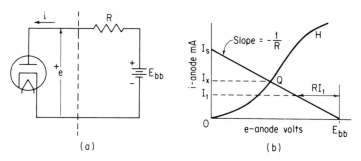

FIGURE 4-2   (a) Diode circuit. (b) *Load-line* graphical analysis.

line, or *load line*. The intersection point of the load line with the diode characteristic at point Q simultaneously satisfies Eqs. (4-1) and (4-2) and is therefore the solution sought. The ordinate I_x gives the operating current, and the abscissa of point Q is the corresponding diode voltage drop.

Suppose that the source voltage in Fig. 4-2a were varying with time. Then selected points on the source voltage wave would be chosen and the same graphical analysis would be applied for each voltage. As a result the wave form of current would be obtained.

4-3
Circuit model for the diode

In the following discussion we introduce the idea of an *incremental* circuit model for a nonlinear device. This model will be most useful for calculating the effects of small changes in current, i.e., small departures from a quiescent point. Our object is mainly to bring in concepts that will shortly be applied to grid-controlled tubes and transistors, rather than to practical diode circuits. The latter will be considered again in later chapters.

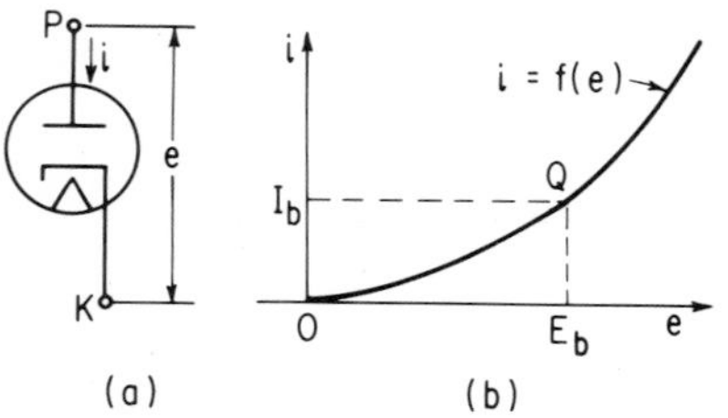

We consider a thermionic diode, though the theory is general and will apply to a semiconductor diode equally well. Assume that the actual diode in Fig. 4-3a has the i versus e characteristic shown in Fig. 4-3b. Since we are concerned with small variations in the current about the value I_b at point Q, we can use Taylor's series to expand i about I_b in

FIGURE 4-3   (a) Diode and (b) diode characteristic curve.

terms of the derivatives taken at point Q; thus

$$i = I_b + \left(\frac{di}{de}\right)_Q (e - E_b) + \left(\frac{d^2i}{de^2}\right)_Q \frac{(e - E_b)^2}{2} + \cdots \qquad (4\text{-}3)$$

Now we shall consider the linear approximation, i.e., we discard the second-order and higher-order terms. Furthermore, we define the *dynamic plate resistance* of the diode r_p by writing

$$\frac{1}{r_p} = \left(\frac{di}{de}\right)_Q \qquad (4\text{-}4)$$

Now Eq. (4-3) reduces to

$$i = I_b + \frac{1}{r_p}(e - E_b) = \left(I_b - \frac{E_b}{r_p}\right) + \frac{1}{r_p}e \qquad (4\text{-}5)$$

This equation is in the form $i = k + me$, where k and m are constants, so we have derived a linear function approximation to $i = f(e)$.

This linear relation is shown by the straight line drawn tangent to the diode characteristic at point Q, whose slope is $1/r_p$ (see Fig. 4-4b). As seen from Eq. (4-5) the line intersects the current axis at the current $I_b - (E_b/r_p)$. It will be more convenient to express the linear function in terms of the voltage intercept E_o and the slope. The reader can show that in these terms

$$i = -\frac{E_o}{r_p} + \frac{1}{r_p}e \quad \text{valid near point } Q \qquad (4\text{-}6)$$

This equation can now be used for approximate circuit calculations using linear circuit theory.

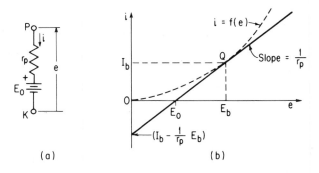

FIGURE 4-4   Linearized model of the diode (a) equivalent circuit, (b) graphical interpretation.

An *equivalent circuit* or *circuit model* for the diode can be obtained from Eq. (4-6). First rearrange the equation to give

$$e = E_o + r_p i \qquad (4\text{-}7)$$

This equation is represented by the dc source E_o and the resistor r_p in series as shown in Fig. 4-4a, which is therefore one possible circuit model of the diode.

4-4
Separation of dc and incremental components of e and i

In the foregoing section a model adequate for total currents and voltages is developed. Often, however, particularly with grid-controlled tubes and with transistors, we are concerned mainly with small variations of e and i

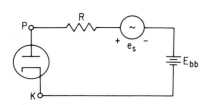

FIGURE 4-5 Diode circuit containing dc and ac sources and a resistance.

caused by a signal voltage. To introduce the concepts needed for such a situation, consider the circuit in Fig. 4-5. Here a direct voltage E_{bb} and a signal voltage e_s are in series with a "load" resistance R and a diode whose characteristic curve is known. With $e_s = 0$ the values of E_{bb} and R are chosen so that a particular Q point results at which the r_p is known. Then the source voltage is excited, but e_s is kept small, so that $e_s \ll E_{bb}$. We want to study the resulting current.

We shall think in terms of the linear approximation but also shall make use of superposition. We think of the total current broken up into two components, one constant and the other varying with e_s. To formalize these ideas, let

$$i_p = i - I_b \tag{4-8}$$

where i is the total current, I_b is the value at the Q point, and i_p is the incremental value (signal component) of the total current. Further, let

$$e_p = e - E_b \tag{4-9}$$

where e is the total diode voltage, e_p the incremental part of this voltage, and E_b the value at the Q point. If (4-8) and (4-9) are solved for i and e, respectively and these values are put in Eq. (4-7), we find

$$e_p + E_b = E_o + r_p i_p + r_p I_b \tag{4-10}$$

Now we assert that, owing to superposition, we may split Eq. (4-10) into two parts, one to represent the cause-effect relation due to E_{bb} and the other due to e_s; thus

$$E_b = E_o + r_p I_b \tag{4-11}$$

and

$$e_p = r_p i_p \qquad (4\text{-}12)$$

Equation (4-11) expresses the dc relations and (4-12) the incremental relation for the diode. These are general and are independent of the particular circuit, except that small variations about a Q point are implied.

Equations (4-11) and (4-12) are the basis for two equivalent circuits *for the diode*, one for dc effects and the other for incremental, or ac, effects. These diode equivalents form a part of each circuit in Fig. 4-6, which shows the equivalents of the actual circuit (Fig. 4-5) for the two kinds of current. Thus, we need to deal only with simple series circuits made up of voltages and resistances.

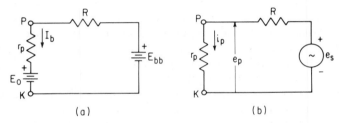

FIGURE 4-6   Equivalent circuit models for (a) dc components, (b) variable components.

To further emphasize the meanings of the various symbols, consider the wave forms in Fig. 4-7. Here e_s has been taken to be a sine wave, and we show the actual wave forms in part *a*, the dc components in part *b*, and the signal components in part *c*. We remark that most of these same symbols, with the same meanings, will be used with grid-controlled tubes. The concepts, but with other symbols, will carry over to the analysis of transistor circuits.

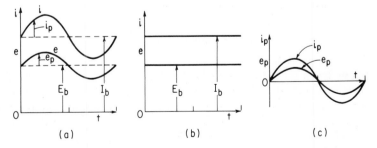

FIGURE 4-7   Illustrating dc and variable components and the standard symbols.

4-5
Grid control of space-charge-limited current, the triode

In Chapter 3 we have studied the difference between temperature-limited and space-charge-limited current in a diode and the conditions in the diode under which the current is controlled by the space charge. The introduction of a *control grid* into the thermionic tube by Lee DeForest in 1907 ushered in the era of the grid-controlled high-vacuum tube. The control grid consists of a latticework or mesh of wires placed between the anode and cathode. As will be explained presently, the charges placed on the grid act to modify the current through the tube by their action on the space charge. When the grid potential is *positive* relative to the cathode, the grid will collect some of the electron stream, but the major portion passes through the gaps between the grid wires and reaches the anode. With a *negative* grid potential of a volt or more the grid still controls the current but no longer collects any of the electrons. Thus, the varying grid potential controls the anode current and can operate some device like a loudspeaker placed in the anode circuit.

An experimental test of the action of the grid can be made using the circuit in Fig. 4-8. Here the conventional representation of a triode is shown.

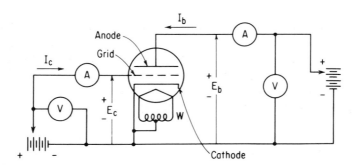

FIGURE 4-8   Circuit for testing a triode.

This triode has a separately heated cathode, with the heater energized by the transformer winding W. Because the cathode temperature is assumed to be constant, the anode current is determined by the anode voltage and the grid voltage. Let us hold the anode voltage fixed, vary the grid voltage, and note the effect on the anode current. The resulting variation is plotted as a curve with the anode current I_b as ordinate and the grid potential E_c as abscissa. The family of curves obtained with different anode voltages (Fig. 4-9) represents the *transfer characteristics* of the triode.

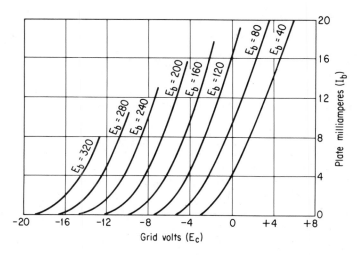

FIGURE 4-9   Transfer characteristics of a triode.

When the voltage drop from grid to cathode is positive, there is a sizable grid current as shown in Fig. 4-10. However, when the grid voltage is negative, the grid current is a fraction of a microampere or less, depending on the type of tube. Thus, if a grid signal voltage is introduced in the grid circuit but the grid is kept negative to the cathode, there is almost no power absorbed by the grid; yet it can control a relatively large power in the anode circuit. Consequently, the grid is usu-

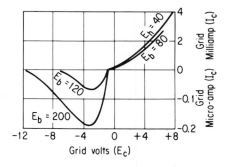

FIGURE 4-10   Grid current curves for a triode.

ally operated in the negative voltage region and the grid current is negligible.

It should be noted that the grid-to-cathode voltage drop E_c must be treated as an algebraic quantity, the sign of this voltage being dependent on the battery connected between cathode and grid. This battery (or other source of direct voltage) is said to supply the *direct grid-bias voltage*, or simply the *grid bias*. There is a certain grid bias for a particular anode voltage called the *cut-off bias*. As its name implies, this is the value of the grid bias just sufficient to reduce the plate current to zero.

If, instead of holding the anode voltage constant, we hold the grid voltage constant and vary the anode voltage, we obtain data for the *anode* or *plate characteristic curves* (Fig. 4-11). The data for these curves can also be read off the curves in Fig. 4-9. For reasons that will become clear later, the anode characteristics are more useful than the transfer characteristics, and these are the curves often published by the tube manufacturer.

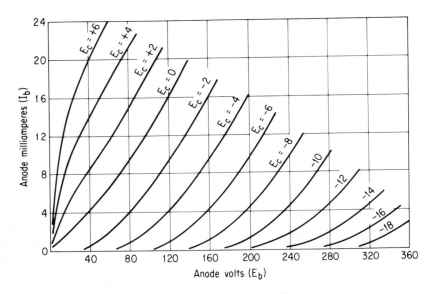

FIGURE 4-11   Plate characteristics of a triode.

The internal conditions in the triode are similar to those in the diode, except that now the electrostatic action of both the grid and the anode on the electronic space charge must be considered. These conditions are illustrated in Fig. 4-12 for a triode having extended plate anode and cathode and grid wires perpendicular to the page. The anode voltage is held constant, so the electrostatic potential diagrams are drawn with the same ordinate E_b in each part of the figure. The potential diagrams show two curves, one that represents conditions on a line through the middle of a grid wire and another that shows conditions along a line midway between the wires. In part (a) of Fig. 4-12 we see that the negative charges at the surface of the grid wire resulting from the grid bias combine with the negative space charge to act as the complementary charge of the anode positive charge. In part (b) the

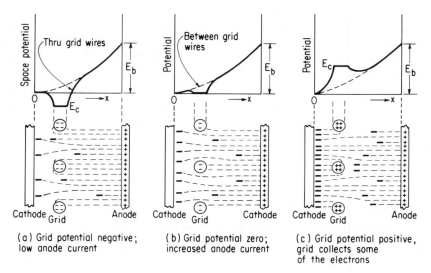

(a) Grid potential negative; low anode current

(b) Grid potential zero; increased anode current

(c) Grid potential positive, grid collects some of the electrons

FIGURE 4-12   Conditions in an idealized triode.

grid potential is zero, though it retains a small negative charge. The space charge must increase, however, to give a combined complementary charge, approximately the same as in part (a). In part (c), the grid has been charged positively. Now the two sets of positive charge—on the grid and on the anode—must be counterbalanced by an equal negative space charge. As a result the density of the space charge is increased in Fig. 4-12c, and the current is also increased. Some of the electrons are collected by the grid and cause grid current, and the remainder move to the anode.

The force on any given electron is in the direction of the lines of force at all times, but the paths of the electrons are not identical with these lines. The electrons tend to deviate from the curved parts of the line of force on account of their inertia, i.e., they tend to fly off the outside of the curve on account of centrifugal force.

The curves of the space potential in Fig. 4-12 may be compared with those in Fig. 3-4. Such a comparison shows that in the region between the cathode and the grid in Fig. 4-12 the effect of the changing grid potential is similar to the effect of the changing anode potential in Fig. 3-4. The combined effect of the grid and anode voltages fixes the flow of the electrons in the triode. As a result, the current leaving the cathode may be expressed approximately as follows, by analogy with the Langmuir-Child law, Eq. (3-2):

$$I = G\left(E_c + \frac{E_b}{\mu}\right)^{\frac{3}{2}} \qquad (4\text{-}13)$$

Here G and μ are constants for a particular triode. The *amplification factor* μ is a number greater than 1 that describes how much more effectively the grid voltage controls the current than the plate voltage does. The tube geometry fixes the values of G and μ. For example, high values of μ are obtained with a closely wound grid of many turns per centimeter placed close to the cathode. Values of μ from about 2 to 100 are encountered in practical triodes.

When E_c is negative, the grid current is negligible, so that in this range Eq. (4-13) may be regarded as an expression for the plate current. In Sec. 4-9 a linearized form of Eq. (4-13) will be developed as a basis for circuit calculations.

4-6
Graphical analysis of a triode amplifier

An elementary amplifier is shown in Fig. 4-13, in which a signal inserted in the grid circuit is amplified and delivered to the load represented by the resistance R in the plate circuit. In this circuit the grid and plate branches return to a common point at the cathode. This point is usually connected to the amplifier chassis as indicated by the "ground" symbol in the diagram, but there may be no conductive path to the earth.

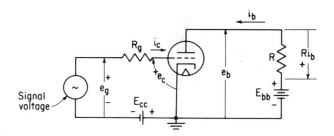

FIGURE 4-13   Elementary triode amplifier.

Let us imagine that a sinusoidal signal voltage is impressed in the grid circuit. This voltage is regarded as the *input* voltage and is expressed by the relation

$$e_g = E_{gm} \sin \omega t \qquad (4\text{-}14)$$

This voltage is in series with the grid-bias voltage E_{cc}, so that the total grid voltage from cathode to grid, designated by e_c, has both a direct and an alternating component. We shall assume that e_c remains negative, so that

i_c will be zero and R_g will have no effect. The total grid voltage e_c acts on the grid of the tube and thereby controls the anode current i_b. The varying anode current through the load resistor R produces the desired result if the output current wave has the same shape as the wave of input voltage and if the available power has been increased. It should be emphasized that it is the varying component of the anode current wave that is useful in the production of an amplified alternating current or voltage.

The graphical analysis used previously for the diode circuits employing the diode characteristic curve and the load line can readily be extended to apply to the triode amplifier circuit. The voltage equation defining the *load line* in the plate characteristic graph is the same as before, since the plate circuit contains the same elements. Thus,

$$e_b = E_{bb} - Ri_b \tag{4-15}$$

The load line in Fig. 4-14 has been drawn for $E_{bb} = 180$ V and $R = 4000\ \Omega$. For any particular grid voltage we assert that the plate current and plate potential will correspond to the intersection point of the load line and the triode curve for that particular grid voltage.

Consider first the *quiescent* condition, when the signal voltage is zero. With $e_g = 0$, we have $e_c = -15$ V, because $-E_{cc} = -15$ V. The intersection of the load line with the -15-V curve is at point Q, the *quiescent point*. If

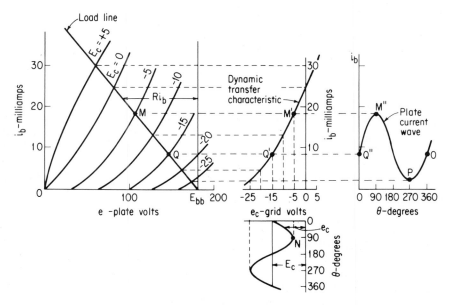

FIGURE 4-14   Construction for the dynamic transfer characteristic and for the wave form of the plate current.

desired, the quiescent values of e_b and i_b can be read off the abscissa and ordinate scales.

Next consider that the signal voltage is active and suppose that $e_g = +10$ V at a particular instant. Then the total grid potential is $(-15 + 10)$ or -5 V and the point on the load line that gives the plate current is point M. To find the plate current for any other instantaneous grid potential, it is only necessary to locate the proper intersection point on the load line.

To find the wave form of plate current produced by a known *input* signal, it is only necessary to find the plate current from the load-line construction at a number of points on the input wave and then plot the results. The auxiliary graphical construction shown in Fig. 4-14 will help us to visualize the technique. From the load-line intersection points the anode current values are projected to the right (as from Q to Q') into a graph with total grid voltage as abscissas. The technical name for the resulting curve is the *dynamic transfer characteristic*. It has a lesser slope than the ordinary transfer characteristic on account of the reduction of the actual anode voltage below the battery voltage E_{bb}; this results from the drop across the load resistor R. Next the total grid-voltage wave is plotted with the time variable (expressed in degrees) extending downward and with the same scale for grid voltage as for the dynamic transfer characteristic. A study of the grid circuit will show that the equation for the grid voltage wave is as follows:

$$e_c = E_c + e_g = E_c + E_{gm} \sin \omega t \qquad (4\text{-}16)$$

After inserting the numerical values used in the construction in Fig. 4-14, we have

$$e_c = -15 + 10 \sin \omega t \qquad (4\text{-}17)$$

As shown in the figure, this wave starts at a value of -15 V when ωt is $0°$, builds up to a maximum value of -5 V when ωt is $90°$, and has a negative maximum of -25 V at $270°$. The wave of anode current can now be drawn by projecting from the grid-voltage wave vertically to the dynamic transfer characteristic and then horizontally to the anode current-time diagram at the right, for example, from point N to M' to M'' for the $90°$ point. As many points on the current wave $Q'' M'' PO$ as are needed for the required accuracy can be found in a similar way.

A study of the wave $Q'' M''PO$ will show that it is a slightly distorted sine wave plus a constant value. The distortion is a result of the curvature of the dynamic transfer characteristic. Since exact calculations dealing with distorted waves are not appropriate at this stage, an approximation will be used, namely, that the anode current can be represented by a constant value plus a sine wave. Thus the equation for i_b becomes

$$i_b \cong I_b + I_{pm} \sin \omega t \qquad (4\text{-}18)$$

where I_b is the average ordinate of the wave and I_{pm} is the maximum amplitude of the sinusoidal component of plate current. The value of I_{pm} will be taken to be half the difference between the ordinates of points M'' and P on the wave (Fig. 4-14). Using the numerical values in Fig. 4-14, we obtain the expression

$$i_b \cong 0.010 + 0.008 \sin \omega t \qquad (4\text{-}19)$$

In some amplifier applications it is the load voltage that is the factor of most interest. An example is the amplifier used in the cathode-ray oscilloscope, where the output voltage acts on the electrostatic deflecting plates. The voltage across the load resistor R can be obtained from Eq. (4-18) by Ohm's law. Thus,

$$Ri_b = RI_b + RI_{pm} \sin \omega t \qquad (4\text{-}20)$$

Let us plot the various wave forms for the amplifier on a common time base. Figure 4-15 shows the total grid voltage wave e_c, the plate current i_b, and the voltage across the tube e_b. The variation of the voltage across R, namely, Ri_b, is shown as the difference between E_{bb} and e_b. We note that as the grid voltage rises, the plate current and also Ri_b rise; therefore the plate voltage e_b falls. A study of the waves will show that there is a 180° phase relation between e_g and the sine-wave component of e_b.

The ratio of the variable (useful) part of the load voltage to the input voltage is termed the *useful voltage amplification*. We introduce the symbol A_v for this ratio† and use Eqs. (4-16) and (4-20) to obtain its value,

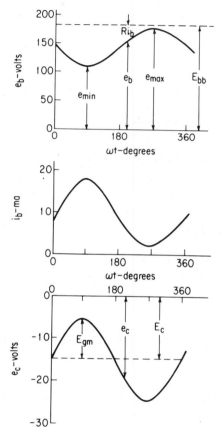

FIGURE 4-15 Voltage and current wave forms in a simple amplifier.

$$A_v = \frac{RI_{pm} \sin \omega t}{E_{gm} \sin \omega t} = \frac{RI_{pm}}{E_{gm}} \qquad (4\text{-}21)$$

The numerical value of A_v can be obtained more directly by calculating the

†An extended definition of voltage amplification in terms of phasor voltages will be given presently.

ratio of the peak-to-peak voltages of the two waves. Using the symbols defined in Fig. 4-15, we have, as an approximation for the distorted waves,

$$A_v \cong \frac{e_{\max} - e_{\min}}{2E_{gm}} \tag{4-22}$$

The numerical values of $e_{\max}$ and $e_{\min}$ can be read off directly from the load line in Fig. 4-14, with the result

$$A_v \cong \frac{175 - 105}{20} = 3.5 \tag{4-23}$$

for the amplifier under discussion. This voltage ratio will remain nearly constant for different levels of input voltage over the straight-line portion of the dynamic transfer characteristic. Over this range the amplifier is said to be a *linear* amplifier.

In the following article the load-line analysis will be applied to the choice of the quiescent point and of the load resistance for an amplifier. A simplified analysis will be used which omits the construction of the dynamic transfer characteristic. This is possible because the required voltages and currents can be taken from the load line itself.

When the load is reactive, the dynamic operation no longer follows a straight line but instead follows a loop similar to a Lissajous figure. Therefore, the method of this article is only applicable to reactive loads as an approximate analysis for situations in which the reactive component is small relative to the resistive (see Sec. 4-8).

4-7
Amplifier design by the
load-line method

The load-line method of analysis is admirably suited to the choice of the quiescent point and of load resistance to obtain a desired voltage amplification and to study possible distortion of the output wave. An example will illustrate the technique. Suppose the triode whose plate characteristics are given in Fig. 4-16 is used in the basic amplifier circuit (Fig. 4-13).

We assume that R_g is of the order of 10,000 Ω or higher. This means that any tendency for the grid potential to go positive will lead to enough grid current to seriously affect the voltage reaching the grid, thereby causing distortion. Consequently, we shall avoid the positive grid region at all times.

Suppose that the signal is a sine wave having a 4-V peak and that the load resistance is to be chosen to obtain a desired value of voltage amplification. Suppose further that E_{bb} has already been fixed by reference to the manufacturer's maximum voltage rating and by the available supply voltage.

Then a trial load line can be drawn for an arbitrarily chosen value of load resistance R_1 as shown in Fig. 4-16. It is logical to place the quiescent point at Q_1 on the -4-V grid level so that the dynamic operation up the load line just reaches $e_c = 0$ when e_g is at its positive maximum. The total *swing* of the grid voltage is between 0 and -8V, i.e., a swing of 8 V. The variation up and down the load line is indicated by the narrow sine wave as shown, but this representation is only qualitative owing to the nonlinear spacing of the

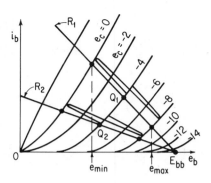

FIGURE 4-16 Amplifier design.

successive plate characteristic curves. To obtain the voltage amplification with the load R_1, we need only read off the extreme values of e_b and then calculate $A_v = (e_{\max} - e_{\min})/8$. If the R_1 line does not produce the desired amplification, a higher load resistance such as R_2 can be tried and the calculation repeated. If the desired amplification is not too high (say, up to 0.8 μ), this procedure will rapidly lead to a solution of the design problem.

In the foregoing example the main interest was in output voltage. In other situations the power output at the signal frequency is of primary importance. This situation will be dealt with later, but a few remarks may be made here. As the load resistance increases, the voltage gain increases, but a study of Fig. 4-16 will show that the plate current variation decreases. Since power depends on the product of voltage by current, it is seen that there must be an intermediate value of load resistance that will maximize the power output.

The effect of the choice of the Q point on the distortion of the output wave is shown in Fig. 4-17. Here three different Q points, i.e., Q, Q_1, and Q_2 are used, but with the same load resistance and an assumed sine-wave signal of 6 V peak value. The resulting wave of e_b for the quiescent point Q is shown in Fig. 4-17b. This wave is a close replica of the signal, with small distortion. Notice that the plate potential drops to the value e_{bo} at the instant when the total grid voltage is zero. In Fig. 4-17c the wave for the higher quiescent point Q_1 (smaller negative bias) is shown. If R_g were zero, the total grid voltage would rise to $+4$ V, but the effect of grid current is to restrict the rise to a fraction of a volt. As a result e_b does not fall much below e_{bo} and a flattened bottom develops on the output wave as shown. Another cause of distortion enters when the Q point is too low, as at Q_2 (or the signal becomes excessively large). Then the negative peak of grid potential is -16 V, but cutoff is at -14 V. As a result the output voltage wave has a flat top at the value $e_b = E_{bb}$ (Fig. 4-17d).

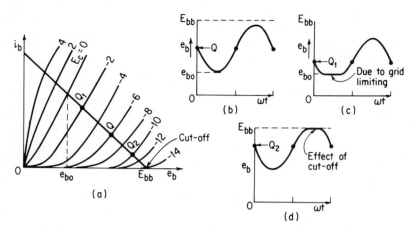

FIGURE 4-17   The effect of the location of the Q-point on the distortion of the output wave.

4-8
Ideal output filter; ideal
output transformer

a. *Output filter*

In the amplifier in Fig. 4-13 the load carries a direct current. Often it is desirable to eliminate the direct current by a capacitor filter, as in Fig. 4-18a. Here R_1 is regarded as the load and capacitor C filters out the direct current.

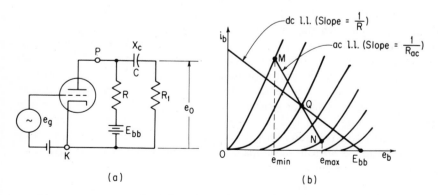

FIGURE 4-18   (a) Amplifier with capacitor output filter. (b) Graphical analysis, showing dc and ac load lines.

A connection like this one is used in the multistage amplifiers to be considered later. For the present we consider a limited aspect of the circuit problem, i.e., if the capacitor is large and the frequency high enough so that $X_c \ll R_1$, how will the circuit behave?

We notice that direct current reaches the tube via resistor R, and that the Q point is established by drawing the *dc load line* having the slope $1/R$.

Upon establishing the signal, we force a variation in the potential e_b, which acts between points P and K. This variation, therefore, acts on the series circuit of C and R_1. At the variational frequency the effect of C is assumed to be negligible. Consequently, resistance R_1 acts as if it were in parallel with R for the variations. Let the parallel resistance be R_{ac}, where

$$R_{\mathrm{ac}} = \frac{RR_1}{R + R_1} \tag{4-24}$$

If now we draw an *ac load line* through point Q, having a slope $1/R_{\mathrm{ac}}$, we have an approximate solution for the locus of the variation of i_b and e_b. For example, the peak-to-peak output voltage for grid signal variation between points M and N will be $e_{\max} - e_{\min}$, where these values are defined in Fig. 4-18b.

b. Output transformer

An output transformer will also filter out the direct current from the load (Fig. 4-19). We shall discuss only the ideal transformer, namely, one

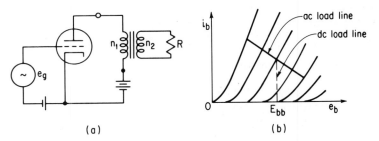

(a)   (b)

FIGURE 4-19   (a) Amplifier with output transformer. (b) Graphical analysis, assuming ideal transformer.

of zero losses and ideal transformation of currents and voltages. In this case the dc load line is vertical, since the dc resistance in the plate circuit is zero. The variational resistance in the plate circuit, call it R_{ac}, is given by

$$R_{\mathrm{ac}} = \left(\frac{n_1}{n_2}\right)^2 R \tag{4-25}$$

Thus, an ac load line can be drawn at the slope $1/R_{ac}$ and the amplifier response can be deduced from this line.

4-9
Triode parameters and equivalent circuits for small-signal operation

We shall, by analogy with the method used with the diode, develop a linear circuit model for the triode. We shall use the symbols e_b and e_c for total plate and grid potentials and i_b and i_c for total plate and grid currents. If we restrict the operation to the negative grid region, then i_c will be zero, and the triode is characterized by the functional expression for the plate current

$$i_b = f(e_c, e_b) \tag{4-26}$$

which describes the plate characteristic curves. Using the same approach as that for the diode, we expand i_b about a quiescent point Q by means of a Taylor's series. Here the Taylor's series for two independent variables applies, with the result

$$i_b = I_b + \left(\frac{\partial i_b}{\partial e_b}\right)_Q (e_b - E_b) + \left(\frac{\partial i_b}{\partial e_c}\right)_Q (e_c - E_c) + \text{higher-order terms} \tag{4-27}$$

Here I_b, E_b, and E_c are values at the Q point. Now introduce symbols for the incremental voltages in the plate and grid circuits, defined as

$$e_p = e_b - E_b \tag{4-28}$$

and

$$e_g = e_c - E_c \tag{4-29}$$

and for the incremental plate current,

$$i_p = i_b - I_b \tag{4-30}$$

We also introduce symbols for the derivatives taken at the Q points, thus introducing the *plate resistance* r_p

$$\frac{1}{r_p} = \left(\frac{\partial i_b}{\partial e_b}\right)_Q \tag{4-31}$$

and the *grid-plate transconductance* (or *mutual conductance*) g_m

$$g_m = \left(\frac{\partial i_b}{\partial e_c}\right)_Q \tag{4-32}$$

Using these symbols and saving only the linear terms, Eq. (4-27) yields

$$i_p = \frac{1}{r_p} e_p + g_m e_g \tag{4-33}$$

This equation expresses the incremental plate current in terms of the incremental plate and grid voltages and is the basic relation of the small-signal theory.

We remark that the dc effects, such as location of the Q point, are calculated separately, usually by graphical analysis.

Notice that Eq. (4-33) represents the current i_p as the sum of the two current terms on the right side. An equivalent circuit for incremental quantities based on Eq. (4-33), therefore, will have a current junction at which the two currents add to produce i_p. This equivalent circuit, known as the *Norton* form, is shown in Fig. 4-20b. Here $g_m e_g$ is a constant-current generator *dependent* on e_g, where e_g is the variable part of the voltage between points G and K. The resistor r_p is the *dynamic plate resistance*.

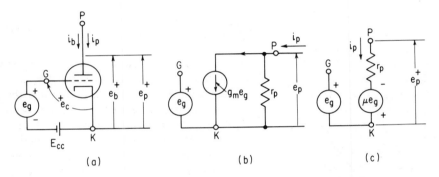

FIGURE 4-20   Symbols and equivalent circuits for the triode.

An alternative equivalent circuit which has a dependent voltage generator, can be derived from that in Fig. 4-20b by the use of Thévenin's theorem, or by rearranging Eq. (4-33). Multiply Eq. (4-33) through by r_p and obtain

$$e_p = r_p i_p - r_p g_m e_g \qquad (4\text{-}34)$$

Now express the dimensionless product $r_p g_m$ as follows:

$$\mu = r_p g_m \qquad (4\text{-}35)$$

The parameter μ, called the *amplification factor* of the tube, will later be expressed in terms of the triode characteristic curves. Now Eq. (4-34) can be written

$$e_p = r_p i_p - \mu e_g \qquad (4\text{-}36)$$

This leads to the equivalent circuit shown in Fig. 4-20c.

How can the foregoing theory be applied to the solution of a circuit that contains a triode? Two approaches are available. One is to represent the triode by Eq. (4-33) or (4-36) and solve the circuit by writing the network equations. The second approach (based on the first) is to redraw the circuit in an equivalent form, using either of the circuit models for the triode, and then solve the resulting circuit by the usual methods. Examples of this technique will follow later.

The triode parameter μ, r_p, and g_m must be obtained for the particular Q point to be used. The manufacturer's data on the tube may provide these data, or the values can be obtained from the plate characteristic curves. For this purpose we express the parameters in terms of increments; thus,

$$\frac{1}{r_p} = \left(\frac{\partial i_b}{\partial e_b}\right)_Q \cong \frac{\Delta i_b}{\Delta e_b}\bigg|_{e_c = \text{const}} \tag{4-37}$$

$$g_m = \left(\frac{\partial i_b}{\partial e_c}\right)_Q \cong \frac{\Delta i_b}{\Delta e_c}\bigg|_{e_b = \text{const}} \tag{4-38}$$

$$\mu = -\left(\frac{\partial e_b}{\partial e_c}\right)_Q \cong -\frac{\Delta e_b}{\Delta e_c}\bigg|_{i_b = \text{const}} \tag{4-39}$$

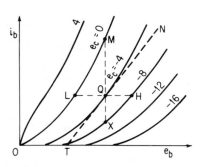

FIGURE 4-21   Illustrating determination of triode parameters.

To illustrate how the parameters are obtained from the plate characteristics, consider Fig. 4-21. In this figure the nonlinear nature of the tube has been emphasized to help clarify the discussion. Because we have i_b as a function of e_b for a constant e_c, we can find r_p by obtaining the partial derivative itself. Thus, we draw the tangent line $\overline{TN}$ to the curve at Q and calculate the reciprocal of the slope of this line to obtain r_p. For g_m we need the increments in i_b for an increment in e_c, but with e_b constant. If we choose the current increment $\overline{XQ}$, our answer will be too low, and if we choose $\overline{QM}$, the result will be too high. Therefore, let us take $\overline{XM}$ as the current increment, and then $\Delta e_c = 8$ V. Thus, $g_m = \overline{XM}/8$. Similarly, μ can be obtained by using the change in e_b from L to H. Then $\mu = \overline{LH}/8$, where $\overline{LH}$ is expressed in volts.

Vacuum triodes are designed with a wide variety of characteristics, but we can classify them roughly as low-μ tubes, medium-μ tubes, and high-μ tubes. Sample values of the parameters for these three types are listed in Table 4-1. Individual types have parameters that depart considerably from the values in the table. For example, some miniature triodes have been developed for high-frequency applications which have parameters in the order of $\mu = 80$, $r_p = 8000$ Ω, and $g_m = 10,000$ μmhos.

Table 4-1 Sample Triode Parameters

Class	μ	g_m, μmhos	r_p, Ω	Remarks
Low μ	4	5,000	800	power tube
Medium μ	20	2,500	8,000	general purpose
High μ	100	1,600	62,500	voltage amplifier

Summary: If we define the triode parameters as

$$\frac{1}{r_p} = \left.\frac{\partial i_b}{\partial e_b}\right|_{e_c=\text{const}} \qquad g_m = \left.\frac{\partial i_b}{\partial e_c}\right|_{e_b=\text{const}} \qquad \mu = -\left.\frac{\partial e_b}{\partial e_c}\right|_{i_b=\text{const}} \qquad (4\text{-}40)$$

then the parameters are related by $\mu = r_p g_m$. The incremental equations, which hold for small signals of any wave form, are as follows:

$$i_p = \frac{1}{r_p}e_p + g_m e_g \qquad (4\text{-}33)$$

and

$$e_p = r_p i_p - \mu e_g \qquad (4\text{-}36)$$

Norton form and Thévenin form equivalent circuits are based on Eqs. (4-33) and (4-36).

We remark that if sinusoidal signals are involved, then Eqs. (4-33) and (4-36) may be written in the forms

$$I_p = \frac{1}{r_p}E_p + g_m E_g \qquad (4\text{-}41)$$

and

$$E_p = r_p I_p - \mu E_g \qquad (4\text{-}42)$$

where I_p, E_p, and E_g are the rms phasor values of i_p, e_p, and e_g. The equivalent circuits, of course, apply for such signals also, within the frequency limitations already mentioned.

4-10
The common-cathode amplifier

There are three different ways that a triode can be connected to serve as an amplifier. The most basic is the *common-cathode* (or *grounded-cathode*) amplifier, which has been discussed in the foregoing articles. The others are the *common-grid* and the *common plate* types.

Let us draw an equivalent circuit for the common-cathode amplifier of Fig. 4-13 and discuss its voltage gain and network properties. Either the Norton form or the Thévenin form of the equivalent circuit will serve here; Fig. 4-22 shows the Thévenin form. The calculation of the voltage gain is left as an exercise for the reader. The result is

$$A_v = \frac{e_o}{e_g} = \frac{-\mu R}{r_p + R} \qquad (4\text{-}43)$$

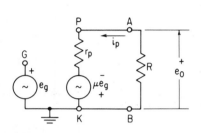

FIGURE 4-22   Equivalent circuit for grounded-cathode amplifier.

The minus sign is noteworthy and shows that the amplifier inverts the signal, or introduces a 180° phase shift. If R could be made very large, so that $R \gg r_p$, then A_v would approach the tube amplification factor μ as a limit. In practice, R is seldom more than 2 or 3 times r_p, so that typical values of A_v range up to 0.7 μ.

Because Fig. 4-22 is already in the Thévenin source form, we conclude that the *output* (Thévenin) impedance equals r_p. Thus, if we vary R, we have a *matched load* when $R = r_p$. For small signals, therefore, the load power is a maximum when $R = r_p$. This means that for most triodes a matched load is rather a high resistance— a few thousand to tens of thousands of ohms.

Owing to our assumptions (zero grid current, negligible tube capacitances), the input impedance to the amplifier is infinite. These assumptions are on the optimistic side, and a more realistic analysis will be made later.

4-11
The common-plate (cathode-follower) amplifier

This amplifier has a low voltage gain—actually less than unity—but it has the useful property of being able to drive low impedance loads. It is also linear over a wide voltage range when properly designed.

The load resistance R is inserted between the cathode and ground (Fig. 4-23a). If the direct current in the load is objectionable, the load is coupled to the cathode resistor through a filter circuit similar to that discussed in Sec. 4-8a.

With zero signal voltage there will be a steady plate current I_b. This will produce a voltage across R that will act as a negative bias voltage between cathode and grid. This voltage may be too large, so that a voltage E_{cc} of

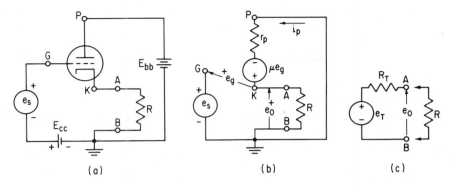

FIGURE 4-23   Circuits for cathode follower amplifier.

opposite sign may be needed. (Practical biasing circuits use networks of resistors and sometimes capacitors.)

The equivalent circuit is developed in Fig. 4-23b by replacing the triode by its Thévenin equivalent, then completing the rest of the external circuit by replacing the dc sources by short circuits. Note that the voltage e_g from G to K is made up of the signal voltage e_s plus the effect of voltage e_o. By Kirchhoff's emf law we write

$$e_g = e_s - e_o \qquad (4\text{-}44)$$

Anticipating the results of the following analysis, we remark that the voltage e_o has the same polarity as e_s and is slightly smaller, so that e_g is small. As e_s varies, the potentials of points G and K vary together, and K follows slightly below G. This explains the reason for the name *cathode-follower* circuit.

To find e_o as a function of e_s, we note that the generator μe_g can be expressed, using (4-44), as $\mu(e_s - e_o)$. This generator acts on a series circuit of R and r_p, and we need e_o across R. Thus, we may think of the voltage-divider action and write

$$\frac{e_o}{\mu(e_s - e_o)} = \frac{R}{R + r_p} \qquad (4\text{-}45)$$

Upon solving this equation for e_o/e_s we obtain

$$A_v = \frac{e_o}{e_s} = \frac{\mu R}{r_p + (\mu + 1)R} \qquad (4\text{-}46)$$

As an example, assume $\mu = 20$, $r_p = 8\,\text{k}\Omega$, and $R = 2\ \text{k}\Omega$. Then $A_v = 20 \times 2/(8 + 21 \times 2) = 40/50 = 0.80$.

Next let us obtain the Thévenin equivalent of the network to the left of terminals AB, that is, referred to the output terminals. First we find the open-circuit value of e_o, i.e., the Thévenin voltage e_T. This can be done by letting $R \to \infty$ in Eq. (4-46), which leads to

$$e_T = (e_o)_{R \to \infty} = \frac{\mu}{\mu + 1}e_s \qquad (4\text{-}47)$$

One method of finding the Thévenin impedance is to calculate the impedance "looking back" into terminals AB, with e_s set equal to zero. However, the dependent generator μe_g will be active, since e_g is partly derived from e_o. We plan to use a different approach. Because no reactive elements are present, the Thévenin impedance will be a resistance R_T (Fig. 4-23c). Then if the load resistance equals the Thévenin resistance, i.e., if $R = R_T$, the load voltage will be $e_T/2$. To use this condition, we replace R in (4-46) by R_T, solve for e_o and place this equal to $e_T/2$ from (4-47)

$$\frac{\mu R_T e_s}{r_p + (\mu + 1)R_T} = \frac{\mu}{2(\mu + 1)}e_s \qquad (4\text{-}48)$$

Solving for R_T, we find

$$R_T = \frac{r_p}{\mu + 1} \qquad (4\text{-}49)$$

Thus, the Thévenin (output) impedance of this amplifier is reduced below that of the common-cathode amplifier by the factor $1/(\mu + 1)$. Using the same numbers as in the example, we obtain $R_T = 8{,}000/21$, or $381\ \Omega$. Thus, a low resistance load can be driven effectively by means of this amplifier.

4-12
The common-grid amplifier

In this circuit (Fig. 4-24a) the grid is common, or grounded, and the signal in effect drives the cathode. The circuit is used to exploit the features of special planar triodes in high-frequency amplifiers.

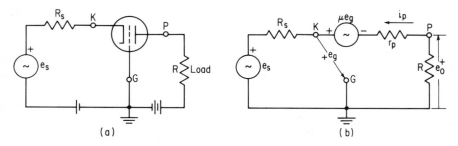

FIGURE 4-24   Grounded-grid amplifier circuits.

An analysis of the equivalent circuit of the amplifier (Fig. 4-24b) will reveal its characteristics. We note that

$$e_g = -e_s - R_s i_p \tag{4-50}$$

Therefore, the loop equation may be written as follows:

$$e_s - \mu(-e_s - R_s i_p) = -i_p(R + r_p + R_s) \tag{4-51}$$

Solving for i_p,

$$i_p = \frac{-(\mu + 1)e_s}{R + r_p + R_s(\mu + 1)} \tag{4-52}$$

But $e_o = -Ri_p$, so using Eq. (4-52), we can calculate the voltage gain

$$A_v = \frac{e_o}{e_s} = \frac{(\mu + 1)R}{R + r_p + R_s(\mu + 1)} \tag{4-53}$$

If the source resistance R_s, is zero, the voltage gain will be slightly higher than for the common-cathode amplifier. However, the output voltage is in phase with the signal.

Equation (4-53) shows that an appreciable source resistance R_s will act to reduce the voltage gain. Inspection of the equivalent circuits shows why this is true. The current i_p is present in R_s, and the resulting voltage across R_s acts in opposition to e_s, thereby reducing the gain.

Notice also that the signal source carries the current i_p. A calculation of the input impedance to the amplifier, taken to be that between terminal K and ground yields

$$Z_{\text{in}} = \frac{R + r_p}{\mu + 1} \tag{4-54}$$

Equation (4-54) shows that Z_{in} is relatively low.

An analysis for the Thévenin impedance yields

$$Z_T = r_p + (\mu + 1)R_s \tag{4-55}$$

which shows that unless R_s is zero, the output impedance is higher than for the grounded-cathode circuit.

4-13
The tetrode, pentode, and beam power tube

The *tetrode*, or double-grid tube, was developed in the search for a tube that would amplify high frequencies without the troubles that occur in triode amplifiers as a result of the electrostatic capacitance between the grid and the plate. The second grid, sometimes called the *screen grid* (Fig. 4-25), is charged to a positive potential of about 100 V. Thus, the screen grid acts

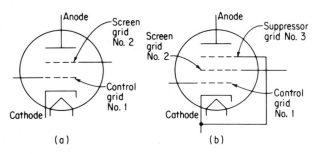

FIGURE 4-25   Symbols for (a) tetrode, (b) pentode.

like the anode of an equivalent triode consisting of the cathode, control grid, and screen grid, except that a large percentage of the electrons pass through the meshes of the screen grid and are collected by the plate. However, when the electrons hit the plate with enough velocity, they may knock out one, two, or even three electrons from the surface of the metal. These are called *secondary electrons*, and this action is called *secondary emission*. The secondary electrons have only small initial velocities, so that the local electric field immediately controls their destinies. Thus, if the screen grid is at a higher potential than the anode, the secondary electrons will move toward the screen grid and will be collected by this grid.

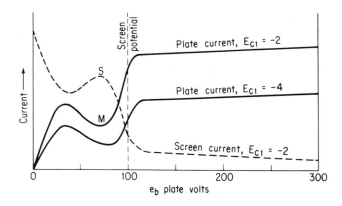

FIGURE 4-26   Curves for a tetrode tube.

The typical plate characteristic curves in Fig. 4-26 illustrate the effect of the secondary emission from the plate. Over the range from about 120 to 300 V the plate collects the electrons that come through the meshes of the screen and also attracts the secondary electrons back to the plate. The resulting curve is nearly flat in this range because the screen grid acts as an electrostatic screen and greatly reduces the effect of changes in the plate voltage on the space charge near the cathode. However, for plate voltages below the screen potential, as in region *M*, the secondary electrons from the plate drift toward the screen grid and are collected thereby to add to the screen current and reduce the plate current. This interpretation is verified by the extra screen current in the region *S*. As the plate voltage reduces still further, the electrons hitting the plate are less and less effective in producing secondary emission; thus the plate current rises again and finally falls to zero.

The control grid can control the magnitude of the plate current much as in a triode, so the tetrode can be used as an amplifier tube. However, the severely distorted plate characteristics seriously limit the range over which the tube can be operated. For this reason the tetrode, except in the modified *beam-tube* form, is nearly obsolete.

The insertion of a third grid between the screen and the plate obviates the difficulties caused by secondary emission. This tube is called the *pentode*, and the third grid is called the *suppressor* grid because it effectively suppresses the effects of secondary emission. The suppressor grid normally is connected to the cathode (Fig. 4-25b) so it is at zero electrostatic potential. Since electrons are forced by the field toward regions of higher potential, it follows that all electrons between the suppressor grid and the anode are forced toward the anode. This is true even though the anode potential may be lower than the screen potential. As a consequence, the secondary electrons that are freed from the anode are driven back to the anode and cause no diminution in the anode current. A wide spacing is used between the suppressor grid wires so that they will not interfere seriously with the main stream of electrons moving to the anode. Typical plate characteristics for a pentode are shown in Fig. 4-27. The wide useful range of these characteristics makes the pentode a desirable tube. It is manufactured in forms suitable for both voltage and power amplifiers.

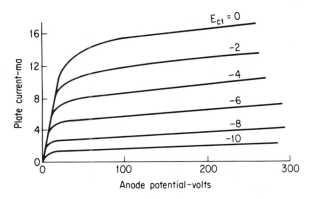

FIGURE 4-27   Plate characteristics for a pentode.

The voltage amplifier pentodes are constructed in two forms. One of these, called a *sharp cutoff* tube, has a uniform spacing of the control grid wires. The other, called a *remote cutoff* tube, has a variable spacing between the control grid wires, varying from close spacing to a fairly open spacing. As a result a large negative bias, say up to -40 V, is required to stop the electron flow completely. This tube's characteristics, therefore, change considerably as the bias changes. This feature is useful in circuits where the amplification must be controlled over a wide range, as in automatic-volume-control circuits in radio receivers.

A modified form of tetrode, called a *beam power tube*, has plate characteristics nearly the same as those of the pentode. For this reason it is sometimes called a beam pentode. The circuit symbol for this tube is the same as for the pentode (Fig. 4-25b), though the symbolic grid 3 really represents a pair of beam-forming electrodes placed between grid 2 and the anode. In this tube the second grid wires are aligned with the control-grid wires. As a result the electron flow is in a flat beam or sheet that passes between the grid wires. The effect of the large number of electrons between the screen and the plate is to lower the space potential at every point in this region. Thus, the secondary electrons from the plate are driven back to the plate just as in the pentode, and the plate characteristic curves are similar to those of the pentode.

A scheme for supplying the screen grid in a pentode or beam tube is shown in Fig. 4-28a. The dropping resistor R_{g2} adjusts the screen grid potential to the level desired at the Q point. Capacitor C acts to hold the screen grid potential nearly constant even though the screen current may vary with the signal. With the screen potential held constant the plate current is dependent on the same variables as for the triode, and the same equations and equivalent circuits apply.

The preferred form of the circuit model is shown in Fig. 4-28b. This will be the equivalent of Fig. 4-28a for small signals, assuming that the react-

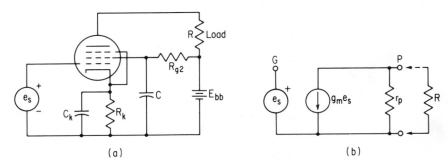

(a)   (b)

FIGURE 4-28

ance of C_k effectively short-circuits R_k at the signal frequency. Consider the voltage gain of the pentode stage having the load resistance R. This is given by Eq. (4-43), repeated here but modified as follows:

$$A_v = \frac{-\mu R}{r_p + R} = \frac{-g_m r_p R}{r_p + R} = \frac{-g_m R}{1 + \dfrac{R}{r_p}} \tag{4-56}$$

Pentodes designed for high voltage gains have values of r_p of the order of 1 $M\Omega$. With these tubes the term R/r_p is only 0.05 or less for values of R up to 50,000 Ω. For this range, therefore, this term can be dropped, and we find $A_v \cong -g_m R$. Thus, pentodes with high values of g_m develop higher gains for a given load resistance. The advantage of the Norton form of the equivalent circuit (Fig. 4-28b) is now obvious, since the approximation consists in omitting r_p from the circuit.

Two types of tube containing five grids should be mentioned. In the *pentagrid mixer tube* grids 1 and 3 both control the electron stream. Grids 2 and 4 act as positive accelerating electrodes, and grid 5 acts as a suppressor grid. This tube is used for combining two separate signals.

In the *pentagrid converter* tube the cathode and first and second grids act like a triode and are used to produce oscillations in an oscillator circuit. A signal placed on grid 4 can control the current, and grid 5 is an accelerating electrode. Thus, a separate signal can be combined with the oscillator output in the manner required in the superheterodyne radio receiver.

REFERENCES

4-1 E. J. Angelo, Jr., *Electronic Circuits*, 2d ed., McGraw-Hill Book Company, New York, 1964.

4-2 R. A. Greiner, *Semiconductor Devices and Applications*, McGraw-Hill Book Company, New York, 1961, Chaps. 1–8.

4-3 J. D. Ryder, *Electronic Fundamentals and Applications*, 3d ed., Prentice-Hall, Inc., Englewood Cliffs, N.J., 1964, Chaps. 3, 4, 8.

4-4 K. R. Spangenberg, *Fundamentals of Electron Devices*, McGraw-Hill Book Company, New York, 1957.

EXERCISES

Note: The device characteristics needed in the solution of a number of the following exercises are given in Appendix B.

4-1 Suppose that the circuit in Fig. 4-2a is set up using one diode of the twin-diode type 6 X 4. If $E_{bb} = 30$ V, find the current in the circuit if R has the values (a) 1500, (b) 1000, and (c) 500 Ω.

4-2 One diode from a 6 X 4 twin diode is used in the circuit of Fig. 4-5. Let $R = 500$ Ω, $E_{bb} = 25$ V, and $e_s = 4 \sin \omega t$. Find (a) the value of the average, or dc, current, and (b) an expression for the varying component of current i_p.

4-3 A triode amplifier as in Fig. 4-13 uses one triode in a twin triode type 12AU7A. Let $R_g = 20{,}000\ \Omega$, $R = 10{,}000\ \Omega$, $E_{cc} = -6$V, and $E_{bb} = 300$V. (a) Find E_b and I_b at the Q point. (b) What is the voltage gain if $e_g = 4 \sin \omega t$? (c) Sketch waves of e_g, i_b, and e_b on a common time axis.

4-4 Consider an amplifier that is the same as that in Prob. 4-3 except that $R = 30{,}000\ \Omega$. (a) Find E_b and I_b at the Q point. (b) What is the voltage gain if $e_g = 4 \sin \omega t$? (c) At what values of signal voltage would distortion due to (1) grid limiting and (2) cutoff be expected to set in?

4-5 Design an amplifier that uses one triode of a twin triode type 12AX7A. The desired voltage gain is 55, and the desired plate voltage peak-to-peak swing is 110 V. The plate supply voltage is not to exceed 300. Specify E_{bb}, E_{cc}, and plate load resistance.

4-6 One triode of a 12AU7A tube is used in the amplifier in Fig. 4-18. Assume that X_c is negligibly small at the signal frequency. Let $E_{bb} = 300$, $E_c = -6$, $R = 30\ k\Omega$, and $R_1 = 30\ k\Omega$. (a) Find the Q point. (b) Find the output voltage e_o if $e_g = 6 \sin 1000t$. (c) Calculate a suitable value for C if the rule of thumb that X_c should be equal to, or less than, $0.1\ R_1$ is followed.

4-7 The circuit in Fig. 4-19 uses one triode of a 12AU7A tube. Let $E_{bb} = 200$, $E_{cc} = -6$, $R = 10\ \Omega$, $n_1/n_2 = 30$, and the peak value of the sine-wave signal be 6 V. Find the output voltage across R and give the result in peak and rms values. The transformer is ideal.

4-8 Design a circuit like Fig. 4-19a that uses one triode of a 12AU7A tube and has an ideal transformer. The load resistance R is 16 Ω and the desired sine-wave voltage across R is 1.5 V rms. E_{bb} is not to exceed 250 V, and the plate dissipation under no-signal conditions is not to exceed 2.5 W. A minimum signal voltage is desirable. Specify E_{bb}, E_{cc}, n_1/n_2, and the required signal voltage.

4-9 Sketch small-signal equivalent circuits for each of the circuits in Fig. 4-29. Let the triode parameters be μ, r_p, and g_m, and neglect tube capacitance effects.

4-10 (a) Derive expressions for e_{o1}/e_s and for e_{o2}/e_s in terms of the tube parameters and circuit constants for the circuit in Fig. 4-29a. (b) This circuit is useful for providing equal but out-of-phase output voltages. Specify how this can be done.

4-11 Consider the circuit in Fig. 4-29c. Derive the equivalent Thévenin source for this circuit relative to terminals AB, assuming that the reactance of capacitor C is zero.

4-12 (a) Obtain the parameters r_p, g_m, and μ from the plate characteristics for one unit of a 12AU7A tube at the Q point given by $E_c = -6$, $E_b = 250$ V. (b) Repeat for the point $E_c = -14$, $E_b = 300$ V.

4-13 (a) Find r_p, g_m, and μ from the plate characteristics for one unit of a 12AX7A tube at a Q point given by $E_c = -2$, $E_b = 250$ V. (b) If the two grids, two plates,

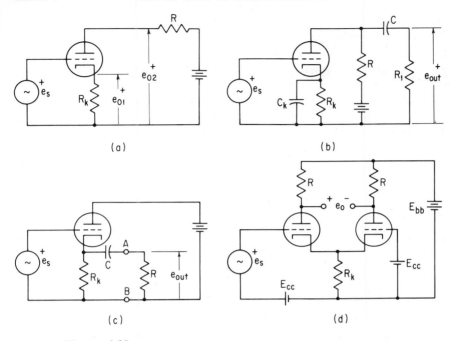

FIGURE 4-29

and two cathodes in the 12AX7A were connected together and the combination used as a triode, what would be the values of r_p, g_m, and μ at the same Q point as in (a)?

4-14 Show that Eq. (4-35) is consistent with Eq. (4-39).

4-15 (a) Rewrite Eqs. (4-33) and (4-36) using delta symbols for increments, i.e., Δi_b for i_p, etc. Sketch two equivalent circuit models for the triode labeled with these symbols. (b) Draw two equivalent circuit models labeled with symbols for the phasor values of sinusoidal currents and voltages.

4-16 Suppose that a triode is to be selected for a grounded-cathode amplifier as shown in Fig. 4-13 from among the three sample triodes in Table 4-1. If maximum small-signal voltage gain is the only basis for selection, which tube should be selected if the load resistance is (a) 10,000 Ω, or (b) 2000 Ω?

4-17 It can be shown that the Thévenin impedance referred to terminals AB in the cathode-follower circuit in Fig. 4-29c is given by $Z_T = R_k r_p / [r_p + (\mu + 1)R_k]$. Suppose that a high mu triode is used, for which $\mu = 100$ and $r_p = 62{,}500$. (a) Choose the value of R_k that will give a matched-load condition with a load of 500 Ω (typical of some transmission lines). (b) What is the voltage gain of this circuit if R_k has the value calculated in (a) and the load R is 500 Ω?

4-18 Suppose that a 12AU7A twin triode is used in the differential amplifier circuit (see Sec. 14-2) in Fig. 4-29d. Let $R = 20$ kΩ, $R_k = 10$ kΩ, and assume that each triode is to have $E_c = -8$ V and $I_b = 10$ mA at the Q point. What values are required for E_{cc} and E_{bb}?

4-19 (a) Derive Eq. (4-54). (b) Derive Eq. (4-55).

4-20 A sharp cutoff pentode, type 6AU6A, is operated in the circuit of Fig. 4-28a. The conditions are: $E_{bb} = 250$ V, grid 2 V $= 125$, $R_k = 100$ Ω, $R = 20,000$ Ω, $I_b = 7.6$ mA, and grid 2 current $= 3.0$ mA. Under these conditions $r_p \cong 1.5$ MΩ and $g_m = 4.5$ mmhos. (a) What is the grid 1 bias? (b) Choose a value for R_{g2}. (c) What is the voltage gain?

5

Physical Principles
of Semiconductor Devices

5-1
The junction transistor

The rapid development of the transistor following its invention† has led to
its application in many circuits in which grid-controlled vacuum tubes were
formerly predominant. Advantages of the transistor are its small size, rug-
gedness, and absence of cathode heating power. The original transistors
consisted of two fine wire points placed in contact with a wafer of n-type
germanium called the *base*. Junction transistors, which are derived from the
pn junction diode (Chapter 3), are used exclusively today and will be discussed in the following sections. Other types of transistors and other semiconductor devices will be mentioned at the end of the chapter.

Two common types of junction transistors are the *grown-junction* and the
alloy-junction types. In the manufacture of the grown-junction transistor
(Fig. 5-1a and b), the single crystal growing process, described in Sec. 3-11,
is used. For reasons that will appear later, the middle section is made extremely thin, of the order of one-thousandth of an inch. The left-hand section,
called the *emitter*, has a lower resistivity than the right-hand section, called
the *collector*. As a result, though the transistor appears to be symmetrical in
the diagram, it is in fact not so, and the emitter and collector electrodes

†J. Bardeen and W. H. Brattain, "The Transistor, A Semi-conductor Triode," *Phys.
Rev.*, **74**, 230 (1948).

111

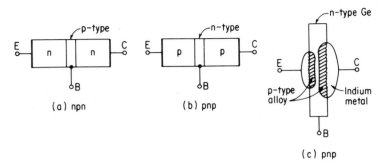

FIGURE 5-1   (a) and (b) Grown junction transistors and (c) alloy junction transistor.

must be identified. The middle section has an intermediate resistivity and is called the *base*.

Two different techniques are used for forming the grown junctions. In one method the impurity added to the melted Ge or Si is controlled to provide the desired type of semiconductor. For example, to produce *npn* layers in succession as the crystal is grown, the high-resistivity collector region is grown first, and a donor impurity is used to produce an *n*-type crystal. Then an acceptor impurity, such as gallium, is added to the melt in sufficient quantity to become predominant and thereby produce the *p*-type layer. After a time needed to grow about a 1-mil layer, a donor material, such as arsenic, is added to the melt in sufficient quantity to produce the low-resistivity *n*-type emitter region. The transistor blank is sawed into many sections about 20 mils square and 250 mils long, and each section is made into a transistor by attaching leads and hermetically sealing it into an enclosure.

A second technique for producing grown junctions is to incorporate nearly equal amounts of donor and acceptor impurities into the melt. Then the percentages of impurities that enter the crystal depend on its rate of growth, and with careful control the growth rates can be adjusted to produce *npn* transistor blanks.

A wafer of germanium or silicon about 100 mils square and 8 mils thick is used in the construction of a small alloy-type transistor (Fig. 5-1c). A small pellet of a metal of valence 3 or 5 is placed on each side of the wafer, and the whole is heated so that an alloy is formed. For example, indium of valence 3 alloys with the germanium to form a layer of *p*-type material. Thus a *pnp* junction transistor is formed. By careful control the gap between the two *p*-type layers is brought down to about 1 mil or even less. The *emitter, base, and collector* material resistivities bear relations similar to those in the grown-junction transistor.

One notices that a crude picture of a transistor consists of two rectifying

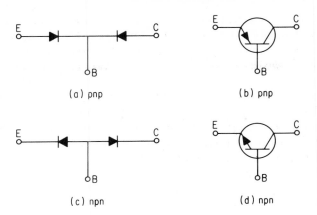

FIGURE 5-2   Representations of *pnp* and *npn* transistors.

pn junctions in series. This leads to an elementary representation in terms of rectifier symbols in Fig. 5-2a and c. The standard conventional representation is shown in Fig. 5-2b and d. As will become evident after reading Sec. 5-4, viewing the transistor as two rectifying junctions in series is only useful for visualizing the forward and reverse directions across the two junctions.

5-2
Experimental evidence of hole motion

Before proceeding to a detailed discussion of the junction transistor let us examine an experiment of Haynes and Shockley.† A relatively long bar of *n*-type germanium is fitted with two point contacts, labeled *E* and *C* in Fig. 5-3.

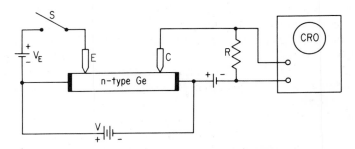

FIGURE 5-3   Arrangement for Haynes-Shockley experiment.

†J. R. Haynes and W. Shockley, *Phys. Rev.*, **75**, 691 (1949). See also W. Shockley, "Transistor Electronics: Imperfections, Unipolar and Analog Transistors," *Proc. IRE,* **40,** 1289–1313 (1952).

A battery V sends an electronic current down the length of the bar. The electrodes at the ends of the bar are of the ohmic type. Means are provided so that contact E can be charged positively through closing switch S and the current collected by the negatively biased contact C can be observed on a CR oscilloscope.

Now consider that switch S is closed for a short time so as to produce a short square-wave pulse of voltage (Fig. 5-4a) on the emitter E. A change in collector current which matches the emitter pulse is observed immediately. However, after a time delay there is a rounded pulse of collector current. If the experiment is repeated with a lower voltage V, then the delayed pulse is spread out more and suffers a longer delay (Fig. 5-4b).

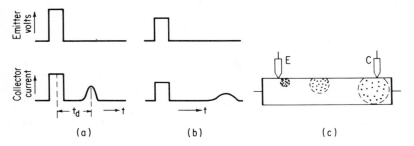

FIGURE 5-4   Results of Haynes-Shockley experiment.

The first pulse is the result of the increase in *electron* current caused by the potential V_E impressed at E. This increase occurs almost instantly owing to the interactions on each other of the electrons in the bar much the same as in a copper wire. The delayed pulse is interpreted as the reaction on the current at C caused by the arrival of the cloud of *holes* which were emitted from E into the n-type material. This cloud diffuses somewhat as it travels down the bar. The time delay t_d is a measure of the time needed for the holes to move from E to C under the force of the electric field. Thus an approximate drift velocity for holes can be measured by this experiment. For example, if the electric field is 10 V/cm and the distance EC is 0.4 cm, the measured time t_d would be about 22 μsec, indicating a drift speed of 18,200 cm/sec.

If the voltage V is reduced, then the drift speed is reduced and the cloud of holes has more time to diffuse, so the pulse received at C comes later (Fig. 5-4b) and is spread out more. Furthermore, the effect is smaller because more holes have disappeared by recombination with electrons during their journey along the bar. A schematic interpretation of the cloud of holes as it moves down the bar is given in Fig. 5-4c.

5-3
Transistor characteristics
with the common-base connection

In Fig. 5-5a are shown the symbols adopted for the designation of the electrode currents and potentials for the dc characteristics of *both* the *npn* and
the *pnp* junction transistors. Since the current symbols, following convention,
all designate assumed positive currents toward the transistor, we realize that
one or two of the currents must actually be negative. Figure 5-5a follows the
practice used with the early point-contact transistor of making the base electrode the *reference* or *common* terminal. In practical circuits the terminal
chosen to be common to both the signal input and the signal output circuits
may be any one of the three electrodes. The most used connection is the
common-emitter arrangement, and the *common-collector* and *common-base*
connections are less often employed.

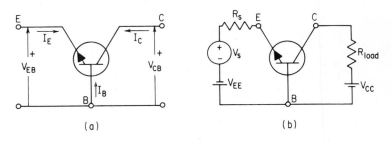

(a)   (b)

FIGURE 5-5   (a) Common-base connection and (b) elementary
common-base amplifier.

Some ideas relating to transistor operation can be introduced by means of
the elementary common-base transistor amplifier shown in Fig. 5-5b, which
incorporates an *npn* transistor. By analogy with the thermionic triode we
might expect that dc bias voltages would also be needed with the transistor
amplifier, as shown at V_{EE} and V_{cc}. If we recall the directions of easy conduction in the two transistor junctions, we note that the dc bias V_{EE} biases the
base-to-emitter path in the *forward* direction, and, V_{cc} biases the collector-
to-base path in the *reverse* direction. One may ask how it is that this circuit
will give a power gain since the collector (load) current would be expected to
be smaller than the emitter current? In part the reason is that the emitter-to-
base voltage and therefore the signal voltage will be small (assuming that
R_s is small), and the collector-to-base voltage and the load voltage can be
relatively large. Additionally, in the junction transistor the design is such that

the collector current nearly equals the emitter current. As a result the amplifier develops useful power and voltage gains.

The foregoing paragraph suggests which voltage and current regions are
of primary interest, namely, the variations of I_E and I_C in the ranges where
V_{EB} is negative and V_{CB} is positive. (For a *pnp* transistor both of these polarities would be reversed.) Typical characteristic curves for a small *npn* transistor are shown in Fig. 5-6. Let us examine first the curve in Fig. 5-6a for
$I_E = 0$. This corresponds to a reverse voltage test of the collector to base
"diode," and I_{CO} is the *reverse saturation* or *cutoff* current (exaggerated in the
figure). When an emitter current flows, as for example $I_E = -2$ mA, a collector current of slightly smaller magnitude than I_E flows which is only slightly dependent on collector voltage. The internal actions that account for this
behavior will be considered in Sec. 5-4.

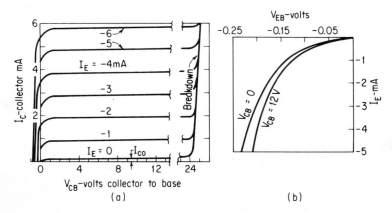

FIGURE 5-6   Common-base characteristics: (a) output characteristics, (b) input characteristics.

The effectiveness of changes in the emitter current in causing changes in
the collector current is described by the parameter α. Because α will later be
used in a similar way for a different circuit and because α is defined for both
small signals and large signals, we use the double subscript notation in the
defining equation

$$\alpha_{fb} = -\frac{\partial I_C}{\partial I_E}\bigg|_{V_{CB}=\text{const}} \tag{5-1}$$

The paramenter α_{fb} is called the *small-signal common-base short-circuit
forward-current transfer ratio* or *common-base short-circuit current gain.*
In junction transistors typical values of α_{fb} range from about 0.90 to 0.995.
For a given unit, the value will depend somewhat on the operating conditions.

The *static value* of the parameter, which applies for dc values, is defined as

$$\alpha_{FB} = -\frac{\Delta I_C}{\Delta I_E}\bigg|_{V_{CB}=\text{const}} \tag{5-2}$$

where it is understood that ΔI_E is the change from zero to a particular value.

If the small effect of changes in V_{CB} on α_{FB} be neglected, we can write a simple linear expression for the common-base collector characteristics in the *active region*, namely,

$$I_C = I_{CO} - \alpha_{FB}I_E \tag{5-3}$$

where I_{CO} is the collector cutoff current with $I_E = 0$, i.e., with the emitter open. The active region in Fig. 5-6a is the region in which the characteristics are approximately parallel straight lines. One application of Eq. (5-3) will be in the discussion of the effect of temperature on transistor characteristics.

5-4
Internal transistor action

The picture of a transistor as two semiconductor diodes is inadequate, primarily because the phenomena in the base region are not properly represented. In Fig. 5-7 the internal actions in an *npn* transistor are shown schematically under the usual bias conditions. For clarity the base width is exaggerated so that the actions in this region can be portrayed. The conditions at the left-hand junction are similar to those shown in Fig. 3-16a. The energy barrier is reduced sufficiently by the bias voltage V_{EE} so that swarms of electrons from the emitter surmount the barrier and are *emitted* as it were into the *p*-type base material. The electric field is nearly zero in the base except near the junctions, but most of the emitted electrons cross the base region by *diffusion*. When they reach the region of the base-collector junction, they are

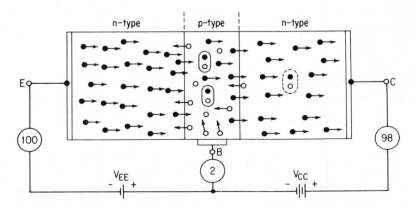

FIGURE 5-7   Internal actions in an *npn* transistor in the active condition. Open circles=holes; solid circles=electrons.

accelerated toward the collector by the internal field, and this electron flow accounts for the major portion of the collector current. Thus the motions of the *minority* carriers in the base predominate in controlling the collector current. Some electrons are lost in the base region by *recombination* with holes, indicated by solid-line ovals. Holes that disappear by this process must be replaced by holes introduced at the base electrode. Thus a portion of the current in the base lead is required to compensate for the recombination of holes in the base. The remaining portion of the base current is needed to compensate for the difference between the hole currents across the two junctions. Holes are emitted from the base into the emitter, but at a low rate relative to the electron emission in the reverse direction, owing to the relatively high impurity content in the emitter. Holes also enter the base region across the collector-base junction. This flow can be minimized by heavy doping of the collector. The base current therefore is primarily dependent on the recombination in the base and on the emission of holes from base to emitter. Typical relative magnitudes of the currents in the emitter, base, and collector leads are shown in Fig. 5-7 by the meter readings 100, 2, and 98.

In summary then, we see that transistor action consists in controlling the collector current by the emission of minority carriers (electrons in the *npn* transistor) into the base from the emitter, the diffusion of these carriers across the base, and their accelerated motion through the base-collector junction. A small base current is needed to compensate for the loss of minority carriers from the base.

These internal actions account in a general way for the shapes of the curves in Fig. 5-6. For example, the collector current is controlled by the emitter current (Fig. 5-6a) and is slightly smaller than the emitter current over most of the range of the curves. The magnitude of the base current is the difference of the magnitudes of the collector and emitter currents, consequently the base current is small. The input characteristic (Fig. 5-6b) is essentially the *forward* characteristic of the emitter-base junction. If the current I_E is held constant while I_C and V_{CB} are increasing, we notice that the magnitude of V_{EB} decreases.

5-5
Energy band picture of the npn transistor

An insight into transistor action can be gained by a study of its electron energy-level diagrams under different bias conditions. These diagrams can be built up from the diagrams already given for the *pn* junction. Figure 5-8 shows a schematic energy level picture for the *npn* transistor with zero bias voltages. We recall that the holes stay in the valence band but tend to rise to higher levels. The electrons, on the other hand, tend to drop to lower energies under

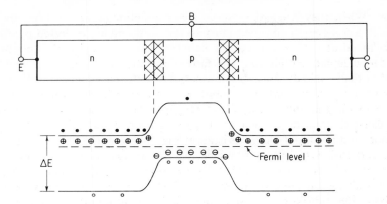

FIGURE 5-8   Energy level diagram of *npn* transistor with zero
bias. Open circles=holes; solid circles=electrons.

the influence of the inner fields. At the junctions the charge depletion region
is indicated by the crosshatching, though its width is much exaggerated.

When forward bias is applied to the emitter-base junction, the barrier
height decreases and the depletion region narrows (Fig. 5-9), so that electrons
are flowing into the base in large numbers. We notice that the edge of the conduction band in the base is drawn horizontally, so that there is no electric
field in the base.† Consequently the electrons move across the base by diffu-

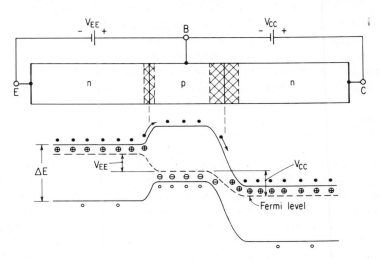

FIGURE 5-9   Energy level diagram of *npn* transistor in the active
region.

†An exception to this state of affairs occurs in the diffused base or drift transistor,
which has improved high-frequency characteristics.

sion. When they reach the collector-base junction, they quickly move into the collector region and then move to the right and are collected by the contact metal at C to constitute the collector current. In actual transistors the widened depletion region extends farther into the base than into the collector, rather than equal distances as shown, because the base material usually has a lower concentration of acceptors than the collector has donors.

Suppose that the voltage V_{EE} is changed. This change would be expected to cause the emitter current to vary in an exponential manner, as for a pn diode, and the input characteristics in Fig. 5-6b confirm this expectation. If the collector-base voltage is varied, we do not expect a change in current, because the carriers that diffuse to the edge of the base-collector junction depletion region are sure to move into the collector region. As Fig. 5-6a shows, the collector current changes only slightly with collector voltage. This small effect will be analyzed in the following section.

5-6
Early effect; punch-through; breakdown

Some discussion of the small effect that the collector voltage exerts on the collector current is in order. This is known as the Early† effect, after the worker who first provided a theoretical analysis of the phenomenon. We recall that the depletion layer varies in thickness as the reverse voltage varies on a junction diode (Sec. 3-11). As the collector voltage *increases* in a transistor, the depletion region invades the base region farther and farther. As a result the effective width of the base *decreases*, because the minority carriers in the base need only reach the inner edge of the depletion region before they are "emitted" into the collector. The decrease in effective base width causes an increased collector current (I_E held constant) owing to the decreased opportunity for recombination and the consequent reduction of loss of minority carriers.

An additional result of the variation in base width is its effect on the emitter voltage for a constant emitter current. The emitter current is primarily a function of the inner barrier height at the emitter-base junction, but the decrease in effective base width as the collector voltage rises tends to raise the emitter current. Thus, if the emitter current is to remain constant as the collector voltage increases, the emitter junction barrier height must increase slightly, with a corresponding decrease in the magnitude of voltage V_{EB}. An added reason for a change in V_{EB} in this situation is the change in the voltage drop in the base where the base current spreads out toward the base terminal. The base current decreases slightly as V_{CB} increases, so the ohmic

†J. M. Early, "Effects of Space-Charge Layer Widening in Junction Transistors," *Proc. IRE*, **40**, 1401 (1952).

resistance drop in the base decreases. The combined effect is to produce an effect on V_{EB} caused by changes in V_{CB}, which may be regarded as a small *feedback* effect.

High values of collector voltage may lead to failure through *breakdown* or *punch-through*. The punch-through occurs when the collector voltage is so high that the effective base width approaches zero. In effect the carriers then spill over directly from emitter to collector. Breakdown is an independent phenomenon which occurs in the collector junction. One cause of breakdown is the multiplication of charge carriers by a process analogous to ionization by collision in gaseous discharges. Another type of breakdown (Zener break-down) is associated with the breaking apart of the covalent bonds in the crystal by the action of the high electric field in the junction. The resulting hole-electron pairs contribute to the current, which may build up sharply with increasing voltage.

5-7
Common emitter characteristics

Many transistor circuits, for example, the amplifier† in Fig. 5-10a, utilize the emitter as the common electrode. Here the output circuit includes the collector-to-emitter path, and the input signal is applied from base to emitter. For the analysis of such circuits the static or dc collector characteristics (Fig. 5-10b) are required. Here the collector-to-emitter voltage is symbolized by V_C rather than V_{CE}, as the reference electrode is understood. Notice that

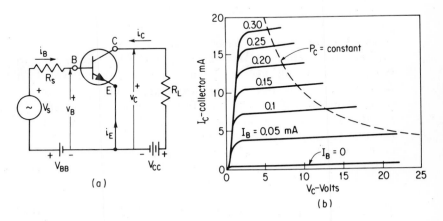

FIGURE 5-10   (a) Elementary common-emitter amplifier and (b) collector characteristics.

†This amplifier incorporates an *npn* transistor, though *pnp* types are also often used.

the *base current* is the parameter chosen for the third variable rather than the base-to-emitter voltage. This choice is consistent with the explanation of the transistor action in terms of the junction currents.

From Fig. 5-10b we see that if the base current is changed by 0.1 mA, the collector current changes by about 6 mA for constant V_C, giving a 60-fold greater change. This observation suggests the high current gain obtainable with the common emitter circuit. We can formalize the relation between base current and collector current as follows. The current law requires that

$$I_E = - (I_B + I_C) \tag{5-4}$$

Upon eliminating I_E between Eqs. (5-3) and (5-4) we obtain

$$I_C = \frac{I_{CO}}{1 - \alpha_{FB}} + \frac{\alpha_{FB}}{1 - \alpha_{FB}} I_B \tag{5-5}$$

We recall that Eq. (5-2) was written for the common-base characteristics, and the approximation was used that V_{CB} had no effect. If we wish to apply Eq. (5-5) to the common-emitter connection, we must assume that changes in V_{CE} have no effect, which is nearly the same assumption as used before, since V_{EB} is small.

In circuit calculations involving incremental currents it is helpful to use the small signal parameter α_{fe}, defined as follows:

$$\alpha_{fe} = \left. \frac{\partial I_C}{\partial I_B} \right|_{V_{CE}=\text{const}} \tag{5-6}$$

This parameter is called the *small-signal forward short-circuit current gain*.

The static value of the common-emitter alpha is defined as

$$\alpha_{FE} = \left. \frac{\Delta I_C}{\Delta I_B} \right|_{V_{CE}=\text{const}} \tag{5-7}$$

Here ΔI_B is the increment measured from $I_B = 0$.

For some purposes, *reverse* current gains such as α_{rb} and α_{re} are defined. If no confusion with these gains will result, then the simplified symbols α_b, α_e, etc. are used for the forward current gains. The symbol α with no subscript is understood to mean α_{fb}. In the transistor literature the symbol β has also been used in place of α_{fe}. We shall later introduce a hybrid parameter that is equal to α_{fe}.

If we apply Eq. (5-7) to (5-5), we obtain

$$\alpha_{FE} = \frac{\alpha_{FB}}{1 - \alpha_{FB}} \tag{5-8}$$

To illustrate the magnitude of the common-emitter short-circuit current gain we note that if, for example, $\alpha_{FB} = 0.98$, then $\alpha_{FE} = 0.98/(1 - 0.98) = 49$. Furthermore, small changes in α_{FB} will produce larger changes in α_{FE} and in the relation of I_C to I_B according to Eq. (5-5). The variations in transistor manufacturing processes lead to small variations in α_{FB}, which cause the values of α_e and of α_{FE} of different transistors of the same type designation to vary over a considerable range, sometimes as much as three to one. Therefore transistor specifications often embody a range of specified values of these parameters or specify their minimum values. The parameter values are also dependent on the collector current and on the junction temperature.

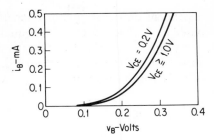

FIGURE 5-11   Input characteristics, common emitter connection.

Though the transistor is viewed primarily as a current-operated device, a knowledge of base-to-emitter voltage as a function of base current is needed in a study of the input circuit phenomena. Typical curves for a germanium transistor are shown in Fig. 5-11. For values of V_{CE} over 1 V, the current-voltage relation is essentially that of the base-emitter diode. Therefore the diode equation given in Chapter 3 will apply; thus,

$$i_B = I_o\left[\exp\left(\frac{eV_B}{kT}\right) - 1\right] \cong I_o \exp\left(\frac{eV_B}{kT}\right) \tag{3-3a}$$

The approximate form is sufficiently accurate for values of V_B larger than $4kT/e$, or for $V_B > 0.10$ V at room temperature. In this range the current varies exponentially with the voltage. At higher temperatures deviations from the exponential variation occur (see Fig. 7-19b), but the relation is always markedly nonlinear. As a result there is an undesirable nonlinear relation between signal voltage and base current which may cause distortion in the output wave.

5-8
Effect of temperature; collector dissipation rating

Transistors are subject to considerable variation in characteristics from unit to unit, particularly in the common-emitter characteristics. Here the base current parameter is in effect the small difference between the two large currents I_E and I_C, and any small change in α_{FB} will cause a relatively large change in the curves.

In Sec. 3-11 we have referred to the physical basis for the saturation current in pn junction diodes I_o and have indicated that thermal effects are largely responsible for its magnitude. Likewise the value of I_{CO}, the collector current for zero emitter current in the common-base connection, is highly dependent on the transistor temperature. The value of I_c for $I_B = 0$ (designated as I_{CEO}) is, by Eq. (5-5), equal to $I_{co}/(1 - \alpha_{FB})$. This value is therefore many times I_{co} and also varies with temperature in the same way that I_{co} varies. Now if the temperature rises, the whole set of collector characteristics is shifted upward by the amount $I_{co}/(1 - \alpha_{FB})$, as illustrated in Fig. 5-12.

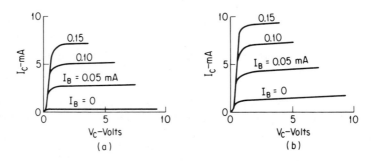

FIGURE 5-12   Effect of temperature on collector characteristics: (a) normal temperature and (b) elevated temperature.

These temperature effects require that careful attention be paid to the dc bias circuits so that replacement of a transistor or a change in its temperature will not throw the operation into undesirable ranges on the characteristics.

As can be seen in Fig. 5-13, transistors are very small compared with vacuum tubes of similar power ratings and have a correspondingly low heat capacity. The losses in the transistor will raise its temperature, and in most circuits the losses rise as the temperature rises, and a tendency arises toward a cumulative or runaway heating effect which may lead to melting and burn-

FIGURE 5-13   Representative transistors. Transistor dissipation ratings, left to right: low-power types (rated in free air at 25°C) 60 mW, 150 mW, 150 mW, 200 mW, 250 mW, 300 mW; power types (rated at case temperature of 25°C) 5W, 100W, 150W. (University of Wisconsin Photographic Laboratory)

out of the transistor. This catastrophe can be prevented if the power dissipation at the collector (the major power loss in the transistor) is limited to a rated value prescribed by the manufacturer. Considering quiescent conditions, we have for this power

$$P_C = V_C I_C \qquad (5\text{-}9)$$

called the *collector* power. Therefore, if P_C is fixed by the rating, I_C and V_C are related by a hyperbola such as the dotted curve in Fig. 5-10b. Furthermore, the transistor should be biased so that the quiescent point lies below this curve. Owing to its low heat storage capacity, a transistor can be ruined by being subjected to excessive heating for even a short time.

5-9
Small signal parameters based
on internal behavior

In the analysis of the application of electronic devices in circuits one finds a great simplification if the device can be represented by a simplified model or equivalent circuit. For example, when dealing with the high-vacuum diode, the dynamic plate resistance based on a linearization of the three-halves power function is used. Similarly, we seek a model of the transistor which will represent its behavior for small signals. This implies that the main concern is with the fluctuating component of voltage or current which results from the impressed signal. For convenience the signal is thought of as a low-frequency sinusoidal wave, though other wave forms can also be analyzed by means of the equivalent circuits.

Consider the common-base circuit in Fig. 5-5. In accord with the Institute of Electrical and Electronics Engineers standards† we adopt lowercase letters for time-varying components or total values and capitals for average, root-mean-square, or maximum values. Furthermore, *lowercase subscripts* indicate the *varying components*, and *capital letter subscripts* mean *dc components* and *instantaneous total values*. Figure 5-14 is intended to illustrate these conventions as applied to the emitter-to-base voltage and the collector current waves. Here the signal is assumed to start operating at instant t_1, so that a short section of the dc or static bias condition is shown. In what follows the *varying components*, e.g., i_c, v_{eb}, and the related quantities of v_{cb} and i_b will be of primary interest. Note that the second subscript in v_{eb} and v_{cb} serves to indicate the base as the reference electrode. When no confusion is caused thereby, the second subscript will be omitted; then the reference electrode must be understood.

As a much oversimplified equivalent circuit consider Fig. 5-15a. Here

---

†"IEEE Standard Letter Symbols for Semiconductor Devices," *IEEE Trans. on Electron Devices*, v. ED-11, No. 8, Aug. 1964, p. 392–397.

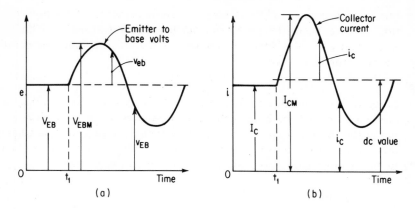

FIGURE 5-14 Illustration of conventional symbols.

the basic transistor action is shown by the constant *current source* of value $\alpha_b i_e$ introduced into the collector circuit. Here α_b is the short-circuit current gain already defined, which has a value of the order of 0.98. Thus a collector current equal to, say, 0.98 of the emitter current would flow, regardless of the load resistance or of collector voltage.

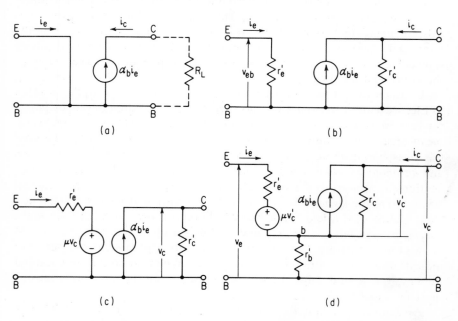

FIGURE 5-15 Development of an equivalent circuit for small signals.

Actually, the varying collector voltage causes a variation in collector current through the base widening effect. Consequently a shunting resistor, r'_c in Fig. 5-15b, is introduced to account for this variation. A second improvement in this diagram is the addition of r'_e, a dynamic resistance required to represent the forward resistance of the emitter-base junction.

A third refinement is needed to include the effect of the collector voltage, acting through the base-widening mechanism, on the emitter current-voltage relationship. This produces an inherent *feedback* effect from output circuit to input circuit. The effect can be represented by the equivalent voltage generator μv_c, as in Fig. 5-15c.

The elements of Fig. 5-15c are intended to represent the *inner* behavior of the emitter-base and base-collector junctions. Therefore an added resistor, r'_b in Fig. 5-15d, is needed to account for the ohmic resistance from the *external* base connection to the effective center of the base region. This resistance is called the *base spreading resistance*. The resistance r'_b is appreciable owing to the thinness of the base region. A modified form of this equivalent circuit will be used in the following chapter. Further modifications of the equivalent circuits are needed to account for junction capacitance and carrier transit time effects, as discussed in Chapter 7.

5-10
The pnpn silicon controlled rectifier (SCR)

A number of semiconductor devices have been developed† which have characteristics similar to those of a gaseous thyratron. As shown schematically in Fig. 5-16a, the *SCR* is a three-terminal device comprising three junctions $J1$, $J2$, and $J3$. The forward direction for the device corresponds to the for-

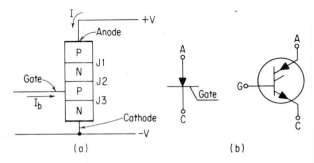

FIGURE 5-16   (a) Schematic diagram of silicon controlled rectifier. (b) Symbols for *SCR*.

†T.P. Sylvan, *Electronics*, **32**, No. 10, p. 50, Mar. 6, 1959.

ward direction for junctions $J1$ and $J3$, i.e, with a positive anode to cathode voltage drop. Consequently junction $J2$ is *reverse*-biased under this condition and would be expected to sustain the impressed voltage. However, when the gate (or base) current I_b increases sufficiently, the device suddenly switches to a low-resistance conducting state. If the impressed voltage is raised with the gate open ($I_b = 0$), the same switching action will occur, but at a higher voltage. Figure 5-17 illustrates this behavior. For example, when the gate current is I_{b1}, the *breakover voltage* is at V_{BO}. Increasing the gate current to I_{b2} would produce a breakover at point N at a lower voltage. In the high conduction condition the V-I characteristic is line GG, which represents a voltage drop of about 1 to 3 V for currents up to 50 A in a typical unit. In this condition the gate current has no control over the anode current. The anode current must be reduced to nearly zero before the gate regains control over the breakover voltage.

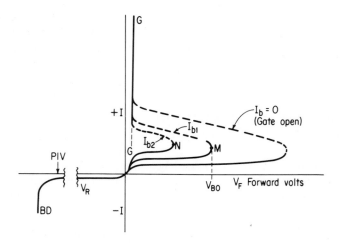

FIGURE 5-17   Control characteristics of silicon controlled rectifier.

Because breakdown voltages up to hundreds of volts can be controlled, the device can control powers well into the multikilowatt range. With reversed impressed voltage V_R an avalanche breakdown will develop at BD, so that a maximum peak-reverse-voltage rating is required.

The *SCR* is applied in a host of circuits for (1) switching currents on or off, (2) controlling the ac power going to a load, (3) converting ac power to a controlled dc power in controlled rectifier applications (Sec. 8-8), (4) voltage regulation, and (5) converting dc power to ac power in so-called *inverter* circuits. In these circuits the gate is called on to control the start of the anode current, but the anode current is reduced to a small value (or the anode voltage is reversed) in order to return the *SCR* to its high resistance condition.

5-11
Additional types of transistor

Several modified types of transistor have been developed and more appear from time to time. One class of modification is in the structural arrangement. For example, in the *mesa* construction the base and emitter are elevated strips or rectangles on one side of a plane pellet which acts as the base. In another arrangement, called a *planar* construction, the emitter and base are formed by diffusing impurities into one side of a silicon pellet, which acts as the collector.

Additional types will be explained by reference to Fig. 5-18.

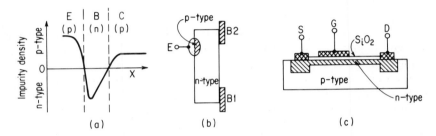

FIGURE 5-18   (a) Impurity density variation in the base region of diffused base transistor. (b) Schematic diagram of unijunction transistor. (c) Diagram of the *MOS*-type field-effect transistor. S = source, G = gate, and D = drain.

a. Diffused base transistor; drift transistor

Several fabrication techniques are used to produce transistors that have an accelerating field in the base region. This result is attained by producing a gradation of impurity in the base, as shown for a *pnp* transistor in Fig. 5-18a. The technique is to produce the base by diffusing the impurity into a *p*-type wafer. In this way a thin, low resistivity base is produced. The gradation of impurity causes a resistivity gradient in the base and a "built-in" electric field. The field acts to accelerate the drifting holes across the base and thus improves the switching speed and the high-frequency response.

b. Unijunction transistor

As shown in Fig. 5-18b, this device has two (ohmic) base connections on a bar of *n*-type material. A *p*-type emitter is provided on the opposite side of the bar. The reader will note a similarity to the device in Fig. 5-3, and in fact the unijunction transistor operates in a similar way. A voltage of, say, 20 V is impressed between the two bases, with $B2$ positive. If the emitter is open-circuited, we may think that the potential divider action between $B2$ and $B1$ will establish a positive emitter potential of, say, 12 V. However, when a positive emitter current is established, the emitter injects holes into the bar. This initially requires an emitter voltage just over 12 V because of the rectifying emitter contact. The emitted holes move downward toward $B1$ and attract electrons to maintain charge neutrality. As a result, the resistance of the bar between E and $B1$ falls, and the potential of E also falls. Thus a falling volt-ampere characteristic results for the emitter-to-base $B1$ path. This negative dynamic resistance characteristic is useful in sawtooth generator, trigger, and pulse circuit applications.

c. Field-effect transistors

In one type of field-effect transistor the variation of the thickness of the depletion region at a *pn* junction is caused to control a transverse current through a channel of *n*-type material. The controlled current enters the channel at a *source* electrode and leaves at a *drain* electrode. The negative voltage on the *p*-type material, which controls the current, is called the *gate* voltage.

In another type of field-effect transistor, known as the *metal-oxide-semiconductor* (MOS) type[†], the control action is similar except that the gate voltage is applied to a metallic electrode on an insulating oxide layer. One form of the device is shown schematically in Fig. 5-18c. The current from the source S to the drain D is carried in the narrow channel of *n*-type silicon formed in the relatively high resistivity *p*-type substrate. An insulating oxide layer on the *n*-type region carries the metallic gate electrode G. A voltage impressed on the gate produces a field which extends into the *n*-type channel. With a negative gate voltage the field terminates on immobile positive space charge produced by depleting the region of electrons. A variation of this voltage will vary the depth of the depletion region and thereby vary the effective depth remaining for electronic conduction in the channel. Thus the channel current can be controlled by the gate voltage.

A positive gate voltage produces mobile electronic space charge in the channel and can thereby increase the channel current. As a result a reasonably linear transfer characteristic between gate-to-source voltage and drain current is achieved. However, curves of channel current versus source voltage are nonlinear, the current approaching saturation values at the higher voltages. The amplitudes of these curves vary with the gate voltage, and the family of curves is similar to the plate characteristics of a pentode tube.

A signal applied to the gate needs to furnish only the small leakage and capacitance currents required by the gate electrode. A typical value of input

†S. R. Hofstein and F. P. Heiman, "The Silicon Insulated-gate Field-effect Transistor," *Proc. IEEE*, **51**, 1190, 1963.

impedance at low frequencies corresponds to about 10^{13} Ω resistance shunted by about 5 pF capacitance. Owing to its high input impedance the device is suitable for the input stages of electrometer and operational amplifier circuits. The device also has good potentialities for high-frequency amplification up to 250 MHz, and modified forms are suitable for switching and logic circuit applications.

REFERENCES

5-1 *General Electric Transistor Manual*, 7th ed., General Electric Co., Syracuse, N.Y., 1964.

5-2 F. E. Gentry, F. W. Gutzwiller, N. Holonyak, Jr., E. E. Von Zastrow, *Semiconductor Controlled Rectifiers*, Prentice-Hall, Inc., Englewood Cliffs, N.J., 1964.

5-3 R. A. Greiner, *Semiconductor Devices and Applications*, McGraw-Hill Book Company, New York, 1961, Chaps. 9, 10, 12.

5-4 M. P. Ristenbatt and R. L. Riddle, *Transistor Physics and Circuits*, Prentice-Hall, Inc., Englewood Cliffs, N.J., 1966.

5-5 A. van der Zeil, *Electronics*, Allyn and Bacon, Inc., Boston, 1966, Chap. 6.

EXERCISES

5-1 In a Haynes-Shockley experiment (Fig. 5-3) the voltage V produces an axial field of 20 V/cm. Assume that the drift velocity in the silicon in centimeters/sec is 500 times the field strength in volts/centimeter. How much time will elapse between an input pulse at E and the received pulse at C? The distance E to C is 0.5 cm.

5-2 Describe the internal actions that occur in a *pnp* transistor. Explain which carriers conduct the current in the various parts of the transistor, the types and origins of the carriers that cross the two junctions, and the actions that account for the magnitude of the base current.

5-3 Consider a *pnp* and an *npn* transistor in each of which the current magnitudes are $I_E = 6$ mA and $I_C = 5.8$ mA, and both have $I_{CO} = 0.01$ mA. (a) List the algebraic values of I_E, I_C, and I_B for both transistors, using the conventional senses shown in Fig. 5-5a. (b) What is the value of α_{FB} for these transistors?

5-4 (a) In Fig. 5-9 the emitter-to-base potential energy barrier height is the same for conduction electrons and for holes. Why is the electron current across the EB junction in the usual transistor much larger than the hole current? (b) Compare the flow rates for electrons to that for holes across the CB junction and interpret in terms of Fig. 5-9.

5-5 What is meant by the terms *breakdown* and *punch-through*? Describe the related physical processes.

5-6 A germanium transistor has values of I_{CO} of 10^{-6} A at 25°C and 8×10^{-6} A at 55°C. Assume that α_{FB} is 0.99. Obtain expressions for I_C as a function of I_B for this transistor when placed in a common emitter circuit and operated at (a) 25°C and (b) 55°C.

5-7 A transistor in a common-emitter circuit has the following input voltage and output current variations: $v_{BE} = 0.45 + 0.1 \sin \omega t$ and $i_C = 6 + 3 \sin \omega t$ mA. List values or expressions for V_{BE}, v_{be}, I_C, and i_c.

6

Small-Signal Analysis
of Transistor Amplifiers

6-1
Introduction

Just as with vacuum-tube circuits, the analysis of transistor circuits is greatly facilitated by the use of linearized (small-signal) models of the device in the form of *equivalent circuits*. This chapter will be concerned with the equivalent circuits suitable for low frequencies and their application to the transistor amplifier.

Both the vacuum triode and the transistor are three-terminal devices, but there is an essential difference in their internal behavior at low frequencies. There is no feedback of signal voltage from the output to the input circuits in the triode, and in a transistor circuit there is a definite feedback effect between the output and the input. This inherent feedback is evidenced by the resistor r'_b and the generator $\mu v'_c$ in Fig. 5-15d. One result of this feedback is that the transistor is a *bilateral* circuit element, that is, it will pass signals in both directions. Another result is that the exact analysis of transistor circuits is likely to be complicated because of the feedback. We shall usually find it useful to reduce the network formulas obtained by exact analysis to more manageable approximate formulas.

Other differences between the tube and the transistor concern the type of input signal and the input power. We have seen that the transistor is basically a *current-operated* device, in contrast to the *voltage-operated* negative-grid vacuum tube. We shall learn that the input impedance to a transistor is

133

usually low, so that the signal current wave develops a low voltage at the transistor input. Owing to the nonlinear *e-i* characteristic at the input, a sine wave of current will produce a distorted voltage wave at the input. Conversely, a sine wave of impressed voltage will produce a distorted current wave. For this reason when the signal comes from a voltage source of low impedance we may find it advisable to add a linear resistor in series with the input to linearize the signal current, i.e., to limit the effect of the nonlinear transistor input impedance.

In the tube amplifier the input power either is zero or there may be a very small dissipation in a high-value grid resistor. In contrast, the transistor requires an input current as well as a voltage, therefore an input power. The concept of *power gain*, which had little importance with the tube, is very important with the transistor. Furthermore, the input circuit, as well as the output circuit, should receive attention with reference to impedance matching and power transfer from the signal source to the transistor.

Of the several equivalent circuits and sets of small-signal parameters used in transistor circuit analysis, we shall first deal with the equivalent-*T* form of circuit and the corresponding parameters. The *h* parameters will be introduced next, but other sets will receive only a brief mention.

6-2
Equivalent-T circuits for the
common-base, common-emitter, and
common-collector connections

There are three ways of connecting a transistor so as to develop a power gain, as shown in Fig. 6-1. These connections are called the *common base* (Fig. 6-1a), the *common emitter* (Fig. 6-1b), and the *common collector* (Fig. 6-1c), depending on which terminal is common to the input and the output. The incremental current magnitudes in the three leads of the transistor are

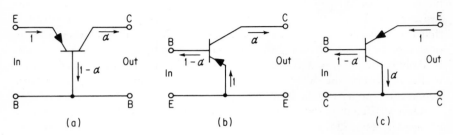

FIGURE 6-1   Transistor connections: (a) common base, (b) common emitter, and (c) common collector.

shown in each diagram relative to an emitter current of unity. Here α is α_{fb}, the common-base short-circuit incremental current gain, which is usually in the range from 0.96 to 0.995. (The use of the same value of α in all three connections is not strictly justified, as a study of later results in this chapter will show, but is a very good approximation.)

In the common-base connection the output current is slightly smaller than the input, so the current gain is approximately unity. As a result, power gain can be achieved only by using a higher load resistance than the transistor input resistance and thereby obtaining a sizable voltage gain.

In the common-emitter and common-collector connections the input current is the base current, of value $1 - \alpha$, which is small; therefore good current gains are realized. These are $\alpha/(1 - \alpha)$ for the common-emitter and $1/(1 - \alpha)$ for the common-collector arrangements. For example, if $\alpha = 0.99$, the common-emitter current gain is 99 and the common-collector current gain is 100. The voltage gain, power gain, and input and output resistances of these two important connections will be analyzed later in the chapter.

Since we have been discussing incremental quantities, the foregoing discussion applies equally to both *pnp* and *npn* transistors, because the bias voltage polarity has no effect on the senses of the incremental currents and voltages. Consideration of the details of biasing is deferred to Sec. 7-10.

In Sec. 5-9 a small signal equivalent circuit was developed (Fig. 5-15d) which contained two dependent generators. This circuit can be converted to the one-generator equivalent circuit shown in Fig. 6-2a. If desired, we

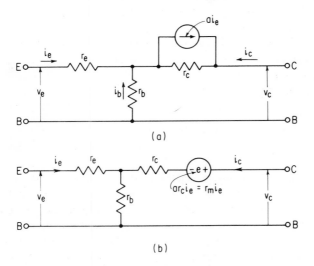

FIGURE 6-2   Common-base equivalent-T circuits (a) with current generator and (b) with voltage generator.

could derive expressions for the new parameters, namely, a, r_c, r_b, and r_e in terms of those used earlier, i.e., α, r'_c, r'_b, and μ. However, we prefer to regard the circuit parameters a, r_c, r_b, and r_e as values obtained by direct measurement on the transistor rather than from a consideration of the physics of the device.

A useful alternative form of the equivalent-T circuit is obtained by converting the current source ai_e and resistor r_c into the equivalent Thévenin source form as in Fig. 6-2b. Here the new symbol r_m is defined as equal to ar_c, the internal current gain times the collector resistance. Parameters r_e and r_b are called the *emitter resistance* and *base resistance*, respectively, and r_c is called the *collector resistance*.

In a common-base amplifier the input signal is applied from E to B, and a resistance across C and B comprises the load. Thus, the amplifier can be analyzed as a two-loop network. This analysis will be considered later; for the present let us calculate the *short-circuit current gain*. We think of terminals C and B short-circuited, with a signal between E and B. Elementary analysis of the circuit yields the result

$$\left(\frac{i_c}{i_e}\right)_{\text{sc}} = -\left(\frac{r_m + r_b}{r_c + r_b}\right) \qquad C \text{ and } B \text{ shorted} \qquad (6\text{-}1)$$

Before discussing this result, we introduce a set of numerical values of the parameters for a small transistor suitable for audiofrequency application: $r_e = 21 \ \Omega$, $r_b = 500 \ \Omega$, $r_c = 2.10 \times 10^6 \ \Omega$, $r_m = 2.04 \times 10^6 \ \Omega$, and $a = 0.9714$. We remark that different transistors of a given type, or a given transistor under different temperatures, show considerable variations in the values of their parameters; consequently in design work these variations must be considered. We have stated a value for a to a precision of 1 part in about 10^4 only in order to have an arithmetically consistent set of parameters. Now, since $r_b \ll r_c$ and $r_b \ll r_m$, Eq. (6-1) becomes, to an accuracy of 0.1 per cent or better,

$$\left(\frac{i_c}{i_e}\right)_{\text{sc}} \cong -\frac{r_m}{r_c} = \frac{-ar_c}{r_c} = -a \qquad C \text{ and } B \text{ shorted} \qquad (6\text{-}2)$$

But i_c/i_e with C and B shorted is the common-base short-circuit current gain $-\alpha_{fb}$ defined in Sec. 5-3. Thus, $a = \alpha_{fb}$ within the accuracy limits specified for Eq. (6-2).

One of the desirable features of the equivalent-T circuit is that the common-emitter and common-collector equivalent circuits can be obtained if desired by merely rearranging the network, keeping the circuit elements the same. For the *common-emitter* connection this procedure leads to the equivalent circuit in Fig. 6-3. We notice, however, that the dependent voltage generator is controlled by i_e rather than by the *input* current, which is now i_b. Let us seek a more useful form of the equivalent circuit in which the generator depends on i_b rather than on i_e. Imagine that the collector branch

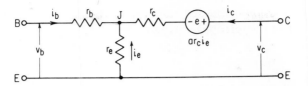

FIGURE 6-3 Common-emitter circuit with generator dependent on i_e.

(J to C in Fig. (6-3)) is tentatively replaced by a series-connected unknown resistor r_x and a voltage generator $a_x i_b$ of the same polarity as e. To test for equivalence, we write the voltage equation for the collector-emitter loop in Fig. 6-3; thus,

$$v_c = ar_c i_e + r_c i_c - r_e i_e \qquad (6\text{-}3)$$

and for the altered circuit,

$$v_c = a_x i_b + r_x i_c - r_e i_e \qquad (6\text{-}4)$$

In Eq. (6-3) replace i_e by its equivalent $-(i_b + i_c)$ and rearrange to find

$$v_c = -ar_c i_b + (r_c - ar_c)i_c - r_e i_e \qquad (6\text{-}5)$$

A term-by term comparison of Eqs. (6-5) and (6-4) shows that they are identical if we require that

$$a_x = -ar_c \qquad (6\text{-}6)$$

and

$$r_x = r_c - ar_c = r_c(1 - a) \qquad (6\text{-}7)$$

Thus, the tentative circuit is proved to be feasible and is shown in Fig. 6-4. Here the polarity of the voltage generator has been reversed to avoid the use of the negative sign in Eq. (6-6). Furthermore, the new symbol r_d is introduced in place of $r_c(1 - a)$.

Figure 6-4 gives the equivalent-T circuit which is convenient to use in

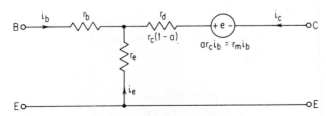

FIGURE 6-4 Common-emitter circuit with generator dependent on i_b.

the calculation of the low-frequency response of the common-emitter amplifier. To summarize the relations among the symbols we write

$$a \cong \alpha_{fb}$$
$$r_m = ar_c \qquad (6\text{-}8)$$
$$r_d = r_c(1 - a) = r_c - r_m$$

For the small transistor whose parameters were listed previously we note that $1 - a = 0.0286$ and by Eq. (6-8) we find that $r_d \cong 60{,}000 \; \Omega$.

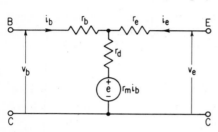

FIGURE 6-5   Equivalent-T circuit for common-collector connection.

The equivalent-T circuit for the *common-collector* connection has the same elements as in Fig. 6-4 but is redrawn in Fig. 6-5 to emphasize the collector as the reference terminal. Usually the reference terminal is grounded for signal-frequency voltages, so the terms *grounded-collector, grounded-emitter*, and *grounded-base* are also used.

In summary we observe that three basic equivalent circuits have been developed, all in terms of the resistance parameters and the common-base short-circuit gain. The voltage and current symbols indicate that the instantaneous values of the incremental quantities, such as i_c and i_b for collector and base currents, are being considered. However, the equivalent circuits are valid only for rates of change (or frequencies in the case of sine waves) low enough to reduce to negligible values the effects of junction capacitance and time delays due to the diffusion of charge. Because these effects have been neglected, there are no reactive elements in the equivalent circuits. Therefore, sine-wave signals will pass through these circuits with phase shifts of either zero or 180°.

The following sections will be concerned with the application of the equivalent circuits to the analysis of the three basic amplifier connections.

6-3
Gain and network properties of the common-emitter amplifier

The common-emitter connection is most frequently used in amplifiers owing to its intermediate values of input and output impedance and its high current, voltage, and power gains. We combine the equivalent-T network for the transistor with a signal source of resistance R_s and a load resistance R_L, as shown in Fig. 6-6. We consider here instantaneous values, but the results will apply for sine-wave quantities also.

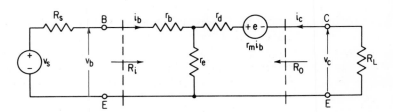

FIGURE 6-6   Small-signal equivalent circuit for common-emitter amplifier.

Whether an amplifier is suitable for its intended purpose can be judged on the basis of the requirements of power gain G_p, current gain A_i, voltage gain A_v, input resistance R_i, and output (Thévenin) resistance R_o. For example, if the amplifier stage is intended to drive another transistor, then the current gain and input and output resistances are most important. For the present analysis we define the gains and network quantities as follows;

$$A_i \equiv \frac{i_c}{i_b} \quad A_v \equiv \frac{v_c}{v_b} \quad G_p \equiv \frac{p_{\text{out}}}{p_{\text{in}}} = |A_v| \times |A_i|$$

$$R_i \equiv \frac{v_b}{i_b} \quad R_o = \text{Thévenin impedance viewed from terminals } C\text{-}E$$

(6-9)

To start the analysis, we write the emf equations for the two loops in Fig. 6-6 in the following forms:

$$v_b = (r_b + r_e)i_b + r_e i_c \tag{6-10}$$

$$v_c = (r_e - r_m)i_b + (r_d + r_e)i_c \tag{6-11}$$

Also, we write

$$v_c = -R_L i_c \tag{6-12}$$

To calculate the current gain, introduce v_c from Eq. (6-12) into (6-11) and solve for the current ratio

$$A_i = \frac{i_c}{i_b} = \frac{r_m - r_e}{R_L + r_d + r_e} \tag{6-13}$$

If we recall the typical parameter values listed earlier, we realize that $r_e \ll r_m$ and $r_e \ll r_d$, so that the r_e terms can be discarded. The resulting approximate formula will be listed later.

The voltage gain can be found by eliminating i_c and i_b among Eqs. (6-10), (6-11), and (6-12), with the result

$$A_v = \frac{v_c}{v_b} = \frac{-(r_m - r_e)R_L}{(r_b + r_e)(R_L + r_d + r_e) + r_e(r_m - r_e)} \tag{6-14}$$

By eliminating v_c and i_c from the three basic equations, we can find

$$R_i = r_b + r_e + \frac{r_e(r_m - r_e)}{r_d + r_e + R_L} \tag{6-15}$$

We recall that the output (Thévenin) impedance may be calculated with reference to terminals C-E by letting v_s go to zero, imagining a voltage v_c applied across C-E and calculating i_c, and finally forming $R_o = v_c/i_c$. We remark that the voltage of the dependent generator $r_m i_b$ will enter this calculation owing to the current i_b present in the circuit. The result of these procedures is

$$R_o = r_d + \frac{r_e(r_m + r_b + R_s)}{R_s + r_b + r_e} \tag{6-16}$$

Note that the source resistance has an effect on the output resistance.

The typical parameter values listed earlier showed that $r_e \ll r_m$, $r_e \ll r_d$, and $r_b \ll r_m$. Thus, Eqs. (6-13) through (6-16) can be expressed with sufficient accuracy by the following approximate relations:

$$A_i \cong \frac{r_m}{R_L + r_d} = \frac{a}{(1 - a)\left(1 + \frac{R_L}{r_d}\right)} \tag{6-17}$$

$$A_v \cong \frac{-r_m R_L}{(r_b + r_e)(R_L + r_d) + r_e r_m} \tag{6-18}$$

$$R_i \cong r_b + r_e + \frac{r_e r_m}{r_d + R_L} \tag{6-19}$$

$$R_o \cong r_d + \frac{r_e(r_m + R_s)}{R_s + r_b + r_e} \tag{6-20}$$

Further simplification may often be made if the range of R_L or of R_s is restricted or if the accuracy requirement is relaxed.

Example : To obtain a feeling for the magnitudes involved, we shall calculate the gains and input and output resistances for an amplifier which uses a transistor having the parameters $r_e = 21$, $r_b = 500$, $r_d = 60,000$, and $r_m = 2.04 \times 10^6 \; \Omega$, as before. Assume that the amplifier is driven by a signal from a 1000 Ω voltage source and delivers an output to a second common-emitter amplifier stage whose input resistance is 1200 Ω. Thus we have $R_L = 1200$ and $R_s = 1000$. Using the approximate formulas, we calculate

$$A_i \cong \frac{2.04 \times 10^6}{1200 + 60,000} = 33.3$$

$$A_v \cong \frac{-2.04 \times 10^6 \times 1200}{520 \times 61,200 + 21 \times 2.04 \times 10^6} = -32.8$$

Consequently the power gain is

$$G_p = 33.3 \times 32.8 = 1092 \text{ (or 30.4 dB)}$$

Furthermore,

$$R_i = 500 + 21 + \frac{21 \times 2.04 \times 10^6}{60{,}000 + 1200} = 1220 \ \Omega$$

and

$$R_o = 60{,}000 + \frac{21(2.04 \times 10^6 + 1000)}{1000 + 500 + 21} = 88{,}200 \ \Omega$$

This common-emitter amplifier develops good current, voltage, and power gains and has a low input resistance and an intermediate ouput resistance.

Next we wish to interpret some of the approximate formulas in relation to the equivalent circuit. For example, Eq. (6-17) for A_i can be derived from Fig. 6-6 by letting r_e go to zero, so that i_c can be calculated by Ohm's law, $i_c = r_m i_b / (r_d + R_L)$, which leads to Eq. (6-17). Thus, for the purpose of calculating A_i, we can regard r_e as negligible. However, r_e must be included in the formulas for A_v, R_i, and R_o. A qualitative reason for this is apparent if we study the numerical example a bit more. Owing to the current gain we note that i_c is 33.3 times the value of i_b. If we think of the current through r_e as $i_b + i_c$, we see that the amplified current produces a sizable voltage drop across r_e, even though r_e is small. Consider the formula for R_i in this light. If the right-hand loop is broken, so that $i_c = 0$, then R_i would equal $r_b + r_e$, the first two terms on the right of Eq. (6-19). With i_c present, the "feedback effect" of the voltage across r_e produces the third term on the right of (6-19). The numerical example shows that this term is of comparable magnitude to the quantity $r_b + r_e$.

A study of Fig. 6-7 will throw further light on the performance of the common-emitter stage. Here the gains and R_i are plotted as a function of

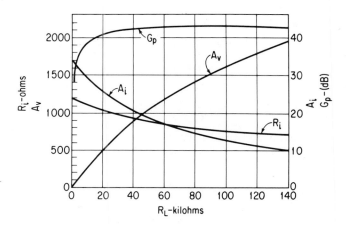

FIGURE 6-7   Characteristics of a common-emitter amplifier.

R_L using the same amplifier parameters as in the example. As Eq. (6-17) shows, the value of A_i for $R_L = 0$ equals $a/(1 - a)$, which is the common-emitter short-circuit current gain α_{fe}. Its value is 33.9 in this example. (The values of α_{fe} for commercial transistors cover a considerable range, say from 15 to 150 for the median values for different types, and a range for a particular type of as much as from 0.4 to 3.0 times the median value.) We note that the curve for power gain goes through a broad maximum and reaches a value of 42.5 dB when $R_L = R_o = 88{,}200\ \Omega$. What is perhaps more important is that the amplifier gives a good power gain for a value of R_L as low as 1000 Ω, so that common-emitter stages can be cascaded to develop a higher over-all gain.

6-4
The common-base amplifier

To form a common-base amplifier, we think of adding a signal source and a dc bias between emitter and base in Fig. 6-1a and a load resistance R_L and a dc bias between collector and base. Since we are dealing only with incremental quantities, we shall use the equivalent-T circuit in Fig. 6-2b for the transistor. Let the source consist of a voltage v_s in series with a resistance R_s. The circuit analysis is similar to that for the common-emitter network; therefore, we write down the results without proof. It is worth noting that when we write, for example, v_c, we mean the collector-to-base voltage, though the same symbol was used previously for collector-to-emitter voltage. (If desired, these voltages can be written v_{cb} and v_{ce}, respectively.) The exact formulas for the gains and input and output resistances are

$$A_i \equiv \frac{i_c}{i_e} = -\frac{r_b + r_m}{R_L + r_b + r_c} \tag{6-21}$$

$$A_v \equiv \frac{v_c}{v_e} = \frac{R_L(r_m + r_b)}{R_L(r_b + r_e) + r_e r_c + r_b(r_d + r_e)} \tag{6-22}$$

$$R_i \equiv \frac{v_e}{i_e} = r_e + \frac{r_b(R_L + r_d)}{R_L + r_b + r_c} \tag{6-23}$$

$$R_o = r_c + r_b - \frac{r_b(r_b + r_m)}{R_s + r_e + r_b} \tag{6-24}$$

The following approximate formulas, based on the relations $r_b \ll r_m$, $r_b \ll r_c$, and $r_e \ll r_d$, are sufficiently accurate for most purposes

$$A_i \cong -\frac{r_m}{R_L + r_c} \tag{6-25}$$

$$A_v \cong \frac{R_L r_m}{R_L(r_b + r_e) + r_e r_c + r_b r_d} \tag{6-26}$$

$$R_i \cong r_e + \frac{r_b(R_L + r_d)}{R_L + r_c} \tag{6-27}$$

$$R_o \cong r_c - \frac{r_b r_m}{R_s + r_e + r_b} \tag{6-28}$$

These equations show that the current gain remains less than unity, as expected from the physical picture of the internal transistor action. The voltage gain is not far different from that of a common-emitter stage with the same R_L. The input resistance is very low, starting at a value close to r_e when $R_L = 0$. The output resistance has a value close to that of the common-emitter stage when $R_s = 0$ but rises markedly as R_s increases. For example, using the same transistor parameters as before, we calculate $R_o = 114{,}000\ \Omega$ with $R_s = 0$, but with $R_s = 1000\ \Omega$, R_o rises to $1{,}430{,}000\ \Omega$. This result indicates that the difficulty of providing a *matched* load will be even greater with the common-base stage than with the common emitter. Figure 6-8 shows how the gains and R_i vary with R_L. With the usual range of R_L's, say up to $10{,}000\ \Omega$, we may for estimating purposes regard $A_i \cong -\alpha_{fb}$. Also A_v varies nearly linearly with R_L over this range, and R_i does not depart greatly from its initial value, $r_e + r_b r_d / r_c$, which may be expressed as $r_e + r_b(1 - a)$.

To conclude, we emphasize that a common-base stage gives best power gain if the source resistance is low, say 30 to 50 Ω, and the load resistance is high, of the order of 50kΩ or higher. The power and voltage gains are more stable or predictable for changes in transistors or in temperature than for the simple common-emitter stage.† This is obvious if we notice that the gains

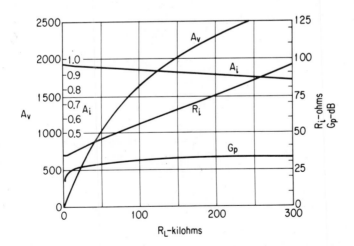

FIGURE 6-8   Characteristics of a common-base amplifier.

†Bias circuits that improve this stability will be discussed in Sec. 7-10.

for the common-base circuit depend on the short-circuit current gain, approximately a in value, while the common-emitter gains depend on the factor $(1 - a)$. Since a is around 0.98, a small percentage change in a becomes a much larger percentage change in $(1 - a)$.

6-5
The common-collector amplifier

This amplifier is derived from Fig. 6-1c by impressing a source between B and C, a load between E and C, and by adding bias voltages. In the analysis of the small-signal properties we use the equivalent circuit in Fig. 6-5 for the transistor. The analysis is similar to that for the other amplifiers, and we write the exact formulas as follows:

$$A_i \equiv \frac{i_e}{i_b} = -\frac{r_c}{R_L + r_d + r_e} \tag{6-29}$$

$$A_v \equiv \frac{v_e}{v_b} = \frac{R_L r_c}{R_L(r_c + r_b) + r_b(r_d + r_e) + r_e r_c} \tag{6-30}$$

$$R_i \equiv \frac{v_b}{i_b} = \frac{R_L(r_c + r_b) + r_b(r_d + r_e) + r_c r_e}{R_L + r_d + r_e} \tag{6-31}$$

$$R_o = r_e + \frac{r_d(R_s + r_b)}{R_s + r_c + r_b} \tag{6-32}$$

R_s is the signal source resistance and R_L is the load resistance. In view of the inequalities $r_b \ll r_c$ and $r_e \ll r_d$ we can write the approximate forms of these formulas

$$A_i \cong \frac{r_c}{R_L + r_d} = -\frac{1}{(1 - a)\left(1 + \dfrac{R_L}{r_d}\right)} \tag{6-33}$$

$$A_v \cong \frac{1}{1 + \left(\dfrac{1}{R_L}\right)[r_b(1 - a) + r_e]} \tag{6-34}$$

$$R_i \cong \frac{(R_L + r_e)\left(\dfrac{1}{1 - a}\right) + r_b}{1 + \dfrac{R_L}{r_d}} \tag{6-35}$$

$$R_o \cong r_e + \frac{r_d(R_s + r_b)}{R_s + r_c} \tag{6-36}$$

These formulas were used to calculate the gains and R_i as a function of R_L, assuming the same parameters as used previously with the results plotted in Fig. 6-9. The power gain maximizes at a low value of R_L, less than 1000

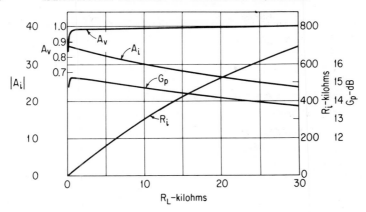

FIGURE 6-9   Characteristics of a common-collector amplifier.

ohms, but reaches a value of only a little over 15 dB. The current gain starts at a value of about 35 for $R_L = 0$ and drops slowly as R_L increases.

Equation (6-33) shows that as R_L approaches zero, the current gain approaches $-1/(1 - a)$. Thus, the magnitude of the short-circuit current gain is a bit higher than for the common-emitter connection; in fact, the ratio of the gains is $1/a$, since $\alpha_{fe} = a/(1 - a)$.

The voltage gain is less than one but approaches unity for R_L's over 1000 ohms. The variation of voltage gain only for low values of R_L is an indication that the circuit has a low output resistance.

The input resistance rises with increasing R_L and is much higher than for the other two amplifiers. Let us relate this behavior to Eq. (6-35). We note first that for $R_L = 0$, $R_i = r_b + r_e/(1 - a)$, which works out to be 1220 Ω in this amplifier. We remark that the R_i for the common-emitter stage has this same value at $R_L = 0$. From Eq. (6-35) we can deduce that if R_L is in the range from about 1000 to 3000 Ω, R_i can be expressed within an accuracy of about 5 per cent as $R_L/(1 - a)$, or 35 R_L. With other transistors the numbers would be different, but it is safe to conclude that the R_i of the common-collector stage is relatively high.

The outstanding feature of this amplifier is its low output resistance. This feature is useful for driving low-impedance loads. A further approximation in Eq. (6-36) will be helpful. If $R_s \ll r_c$, then Eq. (6-36) can be converted to the form

$$R_o \cong r_e + (1 - a)(R_s + r_b) \qquad (6\text{-}37)$$

Thus, the actual resistance of the input branch $R_s + r_b$ is reduced by the factor $(1 - a)$ owing to the internal feedback. In the numerical example, if $R_s = 1000$, then $R_o = 64\ \Omega$, and if $R_s = 10,000$, then $R_o = 321\ \Omega$.

Thus, low impedance loads can be driven with satisfactory impedance matching and power gain.

6-6
Further comparison of the basic amplifiers and some practical considerations

In the foregoing articles we have developed the network relations for the common-base (*CB*), common-emitter (*CE*), and common-collector (*CC*) amplifiers in a formal way. The basic assumptions were that (1) the signals are small and that (2) the frequency is low. Only the transistor itself was considered in the analysis, that is, the effect of biasing resistors and of coupling networks (at input or output) was neglected, and no *external* feedback connections were considered. We now make a start toward the analysis of practical amplifiers, and make further comparisons of the basic amplifiers.†

a. *Comparison of output resistance for CB, CE, and*
    CC amplifiers

We shall emphasize the influence of the network properties on the performance of the amplifier circuits. Consider first a comparison of the output resistance as a function of the source resistance for the three amplifiers

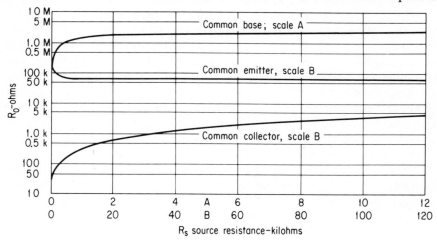

FIGURE 6-10 Comparison of output resistance of transistor amplifiers.

†See Chapter 7 for treatments of biasing and of frequency effects.

(Fig. 6-10) using the same numerical values as before. As was noted earlier, the *CC* stage exhibits the lowest values, the *CE* stage intermediate, and the *CB* stage the highest values. Suppose that an amplifier is needed to drive a specified load resistance with a known source resistance. It is extremely unlikely that the load resistance will equal the R_o of one of the basic amplifier stages. In some cases the load resistance can be *matched* to the amplifier R_o through the use of the impedance transforming property of an iron-core transformer. However, this method is not practical for high R_o's, such as for a *CB* stage, and has other limitations. In the following discussion we assume that transformers are *not* used, which means that there is likely to be a *mismatch* between R_L and R_o.

b. A practical CE amplifier

Some factors which enter the analysis can be illustrated by a study of the practical *CE* stage in Fig. 6-11a. Here we think of the input signal as an audiofrequency sine wave. The resistors R_1, R_2, and R_3 determine, with R_L, the bias condition for zero signal, as will be explained later. The coupling capacitor C_1 prevents the diversion of direct current into the source, and the bypass capacitor C_3 is intended to short-circuit R_3 as far as the signal-frequency currents are concerned. Only one dc source is required.

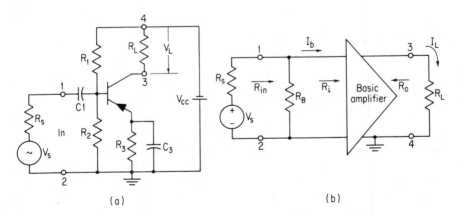

(a)   (b)

FIGURE 6-11   (a) Transistor amplifier and (b) network for signal frequency currents.

The relation of the basic *CE* amplifier to the rest of the circuit, considering only signal-frequency current, is shown in Fig. 6-11b. Here R_B represents the value of R_1 and R_2 in parallel, i.e., $1/R_B = 1/R_1 + 1/R_2$. Symbols R_i and R_o refer to the basic amplifier. How does the presence of R_B affect the analysis of the complete system? With R_L known, R_i can be calculated by Eq. (6-15). However, with R_B present, we must use the parallel-value resistance of R_s and R_B in the calculation for R_o. Let this value be R'_s, i.e., $1/R'_s = 1/R_s + 1/R_B$. Furthermore, the current I_b is less than the current supplied by the source, owing to the current division between R_i and R_B. As a result, the current gain from source to load and actual power gain will be less than for the basic amplifier alone.

Example: In Fig. 6-11b let $R_L = 5000$, $R_B = 8000$, and $R_s = 1000$ and assume that the transistor is the same as before. Then R'_s is $889\ \Omega$. The amplifier properties as calculated by the approximate formulas are compared with those of the basic amplifier in Table 6-1.

Table 6-1

Characteristic	Over-all system	Basic amplifier
Current gain	27.4	31.4
Voltage gain	−137	−137
Power gain	3,750	4,300
Input resistance	1,005	1,150
Output resistance	89,000	86,840

We see that the shunt resistance R_B reduces the current gain, the power gain, and the input resistance.

c. Effect of bias circuit on the gain of a CC stage

The effect of the bias circuits on the current gain is even more striking in the case of the common-collector amplifier. Figure 6-11b can be used for this case without change, but in Fig. 6-11a the load R_L would be moved to the emitter branch. The resistance R_B would be about the same size as for the CE stage, but now R_i would be high—about $160,000\ \Omega$ in this example. Thus, if R_B is $8000\ \Omega$, only a small fraction of the signal current (0.048) will enter the base of the inner amplifier, and the current and power gains of the complete amplifier are severely reduced.

d. Transducer power gain

Thus far we have defined the *actual* power gain G_p as the ratio of the power in the load to the power entering at the input terminals. This gain does not tell us how effective the amplifier is when used between a *particular* source and a load. The *transducer power gain* is defined as the ratio of the actual output power to the maximum power which the source could *theoretically* deliver if the source were connected directly to a *matched* load. This theoretical maximum power equals $V_s^2/4R_s$, thus G_t, the transducer power gain, equals

$$G_t = \frac{\text{power in load for signal voltage } V_s}{\dfrac{V_s^2}{4R_s}} \qquad (6\text{-}38)$$

In terms of the symbols in Fig. 6-11b this is given by

$$G_t = \frac{4R_s}{R_L}\left(\frac{R_{\text{in}}}{R_s + R_{\text{in}}}\right)^2 (A_v')^2 = \frac{4R_sR_L(A_i')^2}{(R_s + R_{\text{in}})^2} \qquad (6\text{-}39)$$

where A_v' and A_i' are the over-all gains of the amplifier. When $R_{\text{in}} = R_s$, the transducer gain will equal the actual power gain, but when $R_{\text{in}} \neq R_s$, the transducer gain will be less than the actual gain. The disparity between the two gains depends on the degree of the mismatch at the input.

For the *CE* amplifier example with the properties given in Table 6-1 the input resistance R_{in} is close to being equal to the assumed source resistance, $R_s = 1000\ \Omega$. Thus $G_t = G_p$, or 3750, in this example. If, however, R_s is changed to $4000\ \Omega$, the transducer gain falls to $G_t = 2400$.

e. Summary

The output resistance characteristics of the three basic amplifiers were compared. The degrading effect of an internal shunting resistor at the input on the amplifier characteristics was discussed, and its large effect on a *CC* stage was noted. Transducer power gain was defined. Table 6-2 gives a qualitative comparison of the characteristics of the three transistor amplifiers.

Table 6-2

Characteristic	Common base	Common emitter	Common collector
Power gain	intermediate	high	low
Voltage gain	high	high	below unity
Current gain	below unity	high	high
Input resistance	very low	low	moderately high
Output resistance	very high	high	low
Phase of output voltage for sine waves (relative to input)	0°	180°	0°

6-7
Equivalent circuits in terms of
h parameters

In Sec. 2-10 the z- and y- and h-parameter equations for the two-port network and their associated equivalent circuits were introduced. One or the other of these parameters and equations is preferable for transistor circuit analysis, depending on the type of problem being undertaken. Of these systems of equations, the h-parameter system has found increasing use in transistor calculations. Furthermore, transistor parameters are often specified in the h-parameter form by the manufacturer, partly because they are easy to measure.

The only alteration in the equivalent circuit in Fig. 2-28 needed to adapt it to transistor circuits is to join the bottom conductors to convert the circuit to a three-terminal one, as shown in Fig. 6-12. In this figure the symbols have been written specifically for a common-emitter connection. For the CB or CC connections the equivalent circuit *remains the same*, but the values of the h-parameters change in each case. The symbols h_{ib}, h_{rb}, h_{fb}, and h_{ob} can be used for the CB connection, and h_{ic}, h_{rc}, h_{fc}, and h_{oc} for the CC connection. Often the second subscript is omitted if the common electrode is understood.

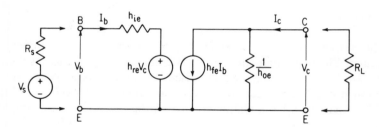

FIGURE 6-12   Equivalent circuit of common-emitter connected transistor amplifier using h parameter representation.

It will be well to review the basic equations and the definitions of the h parameters. Using the symbols for the phasor voltages and currents, and for the h parameters for the common-emitter connection (Fig. 6-12), these are

$$\mathbf{V}_b = \mathbf{h}_{ie}\mathbf{I}_b + \mathbf{h}_{re}\mathbf{V}_c \tag{6-40}$$

$$\mathbf{I}_c = \mathbf{h}_{fe}\mathbf{I}_b + \mathbf{h}_{oe}\mathbf{V}_c \tag{6-41}$$

$$\mathbf{h}_{ie} = \left(\frac{\mathbf{V}_b}{\mathbf{I}_b}\right)_{\mathbf{V}_c=0} = \text{input impedance with output short-circuited} \tag{6-42}$$

$$\mathbf{h}_{re} = \left(\frac{\mathbf{V}_b}{\mathbf{V}_c}\right)_{I_b=0} = \text{reverse voltage gain with input open} \qquad (6\text{-}43)$$

$$\mathbf{h}_{fe} = \left(\frac{\mathbf{I}_c}{\mathbf{I}_b}\right)_{V_c=0} = \begin{array}{l}\text{forward current gain with output} \\ \text{short-circuited}\end{array} \qquad (6\text{-}44)$$

$$\mathbf{h}_{oe} = \left(\frac{\mathbf{I}_c}{\mathbf{V}_c}\right)_{I_b=0} = \text{output admittance with input open} \qquad (6\text{-}45)$$

If the h parameters of a transistor are known for the connection under study we can immediately calculate the network quantities $\mathbf{A}_i$, $\mathbf{A}_v$, $\mathbf{Z}_i$, and $\mathbf{Z}_o$ for the terminated transistor by the formulas in Sec. 2-11. If the h parameters are known for a *different* connection, then the conversion relations in Appendix C-2 may be used to find the ones that are needed. Similarly, conversion from the equivalent T to the h parameters or vice versa can be effected by reference to Appendix C-2. Figure 6-13 shows the numerical values of the h parameters in the three configurations for the transistor used in the previous examples. A study of the figure will reveal some interesting comparisons, for example, of the short-circuit current gains and of the reverse "internal feedback" voltages $h_r V_c$. In the CE and CB cases these feedback voltages are small, but in the CC circuit this voltage is large and largely accounts for the unique properties of this connection.

A comparison of the forward short-circuit current gains defined here with those defined in Chapter 5 will show that they are identical in magnitude, but h_{fb} is opposite in sign; thus $h_{fe} = \alpha_{fe}$, and $h_{fb} = -\alpha_{fb}$.

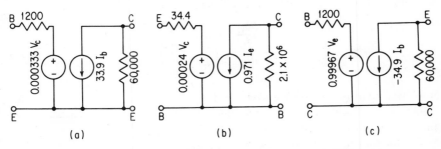

FIGURE 6-13 h parameter equivalent circuits for a small transistor in (a) CE, (b) CB, and (c) CC connections.

6-8
Low-frequency h parameters from transistor characteristics

Our aim is to show how the low-frequency h parameters can be calculated from the characteristic curves of a nonlinear device, in this case a transistor. The two-port device is shown in Fig. 6-14. We need to distinguish clearly between *total instantaneous* values of currents and voltages and their *variational* or *incremental* components. Therefore, let

$$v_{1t}, v_{2t}, i_{1t}, i_{2t} \quad \text{be total instantaneous values}$$
$$v_1, v_2, i_1, i_2 \quad \text{be incremental values near a}$$
$$\text{specified quiescent point}$$

FIGURE 6-14   Two-port   nonlinear device.

The total quantities may be expressed by the nonlinear functional relations that characterize the device. We choose v_{1t} and i_{2t} as the dependent variables so that these relations are

$$v_{1t} = f_1(i_{1t}, v_{2t}) \qquad (6\text{-}46)$$
$$i_{2t} = f_2(i_{1t}, v_{2t}) \qquad (6\text{-}47)$$

Next we obtain linearized versions of these equations that will apply for small increments about the Q point. To do this we take the total differential of Eqs. (6-46) and (6-47)

$$dv_{1t} = \frac{\partial v_{1t}}{\partial i_{1t}} di_{1t} + \frac{\partial v_{1t}}{\partial v_{2t}} dv_{2t} \qquad (6\text{-}48)$$

$$di_{2t} = \frac{\partial i_{2t}}{\partial i_{1t}} di_{1t} + \frac{\partial i_{2t}}{\partial v_{2t}} dv_{2t} \qquad (6\text{-}49)$$

As abbreviations, we define the coefficients to be the h parameters; thus,

$$h_i \equiv \frac{\partial v_{1t}}{\partial i_{1t}} \qquad h_r \equiv \frac{\partial v_{1t}}{\partial v_{2t}}$$
$$h_f \equiv \frac{\partial i_{2t}}{\partial i_{1t}} \qquad h_o \equiv \frac{\partial i_{2t}}{\partial v_{2t}} \qquad (6\text{-}50)$$

Now we identify the differentials in Eqs. (6-48) and (6-49) with the incremental quantities, that is, we replace dv_{1t} by v_1, di_{1t} by i_1, etc, and use the abbreviations in Eq. (6-50) in (6-48) and (6-49) to obtain

$$v_1 = h_i i_1 + h_r v_2 \qquad (6\text{-}51)$$
$$i_2 = h_f i_1 + h_o v_2 \qquad (6\text{-}52)$$

Next we apply the foregoing relations to the common-emitter transistor (Fig. 6-15) with the result

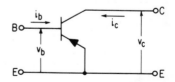

FIGURE 6-15 Defining symbols for small-signal analysis of common-emitter connection.

$$v_b = h_{ie} i_b + h_{re} v_c \qquad (6\text{-}53)$$
$$i_c = h_{fe} i_b + h_{oe} v_c \qquad (6\text{-}54)$$

Here the h parameters are defined as follows (see Eqs. (6-50)):

$$h_{ie} = \left.\frac{\partial v_{bt}}{\partial i_{bt}}\right|_{v_{ct}=\text{const}} \qquad h_{re} = \left.\frac{\partial v_{bt}}{\partial v_{ct}}\right|_{i_{bt}=\text{const}}$$

$$h_{fe} = \left.\frac{\partial i_{ct}}{\partial i_{bt}}\right|_{v_{ct}=\text{const}} \qquad h_{oe} = \left.\frac{\partial i_{ct}}{\partial v_{ct}}\right|_{i_{bt}=\text{const}} \tag{6-55}$$

These relations show how the h parameters can be obtained from the characteristic curves of the transistor. For example, h_{oe} is the slope of the collector current versus collector voltage curve at the Q point. In practice, however, the h parameters are obtained by measurement in special test circuits.

6-9
Amplifier calculations using
h parameters

As an illustration of the use of the h parameters let us use the transistor of Fig. 6-13a in a *CE* amplifier stage, driven by a source of V_s V and R_s Ω and driving a load R_L as in Fig. 6-12. Using the formulas in Sec. 2-11 we shall calculate the amplifier properties. First calculate Δ_h as follows:

$$\Delta_h = h_i h_o - h_r h_f = \tfrac{1200}{60,000} - 0.000333 \times 33.9 = 0.0087 \tag{6-56}$$

We use Eq. (2-146) to find $\mathbf{A}_i$

$$A_i = \frac{h_f \mathbf{Y}_L}{h_o + \mathbf{Y}_L} = \frac{\dfrac{33.9}{R_L}}{\dfrac{1}{60,000} + \dfrac{1}{R_L}} = \frac{33.9}{1 + \dfrac{R_L}{60,000}} \tag{6-57}$$

This form clearly shows that $\mathbf{A}_i \cong \mathbf{h}_f$ for values of R_L up to a few thousand ohms. Next calculate $\mathbf{A}_v$ by Eq. (2-147)

$$A_v = \frac{-h_f \mathbf{Z}_L}{h_i + \Delta_h \mathbf{Z}_L} = \frac{-33.9 R_L}{1200 + 0.0087 R_L} \tag{6-58}$$

For small values of R_L the second term in the denominator is small compared with 1200, so A_v increases approximately linearly with R_L in this range. This result correlates with Fig. 6-13a, that is, the shunting effect of the 60,000-ohm resistor and the feedback effect of $h_r V_c$ are small when R_L is low. Finally, we calculate R_i and R_o by Eqs. (2-144) and (2-145)

$$R_i = \frac{\Delta_h + h_i \mathbf{Y}_L}{h_o + \mathbf{Y}_L} = \frac{0.0087 + \dfrac{1200}{R_L}}{\dfrac{1}{60,000} + \dfrac{1}{R_L}} = \frac{1200 + 0.0087 R_L}{1 + \dfrac{R_L}{60,000}} \tag{6-59}$$

$$R_o = \frac{h_i + Z_s}{\Delta_h + h_o Z_s} = \frac{1200 + R_s}{0.0087 + \dfrac{R_s}{60,000}} \tag{6-60}$$

The reader can readily analyze these formulas for the limiting cases of very small or very large values of R_L or R_s. The variation of R_i with R_L has already been plotted in Fig. 6-7, and of R_o with R_s in Fig. 6-10.

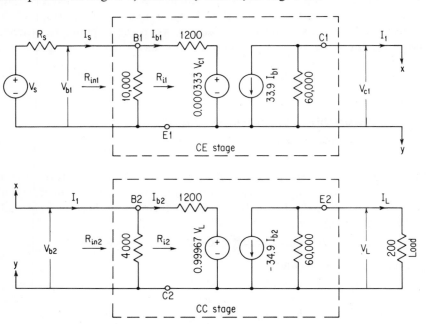

FIGURE 6-16   Equivalent circuit for a two-stage amplifier.

As a second example we calculate the properties of the two-stage cascade amplifier whose equivalent circuits are shown in Fig. 6-16. The signal source V_s drives a *CE* stage, whose output drives a *CC* stage having the 200 Ω load. The *RC* interstage coupling network between stages, to be described in Chapter 7, is assumed to add no impedances to the network. The h parameters are taken from Fig. 6-13. The 10,000-Ω resistance from base $B1$ to ground represents the effect of the biasing resistors of the *CE* stage. The 4000-Ω resistor from $B2$ to ground represents the combined effect of the collector feed resistor of the *CE* stage and the bias resistors of the *CC* stage. Let us approach this problem as follows. First, assume a numerical value of the load voltage V_L. Then use the network formulas to calculate the conditions at the input to the second (*CC*) stage, thus finding I_1, V_{c1}, and R_{in2}. Noting that R_{in2} acts as the load on the first stage, we can use the network formulas again to find the conditions at the input of the *CE* stage.

Assume that $V_L = 1$ V; then $I_L = 5$ mA, both regarded as rms values of sine waves.† First use Eq. (2-146) to find the current gain of the CC stage, A_{i2} but reverse the sign since I_L is taken positive toward the load and find 34.8. Thus, $I_{b2} = 5/34.8 = 0.1437$ mA. Next use Eq. (2-144) to calculate R_{i2} and find $R_{i2} = 8150 \, \Omega$. Taking into account the effect of the $4000 \, \Omega$ resistor, we find that $R_{in2} = 2680 \, \Omega$, $I_1 = 0.436$ mA, and $V_{c1} = V_{b2} = 1.17$ V. Next consider the CE stage. Using the same formulas as before, we calculate $R_{i1} = 1170 \, \Omega$, $R_{in1} = 1050 \, \Omega$, $I_{b1} = -0.0135$ mA, $I_s = -0.0151$ mA, and $V_{b1} = -15.8$ mV. The over-all gains then are: $|A_v| = 1/0.0158 = 63.2$, and $|A_i| = 5/0.0151 = 331$. Thus, $G_p = 63.2 \times 331 = 20{,}920$, or 43.2 dB. If desired, the output for particular values of V_s and R_s can now be calculated, since R_{in1} is known. Of course, the linear theory used here will apply accurately for only small signals, but it is useful as an approximation up to the point where distortion due to cutoff or saturation sets in.

6-10
Approximate calculations using
h parameters

The effect of one or more of the h parameters is often small enough to be neglected, particularly when the load resistance is low. Consider the CE amplifier stage in Fig. 6-12 for values of load resistance such that R_L is small compared with $1/h_{oe}$. Then the shunting effect of h_{oe} is small. Furthermore, with low load resistance the load voltage V_c is small and the voltage $h_{re}V_c$ may be small compared with V_b. Thus, if we let $h_{oe} = 0$ and $h_{re} = 0$, we obtain an approximate equivalent circuit accurate enough for many calculations. This approximation yields the following CE amplifier properties: $|A_i| \cong h_f$, $|A_v| \cong h_f R_L/h_i$, and $R_i \cong h_i$. For the transistor used in the numerical example the values are $|A_i| = 33.9$, $|A_v| = 0.0282R_L$, and $R_i = 1200 \, \Omega$. The degree of approximation depends on the value of R_L. For example, with $R_L = 3000$ ohms, the approximate A_i is about 5 percent too high, while the approximate A_v is about 2 percent too high.

A study of the two-stage amplifier in Fig. 6-16 will show that the approximations $h_{re} = 0$, $h_{oe} = 0$, and $h_{oc} = 0$ may be used with little error. These approximations simplify the equivalent circuit considerably and simplify

---

†Since no reactive elements are present, the signals could be considered to be instantaneous values, if desired. It should be pointed out that the CC stage transistor would have to operate, under the assumed conditions, at a quiescent current of somewhat greater than $\sqrt{2}$ 5 mA for the linear theory to apply.

the calculations. Upon recalculating the gains, we find $|A_v| = 64.8$ and $|A_i| = 347$—values which are in error by 2.3 and 4.8 per cent respectively.

6-11
Determination of transistor parameters

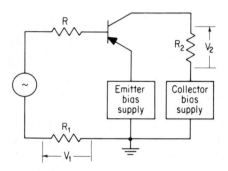

FIGURE 6-17   Circuit for the measurement of h_{fe} and h_{ie}.

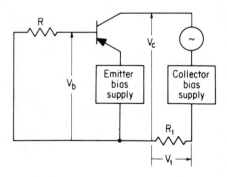

FIGURE 6-18   Circuit for the measurement of h_{oe} and h_{re}.

The low-frequency h parameters are readily measured in the laboratory. A method† for measuring h_{fe} is shown in Fig. 6-17. In this circuit R_2 should be small compared with $1/\mathbf{h}_{oe}$ so that the output is, in effect, short-circuited. The resistor R in the base circuit should be large enough so that the input source approximates a constant-current generator. Then $\mathbf{h}_{fe} = \mathbf{I}_c/\mathbf{I}_b = (\mathbf{V}_2 R_1)/(\mathbf{V}_1 R_2)$. The same circuit can be adapted to the measurement of the input impedance with the output shorted, i.e., $\mathbf{h}_{ie}$, merely by measuring the base-to-ground voltage in addition to $\mathbf{V}_1$ and $\mathbf{V}_2$.

To measure the output admittance $\mathbf{h}_{oe}$ with the input current approximately zero the signal generator is inserted in the collector circuit (Fig. 6-18). The resistance R is chosen high enough so that the input circuit may be regarded as an open circuit. Then $\mathbf{h}_{oe} = \mathbf{V}_c/\mathbf{I}_c = \mathbf{V}_c R_1/\mathbf{V}_1$. This circuit can also be used to measure $\mathbf{h}_{re}$ by measuring $\mathbf{V}_b$ and then calculating $\mathbf{V}_b/\mathbf{V}_c$.

Because the different parameters refer to the same device, we expect that the values of one set can be calculated from those of another. Formulas for this purpose are listed in

† "IRE Standards on Solid-state Devices: Methods of Testing Transistors," *IRE Proc.*, **44**, 1543, 1956.

Appendix C-2. These allow us to convert the values from a set obtained by measurement or from the manufacturer's data to another set for use in circuit calculations.

6-12
Measurement of the small-signal
short-circuit forward-current gain
cutoff frequency

At the higher frequencies the short-circuit current gain falls off with increasing frequency. For a given transistor this effect occurs at a much lower frequency for the common-emitter connection than for the common-base connection. Generally the effect is measured and reported for the common-base connection. A circuit similar to that in Fig. 6-17 is used for the measurement, except that the grounded-base connection is employed, with corresponding changes in the bias and drive arrangements.

By definition, the *common-base forward-current gain cutoff frequency* (sometimes called the *alpha cutoff frequency*) is that frequency at which h_{fb}(or α_{fb}) reduces to $1/\sqrt{2}$, or 0.707, of the value measured at 1 kHz. This frequency, labeled $f_{h_{fb}}$ or $f_{\alpha b}$, is an approximate measure of the usefulness of a transistor at the higher frequencies. The values of $f_{h_{fb}}$ vary over a great range, depending on the design of the transistor. Order of magnitude values are as follows: small audio type, 5MHz; audio power type, 1.0MHz; rf type, 35MHz; and VHF-UHF type, 500MHz and higher.

The common-emitter cutoff frequency, $f_{h_{fe}}$ or $f_{\alpha e}$, is much lower than $f_{h_{fb}}$ for the same transistor. As outlined in Sec. 7-12, the value of $f_{h_{fe}}$ is somewhat less than $(h_{fb}/h_{fe})f_{h_{fb}}$, where h_{fb} and h_{fe} are the low-frequency values. Thus, typically, $f_{h_{fe}}$ may be one-fiftieth or one one-hundredth of $f_{h_{fb}}$.

In principle, the h or y parameters can be measured at frequencies at which effects due to transistor junction capacitance and carrier transit time become important. Then the parameters are complex quantities and are functions of the frequency. An alternative approach, outlined in Chapter 7, is to develop modified equivalent circuits that will represent the transistor over the higher range of frequencies.

REFERENCES

6-1 D. Dewitt and A. L. Rossoff, *Transistor Electronics*, McGraw-Hill Book Company, New York, 1957.

6-2 K. W. Cattermole, *Transistor Circuits*, 2d ed., Temple Press Books Ltd., London, 1964.

6-3 R. A. Greiner, *Semiconductor Devices and Applications*, McGraw-Hill Book Company, New York, 1961.

6-4 J. D. Ryder, *Electronic Fundamentals and Applications*, 3d ed., Prentice-Hall, Inc., Englewood Cliffs, N.J., 1964.

EXERCISES

6-1 Consider a common-base amplifier which has a source resistance R_s and load resistance R_L. Derive formulas for this circuit to verify (a) Eq. (6-21), (b) Eq. (6-22), (c) Eq. (6-23), and (d) Eq. (6-24).

6-2 Consider a common-collector amplifier which has a source resistance R_s and a load resistance R_L. Use the appropriate equivalent-T circuit as a basis and derive formulas for this circuit to verify (a) Eq. (6-29), (b) Eq. (6-30), (c) Eq. (6-31), and (d) Eq. (6-32).

6-3 A small general-purpose alloy transistor is listed as having the following parameters in the *common-base* connection: $h_i = 60\ \Omega$, $h_r = 3.0 \times 10^{-4}$, $h_f = -0.965$, and $h_o = 0.4 \times 10^{-6}$ mho. The calculated elements of the equivalent-T circuit are: $r_e = 36\ \Omega$, $r_b = 660\ \Omega$, $r_c = 2.54 \times 10^6\ \Omega$, $r_d = 88,900$, and $a = 0.965$. This transistor is used in a common-emitter amplifier that can be represented by the equivalent circuit in Fig. 6-6. (a) Show that the voltage gain for values of R_L up to 6000 Ω equals approximately $-R_L/61.3$ to an accuracy of better than 3 per cent. (b) If $R_L = 5000\ \Omega$, what are the values of A_i and of R_i? (c) What is R_o for $R_s = 0$?

6-4 The transistor described in Prob. 6-3 is used in the circuit of Fig. 6-11a. Let $R_L = 3000$, $R_1 = 40,000$, $R_2 = 8000$, and $R_3 = 1000$, all in ohms. Assume that the capacitors have a negligible reactance. Let $R_s = 1000\ \Omega$. (a) What is R_{in} at terminals 1–2? (b) What is R_o? (c) What is the current gain defined as I_L/I_s, where I_s is the current delivered by the source? (d) Calculate V_L/V_s, where V_L is the rms value of the sine component of voltage across R_L.

6-5 Use the approximations discussed in Sec. 6-10 for the amplifier in Fig. 6-16 as the basis for calculating the approximate over-all gains A_v and A_i and compare with the values given in the text. Also calculate the approximate value of R_{in1} and compare with the exact result.

6-6 Two transistors as described in Prob. 6-3 are used in an amplifier having two *CE* stages in cascade. The coupling network between the two stages is such that it adds no impedances to the network. The load is transformer-coupled into the output by an ideal transformer and equals 3000 Ω (equivalent) from collector to emitter. Each stage has a biasing network equivalent to an 8000 Ω resistor from base to ground. Calculate the over-all gains (a) A_v, (b) A_i, and (c) G_p. (d) What value of source resistance would provide an impedance match at the input?

6-7 In the amplifier in Fig. 6-19 assume that the transformer is ideal and that X_c

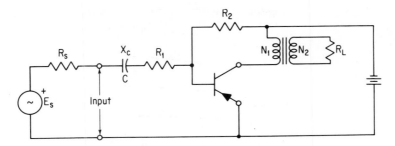

FIGURE 6-19   *CE* amplifier with transformer-coupled load.

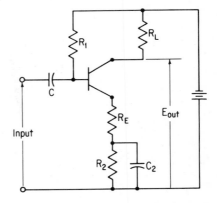

is very small. Let $E_s = 0.01$ V rms, $R_s = 600$, and $R_1 = 1000 \, \Omega$. Let $N_1/N_2 = 2.0$ and assume that $R_L = 800 \, \Omega$. The bias resistor R_2 is adjusted so that the transistor has equivalent-*T* parameters as follows: $r_b = 970$, $r_e = 34$, $r_c = 3.45 \times 10^6$ and $r_m = 3.39 \times 10^6 \, \Omega$. Assume that R_2 is so large that its effect on the amplifier input resistance is negligible. (a) Draw an equivalent circuit for this amplifier. (b) Find the voltage across R_L and the signal power delivered to R_L.

FIGURE 6-20   *CE* amplifier with emitter resistor feedback element.

6-8 The amplifier in Fig. 6-20 has the unbypassed resistor R_E in the emitter branch. (a) Draw the ac equivalent circuit based on the equivalent-*T* circuit of the transistor. Assume that the capacitors have negligible reactances and that the effect of bias resistor R_1 is also negligible. (b) Using the development in Sec. 6-3 as a basis, obtain approximate formulas for A_v, A_i, and R_i. Assume that $r_e \ll r_m$, $r_e \ll r_d$, $R_E \ll r_m$, and $r_b \ll r_m$.

6-9 Find the common-emitter h parameters for the transistor whose characteristics are given in Fig. 6-21 at a point defined by $V_{\text{CE}} = -10$ V and $I_B = -75 \, \mu\text{A}$.

6-10 (a) Draw an ac equivalent circuit for the amplifier in Fig. 6-20 based on the h parameters of the transistor and assuming that C and C_2 act as short-circuits and that R_1 is so high as to act as an open circuit. (b) Derive approximate expressions for the gains A_i and A_v on the assumption that $h_r = h_o = 0$. Calculate these gains if $R_E = 1000$, $R_L = 4000$, and if the transistor has the parameters given in Fig. 6-13a. (c) Repeat (b) but use the complete equivalent circuit. Compare the results with those of (b).

6-11 Repeat Prob. 6-6, but use the h parameter equivalent circuit and parameters for the transistor. These parameters are: $h_{ie} = 2925 \, \Omega$, $h_{re} = 5.65 \times 10^{-4}$, $h_{fe} = 56.5$, and $h_{oe} = 16.7 \times 10^{-6}$ mho.

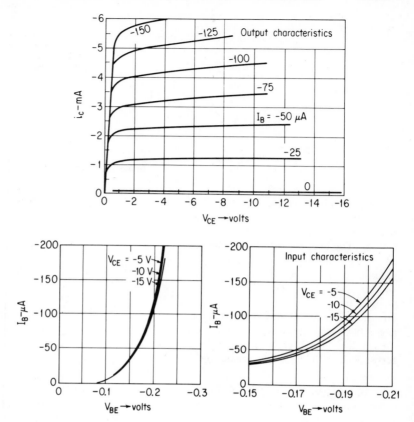

FIGURE 6-21   Characteristics of transistor in *CE* configuration.

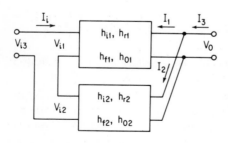

FIGURE 6-22

6-12 Two networks whose *h* parameters are known are connected in series-parallel as shown in Fig. 6-22. Show that the *h* parameters of the combined circuit equal the sums of the individual *h* parameters, e.g., $h_{i3} = h_{i1} + h_{i2}$, etc., where h_{i3} refers to the combined circuit.

7

Voltage Amplifiers

7-1
Introduction

Although the purpose of an amplifier basically is the production of an output power larger than the power available from the signal source, it is common to speak of a *voltage* amplifier, a *current* amplifier, or a *power* amplifier. These terms specify the aspect of the output that is of most interest in the particular application.

We shall discuss some practical aspects of voltage amplifiers, such as bias circuits, cascade or multistage connections, and operation over a wide frequency range. Power amplifiers will be discussed in the following chapter.

The desirable features of an amplifier depend on its application. Some instrument amplifiers must maintain a specified voltage amplification over long periods of time and over a wide frequency range and must not be sensitive to changes of transistors or tubes. Pulse amplifiers may have to amplify the pulse without appreciable change in shape or delay in time. In other applications a narrow band of frequencies should be amplified, and other frequencies should be suppressed.

Important aspects of amplifier performance include the *power gain*, the *voltage amplification*, and the *current amplification*. Further, the amplification-frequency and the phase shift-frequency characteristics are often important. The *input impedance* determines the loading of the signal source, and the *output* (Thévenin) *impedance* determines the suitability for a parti-

161

cular load impedance. Other items which may be important are the *distortion* introduced by the amplifier, the *stability* against changes in line voltage or ambient temperature, and the *power sensitivity*, i.e., the ratio of power output to signal voltage input. We remark that when more stringent requirements are placed on an amplifier, its circuit complexity and cost generally increase.

7-2
Class A, class AB, class B, and class C operation

As we shall explain in Chapter 8, there is a distinct improvement in the efficiency of a power amplifier if the collector or plate current flows in half-cycle pulses in response to a sine-wave signal. For the present we merely define the several classes of amplifier element operation in terms of the fraction of the time that the transistor or tube carries current, as follows:

class A	current flows during complete cycle
class AB	current flows more than one-half cycle but less than the full cycle
class B	current flows approximately one-half of the cycle
class C	current flows less than one-half of the cycle

We recall that the tube and transistor amplifiers discussed in the foregoing chapters operated in the class A mode. The present chapter will also treat only class A amplifiers.

7-3
The amplifier as a network element; cascade connection

In Chapter 6 we introduced the concept of the Thévenin equivalent of an amplifier circuit but treated the equivalent impedances as resistances. At higher frequencies the more general circuit (Fig. 7-1) which contains the complex input impedance $\mathbf{Z}_{\text{in}}$ and the complex Thévenin impedance $\mathbf{Z}_o$ is usually required. We review the definitions of gain in terms of the symbols in Fig. 7-1; thus

$$\mathbf{A}_v \equiv \frac{\mathbf{E}_L}{\mathbf{E}_i} \quad \text{and} \quad \mathbf{A}_i \equiv \frac{\mathbf{I}_L}{\mathbf{I}_i} \tag{7-1}$$

and

$$G \equiv \frac{P_L}{P_{\text{in}}} = \frac{I_L^2 R_L}{I_i^2 R_{\text{in}}} \tag{7-2}$$

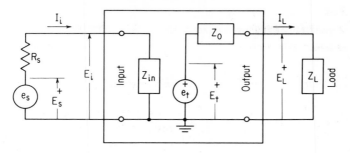

FIGURE 7-1   Amplifier as network element.

where R_L and R_{in} are the resistive components of the load and input impedances, respectively. The transducer gain G_T (see Sec. 6-6d) is given by

$$G_T = \frac{4R_L R_s}{(R_s + R_{in})^2} A_i^2 \qquad (7\text{-}3)$$

This relation is useful when the generator and load resistances are specified
and a transistor stage is to be designed to give maximum output power.

Often the required voltage gain cannot be developed in a one-stage
amplifier. Then a two-stage (Fig. 7-2) or a multistage amplifier is used. We
shall study some of the coupling networks used to couple cascaded stages
and the frequency response of such amplifiers.

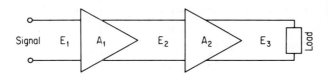

FIGURE 7-2   Amplifier stages in cascade.

If the voltage gain of the individual stages is known, it is a simple matter
to calculate the over-all gain

$$\mathbf{A} \equiv \frac{\mathbf{E}_3}{\mathbf{E}_1} = \frac{\mathbf{E}_2}{\mathbf{E}_1}\frac{\mathbf{E}_3}{\mathbf{E}_2} = \mathbf{A}_1 \mathbf{A}_2 \qquad (7\text{-}4)$$

In view of the definition of the decibel voltage ratio in Eq. (2-122), we can
write the total gain in dBv as follows:

$$A_{dBv} = A_{1dBv} + A_{2dBv} \qquad (7\text{-}5)$$

The over-all power gain is also the sum of the individual decibel gains. Thus,
gains (both positive and negative) may be added algebraically in the decibel
system. The convenience of this calculation is one of the prime advantages
of the decibel notation.

7-4
Q-point determination in triode circuits

a. Grounded-cathode amplifier with self-bias circuit

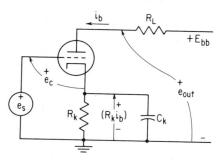

FIGURE 7-3 Triode amplifier with self-bias circuit.

The self-bias circuit consists of the resistor R_k shunted by the capacitor C_k as shown in Fig. 7-3. At the signal frequency the reactance of C_k is generally low compared with R_k; therefore the impedance from cathode to ground is small and the circuit behaves like the grounded-cathode amplifier. (The effect of the bias circuit on the gain will be examined later.)

To study the bias condition we assume $e_s = 0$ and focus our attention on the $R_k i_b$ voltage drop across R_k. This voltage causes the grid to be negative to the cathode, i.e., it provides a negative bias.

We consider the following problem. Suppose that R_L, R_k, E_{bb}, and the tube type are all specified and we wish to find the Q point. Since the grid current is zero, the applicable voltage equations are, for $e_s = 0$,

$$e_c = -R_k i_b \tag{7-6}$$

and

$$e_b = E_{bb} - (R_L + R_k)i_b \tag{7-7}$$

The last equation represents a *resistance line* that corresponds to the resistance $R_L + R_k$. Let this line be drawn on the plate characteristics as shown in Fig. 7-4. Now the constraints on the problem are (1) the resistance line, (2) the tube characteristics, and (3) Eq. (7-6). In a numerical problem we draw a curve, called the *bias curve*, which satisfies constraints 2 and 3, and find where the bias curve intersects the resistance line so that all three constraints are finally satisfied. To draw the bias curve we *assume* values of e_c the same as on the plate characteristics, e.g., -4, -6, -8, etc. in Fig. 7-4, and then calculate the i_b values that *would be* required to give the assumed e_c. For example, if $R_L = 25$ k and $R_k = 4$ k, we would get the following pairs of values:

e_c (assumed):	-4	-6	-8	-10 V
i_b (required):	1.0	1.5	2.0	2.5 mA

When these i_b values are plotted on the plate characteristics and connected

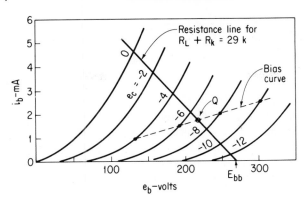

FIGURE 7-4   Graphical analysis of amplifier with self-bias circuit.

by a curve, we get the bias curve shown dotted in Fig. 7-4. All points on this line satisfy Eq. (7-6) *and* the tube characteristics, but only *one* point also satisfies the 29-k resistance line constraint, namely, the intersection point Q. This point gives the bias value of -7 V.

If the values of R_L, E_{bb}, and the bias voltage are specified and we wish to find R_k, we have posed a different problem, which we leave as an exercise for the reader.

b. Triode with R_k returned to $-E_{cc}$

In some circuits, for instance in a cathode follower amplifier, it is sometimes desirable to provide a negative potential of as much as 2 or 3 hundred volts and return the R_k connection thereto. The arrangement is shown in Fig. 7-5, where a resistor R_L is included in the plate lead to give a more generally useful circuit.

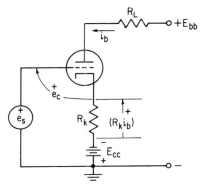

FIGURE 7-5   Amplifier with R_k returned to $-E_{cc}$.

We make the same assumptions as before, i.e., $e_s = 0$ and $i_c = 0$, and use the same approach to find the Q point. The emf equations now are

$$e_c = E_{cc} - R_k i_b \qquad (7\text{-}8)$$

and

$$e_b = E_{bb} + E_{cc} - (R_L + R_k)i_b \qquad (7\text{-}9)$$

Equation (7-9) can be represented by a resistance line, which has the intercept $E_{bb} + E_{cc}$ on the voltage axis. The *bias curve* is found by assuming values of e_c and calculating i_b values by the use of Eq. (7-8). Let $E_{cc} = 100$, $E_{bb} = 300$, $R_k = 16$ k, and $R_L = 16$ k. The resistance line for 32 k is shown in Fig. 7-6. Next compute corresponding values of e_c and i_b by Eq. (7-8) and find

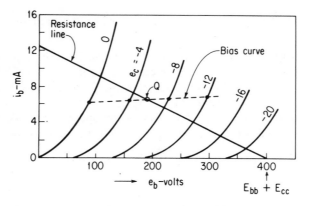

FIGURE 7-6   Analysis of circuit in Fig. 7-5.

e_c (assumed):	0	−4	−8	−12	V
i_b (calculated):	6.25	6.50	6.75	7.00	mA

These points are plotted to give the *bias curve* (Fig. 7-6). We notice that the curve is rather flat, owing to the large value of E_{cc}. As before, the intersection with the resistance line gives the Q point.

7-5
The effect of the cathode bias circuit on voltage gain

An analysis of the amplifier circuit in Fig. 7-3 will give us a better understanding of the action of the bias circuit. The first step is to draw the small-signal equivalent circuit (Fig. 7-7). We note that the grid-to-cathode voltage

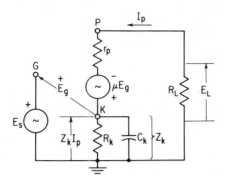

FIGURE 7-7 Small-signal equivalent circuit of amplifier in Fig. 7-3.

E_g differs from the signal voltage by the drop across the cathode bias imped-ance $\mathbf{Z}_k$; therefore,

$$\mathbf{E}_g = \mathbf{E}_s - \mathbf{Z}_k\mathbf{I}_p \qquad (7\text{-}10)$$

where $\mathbf{I}_p$ is the phasor plate current. The voltage equation for the loop carry-ing $\mathbf{I}_p$ is

$$\mu\mathbf{E}_g = (R_L + r_p + \mathbf{Z}_k)\mathbf{I}_p \qquad (7\text{-}11)$$

If we replace $\mathbf{E}_g$ in (7-11) by its value from (7-10) and solve for $\mathbf{I}_p$, we find

$$\mathbf{I}_p = \frac{\mu\mathbf{E}_s}{R_L + r_p + (\mu + 1)\mathbf{Z}_k} \qquad (7\text{-}12)$$

But $\mathbf{E}_L = -R_L\mathbf{I}_p$; so using (7-12), we calculate

$$\mathbf{A}_v = \frac{\mathbf{E}_L}{\mathbf{E}_s} = \frac{-\mu R_L}{R_L + r_p + (\mu + 1)\mathbf{Z}_k} \qquad (7\text{-}13)$$

Because $\mathbf{Z}_k$ is multiplied by the factor $(\mu + 1)$, we expect that this term will have a substantial effect on the gain, unless $\mathbf{Z}_k$ is very small.

To find the effect of frequency on the gain we need to replace $\mathbf{Z}_k$ by its value; thus, for the parallel-connected R_k and C_k we write

$$\mathbf{Z}_k = \frac{\dfrac{R_k}{j\omega C_k}}{R_k + \dfrac{1}{j\omega C_k}} = \frac{R_k}{1 + j\omega R_k C_k} \qquad (7\text{-}14)$$

Next we replace $R_k C_k$ by the parameter $1/\omega_1$ and then substitute $\mathbf{Z}_k$ into (7-13)

$$\mathbf{A}_v = \frac{-\mu R_L}{R_L + r_p + \dfrac{(\mu + 1)R_k}{1 + j\dfrac{\omega}{\omega_1}}} \qquad (7\text{-}15)$$

Multiplying numerator and denominator by $1 + j\omega/\omega_1$, we find

$$\mathbf{A}_v = \frac{-\mu R_L\left(1 + j\dfrac{\omega}{\omega_1}\right)}{(\mu + 1)R_k + (R_L + r_p)\left(1 + j\dfrac{\omega}{\omega_1}\right)} \tag{7-16}$$

If desired, this relation can be manipulated into the form of Eq. (2-130) for the phase-lead network. Therefore, the magnitude and phase of $\mathbf{A}_v$ will vary with frequency, as shown in Fig. 2-24.

A numerical example will serve to show this variation. Let $\mu = 20$, $r_p = 10\,\mathrm{k}$, $R_L = 50\,\mathrm{k}$, $R_k = 2\,\mathrm{k}$, and $C_k = 25\,\mu\mathrm{F}$. Substitution in (7-16) yields

$$\mathbf{A}_v = \frac{-9.8\left(1 + j\dfrac{\omega}{20}\right)}{1 + j\dfrac{\omega}{34}} \tag{7-17}$$

Thus, as $\omega \to 0$, the voltage gain approaches -9.8, and as $\omega \to \infty$, it approaches $-9.8 \times 34/20$, or -16.7. In the terminology of Fig. 2-24, the lower corner frequency is 20 rad/s and the upper corner frequency is 34 rad/s (5.4 Hz). Substitution in Eq. (7-17) will show that when $\omega = 34$, then $\mathbf{A}_v = -13.7\underline{/14.5°}$, and when $\omega = 68\,(f = 10.8)$, then $\mathbf{A}_v = -15.5\underline{/9.5°}$. Thus, at a frequency of 10.8 Hz the magnitude of the gain is within 7 per cent of its high-frequency value and the phase displacement is 9.5°.

A rule of thumb sometimes advanced for the design of a bias circuit is to require that $1/\omega C$ be equal to $R_k/10$ at the lowest frequency of interest. In the example, this ratio would obtain at an ω of 200. At this frequency we calculate $\mathbf{A}_v = -16.5\underline{/3.8°}$, a value within 1.2 per cent of the high-frequency gain.

7-6
The effect of an output filter on the voltage gain

A load of resistance R_L that cannot tolerate the direct-current component can be fed through a capacitor as in Fig. 7-8a. The resistor R_1 is needed to supply the direct current to the tube. Let us analyze the circuit to find how the voltage gain varies with frequency.

We first replace the tube by its equivalent circuit (Fig. 7-8b) using the Norton form. We note that r_p and R_1 are in parallel, so we designate their parallel value by R_{eq} and for later application introduce the symbol $r_p \| R_1$ to mean the parallel value of r_p and R_1; thus

$$R_{eq} = r_p \| R_1 = \frac{r_p R_1}{r_p + R_1} \tag{7-18}$$

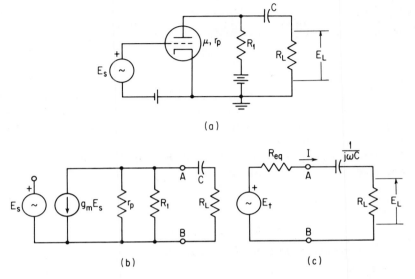

FIGURE 7-8 (a) Amplifier with output filter. (b) Tube replaced by equivalent circuit. (c) Circuit in (b) modified by application of Thévenin's theorem.

Next we replace the circuit to the left of terminals AB in Fig. 7-8b by its Thévenin equivalent, as in Fig. 7-8c. The source voltage $\mathbf{E}_t$ equals $-g_m R_{eq} \mathbf{E}_s$. To calculate $\mathbf{E}_L$ in terms of $\mathbf{E}_t$ we observe that $\mathbf{E}_L/\mathbf{E}_t$ equals the ratio of R_L to the total series impedance

$$\frac{\mathbf{E}_L}{\mathbf{E}_t} = \frac{\mathbf{E}_L}{-g_m R_{eq} \mathbf{E}_s} = \frac{R_L}{R_L + R_{eq} + \dfrac{1}{j\omega C}} \tag{7-19}$$

Therefore,

$$\mathbf{A}_v = \frac{\mathbf{E}_L}{\mathbf{E}_s} = \frac{-g_m R_{eq} R_L}{R_L + R_{eq} + \dfrac{1}{j\omega C}} \tag{7-20}$$

A comparison of (7-20) with (2-126) will show that both are the same function of $j\omega$, so we conclude that the amplifier circuit behaves like a *high-pass RC filter*.

Equation (7-20) can be manipulated as follows:

$$\mathbf{A}_v = \frac{\dfrac{-g_m R_{eq} R_L}{(R_L + R_{eq})}}{1 + \dfrac{1}{j\omega(R_L + R_{eq})C}} = \frac{-g_m R}{1 - j\dfrac{\omega_1}{\omega}} \tag{7-21}$$

in which $R = R_{eq} \| R_L = r_p \| R_1 \| R_L$ and where

$$\omega_1 = \frac{1}{(R_L + R_{eq})C} \qquad (7\text{-}22)$$

Thus, the corner frequency is ω_1 and the asymptotic gain at high frequencies is $-g_m R$.

Example: Let $\mu = 20$, $r_p = 10$ k, $g_m = 2 \times 10^{-3}$, $R_1 = 40$ k, $C = 0.5 \ \mu$F, and $R_L = 20$ k. Then $R_{eq} = 8$ k, $R = 5.7$ k, the high-frequency gain is -11.4, and the corner frequency is 71.5 rad/s (11.4 Hz). At the corner frequency the complex gain is $-(11.4/\sqrt{2})\underline{/45°}$.

Sometimes a CR filter is also needed at the amplifier input. Its effect can be analyzed by the usual methods.

7-7
The effect of stray capacitances on gain and input impedance of tube amplifiers

The analyses thus far have neglected the effect of the small capacitances due to the wiring and the capacitances between the tube electrodes. Total capacitance values of 10 pF† may be involved, and these may act in shunt or in series with the circuit resistances. As the frequency is raised, the capacitance may become significant or even controlling in its effect. For example, a 10-pF capacitance has a reactance of only 15,900 Ω at $f = 10^6$ Hz.

As shown in Fig. 7-9a, there are three interelectrode capacitances involved in a triode: from grid to cathode, C_{gk}; from grid to plate, C_{gp}, and from plate to cathode, C_{pk}. The connecting wires may add a few picofarads to the tube capacitances.

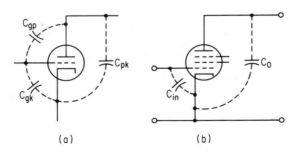

(a)   (b)

FIGURE 7-9 Interelectrode capacitances (a) for a triode and (b) approximate effective capacitances for a pentode.

†1 picofarad (pF) = 1 micromicrofarad = 10^{-12} farad.

When a triode is used in an amplifier, the grid-to-plate capacitance causes a larger input current than might be expected and thereby lowers the input impedance. In some circuits the grid-to-plate capacitance can cause unwanted oscillations.

In pentode amplifier circuits the screen and suppressor grids are effectively at cathode potential for signal voltages. These grids act as an electrostatic shield between the control grid and the plate, so the grid-to-plate capacitance is small, of the order of 0.01 pF. Therefore the capacitances in the pentode (and beam tube) can be represented in an equivalent circuit by two capacitances, (1) an input capacitance that includes the capacitance from control grid to cathode and from control grid to screen, and (2) an output capacitance that includes the plate-to-suppressor and plate-to-screen capacitances and plate-to-cathode or to shield capacitance (Fig. 7-9b).

First we discuss the gain and input impedance of a grounded-cathode triode amplifier which has a load impedance $\mathbf{Z}_L$. Its small-signal equivalent circuit is drawn in Fig. 7-10 with the capacitances included. If this network is solved for the complex voltage gain, we find

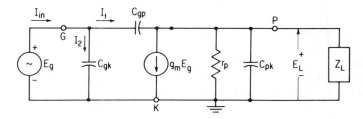

FIGURE 7-10 Equivalent circuit of grounded-cathode triode stage including interelectrode capacitances.

$$\mathbf{A}_v = \frac{-g_m + \mathbf{Y}_{gp}}{\mathbf{Y}_{pk} + \mathbf{Y}_{gp} + \mathbf{Y}_L + \dfrac{1}{r_p}} \qquad (7\text{-}23)$$

where

$$\mathbf{Y}_{gp} = j\omega C_{gp}, \quad \mathbf{Y}_{pk} = j\omega C_{pk}, \quad \text{and} \quad \mathbf{Y}_L = \frac{1}{\mathbf{Z}_L}.$$

With typical triodes and the usual load resistance values, the effect of the capacitances is small up to the lower radio frequencies.

Example: Consider a triode for which $\mu = 20$, $r_p = 8$ k, and $g_m = 0.0025$ loaded with 50 k. Also let $C_{gp} = 5$ pF, $C_{pk} = 6$ pF, and $C_{gk} = 6$ pF. The low-frequency gain is $17.2\underline{/180°}$. If the gain is calculated by Eq.

(7-23) for a frequency of 10^5 Hz, we find $\mathbf{A}_v = 17.2\underline{/177.3°}$, which differs from the low-frequency gain only by a small phase shift. However, a calculation for $f = 10^6$ Hz gives $\mathbf{A}_v = 15.6\underline{/153.8°}$, which indicates significant changes in both gain and phase.

To calculate the *input impedance* $\mathbf{Z}_{\text{in}}$, we note that $\mathbf{I}_{\text{in}} = \mathbf{I}_1 + \mathbf{I}_2$; therefore,

$$\mathbf{Z}_{\text{in}} = \frac{\mathbf{E}_g}{\mathbf{I}_{\text{in}}} = \frac{\mathbf{E}_g}{\mathbf{I}_1 + \mathbf{I}_2} \tag{7-24}$$

But the currents can be expressed as

$$I_1 = -j\omega C_{gp}\mathbf{E}_{pg} \quad \text{and} \quad I_2 = j\omega C_{gk}\mathbf{E}_g \tag{7-25}$$

where $\mathbf{E}_{pg}$ is the drop from P to G. Next express $\mathbf{E}_{pg}$ in terms of $\mathbf{E}_g$ and $\mathbf{A}_v$ through the voltage relation

$$\mathbf{E}_L = \mathbf{A}_v\mathbf{E}_g = \mathbf{E}_g + \mathbf{E}_{pg} \tag{7-26}$$

From (7-26) we see that

$$\mathbf{E}_{pg} = \mathbf{E}_g(\mathbf{A}_v - 1) \tag{7-27}$$

Upon combining (7-24), (7-25), and (7-27) we find

$$\mathbf{Z}_{\text{in}} = \frac{1}{j\omega[C_{gk} + C_{gp}(1 - \mathbf{A}_v)]} \tag{7-28}$$

The input impedance is obviously a function of frequency through ω but also through the gain $\mathbf{A}_v$.

In the numerical example we found that up to 10^5 Hz there was only a small change in the angle of $\mathbf{A}_v$ for the resistance-loaded amplifier. Up to this frequency, therefore, we could say that $\mathbf{A}_v \cong -A_r + j0$, where A_r is real and positive. If this value is introduced into Eq. (7-28) we get

$$\mathbf{Z}_{\text{in}} \cong \frac{1}{j\omega[C_{gk} + C_{gp}(1 + A_r)]} \tag{7-29}$$

This relation shows that the effect of capacitance C_{gp} is multiplied by the large factor $(1 + A_r)$. We may think of the square-bracketed quantity as an equivalent *input capacitance* of value $C_{gk} + C_{gp}(1 + A_r)$. Thus, the grid-to-plate capacitance has a large influence on the input capacitance—a phenomenon known as the *Miller effect*. The calculated value of Z_{in} at 10^5 Hz in the amplifier in the example is 16,400 Ω—a relatively low value.

If $\mathbf{Z}_{\text{in}}$ is calculated by Eq. (7-28) for the conditions of the example for $f = 10^6$ Hz, we obtain $\mathbf{Z}_{\text{in}} \cong 1810\underline{/-56.9°}$. This impedance is equivalent to a *parallel* connection of a 3310 Ω resistor and a 73.7-pF capacitor at 10^6 Hz. Thus, the input impedance may have a resistive, as well as a capacitive, component at the higher frequencies. With an *inductive* load in the plate circuit, the calculated input resistance can turn out to be *negative*, which means that the tube circuit can cause power to flow back into the "source" E_g. In this situation steady oscillations may build up.

In a pentode amplifier additional interelectrode capacitances are present, but the capacitance C_{gp} can be neglected, as explained in the following sections.

7-8
RC-coupled pentode amplifier stage

Generally a single dc power supply is used for all the stages of a multistage amplifier. Therefore the coupling circuit from one stage to the next must convey the signal at the first plate but not the direct voltage. The separation of the signal from the dc component was effected by the CR_L output circuit in Fig. 7-8a. This coupling circuit is also commonly used between stages, as shown by CR_g in Fig. 7-11. For simplicity, the screen supply circuits and the

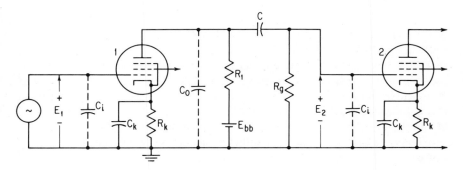

FIGURE 7-11 Pentode amplifier stage.

load on the second tube have been omitted, but the stray capacitances are accounted for by the *input capacitance* C_i and the *output capacitance* C_o.

This type of amplifier is usually designed to give nearly constant amplification over a wide frequency range, as shown by the gain-frequency curve in Fig. 7-12. Here the voltage gain of one stage is defined as E_2/E_1, i.e., the ratio of the signal voltages at the grids of successive tubes. We define the *lower half-power frequency* f_1 as the frequency at which the gain drops to $A_M/\sqrt{2}$, where A_M is the mid-band gain shown in the figure. Similarly, the *upper half-power frequency* f_2 is the upper frequency at which the gain drops to $A_M/\sqrt{2}$, or a drop of 3 dBv.

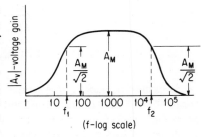

FIGURE 7-12 Gain *vs.* log frequency for an *RC*-coupled stage.

As mentioned earlier, the series circuit CR_g acts as a filter to convey the signal to the grid of tube 2, but to prevent the dc plate potential of tube 1 from affecting the second tube's grid. At low frequencies some of the signal voltage is lost across C, so the gain decreases as the frequency decreases. The resistor R_g is needed to carry any charges collected by the grid away to ground, or in other words to maintain a definite direct voltage bias on tube 2. A typical set of values for the load and coupling components might be $R_1 = 0.2$ MΩ, $R_g = 0.5$ MΩ, and $C = 0.01$ μF, though these values vary widely depending on the frequency band width and the gain desired.

7-9
Frequency response of RC-coupled amplifier

A natural approach to the analysis of the RC-coupled amplifier is to start with the small-signal equivalent circuit. To simplify this circuit let us assume that C_k is large enough relative to R_k so that the bias circuit has no effect on the gain over the range of frequencies of interest. Then the equivalent circuit takes the form in Fig. 7-13. While the exact voltage gain can be derived from this circuit, the resulting equations are cumbersome and contain terms that are negligible over portions of the frequency range. Therefore, we seek approximations that will hold with sufficient accuracy over specified frequency ranges.

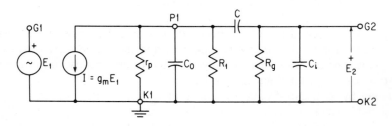

FIGURE 7-13   Equivalent circuit for pentode amplifier stage.

Because the gain curve varies only slightly over a 100 to 1 frequency range (Fig. 7-12), it can be inferred that none of the capacitances have an appreciable effect on the gain in this middle range. If we take $C = 0.01$ μF, $C_i = 10$ pF, and $C_o = 8$ pF, then the corresponding reactances at $f = 1$ kHz are $X_c = 15{,}920$ Ω, $X_i = 15.9$ MΩ, and $X_o = 19.9$ MΩ. Thus, X_c is small compared with the usual values of R_1 and R_g, and X_i and X_o are large shunting reactances across R_1 and R_g. As an approximation, therefore, we assume that $X_c = 0$ and $X_i = X_o \to \infty$ for the mid-band frequencies, so that the equivalent circuit reduces to the form in Fig. 7-14. For convenience, we define the resistance of the parallel combination in this figure to be R, i.e., $R = r_p \| R_1 \| R_g$, or

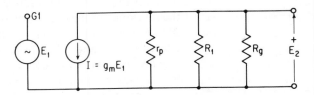

FIGURE 7-14   Approximate equivalent circuit for mid-band frequency.

$$\frac{1}{R} = \frac{1}{r_p} + \frac{1}{R_1} + \frac{1}{R_g} \qquad (7\text{-}30)$$

Then we can write $\mathbf{E}_2 = -g_m R \mathbf{E}_1$, or

$$\mathbf{A}_M = \frac{\mathbf{E}_2}{\mathbf{E}_1} = -g_m R \qquad (7\text{-}31)$$

Usually R is mainly dependent on R_1 and R_g because r_p for a pentode is high.

Next we consider the *high-frequency* approximate circuit. Here X_c must still be negligible, but the capacitances C_i and C_o cause a shunting effect, so the circuit reduces to that in Fig. 7-15a. This circuit can be further reduced to the form in Fig. 7-15b, where R has the value already given, and C_p equals $C_o + C_i$. Circuit analysis applied to this circuit yields

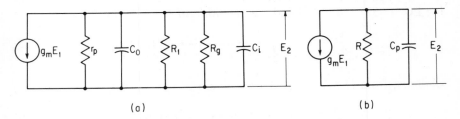

(a)   (b)

FIGURE 7-15   Equivalent circuits for high frequencies.

$$\mathbf{A}_H = \frac{-g_m R}{1 + j\omega R C_p} \qquad (7\text{-}32)$$

Comparison of this relation with Eq. (2-118) for the low-pass RC filter shows that they are the same except for a constant factor. Thus, the upper corner, or half-power, frequency is given by

$$f_2 = \frac{1}{2\pi R C_p} \tag{7-33}$$

At this frequency the denominator of (7-32) reduces to the value $1 + j1$, so the gain is down by the factor $1/\sqrt{2}$ or 0.707.

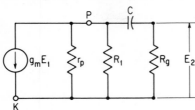

FIGURE 7-16   Equivalent circuit for low frequencies.

Over the lower range of frequencies the reactance of the coupling capacitor X_c becomes important, whereas the effects of C_o and C_t are negligible. The approximate equivalent circuit for low frequencies is given in Fig. 7-16. The voltage E_2 is less than the voltage at the plate of tube 1 owing to the voltage divider effect of C and R_g in series. The circuit in Fig. 7-16 is identical with that in Fig. 7-8a, so that we can use Eq. (7-21) for the low-frequency gain

$$\mathbf{A}_L = \frac{-g_m R}{1 - j\frac{\omega_1}{\omega}} \tag{7-34}$$

except that here $R = r_p \| R_1 \| R_g$ and $\omega_1 = 1/(R_g + R_{eq})C$, where $R_{eq} = r_p \| R_1$. As already explained in Sec. 7-6, this relation shows the same variation with ω as that of a high-pass RC filter. The lower corner frequency is ω_1 or $f_1 = \omega_1/2\pi$. A knowledge of f_1 is useful as a measure of the low-frequency characteristic of the stage.

Before discussing the amplifier frequency response characteristics we wish to obtain normalized formulas that show how the gain and phase vary relative to the gain and phase at mid-band. Thus, we calculate $\mathbf{A}_H/\mathbf{A}_M$ by combining Eqs. (7-32) and (7-31) and the definition of f_2 to obtain

$$\frac{\mathbf{A}_H}{\mathbf{A}_M} = \frac{1}{1 + j\frac{f}{f_2}} = \frac{1}{\sqrt{1 + \left(\frac{f}{f_2}\right)^2}} \left| \underline{-\tan^{-1}\frac{f}{f_2}} \right. \tag{7-35}$$

similarly, from (7-34) and (7-31) we obtain

$$\frac{\mathbf{A}_L}{\mathbf{A}_M} = \frac{1}{1 - j\frac{f_1}{f}} = \frac{1}{\sqrt{1 + \left(\frac{f_1}{f}\right)^2}} \left| \underline{\tan^{-1}\frac{f_1}{f}} \right. \tag{7-36}$$

These formulas will help us to gain an insight into the amplifier gain and phase frequency characteristics.

A polar diagram of $\mathbf{A}_f/\mathbf{A}_M$, where $\mathbf{A}_f$ is the gain at frequency f, is easy to construct because its locus is a circle (Fig. 7-17). Several complex gain ratios are shown, and the frequency for each is labeled in terms of the half-power frequencies f_1 or f_2. For example, the gain ratio is $0.707/\underline{45°}$ at the frequency

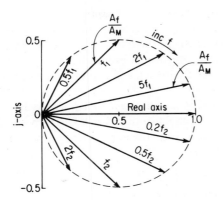

FIGURE 7-17   Locus diagram of A_f/A_M as the frequency varies.

f_1. This means that if $\mathbf{E}_1 = 1.0\underline{/0°}$ and if $\mathbf{A}_M = 20\underline{/180°}$, then at $f = f_1$ the phasor $\mathbf{E}_2 = 0.707 \times 20\underline{/180 + 45°} = 14.14\underline{/225°}$. This calculation calls attention to the 180° phase angle inherent in $\mathbf{A}_M$. Because the phase angles in Fig. 7-17 are based on $\mathbf{A}_M$ as a reference, we must think of the output volt-age leading or lagging its phase position *for the mid-band frequency†* by the angles shown in the figure.

Another rapid method of plotting the frequency characteristic is to plot the log of the magnitude of the gain against a log-frequency scale as discussed in Sec. 2-9. This form, called a Bode plot, is useful in the application of an amplifier to a feedback control system. As shown in Fig. 7-18, the gain

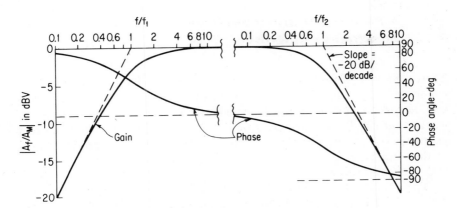

FIGURE 7-18   Bode plot of gain and phase of RC-coupled stage. f_1 = lower corner frequency, f_2 = upper corner frequency, and ϕ = phase of $\mathbf{A}_f$ relative to that of $\mathbf{A}_M$.

†The mid-band frequency may be taken to be $\sqrt{f_1 f_2}$.

variation can be plotted rapidly by first sketching the straight-line asymptotes and then locating one or more points on the actual curve. Two convenient points are at the corner frequencies where the gain ratio is down 3 dBv. The figure also shows the variation of phase, which ranges from nearly 90° lead at low frequencies to 90° lag at high frequencies. The phase is changing most rapidly at the corner frequencies.

The amplifier *frequency bandwidth* or *passband* is defined to be $f_2 - f_1$. However, in wide-band amplifiers, $f_1 \ll f_2$; so that f_2 is taken to be the bandwidth. A criterion for the choice of a tube for a wide-band amplifier is the so-called *gain-bandwidth product*, i.e.,

$$\text{gain} \times \text{bandwidth} = |\mathbf{A}_M| \times f_2 \qquad (7\text{-}37)$$

but $\mathbf{A}_m$ and f_2 are given in (7-31) and (7-33); so we get

$$\text{gain} \times \text{bandwidth} = g_m R \times \frac{1}{2\pi R C_p} = \frac{g_m}{2\pi C_p} \qquad (7\text{-}38)$$

Thus the tube should have a high g_m and the shunt capacitance C_s should be low.

If R_1 and R_g are increased, the mid-band gain increases, but according to (7-38) the gain-bandwidth product stays the same, so the bandwidth decreases. As an example we take $R = 0.2$ MΩ, $g_m = 0.004$ mho, and $C_p = 14$ pF. Then $A_M = 800$ and the gain-bandwidth product is 45.5×10^6, which gives a bandwidth of 57,000 Hz. If the resistances R_1 and R_g are lowered enough to cut A_M to 80, then the bandwidth rises to 570,000 Hz.

7-10
Bias circuits for transistor amplifiers; stability

There are several reasons for the greater difficulty of maintaining a proper bias condition, or Q point, in transistor circuits than in tube circuits. The important factors in common-emitter circuits are: (1) the variation of collector leakage current I_{co} with temperature, (2) the variation of the static current gain h_{FE} with the temperature, (3) the variation of h_{FE} between transistors of the same type, and (4) the variation of the base-to-emitter voltage V_{BE} with the temperature.

These factors have a different importance depending on whether germanium or silicon transistors are used. For example, the effect of I_{co} is important in a germanium transistor, but in a silicon transistor is of much lesser importance owing to its small value. The variation of V_{BE} is important in both types, but the variation of h_{FE} is more important in the Si transistor.

The types of variations that may be expected for a small Ge transistor are

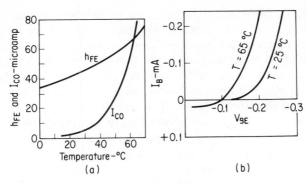

FIGURE 7-19   Effect of temperature on h_{FE}, I_{CO}, and input characteristics, for a germanium transistor.

shown in Fig. 7-19. The variation of I_{CO} is exponential, and I_{CO} doubles for a temperature increase of about 8 to 11°C. The input curves in Fig. 7-19b, which assume $|V_{CE}| > 0.5$ V, show a considerable temperature effect on V_{BE} for a fixed value of I_B.

The object of the bias circuit is to keep the operation within the linear region of the output characteristics. As illustrated in Fig. 7-20, this region is bounded on the right by the safe maximum voltage V_{max}, on the top by the power dissipation limit, on the left by the line PQ due to saturation, and by cutoff near the horizontal axis. The figure shows two curves, 1 and 2, which could represent two different temperatures for the same bias current (I_B or I_E), or two different transistors of the same type for the same bias current. We first note that if I_C were held constant (as by a current generator source in the collector circuit) at the level of line ST, then the operation would be highly unsatisfactory. However, if V_C is maintained constant, as along line MN, the displacement of the Q point from line 1 to line 2 would be much reduced.

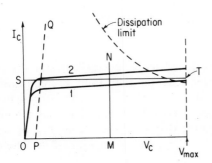

FIGURE 7-20   Transistor output characteristics.

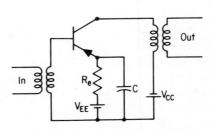

FIGURE 7-21   Two-battery bias circuit.

Better yet would be to constrain *both* V_C *and* I_C to nearly constant values. But I_C can only be controlled indirectly through a constraint on I_E. In good transistors I_C is within several per cent of I_E, so controlling I_E also controls I_C.

A circuit based on this reasoning is the two-battery bias circuit in Fig. 7-21. If we regard the base-to-emitter voltage as low, then the voltage V_{CE} is held constant by V_{CC}. For the same reason the dc emitter current is approximately V_{EE}/R_e, and therefore constant. The capacitor C bypasses the signal-frequency currents. This circuit has good stability, but the dc power loss in R_e and the need for two batteries are disadvantages.

The bias circuit in Fig. 7-22a makes use of V_{CC} and requires only one resistor R_1, but it has poor stability. For the usual range of V_{CC} the voltage from base to emitter is relatively small. As a result, $I_B \cong -V_{CC}/R_1$, and is a constant. Any large change in the I_C versus V_{CE} characteristics will therefore lead to undesirably large changes in the Q point, so this is a poor circuit.

Some improvement can be made by connecting the bias circuit to the collector instead of to V_{CC} as in Fig. 7-22b. The base bias current is approximately equal to $-V_{CE}/(R_1 + R_2)$, and if I_C tends to rise for any reason, then V_{CE} falls and the bias current falls and thereby partially limits the degree of the change. The network of two resistors and the capacitor C is used to prevent the signal feedback effect that would occur with a single bias resistor.

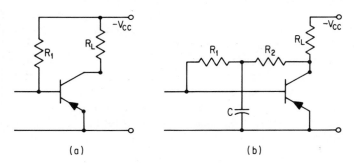

(a)   (b)

FIGURE 7-22   (a) Simple bias circuit and (b) improved bias circuit.

A bias circuit which can be proportioned to have excellent stability is shown in Fig. 7-23a. The voltage divider R_1R_2 tends to hold V_{CB} constant, and an emitter resistor R_e has been added. In practice, this resistor is bypassed by a capacitor to avoid signal-frequency feedback. The bias circuit analysis is begun by replacing the voltage divider supply from V_{CC} by an equivalent Thévenin voltage source, labeled V_B and R_b in Fig. 7-23b. These values are

$$R_b = \frac{R_1 R_2}{R_1 + R_2} \quad \text{and} \quad V_B = \frac{R_2}{R_1 + R_2} V_{CC} \tag{7-39}$$

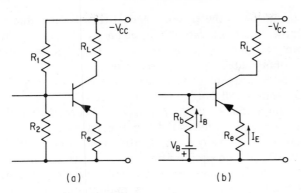

FIGURE 7-23   (a) Bias circuit with emitter resistor and (b) base supply replaced by a Thévenin source.

In a qualitative way it can be seen that to try to hold V_{CB} constant as I_B varies we should make R_b small, i.e., use low values of R_1 and R_2. But R_b acts as a shunt on the signal input, and to avoid an excessive loss of signal we must make R_b several times as large as the input impedance at the base.

Let us discuss the effect of R_e on the circuit behavior in a restricted problem. Since R_L is often below a few kilohms, it has little effect on the currents, since the output resistance is high, so we shall assume $R_L = 0$. Further, we consider only the effect of a change in h_{FE}, such as caused by changing transistors. We assume a Ge transistor, let $V_{BE} = -0.2$ V, and assume that this value is independent of I_B. The voltage equation around the base circuit in Fig. 7-23b is

$$V_B = R_e I_E + 0.2 - R_b I_B \qquad (7\text{-}40)$$

Next we use the relations $I_E = -(I_C + I_B)$ and $I_C = h_{FE} I_B$ with (7-40) and solve for I_C to find

$$I_C = \frac{-V_B + 0.2}{\dfrac{R_b}{h_{FE}} + R_e \left(1 + \dfrac{1}{h_{FE}}\right)} \qquad (7\text{-}41)$$

A numerical example will show the stabilizing effect of R_e against changes in h_{FE}. Let $R_1 = 50$ k, $R_2 = 12.5$ k, and $V_{CC} = -12$ V. Then $R_b = 10$ k and $V_B = 2.4$ V. Also let $R_e = 1$ k and consider two transistors: 1 with $h_{FE} = 40$, and 2 with $h_{FE} = 80$. Substitution in (7-41) yields $I_C \cong -1.73$ mA for transistor 1 and $I_C \cong -1.94$ mA for transistor 2. Thus, the increase in I_C at the Q point is only 12 per cent for a 100 per cent increase in h_{FE}!

As Eq. (7-41) shows, a larger value of R_e would produce a greater stabilization. But the voltage drop across R_e subtracts from the voltage available across the transistor and the power loss in R_e is objectionable, so R_e cannot be made too large.

This bias circuit stabilizes the Q point against temperature changes also. Equation (7-41) shows that temperature induced changes in V_{BE} are swamped out by the relatively large V_B. Changes in h_{FE} and I_{CO} due to temperature changes are also counteracted by the presence of R_e.

For design purposes a quantitative treatment of bias stability is needed, and the following section will outline the basic analysis.

A related problem is that of *thermal runaway*. This condition may arise when the self-heating due to the internal dissipation increases the dissipation. Normally, the heat is carried away to the surroundings (to the metal chassis or to a special *heat sink*), and an equilibrium temperature is attained. But if the dissipation rises too rapidly, a cumulative effect may develop, and the transistor may be destroyed. Thermal runaway is mainly important in power output stages, rather than in low-level stages.

7-11
Bias stability analysis

An analysis of stability is needed for design purposes. Germanium and silicon transistors, as we have seen, are sufficiently different to warrant separate treatment. We shall analyze the circuit of Fig. 7-23 and follow the approach of Searle *et al.*†

a. Germanium transistors

We consider only the active region. In this region we may replace the transistor by a model in which V_{BE} is a function of temperature and in which the collector current is assumed to be given by

$$I_C = I_{CO} - \alpha_F I_E \tag{7-42}$$

where I_{CO} is a function of temperature, but α_F is not. Then the voltage equation around the input loop is

$$V_B = R_e I_E - V_{BE} - R_b I_B \tag{7-43}$$

We use the relation $I_C = -(I_B + I_E)$ and the two preceding equations to eliminate I_B and I_E to obtain

$$I_C = -\frac{\alpha_F V_B + \alpha_F V_{BE} + (R_e + R_b) I_{CO}}{R_e + (1 - \alpha_F) R_b} \tag{7-44}$$

Since we have taken α_F and V_B to be independent of temperature we can take increments to obtain

$$\Delta I_C = -\left[\frac{R_e + R_b}{R_e + (1 - \alpha_F) R_b}\right] \Delta I_{CO} - \left[\frac{\alpha_F}{R_e + (1 - \alpha_F) R_b}\right] \Delta V_{BE} \tag{7-45}$$

†Searle, Boothroyd, Angelo, Gray, Pederson, *Elementary Circuit Properties of Transistors*, John Wiley & Sons, Inc., 1964, Chap. 5.

It will aid the discussion to make both square-bracketed factors the same, as follows:

$$\Delta I_C = -\left[\frac{R_e + R_b}{R_e + (1 - \alpha_F)R_b}\right]\Delta I_{CO}$$

$$-\left[\frac{R_e + R_b}{R_e + (1 - \alpha_F)R_b}\right]\frac{\alpha_F \Delta V_{BE}}{(R_e + R_b)} \qquad (7\text{-}46)$$

Let the square-bracketed factors equal S, called the *stability* or *sensitivity factor;* then

$$\Delta I_c = -S\Delta I_{co} - S\frac{\alpha_F \Delta V_{BE}}{R_e + R_b} \qquad (7\text{-}47)$$

We remark that a *small* value of S is needed to give *good* stability.

The factor S may be regarded as a function of R_e/R_b and of α_F. For a given value of α_F the value of S decreases (desirable) as R_e/R_b increases. Thus, larger R_e's are desirable, but as the earlier discussion brought out, limiting factors prevent the use of too large an R_e.

To gain some familiarity with the relations, we calculate the effect of a temperature change from 25 to 75°C on the Q point of a *pnp* transistor in a typical circuit. Let $V_{CC} = -14$ V, $R_L = 5$ k, and $\alpha_F = 0.98$. As a trial bias network (based on experience) we arbitrarily take $R_1 = 60$ k, $R_2 = 10$ k, and $R_e = 2$ k. Let I_{co} be $3\mu A$ at 25°C and assume that I_{co} doubles every 10°C. Let V_{BE} be -0.20 V at 25°C and $\Delta V_{BE}/\Delta T$ be $3mV/°C$. First we calculate and find $V_B = 2.0$ V, $R_b = 8.6$ k, and $S = 4.9$. Next calculate I_C by Eq. (7-44) at $T = 25$°C and find $I_C = -0.81$ mA. With an I_C of -0.81 mA we have a 4.0 V drop across R_L, a 1.6 V drop across R_e, and $V_{CE} = 14 - 4.0$ $-1.6 = 8.4$ V. Thus, the operating point could swing along the load line by about $14 - 8.4$ or 5.6 V maximum before $i_C \to 0$ at cutoff.

Next we calculate ΔI_C for a change from 25 to 75°C. First note that $\Delta I_{co} = 3 \times 2^5 = 96 \mu A$ and that $\Delta V_{BE} = 3 \times 50$ mV $= 0.15$ V. Next we use (7-47) to calculate ΔI_C and find $\Delta I_C \cong -0.47 - 0.07 = -0.54$ mA. Therefore, I_C at 75°C becomes $(-0.81 - 0.54)$, or -1.35 mA. The Q point has moved up on the load line so the drop across R_L is now 6.65 V, across R_e is 2.7 V, and V_{CE} is 4.65 V. Now the limitation on the output swing is due to the approach to saturation. If we use $V_{CE} = 0.5$ V as a minimum value, then the available peak swing is 4.1 V.

Some guidelines for the choice of R_1, R_2, and R_e can be laid down. The example shows that the Q point at the low temperature limit should be as low a value of I_C as the required output swing permits. For a given initial choice of R_b and R_e the low-temperature Q point can be adjusted by changing the voltage divider ratio and thus changing V_B in Eq. (7-44), while keeping R_b constant. If the high-temperature Q point comes out at too high a value of I_C, the most effective way of lowering it is to increase R_e, though a decrease in R_b will help.

When specified values of R_L, output voltage swing and temperature limits are to be met by a bias circuit design, an initial trial plus a few repetitive calculations will show whether or not the specifications can be met.

b. Silicon transistors

The calculations should reflect the facts that I_{co} is so small that its changes are not important, and that changes in h_{FE} with temperature are relatively large. We consider the same bias circuit and use the same approach as for the Ge transistor. In Eq. (7-44) we use the relation $h_{FE} = \alpha_F/(1 - \alpha_F)$ to obtain

$$I_C = -\left[\frac{V_B + V_{BE} + \dfrac{I_{co}}{\alpha_F}(R_b + R_e)}{\dfrac{R_e}{\alpha_F} + \dfrac{R_b + R_e}{h_{FE}}}\right] \qquad (7\text{-}48)$$

We shall neglect the I_{co} term and use the relation $\alpha_F = h_{FE}/(h_{FE} + 1)$ to find

$$I_C = -\frac{(V_B + V_{BE})h_{FE}}{R_b + R_e + R_e(h_{FE} + 1)} \qquad (7\text{-}49)$$

A bias circuit can be designed by applying Eq. (7-49) in the repetitive calculation method.

Example : Let $V_{CC} = -14$ V, and $R_L = 5$ k. At 25°C we assume that $I_{co} \cong 10^{-9}$ A, $V_{BE} = -0.70$ V, and $\Delta V_{BE}/\Delta T = 3$ mV/°C. We calculate I_{co} at 75°C, assuming that I_{co} doubles every 7°C and find 0.13 μA, which is small enough to neglect. At 75°C we calculate V_{BE} and obtain -0.55 V. Assume that $h_{FE} = 30$ at 25°C and equals 90 at 75°C. As a first trial let the bias circuit values be the same as before; $R_1 = 60$ k, $R_2 = 10$ k, and $R_e = 2$ k. Then $V_B = 2.0$ V and $R_b = 8.6$ k. First use (7-49) at 25°C

$$I_{C25} = -\frac{(2.0 - 0.7)30}{8.6 + 2 + 2(30 + 1)} = -0.54\text{mA}$$

Then at 75°C,

$$I_{C75} = -\frac{(2.0 - 0.55)90}{8.6 + 2 + 2(90 + 1)} = -0.68\text{mA}$$

A study of the load circuit voltages will show that these points are too low. It is left for the reader to repeat the calculations to obtain a better design.

In the foregoing analysis the well-known variation of h_{FE} with collector current has been ignored. This variation, as well as the effect of changing the transistor, can be considered if we use the principle of *worst case design*, Thus, at the low-temperature limit we would use the lowest h_{FE}, and at the high temperature the highest h_{FE} expected, considering temperature, current, and device changes. Of course, iterative calculations would be needed here also.

Mention should be made of the application of compensating nonlinear devices in bias circuits. Thermistors† or diodes may be incorporated in the bias network to partially compensate for the temperature effects in the transistor.

7-12
Transistor behavior at higher frequencies

Factors which affect the high-frequency or transient response of a transistor include (1) the depletion layer junction capacitances at emitter and collector junctions, (2) the minority carrier charge storage in the base region, and (3) the transit time of the carriers across the base. In the simple junction transistor the transit time depends on the rates of diffusion of the carriers across the base without assistance from an electric field. The carriers are emitted into the base by the emitter and diffuse across the base and arrive at the collector junction after traveling various paths, and after various delays. Any time delay of response of a device corresponds to a reduction of its high-frequency response and to a phase shift, so that the transit time will produce these effects. Their mathematical analysis is beyond the scope of this book, but we shall describe the result as giving a complex alpha that is frequency-dependent. Let us indicate this dependence by the notation $\alpha_b(\omega)$. An approximate expression for the complex alpha is

$$\alpha_b(\omega) = \frac{\alpha_b(0)}{1 + j\dfrac{\omega}{\omega_{ab}}} \tag{7-50}$$

Here $\alpha_b(0)$ is the low-frequency common-base alpha and $\omega_{ab} = 2\pi f_{ab}$, where f_{ab} is a parameter for a given transistor called the *alpha cutoff frequency*. Thus, when the frequency reaches f_{ab}, the magnitude of $\alpha_b(\omega)$ has dropped to 0.707 of its low-frequency value.

We recall from the discussion in Chapter 5 that the width of the depletion region at the collector junction varies with the voltage. At the same time, the quantity of the equal and opposite uncompensated charges on the two sides of the junction in the depletion region varies, as in a capacitor, but *not* in direct proportion to the voltage. The incremental variation dQ/dV defines the *capacitance* of the junction effective for small signals. This capacitance, called the *depletion* or *transition* capacitance, varies directly as the area of the junction, and in an alloy junction varies inversely as the square root of the bias voltage across the junction. Its value in a high-frequency transistor may be a few picofarads or less, or in a low-frequency power transistor may be several hundred picofarads.

†Temperature sensitive resistors, usually semiconductors.

At the forward-biased emitter junction is the built-in potential barrier which varies in height with the variation of the emitter-to-base voltage. Therefore the emitter junction has a *transition* capacitance similar to that of the collector junction. Of greater importance is a capacitance that owes its origin primarily to the diffusion mechanism of the minority carrier motion in the base, therefore called the *diffusion* capacitance. One approach to the visualization of the diffusion capacitance is to recall the picture of the minority carrier injection at the emitter-base junction and the variation of the carrier density across the base. If the emitter-to-base voltage is changed, say by a positive step, the carrier density rises suddenly at the junction, but some time elapses before a new equilibrium density variation across the base is reached. Thus we expect a sudden rise of emitter current as the carrier density rises but a decay of the current as the density equilibrium is regained at the higher level. The current variation during the transient period is of the same general form as that of a resistance-capacitance network. One method of calculating the diffusion capacitance is to assume a sinusoidal emitter-to-base voltage and then calculate† the time-dependence of the current, and calculate the emitter-base admittance. The diffusion capacitance is obtained from the imaginary part of this admittance. The diffusion capacitance is found to vary directly with the emitter bias current.

The detailed analysis of transistor high-frequency behavior in terms of the internal processes is rather complex and will not be attempted here. For application purposes equivalent circuit models are used to approximate the actual behavior, but models that will apply over the wider frequency ranges become increasingly complex. A relatively simple circuit for the common-base connection, which is based on the equivalent-T circuit of Fig. 6-2a, is given in Fig. 7-24. Here the emitter capacitance (diffusion plus transition)

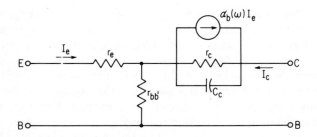

FIGURE 7-24   Complex $\alpha_b(\omega)$ and collector junction capacitance C_c.

†A rigorous calculation requires the solution of the time-dependent diffusion equation subject to the condition of a variable base width. See, for example, R. P. Nanavati, *An Introduction to Semiconductor Electronics*, McGraw-Hill Book Company, New York, 1963, Chaps. 7, 8, 9.

has been neglected because it would be in shunt with the low resistance r_e. We note that the base resistance $r_{bb'}$ is the ohmic resistance as in Fig. 5-15d.

We think of short-circuiting terminals C and B in Fig. 7-24 so as to examine the effect of frequency on the short-circuit current gain of this model. For frequencies up to $f_{\alpha b}$ the reactance of C_c remains high compared with $r_{bb'}$ and to r_e. Since r_c is very large, the short-circuit current gain is given closely by $\alpha_b(\omega)$. Some relative values of the current gain based on the approximate formula (7-50) are given in Table 7-1. We note that this variation is the same mathematically as the high-frequency gain variation of the RC-coupled amplifier (Fig. 7-18). In high-frequency amplifiers the load impedance is kept low, consequently the variation of the short-circuit gain gives a fair indication of the high-frequency performance. The amplitude of the gain may be reasonably accurate up to a frequency of about $f_{\alpha b}$, but the phase angle at this frequency and above is increasingly in error.

Table 7-1

$\omega/\omega_{\alpha b}$	$\alpha_b(\omega)/\alpha_b(0)$	$\begin{pmatrix} relative\ short\text{-}circuit \\ current\ gain \end{pmatrix}$
0.1	$0.995\underline{/-5.7°}$	
0.2	$0.980\underline{/-11.3°}$	
0.5	$0.912\underline{/-26.6°}$	
1.0	$0.707\underline{/-45°}$	
2.0	$0.455\underline{/-63.4°}$	

7-13
Common-emitter circuit at higher frequencies

The question arises about the high-frequency characteristics of the common-emitter circuit relative to those of the common-base amplifier. If we start with Eq. (5-8), i.e., $\alpha_e = \alpha_b/(1 - \alpha_b)$ and introduce the frequency variation from Eq. (7-50), we can obtain

$$\alpha_e(\omega) = \frac{\alpha_{e0}}{1 + j\dfrac{\omega}{\omega_{\alpha e}}} \qquad (7\text{-}51)$$

where $\omega_{\alpha e}$ is the *cutoff frequency* for the common-emitter circuit, which can be expressed as

$$\omega_{\alpha e} \cong \frac{\alpha_{b0}}{\alpha_{e0}}\omega_{\alpha b} \qquad (7\text{-}52)$$

Measurements show that the form of (7-51) gives good agreement with experiments on both diffusion and drift-type transistors, but that (7-52) is only a rough approximation. However, Eq. (7-52) correctly shows that a high-gain transistor will have a relatively low common-emitter cutoff frequency. For example, an alloy transistor for audiofrequency applications that has an $f_{\alpha b}$ of 1.5 MHz and has $\alpha_{e0} = h_{fe0} = 44$ and $\alpha_{b0} = -h_{fb0} = 0.978$, has $f_{\alpha e} \cong 33$ kHz according to (7-52). Transistors for high-frequency applications may have values of $f_{\alpha b}$ of several hundreds of megacycles up to one gigacycle (10^9 Hz) or higher.

In high-frequency applications the common-emitter circuit is often used at frequencies above $f_{\alpha e}$, since sizable power gains can still be achieved in this range. When the frequency is above about $5f_{\alpha e}$, we can use the high-frequency asymptote in place of (7-51); thus

$$|\boldsymbol{\alpha}_e(\omega)| \cong \frac{\alpha_{e0}\omega_{\alpha e}}{\omega} \qquad (7\text{-}53)$$

In this range the short-circuit current gain varies at the rate of 20 dB per decade. A characteristic frequency called the *gain-bandwidth product* and designated ω_T or f_T, is defined to be that value for which the gain falls to unity, so we set $|\boldsymbol{\alpha}_e(\omega)| = 1$ in (7-53) and obtain

$$\omega_T = 2\pi f_T = \alpha_{e0}\omega_{\alpha e} \qquad (7\text{-}54)$$

Often ω_T or f_T is included in the specification of a high-frequency transistor. These values are, however, dependent on the operating conditions, for example, ω_T increases as I_E increases.

7-14
The hybrid-π equivalent-circuit

Three alternative approaches to the quantitative analysis of the high-frequency behavior of the common-emitter circuit can be mentioned: (1) to derive a new equivalent circuit based on the approximate common-base circuit in Fig. 7-24, (2) to measure the complex h or y parameters over the frequency range of interest and use these directly, and (3) to devise a new equivalent circuit. The first approach is not very productive. Method 2 requires data that is sometimes provided by the manufacturer of high frequency transistors. Let us follow method 3 and give a brief and intuitive development of a new equivalent circuit.† This circuit, called the *hybrid-π* circuit, is based on Fig. 5-15d, but with the two-generator upper portion replaced by a π equivalent. This change gives the *low-frequency* hybrid-π circuit (Fig. 7-25a). To account for the junction capacitances and other causes of delay, two capacitors are

†See, for example, Searle *et al.*, *op. cit.*, Chap. 1.

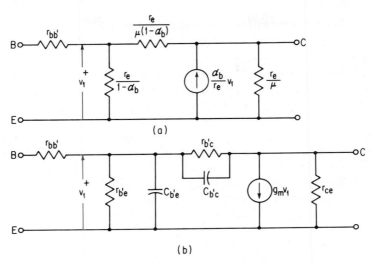

FIGURE 7-25 (a) Low-frequency hybrid-π equivalent circuit. Symbols as in Fig. 5-15d. (b) Medium and high frequency hybrid-π circuit.

added as shown in Fig. 7-25b. Also, the resistor designations are modified and the reference direction for the generator is reversed. The capacitance $C_{b'e}$ represents the combined effect of (1) changes in stored charge in the base due to the "inner" voltage v_1, (2) transit time effects, and (3) emitter junction capacitance, and $C_{b'c}$ gives the sum of the effects of (1) base width modulation due to v_{ce}, and (2) the collector junction capacitance. In this circuit the active generator $g_m v_1$ is frequency-dependent through the effect of frequency on the voltage v_1. However, none of the parameters are functions of the frequency, though they do depend on Q point and temperature.

A set of values of the parameters for a small radio-frequency transistor is given below†

$$r_{bb'} = 50 \ \Omega \qquad r_{b'c} = 10^6 \ \Omega \qquad g_m = 0.08 \ \text{mho}$$
$$r_{b'e} = 1200 \ \Omega \qquad C_{b'c} = 5 \ \text{pF} \qquad r_{ce} = 12{,}000 \ \Omega$$
$$C_{b'e} = 200 \ \text{pF}$$

A study of these parameters will show that simplified approximate equivalent circuits may be used over certain frequency ranges. At sufficiently low frequencies the capacitances may be ignored completely. At medium and high frequencies the reactance of $C_{b'c}$ is small compared with $r_{b'c}$, so that $r_{b'c}$ is omitted in this range.

†Searle *et al.*, *op. cit.*, pp. 1–32.

7-15

Common-emitter stages in cascade

Often two or more transistor amplifier stages are needed to furnish the required gain. The stages can be coupled by the same methods as used with tubes, i.e., direct-coupled, RC-coupled, and transformer-coupled. We shall find that there is a greater interaction between stages with transistors than with tubes.

We shall study a two-stage RC-coupled common-emitter ac amplifier. The main function of the first stage is to provide current gain, while the second stage provides the power output. We shall calculate the current gain over the individual stages, and the effect of the coupling circuit and the emitter resistor and by-pass capacitor on the low-frequency transmission of one stage. Approximate methods will be used where appropriate to simplify the analysis.

A practical form of a two-stage amplifier that drives the load resistance R_L is shown in Fig. 7-26. To permit certain approximations in the analysis we regard R_L as of the order of 1 or 2 kΩ, as would be true if R_L represented the input impedance of a possible third common-emitter stage. Resistors R_1, R_2, and R_e are chosen to provide the needed stability of Q point as explained in Sec. 7-10. Resistors R_3 feed the collectors, but also act as shunts on each stage output.

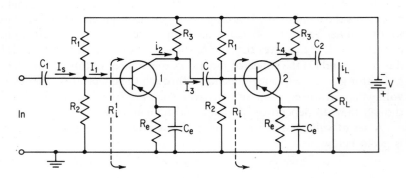

FIGURE 7-26   Two-stage common-emitter amplifier.

At sufficiently low frequencies the effect of the coupling capacitors C_1, C, and C_2, and also of the bypass capacitor C_e will be felt. At medium frequencies the gain will be virtually constant as the frequency is raised. At higher frequencies the effects discussed in the foregoing articles will act to reduce the gain.

We take up first the current gain of stage 1 at mid-band frequency and the low-frequency variation of this gain.

At mid-band frequency all capacitors act as short circuits, and the equivalent circuit for stage 1 takes the form in Fig. 7-27. Here R_i is the input resistance of stage 2, which depends on the load resistance on stage 2. This load consists of R_L and R_3 in parallel. As mentioned before, we regard R_L as a low resistance of up to 2000 Ω. Under this proviso, the feedback generator voltage $h_{re}V_c$ will be small, and therefore R_i of stage 2 will be approximately equal to h_{ie} of transistor 2.

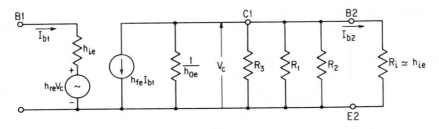

FIGURE 7-27   Equivalent circuit for first stage at mid-band frequency.

Because h_{ie} is about 1200 Ω, stage 1 also has a low load resistance dominated by h_{ie}. Consequently, within a few per cent error, the effects of $1/h_{oe}$ and of generator $h_{re}V_c$ in stage 1 can be neglected. Let us calculate the current gain I_{b2}/I_{b1} to this approximation. First, define R_p as the combined resistance of R_1, R_2, and R_3 all in parallel, i.e., let $R_p = R_1 \| R_2 \| R_3$. Now the equivalent load on the current generator in Fig. 7-27 consists of R_p and h_{ie} in parallel. The current divides according to the usual rule, so we find

$$A_i = \frac{I_{b2}}{I_{b1}} \cong h_{fe}\frac{R_p}{R_p + h_{ie}} \qquad (7\text{-}55)$$

Here the ratio of base currents is defined as the current gain, rather than the more conventional ratio I_3/I_s (Fig. 7-26), but our definition will simplify the study of frequency effects.

For a numerical example we let $R_e = 0.8$ k, $R_1 = 50$ k, $R_2 = 5$ k, $R_3 = 3.8$ k, $h_{ie} = 1500$, $h_{oe} = 20 \times 10^{-6}$, and $h_{fe} = 46$. Then $R_p = 2.07$ k and the mid-band current gain is 26.7.

The low-frequency response will be influenced by capacitors C and C_e. The equivalent circuit could be modified to include these effects and a complete analysis could be made. But it is much simpler to separate the calculation into two parts, i.e., to calculate the effect of one capacitor while assuming that the other effect has been relegated to a lower frequency range by suitable choice of capacitor size. Experience shows that usually C can be chosen to shift its effect to a lower range than that of C_e.

First we consider the effect of C alone by means of the equivalent circuit in Fig. 7-28. As the frequency decreases, the reactance of C increases, so I_{b2} and therefore the current gain decreases. We need symbols for the parallel combinations, so we let $R' = R_1 \| R_2 \| h_{ie}$ and $R'' = (1/h_{oe}) \| R_3$. If we now think of the circuit to the left of terminals MN as a Thévenin equivalent source, we can visualize the circuit as a voltage source with a series load circuit comprising R'', C, and R' in series. Now think of the frequency for which the reactance of C equals $R' + R''$. At this frequency the total series impedance has the magnitude $\sqrt{2}\,(R' + R'')$, so the current through C (and therefore also I_{b2}) is 0.707 of its mid-band value. This frequency is the lower corner frequency, and is given by

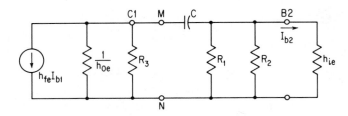

FIGURE 7-28 Equivalent circuit for calculation of effect of coupling capacitor C.

$$f_1 = \frac{1}{2\pi C(R' + R'')} \tag{7-56}$$

The similarity between this situation and that in the RC-coupled tube amplifier is obvious. In fact, the ratio of current gain at frequency f to the mid-band current gain is given by the right side of Eq. (7-36), and its variation is shown in the left half of Fig. 7-18.

To continue the numerical example we let C be 10 μF and calculate $R' = 1.13$ k, $R'' = 3.53$ k, and use (7-56) to calculate $f_1 = 3.4$ Hz.

Now we assume that the coupling capacitors are so large as to have no effect and calculate the effect of the bypass capacitors, in particular of C_e in the emitter circuit of transistor 2. When the frequency is low enough, an appreciable signal-frequency voltage builds up across R_e and C_e. This voltage acts as a *feedback* voltage, which will influence the gain of the stage. Our approximate calculation of its effect will be carried out in two steps.

First we calculate the input impedance to the base transistor 2. Refer to Fig. 7-29, which shows an *approximate* form of the h-parameter equivalent circuit of transistor 2 plus the R_eC_e network. The omissions of resistor $1/h_{oe}$ and of generator $h_{re}V_e$ are permissible in view of the assumed low value of R_L and because the impedance $\mathbf{Z}_e$ of the R_eC_e network is also low. Almost by inspection we can write

$$\mathbf{Z}_i = \frac{\mathbf{V}_{b2}}{\mathbf{I}_{b2}} = h_{ie} + (1 + h_{fe})\mathbf{Z}_e \qquad (7\text{-}57)$$

where

$$\mathbf{Z}_e = \frac{R_e}{1 + j\omega C_e R_e} \qquad (7\text{-}58)$$

Equation (7-57) shows that $\mathbf{Z}_i$ is increased markedly by the presence of $\mathbf{Z}_e$.

Next we modify the equivalent circuit of Fig. 7-27 to show the effect of R_e and C_e. The feedback voltage generator and $1/h_{oe}$ are again omitted, and a network to represent $\mathbf{Z}_i$ as given by (7-57) is introduced to obtain Fig. 7-30. Upon calculating the current gain by applying circuit theory to this figure we find

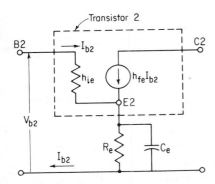

FIGURE 7-29   For the calculation of the input impedance to the base of transistor 2.

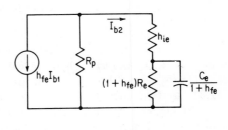

FIGURE 7-30   Equivalent circuit showing effect of R_e and C_e.

$$\mathbf{A}_i = \frac{\mathbf{I}_{b2}}{\mathbf{I}_{b1}} = \frac{-h_{fe}R_p(1 + j\omega C_e R_e)}{[(1 + h_{fe})R_e + R_p + h_{ie}] + j\omega C_e R_e(R_p + h_{ie})} \qquad (7\text{-}59)$$

A study of Eq. (7-59) will show that the frequency variation can be expressed in the following forms:

$$\mathbf{A}_i = \frac{K'\left(1 + \dfrac{j\omega}{\omega_2}\right)}{1 + \dfrac{j\omega}{\omega_3}} = \frac{K\left(1 + \dfrac{\omega_2}{j\omega}\right)}{1 + \dfrac{\omega_3}{j\omega}} \qquad (7\text{-}60)$$

where K' and K are constants and ω_2 and ω_3 are characteristic frequencies given by

$$\omega_2 = \frac{1}{R_e C_e} \quad \text{and} \quad \omega_3 = \omega_2\left[\frac{R_e(1 + h_{fe})}{R_p + h_{ie}} + 1\right] \qquad (7\text{-}61)$$

Analysis will show that K is the mid-band current gain. The gain decreases toward an asymptote of $K\omega_2/\omega_3$ as the frequency decreases with a variation as shown in Fig. 7-31. As Eq. (7-60) shows, the variation is the same as that of the phase advance circuit (Fig. 2-24.).

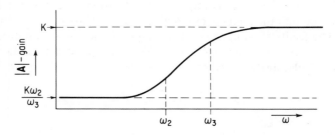

FIGURE 7-31   The effect of R_e and C_e on the frequency response.

As an example, let the stage have the parameters listed earlier and in addition let $C_e = 125 \ \mu\text{F}$. Then we calculate $\omega_2 = 10 \ (f_2 = 1.59 \ \text{Hz})$ and $\omega_3 = 115 \ (f_3 = 18.3 \ \text{Hz})$. The value of K is 26.7, so the asymptote $K\omega_2/\omega_3$ is 2.32. At frequency f_3 the gain calculated by Eq. (7-58) is $19\underline{/40°}$.

At higher frequencies the gain will drop owing to the effects discussed in Secs. 7-12 and 7-13. A detailed analysis would take us too far afield, but a few comments can be made. The common-emitter "cutoff" frequency $f_{\alpha e}$ is some measure of the suitability of a transistor for high-frequency amplification. However, considerable gain can be achieved with a high h_{fe} transistor at frequencies higher than $f_{\alpha e}$. Some manufacturers give the parameter f_T, which we have defined as the frequency at which $|\mathbf{h}_{fe}|$, or $|\boldsymbol{\alpha}_e(\omega)|$, reduces to unity and is called the *gain-bandwidth product*. We recall that in a pentode amplifier the effect of a change in R_L was to change the gain and the bandwidth so as to keep gain × bandwidth constant. In a transistor stage the same relation holds, but only over the limited range where the gain is high. As R_L is decreased, the bandwidth tends toward a limit. Furthermore, the location of the Q point has an effect on bandwidth. When I_E is changed, the gain and bandwidth change in opposite directions.

Next we ask whether it is possible to connect additional stages in cascade, each with lower gain and greater bandwidth, so as to improve the over-all amplifier. With n stages in cascade the over-all gain is the product of the stage gains, so

$$\mathbf{A}_{\text{tot}} = \frac{A_M}{\left(1 + j\dfrac{f_n}{f_2}\right)^n} \tag{7-62}$$

where f_2 is the cutoff frequency of one stage and A_M is the nth power of the mid-band gain per stage. To find the -3-dB point, we set the absolute value of the denominator equal to $\sqrt{2}$; thus

$$\left| \left(1 + j\frac{f_{n2}}{f_2} \right)^n \right| = \sqrt{2} \tag{7-63}$$

where f_{n2} is the frequency for the -3-dB point with n stages. From (7-63) we find

$$f_{n2} = f_2 \sqrt{2^{1/n} - 1} \tag{7-64}$$

Some corresponding values of n and f_{n2}/f_2 follow:

n	= 2	3	4	5	6
f_{n2}/f_2 =	0.644	0.51	0.435	0.386	0.35

Thus, the f_2 of an individual stage may be increased at the expense of the gain, and additional stages may be used to produce the desired over-all gain.

REFERENCES

7-1 E. J. Angelo, Jr., *Electronic Circuits*, 2d ed., McGraw-Hill Book Company, New York, 1964.

7-2 J. J. Corning, *Transistor Circuit Analysis and Design*, Prentice-Hall, Inc., Englewood Cliffs, N.J., 1965.

7-3 A. J. Cote, Jr., and J. B. Oakes, *Linear Vacuum-tube and Transistor Circuits*, McGraw-Hill Book Company, New York, 1961.

7-4 M. V. Joyce and K. K. Clarke, *Transistor Circuit Analysis*, Addison-Wesley Publishing Company, Inc., Reading, Mass., 1961.

7-5 J. M. Pettit and M. M. McWhorter, *Electronic Amplifier Circuits, Theory and Design*, McGraw-Hill Book Company, New York, 1964.

EXERCISES

7-1 One of the triodes in a type 12AU7A twin triode (Appendix B) is used in the cathode follower circuit in Fig. 4-23a, except that E_{cc} is zero. (a) Calculate points for, and plot a graph of, instantaneous output voltage versus signal voltage. The load resistance is 20 kΩ and E_{bb} is 300 V. Cover the range from cutoff to the point at which grid current starts. Suggested procedure: Plot the resistance line. Assume a value of e_c, obtain i_b from the resistance line, and calculate corresponding values of e_o and e_s. Repeat with enough values of e_c to cover the desired range. (b) Suppose that e_s is an ac signal and that we desire to use the maximum amplitude of e_s consistent with good linearity. What conclusions can be drawn from part (a) about a desirable value of E_{cc}? (c) Devise alternative biasing schemes for the situation in part (b).

7-2 One triode in a 12AU7A twin triode (Appendix B) is used in the circuit in Fig. 7-3 with $E_{bb} = 300$ V and $R_L = 29$ kΩ. (a) If $R_k = 1.0$ kΩ, what is the value of the grid bias at the Q point? (b) Choose a value of R_k to give a Q point bias of -10 V.

7-3 One triode in a 12AU7A twin triode (Appendix B) is used in the circuit in Fig. 7-5 with $E_{bb} = 320$ V, $E_{cc} = 80$ V, $R_L = 10$ kΩ, and $R_k = 10$ kΩ. (a) Find the values of e_c and of e_b at the Q point. (b) Use a technique like that suggested in Prob. 7-1a to obtain values for a plot between e_{out}, taken from plate to ground, versus e_s, and plot the curve. (c) Repeat part (b) except for the voltage from cathode to ground.

7-4 Sketch approximate curves for the magnitude of the voltage gain in dBv and the phase versus log ω for the numerical example in Sec. 7-5 in the manner of Fig. 2-24. Suggestion: Calculate the gain and phase at the geometric mean of the upper and lower corner frequencies, i.e., at $\omega = \sqrt{\omega_1 \omega_2}$.

7-5 The amplifier in Fig. 7-8a has the following parameters: $\mu = 96$, $r_p = 60$ k, $g_m = 0.0016$ mho, $R_1 = 140$ k, and $R_L = 40$ k. (a) Choose a value for capacitor C so that the corner frequency will be 20 Hz. (b) What is the value of E_L at 10 Hz if $E_s = 0.1\underline{/0°}$ and C has the value chosen in part (a)? (c) Repeat part (b) for $f = 100$ Hz.

7-6 An additional capacitor C_1 is connected between plate and ground in the circuit in Fig. 7-8a with the object of reducing the gain at the high frequencies. Obtain an expression for E_L/E_s for this circuit.

7-7 Consider a grounded cathode triode amplifier that has the parameters used in the example in Sec. 7-7. (a) What are the values of the effective input capacitance and of input impedance at $f = 20$ kHz? (b) What are these values if the load resistance is reduced to 20 k?

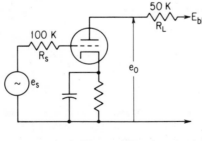

FIGURE 7-32

7-8 The triode in Fig. 7-32 has the parameters $\mu = 20$ and $r_p = 8$ k at the Q point. The tube plus wiring capacitances are $C_{gk} = 5$ pF, $C_{gp} = 4$ pF, and $C_{pk} = 3$ pF. Let $e_s = 1.0 \sin 2 \times 10^5 t$. Assume that the bias filter capacitor is very large. (a) What is the ac component of e_o if the capacitances are neglected? (b) Show that the voltage gain from grid to plate including the capacitance effects at $\omega = 2 \times 10^5$ is very nearly equal to $-\mu R_L/(r_p + R_L)$. (c) What is the ac component of e_o if the capacitance effects are included?

7-9 Two identical pentodes are used in an RC-coupled amplifier. The plate load resistors are 100 k and the grid resistor is 250 k. These tubes have a g_m of 0.002 and an r_p of 1.0 MΩ at the Q point. Assume that the input capacitance is 7 pF and

that the output capacitance is 9 pF, both including the wiring. The coupling capacitor is 0.02 μF. Calculate data for and plot the approximate gain versus frequency
curve for one stage of amplification (first grid to second grid) using a dBv versus
log f plot. Also sketch a phase angle curve.

7-10 (a) Redraw the pentode amplifier circuit in Fig. 7-11 but add screen dropping
resistors and filter capacitors and a load on the second tube. (b) This amplifier is
intended for a frequency range from 100 Hz to 100 kHz. At the desired Q point
for the first stage: $E_{c1} = -2$ V, $E_{c2} = +100$ V, $E_b = +100$, $i_b = 5$ mA and
$i_{c2} = 1.0$ mA. Assign exact values to R_1, R_k, and the screen-dropping resistor, and
choose a value for C_k, if the plate and screen supply is 300 V.

7-11 Consider a pentode amplifier stage as shown in Fig. 7-11 with $R_1 = 40$ k,
$R_g = 250$ k, $C = 0.02$ μF, $C_i = 10$ pF, $C_o = 10$ pF, $r_p = 1$ MΩ and $g_m = 0.004$
mho. (a) What is the effect on the mid-band gain and on the bandwidth of doubling
R_1? Calculation of the ratio of the altered to the original value is suggested. (b)
What is the effect on the lower half-power frequency of doubling R_g? (c) Repeat
(b) for doubling C. (d) What is the effect on the upper half-power frequency of
doubling C_i?

7-12 In some studies of transistor biasing the following sensitivity factor is defined:

$$S_I = \frac{dI_C}{dI_{CO}}$$

On the basis of the approximate expressions (5-3) and (5-5) what are the values of
S_I for: (a) a common-base circuit in which I_E is held constant, and (b) a common-
emitter circuit in which I_B is held constant? (c) Compare the numerical values of
S_I in parts (a) and (b) if α_{FB} be taken as 0.98.
Note: Values of S_I above about 15 are considered unsatisfactory for practical
circuits.

7-13 A certain type of *pnp* transistor is used in the circuit of Fig. 7-23a. The circuit
values are: $R_L = 0.75$ k, $R_e = 0.25$ k, $R_1 = 68$ k, and $R_2 = 12$ k. Figure 7-33

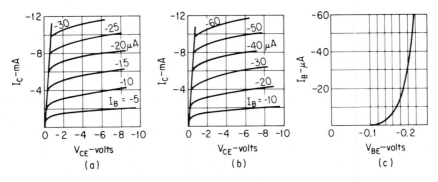

FIGURE 7-33   Collector characteristics for (a) transistor A, and
(b) transistor B, and (c) input characteristics for A and B for
$V_{\text{CE}} < -1$ V.

shows the collector characteristics of two samples, A and B, of this transistor and the input characteristics at 30°C, assumed to be the same for both A and B. Find the Q point values for samples A and B if placed in this circuit and if $V_{CC} = -10$V. *Suggestions:* Replace the base supply network by its Thévenin equivalent. Draw dc resistance lines in the collector characteristics (neglecting the component I_B as a part of I_E). Use trial and correction calculations to satisfy simultaneously both Kirchhoff's emf law around the base circuit and the resistance line constraint.

7-14 A *pnp* germanium transistor is used in the biasing circuit in Fig. 7-23a. Assume that $I_{CO} = 1.0 \ \mu A$ at 25°C and that it doubles for each 10°C rise in temperature. The value of V_{BE} is -0.20 V at 25°C at the initial Q point and $\Delta V_{BE}/\Delta T = 3$mV/°C. Assume that α_F is 0.99 and is independent of the temperature. The circuit values are: $V_{CC} = 10$ V, $R_L = 0.75$ k, $R_e = 0.25$ k, $R_1 = 68$ k, and $R_2 = 12$ k. (a) Calculate the value of I_C at 25°C. (b) Obtain linear expressions with numerical coefficients for ΔI_C as a function of ΔI_{CO} and of ΔV_{BE} as the temperature varies. (c) Calculate values of I_C for 45°C and for 65°C. Is the biasing circuit satisfactory?

7-15 Repeat Prob. 7-14 except to alter R_L to 0.88 k and R_e to 0.12 k.

7-16 Refer to the example in Sec. 7-11b. Redesign the bias circuit so that the 25 and 75°C values of I_C are higher on the dc load line. *Suggestion:* Change R_e only.

7-17 Consider the hybrid-π circuit model in Fig. 7-25b at such a high frequency that $r_{b'c}$ can be omitted. (a) Show that the short-circuit current gain is given by

$$\mathbf{A}_{isc} = \frac{g_m - j\omega C_{b'c}}{\dfrac{1}{r_{b'e}} + j\omega(C_{b'c} + C_{b'e})}$$

(b) Calculate values of A_{isc} for values of ω of 10^7, 10^8, and 10^9. Use the transistor circuit parameters given in Sec. 7-14.

7-18 Assume that the hybrid-π circuit model in Fig. 7-25b is used for a *CE* amplifier loaded with $R_L \ \Omega$. Consider a range of R_L such that $r_{ce} > R_L$ and a high frequency range so that $r_{b'c}$ can be omitted. (a) Show that the voltage gain then is given by

$$\mathbf{A}_v = \frac{-(g_m - j\omega C_{b'c})}{\left(\dfrac{1}{R_L} + j\omega C_{b'c} \right)\left(1 + \dfrac{r_{bb'}}{r_{b'e}} + j\omega C_{b'e}r_{bb'} \right)}$$

(b) Calculate $\mathbf{A}_v$ for $\omega = 10^7$, 10^8, and 10^9 if the transistor has the parameters given in Sec. 7-14.

7-19 What is the input impedance to the base of the stage 2 transistor in the example in Sec. 7-15 at radian frequencies of (a) 10, (b) 40, and (c) 115 rad/s?

7-20 The transistors in the amplifier in Fig. 7-26 are operated so that $h_{ie} = 2000 \ \Omega$, $h_{re} = 5.0 \times 10^{-6}$, $h_{fe} = 100$, and $h_{oe} = 40 \times 10^{-6}$ mho. The circuit constants are: $R_1 = 20$ k, $R_2 = 4$ k, $R_e = 1.0$ k, $R_3 = 5$ k, $R_L = 2$ k, $C_e = 50 \ \mu F$, and $C = 10 \ \mu F$. Assume that C_1 and C_2 have negligible effects on the ac response. (a) What is the approximate current gain I_L/I_s at the mid-band frequency? (b) What is the approximate overall voltage gain at mid-band frequency? (c) How much different is the exact value of the input impedance to the base of transistor 2 compared with

h_{ie}? (d) To what value should R_L be changed in order to match the Thévenin impedance of the output stage? (e) Analyze the effects of C and C_e (as if each were acting alone) on the low-frequency characteristics of the current gain of the first stage in the manner of Sec. 7-15.

7-21 Assume that the voltage gain per stage of a multistage transistor amplifier can be expressed as $A_m/[1 + j(f/f_2)]$ over the high frequency range. Also assume that $A_m f_2$ is a constant and has the value 1000 if f_2 is in megacycles per second. Suppose that the over-all voltage gain for n stages is to be kept constant at 1000. What would the upper -3-dB frequencies be for (a) $n = 2$, (b) $n = 3$, and (c) $n = 5$?

7-22 Two amplifiers, numbered 1 and 2, are connected in cascade as shown in Fig. 7-2. Amplifier 1 has a mid-band voltage gain of 100, a lower -3-dB frequency of 50 Hz, and an upper -3-dB frequency of 20 kHz; and amplifier 2 has the following corresponding values: 200, 100 Hz, and 5 kHz. What is the over-all complex voltage gain (E_3/E_1) at (a) 5 kHz and (b) 50 Hz?

8

Power Amplifiers

8-1
Introduction

8-1
Introduction

In this chapter the emphasis is on amplifiers that develop considerable output power, say from a few watts to hundreds of watts. Such amplifiers are needed in the output stages of audio systems, radio transmitters, and servo systems, and as relay and solenoid drivers.

A wide variety of devices are used as power amplifiers, including transistors, silicon-controlled rectifiers, vacuum and gas tubes, magnetic amplifiers, and rotating electromagnetic machines. The factors that may be important in the application of a power amplifier include: (1) the *maximum power output*, (2) the *efficiency*, (3) the *speed of response* (or the frequency range), (4) the *distortion* in the output wave, (5) the *power sensitivity*, defined as the ratio of power output to input voltage or current, and (6) the *power gain*. Some of these factors will be considered for transistor and tube amplifiers. The transistor operating in the *switching* mode, the controlled rectifier, and the magnetic amplifier will be described.

Transistor and tube amplifier stages were classified in Sec. 7-2 as class A, AB, B, or C according to the duration of the collector or plate current wave on a sine wave input. In a class A stage the current remains above zero for the full 360° of the input wave. Typical class A voltage and current waves were shown in Fig. 4-15. In a class B stage the current flows in pulses of approximately 180° duration, as shown in Fig. 8-1a. Thus the Q point

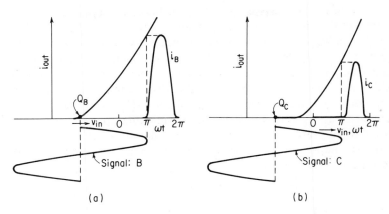

FIGURE 8-1 Q-point, signal wave, and output current wave for (a) class B operation, and (b) class C operation.

is near the cutoff bias. In a class AB stage the current flows for more than 180° but less than 360°. For the class C stage the Q point is set beyond cutoff (Fig. 8-1b); therefore current flows for less than 180°.

Class A stages are used typically in voltage amplifier stages where the power level is low. The output stage of a high-quality audio amplifier may use a class AB stage. Class B stages are used as the output stage in audio amplifiers and in higher frequency amplifiers. Class C stages generally work into tuned load circuits and are found in selective amplifiers, modulators, and oscillators.

8-2
Class A power amplifier

Our interest is mainly in the power output and plate-circuit efficiency of the class A amplifier. To obtain maximum power output we need a combination of large voltage and large current swings in the output, consequently as large a dc supply voltage and input signal as possible. We discuss primarily the *large signal* sine wave input behavior, but similar considerations apply with large signal pulses. For the present, wave distortion is disregarded. Though operation under maximum output conditions depends basically on transistor or tube heating, this aspect of the subject will also be ignored.

A graphical analysis is applicable if we have a nonreactive load. Specifically, we consider a transistor or pentode amplifier which has an ideal output transformer coupling to the load. Figure 8-2a shows a typical ac load line, with the bias point at Q determined by the dc supply voltage V_{cc}

and the base bias current (or tube grid bias). First we obtain approximate formulas for signal power output and plate circuit efficiency. We assume that the collector current is a sine-shaped wave that varies between i_{Cmx} and zero (I_{CEO} is neglected). The voltage varies from the maximum, v_{Cmx}, to a minimum, v_{Cmn}, also in a sinusoidal manner, disregarding the distortion which may exist in practice. The value of v_{Cmx} must be chosen so as not to approach the transistor breakdown voltage, BV_{CE}, too closely. The minimum voltage, v_{Cmn}, is determined by the permissible approach of the operating point to saturation, as at point S, in order to avoid excessive distortion. Further, the load line should not pass through the region above the device power dissipation limit curve.

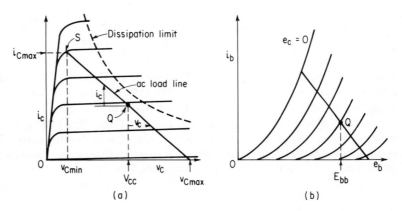

FIGURE 8-2   (a) Transistor (or pentode) graphical analysis and (b) load line in triode characteristics.

We need the rms values of the ac components, i.e., of i_c and v_c, to calculate the average power output. The rms value of i_c is

$$I_c = \frac{i_{Cmx}}{2\sqrt{2}} \tag{8-1}$$

and of v_c is

$$V_c = \frac{v_{Cmx} - v_{Cmn}}{2\sqrt{2}} \tag{8-2}$$

The load is resistive, so the power is

$$P_{\text{out}} = V_c I_c = \frac{i_{Cmx}(v_{Cmx} - v_{Cmn})}{8} \tag{8-3}$$

This formula has a simple geometrical interpretation, namely, the power equals one-fourth of the *area* between the ac load line and the voltage axis.

To calculate the efficiency we need the dc power input. Under our assumption this will be

$$P_{dc} = V_{CC}I_C = V_{CC}\frac{i_{Cmx}}{2} \qquad (8\text{-}4)$$

Therefore, the efficiency is

$$\eta = \frac{P_{out}}{P_{dc}} = \frac{v_{Cmx} - v_{Cmx}}{4V_{CC}} \qquad (8\text{-}5)$$

But $V_{CC} = (v_{Cmx} + v_{Cmn})/2$, so (8-5) may be written

$$\eta = \frac{1}{2}\frac{v_{Cmx} - v_{Cmn}}{v_{Cmx} + v_{Cmn}} \qquad (8\text{-}6)$$

What is the maximum possible value of η? If we allow v_{Cmn} to be zero, we get $\eta = 0.50$, or if $v_{Cmn} = 0.2\, v_{Cmx}$, a more realistic figure, then $\eta = 0.32$. In the triode amplifier (Fig. 8-2b), this limit would be considerably smaller. Thus, the class A output stage has a poor efficiency.

We have remarked on the choice of v_{Cmx} and the limitation on v_{Cmn} in an attempt to obtain maximum power. What of the choice of R_L and Q point? Since the voltage range is relatively fixed, we can let the ac load line swing upward until it approaches the device dissipation curve. Then the thermal conditions in the device would become the limiting factor—the junction temperature or thermal runaway in a transistor or the plate loss in a tube. Often the device manufacturer provides typical operating conditions for a device that will serve as a guide to circuit design.

8-3
Large-signal analysis of a class A
common-emitter stage

A graphical analysis of the common-emitter amplifier in Fig. 8-3 will reveal possible sources of distortion of the output wave. The bias circuit V_B and R_b is conceived to represent a divider circuit as shown in Fig. 7-23a. The coupling capacitor C is considered to be so large as to have no effect at the signal

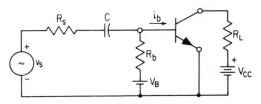

FIGURE 8-3   Common-emitter amplifier circuit.

frequency. We desire the wave of collector current due to a sine-wave signal
voltage.

The first step is to draw a load line on the collector characteristics. From
the intersection points on this line we get data for the *dynamic collector
curve*, i.e., the curve between i_C and i_B for the known values of V_{CC} and R_L.
This curve, shown as $ONQM$ in Fig. 8-4, is likely to be nonlinear owing to the
variation of h_{FE} over the range of currents.

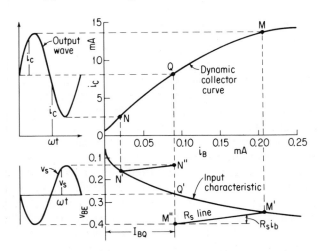

FIGURE 8-4   Graphical analysis of common-emitter amplifier
stage.

The other basic information needed is the curve of i_B as a function of v_{BE},
which is drawn to the same i_B scale, i.e., curve $ON'Q'M'$. We assume that
the bias circuit is proportioned to furnish the quiescent base current I_{BQ},
thereby establishing points Q' and Q.

As an approximation, since R_b is large compared with the base input
resistance, we assume that

$$v_{BE} = V_{BQ} + v_s - R_s i_b \qquad (8\text{-}7)$$

where V_{BQ} is the value of v_{BE} at point Q' and i_b is the variable part of the
base current. Now we can use the graphical construction in Fig. 8-4, as follows.
A reference wave of v_s is drawn as shown. To implement Eq. (8-7) we take
a particular value of v_s, for example, the negative peak, and project horizontally to point M'' on the vertical reference line through point Q'. Then
a line at a slope of R_s is drawn and extended until it intersects the input
characteristic at point M'. This fixes the base current; therefore we can
project upward to point M to find the collector current at this instant. As
many points as desired can be found similarly, but the projections only for
the positive and negative peaks and zero values of v_s are shown.

The output wave is not seriously distorted, though the nonlinearities of both the input characteristic and of the dynamic output characteristic contribute to the distortion. Luckily, the effects of these nonlinearities tend to cancel each other.

However, if the signal voltage is increased or if the Q point shifts appreciably, serious distortion can ensue, For example, if the operating point on the input characteristic falls below about $v_{BE} = 0.1$ V, the bottom part of the i_c wave would become flattened. Furthermore, if operation goes beyond point M on the collector curve, the top of the i_c wave would be flattened. Point M indicates an approach to saturation in the transistor.

The graphical analysis provides guidance on the choice of Q point and on the allowable signal level. Further study of the effect of junction temperature change on the characteristics, or of the substitution of a different transistor, could be carried out by the graphical technique.

8-4
Harmonic distortion in the output wave

In power amplifiers, where the operation ranges over the nonlinear regions of the transistor or tube characteristics, a distorted output wave is likely. The output wave is said to contain *harmonics* of the signal frequency in addition to the fundamental frequency component.

We shall briefly discuss harmonics in general and shall give a method of analysis for the dc, fundamental, and second harmonic components of a distorted wave. We assume that the signal voltage driving the amplifier has the form $E_m \cos \omega t$, and that we can obtain the collector current (or plate current) wave. The distorted wave in Fig. 8-5a will be used as a basis for the discussion.

The well-known† Fourier analysis of periodic waves can profitably

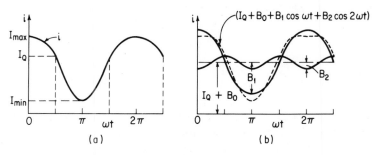

FIGURE 8-5   Analysis of distorted wave.

†See Appendix D and the references listed there.

be applied to the current wave. In general, a constant term plus two infinite series of cosine and sine terms are needed to represent the function. However, the wave in Fig. 8-5a is symmetrical about the origin and thus is an even function $f(\omega t) = f(-\omega t)$, so that only a constant term plus a series of cosine terms is needed, as follows:

$$i = I_Q + B_0 + B_1 \cos \omega t + B_2 \cos 2\omega t + \cdots \qquad (8\text{-}8)$$

Here the constant term is written $I_Q + B_0$ where I_Q is the quiescent current. Generally speaking, the amplitudes of the cosine terms diminish as the harmonic frequency increases.

If a measure of the distortion due to the second harmonic component is wanted, then the definition of the term *second harmonic distortion*

$$D_2 = \frac{|B_2|}{|B_1|} \qquad (8\text{-}9)$$

is useful.

Sometimes the *total distortion factor* D is needed to indicate the effect of all the harmonics. This definition is

$$D = \frac{1}{B_1}(B_2^2 + B_3^2 + B_4^2 + \cdots)^{1/2} \qquad (8\text{-}10)$$

The quantity D^2 is the ratio of the total power in all the harmonics to the power at the fundamental frequency.

If no harmonic higher than the second is required, then we need to find B_0, B_1, and B_2 for the known wave. Three points on the wave are sufficient for this purpose. Let us use the known values of current as follows: $i = I_{mx}$ at $\omega t = 0$, $i = I_Q$ at $\omega t = \pi/2$, and $i = I_{mn}$ at $\omega t = \pi$ (Fig. 8-5a). Each of these values is substituted in Eq. (8-8), but the terms having higher frequencies than the $B_2 \cos 2 \omega t$ term are neglected, with the result

$$\begin{aligned} I_{mx} &= I_Q + B_0 + B_1 + B_2 \\ I_Q &= I_Q + B_0 - B_2 \\ I_{mn} &= I_Q + B_0 - B_1 + B_2 \end{aligned} \qquad (8\text{-}11)$$

Upon solving these equations for B_0, B_1, and B_2 we find

$$B_1 = \frac{I_{mx} - I_{mn}}{2} \qquad (8\text{-}12)$$

and

$$B_2 = B_0 = \frac{I_{mx} + I_{mn} - 2I_Q}{4} \qquad (8\text{-}13)$$

Thus, the fundamental wave amplitude B_1 is half of the peak-to-peak swing of the current.† Another point to notice is that the second harmonic amplitude equals the change B_0 in the direct current caused by impressing the signal.

†This value was used to obtain the approximate sine wave in Sec. 4-6.

Figure 8-5b shows the component waves that result from the analysis of the rather severely distorted wave in part (a) of the figure. For convenience, the fundamental and second harmonic components are drawn about the ordinate $I_Q + B_0$. The dotted curve shows the sum of the components and can be compared with the original wave. The value of D_2 in this example is 0.20, which would be excessive for many applications.

The foregoing example shows that an analysis including the second harmonic is fairly adequate to represent a wave that is flattened on one side and peaked on the other. If both halves are flattened (or peaked), then the third harmonic is important, and an analysis† that yields B_3 and B_4 may be required.

8-5
Balanced amplifier; class B operation

a. Balanced connection

Figure 8-6 shows a transistor amplifier that uses balanced input and output connections. If we disregard the bias network resistors R_1, R_2, and R_e for the present, we see that the signal voltages fed to the two bases are equal but 180° out of phase. First we assume class A operation. Then collector current i_{C1} is *increasing*, while i_{C2} is *decreasing*, but the senses are such that *both* changes cause load current changes in the *same* direction. In effect the magnetic coupling in the output transformer develops a load current i_L equal to a turns ratio times the quantity $(-i_{c1} + i_{c2})$. We recall that i_{c1} is the variable part of i_{C1}. Thus, except for the turn ratio factor, the two

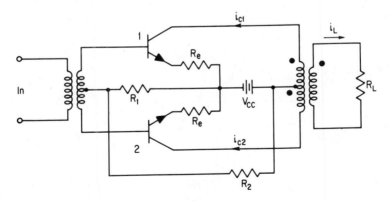

FIGURE 8-6   Balanced amplifier circuit.

†See, for example, Jacob Millman, *Vacuum-tube and Semiconductor Electronics*, McGraw-Hill Book Company, New York, 1958, pp. 405 ff.

transistors act as if they were in parallel (with one reversed) to furnish current to the load.

A study of the distortion of the load current wave shows that the distortions in the two collector current waves partially compensate. The even harmonics in the two collector current waves cancel in the output, but the odd harmonics add. For example, let the second harmonic component in i_{c1} vary as $\cos 2\,\omega t$. Then the second harmonic in i_{c2}, assuming perfect symmetry, will vary as $\cos(2\,\omega t + 360°)$, because the 180° phase displacement of i_{c2} relative to i_{c1} becomes 360° at the second harmonic frequency. Thus, when these two typical terms are placed in the expression $(-i_{c1} + i_{c2})$, which is proportional to i_L, they will cancel exactly. Similar reasoning shows that the odd harmonics will add in the output, but their magnitude relative to the fundamental is the same as in a one-sided amplifier. Thus, the cancellation of the even harmonics results in a much improved wave form in the output.

The efficiency of a class A stage is low, so the main appeal of the balanced circuit is for class B operation.

b. Transistor class B stage; crossover distortion

Ideally, the collector current waves in each transistor should be half-sine waves, i.e., should give 180° conduction. However, if the class B stage is biased at zero volts, the nonlinear input characteristic will cause serious distortion. The voltage-current transfer characteristics are plotted for transistors 1 and 2 in the first and third quadrants as shown in Fig. 8-7a. Then a sine wave signal will give the distorted wave in Fig. 8-7b. Figure 8-7c shows a scheme for eliminating the crossover distortion by shifting the bias on both transistors so that the linear portions of their characteristics line up. During a portion of the cycle both transistors conduct simultaneously. Their

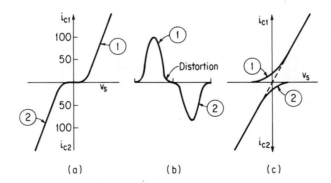

(a)   (b)   (c)

FIGURE 8-7   (a), (b) Cross-over distortion; (c) bias shift to eliminate cross-over distortion.

combined effect is proportional to $i_{c1} - i_{c2}$, so the combined effect is shown by the nearly linear dotted line segment near the origin. As a result the cross-over effect is nearly eliminated.

One scheme for providing the needed bias is shown in Fig. 8-6. The voltage across R_1 provides the few tenths of a volt of forward bias needed to align the characteristics. Resistors R_e are included to provide the required bias stability.

c. Power output and efficiency of ideal class B stage

Let us analyze the efficiency on the basis of the following idealizing assumptions: (1) the output transformer is ideal, (2) the current waves on each side are half-sine waves, (3) the voltage at collector or plate varies in the form of a displaced sine wave, with values varying between zero and $2V_{cc}$, and (4) I_{co} is neglected in the transistors and all bias losses are neglected. Assumption 3 may need further explanation. In terms of the transistor circuit, the voltage from collector to the negative side of V_{cc} consists of V_{cc} plus the voltage across half of the transformer primary. The wave across the half primary is assumed to be a sine wave of peak value V_{cc}; therefore the collector voltage goes from zero to $2V_{cc}$. We remark that the saturation voltage is considered to be negligible.

Let the peak of i_{c1} be I_m. For simplicity assume that the secondary turns equal the turns on half of the primary. Then the load will receive a sine current of peak value I_m and a sine voltage of peak value V_{cc}, so that the average power will be

$$P_L = \frac{I_m V_{cc}}{\sqrt{2}\sqrt{2}} = \frac{I_m V_{cc}}{2} \tag{8-14}$$

Comparison with Eq. (8-3) for class A operation shows that the output per transistor has been about doubled.

To find the efficiency, we need the dc power supplied by V_{cc}. This will be $V_{cc}I_{dc}$, where I_{dc} is the average value of $i_{c1} + i_{c2}$. Since there are two half-sine pulses per cycle, we have $I_{dc} = 2I_m/\pi$, or $P_{dc} = 2I_m V_{cc}/\pi$. Using (8-14), we find

$$\eta_{max} = \frac{P_L}{P_{dc}} = \frac{\pi}{4} = 0.785 \tag{8-15}$$

Thus, an efficiency of about 75 per cent is attainable in a class B balanced (or push-pull) output stage.

d. Complementary symmetry push-pull circuit

We conclude our survey of push-pull transistor amplifiers by referring to a circuit which has no counterpart in vacuum-tube amplifiers. This circuit

(Fig. 8-8) uses a pair of transistors that have matched characteristics, but one is *npn* and the other *pnp*. As a result, when the bases are driven in parallel, one transistor is active on one half-cycle and the other on the alternate half-cycle. The outputs of the two transistors are also in parallel, so the load carries alternate half-cycles in opposite directions. This circuit is said to have *complementary symmetry*. Obvious economic advantages accrue from the elimination of the input and output transformers. If one input terminal and one battery terminal are to be grounded, then the common-collector circuit shown can be employed.

Modified complementary symmetry circuits have been devised to give class AB operation and also to exploit the common-emitter arrangement.

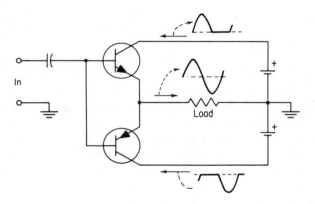

FIGURE 8-8   Amplifier that illustrates the application of complementary symmetry.

8-6
Class C amplifier

As explained in Sec. 8-1, class C amplifiers operate with values of dc bias that result in narrow pulses of plate or collector current that have a duration of less than one half-cycle. Class C operation is advantageous owing to the high efficiency of power conversion from the dc source to the ac output, which may reach a value up to 90 per cent. A tuned circuit, such as the *LC* circuit shown in Fig. 8-9, serves to maintain a quasisinusoidal output voltage, even though the plate current comes in pulses. Thus, the output wave form depends on the characteristics of the tuned circuit, rather than on the form of the signal voltage, and therefore the class C amplifier can not be used for the direct amplification of a signal having a complex wave form.

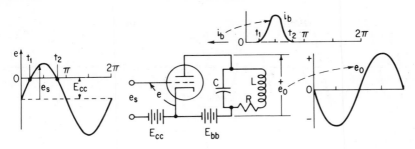

FIGURE 8-9   Class-C amplifier circuit and waveforms.

However, class C operation is useful in (1) some types of amplifiers in radio transmitters, (2) modulators (Chapter 13), (3) frequency-multiplying amplifiers, and (4) power oscillators (Chapter 12).

A qualitative account of the behavior of the circuit in Fig. 8-9 will serve for the present, and a quantitative treatment of class C operation will be given in Chapter 12. A triode circuit is used here, though it is understood that multigrid tubes or transistors could also be used with suitable circuit modifications.

As suggested by the wave forms in the figure, the grid bias E_{cc} is relatively large, but with a large input voltage e_s, the total grid voltage rises to the cutoff value at instant t_1 and goes positive before it recedes to high negative values. Of course, the cutoff value is dependent on the variation of the instantaneous plate potential caused by the presence of the output voltage e_o. For the present we assume that plate current flows in the interval from t_1 to t_2 with the wave form shown.

How can such pulses of current produce a nearly sinusoidal output voltage? One approach is to think of the pulses as giving a sort of shock excitation to the tuned circuit (often called the *tank circuit*) during a portion of the cycle and think of the LC circuit as oscillating freely in a decaying oscillatory manner during the rest of the cycle. Before pursuing this idea further, consider the experiment illustrated in Fig. 8-10. The first two periods, up to $t = 2T$, show the steady oscillating condition. Then the signal is cut off for three periods and then reapplied. From time $2T$ to $5T$ the LC circuit is oscillating freely, but the oscillations are dying out owing to the losses in the load resistance R. Now when the signal is reapplied, each plate current pulse tends to raise the level of the oscillation, and the output voltage amplitude rises. However, the average power going to the load rises also, and, in fact, rises until the average power supplied to the tuned circuit by the plate current pulses just equals the output power. Then equilibrium is re-established, and a constant amplitude output will be maintained.

In the equilibrium condition we may think of a narrow plate-current pulse as charging the capacitor to a higher (negative) voltage and thus storing

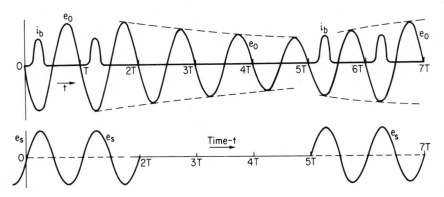

FIGURE 8-10   Intermittent signal applied to class C amplifier.

extra energy in the capacitor. The pulse will mostly pass into the capacitor rather than the inductive branch because the inductor opposes a sudden change in its current. The extra energy stored in the capacitor is released during the remainder of the cycle to maintain the oscillation. The reader can readily devise a mechanical system based on a clock pendulum that will be analogous to the electrical circuit.

Quantitative relations for class C operation will be developed in Chapter 12, where a somewhat different approach to the circuit calculation will be employed.

8-7
Transistor in the switching mode; ON-OFF *control*

Transistors are used as high-speed repetitive switches in modulators, inverters, and in the bi-stable circuits that are the building blocks of digital computers. They are also used in simple ON-OFF control applications or as a relay for turning on lamps, energizing solenoids, etc. We shall examine some of the basic concepts relating to the switching mode but must defer such topics as the speed of response of the device and other details.

We think of the collector to emitter in Fig. 8-11a as the switch that is under the control of the voltage e. Ideally, when the switch is ON, the voltage V_{CE} should be zero and the base current I_B should not influence the load current I_C. Likewise, when the switch is OFF, the load current should be zero, that is, the switch should pass no current.

The actual switch fails to live up to the ideal, as will be explained by

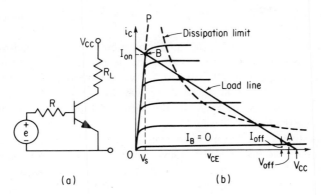

FIGURE 8-11   (a) Circuit of transistor switch and (b) graphical analysis.

reference to Fig. 8-11b. Assume that the control voltage e is a square wave that causes I_B to be zero half of the time (operation at point A), and causes a value of I_B large enough to drive the transistor to saturation at point B during the other half of the time. The diagram shows two respects in which the real switch departs from the ideal. In the OFF condition, at point A, there is a small current through the load, of value equal to $I_{co}/(1 - \alpha_{FB})$. In the ON condition, at point B, a voltage V_s remains across the transistor, so the load current does not quite reach the short-circuit value, V_{cc}/R_L. The saturated condition is characterized approximately by the line OP. The inverse slope of this line is called the *saturation resistance* and is symbolized by R_s. These deficiencies are small, particularly in germanium transistors designed for switching service, and if compared with those of vacuum tubes.

Switching transistors are made in small, high-speed types used in computers, which may dissipate about 250 mW, and in power switching types which may dissipate 1, 5, 50 or more watts. To illustrate the discussion, we assume a power transistor of about 5-W dissipation rating and make some rough calculations. Let $V_{cc} = 50$ V, and $R_L = 34\,\Omega$, then the short-circuit current is 1.47 A. In the ON condition, assuming that $R_s = 1.25\,\Omega$, we calculate $V_s = 1.77$ V and $I_{ON} = 1.42$ A. The collector power dissipation during the ON time is therefore 1.77×1.42 or 2.52 W, as contrasted with a load power of $(1.42)^2 \times 34$, or 68.5 W. We can deduce that the saturated state must be considered carefully in a circuit design to insure that the base current drive is adequate to produce saturation and to reduce the dissipation in the ON state.

If we assume that I_{co} is 0.4 mA at the operating junction temperature, and that $1/(1 - \alpha_{FB})$ is 20, then $I_{OFF} = 0.4 \times 20$ or 8 mA. The voltage across the transistor is very nearly 50 V, so the transistor loss in the OFF state is 0.008×50, or 0.4 W. This value would be strongly dependent on the junction temperature.

An additional power loss occurs in the base circuit. Let us estimate the additional loss in the transistor due to I_B in the ON state. We estimate I_B to equal I_C/h_{FE}, and find 1.42/20 or 0.070 A. We assume that the input characteristic shows that $V_{BE} \cong 0.6$ V, so the power loss is 42 mW. This power controls a load power of 68.5 W, so the ratio of load power to control power (neglecting the loss in R) is 1630.

Often transistors are called upon to switch repetitively, at multimegacycle rates in computers or up to multikilocycle rates in power controllers and inverters. We shall defer a study of the delays involved in switching, but a calculation of the transistor losses for an idealized switching cycle will reveal some of the factors involved. The circuit is that in Fig. 8-11a, and the voltage e is assumed to be a square wave that drives the operating point back and forth between points A and B on the load line in Fig. 8-11b. In the absence of any reactance (parasitic and internal capacitance would enter at high switch speeds) the operating point will move along the resistive load line. A finite time is needed to produce the change of current, mostly owing to the charge stored in the base of the transistor. The actual time variation is more complex, but we assume the idealized linear variations shown in Fig. 8-12. For simplicity, the *turn-on* time and *turn-off* time are taken to be equal at the value T_1. The transistor voltage drops, V_{OFF} and V_s in the two states, as well as the collector currents I_{ON} and I_{OFF} are assumed to be known.

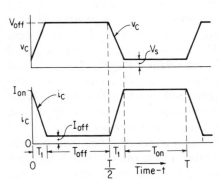

FIGURE 8-12 Collector voltage and current waves in the transistor switch.

We want to calculate the average power loss in the transistor. To do this we first calculate the energy loss during T_1 and then double this value since the two transitions are symmetrical. To this value we add the loss during the OFF time and the loss during the ON time. The total energy loss divided by the period T will give the average power. During the interval $0 < t < T_1$ we can express the collector voltage as $v_C = V_s + b_1 t$ and the collector current as $i_C = I_{ON} - b_2 t$, where b_1 and b_2 are the *magnitudes* of the slopes. Upon integrating the expression $W_{T_1} = \int_0^{T_1} v_C i_C \, dt$ to obtain the energy loss we find

$$W_{T_1} = V_s I_{ON} T_1 + (b_1 I_{ON} - b_2 V_s)\frac{T_1^2}{2} - b_1 b_2 \frac{T_1^3}{3} \qquad (8\text{-}16)$$

On account of symmetry, the loss during the two transitions W_{SW} will be double W_{T_1}; thus,

$$W_{SW} = 2V_s I_{ON} T_1 + (b_1 I_{ON} - b_2 V_s)T_1^2 - \frac{2}{3}b_1 b_2 T_1^3 \qquad (8\text{-}17)$$

The loss during the ON time is

$$W_{ON} = V_s I_{ON} T_{ON} \qquad (8\text{-}18)$$

and during the OFF time

$$W_{OFF} = V_{OFF} I_{OFF} T_{OFF} \qquad (8\text{-}19)$$

Thus, the average power will be

$$P_{dis} = \frac{W_{SW} + W_{ON} + W_{OFF}}{T} \qquad (8\text{-}20)$$

We can see that to keep the dissipation down we need low values of V_s, I_{OFF} (and, therefore I_{CO}), and T_1.

A numerical example will be helpful. Imagine a 4-W transistor operating on an 0.5-kHz repetition rate. We assume the following values:

$$T = 2 \text{ ms} \qquad V_s = 1.0\text{V} \qquad I_{ON} = 1.0 \text{ A}$$
$$T_1 = 0.1 \text{ ms} \qquad V_{OFF} = 50 \text{ V} \qquad I_{OFF} = 2 \text{ mA}$$

Further, let $T_{ON} = T_{OFF}$, which are then each 0.9 ms. We calculate W_{SW} and find 1.75 mJ(millijoules), and find $W_{ON} = 0.90$ mJ and $W_{OFF} = 0.09$ mJ. Therefore

$$P_{dis} = \frac{1.75 + 0.90 + 0.09}{2} = \frac{2.74 \text{ mJ}}{2 \text{ ms}} = 1.37 \text{ W}$$

The point to notice is that the major loss occurs during the transitions. A faster transistor will reduce the loss. If, as an added approximation, V_s and I_{OFF} are considered to be zero in calculating the slopes b_1 and b_2, then (8-17) reduces to

$$W_{SW} \cong \tfrac{1}{3} V_{OFF} I_{ON} T_1 \qquad (8\text{-}21)$$

This relation emphasizes the importance of a short switching time.

Suppose that we calculate the *instantaneous* power dissipation at the instant $t = T_1/2$, i.e., halfway through the transition. In the example this gives $p_{inst} = v_c i_C \cong 25.5 \times 0.5 = 12.75$ W. This value is far above the average power of 1.37 W and is above the assumed dissipation limit of 4 W. In terms of Fig. 8-11b, this means that the load line passes considerably above the dissipation limit curve. Whether the transistor could tolerate this type of service or not depends on the thermal time constant of the transistor, on the switching time T_1, and on the maximum safe junction temperature. To conclude the discussion of the example, we note that the load instantaneous power during the ON interval is approximately 50 W and the average load power is roughly 25 W.

8-8
Controlled rectifier as a power amplifier

In a very real sense a controlled rectifier circuit acts as a power amplifier. The insertion of a small control power can vary the output going to the load. As we shall see presently, the control or amplification acts to change the size of the current pulses going to the load and therefore is not exactly comparable to a linear amplifier.

We have mentioned the silicon controlled rectifier and shall later discuss the gaseous thyratron and ignitron, which serve in the same capacity. For the present we shall discuss the behavior of a generalized (and idealized) controlled rectifier circuit that has a resistance load (Fig. 8-13). The details

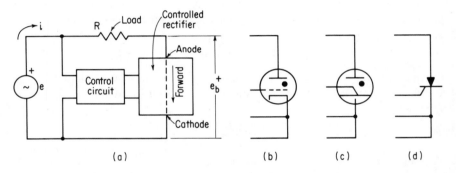

FIGURE 8-13   (a) Generalized controlled rectifier circuit, (b) thyratron, (c) ignitron, and (d) silicon controlled rectifier.

of the control circuits depend upon the device used, so we show only a "black box" in the diagram. This black box has the function of feeding a current or voltage wave or pulse to the controlled rectifier that causes the rectifier to *break down* or to *fire* at some angle ϕ_1 on the positive source voltage half-cycle. Up to this instant the rectifier passes zero current, i.e., is insulating. After the device fires, its anode to cathode drop is low—about 1 or 2 V in SCR's and 9 to 15 V in the gaseous devices—and it conducts the whole load current.

To analyze the circuit in Fig. 8-13a, we let the source voltage be $e = E_m$ sin ωt. For simplicity, we assume that the voltage across the rectifier drops to zero during the conducting condition. During the nonconducting half-cycle the rectifier becomes insulating again and the control circuit regains control.

We see that current i is zero up to the *cut-in* (or *firing*) angle ϕ_1 and then jumps to the wave given by

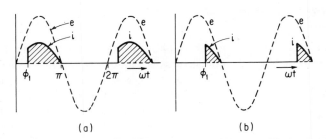

FIGURE 8-14 The effect of a change in the cut-in angle ϕ_1.

$$i = \frac{E_m}{R} \sin \omega t \qquad \phi_1 < \omega t < \pi \qquad (8\text{-}22)$$

This wave is shown in Fig. 8-14 for two different firing angles.

Two aspects of the current wave may be of interest, (1) the average or dc value, or (2) the rms value. For instance, the latter value would be used to calculate the heating produced in the load by calculating $I_{\text{rms}}^2 R$. The dc value is obtained by averaging over a complete period; thus,

$$I_d = \frac{1}{2\pi} \int_{\phi_1}^{\pi} \frac{E_m}{R} \sin \omega t \, d(\omega t) = \frac{E_m}{2\pi R}(1 + \cos \phi_1) \qquad (8\text{-}23)$$

The resulting control characteristic, which has the shape of a cosine wave displaced one unit upward, is shown in Fig. 8-15. Over a considerable range the characteristic has approximately the desirable linear form.

Upon calculating the rms value of the wave, we obtain the result

$$I_{\text{rms}} = \frac{E_m}{2R}\left[1 + \frac{1}{\pi}\left(\frac{\sin 2\phi_1}{2} - \phi_1\right)\right]^{1/2}$$

(8-24)

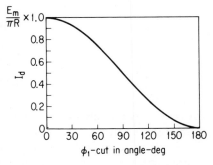

FIGURE 8-15 Direct load current vs. cut-in angle in controlled rectifier circuit.

This value is, of course, higher than the value of I_d for the same wave.

When output powers greater than a few hundred watts are required, other controlled rectifier circuits are often used. These are similar to the rectifier circuits shown in Chapter 11 and include full-wave and polyphase networks. Owing to their low forward voltage drop the silicon controlled rectifiers are often chosen in preference to the other devices. The ignitron is chosen when the load current is very large, say, in the hundreds or thousands of amperes, and the circuit voltage is also high.

8-9
Magnetic amplifier

The magnetic amplifier is a power amplifier in which a current in a *control* coil on one or more magnetic cores controls a load current that flows through

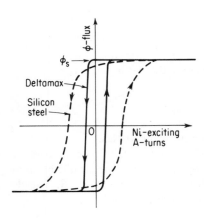

so-called *gate* coils on the same core. The high power sensitivity of the modern magnetic amplifier is due to the advent of magnetic materials that have sharply saturating hysteresis loops (Fig. 8-16) and low coercive force. We shall describe one class of this interesting device, namely, the *self-saturation* or *intrinsic feedback* magnetic amplifier.

Consider first a closed core of the sharply-saturating material wound with a *gate coil* of N_g turns, upon which is impressed a sine voltage e. It is best not to think of the coil as an inductance, owing to the extreme nonlinearity of flux versus current, but to think in terms of induced voltages and resistance drops directly. If the core does *not* go into saturation, the magnetizing currents are small and the induced voltage far exceeds the coil iR drops. Then the gate-coil voltage is given by

FIGURE 8-16 Hysteresis loops of Deltamax* (a grain oriented nickel-iron alloy) and of silicon transformer steel.
*Tradename of the Arnold Engineering Co., Marengo, Illinois, U. S. A.

$$e_g = N_g \frac{d\phi}{dt} \tag{8-25}$$

where N_g is the number of turns and ϕ is the flux in the core. If the sine wave of impressed voltage is increased until the flux tends to exceed the *saturation flux* ϕ_s, then (8-25) will no longer be adequate, as $d\phi/dt$ is nearly zero in saturation, and then the resistance voltages around the circuit must absorb the source voltage.

Equation (8-25) is, however, adequate as a basis for the definition of the *rated value* of peak ac source voltage. This is defined as the value which just drives the flux between $-\phi_s$ and $+\phi_s$, that is, just to saturation. For an assumed wave of form $E_m \sin \omega t$ the *rated voltage* works out to be

$$E_{mr} = N_g \omega \phi_s \tag{8-26}$$

Next we consider the elementary magnetic amplifier circuit in Fig. 8-17a. The ac circuit contains the gate coil N_g, the load resistor R, and a diode D. The control coil N_c is assumed to be driven by a current source I_c. The ac

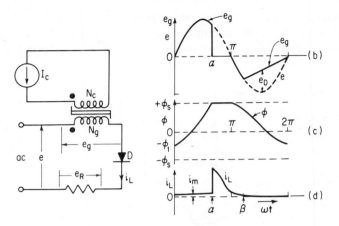

FIGURE 8-17   Sharply saturating saturable reactor with blocking rectifier in the load circuit.

voltage is assumed to be the rated value E_{mr} peak volts for the coil N_g. The circuit behavior can best be explained by reference to the typical wave forms in Fig. 8-17b, c, and d. The flux variations are all-important, so we note that ϕ starts at an assumed initial (but steady state) value of $-\phi_1$. Then the source voltage e tends to cause the flux to rise, because the magnetizing current and Ri drop are small while the flux is rising. If the Ri drop be neglected during this first interval, then Eq. (8-25) can be rearranged and integrated to give

$$\Delta\phi = \phi_t - \phi_i = \frac{1}{N_g}\int_0^t e\, dt \qquad (8\text{-}27)$$

Here $\Delta\phi$ is the change in flux, ϕ_t is the flux at time t, and ϕ_i is the initial flux at $t = 0$. In Fig. 8-17c the flux can change from $-\phi_1$ only to ϕ_s, so this fixes $\Delta\phi$. Thus, $\int_0^t e\, dt$ is also determined and thereby fixes the instant at which the core goes into saturation. This is indicated in the diagram as the angle $\omega t = \alpha$. The flux stays in saturation from α to π. During this interval there is zero $d\phi/dt$, so the current must jump up so that the Ri drop can absorb the source voltage (diode drop is neglected). The resulting current pulse is much like that in a controlled rectifier circuit, so it is common to speak of α as the *firing* angle or *saturation* angle.

In the second half-cycle the flux starts dropping and the gate coil absorbs the line voltage as before. However, at the angle β the circuit current tends to reverse but cannot do so on account of the diode. Therefore, the diode absorbs part of the line voltage and the flux returns to its initial value $-\phi_1$.

The level of the initial flux $-\phi_1$ can be changed by changing the control current I_c, and thus I_c has control over the saturation angle α and the size of the load current pulse.

An objection to the single-core circuit is that the voltage induced in the control coil by transformer action can cause losses in the control circuit. An improved circuit, which uses two identical cores, is shown in Fig. 8-18.

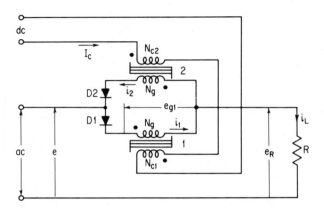

FIGURE 8-18 Self-saturating (intrinsic feedback) magnetic amplifier circuit.

In this circuit the voltages induced in the control coils largely cancel out in the series-connected control circuit.

The wave forms in Fig. 8-19 will aid a brief explanation of the action in the circuit. The assumptions are that the ac source voltage equals the rated voltage for the gate coils and that the control circuit source impedance is zero. In actual amplifiers the control circuit has some resistance, which will alter the behavior somewhat. The first exciting interval from 0 to α is similar to that in the single-core circuit, as far as core 1 flux and the voltage and load current waves are concerned. Thus, the supply voltage, acting on coil N_g on core 1, causes the flux to rise from $-\phi_1$ to $+\phi_s$. But what of core 2 during this interval? A detailed study will show that core 2 is excited via the two control coils N_{c1} and N_{c2}. That is, the voltage induced in N_{c1} is impressed on N_{c2}, since the dc source impedance was taken to be zero. The effect on core 2 is to lower the flux (which starts in saturation) by the same amount that the flux rises in core 1. During this interval the flux in core 1 is moving from B to C on the hysteresis loop (Fig. 8-19f), while the flux in core 2 is moving from F to A. This explains why the control current is nearly constant during the excitation interval.

During the saturation interval the load current flows via diode $D1$ and coil N_g on core 1.

The second half-cycle is similar to the first, except that cores 1 and 2 exchange roles. As a result, the load carries an ac current as in Fig. 8-19e.

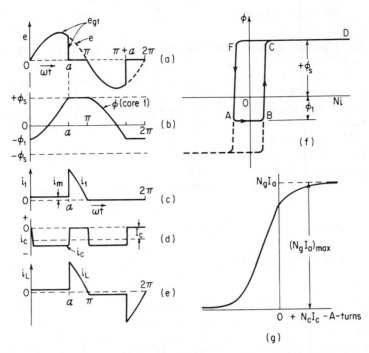

FIGURE 8-19   Waveforms, hysteresis loop and control characteristic for the circuit in Fig. 8-18.

The exact variation of load current with control current depends on the shape of the dynamic hysteresis loop, but a typical form is shown in Fig. 8-19g. Here I_a is the *rectified average* value of the load current. The maximum value of I_a, then, is the value for a full sine wave, which obtains when one core or the other is saturated over the full cycle. This maximum value is given by

$$I_{a,\max} \cong \frac{2E_{mr}}{\pi R} \qquad (8-28)$$

if diode drop and coil resistance be neglected.

At negative values of control current the output current reaches a minimum value and then rises again. This minimum depends on the magnetizing current of the cores and becomes smaller if the hysteresis loop is narrower.

The value of $\Delta N_c I_c$ needed to produce the change of output from maximum to minimum also depends on the width of the hysteresis loop and is approximately equal to the width as expressed in Ni values (Fig. 8-19f). The ratio of the change of the power in the load to that in the control coil is of the order of 5000 to 1 in a high-quality amplifier.

REFERENCES

8-1   G. M. Attura, *Magnetic Amplifier Engineering*, McGraw-Hill Book Company, New York, 1959.

8-2   E. J. Angelo, Jr., *Electronic Circuits*, 2d ed., McGraw-Hill Book Company, New York, 1964, Chaps. 11, 12.

8-3   Engineering Staff of Texas Instruments, Inc., *Transistor Circuit Design*, J. A. Walston and R. J. Miller, eds., McGraw-Hill Book Company, New York, 1963, Chaps. 16, 17, 18.

8-4   R. A. Greiner, *Semiconductor Devices and Applications*, McGraw-Hill Book Company, New York, 1961, Chap. 14.

8-5   A. G. Milnes, *Transductors and Magnetic Amplifiers*, Macmillan & Co., Ltd., London, 1957.

EXERCISES

8-1 A type 2N1100 *pnp* transistor (Appendix B) is operated at a case temperature of 25°C in a class A common-emitter amplifier with a transformer-coupled load. The collector circuit source voltage is 15 V, and the load resistance referred to the collector circuit is 6 Ω. (a) Estimate the ac power output and the efficiency if the base current varies from 0 to −300 mA (peak to peak). Use the methods of Sec. 8-2. The Q point is defined by $I_B = 150$ mA. (b) Assume that the transistor collector power is to be limited to 5 W. Is the collector power within the safe range? Does the margin of safety increase or decrease when the signal is applied?

8-2 A type 2N2338 *npn* transistor (collector characteristics in Appendix B) is operated in the circuit of Fig. 8-3 with $V_{CC} = 40$ V, $R_L = 8$ Ω, and $R_s = 2$ Ω. The transistor input characteristic data follows:

I_B mA =	0	10	50	100	200	300
V_{BE} V =	0.40	0.58	0.78	0.98	1.27	1.5

The bias circuit provides $I_B = 125$ mA at the Q point. Assume that $v_s = 0.7$ sin ωt. Use a graphical method to find the wave of i_C versus ωt and plot the wave.

8-3 A type 2N2338 transistor (Appendix B) is operated in the common-emitter stage shown in Fig. 8-3 with $V_{CC} = 30$ V and $R_L = 5$ Ω. Assume that I_B is 200 mA at the Q point and that a sine-wave base current signal having a peak value of 150 mA is forced into the base. Analyze the resulting collector current wave to find (a) its average value, (b) the peak value of the fundamental frequency term, and (c) the peak value of the second harmonic component.

8-4 Consider a known current wave that is symmetrical about the origin and therefore is an even function of ωt. This wave is to be expressed in the form of Eq. (8-8), retaining terms up to and including the B_3 cos $3\omega t$ term. Obtain a set of formulas for B_0, B_1, B_2, and B_3 in terms of selected ordinates of the wave. Suggestion: Use the ordinates at $\omega t = 0$, $\pi/3$, $2\pi/3$, and π.

8-5 Discuss the possibility of distortion in the output current wave in the circuit in Fig. 8-8, particularly near the current zeros. Under what conditions is distortion likely, and how can it be minimized?

8-6 A type 2N1100 transistor (Appendix B) is used in the switching circuit in Fig. 8-11a. Let $V_{CC} = +20$ V, $R_L = 1.8\ \Omega$, and the saturation resistance be $0.4\ \Omega$. Assume that the switching takes place in the idealized way shown in Fig. 8-12, but let $I_{\text{OFF}} = 0$, $T_1 = 0.1$ ms, and $T_{\text{ON}} = T_{\text{OFF}} = 1.2$ ms. (a) What is the average power dissipation in the transistor due to the collector current? (b) What is the instantaneous power input to the collector at an instant halfway through the transition? (c) What is the average power going to R_L?

8-7 Show the detailed steps by which Eq. (8-24) is obtained from the known current wave form given by Eq. (8-22).

8-8 Calculate numerical values of the ratio $I_{\text{rms}}/I_{\text{dc}}$ for the current wave given in Eq. (8-22) for cut-in angles of (a) $\pi/4$, (b) $\pi/2$, and (c) $3\pi/4$.

8-9 A controlled rectifier device has current ratings as follows: maximum recurring peak = 40 A and maximum average value = 5 A. This device is used in the circuit of Fig. 8-13a. Assume that $e = 300 \sin \omega t$ and that the cut-in angle will always remain in the range from $\pi/2$ to π rad. What is the lowest safe load resistance?

8-10 Two cores, which consist of 50% Ni–50% Fe grain-oriented alloy that has a rectangular hysteresis loop, are used in the magnetic amplifier circuit in Fig. 8-18. The alloy has a saturation flux density of 1.4 Wb/m² and a coercive force of 40 amp-turn/m. The tape-wound cores are ring-shaped and have a mean circumference of 16 cm and a net cross sectional area of 1.5 cm². Each core is wound with a gate coil having N_g turns and a control coil of 800 turns. The ac source voltage is 80 V peak at 400 Hz, and the load resistance is 40 Ω. (a) What value should N_g have so that 80 V will be the rated value for the coils? (b) What is the maximum rectified average current through the load for positive control circuit current? (c) Estimate the *change* in control circuit current needed to change the load current from maximum to minimum average value.

9

Feedback Theory;
Feedback in Amplifiers

9-1
Introduction

In the earlier chapters some instances of *feedback* (an added input current or voltage that depends on an output current or voltage) appeared. For example, inherent feedback effects appeared in the equivalent circuits of transistors. In the following discussion we are concerned with the intentional addition of a feedback path around one or more stages of an amplifier which is intended to enhance some of the desirable characteristics of the over-all system.

It is well to mention at the outset that different feedback connections produce different results, so that we cannot generalize about the effect of feedback on output impedance, input impedance, constancy of gain, etc. These effects will be examined for the more important feedback connections.

Let us make a qualitative distinction between *positive* and *negative* feedback. In *positive* feedback, or *regeneration*, the quantity (current or voltage) fed back to the input reinforces the original signal; whereas in *negative* feedback, or *degeneration*, the reverse is true. If a strong positive feedback is provided, the circuit is likely to produce an output wave even if the signal is zero, i.e., self-oscillation may occur. Such circuits will be discussed in Chapter 12. Negative feedback can have remarkably beneficial effects, such as improvement of constancy of gain and reduction in certain types of noise, but with attendant loss of gain and with some risk of the development of self-

224

oscillation. These drawbacks can be overcome by providing additional gain and by careful design. The importance of feedback can be judged by the assertion that without the negative feedback amplifier several precision electronic instruments would be impractical.

9-2
Basic feedback analysis

An elementary feedback system, such as a feedback amplifier or a feedback control (servo) system, has a forward transmission channel G and a feedback path H, as shown in the one-line diagram in Fig. 9-1. If the diagram represents a tube amplifier, the X's represent sinusoidal voltages, G represents the gain of the *internal* amplifier from X_2 to X_o, and H represents the voltage transfer function of the feedback circuit network. The small circle at the left with the adjacent $+$ and $-$ signs indicates that

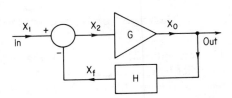

FIGURE 9-1   Basic feedback system.

X_f is subtracted (algebraically) from the signal X_1 to produce X_2. The phase and magnitude of the voltage X_f in relation to the phase and magnitude of X_1 determine whether we shall have positive or negative feedback. In the case of a transistor amplifier, the X's could be currents, G would be a current gain, and H a current transfer function. We remark that additional specifications will be needed for the particular systems to be treated subsequently to clarify the assumptions regarding loading conditions and interactions between the circuit elements.

Often we are concerned with the steady-state response to sine-wave signals: then we treat the X's as phasors, and G and H as functions of $j\omega$. However, if a Laplace transform solution for transient response is desired, then the X's are the transformed variables and G and H are the transfer functions $G(s)$ and $H(s)$.

Let us consider the steady-state sinusoidal behavior of the system, in particular let us find $\mathbf{X}_o/\mathbf{X}_1$, the over-all gain in the presence of feedback. By definition,

$$G(j\omega) = \frac{\mathbf{X}_o}{\mathbf{X}_2} \tag{9-1}$$

and

$$H(j\omega) = \frac{\mathbf{X}_f}{\mathbf{X}_o} \tag{9-2}$$

Furthermore,

$$\mathbf{X}_2 = \mathbf{X}_1 - \mathbf{X}_f \tag{9-3}$$

If we solve for $\mathbf{X}_2$ in (9-1) and for $\mathbf{X}_f$ in (9-2), insert these values in (9-3), and rearrange, we find

$$\frac{\mathbf{X}_0}{\mathbf{X}_1} = \frac{\mathbf{G}(j\omega)}{1 + \mathbf{G}(j\omega)\mathbf{H}(j\omega)} \tag{9-4}$$

This is the basic relation for the analysis of single-loop feedback systems.†

Let us next examine the properties of the so-called *voltage* feedback connection.

9-3
Voltage (series-parallel) feedback

The conventional amplifier G in Fig. 9-2a is converted into a *voltage feedback* amplifier by connecting the feedback network in *parallel* at the output and in *series* at the input. In the following we write simply **G** for **G**($j\omega$) and **H** for

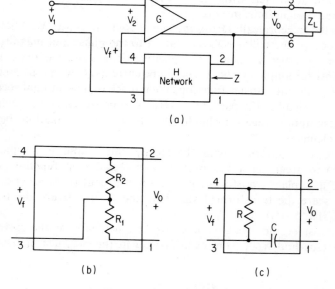

(a)

(b)   (c)

FIGURE 9-2   (a) Voltage feedback connection, (b) resistive feedback network, and (c) reactive feedback network.

†This relation has been written with the symbols and sign conventions usually used in control system theory. In the electronics literature Eq. (9-4) is usually expressed in the form $\mathbf{A}_f = \mathbf{A}/(1 - \boldsymbol{\beta}\mathbf{A})$. Thus, if **G** is identified with **A** and **H** with $-\boldsymbol{\beta}$, the two relations are the same.

$H(j\omega)$. Two possible feedback networks are shown in parts (b) and (c) of the figure. The voltage divider in Fig. 9-2b would give a *negative* real number for H, whereas the network in Fig. 9-2c would require a complex number for H.

To apply Eq. (9-4) to this situation, we specify that G is defined under the conditions of loading shown, i.e., including the load Z_L and the input impedance to the feedback network Z, acting in parallel. For simplicity, we assume temporarily that the input impedance to amplifier G at terminals V_2 is very large,† so that Z is determined solely by the elements of the feedback network. Now the over-all gain G_f can be written

$$G_f = \frac{V_0}{V_1} = \frac{G}{1 + GH} \qquad (9\text{-}5)$$

Here G_f, the over-all gain with feedback, is often called the *closed-loop gain*. For some purposes it is useful to refer to the gain from V_2 around through G and H to V_f as the *open-loop gain*. Its value is GH.

An examination of Eq. (9-5) shows that if the magnitude of the denominator is greater than unity, i.e., if $|(1 + GH)| > 1$, then $|G_f| < |G|$. This is defined to be the condition for *negative* feedback. In the converse situation $|G_f| > |G|$ and we have *positive* feedback. Positive feedback sometimes occurs as an unwanted side effect in a feedback amplifier or is deliberately introduced to produce an *oscillator*.

In a conventional amplifier the gain may change with time owing to changes in the parameters of the transistors or tubes with temperature or age or change in supply voltage. A negative feedback amplifier can be designed to reduce these changes to negligible proportions. How is this possible? Consider first a numerical example. Let a conventional resistance-loaded amplifier have a gain G that in the course of time changes from -50 to -45, a change of 10 per cent. Now suppose that this same amplifier is provided with the feedback network in Fig. 9-2b such that $H = -0.1$. Now calculate the two gains with feedback by Eq. (9-5).

$$\frac{-50}{1 + (-0.1)(-50)} = -8.33 \qquad \frac{-45}{1 + (-0.1)(-45)} = -8.18$$

Thus instead of a 10 per cent change, the change in gain, 8.33 to 8.18, is now only 1.8 per cent. In practice, the reduction in gain can be made up by providing additional amplification in G, and the improvement in gain stability can be increased by increasing the open-loop gain GH.

Suppose that the gain G is increased without limit, then Eq. (9-5) shows that

$$(\lim G_f)_{|G|\to\infty} = \frac{1}{H} \qquad (9\text{-}6)$$

Therefore, in the limiting conditions, the gain with negative feedback depends *only* on the feedback factor H. Since this factor depends only on the feedback

† Usually valid at low frequencies for tube amplifiers but not for transistor amplifiers.

network, which can be constructed of very stable and precise passive components such as resistors, the over-all gain can likewise be stabilized to a high degree. This feature is used to advantage in precision electronic instruments.

9-4
Effect of voltage feedback on input and output impedances

What is the effect of voltage feedback on the input and on the output (Thévenin) impedance of the amplifier? First we find the Thévenin equivalent of the internal amplifier with reference to terminals 5 and 6 in Fig. 9-2a and show this equivalent as a part of the feedback system (Fig. 9-3). Here the generator $V_2 G_t$ and the impedance Z_t are the Thévenin equivalents of amplifier G, including the effects of the input impedance Z to the feedback network as well as any internal impedances in G. (Note that Z should include the loading effect of the loop connected to terminals 3 and 4 in Fig. 9-2a, though the loop is not considered closed for the determination of Z_t.)

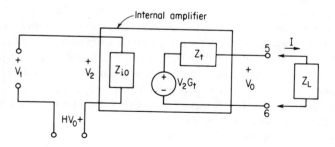

FIGURE 9-3   Thévenin equivalent of internal amplifier as a part of the feedback system.

We seek the Thévenin equivalent of the *over-all amplifier with feedback*, again referred to terminals 5 and 6. In Fig. 9-3 we think of connecting the load Z_L and seeking a relation of the form $V_o = K V_1 - Z_x I$. Then $K V_1$ will be the required Thévenin voltage and Z_x will be the required output impedance. The input circuit gives

$$V_2 = V_1 - H V_o \qquad (9\text{-}7)$$

The output circuit yields

$$V_o = V_2 G_t - Z_t I \qquad (9\text{-}8)$$

Replace $\mathbf{V}_2$ in (9-8) by its value from (9-7) and solve for $\mathbf{V}_o$ to find

$$\mathbf{V}_o = \left(\frac{\mathbf{G}_t}{1 + \mathbf{G}_t \mathbf{H}}\right)\mathbf{V}_1 - \left(\frac{\mathbf{Z}_t}{1 + \mathbf{G}_t \mathbf{H}}\right)\mathbf{I} \tag{9-9}$$

which is in the required form. Thus the feedback amplifier can now be represented as in Fig. 9-4, where

$$\mathbf{G}_{ft} = \frac{\mathbf{G}_t}{1 + \mathbf{G}_t \mathbf{H}} \tag{9-10}$$

$$\mathbf{Z}_{ft} = \frac{\mathbf{Z}_t}{1 + \mathbf{G}_t \mathbf{H}} \tag{9-11}$$

Thus with negative feedback, where $|(1 + \mathbf{G}_t \mathbf{H})| > 1$, the output impedance is *reduced* by the feedback action. In other words, the output voltage is more nearly constant as the load is varied.

The input impedance referred to the V_1 terminals, labeled Z_{if} in Fig. 9-4, is different from the impedance Z_{io} of the basic amplifier. Let us assume that the impedance looking back into the terminals HV_o in Fig. 9-3 is small compared with Z_{io}. Then we can equate the input currents for the two circuits, Fig. 9-3 and 9-4, to find

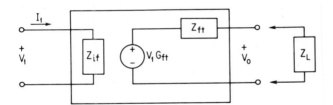

FIGURE 9-4   Thévenin equivalent of feedback amplifier.

$$\mathbf{I}_1 = \frac{\mathbf{V}_1 - \mathbf{H}\mathbf{V}_o}{\mathbf{Z}_{io}} = \frac{\mathbf{V}_1}{\mathbf{Z}_{if}} \tag{9-12}$$

Solve for $\mathbf{Z}_{if}$ and replace $\mathbf{V}_o/\mathbf{V}_1$ by $\mathbf{G}_f$ to obtain

$$\mathbf{Z}_{if} = \frac{\mathbf{Z}_{io}}{1 - \mathbf{G}_f \mathbf{H}} \tag{9-13}$$

Replacing $\mathbf{G}_f$ by means of Eq. (9-5), we obtain

$$\mathbf{Z}_{if} = \mathbf{Z}_{io}(1 + \mathbf{GH}) \tag{9-14}$$

Thus the effect of negative voltage feedback is to *increase* the input impedance in the same ratio as the voltage gain is reduced. This feature may be of importance in both transistor and tube amplifiers.

In summary, the effects of negative voltage feedback are to (1) stabilize the gain, (2) reduce the output impedance, and (3) increase the input impedance.

9-5
Effect of negative voltage feedback on noise and distortion

Let us think of a *noise voltage* which may be introduced anywhere in the system. If we interpret the term "noise" in a broad sense, we can encompass such items as resistor noise, power-supply hum, and the harmonic voltages due to nonlinear distortion. If we assume that the noise voltage is present in series with the signal at the *input* of the amplifier, then the application of negative feedback will *not* have a beneficial effect because the noise and signal voltages are affected equally. However, if the noise voltage enters in a stage beyond the input, or if an *ideal* (noisefree) *preamplifier* can be added ahead of the noise source (Fig. 9-5), then negative feedback will improve the signal-to-noise ratio.

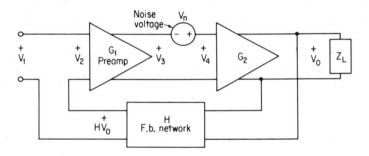

FIGURE 9-5   Effect of feedback on noise voltage.

Let us analyze the system in Fig. 9-5. Let G_1 represent the ideal preamplifier. For simplicity we regard the noise voltage $\mathbf{V}_n$ as harmonic in nature. First assume that the signal $\mathbf{V}_1$ is zero and calculate the noise voltage component at $\mathbf{V}_o$, which we designate $\mathbf{V}_{on}$. Note that $\mathbf{V}_4 = \mathbf{V}_3 + \mathbf{V}_n$; therefore

$$\mathbf{V}_{on} = \mathbf{G}_2(\mathbf{V}_3 + \mathbf{V}_n) \qquad (9\text{-}15)$$

But the feedback path develops a voltage $\mathbf{V}_3$, given by

$$\mathbf{V}_3 = -\mathbf{G}_1\mathbf{H}\mathbf{V}_{on} \qquad (9\text{-}16)$$

If we eliminate $\mathbf{V}_3$ between (9-15) and (9-16), we find

$$\mathbf{V}_{on} = \frac{\mathbf{G}_2\mathbf{V}_n}{1 + \mathbf{G}_1\mathbf{G}_2\mathbf{H}} \qquad (9\text{-}17)$$

If there were no feedback, then the output due to $\mathbf{V}_n$ would be $\mathbf{G}_2\mathbf{V}_n$. Eq. (9-17) shows that the feedback modifies this output by the factor $1/(1 + \mathbf{G}_1\mathbf{G}_2\mathbf{H})$. With negative feedback the denominator of this fraction exceeds unity, so the effect is to reduce the noise voltage in the output.

Now let the signal voltage $\mathbf{V}_1$ become active. Then the output voltage has an added term at the signal frequency, so the *total* output becomes

$$\mathbf{V}_o = \frac{\mathbf{G}_1\mathbf{G}_2\mathbf{V}_1}{1 + \mathbf{G}_1\mathbf{G}_2\mathbf{H}} + \frac{\mathbf{G}_2\mathbf{V}_n}{1 + \mathbf{G}_1\mathbf{G}_2\mathbf{H}} \qquad (9\text{-}18)$$

Suppose that we discuss the effect of the location of $\mathbf{V}_n$ in terms of the relative values of $\mathbf{G}_1$ and $\mathbf{G}_2$. To keep the over-all signal gain constant, with $\mathbf{H}$ fixed, the product $\mathbf{G}_1\mathbf{G}_2$ must be kept constant. The second term on the right in Eq. (9-18) shows that under this assumption the noise voltage varies directly as $\mathbf{G}_2$. Therefore, $\mathbf{G}_2$ should be small and $\mathbf{G}_1$ large. In other words, negative feedback is most beneficial when the noise or distortion enters near the output of the amplifier.

9-6
Current (series-series) feedback

Connecting the feedback network in *series* at both input and output gives a system in which the feedback voltage is proportional to the *current* through the load, as shown in Fig. 9-6. Here $\mathbf{H}$ is defined to equal $\mathbf{V}_f/\mathbf{I}$ and therefore represents a transfer impedance. The expression for $\mathbf{I}$ as a function of $\mathbf{V}_1$ and the circuit parameters can be found by writing the voltage equations for the input and output loops and manipulating to obtain

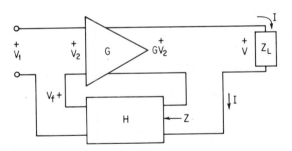

FIGURE 9-6   Current feedback circuit.

$$\mathbf{I} = \frac{\mathbf{G}\mathbf{V}_1}{\mathbf{Z}_L + \mathbf{Z} + \mathbf{G}\mathbf{H}} \qquad (9\text{-}19)$$

where $\mathbf{G}$ is the loaded gain of the internal amplifier. This amplifier is primarily valuable as a *current regulating* circuit, under the following conditions. If the gain $\mathbf{G}$ is large and the quantity $(\mathbf{Z} + \mathbf{G}\mathbf{H})$ is large compared with $\mathbf{Z}_L$, we see that variations in $\mathbf{Z}_L$ will have little effect on the current $\mathbf{I}$. For example, if $\mathbf{G}$ is negative and real, of value -100, $\mathbf{H}$ is $-100 + j0$ Ω, and $\mathbf{Z} = 100$

$+j0 \; \Omega$, then Eq. (9-19) gives $I = -100V_1/(Z_L + 100 + 10{,}000)$. If Z_L is initially 1000 Ω and then changes by 10 per cent, we see that the current will change by only 0.9 per cent. By increasing G and H this stabilizing effect can readily be improved.

It can be shown† that the output impedance of this circuit, referred to the load terminals, is given by

$$Z_{tf} = Z_t + Z + G_tH \qquad (9\text{-}20)$$

where Z_t and G_t are the Thévenin source impedance and voltage gain of the basic amplifier. When the product G_tH is large, the output impedance is high, as one would expect from the current-regulating property of the circuit.

9-7
Shunt (parallel-parallel) feedback

In another class of feedback connection the feedback network is connected in *parallel* at both input and output. Fig. 9-7 shows a special case of this class of connection in which an impedance Z_f is shunted from the output to the input. This connection is used in some transistor and tube amplifiers. It is exploited particularly in the operational amplifiers used in analog computers. This application is discussed at some length in Chapter 14.

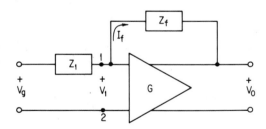

FIGURE 9-7   Shunt feedback.

For the present we consider only the effect of current I_f on the input impedance at terminals 1 and 2. The current I_f is equal to $(V_1 - V_o)/Z_f$. If we replace V_o by GV_1 and solve for V_1/I_f, we obtain the contribution of I_f to the input impedance. The result is

$$\frac{V_1}{I_f} = \frac{Z_f}{1 - G} \qquad (9\text{-}21)$$

In the mid-band range the gain G must be a *negative* real number for stable

†Jacob Millman, *Vacuum-tube and Semiconductor Electronics*, McGraw-Hill Book Company, New York, 1958, p. 448.

operation. Thus an impedance much lower than Z_f appears at the input. A special case of this phenomenon is the Miller effect (Sec. 7-7).

9-8
Feedback in transistor amplifiers

Negative feedback may be used in transistor amplifiers with the same objectives as for tube amplifiers, e.g., to improve constancy of gain, reduce distortion and noise, increase frequency bandwidth, or to adjust the input or output impedances. Since transistor parameters are variable, the use of feedback to stabilize gain is particularly important.

a. *The effect of source resistance*

The general theory in the foregoing articles shows what kind of results can be expected through the use of feedback. However, the general theory did not consider the effect of the resistance of the source, and with transistor amplifiers this should be included. We wish to find the relation of V_o to V_s in the voltage feedback amplifier in Fig. 9-8. Here we use resistance circuit

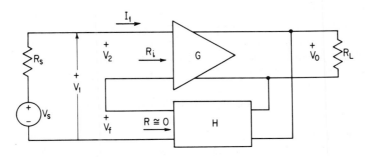

FIGURE 9-8   Voltage feedback amplifier.

elements, though impedances could be substituted if desired. The assumptions regarding **G** and **H** are the same as before, e.g., **G** is the loaded voltage gain and **H** is the loaded voltage transfer function. Furthermore, the impedance looking back into **H** is considered negligible. Then $V_o = V_2 G$, and $V_2 = I_1 R_i$; so

$$V_o = GI_1 R_i \tag{9-22}$$

Also

$$I_1 = \frac{V_s - V_f}{R_s + R_i} = \frac{V_s - HV_o}{R_s + R_i} \tag{9-23}$$

Combine (9-22) and (9-23) and solve for $\mathbf{V}_o/\mathbf{V}_s$ to find

$$\frac{\mathbf{V}_o}{\mathbf{V}_s} = \frac{\mathbf{G}R_i}{(R_s + R_i)} \frac{1}{\left[1 + \dfrac{\mathbf{G}\mathbf{H}R_i}{R_s + R_i} \right]} \qquad (9\text{-}24)$$

The factor which contains $\mathbf{H}$ in the square brackets is the feedback factor, which goes to zero if $\mathbf{H}$ goes to zero. Thus the effective feedback depends on the relation of R_i to R_s. In tube amplifiers, usually $R_i \gg R_s$, in which case Eq. (9-24) reduces to the earlier form in Eq. (9-5). With transistor amplifiers, however, the effect of the source resistance on the feedback is likely to be important.

b. Some general observations

A few general observations may be in order. It can be shown† that in multistage amplifiers it is more effective to use feedback around the whole amplifier, rather than only over the individual stages. Analysis shows that an n-stage amplifier with over-all feedback, which is designed to have the same effective gain as n stages with individual feedback, will have an improvement in the stability of effective gain by a factor of $(GH)^{n-1}$. Nevertheless, in transistor amplifiers some feedback is often provided over individual stages to stabilize the stage gain, as well as over the whole amplifier. Feedback over multiple stages is usually limited in practice to two or three stages, owing to the possibility of self-oscillation. As will become evident in Sec. 9-10, self-oscillation is likely in a feedback amplifier when there are large phase shifts through the amplifier at frequencies where there is still considerable gain. The internal phase shift in the transistor itself is likely to contribute to this effect at the higher frequencies.

The general feedback theory of the foregoing sections does not always apply to particular circuits. For example, it may not be possible to identify an isolated feedback path. In this event one can apply Kirchhoff's laws to the network to obtain the desired relationships. A more sophisticated approach is to apply the four-terminal network theory of Sec. 2-10 to the over-all network. Some typical feedback connections will next be presented, though with a minimum of circuit analysis.

c. CE stage with current (series-series) feedback

The addition of an unby-passed resistor R_E in the emitter branch of a common-emitter stage (Fig. 9-9a) will provide negative feedback. At midband the ac behavior of the circuit will conform to the network in Fig. 9-9b, if

†David DeWitt and Arthur L. Rosoff, *Transistor Electronics*, McGraw-Hill Book Company, New York, 1957, p. 225.

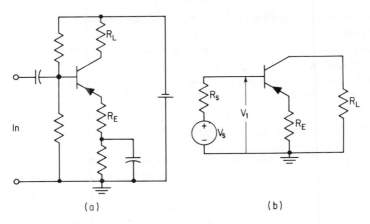

FIGURE 9-9   Feedback due to emitter resistor. (a) Circuit diagram; (b) circuit for ac behavior.

the base biasing resistances are high enough to be neglected (or are accounted for by altering R_s and V_s by means of Thévenin's theorem applied between the base and ground). This network can be analyzed by using the equivalent-T representation of the transistor, as shown in Fig. 6-4. Thus R_E is in series with r_e, so it simply adds to r_e in the formulas for the network behavior. If we restrict the range of R_E to values such that $R_E \ll r_m$, as is generally true, and also use the approximations that $r_e \ll r_m$, $r_e \ll r_d$, and $r_b \ll r_m$, then Eqs. (6-13) through (6-16) lead to the following formulas:

$$A_i \cong \frac{r_m}{R_L + r_d + R_E} \tag{9-25}$$

$$A_v \cong \frac{-R_L}{\dfrac{1}{r_m}(r_b + r_e + R_E)(R_L + r_d + R_E) + r_e + R_E} \tag{9-26}$$

$$R_i \cong r_b + r_e + R_E + \frac{(r_e + R_E)r_m}{(R_L + r_d + R_E)} \tag{9-27}$$

$$R_o \cong r_d + \frac{(r_e + R_E)(R_s + r_m)}{R_s + r_b + r_e + R_E} \tag{9-28}$$

In the formula for current gain R_E enters as an addition to $R_L + r_d$. But practical values of R_E are small compared with $R_L + r_d$; therefore the current gain is only slightly reduced by the addition of R_E. Next consider the voltage gain. The large value of r_m tends to reduce the first term in the denominator of (9-26) to a small value, so that the voltage gain can be approximated by $-R_L/(r_e + R_E)$. Therefore the voltage gain depends primarily on R_L and R_E rather than on the transistor parameters (usually $r_e < R_E$). Thus the voltage gain is stabilized against changes in transistor parameters.

As shown in Eq. (9-27), R_i is increased by the value of R_E and is also increased due to the effect of R_E in the last term on the right. Sample calculations will show that this term is the more important one and has the effect of increasing R_i considerably. This can be a useful feature since it is often desirable to have a higher input resistance. The value of R_o (Eq. (9-28)) is similarly increased markedly by the addition of moderate values of R_E.

d. CE stage with shunt (parallel-parallel) feedback

The principle of this connection is shown in Fig. 9-10a, in which the details of bias and coupling schemes have been omitted. (A capacitor would be placed in series with R_F to avoid its effect on the bias, if this were desired.) An approximate analysis of this amplifier can be based on the use of the h parameters, but neglecting the effect of the $h_r V_c$ voltage (Fig. 9-10b). This approximation will be sufficiently accurate for most purposes if R_L is not too high and if R_F is within the practical range.

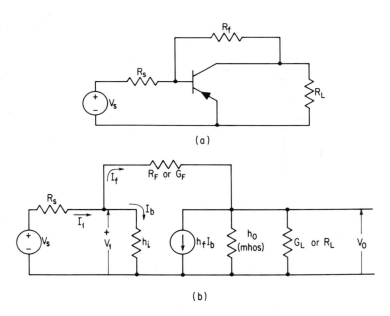

FIGURE 9-10 Shunt feedback circuits: (a) for ac behavior, and (b) including approximate equivalent circuit for the transistor.

Elementary circuit analysis permits the derivation of the network functions for this circuit. The analysis and the resulting formulas are simplified by using conductances (e.g., $G_F = 1/R_F$) where appropriate. Also we define the effective parallel conductance of h_o and G_L by the symbol

$$G'_L = h_o + G_L \tag{9-29}$$

The resulting formulas follow:

$$A_v \equiv \frac{V_o}{V_1} \cong -\frac{\dfrac{h_f}{h_i} - G_F}{G'_L + G_F} \tag{9-30}$$

$$A_i \equiv \frac{I_L}{I_1} \cong \frac{-(h_f - G_F h_i)}{R_L G'_L + G_F R_L (h_f + 1 + G'_L h_i)} \tag{9-31}$$

$$R_i \equiv \frac{V_1}{I_1} \cong \frac{h_i}{1 + \left(\dfrac{h_f + G'_L h_i}{G'_L R_F + 1}\right)} \tag{9-32}$$

$$G_o \cong h_o + \frac{R_s(1 + h_f) + h_i}{R_s(R_F + h_i) + R_F h_i} \tag{9-33}$$

These formulas are approximate because the effect of $h_r V_c$ has been neglected, but no further approximations have been made. Further approximations can be made, depending on the values of R_s, R_F, and R_L and on the accuracy desired, as the following example will show:

Example:

Let

$h_i = 1200 \ \Omega$	$R_L = 2000 \ \Omega$
$h_f = 34$	$R_F = 20{,}000 \ \Omega$
$h_o = 16.7 \times 10^{-6} \ \text{mho}$	$R_s = 1000 \ \Omega$

Then $G'_L = 517 \ \mu$mhos and $G_F = 50 \ \mu$mhos. Calculating A_v by Eq. (9-30), we find, using μmhos in both numerator and denominator, $A_v \cong -(28350 - 50)/(517 + 50) = -50$. Thus the G_F term in the numerator is negligible in this example. Similarly calculate A_i by (9-31), $A_i \cong -(34 - 0.06)/[1.034 + 0.1(34 + 1 + 0.62)] = -34/(1.034 + 3.56) = -7.4$. Again, one or two terms are negligible. Also, calculate R_i by (9-32) and find $R_i \cong 1200/[1 + (34 + 0.62)/(10.34 + 1)] = 296 \ \Omega$. Finally, calculate G_o by (9-33), using μmhos, $G_o \cong 16.7 + (35{,}000 + 1200)/(21.2 + 24) = 817 \ \mu$mhos, or $R_o = 1220 \ \Omega$. These results should be compared with the values obtained with no feedback, i.e., $G_F = 0$. If these are calculated on the same basis ($h_r = 0$), we obtain: voltage gain $= -54.7$, current gain $= -32.8$, input resistance $= 1200 \ \Omega$, and output resistance $= 60{,}000 \ \Omega$. This example illustrates the general effects of shunt feedback, to wit: a small effect on A_v; a reduction (and stabilization) of A_i, and reductions of R_o and R_i.

e. *Multistage feedback connections*

The simple series-series or shunt feedback cannot be applied to two *CE* stages in cascade owing to the incorrect phase relation. However, shunt feedback can be applied around two stages consisting of a *CC* stage followed by a *CE* stage (Fig. 9-11). Owing to the greater "internal" current gain, the effective current gain with feedback can be substantial, yet can be satisfactorily stabilized.

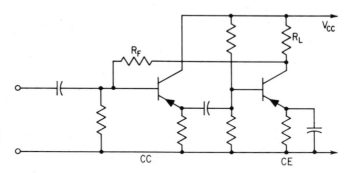

FIGURE 9-11   Two-stage amplifier with shunt feedback.

Figure 9-12 shows one scheme of adding feedback to a two-stage *CE* amplifier. The resistor R_E develops a voltage at the second emitter which is out of phase compared with its collector. Therefore the connection through R_F to the first base will give negative feedback. Although this circuit combines series and shunt feedback, its behavior is primarily that of a shunt feedback circuit.† Thus the current gain will be stabilized and the input resistance will be low. If a current amplifier is desired, the resistor R_1 can be removed, or retained for application as a voltage amplifier.

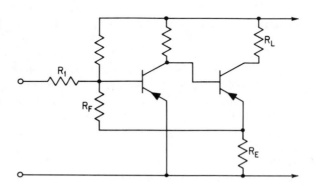

FIGURE 9-12   Two-stage *CE* amplifier with second emitter to first base feedback (diagram for ac behavior).

†See approximate formulas in R. A. Greiner, *Semiconductor Devices and Applications*, McGraw-Hill Book Company, New York, 1961, p. 273.

In a three-stage *CE* amplifier the gain is great enough so that a combination of shunt and series feedback can be used (Fig. 9-13). Owing to the greater tendency to oscillate, the amount of feedback that can be used is limited.

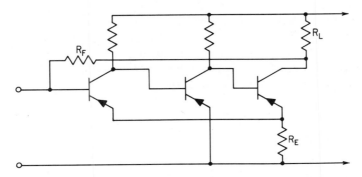

FIGURE 9-13   Amplifier with three *CE* stages, and with compound feedback (simplified diagram).

9-9
Gain versus frequency

The foregoing theory applies to the general situation in which the gain and feedback transfer functions are complex quantities that are functions of the frequency. However, the discussion and examples thus far largely referred to the *mid-band* frequency range in which the gain is a positive or negative real quantity, and to real values of **H**. We turn now to a brief study of the behavior over a wide range of frequencies where phase shifts must be considered, partly to learn what effect feedback will have on the amplifier bandwidth. In the following article we discuss the possibility that the feedback will become sufficiently positive at some frequency to cause undesired effects such as steady oscillations (instability).

Consider the voltage feedback system in Fig. 9-2a, which is governed by Eq. (9-5),

$$\mathbf{G}_f = \frac{\mathbf{G}}{1 + \mathbf{G}\mathbf{H}} \tag{9-5}$$

We remark that our discussion will apply to any system, like some basic servomechanisms which are governed by an equation of the form of Eq. (9-5). First we recall the relation among $\mathbf{V}_1$, the signal; $\mathbf{V}_2$, the inner amplifier input; and $\mathbf{V}_f$, the feedback voltage

$$\mathbf{V}_1 - \mathbf{V}_f = \mathbf{V}_2 \tag{9-34}$$

or

$$\mathbf{V}_1 = \mathbf{V}_2 + \mathbf{V}_f \qquad (9\text{-}35)$$

A typical phasor diagram relating these voltages is shown in Fig. 9-14a. For a reason that we shall see presently, $\mathbf{V}_2$ (the reference phasor) is drawn with its tip at the origin of the complex plane coordinate system. We note that in the figure $|\mathbf{V}_2|$ is smaller than $|\mathbf{V}_1|$, and therefore the phasor diagram illustrates a *negative* feedback condition. The diagram can be simplified and made more useful by letting $\mathbf{V}_2 = 1$, as in Fig. 9-14b. Then the $\mathbf{V}_f$ phasor equals $\mathbf{GH}$, the open-loop transfer function. Furthermore, if $\mathbf{V}_2 = 1$, then $\mathbf{V}_1 = 1 + \mathbf{GH}$ as in Fig. 9-14b (with the origin for $\mathbf{V}_1$ taken at the point $-1 + j0$).

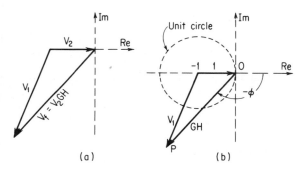

FIGURE 9-14   Phasor diagrams relating $\mathbf{V}_1$, $\mathbf{V}_2$, $\mathbf{V}_f$ and $\mathbf{GH}$.

Now we are in a position to analyze Eq. (9-5) by a study of its denominator, $1 + \mathbf{GH}$. The effect of feedback in modifying the inner gain $\mathbf{G}$ will depend on the magnitude and phase of $1 + \mathbf{GH}$, or of $\mathbf{V}_1$. Recalling the definition of negative feedback, we see that if $|\mathbf{V}_1| > 1$, we have negative feedback. Thus if the tip of the phasor $\mathbf{V}_1$ falls *outside* of the dotted unit circle centered on the point $-1 + j0$, then the feedback is negative.

Suppose that the tip of the $\mathbf{V}_1$ phasor travels along a locus like the curve MN in Fig. 9-15, as the frequency varies. Then phasor $\mathbf{V}_1$ represents a condition of negative feedback, $\mathbf{V}_1'$ represents the dividing line case between negative and positive feedback ($|1 + \mathbf{GH}| = 1$), and $\mathbf{V}_1''$ represents positive feedback. Thus the effect of feedback on the over-all gain can be obtained from the variation of the quantity $1 + \mathbf{GH}$.

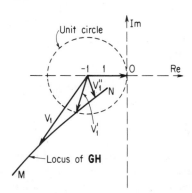

FIGURE 9-15   Illustrating positive and negative feedback in relation to $\mathbf{GH}$.

Let us think now of the effect of widely varying frequencies on the locus of **GH**. It would be desirable if this locus would remain in the first and fourth quadrants (the right-hand half-plane), for then there would be no risk of positive feedback or of instability. However, only the simplest amplifiers have loci that remain in the right half-plane. In general, the locus of **GH** extends into the left-hand half-plane, and is likely to pass within the unit circle. Under such conditions the amplifier is likely to become unstable, as discussed in the following article. Next we briefly examine the forms of the **GH** loci (often called the *Nyquist plots*) for some particular amplifiers.

First consider a one-tube pentode amplifier with *RC* coupling to the load, similar to the triode amplifier in Fig. 7-8a, but with a resistance voltage divider feedback circuit added. As shown in Fig. 7-17, **G** varies in a circular locus in a polar plot, with the mid-band gain along the negative real axis. The function **H** for this connection will be a negative real number, independent of frequency. Thus **GH** will plot as a circle in the right-hand half-plane as sketched in Fig. 9-16a. Further, the variation of the quantity $1 + $ **GH** can be visualized by noting the variation of the phasor labeled V_1. Thus $|1 + $ **GH**$| \geqslant 1$ for all frequencies, so the feedback remains negative over the whole range. The effect on the over-all gain is sketched in Fig. 9-16b. Thus the result is a wider passband but a lower gain. In effect, gain is traded for bandwidth.

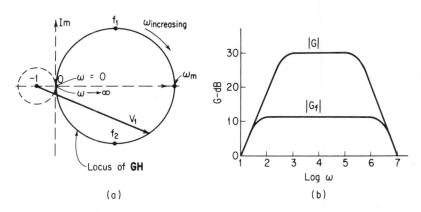

(a)   (b)

FIGURE 9-16   (a) Nyquist plot for one-stage RC-coupled pentode amplifier. (b) Gain *vs.* log ω with and without feedback.

Let us discuss the *two-stage* RC-coupled amplifier without going into much detail. Here **H** would have to be positive in the mid-band range, since **G** is a positive real number here. A possible feedback connection would be a voltage divider across the output which feeds an ideal one-to-one transformer to correct the phase of the feedback voltage. Then the form of the Nyquist plot will follow that of the locus of **G**. We can easily see that the

GH locus will enter the second and third quadrants. For example, at the lower half-power frequency for *one stage* f_1, the first-stage output lags its signal by 135°. The effect of the second stage is to add a lag of another 135° (assuming identical stages), giving 270° in all. Thus at f_1 the locus passes across the $+\text{Im}$ axis. At lower frequencies the locus enters the unit circle and finally approaches the origin as $\omega \to 0$. Thus *positive* feedback arises at low frequencies, and also at the edge of the pass band at high frequencies.

In the *three-stage RC*-coupled amplifier these effects are even more pronounced, again assuming identical stages. In this amplifier the Nyquist plot takes the typical form shown in Fig. 9-17a. The locus is inside the unit circle over a range of frequencies, both at low and at high frequencies. This indicates the presence of positive feedback, and accounts for the humps in the $\mathbf{G}_f$ versus log ω graph in Fig. 9-17b. Furthermore, the positive feedback will lead to sustained oscillations except with rather moderate gains and feedback ratios, as discussed in the following article. The need for careful design† is obvious.

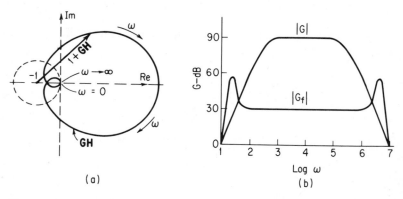

(a)   (b)

FIGURE 9-17   (a) Nyquist plot for three-stage *RC*-coupled pentode amplifier. (b) Gain *vs.* log ω with and without feedback.

9-10
Stability considerations

The foregoing discussion has laid the basis for the analysis of feedback system stability. In Fig. 9-17a, for example, a range of frequencies which gives positive feedback and higher than normal gain was identified.

†A better design is to use two wide-band stages and one with a bandwidth only great enough for the signal frequencies. See, for example, Vincent C. Rideout, *Active Networks*, Prentice-Hall, Inc., Englewood Cliffs, N. J. 1954, p. 176 ff.

Let us examine the Nyquist plots of **GH** a little more closely in the positive feedback region, as in the examples in Fig. 9-18a. These could represent the curves for a direct-coupled amplifier, as the open-loop gain has a finite value at $\omega = 0$, The curves A, B, and C show the effect of increasing the *magnitude* of the gain. We have shown that the close approach of curve A to the point $-1 + j0$ means that positive feedback occurs over the corresponding frequency range. Intuitively, we can predict that curve B, which passes through the point $-1 + j0$, represents an *unstable* condition. From the mathematical viewpoint this situation means that **GH** $= -1$, so the denominator in Eq. (9-5) goes to zero, and the over-all gain goes to infinity. Actually, at the critical point oscillations will begin and grow in amplitude to such a degree that the elementary linear mathematical theory will no longer apply.

a. The Nyquist criterion

A further increase in the gain will lead to curve C, which partially encloses the point $-1 + j0$. We might guess that this also represents an unstable condition. Nyquist[†] has derived a criterion for stability based on the locus of **GH**. A limited form of the Nyquist criterion states that the system *is unstable if the* **GH** *locus for the frequency range* $-\infty < \omega < +\infty$ *encloses the point* $-1 + j0$ *and is stable if the curve does not enclose this point.* In the example in Fig. 9-17a the locus forms a closed curve for values of ω from zero to infinity. However, in the example in Fig. 9-18 the locus must be plotted for values of ω from negative infinity to positive infinity to obtain

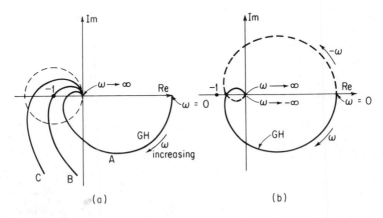

FIGURE 9-18   Nyquist plots: (a) for increasing gain, and (b) for $-\infty < \omega < \infty$.

[†]H. Nyquist, "Regeneration Theory," *Bell Syst. Tech. J.*, **11**, 126, 1932.

a closed curve. Actually, the value of **GH** with $j\omega$ replaced by $-j\omega$ is the conjugate of the first value. Therefore, only the locus for $0 < \omega < \infty$ need be plotted, and the curve for $0 > \omega > -\infty$ will be this curve reflected about the real axis. The limited form of the Nyquist criterion holds for systems for which the quantity **GH** is itself stable,† which is true in the simpler feedback systems.

b. Bode plots

H. W. Bode‡ analyzed the relationship of the forms of two curves: (1) the log of the magnitude of **GH** versus log of frequency and (2) the phase of **GH** versus log of frequency to each other and to the characteristics of the feedback system. The reader can discern that these two curves contain the same information as in a single Nyquist plot. However, the Bode plots are useful because (1) considerable information can be gleaned from the log-magnitude plot alone, which means that the work of computation or experimental test is reduced, (2) the design of systems with desirable characteristics is facilitated, and (3) wider ranges of values are graphed more readily than with the Nyquist plot.

Qualitative examples of log magnitude (gain in dB) versus log ω plots have already been shown in Figs. 9-16b and 9-17b as applied to voltage gains. Here we are concerned with the open-loop gain **GH**. Let us examine the variation of **GH** in the important region near the point $-1 + j0$ in both the Nyquist and Bode plots (Fig. 9-19). The condition of interest is the point at which $|\mathbf{GH}| = 1$ (or 0 dB), as at point M in Fig. 9-19a and M' in the attenuation plot. The angle δ by which the phase angle ϕ of **GH** fails to equal $-180°$ is a measure of the stability of the system. This angle is called the *phase margin*. The point N in the Nyquist plot, where the **GH** locus crosses the negative real axis, likewise is an indication of the stability. The closer point N approaches to the point $-1 + j0$, the closer the system will be to an unstable condition. The term *gain margin* has been applied to the difference between a gain of 0 d**B** and the open loop gain at the 180° crossover point, as shown in Fig. 9-19b. In these terms, the system becomes unstable when the gain margin become zero or negative.

It would take us too far afield to investigate in detail the principles of the Bode plots that relate to the design of feedback systems. However, a numerical example will serve to illustrate some of the techniques involved. Consider a three-stage RC coupled pentode amplifier in which two of the stages have an upper half-power ω of 10^7 and in which the third stage is designed for a

†For the general Nyquist criterion and its application see Harold Chestnut and Robert W. Mayer, *Servomechanisms and Regulating System Design*, 2d ed., John Wiley & Sons, Inc., New York, 1959, pp. 142–160.

‡H. W. Bode, *Network Analysis and Feedback Amplifier Design*, D. Van Nostrand Company, Inc., Princeton, N.J., 1945.

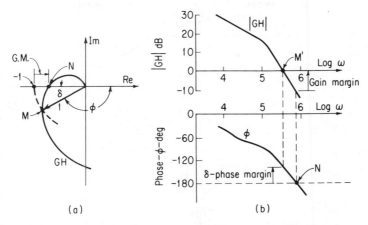

FIGURE 9-19   Phase margin, δ, and gain margin in (a) Nyquist plot, and (b) Bode plots.

higher gain and a smaller upper half-power ω of 10^5. Assume that the amplifier is direct-coupled so that we are not concerned with the low-frequency behavior. Further assume that the mid-band stage gains are 20 for the two identical stages and 40 for the third stage. The feedback network is resistive and such that $\mathbf{H} = 0.0025\underline{/0°}$. Thus the expression for $\mathbf{GH}$ becomes

$$\mathbf{GH} = \left(\frac{20}{1+j\frac{\omega}{10^7}}\right)^2\left(\frac{40}{1+j\frac{\omega}{10^5}}\right)0.0025 = \frac{40}{\left(1+j\frac{\omega}{10^7}\right)^2\left(1+j\frac{\omega}{10^5}\right)} \qquad (9\text{-}36)$$

Since we are interested in wide ranges of frequency, we can use the "corner frequency and asymptote" plotting technique discussed in Chapter 2 for *RC* networks. The term $[1 + j(\omega/10^5)]^{-1}$ has a *corner* frequency of $\omega = 10^5$, and the decibel attenuation of the asymptote in Fig. 9-20 is horizontal at first, and then starts dropping at the 20 dB per decade rate at $\omega = 10^5$. This continues up to the second corner frequency $\omega = 10^7$ ascribed to the two identical stages. Beyond $\omega = 10^7$ there are *three* stages, *each* of which cause a 20-dB per decade drop, so the total rate is 60 dB per decade. Thus the whole asymptotic curve is easily obtained by locating two points and drawing three straight lines. The *actual* curve falls 3 dB below the corner at $\omega = 10^5$ and 1 dB below the straight lines at $\omega = 5 \times 10^4$ and 2×10^5. The correction at $\omega = 10^7$ is -6 dB and is -2 dB at $\omega = 5 \times 10^6$ and 2×10^7. To complete the Bode diagram, we calculate and plot the phase of the $\mathbf{GH}$ function, with the result shown in the figure. Up to $\omega = 10^5$ the two wide-band stages have little effect on the phase. At $\omega = 10^6$ the phases of the three stages add as follows: $84.3 + 5.7 + 5.7 = 95.7°$. At $\omega = 10^7$ the summation is $89.4 + 45 + 45 = 179.4°$. Thus the important 180° crossover point is very

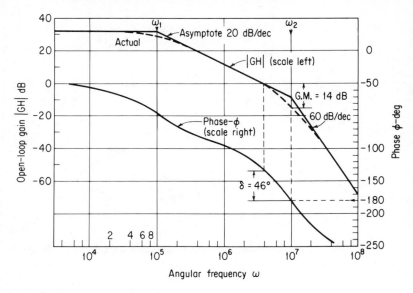

FIGURE 9-20   Bode curves for a 3-stage amplifier.

nearly at $\omega = 10^7$. At this frequency the gain (actual) is -14 dB; thus the amplifier is *stable* with a gain margin of 14 dB. The phase margin is found by noting the point on the phase curve that corresponds to a gain of 0 dB and observing the distance from this point to the $-180°$ level, with the result $\delta = 46°$.

In the passband **GH** is 32 dB, or a value of about 40. Since **G** in this range is $-16,000$ we find that $\mathbf{G}_f = \mathbf{G}/(1 + \mathbf{GH}) = -16,000/(1 + 40) = -390$, or 41.8 dB.

The Bode diagram, like the Nyquist locus, clearly indicates how close the system is to an unstable condition. For example, if the feedback were to be strengthened in this amplifier, the $|\mathbf{GH}|$ plot would move upward, parallel to itself. To preserve a safe gain margin, a rise of perhaps 6 dB would be safe (14 dB would lead to instability). With a 6-dB rise, **H** increases to $0.0024 \times 2 = 0.005$, and **GH** in the passband rises to 38 dB or nearly 80. Then $|\mathbf{G}_f|$ is calculated to be 198.

If stronger feedback is desired, additional design techniques must be used. One of these is to add corrective networks† which alter the gain and phase curves, particularly in the neighborhood of the 0-dB and 180° points. The same techniques are employed extensively in the design of feedback control (servo) systems and are developed in detail in the standard works on the subject. Additional methods used in stability studies are the so-called *root-locus method* and certain stability tests applied to the mathematical

†F. E. Terman, *Electronic and Radio Engineering*, 4th ed., McGraw-Hill Book Company, New York, 1955, pp. 379–390.

forms of the transfer function of the system. The Bode plots, and to some extent also the Nyquist diagram, lend themselves to the study of systems not completely characterized by transfer functions. In this event an experimental technique can be used to obtain the Bode or Nyquist diagram of the open-loop system. Alternatively, the data for a portion of the system can be combined with the known transfer function for the remainder of the system. For example, in amplifiers it may be difficult to characterize the effective parameters with sufficient accuracy, so experimental methods are needed to guide the design.

Considerable information concerning the phase variation of a transfer function can be gleaned from the Bode gain plot,† without any measurement of the phase. Elementary examples are the following. A gain curve that is flat to a single corner frequency and then drops at 20 dB per decade means that there will be a total ultimate phase shift of 90° lagging, most of which takes place within one decade above and below the corner frequency. If the situation is the same, except that the rate of drop is 40 dB per decade the total phase shift will be 180°, and if the rate is 60 dB per decade the total phase shift will be 270°. The phase shift follows somewhat more involved relations when more than one corner frequency, or an added resonant frequency, is present.‡

REFERENCES

9-1 E. J. Angelo, Jr., *Electronic Circuits*, 2d ed., McGraw-Hill Book Company, New York, 1964, Chap. 19.

9-2 A. J. Cote, Jr., and J. B. Oakes, *Linear Vacuum-tube and Transistor Circuits*, McGraw-Hill Book Company, New York, 1961, Chap. 8.

9-3 K. J. Dean, *Transistors: Theory and Circuitry*, McGraw-Hill Book Company New York, 1964, Chap. 4.

9-4 M. S. Ghausi, *Principles and Design of Linear Active Circuits*, McGraw-Hill Book Company, New York, 1965, Chap. 14.

9-5 S. S. Hakim and R. Barrett, *Transistor Circuits in Electronics*, Hayden Publishing Company, New York, 1964, pp. 145–167.

EXERCISES

9-1 An electronic voltmeter contains an amplifier, which, without feedback, has a voltage gain of -4×10^4. What value of voltage feedback factor **H** is needed if

† F. E. Terman, *loc. cit.*

‡ See, for example, Harold Chestnut and Robert W. Mayer, *op. cit.*, pp. 322–343 and Chap. 12.

the resultant gain with feedback should not change more than 0.1 per cent for a decrease of 20 per cent in the magnitude of the inner amplifier voltage gain?

9-2 A high-μ triode has a μ of 100 and an r_p of 75,000 Ω. This tube is used in a grounded-cathode circuit, and the grid-to-ground resistance is 500,000 Ω. Assume that negative feedback is added so that 10 per cent of the output voltage is fed back. (a) Find the output impedance and the Thévenin gain of the feedback amplifier. (b) What is the actual voltage gain if the load resistance is 50,000 Ω? (c) What is the input impedance of the feedback amplifier under the conditions of (b)?

9-3 Assume that the internal amplifier in Fig. 9-3 is a common-emitter transistor stage and that this stage has the parameters $Z_{io} = R_{io} = 1200\ \Omega$, $G_t = -400$, and $Z_t = 22,000\ \Omega$ resistive for $R_s = 0$. Let voltage feedback be added by means of the network in Figs. 9-2a and b. (a) What value of **H** should be chosen to reduce the output impedance to 2000 Ω? (b) If the feedback factor is **H** $= -0.04$, what are the values of $\mathbf{G}_{ft}$ and $\mathbf{Z}_{ft}$? (c) With the conditions as in (b), what are the values of the actual voltage gain, current gain, and input impedance for a resistive load of 3000 Ω?

9-4 Consider a voltage feedback amplifier operating in the passband of frequencies in which the gains are real. Assume that the feedback factor is real. The sensitivity of G_t to changes in G can be evaluated in terms of $(dG_f/dG)(G/G_f)$, which gives the relative change in G_f per unit change in G. (a) Show that this quantity has the value $1/(1 + GH)$. (b) Suppose that a feedback amplifier is to be designed to have $G_f = 50$. Also, it is desired that a 10 per cent change in G will produce only a 0.1 per cent change in G_f. Choose suitable values of G and H for this amplifier.

9-5 In Fig. 9-8 assume that the gain and feedback factors are real. Define $\mathbf{G}'_f = \mathbf{V}_o/\mathbf{V}_s$. Derive a formula for the relative gain sensitivity, i.e., for $(dG'_f/dG)(G/G'_f)$.

9-6 A current (series-series) feedback amplifier circuit contains an inner amplifier having a voltage gain of -1000. The load impedance is a 100-Ω resistance, and the series feedback element in the load circuit is a 10-Ω resistance. Assume that the signal voltage remains constant. (a) If the inner amplifier gain drops by 10 per cent, what is the percentage change in the load current? (b) If the inner amplifier gain remains constant but the load resistance increases by 10 per cent (as due to the heating of a copper magnet coil), what is the percentage change in the load current?

9-7 Refer to the feedback amplifier in Fig. 9-10. Analyze the approximate equivalent circuit in Fig. 9-10b with the object of finding formulas for (a) A_v, (b) A_i, (c) R_i, and (d) G_o, and compare with formulas (9-30) through (9-33).

9-8 Consider the feedback connection shown in Fig. 9-21. Assume that at the frequency of interest the internal amplifier gain is real. Let the h parameters of the internal amplifier be real quantities designated by h'_i, h'_r, h'_f, and h'_o. (a) Show that the h parameters of the combined network, from the terminals AA to BB, can be expressed by: $h_i = h'_i + \beta(1 - \beta)R$, $h_r = h'_r - \beta$, $h_f = h'_f + \beta$, and $h_o = h'_o + (1/R)$. Suggestion: See Exercise 6-12. (b) Calculate the input impedance (resistive) and output impedance of both the internal amplifier and the feedback amplifier, assuming the following parameters: $h'_i = 800\ \Omega$, $h'_r = 5 \times 10^{-4}$, $h'_f = 40$, $h'_o = 5 \times 10^{-5}$ mho, $\beta = 0.2$, $R = 10,000\ \Omega$, $R_L = 5000\ \Omega$, and $R_s = 600\ \Omega$.

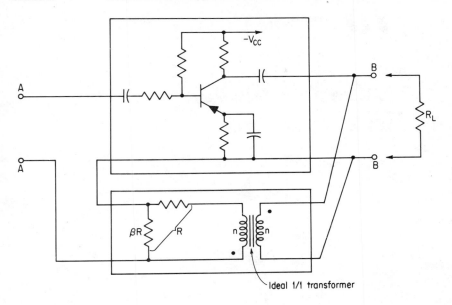

FIGURE 9-21

9-9 Assume that the gain of *one stage* of a three-stage, RC coupled pentode amplifier can be expressed over the upper frequency range by $\mathbf{G} = -g_m R/[1 + j(\omega/\omega_o)]$, where R is the effective resistance from plate to ground and ω_o is the upper half-power frequency. Voltage feedback is applied over the whole amplifier. Show that, if only the upper range of frequencies need be considered, the feedback factor at which instability will set in is $H = -8/(g_m R)^3$. *Suggestion:* Find the frequency ratio and gain needed to reduce the gain margin to zero.

10

Gaseous Diodes
and Triodes

10-1
Electrical discharges in gases

In a high-vacuum tube the current is carried by virtue of the flow of free electrons. The residual gas molecules are so few and far apart that the electrons seldom strike a molecule in their flight from cathode to anode. In a gas-filled tube the situation is different. Here the presence of the gas has such profound effects as to produce sudden changes from the nonconducting to the conducting state, to reduce the voltage required to maintain the current and to give off light from the gaseous *discharge*. We shall give a brief outline of the discharges of interest in electronic tubes, in particular the *Townsend* discharge, *breakdown* or *spark* discharge, and *glow* and *arc* discharges.

To distinguish among these discharges, we discuss the behavior of the gap in the experimental arrangement in Fig. 10-1. Here cold metal electrodes are tested in a gas at a reduced pressure, say, at 0.01 atmosphere. Some general features of a current-voltage characteristic for this kind of test are shown. The actual characteristic would vary in detail, depending on the kind of gas, the pressure, the area and spacing of the electrodes, etc. The dotted portions of the curve are intended to suggest that with the usual values of E and R available in the laboratory no actual data can be obtained over these ranges, owing to sudden transitions from one kind of discharge to the next. Over the range $OABC$ the currents are so small that no light is given off, and this range corresponds to the *dark discharge*, or the *Townsend discharge*. Then a transition, or *breakdown*, occurs, and the dark discharge changes to

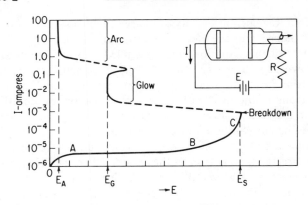

FIGURE 10-1   Generalized current-voltage characteristic.

a *glow* discharge. When the current rises still more, another transition to a lower-voltage, higher-current discharge called an *arc* takes place.

Each of the regions of the characteristic merits further discussion. Starting at the origin we note a gradual increase of current from O to A, then a nearly constant range from A to B. If we postulate a constant rate of generation of free electrons and positive ions in the gas space, say, due to cosmic radiation or to photoelectric effect, these variations become understandable. Thus, over the range O to A the accumulated ions (using this term to mean both ions and electrons) will be moving in greater and greater numbers to the electrodes, giving an increasing current. However, when the ions are swept out so rapidly that as many reach the electrodes per second as are generated, then additional voltage will not cause a higher current.

What then causes the rise from B to C? Here the ions, in this case electrons, are being accelerated so strongly by the field that they are able to knock off electrons from neutral gas molecules, an action called *ionization by collision*. This action is rapidly cumulative, so that the gap will sustain only a certain maximum voltage E_s before the discharge changes into a different form at a lower voltage, i.e., into a glow discharge. The voltage E_s is called the *sparking* or *breakdown* potential.

The glow and arc are characterized by successively lower voltages and higher currents. Values for the glow voltage E_G may range from 70 to 400 V, and for the arc voltage E_A, from 9 to 80 V for short discharges.

10-2
Mechanism of gaseous conduction

Even in the most highly ionized discharges, excepting such extreme conditions as in the plasmas in thermonuclear fusion experiments, the gas space is mostly filled with neutral molecules and with only a small proportion of electrons and molecular ions. In a low-current-density discharge the proportion of charged particles is small indeed and the electric field is not altered by their space charge. An example of this situation is the gas-filled phototube, which is an instance of a Townsend discharge. Here the basic mechanisms are the release of the electrons from the cathode by the incident light and the acceleration of the electrons in the field with resultant ionization by collision. A particular electron may ionize several molecules in its passage across the gap, so that the initial current can be multiplied several fold.

In the phototube the electric field is rather strong and as a result the electron motions are directed mainly toward the anode. When the field is weaker, as in the *plasma* regions in glows and arcs, the electron and ion motions are more nearly random in character. The swarms of ions and electrons are bouncing off the neutral molecules and only occasionally produce extra ions by ionization by collision. The instantaneous electron and ion velocities will vary over a considerable range both in magnitude and direction. On the average, however, the electrons are drifting toward the anode and the positive ions toward the cathode. Owing to their relatively small mass and size, the electrons drift much more rapidly than the ions and carry the major portion of the current in a plasma. A striking feature of a plasma is that the numbers of electrons and ions per unit volume are very nearly equal. As a result, the net space charge is nearly zero and the voltage drop along the length of the tube is low.

A generalized view of the mechanism of conduction in any discharge or portion of a discharge can be based on the rates at which ions enter and leave the region and their rates of formation or disappearance from the region. With steady conditions there must be a balance between the numbers of ions coming into the region plus those being formed, and the numbers leaving or being lost for other reasons. Losses may occur in some gases by *recombination*, in which a negative and a positive particle join to form a neutral gas molecule. In the plasma, for example, ions and electrons are diffusing to the walls, where recombination takes place. In a long tube this loss must be made up by a small amount of ionization by collision.

10-3
Breakdown voltage; glow and
arc discharges and tubes

An understanding of the breakdown voltage of a gap and its variation is fundamental to an appreciation of the limitations of gaseous tubes. First we inquire about the effect of varying the gas pressure in the parallel-plane electrode arrangement. Figure 10-2a shows the form of the experimental results that would be obtained with three different gap settings d_1, d_2, and d_3.

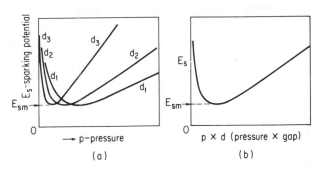

FIGURE 10-2   Sparking voltage as a function of (a) pressure and
(b) pressure times gap.

These gaps are in increasing order of magnitude, that is, $d_1 < d_2 < d_3$. It is noteworthy that the breakdown voltage drops to a minimum as the pressure is lowered and then rises again as the pressure is reduced further. A physical explanation of the shape of this curve can be based on the changes of the spacing of the molecules and of the lengths of the free flights of the electrons. At first as the pressure is reduced and the length of the free paths increases, the preponderant effect is that the voltage can be reduced and yet the electric field can cause adequate ionization over the longer free paths. This ionization must build up cumulatively to a certain level to produce instability and a spark. As the pressure is lowered still farther, however, a condition is reached in which the number of impacts that a single electron makes in crossing the gap becomes rather small. This reduces the multiplication effect of the successive ionizations. Consequently at lower pressures the voltage must be raised to increase the energy of the electrons and thereby produce an adequate number of ionizing collisions while crossing the gap.

A peculiar condition results when the pressures are below the value for the minimum breakdown voltage, namely, that the longer gap d_3 will only sustain a lower voltage than the shorter gaps d_2 or d_1. This result is contrary to our offhand expectations and opposite to the situation for the higher pressures.

When the breakdown voltage is plotted as a function of the pressure multiplied by the gap length a single curve results as shown in Fig.10-2b. This curve is an embodiment of *Paschen's law*, which states that the breakdown voltage is a function only of the product of pressure by gap length. The kind of gas and, to a lesser extent, the material of the electrodes has an effect on the sparking potential curve. For example, the minimum sparking potential for air is about 330 V, while for neon it is about 240 V, with ordinary metals for electrodes.

When the voltage-current characteristic of a medium-length glow tube

(Fig. 10-3) is tested, the prebreakdown current is so small as not to be visible on the graph. At first the voltage falls as the current increases but later rises again. Light characteristic of the gas is given off from the *positive column* and from the negative *glow* as shown in the figure. Investigations have shown that the voltage drop between the cathode and the negative glow is approximately equal to the minimum breakdown voltage of the gas and that the voltage drop along the positive column is typically rather low. In fact, the positive column consists of a plasma region which will carry considerable current with a small voltage drop.

A glow tube specifically designed to produce a nearly constant voltage as the current is varied is shown in Fig. 10-4. This result is obtained by provid-

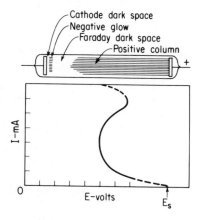

FIGURE 10-3   Glow discharge.

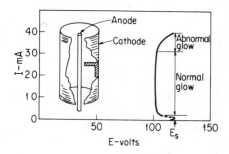

FIGURE 10-4   Voltage regulator tube and its characteristic.

ing a relatively small gap between the anode and the cathode and by providing a cathode of large area. What occurs as the current is varied over the range labeled *normal glow* is that the negative glow spreads over a greater and greater area of the cathode. After the negative glow completely covers the cathode and the current is increased still further, the so-called *abnormal glow* sets in. In this range the tube voltage rises with increasing current owing to an increasing cathode fall of potential.

The useful range of the tube as a voltage regulator device covers the normal glow range except for a short range at low currents. A small projection is welded onto the cathode to provide a variable length gap so that the tube is sure to break down at the minimum breakdown voltage. Voltage regulator tubes are applied in simple voltage regulating circuits and also are used to provide a reference voltage in some electronic voltage regulators.

Arcs take a variety of forms, such as the atmospheric-pressure welding arcs, or arcs in powerful searchlights, and the low-pressure arcs in fluorescent lamps and in hot-cathode and mercury-pool cathode rectifier tubes. An arc can be distinguished from a glow in terms of the voltage drop near the cathode. If this drop is below the minimum breakdown voltage for the gas, then the discharge is defined to be an arc. A typical voltage-current curve for a hot-cathode arc tube is shown in Fig. 10-5. Here the electron-emitting cathode labeled K is heated by an internal heater HH and the emitted electrons enter the plasma, which fills most of the space between the cathode and the anode. In this tube the voltage drop is nearly constant until the current exceeds the normal electron emission capability of the cathode. For a larger current demand the tube drop increases and thereby draws additional electrons from the cathode. If the current forced through the tube becomes too high, however, the tube drop may become high enough to lead to damage to the cathode. This occurs through the bombardment of the cathode by the positive ions from the plasma and leads to rapid disintegra-

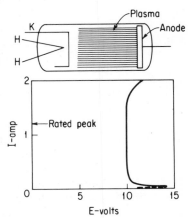

FIGURE 10-5   Hot-cathode gas diode.

tion of the oxide coating. This phenomenon accounts for the *peak current* rating of the tube and also for the necessity of heating the cathode before anode current is passed through the tube. Thus a *rated cathode heating time* must be observed before anode current may flow.

In rectifier circuits the gas diode has a great advantage over the high-vacuum diode in that its tube drop is lower. However, the presence of the gas tends to increase the possibility of a breakdown during the part of the cycle when the anode is negative, i.e., while the tube should act as an insulator. Such a breakdown is called an *arc back* or a *backfire* and is a special case of the spark discharge. In gaseous tubes containing a rare gas the voltage required to produce arc back is usually not over about 1200 V, but in tubes containing mercury vapor the arc back voltage is much higher. In mercury tubes the vapor pressure is highly dependent on the temperature in the coolest part of the tube, called the *condensed mercury temperature*. The arc back voltage decreases as this temperature increases, so the condensed mercury temperature is limited to a rated maximum value.

A decrease in the pressure in a mercury-vapor tube produces a pronounced increase in the tube drop while the tube is conducting; therefore it is necessary to specify a certain *minimum condensed mercury temperature* to avoid possible damage due to positive ion bombardment of the cathode.

10-4

The gas-filled triode (thyratron)

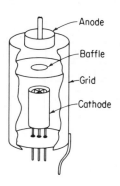

FIGURE 10-6 Electrode structure of negative-grid thyratron.

The thyratron combines the low tube-voltage drop of the arc tube with the grid control feature of the high-vacuum triode. But the function of the grid is very different in the thyratron than in the high-vacuum triode. The thyratron grid can only control the *start* of the arc or the instant of breakdown of the tube and cannot control the arc current after the discharge has started.

The grid structure in the thyratron is usually different from that of the triode (Fig. 10-6). The grid acts as a complete electrostatic shield between the anode and the cathode except for the hole, or holes, in the grid baffle. The internal action of the grid can best be described after an experimental method for the determination of the *grid-control* or *breakdown* characteristic has been explained. A suitable circuit for a test of a typical negative-grid thyratron is shown in Fig. 10-7. We assume that the voltage V_b is initially zero and that the grid bias V_c is -20 V. Then we adjust slider S_a so that V_b indicates 100 V. The anode current will still be zero. Now if the grid bias is gradually reduced, we shall observe the sudden appearance of a glow in the tube and an indication of an anode current. The reading of V_c at the point of breakdown (or just before the breakdown) is called the *critical grid voltage*. If, now, the slider S_g is varied, there will be no effect on the appearance of the discharge or on the anode current. Before the test can be repeated, the discharge must be stopped by removing the anode supply voltage.

If the test is repeated with a higher anode voltage, a somewhat larger negative critical grid voltage will be obtained. A curve showing anode voltage for breakdown versus grid voltage is called the *grid-control* or *breakdown*

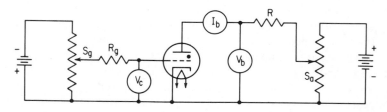

FIGURE 10-7 Circuit for determining thyratron grid-control characteristic.

characteristic of the thyratron. A single curve will suffice for an inert-gas-filled tube (Fig. 10-8a), but for mercury-vapor thyratrons the condensed mercury temperature has an effect (Fig. 10-8b). The catalog data furnished by the manufacturer shows a range for the control characteristic (Fig. 10-8c) within which the curve should fall over the rated range of temperature and for different tubes.

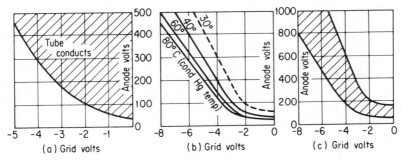

FIGURE 10-8   Grid control characteristics. (a) Inert gas-filled thyratron, (b) negative-grid, mercury thyratron, and (c) typical manufacturer's catalog data.

At the start of the foregoing experiment the grid potential is so far negative that the positive anode potential does not influence the electrons near the cathode. As the grid potential rises, the anode potential begins to have an effect, so that an occasional electron from the cathode can pass through the hole in the grid baffle. These electrons will begin to produce extra electrons and ions through ionization by collision. A slightly higher grid potential will allow an electron flow large enough to initiate an arc. The cathode-to-anode space is filled with a typical plasma, and the current is limited by the external anode-circuit resistance, such as *R* in Fig. 10-7. The tube drop is about the same as in a comparable gas diode.

The negatively charged grid tends to repel electrons and to attract positive ions. The relative sluggishness of the ions results in the formation of a positive *ion sheath* on the grid surfaces, in which a positive space charge predominates. This sheath is rather thin, extending only a fraction of a centimeter into the plasma. As the grid potential varies, the sheath thickness varies also. The net result is that the charges on the grid itself are effectively neutralized by the neighboring space charge; thus the grid voltage has a negligible control over the electrons and ions in the plasma.

If the grid were charged a few volts positive, an electronic space-charge sheath would develop on the grid, which would again shield the plasma from the action of the grid. If the grid potential is raised more than a few volts positive, the grid will act as an anode and an arc current may flow. This possibility can easily be prevented by inserting a resistance of about 50,000 Ω in series with the grid.

Thyratrons have cathode and anode current and voltage ratings like those of gas diodes. In addition, they have an anode voltage rating called the *peak forward voltage*. This is the maximum positive voltage on the anode which still permits consistent control of the breakdown by the grid.

The principal field of application of thyratrons is in controlled rectifiers in which a small amount of control power fed to the grids can control a large power going to the load. In this application the discharge in the tube is extinguished once in each cycle so that the grid regains control for the following cycle. An important factor here is the *time* required for the residual ions to disappear after the anode current goes to zero. For practical purposes, the *deionization time* of a thyratron is defined as the time required after the anode current interruption for the grid to regain control. If the anode voltage is reapplied too soon, the grid will not be able to prevent conduction. Though the deionization time depends on the circuit conditions and on the tube design, a typical value for a power type thyratron is 1000 μsec. It is the relatively long deionization time that prevents the application of a power thyratron when the frequency is above a few hundred cycles per second.

10-5
Grid current in thyratrons; shield-grid thyratron

The magnitude of the grid current is important in the operation of thyratrons, particularly when the grid is controlled from a high impedance source. Besides the current caused by insulation leakage current, it is possible to have grid current caused by the presence of positive ions in the tube even before breakdown occurs. This current typically increases to a maximum of a few tenths of a microampere at the point of breakdown. After the tube breaks down, the grid current increases enormously. In the conducting state at a negative grid potential of several volts, the grid current is a result of the discharge of positive ions on the grid, which come from the surrounding positive ion sheath. When the grid potential approaches zero, the electrons from the plasma begin to penetrate the sheath so that the grid is collecting positive ions and electrons simultaneously. For positive grid potentials the grid current rises rapidly owing to the rapid increase in the number of electrons attracted to the grid.

An important reduction in the value of the grid current is effected in the *shield-grid* thyratron by the introduction of a second grid. The shield grid

surrounds the anode and cathode, whereas the control grid is a smaller structure, in the form of a ring or elongated loop, which is placed opposite a hole
or slot in a baffle in the shield grid. The control grid can initiate the discharge
with a prebreakdown grid current of the order of 10^{-8} A.

10-6
Phase-shift circuit
for thyratron control

The basic idea of thyratron control of load current was explained in Sec.
8-8, without, however, showing how the firing angle can be controlled. One
grid-control circuit for this purpose is shown in Fig. 10-9a. This is a bridge

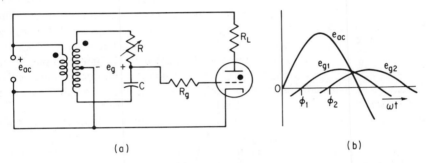

(a)   (b)

FIGURE 10-9   Phase-shift circuit for control of thyratron grid.

circuit which has the property of delivering a lagging grid signal wave e_g
whose phase lag can be varied by varying the resistance R. The magnitude
of the wave does not change, as illustrated by waves e_{g1} and e_{g2} in Fig. 10-9b,
where the angles of lag are labeled ϕ_1 and ϕ_2. The thyratron will fire when the
grid wave rises above the critical value, which is a slowly varying function
of the anode voltage. If e_g has a peak value of about 40 to 50 V and if the
critical grid voltages are a few volts negative, then the thyratron will fire
at angles a little earlier than ϕ_1 and ϕ_2 in the figure. It can be shown that e_g
lags e_{ac} by the angle

$$\phi = 2 \tan^{-1} \omega CR \qquad (10\text{-}1)$$

Another useful scheme of grid control is to combine a 90° lagging constant
ac wave with a variable dc signal. This control scheme and a number of others
are described by Ryder.†

†J. D. Ryder, *Engineering Electronics*, McGraw-Hill Book Company, New York, 1957.

10-7
The ignitron

The power industry has used glass-bulb or metal-tank mercury-pool-cathode arc rectifiers for many years. The ignitron was developed as an improved

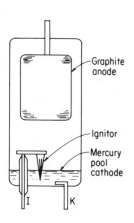

pool-cathode rectifier. In this tube (Fig. 10-10) the arc must be started anew every time conduction is to take place. For example, if the ignitron is used in a 60-cycle rectifier circuit the arc must start and stop 60 times each second. The arc is started by sending a positive pulse of current from the ignitor into the mercury pool. The ignitor consists of a tapered pencil of crystalline semiconductor material like silicon carbide. When a current of about 30 A at, say, 150 V is passed from ignitor to the mercury, a small arc starts at the point where the ignitor dips into the mercury. If the anode is positive to the cathode, the arc started by the ignitor will be transferred to the anode and thereby permit load current to pass from anode to cathode during the remainder of the positive part of the cycle. When the anode becomes negative, the arc goes out and the tube rapidly deionizes. The arc must be restarted by means of the ignitor at the beginning of each period of conduction.

FIGURE 10-10 Schematic diagram of an ignitron.

Ignitron tubes are used mainly in the control of resistance welders and in high-power polyphase rectifiers but are also used to control high-current

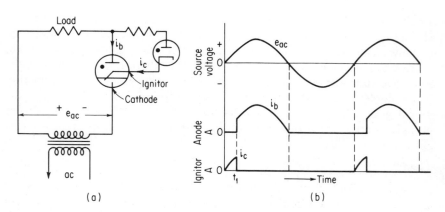

(a)

(b)

FIGURE 10-11   Elementary ignitron rectifier, (a) Circuit diagram and (b) waveforms.

capacitor discharges of many thousand amperes in thermonuclear fusion experiments.

An explanation of the elementary ignitron rectifier circuit in Fig. 10-11 will illustrate the function of the ignitor. In this circuit an alternating voltage is impressed on a series circuit containing a load resistor and the ignitron tube. The ignitor is supplied through a gas diode so that current can flow only from the ignitor to the mercury pool.

At the beginning of the positive half-cycle of voltage there is no current to the anode of the ignitron i_b, but there will be a current through the diode to the ignitor, as shown by the wave form i_c. However, when the ignitor current is large enough to start an arc, for example at instant t_1, the tube starts to conduct; thus the anode current i_b starts and continues to the end of the positive half-cycle. During this interval the voltage across the ignitron is only the relatively low arc drop. This voltage is insufficient to force an appreciable current through the diode into the ignitor, so the ignitor current i_c goes to zero while the tube is conducting. When the voltage reverses, neither the ignitron nor the diode will conduct, so the resulting load current wave represents a unidirectional pulsating current.

REFERENCES

10-1 James D. Cobine, *Gaseous Conductors*, Dover Publications, Inc., New York, 1958.

10-2 Jacob Millman, *Vacuum-tube and Semiconductor Electronics*, McGraw-Hill Book Company, New York, 1958, Chaps. 12 and 13.

EXERCISES

10-1 What is the relative importance of the positive and negative charges in carrying the current in a plasma? How does the situation in the plasma compare with that in a semiconductor?

10-2 What is the distinguishing feature between a normal glow and an abnormal glow?

10-3 What distinguishes a glow discharge from an arc discharge?

10-4 Why must the cathode of a power thyratron tube be heated for a definite time before anode current is allowed to flow?

10-5 Why does the variation of the grid potential in a conducting thyratron have little or no effect on the anode current?

10-6 Discuss the variation of thyratron grid current with the grid voltage (a) before breakdown and (b) in the conducting state.

10-7 Analyze Fig. 10-9a with the object of the verification of Eq. (10-1). Suggestion: Label the branches of the bridge network with voltage and current symbols and develop a phasor diagram that derives E_g from E_{ac}.

11

Rectifier Circuits, Filters, and dc Power Supplies

11-1
Half-wave and full-wave rectifier circuits

Nearly all electronic systems require one or more dc power supply circuits, which generally take power from the ac line, then rectify it and pass it through a smoothing filter. In this chapter we shall consider the circuits used in these power supplies.

In Chapter 3 a number of thermionic and semiconductor rectifying devices were described. Of these, the semiconductor junction diode is predominant today on account of its small size, low forward voltage drop, and small reverse leakage current. In the circuit diagrams in this chapter we shall use the symbol for a semiconductor diode, but of course thermionic devices may be substituted. To simplify the circuit analysis we shall treat the diode as an ideal device. Thus we assume that it acts like a switch, with zero voltage drop while conducting and zero reverse leakage in the reverse direction. More specialized works can be consulted if the small effects of the nonideal rectifier action need to be considered.

a. Half-wave rectifier circuit with resistance load

Consider the elementary circuit in Fig. 11-1a showing a source voltage

263

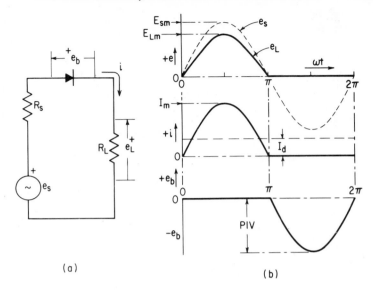

FIGURE 11-1   Half-wave rectifier, (a) circuit diagram and (b) waveforms.

e_s which supplies current through the source resistance R_s and the diode to the resistance load R_L. The wave forms of voltage and current in this circuit are illustrated in Fig. 11-1b. The load current and voltage waves have a sinusoidal shape for the first half-cycle and are zero during the second half-cycle. During the reverse half-cycle all the source voltage appears across the diode. Then the peak reverse voltage (PRV) for this circuit is E_{sm}, i.e., the peak value of the source voltage.

Let the source voltage be expressed as

$$e_s = E_{sm} \sin \omega t \qquad (11\text{-}1)$$

During the conducting half-cycle this voltage is consumed by the drops across R_s and R_L in series, so the current wave is expressible as

$$i = \frac{E_{sm}}{R_s + R_L} \sin \omega t = I_m \sin \omega t \qquad (11\text{-}2)$$

Now we inquire about the *average* or *dc value* of the load current wave, This wave consists of a sine-shaped half-cycle plus a half-cycle of zero current. Recalling that the average value is the area under the curve divided by the period and using angular measure in the calculation, we find

$$I_{dc} = \frac{1}{2\pi} \int_0^{\pi} I_m \sin \omega t \, d(\omega t) = \frac{I_m}{\pi} = 0.318 \, I_m \qquad (11\text{-}3)$$

Because the load voltage also has a half-sine wave shape, having a peak value given by

$$E_{Lm} = \frac{R_L}{R_s + R_L} E_{sm} \qquad (11\text{-}4)$$

the direct load voltage is given by

$$E_{dc} = \frac{1}{\pi} E_{Lm} \qquad (11\text{-}5)$$

Usually the rms value of the source voltage, designated by E_s, is known, so we need to recall that $E_{sm} = \sqrt{2}\,E_s$ in order to calculate the load voltage and current.

b. Full-wave rectifier circuit with resistance load

This circuit, which is also called the bi-phase, half-wave circuit, is shown in Fig. 11-2a. The secondary winding on the transformer is a continuous winding from point P to point M. At an instant when M is positive compared with the center tap at point N, then point P is negative to N. As shown in Fig. 11-2b, the current i_1 flows during the first half-cycle, while e_{s1} is positive.

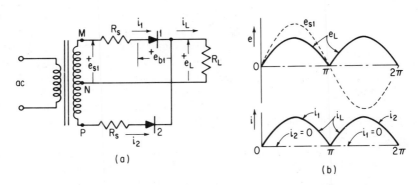

FIGURE 11-2   Full-wave rectifier, (a) Circuit diagram and (b) waveforms.

During the second half-cycle the other end of the winding at P becomes positive to the neutral at N, so that current i_2 flows as shown in the figure. The result is a pulsating direct load current wave that consists of the sum of i_1 and i_2.

The average current in the load will obviously be twice as great as for the half-wave rectifier for the same maximum values, so we have

$$I_{dc} = \frac{2}{\pi} I_m = 0.636 I_m \qquad (11\text{-}6)$$

Similarly the average load voltage will be

$$E_{\text{dc}} = \frac{2}{\pi} E_{Lm} \qquad (11\text{-}7)$$

where E_{Lm}, the peak of the load voltage, is given by Eq. (11-4).

To simplify the analysis for the peak reverse voltage, we assume that R_L is high compared with R_s so that the peak of the voltage across the load can be taken to be E_{sm}. Now consider the instant when e_{s1} is at its negative peak. At this instant the current i_2 through diode 2 produces a voltage E_{sm} across the load. If, now, we apply Kirchhoff's voltage law around the circuit that includes e_{s1}, diode 1, and the load, we find that there are two voltages, each of value E_{sm}, that are additive in polarity. As a result, the voltage across the nonconducting diode 1 is $2E_{sm}$, which is the peak reverse voltage sought.

c. *Single-phase bridge circuit*

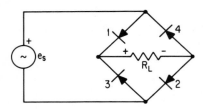

FIGURE 11-3   Single-phase bridge rectifier circuit.

A diamond or bridge arrangement of four diodes as shown in Fig. 11-3 provides a full-wave output current to the load R_L from the ac source e_s. On the half-cycle when e_s is positive, current passes through diode 1, then through the load, and returns through diode 2 to the source. On the other half-cycle the path of the current is through diode 3, the load, and diode 4. The nonconducting diodes are subjected to the ac source voltage, so the peak reverse voltage equals the peak of the source voltage wave.

A simple rectifier-type ac voltmeter uses the bridge circuit arrangement of semiconductor diodes. In this application the load resistance R_L is replaced by a microammeter and a high-value resistor is placed in series with the bridge on the ac side.

11-2
Elementary polyphase
rectifier circuits

When dc power outputs above 1 or 2 kW are required, it is often more economical to use a polyphase rectifier circuit. These give a higher number of pulsations per second in the output, so that filtering the output to smooth the wave is easier. Such circuits are found in high-power oscillators, radio and TV stations, electrochemical plants, and the like.

a.   Three-phase delta-wye connection

This circuit is shown in Fig. 11-4. The diagram uses the conventional scheme in which a secondary winding of a particular phase, say $S3$, is shown in a position parallel to the primary winding, $P3$, of the same phase. There-

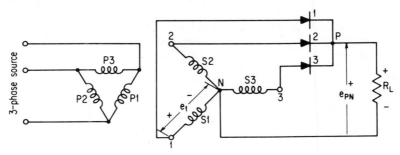

FIGURE 11-4   Three-phase delta-wye rectifier connection.

fore, assuming a phase order of 1, 2, 3, the secondary voltage waves e_1, e_2, and e_3 will follow in the order 1, 2, 3, with a 120° phase difference between successive waves (Fig. 11-5). The load is connected from the common cathode

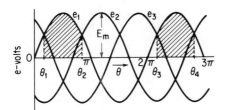

FIGURE 11-5   Three-phase voltage waves.

connection, point P, to the transformer secondary neutral, point N. If we regard point N as the reference point for potentials, then the wave e_1 gives the instantaneous potential of point 1 (relative to point N). We assert that during the interval from θ_1 to θ_2 point 1 has a potential more positive than points 2 or 3, so that diode 1 will conduct the load current during this interval. Since the diode forward drop is assumed to be small, the potential of point P will follow very closely below wave e_1. At instant θ_2 point 2 becomes more positive than point 1, so diode 1 ceases to conduct and diode 2 starts to conduct at this instant. The current is said to *commutate* or switch from the path through winding $S1$ and diode 1 to winding $S2$ and rectifier 2 at instant θ_2. For the present discussion we assume that this transfer occurs instantly, though it actually takes a brief time to complete, owing to the transformer inductance. If transformer and diode voltage drops are ignored, the load voltage e_{PN} will take the shape of a pulsating wave that follows the most positive portions of waves e_1, e_2, and e_3.

Figure 11-6a shows the load voltage wave and also wave e_1. We want to calculate the dc value of the load voltage. For this purpose it is convenient to take the zero of time at the peak of wave e_1, so that $e_1 = E_m \cos \theta$. The pulsations are identical, so the average ordinate of one pulsation gives the dc voltage; thus

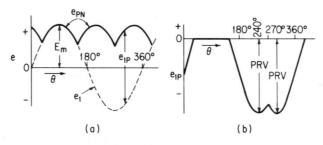

FIGURE 11-6   (a) Load voltage wave and (b) voltage wave across diode 1.

$$E_d = \frac{1}{\frac{2\pi}{3}} \int_{-\pi/3}^{\pi/3} E_m \cos \theta \, d\theta = \frac{3E_m}{\pi} \sin \frac{\pi}{3} = 0.827 E_m \qquad (11\text{-}8)$$

In comparison with the full-wave rectifier, the output wave has a higher dc value relative to the peak and a smaller ripple at a higher frequency and therefore is easier to filter to produce smooth direct current.

Next we examine the duty on the diodes as far as peak reverse voltage is concerned. The voltage across diode 1, call it e_{1P}, can be expressed in terms of the load voltage, e_{PN}, and the source voltage e_1; thus

$$e_{1P} = e_1 - e_{PN} \qquad (11\text{-}9)$$

This relation holds whether diode 1 is conducting or not. The wave obtained by the application of (11-9) is plotted in Fig. 11-6b. The two negative peaks give the peak reverse voltage. Analysis of the wave shows that the value of these peaks is

$$\text{PRV} = \sqrt{3}\, E_m \qquad (11\text{-}10)$$

and that they occur 30° on each side of the negative peak of wave e_1.

Because the load is resistive the load current wave is identical in form to that of e_{PN}. Thus the average current is 0.827 times the peak as obtained for the voltage in Eq. (11-8). Conversely, the peak current is 1.21 times the dc load current. An individual diode carries one-third of the dc load current, so it is subjected to a peak current that is 3×1.21 or 3.63 times the average current in the diode.

The current waveform, and therefore the quantitative relations, change when inductance or capacitance is associated with the load, as in the filter circuits to be considered presently.

b. Multiphase secondary connections

Sometimes four-phase or six-phase secondary connections are used. The greater the number of phases, the easier the output is to filter. However, the pulses of current in the transformer secondary windings become narrower. The narrower pulses have a higher rms value, so that the I^2R losses in the coils increase and the efficiency is lowered.

c. Three-phase wye, double-way (bridge) circuit

This circuit (Fig. 11-7a) is called a *double-way* circuit because the current in the transformer secondary coils flows alternately in both directions. Diodes

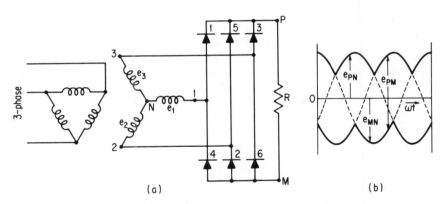

FIGURE 11-7   Three-phase bridge rectifier, (a) circuit and (b) waveforms.

1, 3, and 5 serve to maintain point *P* at the *most positive potential* of terminals 1, 2, or 3, just as in the three-phase one-way circuit. By adding diodes 2, 4, and 6 directed as shown, point *M* is maintained at the *most negative potential*

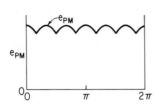

FIGURE 11-8   Load voltage wave in three-phase bridge rectifier circuit.

of the secondary terminals. The waves in Fig. 11-7b, which use the neutral point N as the reference, show how the potential at point P, e_{PN}, varies with reference to the neutral, and likewise at M, by the wave e_{MN}. The load voltage e_{PM} equals $e_{PN} - e_{MN}$, so that it equals the vertical distance between the heavy curves. The wave has six pulsations per cycle as shown in Fig. 11-8.

Further analysis will show that the peak of the load voltage equals $2E_m \cos 30°$, where E_m is the peak of one secondary coil voltage. Also the average, or dc, value of the load voltage is

$$E_d = \frac{12}{\pi} E_m \sin 30° \cos 60° = \frac{3\sqrt{3}}{\pi} E_m = 1.65 E_m \qquad (11\text{-}11)$$

Each diode is subjected to a peak reverse voltage of $2E_m \cos 30°$; therefore PRV $= 1.05 E_d$. This circuit is attractive owing to its relatively low PRV and its high ripple frequency.

11-3
Simple inductor or capacitor filters

The fluctuations of the output voltage are objectionable in most rectifier applications. When the requirements are not severe, simple single inductor or capacitor filters may reduce the fluctuation, or ripple, to a tolerable level. More elaborate filters are discussed in Sec. 11-5. The following treatment is restricted to the full-wave rectifier circuit which has zero source impedance.

a. Inductor filter

Assume that an inductor L of negligible resistance is connected in series with the load R (Fig. 11-9a). If we recall that an inductor tends to oppose changes in the current, we should expect that the current wave will be smoother than without the inductor, somewhat as shown in Fig. 11-9b.

A quantitative analysis for the current wave can be based on the Fourier expansion of the rectified voltage wave. Taking the origin for the ωt axis at the peak of the source voltage wave, the following infinite series of voltage terms results

$$e = \frac{2}{\pi} E_m + \frac{4}{3\pi} E_m \cos 2\omega t - \frac{4}{15\pi} E_m \cos 4\omega t + \cdots \qquad (11\text{-}12)$$

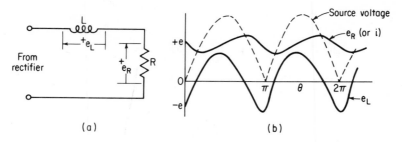

FIGURE 11-9   (a) Inductor and resistor in series. (b) Waveforms with single-phase, full-wave rectifier.

where E_m is the peak of the source voltage. On the basis of the *superposition principle* we say that each voltage term will cause a current component as if it were acting alone. For our purposes it will suffice to calculate the dc component plus the double frequency component, because the higher harmonic components rapidly approach zero. In this way we obtain the approximate current wave

$$i \cong \frac{2E_m}{\pi R} + \frac{4E_m}{3\pi[R^2 + (2\omega L)^2]^{1/2}} \cos(2\omega t - \psi) \qquad (11\text{-}13)$$

where

$$\psi = \tan^{-1}\frac{2\omega L}{R}$$

Now we can calculate the approximate fluctuation or ripple in the current wave. For example, if $R = 200\ \Omega$ and $\omega L = 400\ \Omega$ (1.06 H and 60 Hz), then the double frequency wave has an amplitude equal to 30 per cent of the dc component. If ωL is ten times as large, or 4000 Ω, then the ripple amplitude is only 3.3 per cent.

If voltage drops in the diode, inductor, and transformer are neglected, the direct voltage across the load resistor will be the average of the rectified source wave, or $2E_m/\pi$, or $2\sqrt{2}\ E_{rms}/\pi$, where E_{rms} is the rms value of voltage over half of the secondary winding.

b. *Capacitor in shunt with resistor*

A capacitor can be placed in parallel with the load resistor (Fig. 11-10a) to provide a simple type of filter. The capacitor stores charge during part of the cycle and releases the charge later in the cycle. The wave e_R in Fig. 11-10b, which represents the load voltage, can also be regarded as showing the form of the load current i_L. During the interval from the *cut-in angle* θ_1 to the *cut-out*

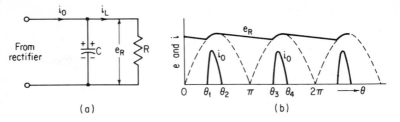

(a)   (b)

FIGURE 11-10   (a) Capacitor and resistor load. (b) Waveforms with single-phase, double-way rectifier.

angle θ_2 the rectifier delivers a pulse of current i_o, which serves to charge the capacitor nearly to the peak of the supply voltage wave (shown dotted in the figure). As the supply voltage falls after the instant θ_2, the capacitor supplies the entire load current until instant θ_3 is reached. Then the cycle of charge and discharge is repeated. With large values of load resistance the load voltage will drop only slightly during the cycle, but under heavy loading the wave will drop sharply between voltage peaks.

During the capacitor discharge the voltage e_R falls according to the exponential relation

$$e_R = E_m \exp\left(\frac{-t}{RC}\right)$$

so that the rate of decay depends on the time constant RC. The wave form of the load voltage and of the diode current can be calculated exactly if necessary, but when the ripple voltage is small, say less than 10 per cent, an

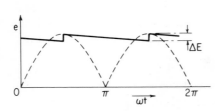

FIGURE 11-11   Approximation to load voltage wave in Fig. 11-10b.

approximate calculation can be made as follows. Let the actual wave (e_R in Fig. 11-10b) be replaced by the wave in Fig. 11-11. Here the voltage is assumed to drop linearly for a half period and then to rise instantly by the amount ΔE. For a wave of amplitude E_m and frequency f, the value of ΔE can be approximated by considering the discharge current to remain constant at the value E_m/R; then,

$$\Delta E = \frac{\Delta Q}{C} = \frac{It}{C} = \frac{E_m}{RC2f} \qquad (11\text{-}14)$$

For example, if $E_m = 400$ V, $R = 20,000\ \Omega$, $C = 20\ \mu$F, and $f = 60$ Hz, then ΔE works out to be 8.3 V. We note that the dc value of the load voltage wave is $E - \Delta E/2$, which in this example equals $400 - 4.1$, or 395.9 V.

Owing to the high peaks of diode current there is danger of damage to the diodes. The effect of transformer impedance is to reduce the peak current. Information can be found in the rectifier manufacturer's handbooks on the minimum allowable source resistance for use with different capacitors and also on the voltage regulation that will be obtained.

11-4
Voltage doubler circuits

Figure 11-12 shows two circuits which develop a dc output voltage approximately twice the peak value of the ac source voltage. In Fig. 11-12a diode 1 charges C_1 to nearly the peak voltage of the source on one half-cycle, and diode 2 does likewise for C_2 on the alternate half-cycle. When the load current is small, the total load voltage is nearly twice the peak of the ac source voltage.

The circuit in Fig. 11-12b operates on a different principle. During the *negative* half-cycle of e_s, diode 1 allows C_1 to charge to the peak of the source voltage with the polarity shown. Near the peak of the *positive* half-cycle of e_s diode 2 conducts to charge C_2. However, at this instant the charge remaining on C_1 causes C_1 to act like a voltage source nearly equal to the peak of the ac source. As a result, C_2 charges to a voltage nearly double the peak of the ac source voltage, assuming small load currents.

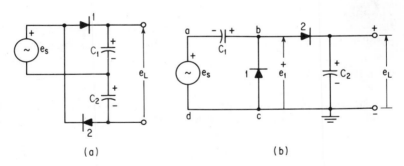

(a)   (b)

FIGURE 11-12   Voltage doubler circuits.

Under load the doubler circuits have an output voltage ripple which restricts their use except with high resistance loads. Circuits related to those in Fig. 11-12 have been devised that produce three, four, or more times the peak source voltage. Voltage doubler and voltage multiplier circuits are used in high-voltage X-ray and particle accelerator supplies.

11-5
Smoothing filters

When the dc output wave must have less ripple than is obtainable with a single inductor or capacitor, the more complex filters shown in Fig. 11-13 are used. The *inductor input* filter in Fig. 11-13a provides smoothing action both because the inductor tends to maintain the current constant and also because the capacitor tends to hold the load voltage constant. Filters similar to these are common in the power supplies for amplifiers and electronic instruments.

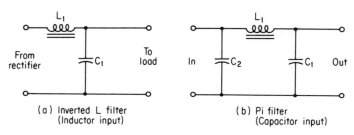

(a) Inverted L filter
(Inductor input)

(b) Pi filter
(Capacitor input)

FIGURE 11-13   Types of smoothing filters.

The effect of capacitor C_2 in the *capacitor input*, or π-*section*, filter (Fig. 11-13b) is to cause the rectifier current to be delivered in pulses similar to those in Fig. 11-10b. These high peaks of current may be detrimental to the rectifier elements. The capacitor input configuration does have the advantage that it delivers a higher output voltage than the other circuit. Typical values of inductance used in these filters are from 5 to 30 H and of capacitance from 8 to 100 μF.

The load voltage falls with increasing load current owing to the effect of the resistance and reactance of the transformer windings, the diode voltage drop and the RI voltage drop in the filter inductor. In low-power rectifiers with filters the drop of voltage may be rather large (see Fig. 11-14), whereas in large polyphase power rectifiers the voltage may remain nearly constant.

Attention should be called to some of the features of the curves in Fig. 11-14. For example, the no-load voltages for the three circuits including filters are all the same. This is evidence of the fact that at no load the filter capacitor charges up to the peak of the ac supply voltage. An explanation of the sudden drop in the load voltage to a value of about $2E_m/\pi$ in the low current range for the inductor-input filter is found in the manner in which the current flows through the inductor L_1. At the higher currents, where the voltage regulation curve is relatively flat, the current flows continuously

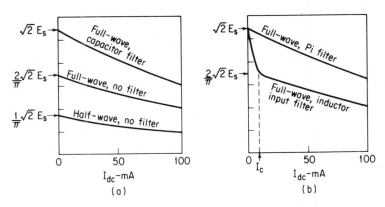

FIGURE 11-14   Voltage regulation curves for low-power rectifiers.

through L_1 with a wave form like that in Fig. 11-9b and with an output voltage about equal to the average of the input voltage wave. At low currents the capacitor tends to charge to the peak of the voltage wave, so the current through L_1 comes in short pulses and the voltage is higher. A *bleeder* resistor is usually connected across the output terminals of this circuit to discharge the filter capacitor upon removal of the load, and this resistor can be chosen to provide enough load to avoid an excessive rise of voltage at no load.

11-6
Analysis of inductor-input filter

Further insight will be gained through an approximate calculation of the magnitude of the ripple in the load voltage and of the critical load current I_c at which the inductor-input filter circuit changes its mode of operation (Fig. 11-14b). Up to this point the current in L_1 passes in pulses with an intervening zero-current interval. As the load current increases, the pulses become wider, until at the current I_c we have a pulsating direct current which barely touches zero at one instant in the cycle.

Our calculation will be based on the same approximation as used in Sec. 11-3, namely, that only the dc and double frequency terms in the Fourier expansion for the voltage need be considered. Thus the reactances of L_1 and C_1, which will enter the calculations, will be those for the second harmonic frequency. For instance, if the supply frequency is 60 Hz and if $L_1 = 15$ H and $C_1 = 20$ μF ,the inductor has a reactance of 11,300 Ω and the capacitor of 66 Ω at 120 Hz. The load resistance shunting C_1 will usually be high compared with the reactance of C_1; for example, it would be 20,000 Ω at the critical condition if $I_c = 0.015$ A and $E_d = 300$ V. If the full load current is 100 mA, the corresponding load resistance would be 3000 Ω. Clearly then, the second harmonic current I_2 follows a path through L_1 and mainly through C_1, with only a small percentage shunted off through the load. Therefore the second harmonic voltage across the load can be approximated by calculating the value of $X_{C1}I_2$, where X_{C1} is the reactance of C_1 to the second harmonic frequency. Thus the effect of the load resistance is neglected.

First we calculate I_c. At the critical condition the peak of the second harmonic current just equals the direct component; so

$$I_c = I_{2m} \qquad (11\text{-}15)$$

The peak second harmonic current I_{2m} can be calculated by noting that the inductive reactance is the major component of the impedance to the second harmonic, so dividing the second harmonic voltage obtained from Eq. (11-12) by the reactance, we obtain

$$I_c = I_{2m} = \frac{4E_m}{3\pi 2\omega L_1} = \frac{2E_m}{3\pi\omega L_1} \qquad (11\text{-}16)$$

where ω is the radian frequency of the supply. Equation (11-16) can be solved for L_1 if it is desired to choose an inductor to give a particular value of I_c. As an example let $E_m = 400$ V, $\omega = 377$, and $I_c = 0.015$ A; then the required value of L_1 obtained from (11-16) is 15 H.

Under the approximations already discussed we see that the ripple voltage for any load current above I_c is constant and has the magnitude $I_{2m}X_{C1}$. Now I_{2m} is given in (11-16) so we obtain

$$E_{2m} = I_{2m}X_{C1} = \frac{E_m}{3\pi\omega^2 L_1 C_1} \qquad (11\text{-}17)$$

Expressed in terms of the direct voltage E_d, this becomes

$$E_{2m} = \frac{E_d}{6\omega^2 L_1 C_1} \qquad (11\text{-}18)$$

Using the values in the former example, we calculate $E_{2m} = 1.0$ V. If the ripple voltage is too high, the values of L_1 and C_1 can be increased, an additional L and C filter section can be interposed between the rectifier and the load, or a voltage regulator circuit (Sec. 11-8) can be added.

11-7
Diode voltage regulator circuits

The output voltage of the dc power supplies described thus far will vary directly with the ac line voltage. Often electronic equipment cannot tolerate the 5 or 10 per cent variations sometimes caused by line voltage changes.

Another problem arises when the load current demànded from the supply changes under different operating conditions, for such changes will cause variations in the direct voltage due to the voltage regulation of the power supply. Both types of variation can be greatly reduced by using a diode voltage regulator circuit or a feedback voltage regulator circuit.

A gaseous voltage regulator diode (Sec. 10-3) or the *breakdown diode* (or *Zener diode*) will hold a nearly constant voltage over a considerable range of current. The curves for two types of breakdown diode in Fig. 11-15 illus-

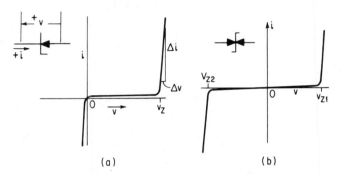

FIGURE 11-15   (a) Breakdown (Zener) diode characteristic. (b) Double breakdown diode characteristic.

trate this characteristic. The diode dynamic resistance in the breakdown region, defined as $r_D = \Delta v/\Delta i$, is a measure of the constancy of the voltage. These diodes are commonly available with breakdown voltages from 2.5 to 200 V. Like all semiconductor devices, they have a maximum temperature limitation, therefore a maximum power dissipation which limits the maximum current. This power limit varies from a fraction of a watt to 10 or more watts.

We want to analyze the regulator circuit in Fig. 11-16 for the situation in which the load resistance R_L can change from a minimum value R_{Lmn} to a maximum value R_{Lmx}. We regard R_s as the source resistance and R_1 as an

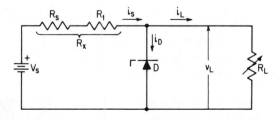

FIGURE 11-16   Shunt diode regulator circuit.

added resistor, so the source branch resistance totals R_x. We inquire how we should choose R_x to obtain good voltage regulation using a diode of known characteristic, if V_s, R_{Lmn}, and R_{Lmx} have been specified. The graphical construction in Fig. 11-17 will give a graphical solution to this problem, but once the relations are understood, the circuit can be designed without actually doing the graphical construction. First note that $i_s = i_L + i_D$ and that the voltage across the diode and across R_L are the same. Therefore we can construct the *combined characteristic* for the diode and R_L in parallel by taking any point on the diode curve, as at N, calculating i_L by Ohm's law, adding the currents and spotting the point N' at the total current value i_s. Using this procedure we obtain the combined characteristic curve $N'P'$ for the maximum load resistance, and $N''P''$ for the minimum load resistance.

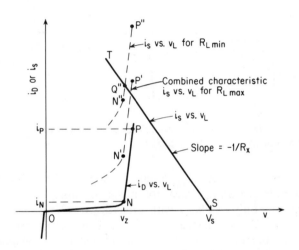

FIGURE 11-17   Analysis of shunt regulator circuit.

The combined characteristics show that the diode should not operate at a current below i_N, if the voltage is to remain nearly constant. The other limit on the operation is at the diode current i_P for the maximum safe diode current. Therefore, on the curve $N'P'$, for example, the desired operation is between points N' and P'.

Next we use the *load line* technique to choose R_x. If a line ST can be drawn from V_s at a slope $-1/R_x$ so as to intersect *both* curves $N'P'$ *and* $N''P''$ between their two limiting points, then we have a solution to the stated problem.

How do the currents vary as the load resistance is changed from R_{Lmn} to R_{Lmx}? With minimum load resistance the current i_L is high and i_D is low. These currents can be measured off in the graph; i_L is the vertical distance from the intersection point Q'' to the curve NP, and i_D is the remaining vertical distance to the voltage axis. As the load resistance increases, i_L decreases but i_D increases so as to keep the total nearly constant.

Practical diodes have such a steep slope on portion NP of their curves that we may assume that the total current remains constant. Thus a short-cut design method is to choose R_x so that i_s equals $i_N + v_z/R_{Lmn}$ and then make a calculation to insure that i_P is not exceeded with minimum load resistance. An example will illustrate the procedure. Let $V_s = 50$ V, $v_z = 30$ V, $i_N = 4$ mA, $i_P = 50$ mA (1.5 W dissipation), $R_{Lmn} = 0.5$ kΩ and $R_{Lmx} = 2$ kΩ. Assuming that v_L remains at 30 V, we calculate $i_s = i_N + v_z/R_{Lmn}$ and obtain $i_s = 4 + 30/0.5 = 64$ mA. Then $R_x = (V_s - v_z)/i_s = (50 - 30)/64 = 0.312$ kΩ. Next we calculate the minimum load current, which is 30/2, or 15 mA. Therefore the maximum diode current is $62 - 15$, or 47 mA, which is within the rating. If this value had exceeded i_P, a higher wattage diode would have to be chosen.

The graphical analysis is also suited to a study of the variation of V_s with a fixed R_L. In this situation R_x should be chosen so that as the load line moves parallel to itself with a varying V_s the intersection point with the combined characteristic remains between the two limit points.

An equivalent circuit model of the diode can also be used in the analysis of the problem of a varying source voltage. The elements r_D and V_z in Fig. 11-18 will represent the diode over small ranges of its characteristic. In this diagram we imagine that V_g represents the ripple voltage of the dc power supply and we ask about the ripple voltage across R_L. Using superposition, we consider only the varying voltage and calculate

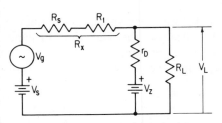

FIGURE 11-18   Regulator circuit incorporating diode model.

$$V_L = \frac{[r_D \| R_L]V_g}{R_x + [r_D \| R_L]} \tag{11-19}$$

For example if $V_g = 1$ V, $R_x = 500$, $r_D = 25$, and $R_L = 500$ Ω, then (11-19) yields a ripple voltage $V_L = 0.045$ V.

11-8
Voltage regulators using amplifiers

We shall discuss examples of two general types of voltage regulator circuits that use transistors or tubes as amplifying elements.

a. Shunt-type voltage regulator circuit

As its name implies, in this type the regulating element is in shunt with the load (Fig. 11-19). The regulating action can be described as follows. Suppose that V_s rises suddenly. Then V_L tends to rise, but V_z remains sensibly constant. As a result V_{BE} rises, which tends to increase I_C. But I_C is drawn through R_1, so the extra I_C gives an added voltage drop across R_1 that counteracts the initial change in V_s. Similar reasoning will show that the circuit tends to keep V_L constant when R_L varies.

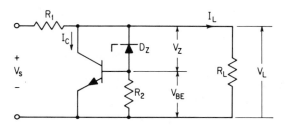

FIGURE 11-19   Shunt voltage regulator. V_s = dc source.

Before giving an analysis of this circuit, we define two factors that measure the efficacy of the regulation. Leaving aside the possible variation of V_L with the ambient temperature, we can think of V_L as a function of V_s and I_L; therefore we can write, for any regulator,

$$\Delta V_L = \frac{\partial V_L}{\partial V_s}\Delta V_s + \frac{\partial V_L}{\partial I_L}\Delta I_L \qquad (11\text{-}20)$$

It is convenient to define the coefficients in (11-20) as follows;

$$H_v \equiv \frac{\partial V_L}{\partial V_s} \quad \text{and} \quad r_0 \equiv \frac{\partial V_L}{\partial I_L} \qquad (11\text{-}21)$$

where H_v is called the *voltage regulation*, and r_0 the *output resistance* or *impedance*. The reciprocal of H_v, called the *stabilization factor*, is also used.

An approximate analysis for H_v and r_0 of the shunt regulator can be

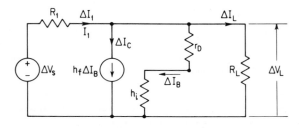

FIGURE 11-20   Incremental equivalent circuit for shunt regulator.

given with the aid of the equivalent circuit in Fig. 11-20. Here the *common emitter h* parameters are used, but h_r and h_o have been neglected. The break-down diode is replaced by its dynamic resistance r_D. We first assume an increment ΔV_s and calculate ΔV_L, assuming R_L remains constant. Applying Kirchhoff's laws,

$$\Delta V_L = \Delta V_s - R_1 \Delta I_1 \tag{11-22}$$

and

$$\Delta I_1 = \Delta I_C + \Delta I_B + \Delta I_L \tag{11-23}$$

By Ohm's law

$$\Delta I_B = \frac{\Delta V_L}{r_D + h_i} \tag{11-24}$$

Combining these relations, and using $\Delta I_L = \Delta V_L/R_L$ and $\Delta I_C = h_f \Delta I_B$ we can, after reduction, obtain

$$H_v = \frac{\Delta V_L}{\Delta V_s} = \frac{1}{1 + \dfrac{R_1}{R_L} + \dfrac{R_1(1 + h_f)}{r_D + h_i}} \simeq \frac{r_D + h_i}{R_1(1 + h_f)} \tag{11-25}$$

As an example assume that a power transistor, for which $h_f = 50$ and $h_i = 20\,\Omega$, is used in a circuit in which $V_s = 50$ V, $V_L \simeq 30$ V and that I_L varies up to 0.5 A. The minimum R_L is then 60 Ω. Also let r_D be 6 Ω. We choose R_1 as 25 Ω so that $I_1 \simeq 0.8$ A, and $I_C \simeq 0.3$ A when $I_L = 0.5$ A. Then substitution in (11-25) gives $H_v \simeq 0.020$. Thus the change in V_L is about 2 per cent of the change in V_s.

To calculate the output resistance r_o, we use the same equivalent circuit, except to assume that ΔV_s is zero and to replace R_L by an auxiliary voltage source of value ΔV_L. Then we write

$$\Delta I_1 = -\frac{\Delta V_L}{R_1} \tag{11-26}$$

Using (11-23) and (11-24) and recalling that $\Delta I_C = h_f \Delta I_B$, we can eliminate ΔI_1, ΔI_C, and ΔI_B, and obtain

$$r_o = -\frac{\Delta V_L}{\Delta I_L} = \frac{1}{\dfrac{1}{R_1} + \dfrac{1 + h_f}{r_D + h_i}} \simeq \frac{r_D + h_i}{1 + h_f} \tag{11-27}$$

Using the same exemplary values, we calculate $r_o = 0.51\,\Omega$. For these values the approximation in the last term in (11-27) would change r_o by about 2 per cent. An r_o of 0.51 Ω would cause a ΔV_L of 51 mV for a 100-mA change in load current.

The shunt regulator suffers from a low power efficiency, and the values of H_v and r_o may not be as low as desired. These factors can be improved by placing an additional transistor between the Zener diode and the regulating transistor to amplify the signal going to its base.

b. Series-type voltage regulator circuits

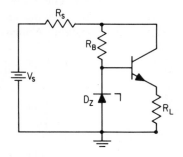

FIGURE 11-21   Emitter follower regulator.

The emitter follower regulator (Fig. 11-21) is a simple form of series regulator. If we recall the action of the emitter-follower (common-collector) amplifier, we can predict that the emitter-to-ground voltage (load voltage) will remain nearly equal to the base-to-ground voltage. In this circuit the latter voltage is stabilized by the breakdown diode D_z, so that the load voltage is also stabilized.

Two other series-type regulator circuits are shown in Fig. 11-22. In these circuits

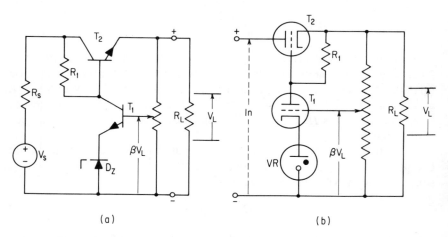

(a)   (b)

FIGURE 11-22   Elementary series regulators.

the voltage drop across the transistor or tube T_2 does the regulating. This drop is controlled by the amplifier stage T_1. In the transistor circuit stage T_1 gets its base-to-emitter voltage as the difference between a portion βV_L of the load voltage and the Zener diode voltage. In the tube circuit the grid-cathode signal is obtained similarly, except that a voltage regulator tube VR may be used for the constant reference voltage. The output of T_1 is applied to T_2 in such a sense as to correct any original disturbance in supply voltage or load current. For example, if R_L is suddenly reduced, V_L tends to fall. A fraction β of the reduction in V_L is applied to change the base or the grid potential of stage T_1. The output of T_1 is opposite in sense to its input.

Therefore T_2 gets a signal that tells it to conduct more freely, i.e., to pass the added current needed by the load, with only a small additional voltage drop. As a result V_L remains nearly constant.

These circuits also permit *adjustment* of the load voltage over a considerable range, say 3 to 1, if properly designed. Practical circuits are often more complex than those in Fig. 11-22. To obtain more precise regulation the stage T_1 is designed to give a greater voltage gain, as by using a multistage arrangement. Temperature effects in the transistor circuit are minimized by using a differential amplifier for stage T_1. Reference 11-4 shows a number of practical regulator circuits. Series regulators are used in the commercial regulated power supplies that are common in electronics laboratories.

c. *Analysis of a series voltage regulator circuit*

The regulator in Fig. 11-22b can be represented in a schematic way as in Fig. 11-23. With some modification the same approach can be applied

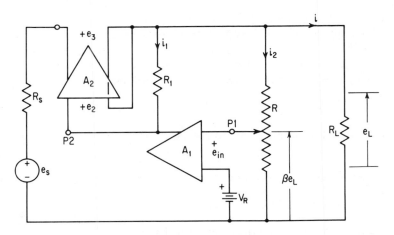

FIGURE 11-23   Schematic diagram of a series regulator.

to the transistor regulator circuit. We shall present an approximate analysis for the voltage regulation. For this purpose we choose to think in terms of a variable source voltage e_s taken to be a sine wave. Then e_L will be a sine wave (superimposed on a dc value in the actual circuit) and the amplifiers A_1 and A_2 will have sine-wave signals. In Fig. 11-24 the amplifiers are represented by their open-circuit (Thévenin) voltage output in series with their Thévenin resistance. For example, the input voltage to amplifier 1 is βe_L, and its *open-circuit* gain is taken as A_1, so that its equivalent circuit consists of the Thévenin generator $\beta A_1 e_L$ in series with the Thévenin resistance R_{01}. Am-

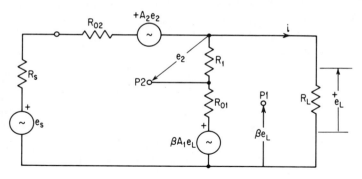

FIGURE 11-24   Diagram for analysis of series regulator.

plifier 2 is represented similarly. Generally the resistances R and R_1 in Fig. 11-23 are large compared with R_L at full load. To simplify the analysis, we neglect the effects of currents i_1 and i_2 in R_1 and R. Then the current in the source and in the load are taken to be the same.

To analyze Fig. 11-24 we first express e_2 in terms of e_L. The net voltage acting in the right-hand loop is $\beta A_1 e_L - e_L$, if we regard e_L as constant. Resistances R_{01} and R_1 form a voltage divider, so we can write a formula for e_2 by means of the voltage divider relation and obtain

$$e_2 = \frac{R_1}{R_1 + R_{01}}(\beta A_1 e_L - e_L) \tag{11-28}$$

The voltage law applied around the outer perimeter of the circuit yields

$$e_s - A_2 e_2 = (R_s + R_{02} + R_L)i \tag{11-29}$$

Next we replace i by e_L/R_L and e_2 by its value from (11-28) and solve for e_s

$$e_s = \left[\frac{A_2 R_1}{R_1 + R_{01}}(\beta A_1 - 1) + \frac{R_s + R_{02}}{R_L} + 1\right]e_L \tag{11-30}$$

Thus the voltage regulation is found to be

$$H_v = \frac{e_L}{e_s} = \frac{1}{\dfrac{A_2 R_1}{R_1 + R_{01}}(\beta A_1 - 1) + \dfrac{R_s + R_{02}}{R_L} + 1} \tag{11-31}$$

If both amplifiers are single triodes then $R_{01} = r_{p1}$ and $A_1 = -\mu_1$, and $R_{02} = r_{p2}$ and $A_2 = -\mu_2$ where the subscript numerals identify the tube. In this case Eq. (11-31) becomes

$$H_v = \frac{1}{\dfrac{\mu_2 R_1}{R_1 + r_{p1}}(\beta \mu_1 + 1) + \dfrac{R_s + r_{p2}}{R_L} + 1} \tag{11-32}$$

Substitution of typical numerical values in Eq. (11-32) shows that the first term in the denominator is the dominant term, so the others can be discarded to obtain the approximate formula

$$H_v \cong \frac{R_1 + r_{p1}}{\mu_2 R_1 (\beta \mu_1 + 1)} \tag{11-33}$$

Tube 2 must carry the full load current and therefore is generally a low-μ, high-current tube. Therefore tube 1 should be a high-μ triode or a pentode to give a low voltage regulation.

If we let $\mu_1 = 100$, $\mu_2 = 4$, $r_{p1} = 80$ kΩ, $\beta = 0.3$, and $R_1 = 120$ kΩ, then (11-33) gives $H_v = 0.0134$ or a 1.34 per cent regulation.

An analysis of Fig. 11-24 to find the output resistance r_o viewed from the load terminals, subject to the same approximations as before, yields the formula

$$r_o = \frac{(R_s + R_{o2})(R_1 + R_{o1})}{R_1 + R_{o1} + R_1 A_2 (\beta A_1 - 1)} \tag{11-34}$$

Replacing the output resistance and gain symbols by those for single tube amplifiers, we find

$$r_o = \frac{(R_s + r_{p2})(R_1 + r_{p1})}{R_1 + r_{p1} + R_1 \mu_2 (\beta \mu_1 + 1)} \tag{11-35}$$

If we substitute the values used before, plus values of $R_s = 1$ kΩ and $r_{p2} = 1$ kΩ, we find $r_o = 26$ Ω. This value is higher than those found in high-grade commercial regulators. We conclude by remarking that because we have used small-signal parameters in the foregoing analysis, the results are really only good for small increments. Actual regulators often require the transistor or tube to work over large ranges of their characteristics. In this event the theory can only give a rough guide to the true behavior.

REFERENCES

11-1 W. D. Cockrell, ed., *Industrial Electronics Handbook*, McGraw-Hill Book Company, New York, 1958, Secs. 3a–3g.

11-2 R. A. Greiner, *Semiconductor Devices and Applications*, McGraw-Hill Book Company, New York, 1961, Chap. 16.

11-3 J. Millman, *Vacuum-tube and Semiconductor Electronics*, McGraw-Hill Book Company, New York, 1958, Chaps. 14, 19.

11-4 *Handbook Preferred Circuits*, by National Bureau of Standards, Dept. of Commerce, for Bureau of Aeronautics, Dept. of the Navy, v. 1: NAVAER 16-1-519, 1955; v. 2: NAVAER 16-519-2, 1962, U.S. Government Printing Office, Washington, D.C.

11-5 Gutzwiller, Bacon, Zastrow, and Rottier, *Rectifier Components Guide*, 2d ed., General Electric Co., Auburn, N.Y., 1962.

11-6 *Silicon Zener Diode and Rectifier Handbook*, 2d ed., Semiconductor Products Div., Motorola, Inc., Phoenix, Ariz., 1961.

11-7 *Zener Diode Handbook HB-20A*, 1960; *Engineering Handbook*, 1959; International Rectifier Corp., El Segundo, Calif.

11-8 J. A. Walston and J. R. Miller, eds., *Transistor Circuit Design*, McGraw-Hill Book Company, New York, 1963, Chap. 9.

EXERCISES

Note: In the following exercises the diodes and transformers are to be considered as ideal, unless specifically stated otherwise.

11-1 A semiconductor diode is to be used in a half-wave rectifier circuit supplied directly by a 60-cycle power line of 120 V rms. The load resistance is 5000 Ω, and the source resistance is negligible. What are the requirements on the diode on (a) average current, (b) peak current, and (c) peak reverse voltage? (d) What is the value of the power delivered to the load?

11-2 A half-wave rectifier is supplied in the same way as in Exercise 11-1. The load resistor is shunted by a large capacitor, so that the ripple voltage at the load is negligible. What is the peak reverse voltage on the diode?

11-3 In the full-wave rectifier circuit in Fig. 11-2 the transformer secondary voltage is 300 *peak* V on each side of the mid-tap and $R_s = 10 \ \Omega$. (a) If the diode maximum average current rating is 200 mA, what is the lowest safe value of R_L? (b) What is the peak reverse voltage sustained by each diode?

11-4 Assume that the source in the circuit in Fig. 11-3 is a 120-rms-V 60-cycle ac line that is grounded on one side. (a) If $R_L = 1000 \ \Omega$, what is the direct current in the load? (b) If the negative end of R_L is accidentally grounded, what would the results be?

11-5 Assume that $e_L = 10,000$ V in the two circuits in Fig. 11-12. (a) What is the required peak value of e_s and what are the peak reverse voltages across diodes 1 and 2 in Fig. 11-12a? (b) Repeat for Fig. 11-12b.

11-6 Sketch waveforms of the currents in diodes 1 and 2 in Fig. 11-4 for two conditions of commutation: (a) instantaneous and (b) slightly delayed owing to transformer inductance.

11-7 (a) Derive an expression for the dc voltage in relation to the peak transformer secondary voltage for a polyphase connection which has a six-phase secondary connection. (b) What is the peak reverse voltage on a diode in this connection?

11-8 Label the diode currents i_1, i_2, etc. in Fig. 11-7 and prepare a diagram that shows all the diode current waveforms on a common time scale.

11-9 (a) Extend Eq. (11-13) to three terms; that is, add the current component of frequency 4ω. (b) What is the ratio of the amplitude of the 4ω term to that of the 2ω term if $R = 200$ and $\omega L = 400\ \Omega$?

11-10 A filter capacitor shunts the resistance load in a half-wave rectifier circuit. Let $E_m = 300$ V, $R_L = 20,000\ \Omega$, and $f = 400$ Hz. Find an approximate value of capacitance required to keep the peak-to-peak ripple voltage below 3 V.

11-11 A full-wave rectifier feeds a resistance $R_L = 2000\ \Omega$ through an inductor input filter of the type in Fig. 11-13a. The peak value of ac source voltage on each side of the transformer center-tap is 50 V and the frequency is 400 Hz. A 2-H inductor is to be used and the ripple voltage should be kept under 0.01 V peak. (a) Choose a value for the filter capacitor. (b) What is the direct load current? (c) What is the value of the critical current I_c?

11-12 A breakdown diode is used in the shunt regulator circuit of Fig. 11-16. The diode data follow: $v_z = 18$ V, $i_N = 1$ mA, slope of characteristic over the range N to $P = 0.05$ A/V, and $P_{\mathrm{dis}} = 1.0$ W. Suppose that the load resistance is to vary from 400 to 4000 Ω and the dc source remains constant at 30 V. (a) Choose a suitable value of R_x for this circuit. (b) Would a 0.5-W diode be satisfactory in this circuit? (c) What is an approximate value for the change of load voltage for the given range of load resistance change?

11-13 A shunt diode regulator circuit as in Fig. 11-16 has a source which includes a ripple voltage of 0.4 V rms. Assume that $R_x = 200\ \Omega$ and $R_L = 400\ \Omega$. Find the dynamic resistance of the diode that is required if the ripple voltage across the load should not exceed 0.020 rms V.

11-14 If the load resistance R_L in Fig. 11-19 is decreased, a condition will be reached beyond which the circuit will fail to regulate. (a) Give a qualitative explanation of this action and of the limiting condition. (b) Estimate the load current at this limiting condition for the circuit used as a numerical example in Sec. 11-8a.

11-15 A high-grade series regulator has nominal voltages of 50 V at the input and 30 V at the load. Up to a load current of 200 mA the values of regulation and output resistance may be taken to be 0.002 and 1.5 Ω respectively. (a) If the input voltage has a 3 per cent ripple, what is the ripple (in millivolts) in the load voltage at 50 mA load current? (b) If the supply voltage is held constant, what is the change in load voltage in millivolts when the load current is increased from 40 to 80 mA?

12

Oscillator and
Inverter Circuits

12-1
Introduction

An oscillator circuit takes power from a dc source and converts it into a fluctuating or oscillating output. The principal classes of oscillators include the (1) relaxation, (2) negative resistance, and (3) feedback types. Type 3 can be further subdivided into *RC* feedback, electromechanical, and *LC* circuit types. An allied type of circuit is the inverter. We shall give a descriptive account of examples of several classes of oscillators, with a minimum of analysis. Most oscillators operate with relatively large voltage swings over the transistor or tube characteristics so that the resulting nonlinearities make exact analysis rather difficult. Often small-signal theory can be used to give some information about the oscillation, but this type of analysis has definite limitations.

12-2
Thyratron sawtooth generator

An example of a *relaxation* oscillator circuit is shown in Fig. 12-1a. In a relaxation oscillator the circuit changes back and forth between two states. These changes are controlled by the discharging or charging of a capacitor, hence the term "relaxation." The output voltage wave is nonsinusoidal and

288

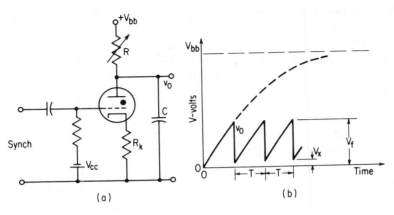

FIGURE 12-1   Thyratron saw-tooth generator.

is rich in harmonics. The oscillation frequency can easily be stabilized at an integral submultiple of another frequency. This is done by feeding a small stabilizing voltage into the oscillator circuit; then the oscillator is said to be *synchronized* with the other frequency.

We focus attention first on the R and C elements in Fig. 12-1a. Assume that C is discharged and then voltage $+V_{bb}$ is applied. The capacitor (and output) voltage v_o will start to rise on the usual exponential curve. Owing to the bias V_{cc} the thyratron will not conduct at first, but when v_o reaches V_f, the thyratron fires. The capacitor C discharges through the tube and the low-value current-limiting resistor R_k. When the capacitor voltage drops to the voltage V_x, of about 20 V, the ionization in the tube disappears, so that the tube becomes insulating again. Then the charging and discharging processes are repeated, as shown in Fig. 12-1b, and the sawtooth wave results.

If we assume that the circuit behavior is as described and we neglect the time taken for C to discharge, we can derive a formula for the period T, or for the frequency f, and find

$$f \cong \frac{1}{RC \ln \dfrac{V_{bb} - V_x}{V_{bb} - V_f}} \tag{12-1}$$

Thus, f can be controlled by means of R, C, V_{bb}, or V_f. With values of V_{bb} of about 300 V, values of R from about 100 kΩ to 3 MΩ, and of C from 0.01 to 0.2 μF may be used. If R is made too small, the tube will fail to de-ionize and the circuit will not oscillate. The upper frequency limit, using thyratrons designed for this service, is about 20 to 30 kHz.

We note that f depends on V_f, so that if the bias V_{cc} is changed, the frequency will change. Alternatively, a small ac signal voltage (1 V) fed in at the terminal marked SYNCH will cause a variation in V_f. This will *synchro-*

nize the sawtooth output to the signal, at least over a limited range of adjustment of the circuit constants.

This sawtooth wave generator is used to produce the linear sweep voltage in some cathode-ray oscilloscopes. In this application V_f is kept low relative to V_{bb} to improve the linearity and an amplifier is added to give the required output.

12-3

Negative resistance oscillators

Perhaps the simplest oscillator comprises a parallel LC-tuned circuit, a bias voltage V_B, and a two-terminal device that has a negative dynamic resistance over a portion of its characteristic (Fig. 12-2). Examples of such devices are the semiconductor *tunnel diode* and the high-vacuum tetrode.

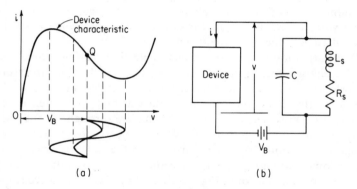

FIGURE 12-2   Negative resistance oscillator.

Our approach will be to use linear theory, notwithstanding its limitations when applied to the nonlinear device. We note that the dynamic resistance r, defined by $r = dv/di$, is *negative* at point Q in the device characteristic. Therefore, an assumed variation in v, as shown at the bottom of Fig. 12-2a, will be accompanied, *not* by a *loss* of power in the device, but by a *generation* of power at the ac frequency. If the reader will visualize the sine waves of v and the corresponding wave of i, he will see that these are 180° out of phase, which corresponds to power output. What becomes of this power? It can only flow into the tuned circuit to maintain the oscillations, that is, to supply the losses in R_s.

Let us develop this idea a bit further. If the frequency is known, the LC circuit can be represented by an equivalent circuit with a parallel resistor R, as in Fig. 12-3. Since we are interested in the ac components, this figure is drawn as an ac equivalent circuit. Let us assume that if the small-signal r is measured at the Q point, we find that $|r| < R$, that is, the negative resistance has a smaller magnitude than R. We assert that the slightest disturbance will start an oscillation at a radian frequency of $1/\sqrt{LC}$. At first, with the small oscillation, more power will

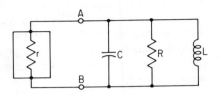

FIGURE 12-3   Linear small-signal equivalent circuit for negative resistance oscillator.

be developed in r than is absorbed in R. The excess goes into building up the level of the oscillation, i.e., into the stored energy circulating between L and C.

What limits the buildup? A consideration of Fig. 12-2a suggests a crude explanation. As the oscillation becomes larger, the operation extends over a range in which the slope of the curve is less. An *average* negative resistance over the cycle, which increases in magnitude as the oscillation amplitude rises, may be defined. On this basis we say that the oscillation stabilizes when $|r| = R$. A more detailed discussion of this phenomenon is given by Arguimbau and Adler.[†]

Let us write down the expressions for L and R in the equivalent circuit in terms of L_s, R_s, and ω; thus,

$$L = \frac{R_s^2 + \omega^2 L_s^2}{\omega^2 L_s} \cong L_s \qquad (12\text{-}2)$$

and

$$R = \frac{R_s^2 + \omega^2 L_s^2}{R_s} \cong \frac{\omega^2 L_s^2}{R_s} \qquad (12\text{-}3)$$

where the approximations are for the case when $R_s^2 \ll \omega^2 L_s^2$, or in terms of the quality factor Q of the inductive branch when $Q^2 \gg 1$.

Suppose that a negative resistance device has $r = -8000\ \Omega$ at point Q and that we desire an ω of 10^7 rad/s and have a coil of $L_s = 40\ \mu\text{H}$. What is the largest value that R_s can have before oscillations will cease and what value should C have? We assume that we can use the approximate formulas in (12-2) and (12-3). First use (12-3) and replace R by $|r|$, or $8000\ \Omega$, and solve for R_s, which yields $20\ \Omega$. If $R_s > 20$, there will be no oscillation; and if $R_s < 20$, there should be vigorous oscillations. We note that ωL_s is $400\ \Omega$, so the approximation is a good one. Using $\omega = 1/\sqrt{LC}$, we find $C = 250$ pF.

The tunnel diode oscillator provides a simple circuit that has excellent

†L. B. Arguimbau, R. B. Adler, *Vacuum-Tube Circuits and Transistors*, John Wiley & Sons, Inc., New York, 1956, pp. 354 ff.

high-frequency capabilities, but it has a severe power limitation owing to the low voltage range of the negative resistance portion of the characteristic. The vacuum tetrode oscillator has a limitation because its characteristic is likely to change with time. An improved negative resistance oscillator, called the *transitron*, depends for its action on a negative resistance region in the screen characteristic of a pentode that results when the plate potential is held constant and the potentials of the screen and suppressor grids vary together. The connection is shown in Fig. 12-4. The direct screen potential is higher than the plate potential, and the suppressor has a negative bias. With these electrode potentials the suppressor strongly influences the electron flow, owing to the effect that its potential has on the fraction of the electron stream that is turned back and collected by the screen. In the oscillator circuit capacitor C' acts to couple the suppressor and screen together, so their potentials go up and down together. Consider a positive increment in their potentials. The rise in suppressor potential lets more electrons go through to the plate so that fewer return to the screen. If this effect is great enough, the screen current *falls* rather than rises as one might expect. Thus, we may have a negative resistance characteristic between the potentials of the two electrodes and their combined current.

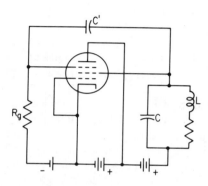

FIGURE 12-4   Circuit of transitron oscillator.

This circuit is suitable for a low-power oscillator, and its frequency of oscillation can be changed from a low audio to about 50 MHz simply by changing the elements of the LC circuit.

12-4
RC feedback oscillator circuits

In Chapter 9 we remarked that positive feedback could produce self-oscillation. If we use the treatment of voltage feedback in Sec. 9-3 as a basis, we can obtain a condition for oscillation as follows. If $\mathbf{G}_f$ in Eq. (9-5) approaches infinity, then the input signal V_1 could approach zero, but there would still be an output. Following this line of reasoning, we set the denominator of Eq. (9-5) equal to zero and obtain

$$1 + \mathbf{GH} = 0 \quad \text{or} \quad \mathbf{H} = -\frac{1}{\mathbf{G}} \tag{12-4}$$

In other words, the open loop gain **GH** should be -1 for oscillations to occur.

A frequency-sensitive feedback path is provided in order to produce sinusoidal oscillations. Perhaps the most common feedback networks contain selective tuned LC circuits, but first we shall discuss two examples of RC feedback networks.

a. A phase-shift oscillator

In the so-called *phase-shift* oscillator in Fig. 12-5 the three-section RC feedback network serves to shift the phase of the wave by 180° before it is applied to the base. Each RC section causes a phase shift, and the phase of

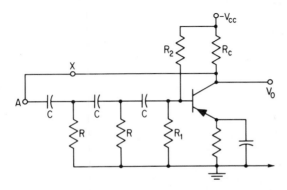

FIGURE 12-5   *RC* phase-shift oscillator.

the voltage wave shifts in a leading sense through each section. The cumulative phase shift must be approximately 180°. Another 180° phase shift occurs through the common-emitter amplifier; therefore the voltage fed back to the input at point A from the amplifier output has the correct phase to maintain the oscillations. How large must the voltage gain be to insure oscillation? This must be great enough so that the magnitude of the open-loop gain is at least unity. Thus, the gain should be the reciprocal of the attenuation through the RC network, or larger. If the condition for oscillation is barely satisfied, the oscillations may be feeble, and with a slight reduction in gain, they would stop. If the gain is larger than the bare minimum, the oscillation will be strong. They will reach a stable amplitude, owing to the nonlinear transistor curves and the reduction in the average gain over the cycle as the amplitude rises. The problem of predicting the oscillation level is not easy to solve, owing to the nonlinearities involved.

In all feedback oscillators we may think of an experiment in which we break the feedback loop and test for the open-loop gain as a function of frequency. For example, we break the feedback circuit at point X in Fig. 12-5 and measure the voltage at V_o while a variable-frequency test voltage is applied between point A and ground. A frequency can be found at which V_o is *in phase* with the input voltage. If V_o is equal to, or greater than, the test voltage at *this frequency*, then the circuit should oscillate when the loop is closed and deliver the same frequency.†

The last section of the feedback network has an equivalent resistance to ground consisting of R_1 in parallel with two other resistances: the bias resistor R_2 and the input resistance to the base of the transistor. For ease in calculation it is better to have the effective resistance of all three sections identical, but this is not a requirement for oscillation.

In the comparable oscillator using a vacuum-tube amplifier and three identical RC feedback sections it can be shown that the voltage gain must be at least 29 and that the frequency of oscillation will be $f = 1/(2\pi\sqrt{6}\,RC)$.

Oscillators of this type are suitable for frequencies from the low audio range up to a few hundred kilocycles per second. Frequency variation can be provided in the higher range by using a ganged triple variable air capacitor for the capacitors.

b. Wien bridge oscillator

The oscillator in Fig. 12-6 is based on the frequency selective property of the Wien bridge circuit, which is drawn at the left of the diagram. A two-stage amplifier is needed to give the correct phase relation. The amplifier output is fed back to energize the bridge. The voltage across the usual balance points of the bridge provides the grid-to-cathode signal applied to the first stage. However, it is preferable to think of this voltage in terms of two separate voltages, first, that from cathode to ground (across R_2) and second, that from grid to ground. The cathode-to-ground voltage provides a *negative* feedback, while the grid-to-ground voltage gives a *positive* feedback at the frequency of oscillation. To function as an oscillator, the positive feedback must be predominant.

In practical circuits the resistor R_2 may consist of a tungsten lamp whose resistance increases with increasing current. Thus, an increasing oscillation amplitude will increase the value of R_2 and thereby give additional negative feedback and tend to stabilize the amplitude. In transistorized versions of the circuit an alternative scheme is used in which a *thermistor* (negative temperature coefficient resistor) is used for R_1, which will stabilize the output level.

The analysis which follows will show that the frequency of oscillation

†This statement is only approximate, owing to the change in the load on the collector when the loop is opened. This will have a slight effect on the gain and phase shift. The test can be improved by providing a temporary load from collector to ground to simulate the input impedance of the RC network.

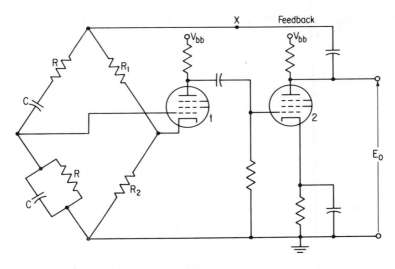

FIGURE 12-6   Wien bridge oscillator circuit.

is $\omega = 1/RC$. In a common form of laboratory oscillator the two capacitors C can be varied since they consist of ganged variable air capacitors. These oscillators generally give a frequency range of about 10 to 1 for one rotation of the dial and have arrangements for switching the resistors to change the frequency ranges in decade steps.

c. Analysis of Wien bridge oscillator

An analysis of the oscillator circuit will give an insight into its operation. We break the feedback loop at point X in Fig. 12-6 and think of applying the test signal E_s as in Fig. 12-7. We shall solve for the conditions for oscillation by equating $\mathbf{E}_o$ and $\mathbf{E}_s$. First note that the stage voltage gains are $\mathbf{A}_1$ and $\mathbf{A}_2$. Furthermore we define

$$\beta = \frac{R_2}{R_1 + R_2} \quad \text{and} \quad \tau = RC \tag{12-5}$$

We shall try to find the frequency and the value of β needed for oscillations to occur. The input voltage to the amplifier $\mathbf{E}_1$ is related to $\mathbf{E}$ and $\beta\mathbf{E}_s$ by

$$\mathbf{E}_1 = \mathbf{E} - \beta\mathbf{E}_s \tag{12-6}$$

if the loading effect of the cathode of tube 1 on the voltage ratio β is negligible. We can write

$$\mathbf{E}_2 = \mathbf{A}_1\mathbf{E}_1 + \beta\mathbf{E}_s \tag{12-7}$$

And since $\mathbf{E}_o = \mathbf{A}_2\mathbf{E}_2$, we can use (12-6) and (12-7) to obtain

$$\mathbf{E}_o = \mathbf{A}_1\mathbf{A}_2\mathbf{E} - \beta\mathbf{A}_2(\mathbf{A}_1 - 1)\mathbf{E}_s \tag{12-8}$$

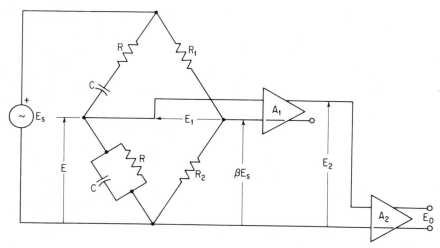

FIGURE 12-7   A circuit for analysis of Wien bridge oscillator.

Next we need to express $\mathbf{E}$ in terms of $\mathbf{E}_s$. Since amplifier A_1 takes a negligible input current, we think in terms of the voltage divider action of the RC circuits. The series combination has an impedance of $R + 1/j\omega C$, and the impedance of the parallel combination can be expressed as $R/(1 + j\omega\tau)$. Therefore

$$\frac{\mathbf{E}}{\mathbf{E}_s} = \frac{\dfrac{R}{1 + j\omega\tau}}{R + \dfrac{1}{j\omega C} + \dfrac{R}{1 + j\omega\tau}} = \frac{j\omega\tau}{1 - \omega^2\tau^2 + j3\omega\tau} \tag{12-9}$$

Replacing $\mathbf{E}$ in (12-8) by its value from (12-9), we can write

$$\mathbf{E}_o = \mathbf{E}_s\left[\frac{j\omega\tau\mathbf{A}_1\mathbf{A}_2}{1 - \omega^2\tau^2 + j3\omega\tau} - \beta\mathbf{A}_2(\mathbf{A}_1 - 1)\right] \tag{12-10}$$

Now we equate $\mathbf{E}_o$ to $\mathbf{E}_s$ and also assume that the $\mathbf{A}$'s are negative and real, so we replace $\mathbf{A}_1$ by $-A_1$ and $\mathbf{A}_2$ by $-A_2$ and find, after rearranging,

$$\beta A_2(A_1 + 1) + 1 = \frac{j\omega\tau A_1 A_2}{1 - \omega^2\tau^2 + j3\omega\tau} \tag{12-11}$$

Both the real and the j parts of (12-11) must be equal. Since the left side is real, the right side must be real. But the only way for this to be true is to have $1 - \omega^2\tau^2 = 0$. Therefore we find

$$\omega = \frac{1}{\tau} = \frac{1}{RC} \tag{12-12}$$

for the frequency of oscillation.

Upon using (12-12) in (12-11) and solving for β, we get

$$\beta = \frac{A_1 A_2 - 3}{3A_2(A_1 + 1)} \cong \frac{A_1 A_2}{3A_2(A_1 + 1)} \cong \frac{1}{3} \qquad (12\text{-}13)$$

The successive approximations are taken on the assumption that $A_1 A_2$ is about 1000 and that A_1 is about 50. Then the error is about 2.3 per cent. If we choose $R_2 = R_1/2$, then β will be 1/3 and the conditions for oscillation will just be satisfied. To be on the safe side, R_2 should be somewhat smaller than $R_1/2$.

12-5
LC feedback oscillator circuits

The most common circuits of this class are one-stage grounded-cathode or common-emitter amplifiers that have an *LC* circuit to control the frequency and a means for providing a 180° feedback voltage. Thus, *positive feedback* or *regeneration* is present. High-power oscillators, say of 1 kW output or above, usually use tube circuits. We shall describe both tube and transistor circuits but shall use a tube circuit to illustrate the method of analysis of a high-power oscillator.

a. Tuned-plate oscillator

An examination of the behavior of the tuned-plate oscillator (Fig. 12-8) will give us a qualitative understanding of the whole class, since the other circuits behave similarly. The actual tuned circuit is more likely to be like that in Fig. 12-2b but it is helpful to think of an equivalent parallel resistance

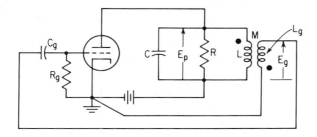

FIGURE 12-8   Tuned-plate oscillator circuit.

R to account for the coil losses and power output. Attention is called to the feedback path via the mutual inductance M and the grid coil L_g through C_g to the grid. Note that the coil polarities put the grid signal 180° from the plate ac voltage. The function of C_g and R_g is to provide a grid bias, as will be explained presently. We assume that C_g and R_g have little effect on the signal reaching the grid, i.e., R_g is relatively high and $1/j\omega C_g$ is low.

A discussion of a possible way that the oscillations start will bring out some important points. In Fig. 12-9 we assume that the circuit is initially

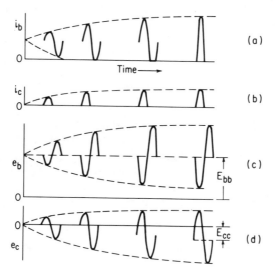

FIGURE 12-9   Start-up of oscillations.

quiescent, with no charge in C_g and with no oscillations in the LC circuit. Then some slight disturbance (such as a switching transient or noise voltage) starts a small oscillation in LC. Of course, we assume that R is high enough so that the *tank circuit* (L, C, R) considered by itself is highly oscillatory as contrasted to overdamped. When the small oscillation starts, the tube operates in a class A mode, with plate current flowing during the full cycle. We call attention to the 180° phase relation of the grid signal relative to the plate ac voltage wave and also to the fact that the ac part of the plate current is *in phase* with the *grid signal*. This is necessary if ac power is to be delivered *to* the tuned circuit.

As the oscillations build up, the operation changes first to class AB, then to class B and finally to class C, as evidenced by the plate current waves. These changes are a result of the growing amplitude and of negative grid bias which stabilizes at the level E_{cc}. The positive grid current pulses drawn through R_g produce a negative grid potential, and the filter capacitor C_g smooths the resulting dc component. In the stabilized condition the potential across C_g varies only slightly over one cycle, since the time constant $R_g C_g$ equals several cycles of the oscillation.

Why do the oscillations stabilize at a particular level? To answer this question let us look at the variations of ac power developed in the circuit in relation to the ac power output (including losses) and to the energy stored in the tank circuit. While the oscillation amplitude is rising, the developed power is greater than the output so there is an excess that goes into building up the energy stored in the LC elements. However, the output goes up as the square of the ac plate voltage. The developed power at first increases at about this same rate, but when class C operation is reached, the power does not rise as fast owing to the narrow pulses of plate current. Eventually, a stable level is reached at which developed power equals output power.

A well-designed circuit operating in class C can convert about 85 per cent of the dc power into ac output power. The major loss is at the plate of the tube, and this limits the output from a particular tube.

We can see that small-signal theory is of little value in oscillator circuit analysis except to find the criterion for oscillation or non-oscillation during the initial class A condition. An analysis of Fig. 12-8 on the basis of small-signal theory yields a radian frequency of $1/\sqrt{LC}$ and the following criterion for oscillation:

$$g_m \geqq \frac{L}{MR'} \tag{12-14}$$

where $R' = [r_p \| R]$. It should be mentioned that if the tank circuit has an L_s, R_s series branch instead of the LR parallel arrangement, then the frequency is shifted slightly and the condition on g_m becomes†

$$g_m \geqq \frac{\mu R_s C}{\mu M - L_s} \tag{12-15}$$

In the derivation of these formulas the effects of the $C_g R_g$ circuit and of inter-electrode capacitances have been neglected.

The design of a power oscillator must be based on an analysis of the class C condition. One technique for this analysis is given in Sec. 12-7.

b. LC oscillator circuits

A number of other oscillator circuits have been devised, some of which are shown in elementary form (dc source and grid bias circuits omitted) in Fig. 12-10. They all have the approximate 180° relation between grid and plate voltages. They also all have oscillatory tank circuits in which energy is surging back and forth between the reactive elements. Some energy is delivered as useful output plus losses during each cycle, and the plate current pulse restores this energy.

The Hartley and Colpitts oscillators are very similar. The tuned-grid oscillator is similar to the tuned-plate circuit. The tuned-grid, tuned-plate circuit needs some explanation. The feedback in this circuit is through the

†T. S. Gray, *Applied Electronics*, 2d ed., John Wiley & Sons, Inc., New York, 1954, p. 666.

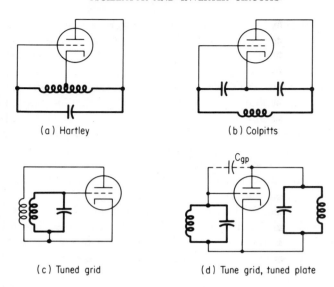

(a) Hartley   (b) Colpitts

(c) Tuned grid   (d) Tune grid, tuned plate

FIGURE 12-10   *LC* oscillator circuits.

grid-plate stray capacitance C_{gp}. The two tuned circuits are adjusted to the same resonant frequency. However, the circuit will oscillate at a slightly lower frequency, so that the tuned circuits will appear inductive at their terminals. The feedback through C_{gp} shifts the phase by the required amount.

Elementary transistor oscillator circuits are shown in Fig. 12-11. The operating principles of the Hartley and Colpitts circuits are similar to those of the tube versions. One difference is that the low transistor impedance from emitter to base tends to damp the tank circuit heavily. For this reason, and also to avoid overdriving the transistor, the ac voltage applied between base and emitter is relatively lower than in the corresponding tube circuit. For example, the tap point *T* in the Hartley circuit is shifted to the left farther than in a similar tube circuit. Both the Hartley and the Colpitts circuits

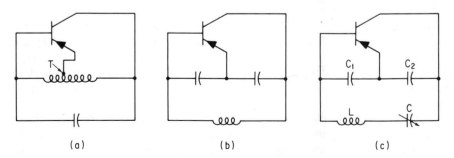

(a)   (b)   (c)

FIGURE 12-11   Elementary (a) Hartley, (b) Colpitts, and (c) modified Colpitts, or Clapp, oscillator circuits.

oscillate readily, and the Colpitts is adapted to somewhat higher frequencies than the Hartley. These circuits, of course, require bias networks to set the dc voltage levels. These generally give class C operation and are designed to avoid collector current saturation, which would degrade the output wave form.

The Clapp oscillator in Fig. 12-11c may be regarded as a variation of the Colpitts circuit. The resonant frequency is determined by the series circuit comprising L, C, C_1, and C_2. But C_1 and C_2 are chosen large compared with C, so that L and C mainly determine the frequency. Then C can be varied to vary the oscillation frequency. Another result is that both the base and the collector are loosely coupled to the tuned circuit, so that the reaction of the transistor on the frequency, and therefore on the frequency stability, is minimized.

A few comments on practical circuits may be made. Trouble is sometimes encountered with *parasitic* oscillations, i.e., unwanted oscillations at either high or low frequencies. For example, in the Colpitts circuit a very high frequency oscillation may arise because the base and collector (or grid and plate) leads act as inductors. Then the transistor or tube capacitances complete a circuit of the tuned-grid, tuned-plate type. Parasitic oscillations can also give trouble in amplifier circuits.

The tuned-plate oscillator in Fig. 12-8 shows the plate dc supply in a connection called *series feed*. In the Colpitts circuit particularly, and in others also, the *parallel feed* arrangement is used. It is shown in Fig. 12-12 applied to the Hartley circuit. The choke coil *RFC* isolates the dc supply from the ac voltage on the plate, while capacitor C_f isolates the tank circuit from the dc source and at the same time allows the ac tank voltage to reach the plate.

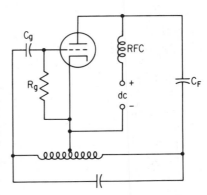

FIGURE 12-12 Hartley oscillator circuit with parallel feed.

12-6
LC feedback power oscillator
analysis

We shall develop a graphical analysis that will enable us to calculate the power output for assumed values of bias voltages and ac voltages. Questions of amplitude stability are, however, not considered in detail. The approach is to assume sine-wave ac voltages on grid and plate that are 180° out of phase. Then the instantaneous plate and grid current pulses are obtained graphically. Next the instantaneous plate loss and average plate loss are found. The law of conservation of power is invoked to obtain an approximate value of ac power output.

We think in terms of the tuned-plate circuit in Fig. 12-8, except that the tank circuit is assumed to have an inductive branch comprising L and R_s in series instead of a parallel resistance R. However, we disregard possible slight deviations from a 180° phase shift between plate and grid voltages. The tube characteristics used in this analysis are the constant plate current curves, drawn with plate voltage as abscissas and grid voltage as ordinates, as shown in the upper portion of Fig. 12-13 for a typical power triode.

If the grid and plate ac voltages are 180° apart, then the locus of the instantaneous total grid and plate voltages e_c and e_b will be a straight line†

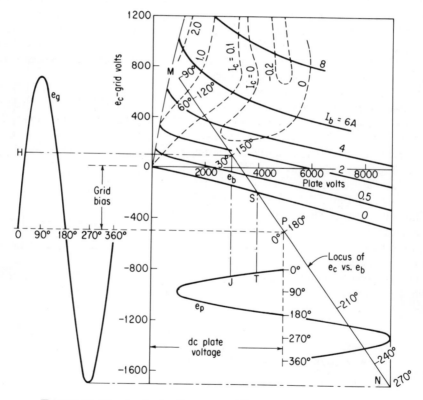

FIGURE 12-13   Analysis of power oscillator.

†To verify the linear relation let $e_p = E_{pm} \sin \omega t$ and $e_g = E_{gm} \sin(\omega t + 180°) = -E_{gm} \sin \omega t$. Upon eliminating $\sin \omega t$ between these equations, we find $e_g = -(E_{gm}/E_{pm})e_p$. This is the equation of a straight line with a negative slope.

such as line NPM in Fig. 12-13. In the figure the grid bias is taken as -500 V, whereas the dc plate-supply voltage is 5000 V. These values locate the point P. The ac grid-voltage wave e_g, drawn at the left about the -500-V line, has a peak value of 1200 V. The ac plate-voltage wave e_p, shown at the lower right with the time scale extending downward, has a peak value of 4000 V. This wave is drawn about the 5000-V dc value as an axis. Thus, when corresponding points on the e_g and e_p waves are considered, as, for example, points H and J at the 30° points, we see that these points determine the ordinate and abscissa values of the 30° point on the total grid versus total plate voltage locus. In a similar way the positive peak of grid voltage and the negative peak of plate voltage locate the limiting point M on the e_c versus e_b locus. It is clear from the construction that the distance from point P to any point on the line PM is proportional to the sine of the corresponding angle. For example, the angle at point S, call it θ_s, can be found from the relation $\theta_s = \sin^{-1}(\overline{PS}/\overline{PM})$.

After the locus NPM has been established and after it has been provided with a scale of degrees corresponding to various points on the locus, it is possible to obtain data for curves of instantaneous plate current and of grid current. For example, if we start at 0° at point P and advance toward M, we see that no plate current flows until we reach cutoff at point S at about 15°. At 30° the plate current is estimated by interpolation to be 1.7 A. In this way the curve of i_b in Fig. 12-14 is obtained. The curve for grid current i_c is obtained in a similar way. The dc or average values of plate and grid currents can now be computed on the basis of the general formula

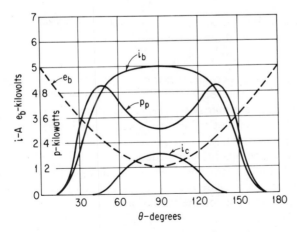

FIGURE 12-14 Curves of plate current i_b, grid current i_c, plate voltage e_b, and instantaneous plate power p_p for the oscillator analyzed in Fig. 12-13.

$$I_{av} = \frac{1}{2\pi} \int_0^{2\pi} i \, d\theta \qquad (12\text{-}16)$$

Here the integral is evaluated graphically as the area under the current curve. If desired, this area can be expressed in degree × ampere units, and in this case the area would be divided by 360 to give the average current. Inasmuch as the current waves are symmetrical about the 90° ordinate, the total area can be computed as twice the area to the left of the 90° line. The curves in Fig. 12-14 give a value of average plate current of 1.5 A and of average grid current of 0.23 A.

The power taken from the dc source in the plate circuit is the product of the average plate current and the dc voltage, or 1.5×5000, or 7500 W. The principal loss of power is at the plate of the tube. An instantaneous plate power curve is obtained by multiplying instantaneous plate voltage by instantaneous plate current and is shown in Fig. 12-14. The *average power* over the cycle works out to be 2.3 kW. Thus with 7.5 kW supplied by the dc source and 2.3 kW lost at the plate, the power converted into the ac form in the tank circuit will be 5.2 kW.

To find the power output, it is necessary to subtract the losses in the tank-circuit elements and the grid-circuit losses. An approximate method of calculation of the total grid loss is based on the idea that the power is delivered to the grid circuit via the grid current i_c and the alternating component of grid voltage e_g. Thus

$$P_g = \frac{1}{2\pi} \int_0^{2\pi} i_c e_g \, d\theta \qquad (12\text{-}17)$$

But the grid-current pulse is short enough so that e_g does not depart greatly from its maximum value E_{gm} while current flows. If a constant value equal to E_{gm} is assumed to act during the grid-current pulse, then the power is the product of the average value of the grid current I_c, and E_{gm}. Thus,

$$P_g \cong I_c E_{gm} \qquad (12\text{-}18)$$

In the numerical example under consideration, a calculation of average grid current gives 0.23 A, and since E_{gm} is 1200 V, P_g is 276 W. This power goes partly to the grid resistor and partly to heat the grid itself. We note that the power available for tank circuit losses and useful output is $5.2 - 0.28$, or 4.92 kW.

To establish the plate-to-cathode impedance of the tank circuit, it is first necessary to find the fundamental frequency component of the plate current. In other words, the pulses of plate current are thought of as analyzed into a Fourier series, which consists of the sum of a dc term, a fundamental frequency sinusoidal term at the operating frequency, and a series of harmonics. In an oscillator, however, the tank circuit acts as a filter so that, though the harmonics in the plate current are large, the harmonic voltages across the tank circuit are small. This unexpected result is due to the rapid drop in the impedance of the tank circuit as the frequency rises above the resonant value. In the circuit example to be given presently, the resonant impedance is 1537 Ω, but the calculated impedance for the second harmonic is only 85 Ω and for the third harmonic is 48 Ω. Thus the harmonic voltage components are small and the total power going into the harmonics is small. Therefore the power converted into the ac form may, without serious error, be regarded as all fundamental frequency power. Furthermore, under the assumptions about phase angles already made, the fundamental component of plate current i_{p1} will be 180° out of phase with the ac plate voltage. Therefore

$$E_p I_{p1} = P_{ac} \qquad (12\text{-}19)$$

where E_p and I_{p1} are effective values. In the numerical example we have a value of E_p of $4000/\sqrt{2}$ and of P_{ac} of 5200 W, so that I_{p1} is 1.84 A.

We recall that we are dealing with a tuned-plate oscillator circuit, so that the circuit between plate and cathode consists of a parallel tuned circuit. The impedance of the circuit will be

$$Z = \frac{E_p}{I_{p1}} \qquad (12\text{-}20)$$

In the example this value is 2828/1.84 or 1537 Ω. An approximate expression for the parallel resonant impedance of this type of circuit, assuming that the resistance is small compared with the reactance, is the following:

$$Z \simeq \frac{X_L^2}{R_s} \qquad (12\text{-}21)$$

where X_L is the reactance of the inductive branch and R_s is its resistance. Thus, a variety of choices can be made of the components X_L and R_s to satisfy the required value of the tank-circuit impedance, but the values chosen will have an important effect on the wave form of the output and on the stability of the oscillations.

If too much load resistance is introduced into the tank circuit, the oscillations may stop. The oscillations must be maintained in the intervals between the plate current pulses by the "flywheel effect" of the tank-circuit inductance and capacitance. The ratio of the energy stored to the energy dissipated per cycle is often used as a criterion of the degree of loading. Let us calculate this ratio for a tank circuit assumed to consist of an inductance L, a capacitance C, and a resistance R_s (including the load) as in a tuned-plate oscillator circuit. The current in the coil is taken as I effective amperes, and the frequency as f cycles per second. The stored energy can be calculated by considering the instant when the energy is all stored in the coil and has the value LI^2. The energy dissipated per cycle is $I^2 R_s/f$, so that we have

$$\frac{\text{energy stored}}{\text{energy dissipated per cycle}} = \frac{f L I^2}{I^2 R_s} = \frac{f L}{R_s} \qquad (12\text{-}22)$$

Experience shows that this value may be as low as 2 at full load without causing instability, and values as high as 8 are used in practical oscillators.

The ratio of the reactive volt-amperes in the tank coil to the power output in watts is closely related to the ratio given in Eq. (12-22), as the following calculation shows:

$$\frac{\text{reactive volt-amperes}}{\text{watts}} = \frac{X_L I \times I}{I^2 R_s} = \frac{2\pi f L}{R_s} \qquad (12\text{-}23)$$

By comparing (12-22) and (12-23) we see that the ratio of reactive volt-amperes to watts is 2π times the ratio of energy stored to energy dissipated per cycle. Typical values at full load therefore range from 12 to 50. A higher ratio gives a more nearly sinusoidal output wave and greater stability but gives a reduced power output owing to increased losses in the tank circuit elements.

To apply these ideas to the numerical example, let us arbitrarily specify a ratio of reactive volt-amperes to watts of 12. Then X_L/R_s is 12, and from Eq. (12-21) we find $1537 = 12X_L$, or $X_L = 128\ \Omega$. Furthermore, R_s equals $128/12$, or $10.67\ \Omega$. This value of resistance is an equivalent resistance that includes the effect of grid-circuit losses and losses in the tank-circuit elements, so that the load resistance referred to the tank-coil branch would be somewhat less than the value calculated. The current in the inductive branch is approximately E_p/X_L, or $2828/128 = 22.1$ A. This value, it will be noted, is relatively high compared with the plate current of the tube.

Several interesting questions remain unanswered. For example, how

Table 12-1 Maximum Ratings and Typical Operation of Type 889 RA as RF Power Amplifier and Oscillator—Class C

Maximum ratings:			
DC plate voltage	8500 max. V		
DC grid voltage	−1000 max. V		
DC plate current	2 max. A		
DC grid current	0.25 max. A		
Plate input	16 max. kW		
Plate dissipation	5 max. kW		
Typical operation:			
DC plate voltage	5000	6000	7500 V
DC grid voltage (fixed bias)	−500	−600	−800 V
Grid resistor (instead of fixed bias)	2600	2900	3300 Ω
Peak RF grid voltage	1240	1460	1830 V
DC plate current	1.5	1.8	2.0 A
DC grid current	0.19	0.21	0.24 approx. A
Driving power to grid circuit	220	290	400 approx. W
Power output	5	7	10 approx. kW

should the operating line be oriented and proportioned to obtain maximum power output or maximum efficiency? If the oscillator were built with the constants obtained in the example, would it operate at the assumed level? Repetitive solutions assuming larger and smaller voltage swings would throw some light on the latter question. However, the situation is complicated by the self-bias arrangement. With a fixed value of R_g the bias will change with the amplitude, so that a "trial and correction" procedure is needed for each new amplitude.

Guidance in the selection of operating conditions that will give the required power output without overloading the tube is often supplied by the tube manufacturer. For example, Table 12-1 gives three different sets of operating conditions for the type 889RA triode in class C service.

We conclude by remarking that class C amplifiers can be analyzed by the same techniques as given in this article, with some obvious modifications.

12-7
Other oscillator circuits

In *electromechanical* oscillators the frequency selection is performed by the vibration of a mechanical element in the feedback system. A simple example is the tuning-fork oscillator. The fork, if of magnetic material, can be excited by a driving coil connected to the output of an amplifier. A pickup coil is placed near the other (magnetized) tine of the fork and the induced voltage is fed to the amplifier input. Frequency stability of a few tenths of a per cent can be achieved without temperature control.

Another example is the magnetostriction oscillator. Some materials such as nickel change their dimensions when placed in a magnetic field. If a circuit like the Hartley is built with separate coils and a nickel rod is used as a common core for the two coils, the oscillations will, under suitable conditions, depend on the natural mechanical vibrations of the rod. One application is in the production of ultrasonic mechanical vibrations.

The *crystal-controlled* oscillator, based on the piezoelectric effect, has been developed to a high degree for purposes of obtaining extremely high frequency stability. The piezoelectric crystal, usually quartz, will change its dimensions when placed in an electric field. When placed in an ac field of just the right frequency one of its natural modes of vibration can be excited. This vibration has an extremely sharp resonance, perhaps one hundred times sharper than that of a high-Q LC resonant circuit. The crystal appears to the external electric circuit like a series resonant circuit of very high Q shunted by a small capacitance. If the crystal is placed between plate elec-

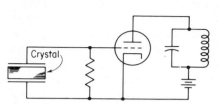

FIGURE 12-15   Crystal-controlled oscillator circuit.

trodes and connected between grid and ground (Fig. 12-15) with a tuned circuit in the plate circuit, the so-called Pierce oscillator results. It acts like a tuned-grid, tuned-plate oscillator. With a proper orientation of the cut of the crystal slab with respect to the crystallographic axes, the temperature dependence of frequency is only 1 or 2 parts per million over 10 or 20°C. Temperature control of the crystal is used for improved frequency stability.

The so-called *beat-frequency* oscillator has some unique features. It really consists of two oscillators. One has a fixed frequency, say 50,000 Hz. The other is variable, say from 50,000 to 70,000 Hz. The two outputs are beat against each other in a "mixer" circuit, and the difference frequency is filtered out and amplified. This oscillator goes to low frequencies and has a wide frequency range for one rotation of the control dial.

Another type of relaxation oscillator, known as the free-running multivibrator, will be discussed in Chapter 16. Special circuits, tubes, and transistors are needed to generate frequencies above 100 MHz or so, and their discussion is beyond the scope of this book.

12-8
Inverter circuits

a. Vibrating contact inverter

The principle of this inverter is shown in Fig. 12-16. The *vibrator* consists of a vibrating reed switch under the control of an exciting coil. In operation the vibrator switches the dc supply voltage V alternately across the two halves of the transformer primary winding. The switching is not instantaneous but may require from 10 to 30 per cent of the entire period. The output voltage, therefore, takes a square-topped form as shown in the diagram.

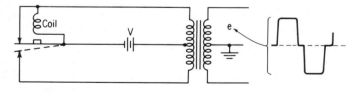

FIGURE 12-16   Vibrating contact inverter.

In practical circuits† a capacitor is added to overcome the inductive surges that would otherwise develop. This type of circuit is useful in battery-operated portable instruments that require a high dc voltage. This can readily be obtained by rectifying the transformer output.

b. Transistor inverter circuit

A two-transistor inverter, which operates on roughly the same principle as the vibrator inverter, is shown in Fig. 12-17. The function of the transistors is to switch the dc source alternately on to the two windings $W1$ and $W2$. As a result a rectangular ac wave of voltage is delivered to the load. The switching is controlled by the voltage fed back from winding $W3$ to the transformer $T2$ and thence to the base connections. Transformer $T2$ has a sharply saturating core such as is used in magnetic amplifiers.

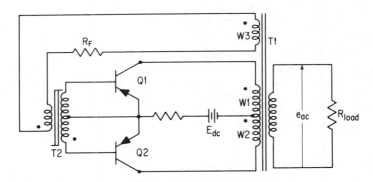

FIGURE 12-17   Transistor inverter circuit.

The base signal, owing to the *positive* feedback, acts to hold one transistor, say $Q1$, in the ON condition and the other transistor in the OFF condition. During this period the magnetic flux in the core of $T2$ is changing, but the magnetizing current drawn by $T2$ is so small that resistor R_F has little effect. However, when $T2$ saturates, its primary current tends to rise owing to the saturation, and the effect of R_F is to drastically lower the voltage developed by $T2$. As a result the base drive diminishes to a point at which the conduction switches over to $Q2$, and $Q1$ stops conducting. This cycle is repeated, and the frequency is determined by the time required for the flux in $T2$ to change from negative to positive saturation. Because the transistors operate as switches, their power loss is low and the circuit provides a useful high-efficiency inverter for low-power applications.

†W. D. Cockrell, ed., *Industrial Electronics Handbook*, McGraw-Hill Book Company, New York, 1958, pp. 3–81 ff.

REFERENCES

12-1 Engineering Staff of Texas Instruments, Inc., *Transistor Circuit Design*, J. A. Walston and J. R. Miller eds., McGraw-Hill Book Company, New York, 1963, Chaps. 12, 22, 34, 35.

12-2 W. A. Edson, *Vacuum Tube Oscillators*, John Wiley & Sons, Inc., New York, 1953.

12-3 H. J. Reich, *Functional Circuits and Oscillators*, D. Van Nostrand Co., Inc., Princeton, N.J., 1961.

EXERCISES

12-1 Derive Eq. (12-1). *Suggestion*: Note that the time required for the capacitor voltage v (Fig. 12-1b) to rise from V_x to V_f on the *first* rising segment is equal to the period T.

12-2 A tunnel diode is operated in the oscillator circuit in Fig. 12-2b. Let $R_s = 4$ Ω, $L_s = 0.02 \ \mu H$, and $\omega = 4 \times 10^8$ rad/s. A suitable Q point is chosen on the negative resistance portion of the diode characteristic. The average dynamic resistance of the diode as a function of the peak oscillating component of current is as follows:

$i_{peak}(mA) =$	2	4	6	8	10
r $(\Omega) =$	-19	-19.6	-20.6	-22	-25

(a) Determine whether the circuit will oscillate, and if so, find the amplitude of oscillation. (b) What is the effective value of capacitance required? (c) What is the approximate ac power delivered to R_s?

12-3 Derive the expression $f = 1/(2\pi\sqrt{6} \ RC)$ for the phase-shift oscillator in Fig. 12-5. Assume that each RC section has identical R values and that the phase shift through the amplifier stage is exactly $180°$.

12-4 In the RC phase-shift oscillator circuit in Fig. 12-5 the input resistance to the base of the transistor is $1800 \ \Omega$, $R_2 = 40 \ k\Omega$, $R_1 = 10 \ k\Omega$, and $C = 0.005 \ \mu F$. (a) What is the equivalent ac resistance from the last (right-hand) capacitor to ground? (b) Assume that the other two phase-shift circuit resistors R have the value calculated in (a), and calculate the frequency of oscillation.

12-5 It is instructive to calculate the output voltage $\mathbf{E}_o$ as a function of ω in the neighborhood of $\omega\tau = 1$ to bring out the frequency selectivity of the network in Fig. 12-7. For this purpose let $A_1 = -50$, $A_2 = -20$, and $\mathbf{E}_s = 1\underline{/0°}$ in Eq. (12-10). Then insert the exact value of β from Eq. (12-13) into (12-10) and calculate $\mathbf{E}_o$ for a range of $\omega\tau$ values from 0.98 to 1.02. Discuss the results. Note that the calculations must be made with more than ordinary precision to avoid error.

12-6 Redraw the circuits in Fig. 12-11 except to include supply and biasing circuits.

12-7 A power triode rated at 4-kW plate dissipation is operated in a tuned-plate oscillator circuit. The dc value of plate voltage is 7000 V and of grid voltage is −700 V. Assume that the ac component of grid voltage is 1200 V peak and of plate voltage is 6000 V peak and that these voltages have a 180° phase relation. A graphical construction like that in Fig. 12-13 using the triode constant-current curves and the stated voltages results in the following data for the instantaneous values of i_b and i_c:

ωt (deg) =	20	24	30	40	50	60	70	80	90
i_b (A) =	0	0.01	0.25	1.30	2.55	3.40	3.90	4.05	4.10
i_c (A) =	0	0	0	0	0.03	0.35	0.65	0.90	1.00

Calculate (a) dc value of plate current, (b) dc value of grid current, (c) power supplied by the plate dc source, (d) plate dissipation, (e) power converted to the ac form, (f) approximate total grid-circuit loss, and (g) ac power available for tank-circuit losses plus output. Also calculate (h) the value of the grid resistor, (i) the tank circuit impedance, and inductive reactance and resistance in the coil branch, assuming a ratio of reactive voltamperes to watts of 20.

13

Modulation, Demodulation, and Related Topics

13-1
Introduction

In the nontechnical sense the term *to modulate* means to vary the characteristics of a sound, for example, to vary the pitch or the volume. Thus we speak of a well-modulated voice. In the technical sense the related term *modulation* may be defined as the process whereby the amplitude (or other characteristic) of one wave is caused to vary as a function of the instantaneous value of a second wave, called the *signal* or *modulating* wave. The first wave, which is usually a high-frequency sine wave, is called the *carrier* wave. The modified carrier wave, which carries the signal information, is called a *modulated* wave.

Modulated waves are basic to radio and television transmission, because the high-frequency carrier is readily radiated through space and because the modulated waves may be selected from a frequency spectrum containing other waves by means of selective electric circuits. Modulated waves are often encountered in electronic instruments, such as strain-gage indicators, and in telemetry (the transmission of instrument readings to a distant receiving center).

The following is a brief treatment of modulation and of *demodulation* or *detection* (the process of recovering the signal information from the modulated wave). In addition, surveys of the related topics of heterodyning, frequency mixing, and phase detection will be included.

312

There are two broad classes of modulated waves, namely, those in which the carrier is a sine wave, and those in which some characteristic of a recurrent pulse train is modulated. The second class is called *pulse* modulation.

Now consider a sine-wave carrier expressed by

$$e = E \sin \theta \tag{13-1}$$

where the angle θ is some function of the time. It is at once clear that this carrier wave can be modulated in either of two ways in response to a signal, namely, (1) in amplitude, by varying E, or (2) in the variation of the angle θ. The first method gives *amplitude modulation* (AM), while the second gives *angle modulation*. Subclassifications of angle modulation include *phase modulation* and *frequency modulation* (FM).

13-2
Amplitude modulation

An example of an AM wave is shown in Fig. 13-1. In the absence of the signal the wave consists of the constant amplitude carrier, of amplitude E. With a signal present, the envelope of the modulated carrier wave should match the form of the signal. While the signal wave can take many forms, it is instructive to study the modulated wave due to a sine-wave signal of radian frequency ω_s. Then the modulated voltage can be expressed as

$$e = (E + E_s \sin \omega_s t) \sin \omega_c t \tag{13-2}$$

where E is the amplitude of the unmodulated carrier, ω_c is its frequency,

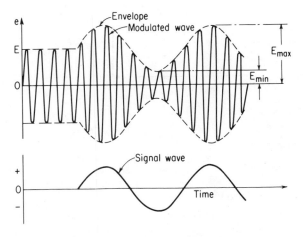

FIGURE 13-1   Amplitude modulated wave.

and E_s and ω_s are the corresponding values for the signal component. If we factor out E and introduce the *degree of modulation m*, we get

$$e = E(1 + m \sin \omega_s t) \sin \omega_c t \qquad (13\text{-}3)$$

where

$$m = \frac{E_s}{E} = \frac{E_{\max} - E_{\min}}{2E} \qquad (13\text{-}4)$$

and $E_{\max}$ and $E_{\min}$ are defined in Fig. 13-1. It is clear that m may vary only from 0 to 1 if the envelope is to represent a sine-wave signal.

Equation (13-3) can be modified as follows:

$$e = E(\sin \omega_c t + m \sin \omega_s t \sin \omega_c t) \qquad (13\text{-}5)$$

Upon expanding the second term in terms of the sum and differences of the angles, we get the important relation

$$e = E\left[\sin \omega_c t + \frac{m}{2} \cos (\omega_c - \omega_s)t - \frac{m}{2} \cos (\omega_c + \omega_s)t \right] \qquad (13\text{-}6)$$

This equation shows that the AM wave can be decomposed into the sum of three fixed-amplitude harmonic voltages, the first having the frequency of the carrier and the other two having frequencies equal to the sum and the difference of the carrier and signal frequencies. The sum and difference frequencies are called the *side-modulation* frequencies. Generally the signal frequency is a small fraction of the carrier frequency, so the three component frequencies are relatively close together, as illustrated in Fig. 13-2a. For example, an AM radio broadcast carrier frequency of 700 kHz with a musical tone signal of 2000 Hz will have components at 700, 698, and 702 kHz.

When the signal wave has a complex form, we may think of its harmonic

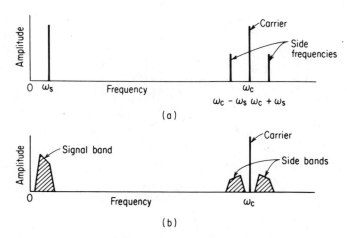

FIGURE 13-2   Frequency components in AM waves.

components as obtained by the Fourier analysis. Then the AM wave will have a number of side frequencies, say, covering a range up to 5000 Hz. The corresponding range of side frequencies is called a *sideband*. Thus a typical radio AM wave comprises a carrier and upper and lower sidebands as suggested in Fig. 13-2b.

At this point mention can be made of a special communication technique that derives from the AM system. Since the signal information is all contained in one sideband, the transmission of the frequencies covering only one sideband is sufficient to carry the signal. This procedure is called *single sideband* transmission. The method conserves frequency bandwidth and potentially can reduce the noise relative to the signal. The carrier may be transmitted at a low level for frequency-controlling purposes, and then a strong carrier wave may be added at the receiver.

A number of interesting questions arise in the design of systems to produce or transmit AM waves, such as the power requirements, or the bandwidth and transient response required in tuned amplifiers to amplify these waves. Moreover, a large number of modulator and detector circuits have been devised. We proceed to a qualitative account of examples of these circuits.

13-3
Examples of AM modulators
and detectors

A simple addition of a signal voltage and a carrier voltage will *not* produce an AM wave. As Eq. (13-5) shows, a product term of the form $\sin \omega_s t \times \sin \omega_c t$ is required. This means that modulators (and detectors) must contain a nonlinear circuit element, such as a diode, to produce the desired result.

The elementary diode modulator circuit in Fig. 13-3 will illustrate this

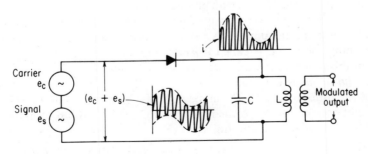

FIGURE 13-3   Diode modulator circuit.

point. The total voltage acting in the circuit is the sum of the signal plus carrier voltages. The diode passes current pulses whose amplitude reflects the variation of the *envelope* of the voltage $e_c + e_s$. The tuned circuit LC is tuned to the carrier frequency. The current pulses excite the tuned circuit, and if the circuit damping is suitable, the voltage across the LC circuit will have the desired amplitude-modulated form. The tuned circuit responds to the current pulses in a manner similar to that of the tank circuit in the class C tuned amplifier discussed in Sec. 8-6. The output wave distortion is reasonably low for low degrees of modulation, and the circuit may be used in low-level modulators.

The plate-modulated class C amplifier (Fig. 13-4) has a high power

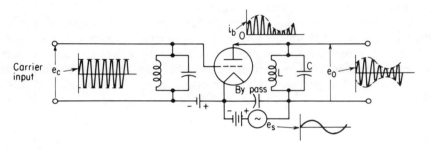

FIGURE 13-4   Plate-modulated class-C amplifier.

efficiency and can be designed for high output and good linearity for high degrees of modulation. The carrier is introduced as a constant-amplitude voltage in the grid circuit, whereas the signal voltage is introduced in series with the dc plate supply. When the signal voltage adds to the dc plate supply, the plate current pulses will be higher and wider, and the tuned circuit will be excited to a higher level. Thus the output voltage envelope will follow the signal wave form. With proper design,† this will be true even with nearly unity (100 per cent) modulation. Similar circuits are used with transistors, and with some modifications with pentodes and beam tubes.

After a modulated wave is transmitted over a wire line or as a radio wave, the original signal must be recovered at the receiving end. The process of regaining the signal is called *demodulation* or *detection*, and the circuits used for this function are called *demodulators* or *detectors*.

The *linear diode* detector circuit is suitable for fairly large AM waves, say, of the order of a few volts in magnitude. The circuit (Fig. 13-5) is essentially that of a half-wave rectifier with an RC load. With an ideal diode the capacitor will charge to the full voltage of each positive peak of the AM

†See, for example, R. W. Landee, D. C. Davis, A. P. Albrecht, *Electronic Designers' Handbook*, McGraw-Hill Book Company, New York, 1957, pp. 5–6 ff.

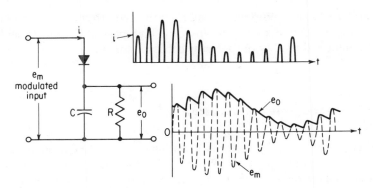

FIGURE 13-5   Diode linear detector.

wave. Then as the modulated voltage falls away from the peak, the charge in the capacitor C tends to maintain the output voltage e_o though this voltage drops along the familiar exponential decay curve with a time-constant RC. The next peak of the AM wave recharges C to a new value, and so forth. The output voltage e_o has the principal characteristics of the original signal wave.

Generally the carrier frequency is forty or more times the signal frequency and therefore the distortion due to the exponential decay between successive peaks will not be as pronounced as in the figure. This distortion is reduced, up to a point, as the time constant is increased. However, if the time constant is made too large, the wave will not fall fast enough on the downgoing side of the AM wave. Instead of following the envelope, the voltage will stay above the envelope and give a distorted output. The maximum value of the time constant that should be used depends on ω_s and on m according to the relation†

$$(RC)_{\max} = \frac{1}{\omega_s}\sqrt{\frac{1}{m^2} - 1} \qquad (13\text{-}7)$$

For example, if $m = 0.8$ and $\omega_s = 2\pi 5000$, then $(RC)_{\max}$ equals 23.8 μs, and if C is chosen to be 150 pF, then R would be 159,000 Ω.

Usually a detector circuit follows an amplifier that has a tuned circuit in its output. The loading effect of the current drawn by the detector is of interest in this situation. The current comes in pulses, so that a kind of average effect is usually calculated.‡ If an effective load resistance is calculated that would draw the same power as the actual circuit, the resulting value is $R/2$, assuming that the diode is ideal.

The output wave e_o in Fig. 13-5 contains a dc component in addition to

†J. D. Ryder, *Electronic Fundamentals and Applications*, Prentice-Hall, Inc., Englewood Cliffs, N.J., 1959, p. 511.
‡J. D. Ryder, *op. cit.*, p. 509.

the signal frequency component (and a small carrier frequency component). The dc can be eliminated by means of a high-pass RC filter, though this added circuit will modify the detector behavior somewhat.

13-4
Square-law modulation

The need for nonlinearity in the modulating device will be brought out by a limited mathematical analysis. We consider the diode modulator of Fig. 13-3 but analyze the operation only for low levels. At high input levels the circuit works as a linear rectifier, but at low levels the operation is over the curved portion of the e-i curve of the diode. This nonlinear characteristic can be represented by a power series expansion about the Q point. We take only the first two terms of the expansion and write

$$i = ae + be^2 \tag{13-8}$$

where a and b are constants and e is the voltage applied to the diode plus the load. But $e = e_c + e_s$, which can be written

$$e = E_c \cos \omega_c t + E_s \cos \omega_s t \tag{13-9}$$

Upon inserting this value in Eq. (13-8), we obtain

$$i = aE_c \cos \omega_c t + aE_s \cos \omega_s t + bE_c^2 \cos^2 \omega_c t$$
$$+ 2bE_c E_s \cos \omega_c t \cos \omega_s t + bE_s^2 \cos^2 \omega_s t \tag{13-10}$$

The first two terms comprise a carrier frequency and a signal frequency term. The cosine squared terms can be expanded by a trigonometric identity, as follows:

$$bE_c^2 \cos^2 \omega_c t = \frac{b}{2} E_c^2 (1 + \cos 2\omega_c t) \tag{13-11}$$

$$bE_s^2 \cos^2 \omega_s t = \frac{b}{2} E_s^2 (1 + \cos 2\omega_s t) \tag{13-12}$$

These terms therefore add constant terms plus double-carrier and double-signal frequency terms. The fourth term in (13-10), upon expansion, yields

$$2bE_c E_s \cos \omega_c t \cos \omega_s t = bE_c E_s [\cos (\omega_c + \omega_s)t + \cos (\omega_c - \omega_s)t] \tag{13-13}$$

This term, then, supplies the desired AM side frequencies.

With a tuned output circuit, as in Fig. 13-3, the carrier and side frequencies will be preserved and the others suppressed; thus the output will be an AM wave. The degree of modulation works out to be

$$m = \frac{2bE_c E_s}{aE_c} = \frac{2b}{a} E_s \tag{13-14}$$

and thus depends on the relative sizes of the linear and squared terms in the power series for the diode current.

If a cubic term is added to the power series and the analysis is extended†
to include this term, it is found that additional side frequencies are generated at the frequencies $\omega_c + 2\omega_s$ and $\omega_c - 2\omega_s$. These components will distort the envelope of the AM output because they are partially or wholly passed by the tuned circuit.

13-5
Frequency modulation and detection

a. Frequency modulation

There are two types of angular modulation called *phase* modulation and *frequency* modulation (FM). In both types the variations take place in the angle θ of Eq. (13-1). In the absence of any modulation the angle θ increases at a uniform rate. With phase modulation the signal voltage causes a variation of the phase of angle θ ahead or behind its normal value, and ideally a direct proportionality between instantaneous relative phase and signal voltage is maintained.

To discuss FM we need a precise definition of instantaneous frequency, which is had by writing

$$2\pi f = \frac{d\theta}{dt} \qquad (13\text{-}15)$$

An FM wave has an instantaneous frequency that varies directly with the instantaneous signal voltage e_s; thus

$$f = f_c + ke_s \qquad (13\text{-}16)$$

The frequency f_c is the *center* (or carrier) frequency and the variable component is ke_s. An FM wave form is given in Fig. 13-6. The FM wave is seen to have a higher frequency at points X and X' where the signal is at its positive maxima and a minimum frequency where the signal is at a negative peak. The amplitude of the signal determines the *amount* of the frequency change, thus information concerning both the size and the periodicity of the signal wave is contained in the FM wave.

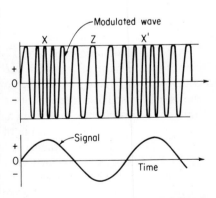

FIGURE 13-6   Frequency-modulated wave.

†See Reference 13-3, p. 300.

The idea of the change of the instantaneous frequency from the center frequency, called the *frequency deviation*, needs further emphasis. A numerical example may be helpful. Let the center frequency be 100 MHz and the maximum signal amplitude be 4 V. Further, assume that the frequency deviation chosen to represent +4 V is +1.0 MHz—a 1 per cent change. Then an instantaneous signal voltage of +2 V would be represented by a frequency of 100.5 MHz; of −2 V by 99.5 MHz; of −4 V by 99.0 MHz, and so on. The *amplitude* variations are converted into *frequency* variations. The magnitude of the largest frequency deviation depends on the design of the system; exemplary values range from a few tenths of 1 per cent of the center frequency in FM radio, to 7.5 per cent in narrow band and 40 per cent in wide-band FM recording on magnetic tape.

When the FM wave is analyzed into its frequency components (Sec. 13-6), the result is more complex than for an AM wave. For a single sine-wave signal there is an infinite series of pairs of side-frequency components at frequencies above and below f_c. The components far removed from f_c become insignificant in amplitude and may be neglected. The number of significant components depends on the ratio of the frequency deviation Δf_c to the signal frequency. For example with $\Delta f_c/f_s = 2$ there are four pairs of significant terms, spaced at $\pm f_s$, $\pm 2f_s$, $\pm 3f_s$, and $\pm 4f_s$ above and below the center frequency. When $\Delta f_c/f_s = 8$, there are about eleven pairs of significant side-frequency terms. These extend beyond the frequency range from $f_c - \Delta f_c$ to $f_c + \Delta f_c$, as explained in the following article. In FM broadcasting the maximum Δf_c is held to 75 kHz; therefore the FM receiver circuits must accept a frequency band 150 kHz wide centered on f_c for each station. This explains why the frequency band allocated to FM broadcasting covers the high frequency range from 88 to 108 MHz.

b. FM modulator

One form of *reactance tube* FM modulator is shown in Fig. 13-7. The circuit to the right of terminals AB acts as a variable capacitance under the control of the signal e_s, and the capacitance change varies the frequency of the Hartley oscillator (details not shown). Assume first that e_s is not active, but that the oscillator generates a sine voltage applied from A to B. With a large coupling capacitor C_c the plate voltage e_p will approximate the oscillator voltage. What is the phase of the grid voltage e_g? The ac voltage-divider action of C and R is proportioned so that most of the voltage is across C, i.e., $1/\omega C > R$. Then the wave of current through the CR branch leads the oscillator voltage by nearly 90°. We recall that a pentode can be represented quite accurately by a current generator $g_m e_g$. Owing to the choke coil RFC the pentode ac plate current must be supplied by the oscillator. But we

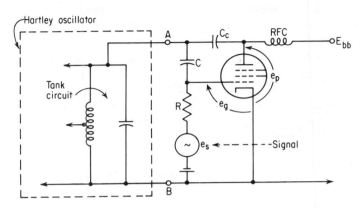

FIGURE 13-7   Reactance-tube FM modulator.

showed that e_g leads by nearly 90°, therefore the current $g_m e_g$ leads by the same angle, and the circuit to the right of AB looks to the oscillator like a capacitor.

The value of g_m can be altered by varying the grid bias. Introducing the signal voltage e_s in the grid circuit will vary g_m accordingly and will vary the effective capacitance and thereby the frequency. In an FM transmitter system the modulation may take place at a low center frequency and then the frequency may be built up through the use of one or more class C frequency multiplier stages. For example, the reactance tube may act on a 5 MHz oscillator and then the frequency may be multiplied 18 times (by a doubler and two triplers) to give a 90 MHz center frequency at the output.

c. FM detector; frequency discriminator

The usual scheme for the recovery of the signal is to convert the FM wave into an AM wave and then use a diode detector. The circuit that converts the FM to AM is called a *frequency discriminator*.

The Foster-Seeley discriminator (Fig. 13-8a) and detector circuit employs coupled resonant circuits tuned to the center frequency. The voltages E_1 and E_2 and also E_1 and E_3 from the primary and the secondary sides are combined (added) and then rectified by the diodes. The rectifier output is zero for the center frequency and varies nearly linearly with frequency on each side of the center over a certain range.

We wish to examine the action of the circuit in more detail. We assume that the coupling capacitor C and the filter capacitors C_1 and C_2 are large. The coupled circuits are tuned to the center frequency and their magnetic

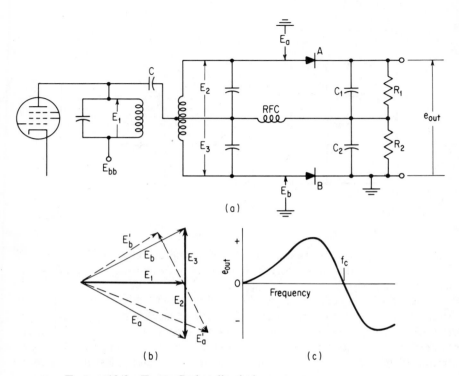

FIGURE 13-8   Foster-Seeley discriminator.

coupling is below the critical value. At the center frequency the voltage induced in the secondary is in phase with $\mathbf{E}_1$. But the terminal voltage $\mathbf{E}_2$ is out of phase with the induced voltage by 90° at resonance, and consequently $\mathbf{E}_2$ is displaced 90° from $\mathbf{E}_1$ as shown in Fig. 13-8b. Next consider the voltages $\mathbf{E}_a$ and $\mathbf{E}_b$ impressed on the diodes. The cathodes of the diodes may be regarded as at *RF* ground potential, owing to C_1 and C_2. If we think of the path from terminal E_{bb} through E_1, through the coupling capacitor C, and through E_2, we see that $\mathbf{E}_a = \mathbf{E}_1 + \mathbf{E}_2$, and likewise $\mathbf{E}_b = \mathbf{E}_1 + \mathbf{E}_3$. Thus at frequency f_c we have $\mathbf{E}_a$ equal to $\mathbf{E}_b$, and the rectified outputs, being opposed, give a total voltage of zero at e_{out}. However, if the frequency is lowered the phases of $\mathbf{E}_2$ and of $\mathbf{E}_3$ shift, and $\mathbf{E}_b$ decreases and $\mathbf{E}_a$ increases as shown by the dashed-line phasors in Fig. 13-8b. As a result the positive component of output exceeds the negative, and e_{out} rises. For higher frequencies the opposite polarity is obtained, and the resulting characteristic curve takes the desired form as in Fig. 13-8c. If the input to the discriminator is an FM wave and the operation remains on the linear part of the characteristic, then e_{out} will be the desired signal wave.

13-6
Analysis of an FM wave

The decomposition of an FM wave that contains an harmonic signal into its frequency components will reveal the effects of (1) signal amplitude, (2) signal frequency, (3) center frequency, and (4) frequency deviation on the frequency components present. This type of information is useful in such applications as radio telemetry and FM tape recording as well as FM radio.

First we modify Eq. (13-16) to read

$$\frac{d\theta}{dt} = \omega = \omega_c + kE_s \cos \omega_s t \tag{13-17}$$

where the signal voltage has been taken to be $E_s \cos \omega_s t$, and k is a constant. Let us define the *peak* frequency deviation to be $\Delta\omega_c$, that is, $\Delta\omega_c = kE_s$. Integration of (13-17) then yields

$$\theta = \omega_c t + \frac{\Delta\omega_c}{\omega_s} \sin \omega_s t + \text{a constant} \tag{13-18}$$

Recalling Eq. (13-1), we see that, except for a phase angle due to the integration constant, the FM wave is given by

$$e = E \sin \left(\omega_c t + \frac{\Delta\omega_c}{\omega_s} \sin \omega_s t \right) \tag{13-19}$$

The ratio $\Delta\omega_c/\omega_s$ is defined to be the *deviation ratio* for the particular signal. For example, the FM wave in Fig. 13-6 has a deviation ratio of roughly four.

Most FM systems have a maximum frequency deviation capability, say, $\Delta\omega_{c\text{max}}$. The *degree of modulation* then is defined to be $\Delta\omega_c/\Delta\omega_{c\text{max}}$. We note that this figure does not depend on the FM wave alone but depends on the capability of the equipment.

The expansion† of Eq. (13-19) to reveal the frequency components makes use of trigonometric identities and Bessel's functions and leads to the following expansion:

$$e = EJ_0\left(\frac{\Delta\omega_c}{\omega_s}\right) \sin \omega_c t$$
$$+ E \sum_{m=1}^{\infty} J_m\left(\frac{\Delta\omega_c}{\omega_s}\right)[\sin (\omega_c + m\omega_s)t + (-1)^m \sin (\omega_c - m\omega_s)t] \tag{13-20}$$

where $J_0(\Delta\omega_c/\omega_s)$ is the Bessel's function of the first kind and of zero order and $J_m(\Delta\omega_c/\omega_s)$ is the corresponding function of the mth order, both of the argument $\Delta\omega_c/\omega_s$. These functions have values in the range from zero to one and are available‡ in the form of tables or curves. Equation (13-20) shows that the side frequencies occur in pairs, but instead of having a single pair as in

†See Reference 13-3 p. 328.
‡E. Janke and F. Emde, *Tables of Functions with Formulae and Curves*, Dover Publications, Inc., New York, 1943.

AM, there now is an infinite series of pairs, each modified in amplitude by a Bessel function coefficient. The side frequencies are spaced at integral multiples of ω_s (or of f_s in terms of actual frequency rather than radian frequency), and thus are somewhat analogous to the harmonics of the signal wave. The importance of a particular component depends on its Bessel coefficient, and these vary in a peculiar way; but eventually, as m increases, the components approach zero. Figure 13-9 shows the amplitudes of the components for

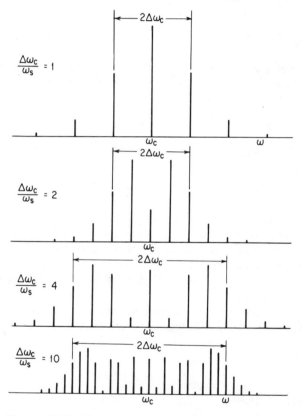

FIGURE 13-9   Frequency spectra of FM waves.

several values of the deviation ratio. The ordinates are all drawn to the same scale, but two different abscissa scales are used in the diagram. If the unmodulated carrier amplitude is taken as unity, then the component of maximum amplitude is 0.765 for $\Delta\omega_c/\omega_s = 1$, and the maximum amplitudes are 0.577, 0.430, and 0.318 for $\Delta\omega_c/\omega_s = 2$, 4, and 10 respectively.

In a practical application, such as in radio telemetry, a knowledge of the bandwidth required to satisfactorily transmit an FM wave is valuable. Corrington† has presented information for different signal wave shapes. He analyzed the magnitudes of the component terms and determined how large a bandwidth is required to pass all terms above a certain magnitude relative to that of the unmodulated carrier. A portion of his results for sine-wave signals is plotted in Fig. 13-10. The symbol f_B gives the bandwidth

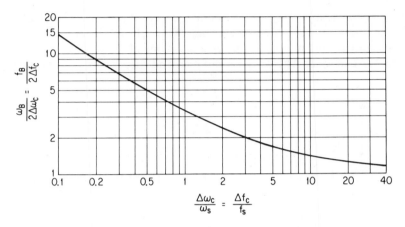

FIGURE 13-10   Bandwidth requirement for FM transmission to retain terms above 0.01 of unmodulated carrier amplitude.

required to retain all terms above a magnitude equal to 0.01 of the unmodulated carrier amplitude. This is said to be a suitable criterion for practical application. The graph shows, for example, that if $\Delta f_c/f_s$ is taken as 10, then $f_B/2\Delta f_c$ is 1.4. That is, the bandwidth needed is 2.8 Δf_c. But if Δf_c remains the same and f_s increases by a factor of 10, then $\Delta f_c/f_s$ is 1.0, and the bandwidth required is 6.8 Δf_c. We see that a practical upper limit on f_s is soon reached, particularly if $\Delta f_c/f_s$ has a value as low as 0.05 or 0.1.

13-7
Superheterodyne receivers;
frequency converter (mixer)

We have seen that in an AM modulator a relatively low frequency signal is combined with a high frequency carrier. When two waves of nearly the same frequency are added, the two waves alternately come "in phase" and rein-

†M. S. Corrington, "Variation of bandwidth with modulation index in frequency modulation," *Proc. Inst. Rad. Eng.*, **35**, 1013–1020 (1947).

force each other and later go "out of phase" and oppose each other. Thus the envelope of the sum has a pulsation at a rate equal to the difference of the two frequencies. The effect is called a *beat* phenomenon, and the difference frequency is called the *beat frequency*.

a. Superheterodyne AM receiver

The *heterodyne* principle is similar, except that the two interacting waves may differ considerably in frequency. This principle is applied in the superheterodyne AM receiver. The general scheme of the receiver is shown in Fig. 13-11. The weak AM wave is amplified and then *heterodyned* against a local

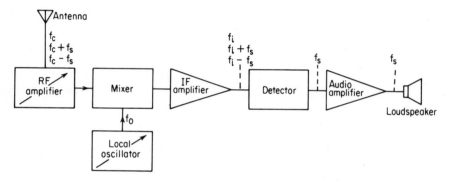

FIGURE 13-11   Block diagram of superheterodyne AM receiver.

oscillator wave of frequency f_o. The two waves are combined in a *frequency converter* or *mixer* stage. The output of the mixer stage contains frequency components consisting of the sum and differences of the component frequencies. The *intermediate frequency* (IF) amplifier selects the difference frequency and amplifies this component. In the case of an incoming AM wave that has a carrier frequency f_c and a signal frequency f_s, the components in the output of the IF amplifier have frequencies f_i, $f_i + f_s$, and $f_i - f_s$, where $f_i = f_o - f_c$, and f_i is called the *intermediate frequency*.

If the AM wave carries a complex signal, such as orchestra music, then there will be sidebands instead of a single f_s. At the output of the IF amplifier these sidebands are preserved as in the original, but now f_i acts as the carrier. The signal is recovered by a detector, with subsequent audio amplification if required.

The advantages of this system are that a high gain together with good selectivity is contributed by the fixed-frequency IF amplifier. The IF amplifier coupling network comprises a double-tuned transformer and the gain versus frequency curve for a properly adjusted stage has a flat top and steep sides.

In AM broadcast receivers generally f_i equals 455 kHz. Thus for a wave having a carrier of $f_c = 800$ kHz, f_o would have to be adjusted to 1255 kHz. If signal frequencies up to 4000 Hz are to be amplified properly, the IF amplifier gain should be flat from 451 to 459 kHz. The receiver is tuned to a different station by simultaneously adjusting the local oscillator and the RF amplifier tuning by means of two variable air capacitors on the dial shaft.

b. A mixer circuit

The mixer stage must contain a nonlinear device to produce the sum and difference frequencies. This may be a diode, a triode, a transistor, etc., but it is often a pentagrid mixer tube. Figure 13-12 shows a mixer circuit

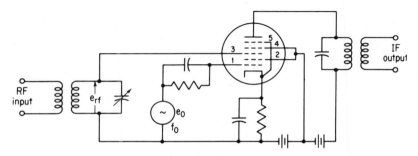

FIGURE 13-12   Pentagrid mixer circuit.

using this tube. The local oscillator f_o drives grid 1 sufficiently hard that the tube current is cut off for part of the cycle and the tube is operated over an extremely nonlinear range. The voltage applied to grid 3 serves to control the division of the space current between the plate and grid 2, which carries a positive potential. Grids 4 and 5 serve the same purpose as the screen and suppressor in a pentode. Now we think of voltages e_{rf} and e_o as sine waves that alternately come "in phase" and "out of phase" owing to their frequency difference. Because e_{rf} is small compared with e_o, we can visualize that the plate current pulse will be increased when the two waves are in phase and decreased when they are out of phase. Thus we would expect a beat phenomenon and an output at the difference frequency. A mathematical analysis† of the case in which e_{rf} is an AM wave with a carrier frequency f_c shows that a number of frequencies appear in the output, including f_c, $f_o - f_c$, $f_o + f_c$ and sums and differences of f_c and the harmonics of f_o, and each type of term retains the amplitude modulated form. The tuned circuit in the

†See Reference 13-1, p. 760.

plate circuit serves as a filter which retains the modulated $f_o - f_c$ term and rejects the others.

The pentagrid tube can also be connected in a circuit that combines the local oscillator and mixer functions. Then it is called a *converter* tube.

c. A receiver for FM

The low-level sections of a typical FM receiver (Fig. 13-13) are similar to

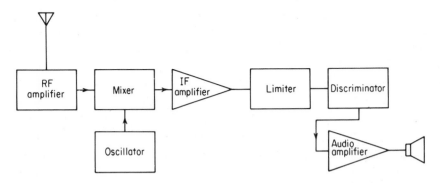

FIGURE 13-13   Diagram of FM receiver.

those of the AM receiver except for design details. However, a *limiter* stage is used to reduce noise and a discriminator circuit is provided to regain the audio signal. The action of the limiter is shown in Fig. 13-14. It clips off

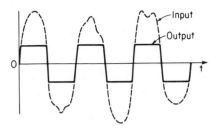

FIGURE 13-14   Limiter action.

the tops and bottoms of the waves beyond a certain level and thereby removes the amplitude modulation which may have inadvertently been added to the waves. One source of such distortion is atmospheric electricity or "static." If the instants of the wave zero crossings have not been shifted by the interference, then a limiter can remove much of the added noise on the FM wave. The tuned circuit in the discriminator that follows the limiter restores the FM wave nearly to its original form. Limiter circuits are based on overdriven amplifiers or on clipper circuits (Chapter 16).

The noise reduction by limiter action is dependent on having at least a minimum signal relative to the noise. If the signal amplitude falls below about 2 or 3 times the peak of the noise component, the noise suppression effect rapidly diminishes.

Actual interference or noise in an FM receiver will contain both amplitude and angle modulation. By using a large frequency deviation the effect of the unwanted angle modulation is reduced. Of course, in commercial FM stations, the frequency deviation is standardized at a compromise value to permit allocation of the frequency spectrum to more stations.

13-8
Switch modulators

Vibrating reed switches called *choppers* are used as modulators and demodulators for low frequency signals. An example of this application is explained in Sec. 14-3.

A semiconductor diode can be viewed as a switch controlled by the polarity of the impressed voltage. In the bridge modulator circuit in Fig. 13-15 the diode switches are under the control of the carrier voltage, which

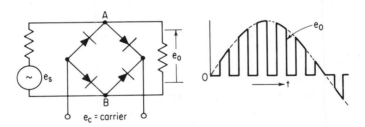

FIGURE 13-15   Bridge or switch modulator.

is assumed to be large compared with the signal e_s. On one carrier half-cycle the diode switches are "closed," thereby shorting terminals A and B. On the alternate half-cycles the diodes are "open," so the load receives a fraction of the signal voltage. The effect is to produce the wave form e_o shown in the figure.

An analysis of the output wave will show that the carrier frequency term is absent, but terms at frequencies f_s, $f_c + f_s$, and $f_c - f_s$, as well as such terms as $2f_c \pm f_s$ are present. The terms at frequencies $f_c \pm f_s$ are representative of the sidebands of an AM wave, and when these are selected by a band-pass filter, the result is a so-called *carrier-suppressed* modulated wave. The signal information is contained in this wave and can be recovered by suitable techniques.

Figure 13-16 shows the circuit of another switch modulator, called the

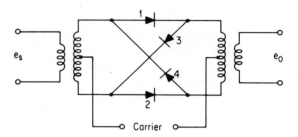

FIGURE 13-16   Diagram of a ring modulator.

ring modulator. With a large carrier voltage diodes 1 and 2 are closed during one half-cycle and 3 and 4 during the other half-cycle by carrier frequency currents that flow via the winding center taps. This, in effect, causes a *reversing switch* action, so that the signal voltage is reversed at carrier frequency. The output wave contains the side frequencies and side frequencies of harmonics of the carrier, but the carrier itself is suppressed.

Switch-type modulators are used in carrier communication systems and in servo systems.

13-9
Phase discriminator;
phase-sensitive detector

In some measurement work it is necessary to obtain an output dependent on the *phase difference* between two signals of the same frequency. Sometimes it is only necessary to discriminate between 0 and 180° phase relations, as in applications of the linear variable differential transformer transducer.

a. Switch-type phase-sensitive detectors

A single-pole, double-throw vibrating reed switch (chopper) can serve as a phase-sensitive detector in the circuit in Fig. 13-17a. The reed is driven by a reference voltage e_r of the same frequency as the signal e_s. For our purposes we think of the switch as ideal, i.e., it reverses instantaneously and has zero

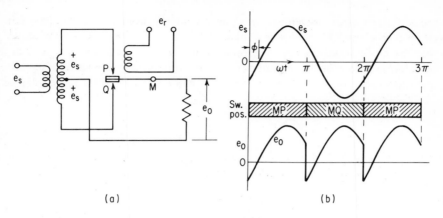

(a)   (b)

FIGURE 13-17 Vibrating switch phase-sensitive detector, (a) circuit diagram and (b) waveforms and switch position.

resistance when closed. Then the output voltage wave consists of segments of the signal voltage one-half cycle in duration but with alternate half-cycles reversed (Fig. 13-17b). The curves in the figure are drawn for a particular value of the angle ϕ between the zero of the e_s wave and the instant of switching.

The average value e_{av} of the output voltage e_o is readily calculated; thus,

$$e_{av} = \frac{1}{\pi} \int_0^\pi E_{sm} \sin(\omega t + \phi)\, d(\omega t) = \frac{2}{\pi} E_{sm} \cos \phi \qquad (13\text{-}21)$$

Thus the average output voltage is a cosine function of the angle ϕ.

A switch-type phase-sensitive detector that can work at higher frequencies is shown in Fig. 13-18. Both the signal and the reference source transformers

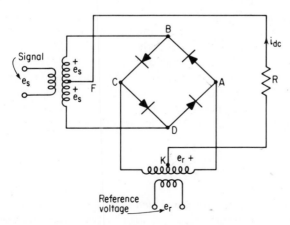

FIGURE 13-18 Switch-type phase-sensitive detector.

have center-tappèd secondary windings, with the load connected between these center taps. The reference voltage should be larger than the signal, so that the diode states depend only on e_r. For example, when e_r is positive, diodes in the path ABC are conducting and the others have a small reverse voltage and so are cut off. The wave forms shown in Fig. 13-19 will aid an explana-

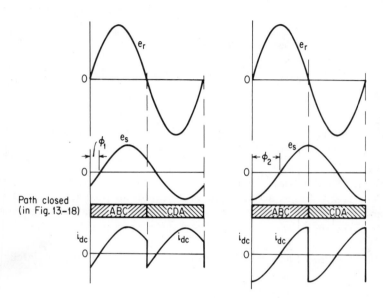

FIGURE 13-19   Waveforms in circuit of Fig. 13-18.

tion of the circuit behavior. During the first half-cycle the circuit path ABC is closed and CDA is open. The signal voltage at point B therefore acts on points A and C simultaneously. As a result current flows from the signal source toward point K via points A and C and the two halves of the reference transformer secondary and thence through the load. During the second half-cycle the path CDA is closed and the lower half of the signal transformer secondary delivers signal current to the load. The load current wave in the ideal case just described has the same form as the switch detector in Fig. 13-17 does. The average value of the output wave then is directly proportional to $\cos \phi$, by analogy with Eq. (13-21). The actual behavior with a current source and a low resistance load approaches the ideal.

b. Phase discriminator

A phase-sensitive detector (or *discriminator*) that works on a different principle is shown in Fig. 13-20. Here e_1 is regarded as a fixed reference and e_2 is the signal whose phase may be varied. Assume first that e_1 and e_2 are

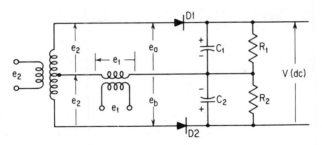

FIGURE 13-20   Phase discriminator circuit.

in phase. Then diode $D1$ receives the sum of the voltages $e_1 + e_2$, and diode $D2$ receives the difference, $e_1 - e_2$. Let $e_1 = E_{1m} \sin \omega t$ and $e_2 = E_{2m} \sin \omega t$. Furthermore, we assume that $E_{1m} \leqq E_{2m}$; that the diodes are ideal, and that the time constants R_1C_1 and R_2C_2 are very long. Each capacitor receives a direct voltage equal to the peak of the voltage impressed in that diode circuit, that is, $E_{1m} + E_{2m}$ appears on C_1 and $|E_{1m} - E_{2m}|$ appears on C_2. Therefore the dc output voltage V, being the difference, is $2E_{1m}$ for the in-phase condition.

If the phase of e_1 is reversed, then $e_1 = -E_{1m} \sin \omega t$, and e_a is diminished and e_b is increased, and the output has the opposite sign, i.e., $V = -2E_{1m}$ for the 180° condition.

Next we consider the more general case of a phase angle ϕ between the reference and the signal, so we let

$$e_1 = E_{1m} \sin \omega t \tag{13-22}$$

$$e_2 = E_{2m} \sin (\omega t + \phi) \tag{13-23}$$

where $E_{1m} \leqq E_{2m}$.

The voltages impressed on the rectifiers are

$$e_a = e_1 + e_2 = E_{1m} \sin \omega t + E_{2m} \sin (\omega t + \phi) \tag{13-24}$$

$$e_b = e_1 - e_2 = E_{1m} \sin \omega t - E_{2m} \sin (\omega t + \phi) \tag{13-25}$$

These relations are illustrated by the phasor diagram in Fig. 13-21. It is clear that the sum and difference voltages depend on the phase angle ϕ as well as on the voltage magnitudes. The output voltage is the difference between the peak values of e_a and e_b. Application of the cosine law to the triangles in Fig. 13-21 yields

$$V = (E_{1m}^2 + E_{2m}^2 + 2E_{1m}E_{2m} \cos \phi)^{1/2}$$
$$- (E_{1m}^2 + E_{2m}^2 - 2E_{1m}E_{2m} \cos \phi)^{1/2} \quad (13\text{-}26)$$

Two special cases are of interest. When $E_{1m} < E_{2m}$, the following approximation holds:

$$V \cong 2E_{1m} \cos \phi \tag{13-27}$$

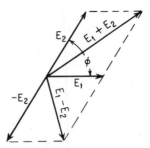

FIGURE 13-21   Phase relations in the circuit in Fig. 13-20.

That is, V is approximately proportional to the component of phasor $\mathbf{E}_1$ that is in-phase with respect to $\mathbf{E}_2$.

In the second case we assume that $E_{1m} = E_{2m} = E_m$, which defines the symbol E_m. Then Eq. (13-26) yields, after some manipulation,

$$V = 2\sqrt{2}\,E_m\left(\cos\frac{\phi}{2} - \sin\frac{\phi}{2}\right) \tag{13-28}$$

The function of ϕ in the parentheses has the value $+1$ at $\phi = 0°$, zero at $\phi = 90°$, and the value -1 at $\phi = 180°$; and the variation in between is not far from linear. However, the function ranges over the same values for $180° < \phi < 360°$. Therefore the value of V does not uniquely determine ϕ, and we must know in which quadrant ϕ lies before its value is definitely determined.

REFERENCES

13-1 Truman S. Gray, *Applied Electronics*, 2d ed., John Wiley & Sons, Inc., New York, 1954, Chap. XII.

13-2 S. S. Hakim and R. Barrett, *Transistor Circuits in Electronics*, Hayden Publishing Company, New York, 1964, Chap. 9.

13-3 V. C. Rideout, *Active Networks*, Prentice-Hall, Inc., Englewood Cliffs, N.J., 1954, Chaps. 10, 11, 12.

13-4 Mischa Schwartz, *Information Transmission, Modulation and Noise*, McGraw-Hill Book Company, New York, 1959.

13-5 F. E. Terman, *Electronic and Radio Engineering*, 4th ed., McGraw-Hill Book Company, New York, 1955, Chaps. 15, 16, 17.

EXERCISES

13-1 A resistance strain-gage bridge circuit is excited by a 5-kHz carrier voltage. The unmodulated carrier voltage at the bridge output has a peak value of 400 mV. Assume that a certain 200-Hz vibration applied to the strain gage structure produces an AM output voltage with a modulation factor of 0.6. (a) What are the amplitudes and frequencies of the components of the modulated wave? (b) What are the instantaneous maximum and minimum values of the modulated wave?

13-2 Suppose that a superheterodyne receiver is receiving an AM wave which has a carrier frequency of 1.1 MHz and a band of audio frequencies from 200 to 2000 Hz. The local oscillator frequency is 1.555 MHz. What are the frequencies of the components present (a) at the input from the antenna, (b) at the output of the IF amplifier, and (c) at the output of the audio amplifier?

13-3 A voltage wave expressible by the following relation:

$$e = 20 \sin 314{,}000t + 2 \cos 308{,}350t - 2 \cos 319{,}650t$$

is impressed on a linear detector. If we assume that the envelope of the wave is recovered without loss, what is the magnitude and frequency of the ac component of the detector output voltage?

13-4 An AM voltage wave has an unmodulated carrier amplitude of 4 V and its degree of modulation is 0.8. The carrier frequency is 10^6 Hz and the signal frequency is 5000 Hz. This wave is applied to a linear diode detector which uses a filter circuit of $C = 150$ pF and $R = 160{,}000 \ \Omega$. (a) Sketch the envelope of the output voltage wave. (b) Repeat (a) on the assumption that C is inadvertently increased to 500 pF.

13-5 The frequency of an oscillator is measured by the following method. A 5.0-MHz standard frequency signal from the National Bureau of Standards station WWV is heterodyned with the oscillator under test. The intermediate frequency is compared with that of an auxiliary laboratory oscillator by means of a cathode-ray oscilloscope and found to be 30,500 Hz. Additional tests show that the test oscillator frequency is lower than that of the standard signal. What is the frequency of the test oscillator, and what is the percentage accuracy of the determination, if the calibration of the laboratory oscillator is accurate to 2 per cent? The standard frequency is accurate to better than one part in 50 million.

13-6 A thermionic diode used in a square-law modulator circuit has the following current-voltage data:

e (V) = 1	2	3	4	5	6
i(mA) = 3.4	7.6	12.6	18.8	25	32.4

Suppose that the diode is biased at 3.0 V, the carrier wave amplitude is 2.0 V and the signal wave amplitude is 1.0 V. (a) What is the amplitude of the side frequency components? (b) What is the degree of modulation in the output?

13-7 Assume that a radiosonde uses an FM telemetry system that employs a center frequency of 10 MHz and has a Δf_c equal to 20 kHz. If the signal frequency is 5000 Hz, what are (a) the frequencies of the important components of the modulated wave and (b) the amplitudes of these components relative to that of the unmodulated carrier?

13-8 The transmission link of an FM telemetry system uses a carrier frequency of 224 MHz and a maximum deviation of 0.1 MHz. Estimate the bandwidth requirement for the FM receiver for sine-wave signals if (a) $f_s = 3$ kHz and (b) $f_s = 30$ kHz.

13-9 Consider a switch-type phase-sensitive detector in which the signal voltage is given by $e_s = E_{sm} \sin(\omega_s + \phi) + E_{2m} \sin(2\omega_s t + \alpha)$. (a) What is the average value of the output voltage? (b) Would the answer to (a) be different if the frequency of the second term in the signal voltage were changed to some other harmonic of the fundamental frequency? (c) Comment on the question whether a phase detector circuit will discriminate against noise voltages introduced with the signal.

13-10 Give a theoretical analysis of a detector system that consists of an electronic multiplier followed by a low-pass filter. Assume that the two voltages feeding the multiplier are the signal voltage $E \sin \omega_s t$ and a reference wave $1.0 \cos \omega_r t$. (a) Show that the output of the multiplier contains components having the radian frequencies $\omega_s + \omega_r$ and $\omega_s - \omega_r$. (b) Consider the case in which $\omega_s = \omega_r = \omega$, but with a phase angle added to the signal, e.g., let $e_s = E \sin (\omega t + \phi)$. What is the output of the low-pass filter? (c) Discuss the noise rejection capability of this detector system.

13-11 The phase discriminator circuit in Fig. 13-20 is used with $e_1 = 20 \sin (2\pi 400t + \phi)$ and $e_2 = 20 \sin 2\pi 400t$. (a) Calculate V for values of ϕ of $0°$, $30°$, $60°$, and $90°$. How nearly linear is the relation of V to ϕ? (b) Choose values for the filter capacitors and resistors for this application.

14

dc Amplifiers and
the Analog Computer

14-1
Elementary dc amplifiers

A need for dc amplification arises in dc vacuum-tube voltmeters, some servo systems, dc voltage regulators, analog computers, and cathode-ray oscilloscopes. By definition, the lower frequency limit is zero, or dc, but the upper frequency limit depends on the application and may be as low as a few cycles per second or as high as the megacycle range. Two general types of high-gain dc amplifiers exist: (1) those having *direct-coupled* (conductively connected) stages, and (2) those that convert (modulate) the signal to an ac signal, then amplify it, and finally regain the original signal by demodulation.

An elementary *direct-coupling* scheme is shown in the two-stage amplifier in Fig. 14.1. Here a sectional plate voltage supply is used and a possible set of electrode potentials relative to ground is shown for the condition $e_i = 0$. By connecting the cathode of tube 2 at a positive potential a few volts higher relative to ground than the quiescent plate potential of tube 1, a direct connection can be made from the plate of tube 1 to the grid of tube 2 and still a negative bias can be provided to the second tube. The output circuit of tube 2 has a balancing voltage, shown as 50 V in the figure, which just balances the $I_b R$ drop of the plate resistor of tube 2 at the *zero-signal* condition. However, with a signal applied at e_i, both the dc and variable signal components are amplified and emerge at e_o.

We might expect that by using high-μ triodes we could realize a voltage

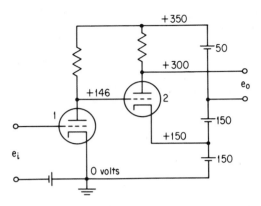

FIGURE 14-1   Two-stage dc amplifier.

gain of about 40 per stage, or 1600 for the amplifier. However, a serious limitation on the practically realizable gain is the tendency of the amplifier output to vary with time, or to *drift*, even though no signal is applied. This drift is mainly caused by temperature variations of tubes or components and to line voltage variations. For example, suppose that a 5 per cent change in line voltage occurs. This will change the heater voltage and cathode temperature and thereby cause a slight shift in the tube characteristics. The shift in the characteristic of tube 1, caused by a change in the initial velocities of the emitted electrons, can produce the same result as about 0.02-V change in grid potential. If the effect of the change in tube 2 be disregarded, we find the change in the output would be 0.02 × 1600, or 32 V. Thus this amplifier would have a fluctuating output with zero input and would be entirely unsuitable in most applications.

Another drawback of this circuit is that both terminals of the output are at dc potentials above ground, and usually a grounded output is required. Other problems are the 150-V stress on the heater-to-cathode insulation of tube 2 if the heater is grounded and the necessity of providing the multiple dc supply voltages.

An improved circuit which has a grounded output and requires only a two section dc supply is shown in Fig. 14-2. In this circuit the resistance voltage divider R_1 and R_2, connected from the plate of tube 1 to a high negative voltage, serves to couple the two tubes. Thus the grid of tube 2 is brought to a suitable negative potential. However, the potential divider action of R_1 and R_2 reduces the incremental signal that reaches the grid of tube 2, thereby cutting down the gain. However, the use of a large value of E_{cc} leads to a relatively large R_2 compared with R_1, and the loss of gain is not too high a price for the advantages gained. A similar voltage divider circuit, comprising R_3 and R_4, serves to bring the output to ground potential.

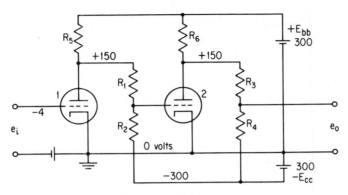

FIGURE 14-2   Improved dc amplifier.

Drift problems similar to those just described are also encountered in transistor dc amplifiers, largely caused by the temperature variation of I_{co}. The low input impedance of the usual transistor stage may be overcome by the circuit design of the input stage or the use of a field-effect transistor. A balanced circuit which reduces the drift will be described in the following article.

In some ways transistors lend themselves more readily to direct coupling than tubes do. For example, both the base and collector dc potentials in a common-emitter stage have the same polarity, which simplifies the coupling problem. Furthermore, in the low-level stages the transistor can be operated satisfactorily at a low collector voltage, so a direct coupling from the collector to the base of the next transistor is feasible. A coupling circuit of this type is shown in Fig. 14-3. In this circuit transistor 1 operates with a lower collector voltage than transistor 2 does, so that adequate collector-to-base voltage

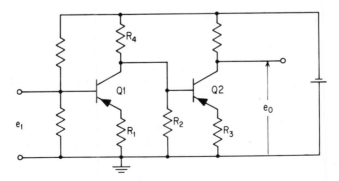

FIGURE 14-3   Transistor dc amplifier.

is available on the output transistor. In a practical design† the resistances are chosen to give suitable Q points for the two transistors and also to provide the needed stability.

14-2
Differential or difference amplifiers

A great improvement in the drift characteristic is achieved by the use of a balanced circuit (Fig. 14-4), which employs two triodes (or pentodes) per stage. The importance of the balanced circuit arises from the fact that if the two triode plate currents change in the same direction, then the changes in plate-to-plate output voltage tend to cancel. Since twin triodes in a single envelope are commonly used, the two triodes will have nearly identical characteristics as well as temperature variations, and therefore will provide nearly exact balance. Thus variations in E_{bb} and E_{cc} are largely compensated, as are the slow changes in contact potentials of the two triodes which cause "zero" drift.

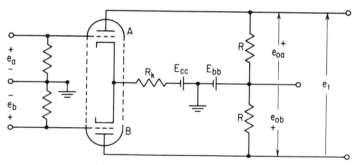

FIGURE 14-4   Difference, or differential, amplifier.

As shown in Fig. 14-4, two separate input signals can be used if desired, or as will be shown presently, a single input signal is also suitable. We discuss the properties of the general circuit first, then proceed to the various modifications.

In the usual application, the cathode resistor R_k is relatively large, requiring a large E_{cc} of, say, -300 V. Thus the amplifier appears to embody high negative feedback, but we shall show that the feedback is only effective in the suppression of the unwanted "*common mode*" voltages. Let us begin

†Transistor Circuit Engineering, Richard F. Shea, ed., John Wiley & Sons, Inc., New York, 1957, p. 60.

the analysis by drawing the small-signal equivalent circuit (Fig. 14-5). Here, for simplicity, the tube parameters and plate load resistors are assumed to be identical on the two sides of the circuit, and capacitance effects are neglected. The sign conventions adopted for the input and output voltages should be noted. These are taken so as to be symmetrical, and their significance will emerge in the subsequent discussion.

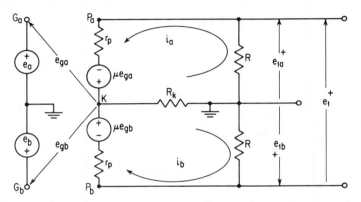

FIGURE 14-5   Small-signal equivalent circuit of difference amplifier.

The loop equations for the circuit are

$$\mu e_{ga} = \mu[e_a - (i_a + i_b)R_k] = i_a(r_p + R_k + R) + i_bR_k \qquad (14\text{-}1)$$

$$\mu e_{gb} = \mu[e_b - (i_a + i_b)R_k] = i_b(r_p + R_k + R) + i_aR_k \qquad (14\text{-}2)$$

By eliminating i_b between these two equations and writing $e_{1a} = -Ri_a$ we find, after simplification

$$e_{1a} = -\mu R \left\{ \frac{e_a\left[1 + \dfrac{r_p + R}{(\mu + 1)R_k}\right] - e_b}{2(r_p + R) + \dfrac{(r_p + R)^2}{(\mu + 1)R_k}} \right\} \qquad (14\text{-}3)$$

The expression for e_{1b} is found in a similar fashion, and it is the same as (14-3) except that e_a and e_b are interchanged.

In the usual circuits R_k is chosen large enough so that $(\mu + 1)R_k \gg (r_p + R)$. Then, as an approximation, the terms containing $(\mu + 1)R_k$ in the denominator can be neglected, so we find

$$e_{1a} \cong -\frac{\mu R}{2(r_p + R)}(e_a - e_b) \qquad (14\text{-}4)$$

and

$$e_{1b} \cong -\frac{\mu R}{2(r_p + R)}(e_b - e_a) \qquad (14\text{-}5)$$

The plate-to-plate output voltage e_1, called the *floating* or *differential* output, is

$$e_1 = e_{1a} - e_{1b} \cong -\frac{\mu R}{r_p + R}(e_a - e_b) \tag{14-6}$$

Equations (14-4), (14-5), and (14-6) show that the output voltages are proportional to the *difference* of the two input signals and thus show why the circuit is called† a *difference* amplifier. The basic amplifier is applied in a number of different modes, as will now be explained.

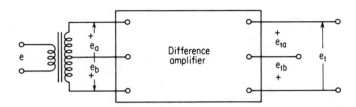

FIGURE 14-6   Balanced input voltage. Note that $e_b = -e_a$.

a. *Balanced input* (Fig. 14-6)

Here $e_b = -e_a$, so by Eqs. (14-4) and (14-6),

$$e_{1a} \cong -\frac{\mu R}{r_p + R}e_a \tag{14-7}$$

and

$$e_1 \cong -\frac{2\mu R}{r_p + R}e_a \tag{14-8}$$

The voltage gain defined as $e_1/2e_a$ is called the *differential mode* gain G_d and has the value

$$G_d = -\frac{\mu R}{r_p + R} \tag{14-9}$$

Thus the gain is the same as for a grounded-cathode stage despite the presence of R_k. This is understandable because a study of Fig. 14-5 shows that the effects of the incremental currents i_a and i_b cancel in R_k.

b. *Common-mode input*

Common-mode voltages are those which act on the two grids equally, or in phase in terms of sinusoids. A common source of such a voltage is

†The circuit is also called the *long-tailed pair*.

illustrated in the strain-gage measurement circuit in Fig. 14-7. Sometimes, as in rocket engine tests, the amplifier and recorder must be placed at some distance from the strain-gage bridge, so that the ground connections are far apart. The local magnetic and electric fields, or the effect of stray currents in the ground circuits, give rise to an equivalent "noise" or interference voltage generator e_n. This acts on the two grids in the common mode and may cause a spurious voltage in the output.

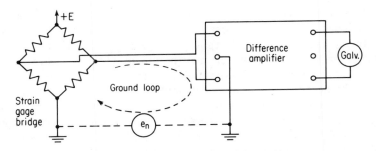

FIGURE 14-7   Source of common-mode noise voltage.

Our analysis will refer to Fig. 14-8. Qualitatively we can see that, since the signals to the two grids are in phase, the currents i_a and i_b in Fig. 14-5 will be in phase. As a result the amplifier operates with cathode resistor feedback, and in fact resistor R_k is twice as effective in producing negative feedback as in a single tube circuit. By placing $e_b = e_a$ in Eq. (14-3) and in the corresponding expression for e_{1b}, we can show that

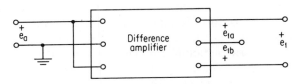

FIGURE 14-8   Common-mode input voltage.

$$e_{1a} = e_{1b} = -\frac{\mu R e_a}{R + r_p + 2R_k(\mu + 1)} \qquad (14\text{-}10)$$

Let us define the common-mode gain G_c as the ratio of the one-sided output voltage to the voltage on the grids with common-mode input; then,

$$G_c = \frac{-\mu R}{R + r_p + 2R_k(\mu + 1)} \qquad (14\text{-}11)$$

Consider an amplifier in which $\mu = 80$, $r_p = 60k$, $R = 100k$, and $R_k = 120k$. Then Eq. (14-11) gives a value of $|G_c|$ of 0.41, showing that the common-mode voltage is attenuated through this amplifier. The same amplifier has a differential gain $|G_d|$, of 50.

c. Discrimination factor; common-mode rejection factor

When a differential amplifier is used with differential signals in the presence of common-mode noise, as in instrumentation, the *discrimination factor*, defined as G_d/G_c, is important. This factor should be as large as possible. In the example in the foregoing paragraph the discrimination factor is 50/0.41 or 122, a value which may be too low for practical work. One method of increasing the discrimination factor is to increase R_k, but this entails a higher E_{cc}, and a practical limit is soon reached. An alternative scheme is to replace R_k by a pentode operated in a nearly constant current region. Thus the incremental resistance is greatly increased without unduly raising the supply voltage requirement. The discrimination factor is also increased by using difference stages in cascade.

In the perfectly symmetrical amplifier discussed thus far the floating output voltage e_1 produced by a common-mode input would be zero (see Eq. 14-10, and note $e_1 = e_{1a} - e_{1b}$). In real circuits there are inevitable differences in the triode parameters on the two sides, with the result that a common-mode input produces a measurable voltage e_1. The *common-mode rejection factor* with respect to e_1 is defined as the ratio:

$$\frac{\text{Common-mode input voltage to produce a specified } e_1}{\text{Differential-mode input voltage to produce the same } e_1}$$

Similar factors are defined in relation to the outputs e_{1a} and e_{1b}. Middlebrook[†] has presented an extensive treatment of the discrimination factor and common-mode rejection factor for tube and transistor differential amplifiers. For example, he points out that the common-mode rejection factor is not a direct function of the discrimination factor. Thus, while a high discrimination factor is helpful in increasing the common-mode rejection factor, the circuit unbalances have a greater effect on the latter factor.

d. Single-ended input to balanced output (Fig. 14-9)

In this connection the lower grid is grounded, then $e_b = 0$, and Eqs. (14-4) and (14-5) give

$$e_{1a} \cong -e_{1b} \cong -\frac{\mu R}{2(r_p + R)} e_a \qquad (14\text{-}12)$$

†Reference 14-4.

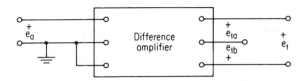

FIGURE 14-9   Single-ended input voltage.

Thus nearly equal and opposite output voltages are developed from a single-ended input. This circuit is also called a *cathode-coupled phase inverter*.

It is of interest to investigate the degree of approximation in Eq. (14-12), in particular to find the ratio of e_{1a} to e_{1b}. For this purpose we put $e_b = 0$ in Eq. (14-3) and manipulate the expression and find

$$e_{1a} = -\frac{e_a}{2}\left[\frac{\mu R}{r_p + R} + \frac{\mu R}{2(\mu + 1)R_K + r_p + R}\right] \quad (14\text{-}13)$$

or, in terms of the differential gain G_d and the common-mode gain G_c,

$$e_{1a} = +\frac{e_a}{2}(G_d + G_c) \quad (14\text{-}14)$$

A similar procedure leads to the value of e_{1b}

$$e_{1b} = -\frac{e_a}{2}(G_d - G_c) \quad (14\text{-}15)$$

To illustrate the difference in magnitudes of the output voltages on the two sides, we use the same constants as in the earlier example and find that $|e_{1a}/e_{1b}| = 1.016$. This degree of unbalance would be acceptable in an audio amplifier but might need to be considered in other applications.

The floating output voltage e_1 is obtained from (14-14) and (14-15)

$$e_1 = e_{1a} - e_{1b} = +G_d e_a \quad (14\text{-}16)$$

and depends only on the differential gain.

e. Differential amplifier stages in cascade

The problem of coupling successive stages is similar to that in other dc amplifiers. If the output can be floating, as in recording work using a high-speed galvanometer, the scheme shown in Fig. 14-10 can be used. In this scheme the potentials at the plates and cathodes of the second-stage triodes are sufficiently raised so that a direct plate-to-grid coupling connection can be made. A study of the quiescent potentials shown in the figure will show how proper grid bias can be provided. In a practical amplifier additional balancing controls would be required, for example, an adjustable balancing resistance in the plate supply connections.

When more than two stages are required, the limitations of the foregoing

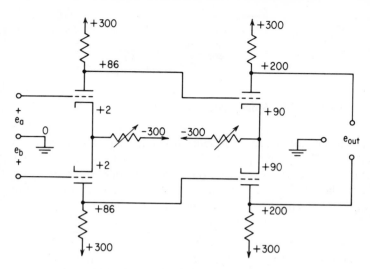

FIGURE 14-10   Two-stage differential amplifier with illustrative voltages to ground.

scheme (limited output voltage, high supply voltage) become serious, and a coupling method like that in Fig. 14-2 can be used to advantage.

f. Transistor differential amplifier

The one-stage amplifier in Fig. 14-11 is seen to comprise emitter coupling by reason of resistor R_3. Differential mode signals are amplified without degeneration in a perfectly symmetrical circuit, whereas the common-mode signals are subject to the degenerating effect of R_3. Therefore R_3 is made relatively large to increase the discrimination factor. The detailed analysis of the effects of small unbalances, of variations in source voltages, and of temperature effects is too involved to include here.† Another factor which

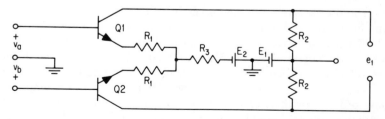

FIGURE 14-11   Emitter-coupled differential amplifier; $R_1 < R_3$.

†Middlebrook, R. D.; Reference 14-4.

enters is the effect of the source impedance, which is greater with the transistor amplifier. If a one-sided output to ground is needed, more sophisticated circuits† are required to achieve the same common-mode rejection factor.

14-3
Instrument amplifiers based on
modulation; chopper amplifier

Some instrumentation and control systems must respond to very low voltages. For example, the output of a thermocouple may be in the microvolt range for small temperature differences. Conventional dc amplifiers would have intolerable drift and adjustment problems in this application. The principle of an amplifying system suitable for such applications is shown in Fig. 14-12. The low-level signal, which may have slowly varying direct voltage or low-frequency ac components, is converted into an ac signal by the modulator, then is amplified in a conventional ac amplifier, and finally demodulated to regain the amplified signal.

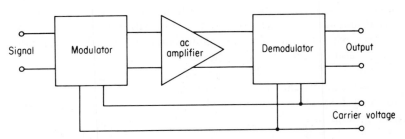

FIGURE 14-12   Modulator-type dc amplifier.

Among the types of low-level modulators which might be selected are the vacuum-tube, transistor, or the switch-type modulator. The switch-type modulators have been favored owing to their low drift and noise. Several switch-types modulators have been used, including mechanical and diode "choppers," second-harmonic magnetic, transistor, and variable-capacitance types. A circuit in which a mechanical chopper performs both the modulation and demodulation function is given in Fig. 14-13.

The chopper consists of a polarized vibrating reed relay, which generally is designed for operation at 60 or 400 vibrations per second. The reed alternately touches contacts 1 and 2 and acts as a single-pole, double-throw switch. Two types are available: (1) the make-before-break type in which

†Middlebrook, R. D., and A. D. Taylor, *Electronics*, **34**, 56–59, (July 28, 1961).

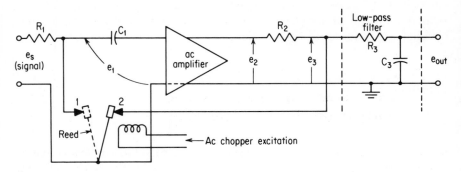

FIGURE 14-13   Chopper-modulated dc amplifier.

there is no open-circuit interval and (2) the break-before-make type. Type 1 is preferable in the application in Fig. 14-13 if the ac amplifier has an even number of stages, so that there is no possibility that the capacitive feedback from contact 2 to contact 1 during the open interval will cause oscillation.

Figure 14-14 illustrates the modulation and demodulation process for a signal e_s which has both a direct and an alternating component. If R_1 is small compared with the input resistance of the amplifier, the voltage at e_1 has an envelope nearly as high as e_s but with alternate segments reduced to zero, while the chopper reed contacts terminal 1. The ac amplifier passes the ac components but not the direct component of e_1 and delivers the amplified wave at e_2 (shown in an idealized form in Fig. 14-14). Since the chopper reed grounds the output while in contact at side 2, alternate segments of the output wave are reduced to zero, with the result shown for e_3. Voltage e_3 is impressed on a low-pass filter which will deliver an output voltage e_{out} whose form is an approximate amplified replica of e_s, except for sign. This amplifier system provides stable and reliable means for amplifying low-level dc signals, but the ac signal frequency range is restricted to an upper limit about one-tenth of the chopper frequency.

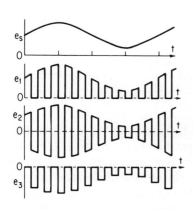

FIGURE 14-14   Illustrating chopper modulation and demodulation.

A number of alternative input switch modulator circuits as well as demodulator circuits are used in practice.†

†See, for example, Reference 14-1, pp. 4–25 ff.

14-4
Chopper-stabilized wide-band
dc amplifier

For such critical applications as in high-quality analog computers the drift of a high-gain conventional dc amplifier is excessive and the frequency bandwidth of a chopper-modulated amplifier is too small. An ingenious scheme† consists in combining the nearly drift-free chopper-modulated amplifier with a wide-band dc amplifier so as to reduce the effective drift of the latter.

Before discussing the actual scheme, let us examine the relative effects of the drift voltages ϵ and ϵ' in the cascade-connected amplifiers in Fig. 14-15. We assume that each amplifier has two inputs which combine the signals in an additive fashion. Thus the output of the amplifier A_2 is $(e_1 + \epsilon')$ A_2, where ϵ' is the drift voltage of this amplifier. The output voltage of A_1 will be

$$e_o = (e_1 + \epsilon')A_2A_1 + \epsilon A_1 = A_1A_2e_1 + A_1A_2\epsilon' + A_1\epsilon \qquad (14\text{-}17)$$

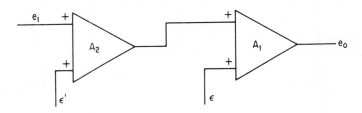

FIGURE 14-15   Cascaded amplifiers with drift voltages.

If we think of forcing the output voltage e_o to zero (in the presence of the drift voltages) by a suitable adjustment of e_1, we find from (14-17)

$$-e_1 = \frac{A_1A_2\epsilon' + A_1\epsilon}{A_1A_2} = \epsilon' + \frac{1}{A_2}\epsilon \qquad (14\text{-}18)$$

Thus the equivalent drift voltage in A_1, namely ϵ, referred to the input has been reduced by the factor $1/A_2$. By making amplifier A_2 a nearly drift-free chopper-modulated amplifier, the effective drift in the whole amplifier chain is reduced.

The actual circuit (Fig. 14-16) embodies the principle just discussed for the dc and low-frequency components of the signal, which pass through the A_2 and the A_1 channels in cascade. However, the input voltage e_1 is impressed directly on one of the inputs on A_1. The two inputs on A_1 are combined,

---

†A. J. Williams, R. E. Tarpley, and W. R. Clark, "dc Amplifier Stabilized for Zero and Gain," *Trans. A.I.E.E.*, **67**, 47, 1948. E. A. Goldberg, "Stabilization of Wide-band Direct-current Amplifiers for Zero and Gain," *R.C.A. Rev.* **11**, 296, 1950.

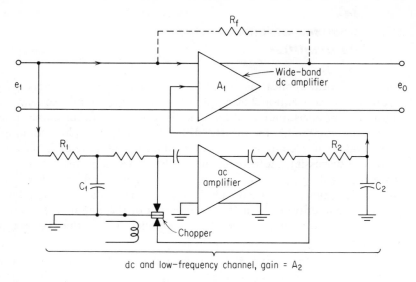

dc and low-frequency channel, gain = A_2

FIGURE 14-16   Chopper-stabilized wide-band dc amplifier system.

usually by using the two inputs of a difference amplifier input stage. Let us recalculate the effect of the drift voltage ϵ of amplifier A_1 in this connection. Assuming that A_2 is drift-free and that there is no sign change in the summing at the A_1 input, we write

$$e_o = A_1 e_1 + A_1 \epsilon + A_1 A_2 e_1 = A_1(1 + A_2)e_1 + A_1 \epsilon \qquad (14\text{-}19)$$

Next solve for the value of e_1 to make $e_o = 0$ and find

$$e_1 = -\frac{A_1}{A_1(1 + A_2)}\epsilon = -\frac{1}{1 + A_2}\epsilon \qquad (14\text{-}20)$$

a result nearly the same as in the foregoing paragraph when A_2 is large. Because the drift voltage ϵ is practically a direct voltage, the gain A_2 must be high only for dc and very low frequencies. The chopper-modulated amplifier satisfies this requirement and has the requisite of a very small inherent drift.

The foregoing discussion concerns the open-loop gains, though the amplifier system is always used with some type of feedback, such as R_f in Fig. 14-16. We have seen that a modulated amplifier needs a filter, such as the low-pass filter R_2C_2, to eliminate frequencies in the range of the chopper frequency. An input filter R_1C_1 serves this same purpose but also attenuates the higher-frequency components of e_1, which might otherwise overload the ac amplifier. In the design† of such an amplifier system its stabil-

†See Reference 14-6, pp. 2–53 ff.

ity against oscillation must also be considered. Stability considerations dictate the number of stages in the two amplifiers and the relative values of the time constants R_1C_1 and R_2C_2, whereas the chopper frequency determines the value of R_2C_2. Typical values are $R_2C_2 = 20$ s and $R_1C_1 = 0.01$ s in a system in which the ac amplifier gain is 10^3. With this value of R_2C_2 the modulated amplifier channel gain versus log-frequency plot would begin dropping at the corner frequency of $1/2\pi R_2C_2$ or at about 0.008 Hz, and at the rate of 20 dB per decade. The R_1C_1 filter begins to add to the attenuation at the corner frequency of 16 Hz, and thereafter the rate of change of the attenuation is 40 dB per decade.

The amplifier A_1 may have a nominal open-loop gain of 10,000 and a 3-dB point at 200 Hz. For frequencies over, say, 100 Hz the Bode diagram of the complete amplifier is dominated by the performance of amplifier A_1. In a typical computer amplifier the gain at the high frequencies drops off approximately as $1/f$, that is, at a rate of 20 dB per decade in the Bode plot. Then the phase shift will approach 90° as the frequency rises and the amplifier will be stable with most feedback connections. In some amplifiers the Bode diagram is shaped by means of compensating networks to shift the 3-dB point to a higher frequency and yet preserve the -20 dB per decade slope in the critical region of unity gain.

As we shall see presently, the computer amplifier is used in a negative feedback connection such as in Fig. 14-19a. Then the gain at the low end of the frequency range is pulled down to a value dependent on the feedback network, for example, to a gain of ten. Then the Bode plot of the feedback amplifier (closed-loop plot) will start with the gain of ten and will remain constant until the high-frequency asymptote of the open-loop Bode plot is approached. The gain curve will then fall along this high-frequency asymptote. Thus the closed-loop bandwidth is much greater than the open-loop value and depends on the level of low-frequency closed-loop gain. For example, if we assume that the open-loop low-frequency gain is 10,000, the 3-dB point is at 200 Hz, and if we assume that the gain drops off as $1/f$; then the new corner frequency for a closed-loop low-frequency gain of ten will be 10,000/10 times 200, or 200,000 Hz. Thus the effective bandwidth for a gain of ten is 200 kHz.

Data and circuit diagrams for several chopper-stabilized commercial amplifiers intended for analog computer application are given in the *Computer Handbook* pp. 2–71 ff. (See Reference 14-6.) A summary of developments on transistor dc amplifiers (differential, modulated, and chopper-stabilized) may be found in Reference 14-5. We remark that transistors operated in the switching mode can be used to replace the mechanical choppers in a modulated amplifier and thereby raise the chopper frequency with consequent increase in the bandwidth.

14-5

Analog computation

An analog method for the solution of a physical problem implies that a system which is different from the original one but which follows the same mathematical relations can be identified. We concern ourselves principally with the solution of physical systems by simulation, though analog computers are also useful as equation-solvers. Though various physical systems (thermodynamic, hydraulic, mechanical, electromechanical) can be simulated by such devices as networks of passive electrical elements or the mechanical differential analyzer, we shall introduce the subject by means of an example of the simulation of a simple mechanical system by means of a generalized analog computer.

In the mass-spring problem pictured in Fig. 14-17a we let $M(d^2x/dt^2)$ equal the inertial force, $B(dx/dt)$ the viscous damping force, and Kx the spring force. Summing these forces (assuming no external force), we obtain the differential equation

$$Mp^2x + Bpx + Kx = 0 \tag{14-21}$$

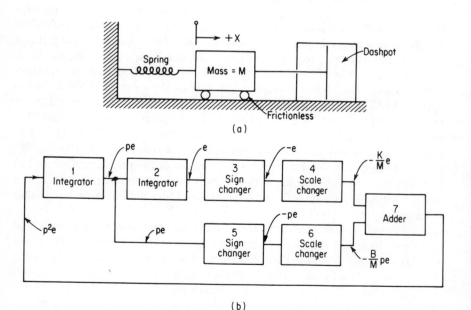

FIGURE 14-17 (a) Mechanical system and (b) analog simulation of mechanical system.

Here operational notation is used.† Let us assume that we possess electric circuits that will accept an input voltage or voltages and deliver an output voltage after performing such mathematical operations as summation, integration, multiplication by a constant, sign changing, or differentiation. We adopt voltage e as the computer analog of the displacement x, so the computer must solve the analogous equation

$$Mp^2e + Bpe + Ke = 0 \qquad (14\text{-}22)$$

Here the *machine* (computer) variables are e and t, while the *problem* variables were x and t. (In general, scale factors will be needed between the machine variables and the problem variables.)

Next we indicate by a block diagram how, in principle, an analog computer setup can solve Eq. (14-22). As we shall learn presently, integrators are preferable to differentiators. Intuitively, we can see that two integrators will be needed to operate in succession on the second derivative terms to give the variable e itself. First rearrange Eq. (14-22) to give

$$p^2e = -\frac{B}{M}pe - \frac{K}{M}e \qquad (14\text{-}23)$$

Let us next build up a possible computer arrangement to represent this equation. (Arrangements using fewer elements will be developed subsequently.) To begin with, assume that we have available a voltage in the machine which represents p^2e. If this voltage is applied to an integrator, the output voltage $\left(\text{of value } \int_0^t \frac{d^2e}{dt^2}\, dt \text{ or } (1/p)p^2e\right)$ will represent pe. A second integration will produce the variable e. Elements 1 and 2 in Fig. 14-17b perform these two steps. To satisfy Eq. (14-22), we need to develop voltages to represent the terms $-(B/M)pe$ and $-(K/M)e$. This is done by the *sign changer* and *scale changer* pairs of elements, 3 and 4, and 5 and 6. Finally, the right-hand terms are added in element 7 and the equality of the two sides of the equation is forced by the *feedback* connection from the output of 7 to the input of 1.

Thus far no mention has been made of any initial disturbance in the system, such as initial values of p^2x, px, or of x; therefore the variables would all be zero. By methods to be discussed later, one or more of these initial conditions can be introduced into the analog. Then the subsequent variations of the voltages which represent p^2e, pe, and e will give the acceleration, velocity, and displacement of the mass in the original problem. These voltage variations can be observed by means of a voltmeter if the variations are slow enough or recorded on a galvanometer recorder, servo recorder, or cathode-ray oscilloscope.

---

†The operator p, operating on $f(t)$, denotes $pf(t) \equiv df(t)/dt$. Further, the operator $1/p$ denotes $(1/p)f(t) \equiv \int_0^t f(t)\, dt$.

The foregoing example is a trivial one in the sense that the analytical solution is known. What, then, are the useful features of analog computers? They can be used for the simulation of complex systems, which are not easily solved by analytical methods, including nonlinear systems. They permit a rapid evaluation of the effects of changes in the system parameters. They assist the engineer or research worker to attain a "feel" for the responses of the system because these are rapidly presented in graphical form. They are sometimes useful as components of control systems. However, digital computers generally have superior capabilities in calculations or problem solutions where high accuracy or extensive tables of numerical output data are required.

14-6
Operational amplifiers

In an electronic analog computer the original physical problem, usually formulated in differential equation form, is solved in terms of the voltages at the outputs of the operational elements, as explained in a general way in the foregoing article. We next consider the characteristics of the combination of high-gain dc amplifier and the *feedback* connections which perform the required mathematical operations.

A generalized form of an operational amplifier is shown in Fig. 14-18.

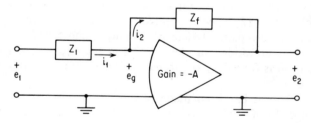

FIGURE 14-18   Generalized operational amplifier connection.

Here e_2 is the output voltage which results after the circuit performs some mathematical operation, such as integration, on the input voltage e_1. We propose to derive a general expression for e_2 in terms of e_1, the operational impedances† Z_f and Z_1, and the gain $-A$; then write an approximate form of this general expression, and finally present the basic networks for computing. The assumptions basic to the derivation follow: (1) the amplifier gain $|A|$ is very high, (2) the input impedance of amplifier A is infinite, (3)

---

†Here Z_f and Z_1 imply $Z_f(p)$ and $Z_1(p)$. For example, for a series circuit of R, L, and C where $Z(j\omega) = R + j\omega L + (1/j\omega C)$ we have $Z(p) = R + pL + (1/pC)$.

the load placed across the output terminals has a high impedance relative to the Thévenin (output) impedance of the circuit, (4) the amplifier is operated over its linear range, and (5) the frequency bandwidth of the operational amplifier network exceeds the highest problem frequency by a suitable margin. In view of assumption 2 we may say that currents i_1 and i_2 are identical, since no current enters the amplifier. Equating the currents, we find

$$\frac{e_1 - e_g}{Z_1(p)} = \frac{e_g - e_2}{Z_f(p)} \tag{14-24}$$

But

$$\frac{e_2}{e_g} = -A \tag{14-25}$$

where A is a large positive number of the order of 10^4 to 5×10^4. Upon eliminating e_g between (14-24) and (14-25), we find

$$e_2 = -\frac{e_1}{\dfrac{Z_1(p)}{Z_f(p)}\left[1 + \dfrac{1}{A}\left(\dfrac{Z_f(p)}{Z_1(p)} + 1\right)\right]} \tag{14-26}$$

If A is large, the term which has $1/A$ as a factor can be neglected† relative to 1, so approximately,

$$e_2 = -\frac{Z_f(p)}{Z_1(p)}e_1 \tag{14-27}$$

The basic mathematical operations obtainable by using certain pairs of impedance elements for Z_f and Z_1 will be given next.

a. Scale changer or coefficient amplifier; sign changer

This circuit uses resistors for both Z_f and Z_1, as shown in Fig. 14-19a in the one-line diagram form (ground conductor omitted). Equation (14-27) yields in this case

$$e_2 = -\frac{R_f}{R_1}e_1 \tag{14-28}$$

We notice a change of sign that is inherent in this circuit. Values of R_f and R_1 can be chosen to give the desired coefficient of an e_1 term in an analog solution. Alternatively, if $R_1 = R_f$, then $e_2 = -e_1$, and we have a *sign changer*, or *inverter*.

b. Integrator

Providing a capacitor for Z_f and a resistor for Z_1 (Fig. 14-19b) leads to an integrating circuit. Here $Z_f = 1/pC$ and $Z_1 = R$, so by (14-27)

†For a study of the errors involved see, for example, Reference 14-9, pp. 162 ff.

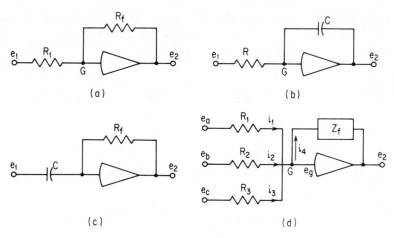

FIGURE 14-19   (a) Scale changer, (b) integrator, (c) differentiator, and (d) multiple input network.

$$e_2 = -\frac{1}{RCp}e_1 \qquad (14\text{-}29)$$

Thus e_2 is the integrated value of e_1, but the sign is reversed and the integral is modified by the constant factor $1/RC$. Because the integrator forms the basis of most analog computer networks, its performance and errors need consideration in precise work. For example, the integrating capacitor has been assumed to be ideal in the derivation, but small leakage and absorption currents may be present. Similarly, the assumptions of zero amplifier input current and infinite gain may need further study.

c. Differentiator

Interchanging the R and the C of the integrator leads to the differentiator (Fig. 14-19c), for which

$$e_2 = -R_fCpe_1 \qquad (14\text{-}30)$$

Differentiators are seldom used in practice, for two reasons, (1) for high rates of change of the variables the derivative becomes so large that the amplifier will overload, and (2) noise voltages are magnified and cause trouble.

d. Circuits using a multiple input

Suppose that three different signals are connected via resistors to the input terminal (Fig. 14-19d). Let us find the output voltage in terms of the input voltages and the network parameters. First observe that, since $e_g = -e_2/A$, and e_2 is normally kept within the range of -100 to $+100$ V, it follows that e_g is close to zero if A is of the order of 10^4 or higher. This observation permits the approximation that $e_g = 0$. The input current to the amplifier is assumed to be zero; therefore

$$i_1 + i_2 + i_3 = i_4$$

and

$$\frac{e_a}{R_1} + \frac{e_b}{R_2} + \frac{e_c}{R_3} = -\frac{e_2}{Z_f(p)}$$

or

$$e_2 = -\frac{Z_f(p)}{R_1}e_a - \frac{Z_f(p)}{R_2}e_b - \frac{Z_f(p)}{R_3}e_c \qquad (14\text{-}31)$$

When $Z_f(p)$ is a resistor R_f, we obtain a *summing amplifier* or *adder*, for which

$$e_2 = -\frac{R_f}{R_1}e_a - \frac{R_f}{R_2}e_b - \frac{R_f}{R_3}e_c \qquad (14\text{-}32)$$

Thus the three voltages are added, though each term has a negative sign and a coefficient.

By using a capacitor for Z_f, we have a *summing integrator*, for which

$$e_2 = -\frac{1}{R_1 Cp}e_a - \frac{1}{R_2 Cp}e_b - \frac{1}{R_3 Cp}e_c \qquad (14\text{-}33)$$

We have mentioned that in precise work the validity of the idealizing assumptions may need examination. Also, care must be exercised so that the amplifier loading is within limits and so that the amplifier output voltages do not exceed the linear range.

14-7
Operational amplifier
in instrumentation

Some features of an operational amplifier that deserve emphasis can be brought out by a discussion of its application to the measurement of current. Consider first the input impedance to the point G in Fig. 14-19a. If we let e_g be the potential at point G, we can express the current through R_f as

$$i = \frac{e_g - e_2}{R_f} = \frac{e_g}{R_f}\left(1 - \frac{e_2}{e_g}\right) \qquad (14\text{-}34)$$

Replace e_2/e_g by $-A$ and solve for e_g/i to find the input impedance Z_{in} at point G.

$$Z_{\text{in}} = R_f\left(\frac{1}{1 + A}\right) \simeq \frac{R_f}{A} \qquad (14\text{-}35)$$

Since A is large, Z_{in} is small. This fact suggests that the operational amplifier with shunt feedback (Fig. 14-19a with $R_1 = 0$) can be used as an ammeter for low currents. The output voltage e_2 is an accurate measure of the current, since replacing e_g by $-e_2/A$ in Eq. (14-34) yields

$$i = -\left(\frac{1}{A} + 1\right)\frac{e_2}{R_f} \cong -\frac{e_2}{R_f} \qquad (14\text{-}36)$$

Let $R_f = 10^6$, $A = 2 \times 10^4$, and assume that $i = 1\ \mu A$. Then $Z_{in} = 10^6/2 \times 10^4 = 50\ \Omega$, and $e_2 = -1$ V, which can readily be observed on a voltmeter or recorder. The resistance in the current-measuring circuit of 50 Ω is low compared with that which would be required across a resistor to produce, say, 1 mV for operating a potentiometer recorder, i.e., $10^{-3}/10^{-6}$, or 1000 Ω. Lower currents can be measured by using higher values of R_f, but below about 10^{-10} or 10^{-11} A errors may arise owing to leakage or amplifier input current.

Next consider how the circuit in Fig. 14-19d can be used to compare two voltages. For this purpose we omit R_3 and let $Z_f = R_f$. Then according to Eq. (14-32), the output voltage becomes

$$e_2 = -R_f\left(\frac{e_a}{R_1} + \frac{e_b}{R_2}\right) \qquad (14\text{-}37)$$

If e_a is an unknown voltage, applying a negative adjustable standard voltage e_b and adjusting this until $e_2 = 0$ would give an accurate measure of e_a.

Another application of a circuit similar to Fig. 14-19d is in the measurement of the sum of two or more currents. For this purpose let $R_1 = R_2 = R_3 = 0$, and let $Z_f = R_f$. An analysis similar to that needed for Eq. (14-36) yields

$$e_2 = -R_f(i_1 + i_2 + i_3) \qquad (14\text{-}38)$$

The voltage at the *summing point* G is low, because it is $-e_2/A$, and A is large.

The concept that the voltage at point G is low is worth further emphasis. For example, the input current in the integrator (Fig. 14-19b) will be e_1/R at all times. We may think of point G as a *virtual ground*, since in *normal* operation its potential remains within a few millivolts of ground potential.

It should be pointed out, however, that when the ampifier is overloaded and saturates so that the output voltage reaches a constant, further increase in input signal will cause point G potential to rise. In effect the amplifier loses control over e_2, and the operational network becomes unreliable.

14-8
Example of an analog
computer solution

We return now to the mass-spring problem of Fig. 14-17, but with the added feature of an applied force in the $+x$ direction which is an arbitrary function of time $f(t)$. The differential equation of the mechanical system is

$$Mp^2x + Bpx + Kx = f(t) \qquad (14\text{-}39)$$

Following the same approach as in Sec. (14-5), we let a voltage in the computer e be the analog of the displacement x. For generality, let *machine* time T in the computer represent the *real* time t. Thus e and T are the *machine variables*.† Converting Eq. (14-39) to machine variables and solving for p^2e, we find

$$p^2e = -\frac{B}{M}pe - \frac{K}{M}e + \frac{1}{M}f(T) \qquad (14\text{-}40)$$

where pe now means de/dT. Each term in the equation will be represented by a voltage, such as in Fig. 14-17b. However, the analog computer network for solving Eq. (14-40) shown in Fig. 14-20 differs in some details from the block diagram in Fig. 14-17b, partly owing to the inherent sign changes in the operational amplifiers.

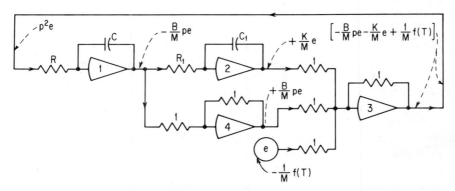

FIGURE 14-20   Analog computer network for mass-spring problem. (Resistor values in megohms.)

The approach is the same, since we solve the equation for the highest derivative and assume that this term is available. Then passing through integrator 1 we choose R and C so as to obtain an output voltage equal to $-(B/M)pe$. A second integration in element 2 gives the voltage $+(K/M)e$. The sign changer, element 4, is needed to develop the voltage $+(B/M)pe$. A voltage generator, which supplies the voltage $-(1/M)f(T)$, is connected to the third input of the adder, element 3, to represent the applied force. Upon connecting the output of the adder back to the input of element 1 ("closing the loop"), the system is forced to conform to Eq. (14-40).

It remains to discuss the choice of the circuit elements R, C, and R_1 and C_1 and to comment on the input and feedback resistors for elements 3

†In general, scale factors will be required, for example, the factor a and a_1 in $e = ax$ and $T = a_1t$. In the present example we let $e = x$ and $T = t$, so that the scale factors are both unity.

and 4. Refer first to the choice of 1-MΩ resistors for both input and feedback resistors in the adder, element 3. Then according to Eq. (14-32) the output will be the sum of the negative of all the input voltages. Similarly, Eq. (14-28) shows that since $R_1 = R_f$ element 4 will produce only a change of sign. Consider next the choice of R and C. The desired output voltage of element 1 is $-(B/M)pe$, but Eq. (14-29) shows that the output voltage will be $-(1/RCp)p^2e$ or $-(1/RC)pe$. Consequently we must choose

$$\frac{1}{RC} = \frac{B}{M} \qquad (14\text{-}41)$$

Similar reasoning for element 2 shows that we must require that

$$\frac{1}{R_1C_1} = \frac{K}{B} \qquad (14\text{-}42)$$

Thus all the elements of the computer can be chosen to fit the constants of the problem, and upon closing the feedback loop, the differential equation must be satisfied.

In this example an applied force excites the system, and we assume that the initial values of px and x are zero. That is, there is no initial energy in the system. The analog network will conform to this assumption if all the internal voltages are zero at the initial instant. Now consider a suddenly applied force, i.e., a step function. The generator in Fig. 14-20 would suddenly have to insert a voltage $-F/M$, where F is the constant force. This would be done by a relay in the slower computers or by an electronic switch in a high-speed repetitive computer. The ensuing variations of acceleration, velocity, or displacement could be observed by recording the voltage p^2e, $-(B/M)pe$ or $(K/M)e$ as a function of time.

If the displacement or the velocity has an initial value, the initial condition can be simulated by setting the appropriate voltage to the proper value. For example, suppose that the initial position has a value x_0, which is simulated by the voltage e_0. Then the output of amplifier 2 in Fig. 14-20 would be set initially at the voltage $(K/M)e_0$, thereby charging capacitor C_1 to this voltage. The output of amplifier 2 is disconnected from the rest of the network during this operation. Upon simultaneously reclosing the circuit and introducing the forcing function, the network will respond to give the combined effects of the initial position and of the forcing function.

Let us consider two examples, one of which will bring out the need for amplitude and time scaling:

Example 1: Let $M = 2$ kg, $K = 50$ N/m, $B = 5$ N·s/m, and $f(T) = F = 20$ N. The initial velocity and position are both zero. The analytical solution is well known so that we could plot the functions in detail if desired. First recall that the analytical solution gives a value of B for critical damping of $2\sqrt{MK}$ or 20. Here B is only 5, therefore the system has an underdamped oscillatory motion, with a damping ratio one-fourth of the critical. For estimating purposes let us calculate the motion for the *undamped* condition but keep in mind that the actual oscillation will reach maximum values slightly smaller than those calculated. The *undamped* response would be given by

$$x = \frac{F}{K} - \frac{F}{K} \cos \omega t$$

where $\omega = \sqrt{K/M}$. Therefore $x = e = 0.4 - 0.4 \cos 5t$; also $px = pe = 2 \sin 5t$, and $p^2x = p^2e = 10 \cos 5t$. The voltage p^2e in the computer network would be a cosine wave having a 10-V amplitude and a frequency of $5/2\pi$ or about 0.8 Hz. The voltage $-(B/M)pe$ would equal $-5 \sin 5t$, and voltage $+(K/M)e$ would equal $10 - 10 \cos 5t$. These amplitudes and frequencies are well within the limits of a medium-speed computer, in fact the amplitudes are lower than the optimum for best accuracy.

Example 2: Let $M = 2$ kg, $K = 5000$ N/m, $B = 50$ N·s/m, and $F = 200$ N. Here the damping is again one-fourth of the critical value. The undamped frequency is now about 8 Hz, and the voltages at the amplifier outputs work out to be $(K/M)e = 100 - 100 \cos 50t$, $-(B/M)pe = -50 \sin 50t$, and $p^2e = 100 \cos 50t$. Thus if the amplifier outputs are limited to ± 100 V, as is common, element 2 would be seriously overloaded. Furthermore, a servo-type recorder (X-Y recorder) would not be fast enough to record the wave. Thus both amplitude and time scaling would be needed.

14-9
Additional computer elements

An extremely useful element is a precision potential divider, or potentiometer (Fig. 14-21), usually of the 10-turn, helical, wire-wound type. The setting

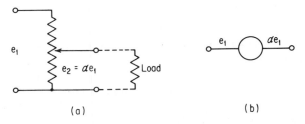

(a)   (b)

FIGURE 14-21   Potential divider (a) circuit and (b) symbol for one-line computer diagrams.

of the potential divider must be determined by test or by calculation so as to account for the effect of the load on the ratio factor. The potentiometer can be used to provide a constant coefficient in the range from zero to unity.

The choice of values for R, R_1, C, and C_1 by Eqs. (14-41) and (14-42) for the setup in Fig. 14-20 would, in general, lead to inconvenient values for these circuit constants, such as 0.285 or the like. (Generally, a stock of fixed R and C units having values such as 0.1, 0.2, 0.5, and 1 are provided in computer laboratories.) This difficulty can often be avoided by the use of potentiometers in the manner shown in Fig. 14-22. Let us think in terms of

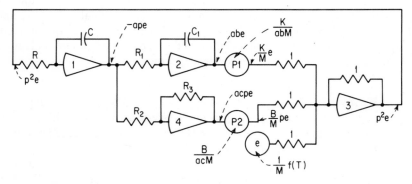

FIGURE 14-22   Alternative network for mass-spring problem.

the numerical values in Example 1. Then $K/M = 25$ and $B/M = 2.5$. Let us choose $R = 1$ MΩ and $C = 0.1$ μF, so that $a = 1/RC = 10$. Choose R_1 equal to R and C_1 equal to C, so that $b = 10$. Then the voltage ratio of potentiometer $P1$ should be

$$\frac{K}{abM} = \frac{50}{10 \times 10 \times 2} = 0.250$$

Finally, let $R_2 = R_3$, so that $c = 1$; then the voltage ratio for $P2$ should be

$$\frac{B}{acM} = \frac{5}{10 \times 1 \times 2} = 0.250$$

The reason for the choices of the coefficients accompanying the integrations in elements 1 and 2 is now evident.

Thus far all the computer elements have been *linear* in nature. One of the useful features of the analog computer is its ability to solve equations having *nonlinear* relations. The so-called *function generator* is an aid in this application. Several forms have been developed, but we only indicate the principle involved by means of Fig. 14-23a. The output is related to the input by the required functional relation.

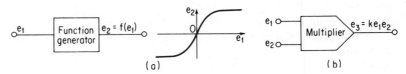

FIGURE 14-23   One-line diagrams of (a) function generator and (b) multiplier.

In some problems the product of two variables appears, so that a multiplier circuit is needed (Fig. 14-23b). As a result of considerable research effort, multipliers have been developed that are accurate and stable, and their use greatly increases the range of equations that can be solved. For example, the solution of van der Pol's equation for the nonlinear theory of oscillations, namely,

$$p^2e - ape + ae^2pe + e = 0 \qquad (14\text{-}43)$$

requires the formation of the term ae^2pe. This could be done with a function generator to form e^2, a multiplier to form e^2pe and with an adjustment of gain to give the constant coefficient a.

14-10
Analog computer techniques

Two general types of computers can be distinguished, though a single computer may operate in both categories. One is the slow-speed computer, in which the solution is traced out over a period of a few seconds to one minute. Here a slow-speed recorder can be used to record the solution, and relays can control the computer functions.

In the high-speed computer the solution is repeated from 20 to 60 times per second and the result is obtained from the screen of a cathode-ray tube. The input function is provided by electronic wave-shaping circuits. This type of computer has the advantage that the elements of the problem can be varied continuously while simultaneously observing the effect on the solution, but the attainable accuracy is less than in the slow-speed type.

The control of the computer functions can be accomplished by switches and relays in the slow-speed type. For example, the initial conditions on the variables are inserted by the following technique. The integrator capacitors are disconnected from their normal circuit by means of relay contacts and charged by an auxiliary circuit to the desired value. Then when the relays switch the charged capacitors back into the integrator circuit (to start the solution), the output voltages immediately take on the values which had been set on the capacitors. The output voltage is equal to the capacitor voltage because the amplifier input is virtually at ground potential.

The solution of a single differential equation has been used as an example of a computer application in the foregoing treatment. Computers can also readily be applied to the solution of a set of simultaneous differential equations and also of a set of simultaneous linear algebraic equations. Some computers are capable of performing iterative procedures, which increase their range of problem solutions. An analog computer may also be coupled to a digital computer, usually through logic circuits. This system, called a *hybrid* computer, exploits the better features of the two types of computers.

Areas where analog computers have been particularly useful include the design of servomechanisms and nuclear reactors, problems of aircraft and rocket stability and control, and in process control studies. In addition, analog computer elements find useful applications in process control and in instrumentation systems.

REFERENCES

14-1   Wm. D. Cockrell, ed., *Industrial Electronics Handbook*, McGraw-Hill Book Company, New York, 1958, Secs. 4b, 6n.

14-2   John E. Gibson and F. B. Tuteur, *Control System Components*, McGraw-Hill Book Company, New York, 1958, Chapter 2.

14-3   George E. Valley, Jr., ed., *Vacuum Tube Amplifiers*, (v. 18, M.I.T. Radiation Lab. Series) McGraw-Hill Book Company, New York, 1948.

14-4   R. D. Middlebrook, *Differential Amplifiers*, John Wiley & Sons, Inc., New York, 1963.

14-5   Lloyd P. Hunter, ed., *Handbook of Semiconductor Electronics*, 2d ed., McGraw-Hill Book Company, New York, 1962, Sec. 13 (D-C Amplifiers).

14-6   Harry D. Huskey, and G. A. Korn, *Computer Handbook*, McGraw-Hill Book Company, New York, 1962.

14-7   Albert S. Jackson, *Analog Computation*, McGraw-Hill Book Company, New York, 1960.

14-8   Clarence L. Johnson, *Analog Computer Techniques*, McGraw-Hill Book Company, New York, 1956.

14-9   Granino A. Korn and Theresa M. Korn, *Electronic Analog Computers*, 2d ed., McGraw-Hill Book Company, New York, 1956.

14-10   J. N. Warfield, *Introduction to Electronic Analog Computers*, Prentice-Hall, Inc., Englewood Cliffs, N. J., 1959.

14-11   Harold Chestnut and R. W. Mayer, *Servomechanisms and Regulating System Design*, v. 1, 2d ed., John Wiley & Sons, Inc., New York, 1959, Chapter 16.

EXERCISES

14-1 Suppose that Type 12AU7A vacuum triodes (Appendix B) are used in Fig. 14-2. Let the dc source voltages and quiescent grid and plate potentials have the values in the figure. Let $R_2 = R_4 = 300$ kΩ. (a) Choose values of R_1, R_3, R_5, and R_6. (b) Find the voltage gain, assuming an infinite impedance load. (c) What is the output impedance of the amplifier?

14-2 Let the amplifier in Fig. 14-4 use high-μ triodes operated so that $\mu = 100$ and $r_p = 75$ k. Let $R = 150$ k, $R_k = 200$ k, and assume that the quiescent conditions are: $E_b = 180$ V, $I_b = 0.8$ mA, and $E_c = -2.0$ V. (a) In this amplifier, what is the percentage error occasioned by the use of Eq. (14-4) compared with (14-3), if a balanced push-pull input is applied? (b) Calculate the following: differential gain, common-mode gain, and discrimination factor. (c) What values of E_{cc} and E_{bb} are needed?

14-3 Assume that the amplifier in Prob. 14-2 is connected for a single-ended input to push-pull output. (a) Calculate the gains for the two sides of the output. (b) How could the amplifier design be changed to minimize the difference in voltage on the two sides at the output?

14-4 Design an amplifier following the circuit in Fig. 14-10. Use Type 12AX7A triodes in the first stage and Type 12AU7A triodes in the second stage. Assume that +300 and −300-V supplies are to be used, but that the quiescent plate and grid potentials do not need to agree with those in Fig. 14-10. Specify the resistance values, quiescent plate and grid potentials, and differential gain.

14-5 Suppose that in the derivation of Eq. (14-3) it is assumed that triode A has a plate resistance $r_p + \Delta r_p$, but that all the other parameters remain unchanged. Find the output voltage e_{1a} under this condition.

14-6 In the system in Fig. 14-13 assume that $R_1 = 200$ k, $C_1 = 0.2$ μF, $R_2 = 500$ k, the gain of the ac amplifier is 4000, its input resistance is 2 MΩ, and its output impedance is negligible. The chopper frequency is 60 Hz. (a) Choose values for R_3 and C_3. (b) Estimate the value of dc signal voltage e_s supplied by a low-impedance source needed to develop $e_{out} = 10$ V. (c) Under the conditions of (b), estimate the value of the 60-Hz component of voltage in the output if R_3 and C_3 have the values chosen in (a).

14-7 Sketch the decibel voltage gain versus log of frequency plot for the system in Fig. 14-16, using the time constants $R_1C_1 = 0.01$ s, and $R_2C_2 = 20$ s. Further assume an ac amplifier gain of 1000 independent of frequency and a gain A_1 of 20,000 with an upper cut-off frequency of 300 Hz.

14-8 In Fig. 14-19b let $R = 500$ k, $C = 2$ μF, and the amplifier gain $= -\infty$. Suppose that the voltage $e_1 = 20 \exp(-0.1t)$ is impressed at $t = 0$, sketch e_o versus t, if $e_o(0) = 0$. If the amplifier dynamic range is ± 100 V, at what time will the amplifier overload?

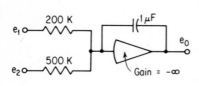

FIGURE 14-24

14-9 Consider the circuit in Fig. 14-24. Let $e_o(0) = 0$ and let e_1 and e_2 be zero up to time $t = 0$, then take on the values $e_1 = 40 \sin 8t$ and $e_2 = 50 \exp(-5t)$. (a) Find $e_o(t)$. (b) What is e_o at $t = 0.1$ s?

14-10 Derive an analog computer setup to solve the following differential equation. Assume that initial values are all zero, and that the right-hand side represents a step function applied at $t = 0$.

$$\frac{d^3 y}{dt^3} + 4\frac{d^2 y}{dt^2} + 2\frac{dy}{dt} + 3y = 10$$

14-11 What differential equation does the circuit in Fig. 14-25 solve? Circuit values are in megohms and microfarads. Initial values are all zero.

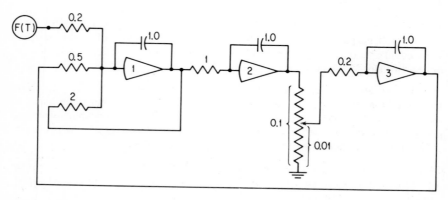

FIGURE 14-25

14-12 Various operational transfer functions relating e_2 to e_1 in Fig. 14-18 have been developed by using combinations of R's and C's for Z_1 and Z_f, or by networks of R's and C's. (a) Let Z_f consist of a parallel combination of R and C, and let $Z_1 = R_1$; find the transfer function. (b) Repeat for the case where Z_f consists of R and C in parallel, and Z_1 consists of R_1 and C_1 in parallel.

14-13 Show a schematic diagram of an analog computer setup for the solution of Eq. (14-43).

15

Servo Systems; Regulators

15-1
Introduction

A *servomechanism* (or *servo*) is an automatic control system in which the controlled quantity is a mechanical position, shaft velocity, or the like. In an *automatic control system* the *controlled variable* (or output) is compared with the *desired value* (or *input*), and the difference, called the *error*, is used to initiate corrective action to try to reduce the error to a small value or to zero. We remark that the term "error" is given a rather broad interpretation, as some of the illustrative examples in the chapter will show. Thus, in some cases the error is the difference between an input and some *function of the output*, rather than the output itself.

The desired value can be a function of time, as in a servo-controlled ship rudder when the pilot changes the course. When the desired value is a *constant*, the system is called an *automatic regulator*.

A comparison of the output with the input to obtain the error requires a measurement of these quantities and a feedback path for performing the comparison. The need for a feedback path is illustrated in the elementary position servo shown schematically in Fig. 15-1. The motor M drives the load J to an angular position θ in response to the input voltage e_i. A transducer T (such as a potential divider energized by a dc voltage with the sliding contact driven by the shaft) translates the angle θ into a voltage e_o. The voltage e_o is fed back and compared to e_i in the comparison device or circuit C, which forms the

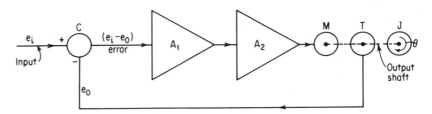

FIGURE 15-1   One-line diagram of a servo.

difference $e_i - e_o$, or the error. The error voltage acts on the preamplifier A_1, the power amplifier A_2, and the motor M in such a sense as to change θ and reduce the error toward zero.

The introduction of a feedback path and electronic amplification into control systems enables the design of systems of great accuracy, high speed of response, and good long-time stability. These systems are the basis for the automatic operation of many industrial processes, i.e., of *automation* in industry. However, just as with feedback in amplifiers, a feedback path can cause unstable operation (oscillation) if not properly designed. For this reason general servo theory lays much stress on the stability problem.

Some servo applications may be cited, including ship steering systems, autopilots for airplanes, automatic potentiometer recorders, X-Y recorders, contour followers for lathes, automatic milling machines, and motor speed controls. Automatic feedback control is applied to a large variety of variables, such as temperature, pressure, flow rate, and the like.

The mathematical analysis of all feedback systems is similar, therefore though we limit our discussion to the simpler servo systems, the analytical methods have a wider significance. We shall begin with the differential equation approach to the analysis of the transient response of elementary servos. Then we shall give a brief account of the transfer function approach and of the application of Bode plots to the stability problem. Finally, a generator voltage regulator will be described.

15-2
Feedback versus
nonfeedback systems

Let us analyze the nonfeedback (or *open-loop*) system in Fig. 15-2 under certain idealizing assumptions. The permanent-magnet-field dc motor M is supposed to stretch the spring by means of the string wound around the pulley P and attached thereto. The motion is opposed by the viscous friction in the dashpot. We ask how the displacement x varies after closing the switch S,

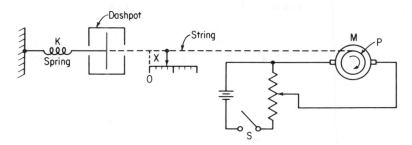

FIGURE 15-2   Nonfeedback system.

if x is zero at $t = 0$, and if the spring force is given by

$$\text{spring force} = Kx \tag{15-1}$$

Let us neglect the inductance in the motor armature and the armature counter emf. Then the current jumps immediately to a constant value and the motor produces a constant torque and a constant force, call it F_m, when measured at the pulley periphery.

For simplicity we also neglect the mass of spring and the inertia of the motor armature and pulley. (The latter assumption is rather extreme but might be an acceptable approximation for conditions of high damping.) The viscous friction force is a constant B times the velocity; thus

$$\text{friction force} = B\frac{dx}{dt} = Bpx \tag{15-2}$$

Summing the forces we have, by Newton's law,

$$Bpx + Kx = F_m \tag{15-3}$$

The solution to this first-order, linear differential equation of the system is well known and may be written

$$x = \frac{F_m}{K}\left[1 - \exp\left(-\frac{K}{B}t\right)\right] \tag{15-4}$$

Thus, the displacement rises on an exponential curve, which has a time constant B/K. Suppose that we wish to increase the speed of response, i.e., reduce the time constant. If K is regarded as fixed, this can be done only by a change in the damping constant B.

Next we convert the open-loop system to an elementary servo system as shown in Fig. 15-3. The output position x is measured by the potentiometer P and is converted into the voltage e_o. This voltage is compared to the input voltage e_i and the error voltage $e_i - e_o$ acts on the amplifier G and the motor M.

In general, e_o is some constant times x, but to simplify matters we let the constant be unity, or let $e_o = x$. Then the input voltage e_i may be equated to a desired value of x, call it x_i, and the error $e_i - e_o$ becomes $x_i - x$. Let us

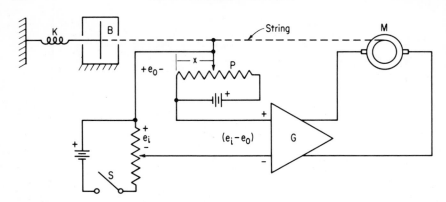

FIGURE 15-3   Elementary servo system in which inertia is neglected.

calculate the response to a suddenly impressed value of x_i, call it X_i, at time $t = 0$, when $x = 0$. We assume that the motor exerts a force on the string in proportion to the error voltage; thus

$$\text{motor force} = K_m(X_i - x) \qquad (15\text{-}5)$$

This means that the amplifier output current is assumed to be a linear function of error voltage. The spring force and the friction force are the same as before, so the differential equation of motion is

$$Bpx + Kx = K_m(X_i - x) \qquad (15\text{-}6)$$

or, putting the terms involving x on the left side,

$$Bpx + (K + K_m)x = K_m X_i \qquad (15\text{-}7)$$

This equation is of the same type as (15-3), and the solution is

$$x = \frac{K_m X_i}{K + K_m}\left[1 - \exp\frac{-(K_m + K)t}{B} \right] \qquad (15\text{-}8)$$

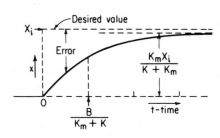

FIGURE 15-4   Response of elementary servo.

Thus, the exponential response, as illustrated in Fig. 15-4, now has a time constant of $B/(K_m + K)$ and an ultimate deflection of $K_m X_i/(K_m + K)$. The time constant has been decreased, but the final deflection is less than the desired value X_i. The speed of response can be increased by increasing the amplifier gain because an increase in gain increases K_m. At the same time the final deflection will approach more closely to the desired value.

Why does x not attain the desired value X_i in the steady state? Some force is needed to keep the spring stretched, and therefore an error signal is needed to produce a motor current and resultant force. The greater the amplifier gain, the smaller the error signal needed to develop a given force.

15-3
A second-order servo

We consider next a modification of the foregoing position control servo that omits the spring and adds a load mass M driven by an endless cable, as in Fig. 15-5. This system is similar to the instrument servos in potentiometers and X-Y recorders.

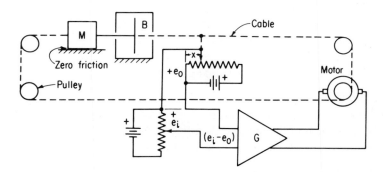

FIGURE 15-5 Elementary servo system which includes inertia.

For simplicity we consider only viscous friction. Actual systems may also be subject to *static* friction, or *stiction*, and to *coulomb* friction, or *dry* friction. Static friction gives a high force just before the sliding parts start to move. Dry friction produces a nearly constant force independent of velocity, which reverses when the velocity reverses.

The mass M is considered to include all inertial effects in the system, such as those due to the cable, pulleys, and the motor armature. The inertial force is therefore Mp^2x.

Using the same assumptions as before, we write the motor force equal to $K_m(x_i - x)$, where x_i is not as yet specified. The motor force equals the sum of the inertial plus viscous friction force

$$Mp^2x + Bpx = K_m(x_i - x) \qquad (15\text{-}9)$$

or

$$Mp^2x + Bpx + K_mx = K_mx_i \qquad (15\text{-}10)$$

Thus, the system is described by a second-order, linear differential equation with constant coefficients. This servo is also called a *proportional* servo, because, as Eq. (15-9) shows, the corrective action is proportional to the error.

As yet we have not specified the time variation of the desired value x_i. In practice a variety of odd-shaped functions are found, such as the example in Fig. 15-6a. However, certain simpler functions are chosen for analyzing servo response, including the constant displacement or step function (Fig. 15-6b), the constant velocity or ramp function (Fig. 15-6c), and a steady sine

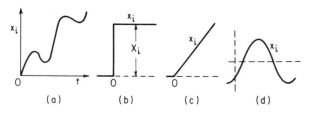

(a)   (b)   (c)   (d)

FIGURE 15-6   Types of forcing functions.

wave. We shall discuss the response of the position x as governed by Eq. (15-10) to the step function and the ramp function and later give some attention to the response of servos in general to harmonic functions.

If the input is a step function X_i, then Eq. (15-10) becomes

$$Mp^2x + Bpx + K_m x = K_m X_i \qquad (15\text{-}11)$$

We divide through by K_m to obtain

$$\frac{M}{K_m}p^2x + \frac{B}{K_m}px + x = X_i \qquad (15\text{-}12)$$

The solution to this equation is well known, and we recall that the natural response of the system may be (1) a damped oscillation, (2) an overdamped, or (3) a critically damped response, depending on the degree of damping. Let us introduce the parameters

$$\text{undamped radian frequency} = \omega_n = \sqrt{\frac{K_m}{M}} \qquad (15\text{-}13)$$

$$\text{damping ratio} = \zeta = \frac{B}{B_c} = \frac{B}{\sqrt{4MK_m}} \qquad (15\text{-}14)$$

where B_c is the critical value of B, which divides the overdamped from the oscillatory responses. Then (15-12) can be written

$$\frac{1}{\omega_n^2} p^2 x + \frac{2\zeta}{\omega_n} px + x = X_i \qquad (15\text{-}15)$$

The roots of the auxiliary equation are

$$-\zeta\omega_n + \omega_n\sqrt{\zeta^2 - 1} \quad \text{and} \quad -\zeta\omega_n - \omega_n\sqrt{\zeta^2 - 1}$$

Upon evaluating the constants in the solutions we find the following functions.

a. *Overdamped case,* $\zeta > 1$

$$x = X_i\left[1 - \frac{(\zeta + \sqrt{\zeta^2 - 1})}{2\sqrt{\zeta^2 - 1}} \exp\left(-\zeta + \sqrt{\zeta^2 - 1}\right)\omega_n t\right.$$

$$\left. + \frac{(\zeta - \sqrt{\zeta^2 - 1})}{2\sqrt{\zeta^2 - 1}} \exp\left(-\zeta - \sqrt{\zeta^2 - 1}\right)\omega_n t\right] \qquad (15\text{-}16)$$

b. *Critical case,* $\zeta = 1$

$$x = X_i[1 - \exp\left(-\omega_n t\right) - \omega_n t \exp\left(-\omega_n t\right)] \qquad (15\text{-}17)$$

c. *Oscillatory case,* $\zeta < 1$

Here the roots are conjugate complex and the transient term is an exponentially decaying oscillation. The total response may be expressed as

$$x = X_i\left[1 - \frac{\exp\left(-\zeta\omega_n t\right)}{\sqrt{1 - \zeta^2}} \sin\left(\omega_d t + \cos^{-1}\zeta\right)\right] \qquad (15\text{-}18)$$

where ω_d is the damped angular frequency and has the value

$$\omega_d = \omega_n\sqrt{1 - \zeta^2} \qquad (15\text{-}19)$$

Thus, the decaying oscillatory component has a frequency lower than the undamped frequency.

The effect of variations in the damping ratio on the response of the system can be seen in the dimensionless curves in Fig. 15-7. Here x/X_i is plotted as a function of $\omega_n t$, with ζ as a parameter. Obviously, if the damping is either very low or very high, the system takes a long time to settle down at or near the desired value. However, if the damping ratio is in the range $0.6 < \zeta < 1$, the system settles rather quickly. In the idealized system under discussion the final displacement agrees with the desired value, so the error approaches zero. However, in real systems that have backlash in gears or dry friction the system settles down at a steady value that departs slightly from the desired value.

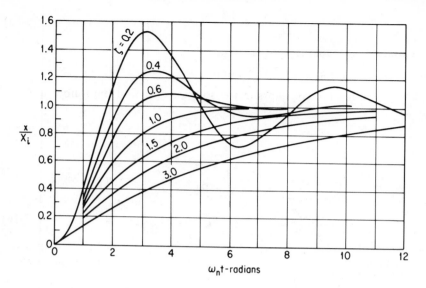

FIGURE 15-7   Response of second-order servo for different values of damping ratio.

In small servos the adjustment of the response by means of the viscous damping, as by introducing an eddy-current brake, may be a practical procedure. But in large servos the lost power and heating would be objectionable, and more sophisticated methods are used.

Some terms used in specifying servo performance are defined in terms of the response to a step input as shown in Fig. 15-8. The meaning of the term *overshoot* is clear from the diagram. The *settling time* is a function of the allowable tolerance and gives the time required before the response remains within the tolerance band. The time to the first peak, and the actual frequency of oscillation may also be matters of specification.

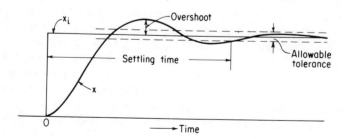

FIGURE 15-8   Servo *overshoot* and *settling time*.

15-4

Response of the second-order

servo to a ramp function

Sometimes the desired motion consists of a suddenly imposed constant velocity. Then the ramp function Fig. 15-6c describes the desired displacement. Suppose that we consider the same servo as in the foregoing article and assume that $x_i = 0$ prior to $t = 0$, and after $t = 0$, let $x_i = v_i t$, where v_i is a constant velocity. The differential equation (15-15) is modified to give

$$\frac{1}{\omega_n^2} p^2 x + \frac{2\zeta}{\omega_n} p x + x = v_i t \tag{15-20}$$

The forms of the transient part of the solution will be the same as before, but the steady state (particular integral) must conform to the driving function. If we assume the form $x_{ss} = x_o + v_s t$ and substitute in (15-20) and evaluate x_o and v_s, we obtain

$$x_{ss} = -\frac{2\zeta v_i}{\omega_n} + v_i t \tag{15-21}$$

Thus, when the transient parts of the response have disappeared, the output will have the desired velocity v_i, but the position will be in error by a constant amount.

We shall discuss the transient response only for the oscillatory case, $\zeta < 1$. If the transient terms are added to the steady-state terms and the constants are evaluated for the assumed initial conditions, the following expression can be obtained:

$$x = v_i t - \frac{2\zeta v_i}{\omega_n} + \frac{v_i}{\omega_n} \left[\frac{(2\zeta^2 - 1)}{\sqrt{1 - \zeta^2}} \sin \omega_d t \right.$$

$$\left. + 2\zeta \cos \omega_d t \right] \exp\left(-\zeta \omega_n t\right) \tag{15-22}$$

where ω_d is defined in Eq. (15-19). Thus, the output comprises the desired variation $v_i t$ minus a constant and plus a decaying oscillation. We rewrite the expression in nondimensional form, as follows:

$$\frac{x}{v_i / \omega_n} = \omega_n t - 2\zeta + \left[\frac{(2\zeta^2 - 1)}{\sqrt{1 - \zeta^2}} \sin \omega_d t \right.$$

$$\left. + 2\zeta \cos \omega_d t \right] \exp\left(-\zeta \omega_n t\right) \tag{15-23}$$

To show an example of the response, we plot the output according to (15-23) for a damping ratio of $\zeta = 0.6$ in Fig. 15-9. The output approaches the steady state asymptotically and eventually has a constant error of 2ζ.

An attempt to reduce the steady-state velocity error might be made by

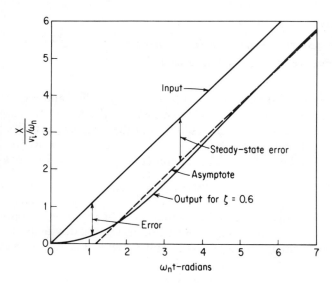

FIGURE 15-9   Response to ramp function.

reducing the damping ratio. However, this course would result in undesirably large oscillations in the response, so a compromise must be made. Servos that eliminate the velocity error will be described in Secs. 15-6 and 15-7.

To summarize, the second-order viscous friction damped servo has zero steady-state position error for a step position input, as explained in the fore-going article, but does have a steady-state velocity error for a ramp input.

15-5
Second-order servo with velocity feedback

Artificial viscous damping can be obtained by the so-called *velocity feedback* (or *derivative control*) method. To illustrate this method we choose a system whose output is the angular displacement of a shaft and represent the system by the one-line diagram in Fig. 15-10. The load is represented by the moment of inertia J, and mechanical friction is neglected altogether. The error is measured by comparing the desired value θ_i and the output θ_o by means of a differential gear. The gear housing drives a transducer TR, such as a potential divider, that translates the error into a voltage e. This voltage provides one input to the differential dc amplifier G. The other input e_v comes from a small

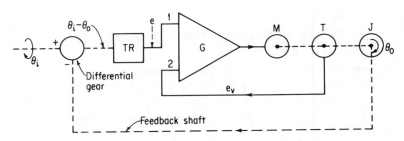

FIGURE 15-10   Second-order servo with velocity feedback.

dc tachometer generator designed to give an output voltage linearly related to the angular speed ω_o. The senses of the two inputs are such that the motor torque is a linear function of $e - e_v$.

Let us write the differential equation of the system. Let J represent the total moment of inertia of all the moving parts and let us neglect motor inductance, counter emf, and all nonlinearities, such as backlash in the differential gear. Then we may write

$$\text{motor torque} = K_m(e - e_v) \qquad (15\text{-}24)$$

We need proportionality constants for the error transducer and for the tachometer; thus let

$$e = K(\theta_i - \theta_o) \qquad (15\text{-}25)$$

and

$$e_v = K_T p\theta_o \qquad (15\text{-}26)$$

Thus (15-24) becomes

$$\text{motor torque} = K_m K(\theta_i - \theta_o) - K_m K_T p\theta_o \qquad (15\text{-}27)$$

We equate motor torque to inertial torque, since friction is neglected

$$Jp^2\theta_o = K_m K(\theta_i - \theta_o) - K_m K_T p\theta_o \qquad (15\text{-}28)$$

or rearranging

$$Jp^2\theta_o + K_m K_T p\theta_o + K_m K\theta_o = K_m K\theta_i \qquad (15\text{-}29)$$

This equation is identical in form to Eq. (15-10). Therefore the constant $K_m K_T$ plays the same role as the viscous friction coefficient B in the earlier discussion.

What are the advantages of velocity feedback? One important advantage lies in avoiding the power loss in a viscous damper. The size of the motor can be chosen to drive the load without regard for the power loss in a viscous damper. Furthermore, the degree of damping can readily be adjusted by providing an adjustment on the velocity feedback voltage.

15-6

Servo with error-rate damping

A servo that uses velocity feedback damping has the same limitation as a viscous-damped system in that it has a steady-state velocity error. In this article we discuss a mode of damping that is proportional to the rate of change of the error. We shall show that this type of damping has a beneficial effect, particularly on the velocity error.

We analyze the system in Fig. 15-11, which is similar to that in Fig. 15-10,

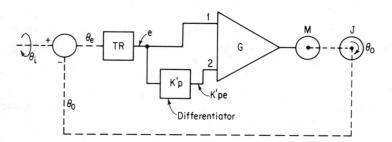

FIGURE 15-11   Servo with error-rate damping.

except for the omission of the velocity feedback and the addition of a differentiator that acts on the error voltage. Amplifier G responds to the *sum* of the voltages at inputs 1 and 2, therefore the amplifier output is $Ge + K'Gpe$. We assume that the motor torque is a constant K_m times the amplifier output, so

$$\text{motor torque} = K_3 e + K_4 pe \qquad (15\text{-}30)$$

where $K_3 = GK_m$ and $K_4 = K'GK_m$. We shall find it convenient to express the equation of the system, using the angular error as the dependent variable rather than output angle. That is, we use the error angle θ_e expressed as

$$\theta_e = \theta_i - \theta_o \qquad (15\text{-}31)$$

Now the error voltage e is a constant times θ_e, i. e., $e = K\theta_e$, and Eq. (15-30) may be written

$$\text{motor torque} = KK_3\theta_e + KK_4 p\theta_e \qquad (15\text{-}32)$$

Now we replace KK_3 by K_1 and KK_4 by K_2 and equate motor torque to inertial torque; thus,

$$Jp^2\theta_o = K_1\theta_e + K_2 p\theta_e \qquad (15\text{-}33)$$

Next we replace θ_o in (15-33) in terms of θ_e and θ_i and obtain

$$Jp^2\theta_e + K_2 p\theta_e + K_1\theta_e = Jp^2\theta_i \qquad (15\text{-}34)$$

Thus, the differential equation connecting error angle and input has the same form of the left-hand side as for the second-order servos already discussed.

The constant K_2, which gives the effect of the rate of change of the error signal, determines the behavior of the system. The magnitude of K_2 determines whether the system is oscillatory or not in the same way as the damping coefficient in the earlier analyses.

Of course, we are here discussing the variation of the error, rather than the output angle. But if we recall that $\theta_o = \theta_i - \theta_e$ and assume that θ_i is a step function or a ramp function, we can see that an oscillatory variation of θ_e will result in an oscillatory component in θ_o.

The right-hand side of Eq. (15-34) represents the second derivative of the input angle. But the second derivative is zero for either a step input or a ramp input, and the right side is zero in the steady state. We conclude that the steady-state value of error angle must also be zero for these inputs! Thus, the system has a zero velocity error in the steady state and exhibits a transient error only during the initial period.

Further analysis would be needed to reveal the details of the transient response and its dependence on the servo parameters. Such analysis would show that the use of error-rate damping may require added amplifier gain and may thereby raise the undamped frequency, which may be objectionable.

Thus far we have ignored the possible need of external load torques. An added load torque that is constant with time will reintroduce a steady-state error. Therefore, error-rate damping may be used when the load inertia is large but the constant load torque is small.

15-7
Servo with error-rate plus integral control

The technique known as *integral control* can be used to control the steady-state error due to a steady torque load. Integral control is obtained by providing a component of motor torque proportional to the integral of the error. Figure 15-12 shows the principle involved. The three signals going to amplifier G are *added* and the sum $e + K'pe + K''(1/p)e$ acts to produce the motor torque. A viscous friction damper B has been incorporated in the system. This can represent an added damper or a load torque proportional to velocity.

The derivation of the differential equation of motion proceeds along the same lines as before. If we assume that the motor torque is given by

$$\text{motor torque} = K_1\theta_e + K_2 p\theta_e + K_3\frac{1}{p}\theta_e \qquad (15\text{-}35)$$

then we can write

$$Jp^2\theta_o + Bp\theta_o = K_1\theta_e + K_2 p\theta_e + K_3\frac{1}{p}\theta_e \qquad (15\text{-}36)$$

By use of the relation $\theta_e = \theta_i - \theta_o$ we can express the error as a function of θ_i and obtain

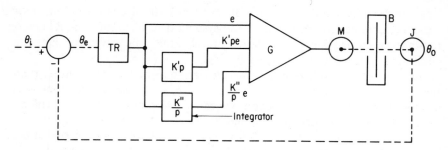

FIGURE 15-12   Servo with error-rate plus integral control.

$$Jp^2\theta_e + (B + K_2)p\theta_e + K_1\theta_e + K_3\frac{1}{p}\theta_e = Jp^2\theta_i + Bp\theta_i \quad (15\text{-}37)$$

as the equation that governs the motion of the system.

Inspection of Eq. (15-37) shows that if the integral term is eliminated by multiplying through by p, the equation becomes a third-order, linear differential equation. It would take us too far afield to consider the complete solution, including the transient components,† but we can draw some conclusions from the form of the basic equation.

Consider that θ_i is subjected to a ramp function $\theta_i = \omega_1 t$, that is, a step of velocity. In the viscous-damped servo the steady state shows a constant error, as in Fig. 15-9, owing to the action of the viscous friction B. With the integral control acting, a constant error would lead to a motor torque that would increase without limit. But because the right side of (15-37) is a constant in the steady state, a constant error is not possible. Analysis of the transient response shows that, if the system is stable, the integral control causes the error to reduce toward zero. After the initial variation of the error, which with low damping is a decaying oscillation plus an exponentially decaying component, the error approaches zero. This type of control is therefore valuable when the load torque demand is large and also when this demand is variable.

15-8
Limitations of the differential
equation approach;
the frequency-response approach

Only the simpler servos are characterized by a second-order or a third-order differential equation, even though simplifying assumptions are made. For example, if the motor armature inductance is included in the analysis of

†See, for example, Reference 15-2, pp. 204ff.

the servo in Fig. 15-12, the order of the equation is increased by one, to the fourth order. The analysis and solution of the higher-order equations becomes increasingly complex and even with numerical coefficients may require an inordinate amount of computation.

For this reason methods have been sought that will give the required information about the system without requiring the complete solution for the transient response. Several techniques have been developed that give indications of the stability of the system and its speed of response and that may be used in design. These include the root-locus techniques, frequency-response methods, and analog computer simulation. Many of the basic ideas for the frequency-response methods have already been discussed under the heading of feedback amplifier analysis, and we shall give a brief account as applied to servos.

The detailed study of feedback amplifiers, particularly by Bode,† led to an understanding of the relations between the amplitude and the phase aspects of the frequency response and to criteria for amplifier stability. These results carry over directly to the analysis of servos.

If a stable linear system is excited by a harmonic driving function, the output, after the transients have died away, will be a harmonic function of the same frequency but in general of different amplitude and phase. Let us assume a sinusoidal excitation of unit amplitude, e. g., of $\sin \omega t$, at the input. Then the steady-state output will have an amplitude and phase that are functions of ω and may be expressed as follows:

$$\text{steady-state output} = G(\omega) \sin [\omega t + \phi(\omega)] \qquad (15\text{-}38)$$

The forms of the gain function $G(\omega)$ and of the phase function $\phi(\omega)$ are characteristic of the system, and they contain the desired information concerning the system response.

What are the most expeditious means of obtaining the functions $G(\omega)$ and $\phi(\omega)$? The methods introduced in Chapter 2 for electric circuits, which included the use of transfer functions involving the complex variable, are applicable when the mathematical description of each part of the system is available. Furthermore, if an actual system, or a model, is available, the functions $G(\omega)$ and $\phi(\omega)$ can be obtained experimentally. Also, the over-all functions for a system can often be constructed from the known frequency-response functions for the components of the system. The components are usually connected in cascade, so the over-all transfer function is the product of the individual functions provided that the loading effect of successive elements is negligible. As a result, log magnitude values are most convenient for the $G(\omega)$ plots, since the component values need merely to be added for a particular frequency. Similarly, the over-all phase is the algebraic sum of the individual phase angles.

†H. W. Bode, *Network Analysis and Feedback Amplifier Design*, D. Van Nostrand Company, Inc., Princeton, N.J., 1945.

15-9
Transfer functions

Our plan is to introduce a transfer function in an operational form and then to convert this to the transfer function in complex variable form that describes the steady-state response to a harmonic driving function. We shall use a second-order servo, as in Fig. 15-5 or Fig. 15-10, as an introductory example and later introduce some more general concepts.

Let us write Eq. (15-15) in the operational form

$$\left(\frac{1}{\omega_n^2}p^2 + \frac{2\zeta}{\omega_n}p + 1\right)x(t) = x_i(t) \tag{15-39}$$

The transfer function in operational form may be obtained by algebraic manipulation; thus,

$$\frac{x(t)}{x_i(t)} = \frac{1}{\dfrac{1}{\omega_n^2}p^2 + \dfrac{2\zeta}{\omega_n}p + 1} \tag{15-40}$$

Now we restrict $x_i(t)$ to a harmonic function, e. g., sin ωt, and inquire about the form of $x(t)$. As our studies of electric circuits in Chapter 2 showed, $x(t)$ will be a harmonic function of the same frequency, but in general of a different magnitude and phase

$$x(t) = G(\omega) \sin\left[\omega t + \phi(\omega)\right] \tag{15-41}$$

It was shown in Chapter 2 to be advantageous to treat harmonic functions as complex quantities, or phasors, and to introduce impedance and transfer functions in the form of complex operators. A study of those techniques will show that the complex transfer function can be obtained expeditiously from the function in operational form simply by replacing p by $j\omega$. Then, for example, p^2 becomes $-\omega^2$, p^3 becomes $-j\omega^3$, etc.

We apply this technique to (15-40) and obtain

$$\mathbf{G}(j\omega) = \frac{\mathbf{x}(j\omega)}{\mathbf{x}_i(j\omega)} = \frac{1}{-\left(\dfrac{\omega}{\omega_n}\right)^2 + j2\zeta\,\dfrac{\omega}{\omega_n} + 1} \tag{15-42}$$

where the symbol $\mathbf{G}(j\omega)$ has been introduced to designate the transfer function. Thus, $G(\omega)$ in (15-41) equals the magnitude of $\mathbf{G}(j\omega)$, and $\phi(\omega)$ is the angle of $\mathbf{G}(j\omega)$.

Equation (15-42) shows that $G(\omega)$ and $\phi(\omega)$ can advantageously be plotted as a function of ω/ω_n, with the damping ratio ζ as a parameter. As already discussed in Secs. 9-9 and 9-10, the two common types of plots are the Nyquist plot, or locus of the complex number in polar form, and the Bode plots of log magnitude and of phase angle versus the log of the frequency ratio. We present the latter type of plots for second-order systems in Fig. 15-13, which covers the same range of damping ratios as in the transient response curves for these systems shown in Fig. 15-7. In accordance with

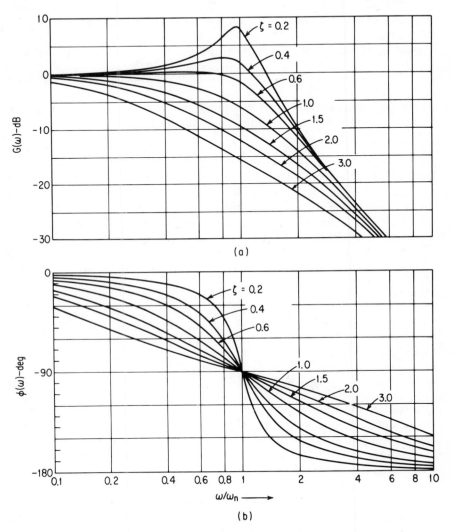

(a)

(b)

FIGURE 15-13　Log amplitude and phase shift curves for the function

$$\frac{1}{-\left(\dfrac{\omega}{\omega_n}\right)^2 + j2\zeta \dfrac{\omega}{\omega_n} + 1}$$

with ζ as the parameter.

custom we use decibels for the log magnitude values and degrees for the phase angles. The maxima of the magnitude curves near $\omega/\omega_n = 1$ for low values of damping show evidence of the effect of *resonance*. If the curves are extended to higher values of ω/ω_n, the function approaches $- 1/(\omega/\omega_n)^2$, and therefore all curves approach an asymptotic slope of $- 40$ dB per decade and the phase approaches $- 180°$.

A general form of the operational transfer function for a servo follows:

$$\frac{a_1 p^m + a_2 p^{m-1} + \cdots a_m p + a_{m+1}}{b_1 p^n + b_2 p^{n-1} + \cdots b_n p + b_{n+1}} \tag{15-43}$$

where the coefficients are real constants and $m \leqslant n$. For our immediate purpose we wish to discuss a limited function, as follows:

$$\frac{a_1 p + a_2}{p(b_1 p^3 + b_2 p^2 + b_3 p + b_4)} \tag{15-44}$$

Let us think of the factored form of the polynomial in the denominator, which can be found by solving for the roots of the polynomial and forming factors like $p + \alpha_1$, where $- \alpha_1$ is one of the roots. The polynomial will have at least one real root and will have two additional roots which may be either both real or both complex. For the purpose of this discussion we assume that the additional pair is complex. If the linear factor corresponding to the real root is factored out, then (15-44) can be written in the form

$$\frac{k_1(k_2 p + 1)}{p(k_3 p + 1)(k_4 p^2 + k_5 p + 1)} \tag{15-45}$$

Here the k's are combinations of the constant coefficients in (15-44).

To obtain the complex transfer function for a sinusoidal input, we replace p by $j\omega$ in (15-45) and obtain

$$\frac{k_1(j\omega k_2 + 1)}{j\omega(j\omega k_3 + 1)(-\omega^2 k_4 + j\omega k_5 + 1)} \tag{15-46}$$

This relation illustrates what types of factors may appear in the numerator or the denominator of a general transfer function. Thus, there may be a factor of the form $j\omega$; linear factors of the form $j\omega k_3 + 1$, and quadratic factors of the form $(- \omega^2 k_4 + j\omega k_5 + 1)$. These factors may also be repeated, giving such factors as $(j\omega)^n$.

To obtain a Bode plot of a function such as (15-46), we think of the product of the several factors in the expression and build up the plot by adding the effects of each factor. For example, for the log-magnitude plot we add the ordinates in decibels for each factor. The factor $(j\omega)^{-1}$ contributes a straight line of negative slope of 20 dB per decade which passes through the point dB $= 0$, $\omega = 1$. The contribution of the linear factors can readily be plotted by the *corner-frequency plus asymptotic lines* technique explained for the plotting of the Bode curves for low-pass and high-pass RC filters in Sec. 2-9. The quadratic factors can be put in the form used in Eq. (15-42), and then the curves in Fig. 15-13 can be used to obtain their contribution to the over-all transfer function. In this way the over-all amplitude and phase plots can be built up with a minimum of labor.

15-10
Open-loop and closed-loop transfer functions; stability

a. Stability

In the foregoing articles our discussion of transfer functions referred to the output/input functions. These are known as the *closed-loop* transfer functions. To extend the discussion, we wish to refer to the block diagram of an elementary servo in Fig. 15-14. This diagram uses the symbol $\mathbf{C}(j\omega)$ for the *controlled* variable, $\mathbf{E}(j\omega)$ for the *error*, and $\mathbf{R}(j\omega)$ for the *reference* (or *command*) variable. The reader can verify that the closed-loop transfer function for this system is

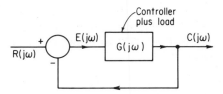

FIGURE 15-14 Block diagram of an elementary servo system.

$$\frac{\mathbf{C}(j\omega)}{\mathbf{R}(j\omega)} = \frac{\mathbf{G}(j\omega)}{1 + \mathbf{G}(j\omega)} \tag{15-47}$$

A similar function relating to the feedback amplifier $\mathbf{G}/(1 + \mathbf{GH})$ was discussed in Sec. 9-9. We recall that the locus of $\mathbf{GH}$ in the Nyquist diagram gave information on the stability of the system. In particular, the behavior of the locus relative to the critical point $-1 + j0$ was crucial in this analysis. Furthermore, we recall that the Bode plots of the function $\mathbf{GH}$ could also be used to obtain stability criteria.

By reasoning similar to that in Sec. 9-9 we can conclude that an analysis of $\mathbf{G}(j\omega)$ in Eq. (15-47) as a function of ω by means of a Nyquist plot or of the Bode plots will be sufficient to determine the stability of this type of system. For example, the Bode plots are examined at the frequency that gives $|\mathbf{G}(j\omega)| = 0$ dB to find the *phase margin* and at the point where $\phi(\omega) = -180°$ to find the *gain margin* in order to judge the degree of stability.

Bode's work† showed that the phase of the transfer function at a particular frequency depends on the rate of change of the log magnitude function over the range $-\infty < \omega < +\infty$. However, the rates of change over a de-

---

†Bode's relations between gain and phase are restricted to the so-called *minimum phase systems*. However, most single-loop servo systems fall into this category.

cade range of frequencies on each side of the particular frequency are predominant in the determination of the phase. This relation between magnitude and phase permits an analysis of stability based on the log-magnitude Bode curve alone, without recourse to the phase curve. For example, if the log-magnitude curve is varying at the rate of $-$ 20 dB per decade for a considerable range on both sides of the frequency at which the gain is unity (0 dB), then the phase is approximately $-$ 90° at this point and the system is surely stable. However, if the rate is $-$ 40 dB per decade in the neighborhood of the 0-dB point, then the phase is close to $-$ 180° and the system stability is seriously in doubt. We conclude that the slope of the log-magnitude plot near the 0-dB point gives a valuable approximate criterion of the stability.

b. Open-loop and closed-loop transfer functions

We wish to define certain transfer functions and will use the systems in Fig. 15-15 (showing compensating schemes to be discussed later) as well as that in Fig. 15-14 as examples. To define the *forward* transfer function, we write

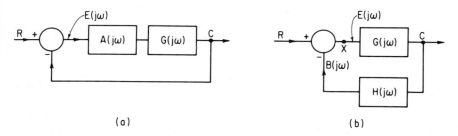

(a)   (b)

FIGURE 15-15 Methods of compensation (a) in the forward path and (b) in the feedback path.

$$\text{forward transfer function} = \frac{\mathbf{C}(j\omega)}{\mathbf{E}(j\omega)} \tag{15-48}$$

In both Figs. 15-14 and 15-15b the forward transfer function is $\mathbf{G}(j\omega)$, but in Fig. 15-15a its value is $\mathbf{A}(j\omega)\mathbf{G}(j\omega)$.

The *open-loop* transfer function is the ratio of the feedback signal to the signal fed into the input of the controller. For example, if the loop is broken at point X in Fig. 15-15b and a unit sine wave is fed in at E, while $R = 0$, the feedback signal is $\mathbf{B}(j\omega)$, and then, for this system,

$$\text{open-loop transfer function} = \frac{\mathbf{B}(j\omega)}{\mathbf{E}(j\omega)} = \mathbf{G}(j\omega)\mathbf{H}(j\omega) \tag{15-49}$$

In the systems in Figs. 15-14 and 15-15a the open-loop transfer function reduces to the forward transfer function, since the feedback is unity.

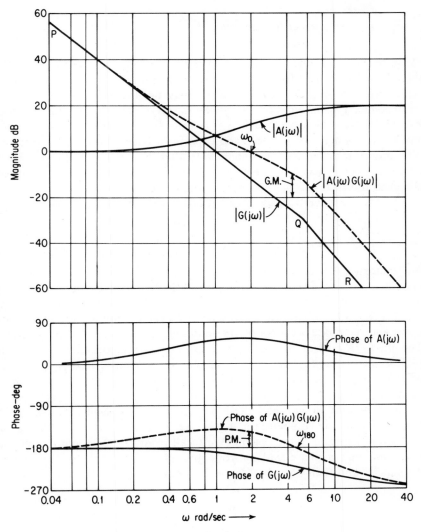

FIGURE 15-16   Log magnitude and phase curves for

$$\mathbf{G}(j\omega) = \frac{1.0}{(j\omega)^2\left(1 + \dfrac{j\omega}{5.5}\right)}$$

and for

$$\mathbf{A}(j\omega)\,\mathbf{G}(j\omega) = \frac{1.0\left(1 + \dfrac{j\omega}{0.5}\right)}{(j\omega)^2\left(1 + \dfrac{j\omega}{5.5}\right)\left(1 + \dfrac{j\omega}{5}\right)}.$$

15-11

A compensated servo

Suppose that an analysis of a servo of the type in Fig. 15-14 shows that the servo is deficient in performance. For example, it may be stable, but its transient response or its steady-state error may be unsatisfactory. Or it may be unstable. Two schemes for improving the servo performance are shown in Fig. 15-15. Here the blocks marked $A(j\omega)$ and $H(j\omega)$ generally represent passive networks made of resistors and capacitors. These networks (sometimes plus added amplifier gain) are intended to alter the Nyquist plot or the Bode curves in such a way as to remove one or more of the system deficiencies. We shall illustrate the method by a numerical example.

We assume a servo whose forward transfer function is given by

$$G(j\omega) = \frac{1.0}{(j\omega)^2\left(1 + \dfrac{j\omega}{5.5}\right)} \qquad (15\text{-}50)$$

The factor $(j\omega)^{-2}$ means that at very low values of ω the phase lag is 180° and the log-magnitude curve is dropping at the rate of 40 dB per decade. The linear term has a corner frequency of 5.5 rad/s. The over-all function is plotted in Fig. 15-16, where the line PQR shows the asymptotic log-magnitude curve and the phase is shown by the solid line at the bottom of the diagram. The line PQR crosses the 0-dB level at $\omega = 1$, and we note that the phase is $-191°$ at this point. Thus, the phase margin is negative (the Nyquist plot would pass the critical point on the "wrong" side), and the system is *unstable* by itself.

Suppose that we consider the insertion of a phase-lead network and a preamplifier as the compensator $A(j\omega)$ in the forward path (Fig. 15-15a) in an attempt to stabilize the system. We recall from Fig. 2-24 and the related discussion that a phase-lead network gives a constant attenuation at low frequencies and then a gradual increase in gain to the 0-dB level. Over this

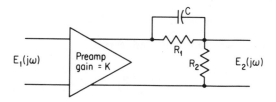

FIGURE 15-17   Preamplifier and phase-advance circuit:

$$\text{Compensation} = A\,(j\omega) = \frac{E_2(j\omega)}{E_1(j\omega)}.$$

range the phase of the output is advanced and the maximum advance occurs midway in the range of gain change.

If a lead network is inserted in the forward path, there would be a decided drop in the forward function amplitude at the low frequencies, which would lower the accuracy of the servo. Therefore, we think of combining a preamplifier with the phase advance circuit, as shown in Fig. 15-17 (or of increasing the gain in the existing amplifier). We recall from Eq. (2-130) that the phase-advance circuit has the transfer function

$$\frac{\alpha\left(1 + \frac{j\omega}{\omega_1}\right)}{1 + \frac{j\alpha\omega}{\omega_1}} \tag{15-51}$$

where

$$\alpha = \frac{R_2}{R_1 + R_2} \quad \text{and} \quad \omega_1 = \frac{1}{CR_1} \tag{15-52}$$

We choose $\alpha = 0.1$ on the assumption that this value will give enough phase advance. The next choice concerns the characteristic frequency ω_1 which also fixes the frequency ω_1/α. The phase advance is a maximum at the midpoint (on a log ω scale) between these two frequencies. We should like to have the maximum phase advance occur at the point where the *modified* log-magnitude curve goes through 0 dB to provide a maximum phase margin. We choose $\omega_1 = 0.5$, which fixes $\omega_1/\alpha = 5$, so the characteristic frequencies are 0.5 and 5 rad/s. Finally, we assume a gain $K = 10$, so that $K\alpha = 1.0$. We remark that our choice of constants is somewhat arbitrary and other choices could be made which would give satisfactory or possibly superior results. Now the transfer function $A(j\omega)$ becomes

$$A(j\omega) = \frac{10 \times 0.1 \times \left(1 + \frac{j\omega}{0.5}\right)}{1 + \frac{j\omega}{5}} \tag{15-53}$$

Therefore, the modified forward transfer function, including the effect of the phase-advance compensation, is

$$A(j\omega)G(j\omega) = \frac{1.0\left(1 + \frac{j\omega}{0.5}\right)}{(j\omega)^2\left(1 + \frac{j\omega}{5.5}\right)\left(1 + \frac{j\omega}{5}\right)} \tag{15-54}$$

The Bode plots of this function are shown by the dotted curves in Fig. 15-16. The figure also shows separately the curves for $A(j\omega)$, and it is easy to see how the ordinates for $A(j\omega)$ and $G(j\omega)$ are added to obtain the combined curves.

The magnitude curve goes through 0 dB at $\omega_0 = 1.9$ rad/s. The phase at this frequency determines the phase margin, labeled P.M. in the figure, which has the value 33°. The gain margin (G.M. in the figure) occurs at $\phi(\omega) = -180°$, and its value is approximately 10 dB. Thus the modified system is stable.

Further study of the system would be needed to obtain information regarding transient response, degree of damping, and accuracy. The servo designer who has extensive experience with open-loop transfer function Bode curves could judge from Fig. 15-16 what the response of the complete system will be, at least in a qualitative way. We shall extend our analysis only to give the closed-loop transfer function, e. g., we shall use the data from the curves in Fig. 15-16 to calculate

$$\frac{C(j\omega)}{R(j\omega)} = \frac{A(j\omega)G(j\omega)}{1 + A(j\omega)G(j\omega)} \tag{15-55}$$

This calculation requires conversion from dB to absolute magnitude and a number of complex algebra manipulations for each frequency of interest. After these tedious calculations† we obtain the curves in Fig. 15-18.‡ Here the amplitude is plotted in actual values, instead of in dB. We notice a rather high resonance peak of 1.85 at about $\omega = 2.4$ rad/s. This indicates that the step-function response will be oscillatory with possibly an inadequate degree of damping, depending on the requirements on the system.

The accuracy of the response for harmonic inputs is of interest. The phase error reaches about 5° at $\omega = 0.4$, and the amplitude error is about 11 per cent at this frequency. At $\omega = 0.1$ the amplitude error is about 1 per cent and the phase error (by calculation) about 0.1°. Thus, the moderate accuracy of this servo might be adequate for low frequency input signals, depending on the requirements.

Other types of compensating network are also used, depending on the particular system. A *lag* network provides attenuation and phase shift over the higher range of frequencies. Thus, the gain at the lower frequencies is maintained at the value needed for the required accuracy, and the frequency response can be altered at the higher frequencies to improve stability. A composite compensator, called a *lag-lead* network provides attenuation over a range of frequencies, and first a phase lag and then a phase lead and finally zero phase shift as the frequency is increased.

---

†The so-called Nichols charts provide a graphical means for calculating the closed-loop from the open-loop function.

‡A check on the calculations can be made for $\omega \to 0$ and $\omega \to \infty$ by writing out the transfer function; thus

$$\frac{C(j\omega)}{R(j\omega)} = \frac{1 + \dfrac{j\omega}{0.5}}{(j\omega)^2\left(1 + \dfrac{j\omega}{5.5}\right)\left(1 + \dfrac{j\omega}{5}\right) + 1 + \dfrac{j\omega}{0.5}}$$

When $\omega \to 0$, this function approaches 1/1 or unity. When $\omega \to \infty$, the function approaches $(5.5 \times 5)/0.5 (j\omega)^3$

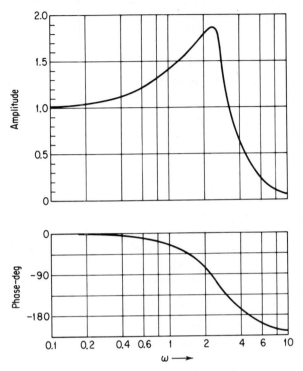

FIGURE 15-18 Amplitude and phase curves of closed-loop transfer function of servo.

Compensating networks can also be introduced into the feedback path in the circuit in Fig. 15-15b. The closed-loop transfer function for this system is

$$\frac{C(j\omega)}{R(j\omega)} = \frac{G(j\omega)}{1 + G(j\omega)H(j\omega)} \tag{15-56}$$

Bode diagrams can also be used for the study of this type of system, but the function in (15-56) is different in form from that in (15-55), so the analysis is somewhat different. Since Eq. (15-56) has the same form as that for the voltage feedback amplifier, the discussion of this amplifier in Chapter 9 can largely be applied to the corresponding servo systems. For example, at the low-frequency end of the range often $|G(j\omega)H(j\omega)| \gg 1$, and consequently (15-56) reduces to

$$\frac{C(j\omega)}{R(j\omega)} \cong \frac{1}{H(j\omega)} \tag{15-57}$$

Thus, the response at low frequencies depends primarily on the elements in the feedback path.

15-12
Servo components and systems

The examples have given an introductory view of servo components and systems, but some additional discussion is desirable.

a. Servo components

In small servos the output element is often a dc motor, however, ac motors are also used, particularly the two-phase induction motor. This motor has two stator windings and a squirrel-cage rotor. One stator winding, called the *reference* winding, is generally energized at a constant level from the ac source. The other winding, called the *controlled* winding, is driven by an ac power amplifier at a phase angle of 90° from the first. The resulting torque is approximately proportional to the voltage impressed on the controlled winding.

When the power requirement is over some tens of watts, other drive systems are used. One of these is the so-called *Ward-Leonard drive*, in which a dc generator, whose field is controlled, supplies the armature of the dc drive motor, which has a constant field. The servo amplifier controls the generator field and indirectly controls the drive motor.

In addition to the power amplifiers discussed in an earlier chapter, there is a family of rotating amplifiers, such as the *amplidyne, metadyne, rototrol,* etc. These are special machines designed to have high power gain between an input to a field winding and the armature output, as well as good speed of response.

Some means are needed for comparing the output with the input and converting the error into an error signal. The earlier examples described a simple potentiometer system; a tachometer generator and adder system, and one using a feedback shaft driving a differential gear with a transducer. We wish to describe another system that uses two identical machines called *synchros*. The circuit diagram is shown in Fig. 15-19. Each machine has three windings distributed over the stator with axes spaced 120° from each other. The two-pole rotor is energized at the power frequency. Imagine first that the two stators are connected as shown but that the rotor coil of the *receiver* is disconnected. The stator coil in the *transmitter*, being energized, will induce single-phase voltages in its three stator coils whose magnitude will depend on the

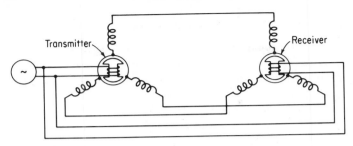

FIGURE 15-19   Synchro pair system.

angular position of the rotor. These voltages will energize the receiver stator coils in the same relative proportions. Therefore, the pattern of magnetic flux in the receiver will match that in the transmitter. Moreover, if the receiver rotor is at the same angle as the transmitter rotor, there will be an induced voltage equal (except for the effect of losses) in magnitude and phase to that impressed on the transmitter. Thus, nothing will happen (no current, no torque) if the receiver rotor coil is now connected to the power supply.

If, however, the transmitter rotor is moved a few degrees, the receiver flux pattern shifts accordingly and the receiver rotor will have an induced current. This current produces a torque which tends to make the receiver coil line up with the transmitter coil. Thus, one application of the synchro pair is to provide an indication of a shaft position at a remote location.

In another application the transmitter is driven by the servo output shaft and the input angle controls the position of the receiver rotor, but only the transmitter rotor is energized. The ac induced voltage in the receiver rotor now varies as the cosine of the angle between the rotors and therefore goes to zero when the angle is 90°. The servo system is designed so that a 90° angular position between the rotors corresponds to *zero error*. A departure from this position will cause an error voltage in the receiver rotor whose magnitude varies as the sine of the error angle and whose phase reverses for a change from positive to negative error. This error detection system, combined with ac amplifiers and an ac servo motor gives a simple, rugged servo system.

b. Servo systems

We have referred to the order of the applicable differential equation as one basis for the classification of servo systems. Another basis for classification is the number of direct integrations present in the transfer function between output and error. These transfer functions (in operational form) have been listed in Table 15-1 for the servos used as examples. The factors of

Table 15-1   Classification of Servo Systems

Refer to figure	Type of system	Transfer function $C(t)/E(t)$	Derived from equation	Type number	Order
15-3	Viscous damping, no mass	$\dfrac{K_m}{Bp + K}$	(15-7)	0	1
15-5	Viscous damping, with mass	$\dfrac{K_m}{p(Mp + B)}$	(15-10)	1	2
15-10	Velocity damping	$\dfrac{K_1}{p(Jp + K_2)}$	(15-29)	1	2
15-11	Error-rate damping	$\dfrac{K_2 p + K_1}{p^2 J}$	(15-34)	2	2
15-12	Error-rate plus integral control	$\dfrac{K_2 p^2 + K_1 p + K_3}{p^2(Jp + B)}$	(15-36)	2	3

the form $1/p^n$ indicate direct integrations. If the function has a factor $1/p^2$, it is classed as a Type 2 servo, if $1/p$, then it is Type 1, and if $1/p^0$, or unity, it is Type 0. Types higher than 2 are seldom used, owing to the difficulty of stabilizing the system.

Step functions of input position and velocity have been used to study the responses of the exemplary servos. These studies could be extended to include a step function of acceleration, which might be important in a high-precision, fast-response servo. Some general conclusions about the steady-state *position* errors for the three types of input are the following. In a Type 0 system the error approaches a constant for a step displacement but increases without limit for a step velocity or step acceleration. In a Type 1 system the ultimate position error is zero for a step displacement, is a constant for a step velocity, but increases with time for a step acceleration. The Type 2 system has a zero ultimate error for both the step displacement and the step velocity, but has a constant final error for a constant acceleration.

15-13
A generator voltage regulator

In the simple voltage regulator circuit in Fig. 15-20 the error voltage e, obtained as the difference between the reference (input) voltage e_r and the output voltage e_o, is used to actuate the generator field through the amplifier G. Because there would be no output voltage if the error voltage were zero, we expect that this is a Type 0 system. Let us verify this estimate by writing down the output/error transfer function.

The amplifier is assumed to act without internal time lags. We let G des-

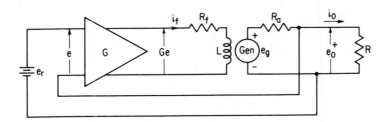

FIGURE 15-20   A generator voltage regulator circuit.

ignate the voltage gain and R_f include the output resistance of the amplifier as well as the field resistance, so we may write

$$\frac{i_f(t)}{e(t)} = \frac{G}{Lp + R_f} = \frac{\dfrac{G}{R_f}}{\dfrac{L}{R_f}p + 1} = \frac{\dfrac{G}{R_f}}{Tp + 1} \qquad (15\text{-}58)$$

where the field circuit time constant L/R_f is written as T. The generated voltage e_g is assumed to be linearly related to the field current, so we write

$$e_g(t) = Ki_f(t) \qquad (15\text{-}59)$$

The load voltage is given by

$$e_o(t) = \frac{R}{R_a + R}e_g(t) = K_1 e_g(t) \qquad (15\text{-}60)$$

where K_1 replaces $R/(R_a + R)$. The error voltage is

$$e(t) = e_r(t) - e_o(t) \qquad (15\text{-}61)$$

We combine (15-58), (15-59), and (15-60) to eliminate $i_f(t)$ and $e_g(t)$ and obtain the differential equation of the system

$$(Tp + 1)e_o(t) = (GK_1K/R_f)e(t) \qquad (15\text{-}62)$$

Or, written as the operational transfer function,

$$\frac{e_o(t)}{e(t)} = \frac{\dfrac{GK_1K}{R_f}}{Tp + 1} \qquad (15\text{-}63)$$

This relation confirms that the regulator is a Type 0 system.

Next we consider the relation of the output voltage to the reference voltage, assuming a constant load resistance. If $e(t)$ in (15-62) is replaced by its value from (15-61) and the terms are rearranged, we get

$$(Tp + 1 + GK_2)e_o(t) = GK_2 e_r(t) \qquad (15\text{-}64)$$

where $K_2 = K_1K/R_f$. Suppose that $e_r(t)$ is a step function of E_r volts. The steady-state value of $e_o(t)$, call it E_o, is found from (15-64) to be

$$E_o = \frac{GK_2}{1 + GK_2} E_r \qquad (15\text{-}65)$$

Thus, E_o will be lower than E_r but will approach E_r when $GK_2 \gg 1$. The response to the step function is as follows:

$$e_o(t) = E_o\left\{1 - \exp\left[-\frac{(1 + GK_2)t}{T}\right]\right\} \qquad (15\text{-}66)$$

This response has a time constant $T/(1 + GK_2)$, which is lower than the field time constant T. An increase in gain will reduce the effective time constant and give a more rapid response.

Example: Let the system constants for a 1-kW, 200-V generator regulator be

$$L = 80\text{H} \qquad K = 800 \text{ V/A}$$
$$R_f = 1250 \ \Omega \qquad K_1 = 0.90$$

Then $K_2 = 0.576$ and $T = L/R_f = 0.064$ s $= 64$ ms. How large must G be if we desire $E_o = 0.99 \ E_r$? Using Eq. (15-65) and solving for G, we find $G = 172$. What is the time constant of the response with this value of gain? The quantity $1 + GK_2$ is 100, so the effective time constant is reduced to 0.64 ms. This low value is approximate for a real system, since the armature inductance would have a comparable effect.

A regulator must also respond quickly to sudden changes in the load. After a sudden increase in the load current, say, of ΔI_o amperes, the generator field current for the first instant remains the same and then begins to respond to the demand of the regulator for more field current. The first result, therefore, is a drop in output voltage in the amount $R_a\Delta I_o$. Then the regulator will more or less rapidly restore the output voltage toward the desired value. To analyze this type of response we formulate the differential equation that connects $e_o(t)$ and $i_o(t)$ and study the effect of an assumed increment in $i_o(t)$. This implies that we no longer are dealing with a load resistance R in the analysis but rather with constant-current loads.

The relation between $e_o(t)$ and $i_o(t)$ is

$$e_o(t) = e_g(t) - R_a i_o(t) \qquad (15\text{-}67)$$

By combining Eqs. (15-58), (15-59), (15-61), and (15-67), we can obtain

$$\left(Tp + 1 + \frac{KG}{R_f}\right)e_o(t) = \left(\frac{KG}{R_f}\right)e_r(t) - R_a(Tp + 1)i_o(t) \qquad (15\text{-}68)$$

We recall that $T = L/R_f$. Next we specify that $e_r(t)$ is a constant E_r and get

$$\left(Tp + 1 + \frac{KG}{R_f}\right)e_o(t) = \left(\frac{KG}{R_f}\right)E_r - R_a(Tp + 1)i_o(t) \qquad (15\text{-}69)$$

To establish the steady-state condition, we assume that $e_o(t)$ and $i_o(t)$ approach the constant values E_o and I_o. These values are substituted in Eq. (15-69), and since the derivative terms go to zero, we solve for E_o to obtain

$$E_o = \frac{\dfrac{KG}{R_f}}{1 + \dfrac{KG}{R_f}} E_r - \frac{R_a}{1 + \dfrac{KG}{R_f}} I_o \qquad (15\text{-}70)$$

The interesting term is the second on the right. This shows that the voltage drop due to R_a is reduced by the factor $1/(1 + KG/R_f)$. If we use the values from the example, except now let $G = 100$, we calculate $1 + KG/R_f$ to equal 65, so that the effective resistance is only 1.54 per cent of its actual value. The reduction in effective resistance should not be surprising, since it is exactly analogous to the reduction in output impedance in the feedback amplifier with voltage feedback which we studied earlier.

Generally the transient of greatest practical importance is that involving a change from a previously established steady state. Therefore, let us write $e_o(t) = E_o + \delta e_o(t)$, and $i_o(t) = I_o + \delta i_o(t)$ in Eq. (15-69). If this is done and the constant and variable parts are separated, we may express the relation between the variable parts as follows:

$$\left(Tp + 1 + \frac{KG}{R_f}\right)\delta e_o(t) = -R_a Tp\delta i_o(t) - R_a\delta i_o(t) \qquad (15\text{-}71)$$

Let us specify $\delta i_o(t)$ to be an increment ΔI_o. Then the first term on the right is an impulse function and the second is a step input. The result is a sudden drop in output voltage of magnitude $R_a\Delta I_o$ and then a relaxation toward the smaller value of drop $R_a\Delta I_o/(1 + KG/R_f)$ on an exponential curve of time constant $T/(1 + KG/R_f)$, as pictured in Fig. 15-21. Thus, the regulator has no effect on the initial drop in voltage but rapidly restores the voltage nearly to its original value.

How can the performance of the regulator be improved? One method is to use a Type 1 or a Type 2 system by providing one or two integrations

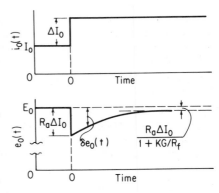

FIGURE 15-21   Voltage regulator response to a change in load current. Note expansion of the voltage scale.

in the control path. A simple method for eliminating the drop in the steady-state voltage with increased load is the following. A small resistance is added in the load circuit. The voltage drop across this resistance, when used as a feedback signal, can be made to compensate for the total resistance drop in the load circuit and thus provide perfect steady-state voltage regulation.

Higher-power systems use a dc machine, called an *exciter*, to supply the field of the main generator. Thus, an electronic amplifier can control the exciter field and thereby the main generator output. Low power dc voltage regulators as used in electronic power supplies have been discussed in Secs. 11-7 and 11-8.

REFERENCES

15-1 H. Chestnut and R. W. Mayer, *Servomechanisms and Regulating System Design*, v. 1, 2d ed., John Wiley & Sons, Inc., New York, 1959.

15-2 H. Lauer, R. N. Lesnick, and L. E. Matson, *Servomechanism Fundamentals*, 2d ed., McGraw-Hill Book Company, New York, 1960.

15-3 P. L. Taylor, *Servomechanisms*, Longmans, Green & Co., London, 1960.

15-4 J. E. Gibson and F. B. Tuteur, *Control System Components*, McGraw-Hill Book Company, New York, 1958.

EXERCISES

15-1 The servo in Fig. 15-5, which is governed by Eq. (15-9), has the constants $M = 0.2$ kg and $K_m = 45$ N/m. (a) If $B = 3.6$ N·s/m, what is the response for a step input of 0.05 m? Sketch the response curve, using Fig. 15-7 as the basis if applicable. (b) What value of B is needed to give a damping ratio of unity? (c) If B is adjusted to give a damping ratio of 0.6 and a step input is applied, what is the percentage overshoot and at what time does it occur?

15-2 Consider the servo shown in Fig. 15-10. Assume that the ratio of motor torque to the quantity $(e - e_v)$ is 1.2 N·m/V, that the error transducer constant is 10 V/rad, and the tachometer constant is 0.08 V·s/rad. Let $J = 0.12$ kg·m². (a) What is the value of the damping ratio of the system? (b) Sketch the response for a step input of angle equal to 10°. (c) Sketch the response for a step input of angular velocity of 5 rad/s.

15-3 Consider a motor that drives a load through a gear train having a reduction factor n. That is, the torque on the load is n times the motor torque, or the motor speed is n times the load shaft speed. Let the motor inertia be J_m and the load inertia be J. We inquire about the total effective inertia referred to the load shaft, call it J_{eff}. (a) Show that $J_{eff} = J + n^2 J_m$. (b) Suppose that the maximum motor torque is T_m. Show that the optimum value of n for maximum load acceleration is $\sqrt{J/J_m}$.

15-4 A portion of a servo that uses a Ward-Leonard control system is shown in Fig. 15-22. Let e be an error voltage that controls the generator field current via

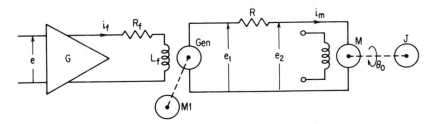

FIGURE 15-22　Motor-generator (Ward-Leonard) control system.

the amplifier G. Auxiliary motor $M1$ drives the generator Gen, which in turn drives the motor M, which has a constant field current. J is the total load plus motor moment of inertia, and R represents the total resistance of the generator-motor armature loop. Armature inductances are assumed negligible, so e_1 and e_2 are the generated voltages in Gen and M, respectively. Show that under these assumptions and assuming linearity the operational transfer function between output and input is given by

$$\frac{\theta_0(t)}{e(t)} = \frac{\dfrac{R_f K_g G}{K_m}}{p(T_f p + 1)(T_m p + 1)}$$

where $T_f = L_f/R_f$, $T_m = JR/K_t K_m$, K_t is the motor torque per unit armature current, K_m is the motor counter emf per unit value of $p\theta_0(t)$, and K_g is the generated voltage in Gen per unit generator field current.

15-5 The self-balancing servo potentiometer shown in Fig. 15-23 is used to measure the emf of the thermocouple TC. The servo motor drives a lead screw which ad-

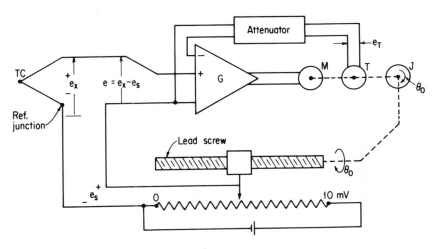

FIGURE 15-23　Servo potentiometer system.

justs the known voltage e_s (obtained from the potential divider) to match the TC voltage e_x. A tachometer generator furnishes a velocity feedback signal, which is added to the error signal in the amplifier G so as to provide damping. Assume that friction effects are negligible, and let e_s be zero when θ_0 is zero. The system constants are J(total) $= 4 \times 10^{-5}$ kg·m². Voltage $e_T = 5$ V at 1000 rpm. Attenuator factor $= 5 \times 10^{-5}$. Lead screw length $= 20$ cm. Lead screw thread $= 30$ threads per cm. Potential divider voltage $= 10$ mV total. The motor torque equals $0.32i_m$ N·m, where i_m is the motor current in amperes.

Suppose that a sudden change in thermocouple voltage occurs. (a) What value of G, expressed in A/V, is required to give a damping ratio of 0.8? (b) How much time is required before the change of potentiometer position is essentially complete under conditions of (a)?

15-6 (a) Derive the differential equation that relates position error to input for the viscous-damped servo in Sec. 15-3, assuming a step input. (b) Repeat (a) for a ramp input.

15-7 (a) Draw a diagram of a motor speed control system that uses the arrangement in Fig. 15-22 plus a dc tachometer generator and a reference voltage input. (b) Derive the differential equation relating output angular velocity ω_0 to the reference voltage e_r. Use the constants defined in Prob. 15-4 and define any new constants required.

15-8 Consider a 1-kW dc generator regulated by the circuit in Fig. 15-20 and having the constants given in the example in Sec. 15-12, except that $G = 100$. Let $E_r = 200$ V and the generator armature resistance be 6 Ω. The system is in the steady state with a 3-A output current when the current jumps to 5 A. Determine and sketch the variation of output voltage for this disturbance.

16

Wave Forming and Shaping;
Pulse Generators

16-1
Introduction

As electronic instruments and industrial controllers become more complex and require a higher speed of response, a greater array of measuring and controlling systems that depend on the formation and manipulation of pulses and wave shapes is being used. These systems include high-speed pulse counters, frequency and time measuring instruments, pulse-height analyzers, digital voltmeters, and the like. This chapter will deal with the circuits that are the basic building blocks for the generation, shaping, and transmission of pulses and other nonsinusoidal wave forms.

16-2
Pulse response of the
series RC circuit

Consider first the response of the RC circuit in Fig. 16-1b to the ideal voltage pulse in Fig. 16-1a. The output voltage e_o has the same variation as the current through the resistor R, since we assume no external load. We can regard the sudden rise of e_i as equivalent to the switching on of a constant voltage E and can calculate the transient current by the methods of Chapter 2. We

401

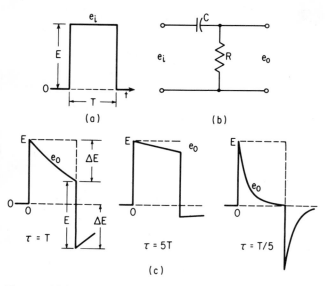

FIGURE 16-1   Pulse response of an RC circuit with the output taken across R.

assume that C initially has zero charge and can express e_o during the pulse length T as

$$e_o = E \exp\left(\frac{-t}{\tau}\right) \tag{16-1}$$

where $\tau = RC$, the *time constant* of the circuit. As shown in Fig. 16-1c, the output voltage jumps to the value E and then decays at a rate that depends on the value of the time constant. The falling voltage across R may be attributed to the rising voltage across C as C accumulates charge.

At the end of the pulse interval, at $t = T$, the input voltage goes to zero, which is equivalent to short-circuiting the input. The accumulated charge in C causes a reverse current; therefore e_o reverses suddenly and dies out on an exponential curve. As shown in Fig. 16-1c, the magnitude of the reverse transient depends on the relation of the time constant to the pulse length. If $\tau \gg T$, there is only a small charge in C and the reverse transient is small, but if $\tau \ll T$, the reverse peak is nearly equal to E. The quantitative relations are shown in the figure for the case of $\tau = T$. At the end of the pulse the voltage falls instantly by the amount E. The negative peak voltage equals ΔE in magnitude, which equals the amount by which the positive voltage fell during the pulse interval T.

Now suppose that the output voltage is taken across the capacitor as shown in Fig. 16-2a. The output voltage is now a rising exponential. The capa-

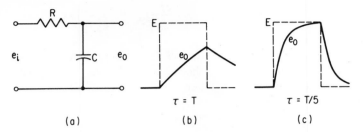

FIGURE 16-2   Pulse response of an *RC* circuit with the output taken across *C*.

citor voltage is the difference between the applied voltage and the resistor voltage; therefore

$$e_o = E - E \exp\left(\frac{-t}{\tau}\right) = E\left[1 - \exp\left(\frac{-t}{\tau}\right)\right] \qquad (16\text{-}2)$$

After the input pulse falls back to zero at the end of the pulse, the capacitor (or output) voltage decays exponentially.

The response to a periodic *square wave* that is symmetrical about the time axis will also be symmetrical after the starting transient has died away. The input wave is shown in Fig. 16-3a; the steady-state output wave

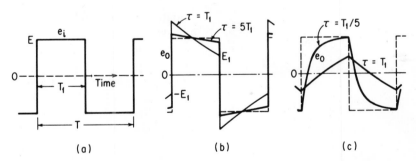

FIGURE 16-3   (a) Input to an *RC* circuit, (b) output across the resistor, and (c) output across the capacitor.

when taken across the resistance is shown in Fig. 16-3b and that when taken across the capacitor is given in Fig. 16-3c. Consider the wave in Fig. 16-3b for the condition $\tau = T_1$, where T_1 is the half-period of the square wave. The wave starts at the level $-E_1$ and then jumps by the amount $2E$ to a level above the input wave and decays to E_1 in the time T_1. The reader can show that

$$E_1 = \frac{2E}{1 + \exp\left(\dfrac{T_1}{\tau}\right)} \qquad (16\text{-}3)$$

which holds for any ratio of T_1 to τ. Thus E_1 approaches E when $\tau \gg T_1$, and the output wave approaches the same form as the input wave.

When the output voltage is taken across the capacitor C (see Fig. 16-3c), the reverse is true. That is, the output wave more nearly approximates the input wave as the time constant is made *small* compared with the half-period.

16-3
The series RC circuit
as an approximate integrator
or differentiator

We consider first a specific example to introduce the concept of the RC differentiator and integrator and to explain the requirements of this application. The input wave, taken to be a single half-wave pulse of sine shape (Fig. 16-4), is impressed across the series circuit of a resistance R and an initially uncharged capacitance C. The series RC circuit can be made to serve as an approximate differentiator or integrator, depending on whether the output is taken across R or across C, and provided that certain restrictions on the output voltages are maintained.

If the circuit time constant is made very short compared with the pulse length T_1, the capacitor voltage e_c will follow the input voltage closely and will be only slightly smaller than e_i. This is equivalent to requiring that

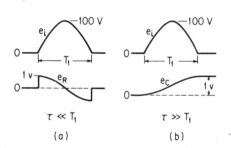

FIGURE 16-4 *RC* differentiator and integrator action.

$$e_c \cong e_1 \qquad (16\text{-}4)$$

at all times. Then the instantaneous current is

$$i = C\frac{de_c}{dt} \cong C\frac{de_i}{dt} \qquad (16\text{-}5)$$

Using Eq. (16-5) and Ohm's law, we find the voltage across R

$$e_R = Ri \cong RC\frac{de_i}{dt} \qquad (16\text{-}6)$$

This result shows that, subject to the restriction in Eq. (16-4), the resistor voltage is the time derivative of the input voltage multiplied by the circuit time constant.

The approximation depends on keeping $e_c \cong e_i$, that is, on keeping $e_R \ll e_i$. Actually, the level of the input voltage as well as the time constant influences the maximum instantaneous value of the derivative that the differentiator can handle. Assume that we require that e_R shall not exceed ke_i for the required accuracy of differentiation where k is perhaps 0.01 or 0.05. Then, using (16-6),

$$(e_R)_{max} = ke_i \cong RC\left(\frac{de_i}{dt}\right)_{max} \tag{16-7}$$

Thus

$$\left(\frac{de_i}{dt}\right)_{max} \cong \frac{ke_i}{RC} \tag{16-8}$$

For example, if $k = 0.05$, $e_i = 100$ V, and $RC = 10^{-6}$s, then $(de_i/dt)_{max} = 5 \times 10^6$ V/s, for roughly 5 per cent error.

To use the RC circuit as an integrator, we take the output across C and require that $e_c \ll e_i$ at all times. Then $e_R \cong e_i$, and the current will be

$$i = \frac{e_R}{R} \cong \frac{e_i}{R} \tag{16-9}$$

We use this current to calculate the capacitor voltage, assuming that the capacitor is initially uncharged

$$e_c = \frac{1}{C}\int_0^t i\,dt \cong \frac{1}{RC}\int_0^t e_i\,dt \tag{16-10}$$

We see that the capacitor voltage is the integral of the input voltage multiplied by the reciprocal of the time constant, provided that we keep $e_c \ll e_i$.

The RC integrator can be applied to produce a desired change in the form of a recurring wave. For example, if the input is a square wave, the output will be a triangular wave. Another application might be the integration of a single pulse or of a group of pulses. Of course, some means may be necessary to discharge the capacitor after each integration. This can be done automatically by a combination of a clamping circuit and a pulse-actuated gate circuit (Secs. 16-5 and 16-6).

16-4
Compensated attenuator

Suppose that an attempt is made to reduce the voltage of a pulse before it is impressed on a *CRO* by means of a simple voltage divider. The equivalent circuit is shown in Fig. 16-5a, which includes the *CRO* input capacitance

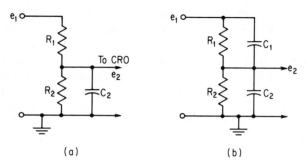

FIGURE 16-5   (a) Voltage divider working into a circuit having input capacitance and (b) compensated voltage divider (attenuator).

C_2. This capacitance will cause a serious distortion of the pulse shape. For example, on a square input pulse the voltage e_2 will rise on an exponential curve of time constant τ rather than rising instantly. Then, when the input pulse terminates, voltage e_2 will collapse with the same time constant rather than instantly. Analysis will show that the time constant is $\tau = C_2[R_1 \| R_2]$, assuming that the source resistance is zero.

Shunting resistor R_1 with a capacitor C_1 of the correct size will correct this difficulty. The circuit which results (Fig. 16-5b) is called a *compensated voltage divider* or a *compensated attenuator*. It can be shown that, if the circuit constants are chosen so that $R_1C_1 = R_2C_2$, then the voltage e_2 will be a faithful replica of e_1. Consider, for example, a step input of value E volts. At the first instant the voltage e_2 across C_2 and $E - e_2$ across C_1 will be determined by the inverse capacitance ratio; thus

$$\frac{e_2}{E - e_2} = \frac{C_1}{C_2} \qquad (16\text{-}11)$$

Solving for e_2, we find

$$e_2 = \frac{C_1}{C_1 + C_2} E \qquad (16\text{-}12)$$

If we use the relation $R_1C_1 = R_2C_2$ to substitute for one of the C's in Eq. (16-12), we obtain

$$e_2 = \frac{R_2}{R_1 + R_2} E \qquad (16\text{-}13)$$

But this is the usual voltage divider formula, so the initial voltage division due to the C's is also the steady-state voltage division due to the R's and the wave of e_2 has the correct step-voltage shape.

In the application of this circuit to the CRO input the capacitor C_1 is made adjustable and is included in a probe that terminates the test cable. The adjustment of capacitor C_1 is made by observing a standard square pulse and changing C_1 until the correct wave shape is seen on the *CRO* screen.

The compensated attenuator concept is extended to multitap attenuators in *CRO* amplifier attenuators and in ac electronic voltmeter input circuits. The *RC* time constant of each section of the attenuator between successive taps must be the same to give an attenuation independent of signal frequency or to preserve the wave form.

16-5
Clipping and clamping circuits

In our study of amplifiers we have found that the nonlinear regions of the device characteristics, such as saturation in a transistor, introduced amplitude distortion into the output. In dealing with pulses and other waves we shall make use of the nonlinear regions to alter the wave form in desirable ways. A multitude of circuits using diodes, vacuum tubes, and transistors are used for wave shaping, but we shall discuss circuits using semiconductor devices primarily. These devices have excellent characteristics for these applications, particularly when the device is called on to change suddenly from a nonconducting to a conducting state, that is, to act as a *switch*.

a. Clipping circuits

A diode circuit that will clip off the tops of voltage waves or pulses above a desired level is shown in Fig. 16-6. If we assume that the diode is ideal, then it acts as a switch which conducts in the forward direction with zero

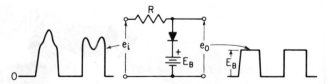

FIGURE 16-6   Diode clipping circuit.

voltage drop and cuts the current off completely as soon as the diode voltage reverses. As long as $e_i < E_B$, the diode is cut off (reverse-biased) and the output wave follows the input wave. However, as soon as e_i exceeds E_B, the diode will conduct, and the current will be limited by the resistor R. Then e_o equals E_B, since the diode forward drop is taken to be zero. As suggested in Fig. 16-6, the clipping circuit can make a series of nonuniform pulses take on a more uniform shape. If desired, the battery and diode can be replaced by a breakdown (Zener) diode that will function to hold the constant voltage E_B.

If the diode is reversed (Fig. 16-7), the portion of the wave during which the input voltage exceeds E_B is transmitted to the output and during the rest of the time the output is constant at E_B. If desired, the battery can be reversed and the constant portion will be below the zero voltage level. In practical circuits the voltage E_B is likely to be derived from a dc supply via a voltage divider, but with a large capacitor across the divider output to help maintain the voltage constant.

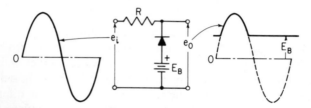

FIGURE 16-7   Modified clipping circuit.

Both the top and the bottom of the wave can be clipped by the circuit in Fig. 16-8. The voltage levels are set by the two breakdown diodes that are placed "back-to-back." As shown in the figure, this circuit can be used to change a sine wave into an approximation to a square wave.

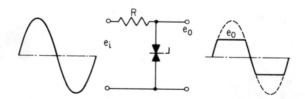

FIGURE 16-8   Clipping circuit using a bi-directional breakdown diode.

b. Square-wave generator

An overdriven transistor amplifier will convert a sine-wave input into an output that approximates a square wave (Fig. 16-9). The values of v_s and R_B must be such as to drive the transistor into saturation very soon after the base current goes positive. During most of the positive half-cycle of v_s the transistor is in saturation and the output is the small saturation voltage

V_{sat}. In the second half-cycle the base current goes negative and both of the transistor junctions are reverse-biased, so that the transistor is in the cutoff region. Only a small collector current (less than I_{CEO}) flows under this condition, and therefore the output voltage is nearly V_{CC}. The transistor operates in the switching mode, as already discussed in Sec. 8-7, and though the base drive is different, much of the earlier discussion applies to the present application.

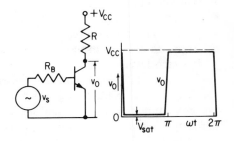

FIGURE 16-9 Overdriven common-emitter amplifier as square-wave generator.

c. Diode clamping circuit

When recurring waves or pulses that have a dc component are impressed on a series RC circuit, the dc component appears across the capacitor. Therefore, as shown in Fig. 16-10a, the voltage across the resistor, e_o or e_o', has a zero dc component. This figure is drawn under the assumption that the RC time constant is very long compared with the pulse length, so that the input pulse shape is retained at the output. However, the dc level of e_i is lost at the output.

If a diode, regarded to be an ideal diode, is added as in Fig. 16-10b, the

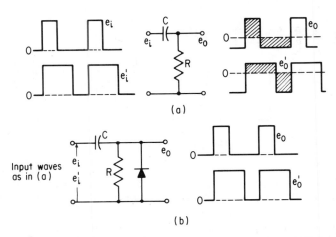

FIGURE 16-10   (a) Square waves passing through an RC circuit and (b) the same as in (a) with a clamping diode added.

output voltage cannot go negative. As a result the pulses are forced to start from the zero level, that is, they are *clamped* to the zero level. In effect, the dc component has been restored, and the circuit is also called a *dc restorer*.

If the diode is reversed, the *most positive* point of the pulse will be clamped to the zero level.

With a real diode the voltage e_o will not be exactly zero during the clamping interval, owing to the diode forward drop. For example, in Fig. 16-10b the waves e_o and e_o' will have small negative peaks just after these waves fall to zero, but this negative voltage will disappear rapidly.

16-6
Gate circuits

A *gate circuit* is one in which a signal is transmitted or rejected under the control of a selector voltage or voltages. When the circuit is designed so as to preserve the amplitude variations of the signal in the output, the circuit is called a *transmission gate*. In the so-called *logic gates*, which will be examined in Chapter 17, the output appears only when certain combinations of input conditions are satisfied and the output amplitude is not required to be directly proportional to a variable signal input.

The transistor gate circuit in Fig. 16-11 is intended to select a certain

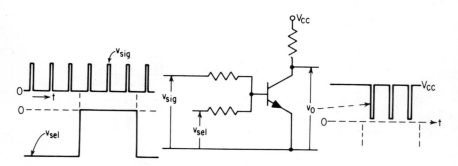

FIGURE 16-11   A transistor gate circuit.

group of pulses from the input pulse train labeled v_{sig}. The selector voltage v_{sel} acts on the transistor base as an additive signal. This voltage is large enough to cut off the transistor except during the time that the pulses are supposed to be transmitted. The output voltage will consist of a group of inverted pulses, which may or may not have a larger magnitude than the signal pulses. In order to qualify as a transmission gate the circuit would have to be designed and operated so that the output would preserve the relative magnitudes of a varying pulse height input signal.

An example of an application of a gate circuit is given in the following article.

16-7
Block diagram of a pulse counter

Several of the wave-forming and control techniques discussed thus far are illustrated in the pulse counter system in Fig. 16-12. We assume that ionizing radiations strike the transducer, such as a Geiger tube, and generate pulses amplified in a pulse amplifier. The resulting pulses are of varying shapes and heights. By passing the pulses through a clipper and differentiator, a more uniform sequence of pulses is formed. The counter is controlled by a gate signal applied to the gate circuit so that the pulses arriving within a definite time, say in one-tenth second, are counted. The systems for the measurement of frequency and of events per unit time described in Chapter 17 use the basic scheme of Fig. 16-12.

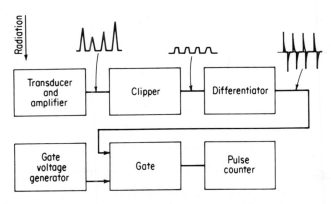

FIGURE 16-12   A pulse-per-unit-time counter system.

16-8
Bistable multivibrator (flip-flop)

The *bistable multivibrator* is one of an extremely interesting and useful group of circuits. Others in this group are the *astable* (free-running) multivibrator, the *monostable* (one-shot) multivibrator, and the *Schmitt trigger* circuit.

These circuits have the common feature of switching back and forth between two states which are either stable or temporarily stable. The bistable multivibrator *MV* has two stable states, but the circuit can be made to change from one state to the other by a suitable trigger pulse. The monostable *MV* has one stable state and one temporarily stable state, while in the astable *MV* both states are only temporarily stable. The two stable states in the Schmitt trigger circuit are controlled by the voltage level of the input signal.

The majority of multivibrator and trigger circuits use two transistors or tubes† in a positive feedback, or regenerative, connection. During the transition from one state to the other the collector or plate current of one device goes from full ON to nearly completely OFF, and the other from OFF to ON. Therefore the action is like that of two switches, and the circuits are also called *switching* circuits.

The superiority of the transistor as a switching device is reflected by its widespread use in electronic counters, digital computers, and the like. We shall discuss only the transistor multivibrator circuits but observe here that the corresponding tube versions of these circuits are available; in fact these were invented first.

The basic bistable *MV* may be regarded as a two-stage, direct-coupled amplifier with regenerative feedback, as shown in Fig. 16-13. If we assume that

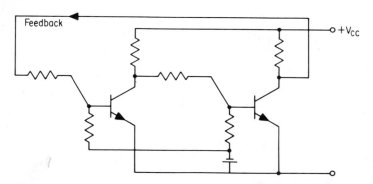

FIGURE 16-13   A bistable circuit viewed as a two-stage common-emitter amplifier with positive feedback.

a signal voltage is inserted at the base of the left-hand transistor, then each stage inverts the signal and the feedback will be regenerative. If we assume that both transistors are operating in the active region and that the open-loop gain is greater than unity, then the circuit is *unstable*. The slightest disturbance that causes one collector current to rise will cause the other collector current

†Single unijunction transistors or tunnel diodes are also used to perform similar functions.

to drop. With the usual circuit constants this transition proceeds at great speed until one transistor is full ON (in saturation) and the other is OFF (in cutoff). This describes one of the stable states of the circuit. The other state is the same except that the transistor that was ON is now OFF, and vice versa. In these states the open-loop gain has fallen below unity (close to zero), thereby insuring that these are stable states.

A closer look at one of these states will be helpful. The circuit is redrawn in Fig. 16-14a to show that it is symmetrical. Typical values of current and

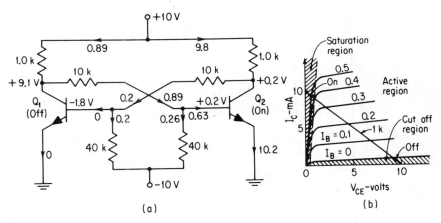

FIGURE 16-14   A stable condition in the bistable circuit. (a) Circuit showing an example of voltages and currents in milli-amperes. (b) Showing the ON and OFF conditions in the collector characteristics. Germanium transistors assumed.

voltage for the ON and the OFF transistor are entered on the diagram. Here Q_2 is assumed to be ON, being driven into saturation by the base current of 0.63 mA. Thus Q_2 acts almost like a closed switch and carries a high current with only 0.2 V from collector to emitter. Because of the voltage divider formed by the 10-k and 40-k resistors the base of Q_1 is placed at a negative voltage of 1.8 V. As a result the base-emitter junction of Q_1 is reverse-biased and Q_1 is operating in the cutoff region.

As an approximation the base and collector currents of Q_1 are taken to be zero. Actually, there will be a small reverse base leakage current and the collector leakage current will be lower than the value for $I_B = 0$, i.e., lower than I_{CEO}. At high transistor temperatures the cutoff current rises and must be considered in the analysis, but for the present we choose to ignore it.

When a bistable MV is used in a counter or computer, the circuit usually is called on to change its state in response to *trigger* signals consisting of short pulses or trains of pulses. Often a single source of trigger pulses must be able to change the state of the circuit regardless of its initial state. In other words, the trigger signal must be able to *initiate* the required *transition* from either state. A variety of triggering methods is in use, since trigger pulses can be applied to the bases, to the collectors, or to the emitters. We limit our discussion to triggering at the emitter and at the collector, though base triggering is also common.

Consider the bistable *MV* in Fig. 16-15. This circuit is derived from that

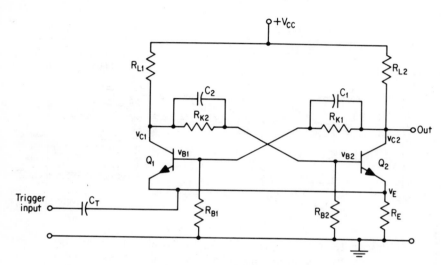

FIGURE 16-15   Bistable *MV* triggered at the emitters.

in Fig. 16-14a by replacing the negative voltage source by the self-bias resistance R_E, by adding the so-called *speed-up capacitors* C_1 and C_2, and by adding a connection through C_T to a source of trigger pulses. Let us first examine the over-all action of the circuit and use the following approximations. We ignore the currents in the OFF transistor and assume that the voltage V_{BE} and V_{CE} of the ON transistor are negligible. Further, we ignore the effect of the charge stored in the base of the ON transistor and the transistor junction capacitance effects.

First we study the wave forms

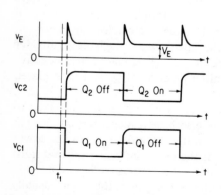

FIGURE 16-16   Wave forms in emitter-triggered bistable *MV*.

in Fig. 16-16, which show voltages v_E, v_{C2}, and v_{C1} referred to ground. In the initial condition, as at instant t_1, transistor Q_2 is ON and Q_1 is OFF. We can calculate the level of V_E, since V_{CE2} (the collector-emitter voltage of Q_2) is taken to be zero, as follows:

$$V_E = \frac{R_E V_{CC}}{R_E + R_{L2}} \qquad (16\text{-}14)$$

What is the effect of the first positive trigger pulse? The sudden rise of emitter voltage tends to cut off *both* Q_2 and Q_1, but Q_1 is already OFF, so only Q_2 will begin to change. Thus as Q_2 comes out of saturation and its collector current starts to fall, its collector voltage v_{C2} will start to rise. This rising value of v_{C2} is transmitted via the coupling circuit C_1, R_{K1}, and R_{B1} to the base of Q_1. As this action proceeds, the base of Q_1 rises out of cutoff so that now both transistors are in their active regions. Then the regenerative action discussed earlier takes hold and a very rapid transition to the other state follows.

The function of the speed-up capacitors C_1 and C_2 deserves added comment. The reader can verify that at instant t_1 the voltage across C_1 is only a fraction of V_E and across C_2 is nearly $V_{CC} - V_E$, so C_2 has a much higher voltage than C_1 does. Since the charge on C_1 cannot change instantaneously, a large part of the rapidly rising voltage v_{C2} is transmitted to the base of Q_1. If C_1 were absent, the change in voltage v_{C2} that reaches the base of Q_1 would be reduced by the voltage divider action of R_{K1} and R_{B1}. The fact that C_2 has a higher initial voltage than C_1 helps to insure that the transition is always completed in the desired direction. For example, a large, fast trigger pulse may cut Q_2 OFF completely, so that momentarily both transistors are cut off. But the difference in the charges in C_1 and C_2 will act to drive v_{B1} more positive than v_{B2} and thereby to turn Q_1 ON as desired.

The *first* pulse turns Q_2 OFF and Q_1 ON. Before the second pulse arrives, the circuit settles into a steady state, since the RC time constants are made small compared with the pulse period. Therefore the *second* pulse will cause the circuit to go through another transition which returns the circuit to the original state. We may say that the first pulse *flips* the circuit over and the second pulse *flops* it back. We notice that *two* trigger pulses are needed to give *one* output pulse at v_{C2}. This feature is applied in the binary counters described in the following chapter.

16-9
Collector triggering circuit
using steering diodes

A collector triggering circuit is shown in Fig. 16-17. The triggering network includes the coupling elements C_T and R_T and the *steering* diodes D_1 and D_2. Otherwise the circuit is the same as the basic bistable *MV*, except that the

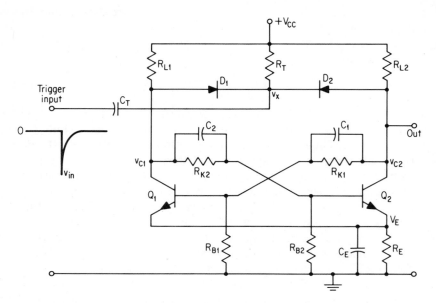

FIGURE 16-17   Bistable *MV* triggered at the collectors, using steering diodes.

emitter resistor is shunted by the relatively large capacitor C_E. Thus the emitter voltage V_E is held at a nearly constant value by the bias elements R_E and C_E.

This circuit is triggered by *negative* pulses, as shown by the wave v_x in Fig. 16-18a. Each trigger pulse causes a change of state, and the resulting collector voltages take on the square-wave forms shown. When a particular transistor, say Q_1, turns ON, its collector voltage drops nearly to V_E. When Q_1 turns OFF, its collector voltage rises nearly to V_{CC}. This value of voltage V_{COFF} can be calculated by considering the voltage divider action of R_{L1} and R_{K2} between V_{CC} and the base of Q_2. While Q_2 is ON, its base is clamped at a small value of voltage V_{BE} above V_E. Therefore we can write

$$V_{COFF} = V_{CC} - \left(\frac{V_{CC} - V_E - V_{BE}}{R_{L1} + R_{K2}} \right) R_{L1} \qquad (16\text{-}15)$$

where V_{COFF} is measured to ground. Usually $R_{L1} < R_{K2}$, so that V_{COFF} approaches V_{CC}.

The action of the trigger pulse and of the steering diodes can be explained with the help of Fig. 16-18b, which shows a portion of the bistable *MV* circuit. The set of voltages given in this diagram is for the instant just before the negative pulse arrives. These voltage are based on $V_{CC} = 8.5\ \text{V}$, and on the assumption that $V_{BE} = V_{CE} = 0$ for Q_2, which is in saturation. Suppose

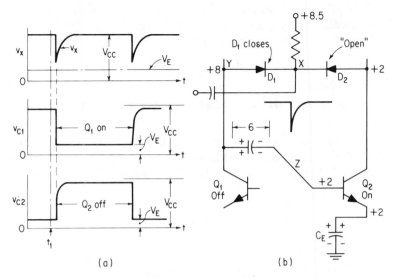

FIGURE 16-18   (a) Wave forms in the collector-triggered bistable *MV* in Fig. 16-17. (b) The portion of the circuit involved in the triggering, with the voltages at time t_1 just before the trigger pulse arrives.

that we assume that the trigger pulse has a peak value of negative 5.5 V. Then the pulse suddenly drives point X down from $+8.5$ to $+3.0$ V. As a result diode D_1 conducts, but diode D_2 remains back-biased, or nonconducting. The pulse is *steered* to the collector of Q_1, and point Y suddenly drops by 5 V. We note that coupling capacitor C_2 has an initial charge of 6 V. When point Y drops in potential, point Z must also drop by 5 V, owing to the capacitor coupling. Thus the base of Q_2 is driven to -3 V, thereby cutting Q_2 off and initiating the transition as described earlier.

The foregoing explanations of triggering and of the transitions have overlooked the presence of junction capacitance and the necessity of removing the charge in the base of the ON transistor. These effects act to slow the transition, as will be analyzed in Sec. 16-14.

The trigger pulse cannot be too small or too short, for the necessity of removing the base charge places a restriction on its minimum magnitude and duration. On the other hand, the trigger pulse cannot be too large, for if the pulse causes both diodes D_1 and D_2 to conduct, the triggering may be unreliable.

An example of the parameters in a high-speed collector-triggered *MV* circuit design† are the following: $V_{CC} = 6.0$ V, $R_{L1} = R_{L2} = 1.0$ k, $C_1 =$

†See Reference 16-1, p. 197.

$C_2 = 15\,\text{pF}$, $R_{K1} = R_{K2} = 9.1\,\text{k}$, $R_{B1} = R_{B2} = 2.0\,\text{k}$, $R_E = 430\,\Omega$, $C_E = 2000\,\text{pF}$, $C_T = 90\,\text{pF}$, and $R_T = 2.7\,\text{k}$. Using high-speed silicon diodes and transistors, the maximum trigger rate using triggers from 4 to 12 V is 5MHz.

16-10
Astable (free-running) multivibrator

In the bistable MV the biasing networks allow the circuit to remain in one state indefinitely unless disturbed by a trigger pulse. In the astable MV, such as shown in Fig. 16-19, the biasing is such that neither transistor can remain

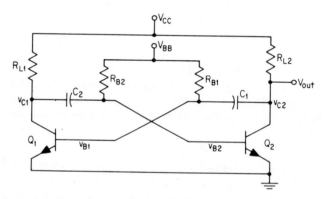

FIGURE 16-19   The basic astable MV circuit.

cut off indefinitely. From another viewpoint the difference in the two circuits may be ascribed to the type of collector to base coupling paths. In the bistable MV these paths are *direct-coupled*, whereas in the astable MV these paths provide only *ac coupling*. Thus a sudden change in voltage in the a-stable MV can be returned through the feedback path, but the ac coupling cannot maintain a constant feedback; therefore the astable MV cannot have a stable state.

The supply voltages V_{CC} and V_{BB} are both positive with *npn* transistors but would be negative with *pnp* transistors. Frequently V_{BB} is made equal to V_{CC} so that only one supply voltage is required.

If the supply voltages are applied gradually, there is a possibility that both transistors will go into saturation and stay there. In this condition the open-loop gain has fallen below unity and the circuit is said to be *locked*. If the voltages are switched on suddenly, the circuit will oscillate with the wave forms depicted in Fig. 16-20. The collector voltages alternately have the low

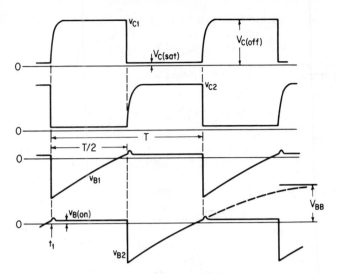

FIGURE 16-20   Wave forms in the astable MV circuit.

value in the ON state, $V_{C\text{sat}}$, and the high value, $V_{C\text{OFF}}$. If the collector leakage current is negligible, then $V_{C\text{OFF}} = V_{CC}$. Let us follow the base voltage v_{B1} during the half-period marked $T/2$. Just prior to the instant t_1 the voltage v_{C1} is low and v_{C2} is high, while v_{B1} and v_{B2} are both slightly positive. Under this condition, therefore, coupling capacitor C_2 has only a small charge, while C_1 is charged nearly to V_{CC}. At instant t_1 the base voltage v_{B2} rises high enough to turn Q_2 ON. The ensuing transition causes v_{C2} to fall sharply. The fall in v_{C2} acts through the coupling capacitor C_1 to drive v_{B1} far negative and thereby to cut off Q_1. Thereafter v_{B1} rises on an exponential curve toward V_{BB}, and when v_{B1} becomes slightly positive, the second transition occurs. At this instant v_{B2} is driven negative and the sequence repeats.

The period is evidently determined by the time required for the base voltage to rise to the next transition level. The half-period $T/2$ can be calculated on the basis of certain simplifications. We assume a symmetrical circuit, i.e., $R_{L1} = R_{L2}$, $R_{B1} = R_{B2}$, and $C_1 = C_2$. Also we let $V_{C\text{ sat}} = 0$, $v_{B\text{ ON}} = 0$, $V_{C\text{ OFF}} = V_{CC}$, and $V_{BB} = V_{CC}$. Under these assumptions v_{B1} drops to $-V_{CC}$ at instant t_1, which we take as a new origin for the time t. At this instant capacitor C_1 is charged to V_{CC} volts with the left-hand terminal negative. The right-hand terminal of C_1 follows v_{C2}, which is at zero volts after the transition. If we neglect the base current of Q_1, we see that C_1 will charge toward V_{BB} through resistor R_{B1}. Since the voltage of capacitor C_1 equals the base voltage v_{B1}, we can write

$$v_{B1} = -V_{CC} + (V_{BB} + V_{CC})\left[1 - \exp\left(\frac{-t}{\tau}\right)\right] \qquad (16\text{-}16)$$

where $\tau = R_{B1}C_1$. We have assumed that $V_{BB} = V_{CC}$, therefore

$$v_{B1} = -V_{CC} + 2V_{CC}\left[1 - \exp\left(\frac{-t}{\tau}\right)\right] \qquad (16\text{-}17)$$

The second transition, at $t = T/2$, occurs when $v_{B1} \cong 0$, so we have a condition on $T/2$

$$0 = -V_{CC} + 2V_{CC}\left[1 - \exp\left(\frac{-T}{2\tau}\right)\right] \qquad (16\text{-}18)$$

from which we obtain

$$\frac{T}{2} = \tau \ln 2 = 0.69 R_{B1}C_1 \qquad (16\text{-}19)$$

The free-running frequency is approximately

$$f = \frac{1}{T} = \frac{0.72}{R_{B1}C_1} \qquad (16\text{-}20)$$

For example, if $R_{B1} = 22$ k and $C_1 = 680$ pF, then $f = 48$ kHz.

Typical applications of the astable MV are in pulse generators, in frequency dividers, and for the generation of harmonics. The term *multivibrator* originated from the concept of the large number of harmonics in the Fourier expansion of the square-wave output. Frequency division is accomplished by feeding a timing, or synchronizing, wave into the circuit in such a manner that it triggers the transition earlier than it would normally occur. Thus the period is determined by the synchronizing sine wave or pulse train.

16-11
Nonlocking astable MV; synchronizing

A circuit that avoids the "locking" difficulty mentioned earlier is shown in Fig. 16-21a. This circuit also shows a provision for synchronizing the MV to a train of negative pulses.

The circuit is different from the standard astable MV in that the timing, or bias, resistors R_{B1} and R_{B2} are returned to the collectors instead of to a positive dc source. In the standard circuit the ON transistor is kept in saturation by the current supplied via the bias resistor R_B, except that during the initial recovery of the *other* transistor a capacitance current is added through the cross-coupling capacitor. In the nonlocking circuit the current furnished via R_B is negligible during the saturated half-period, therefore the charging current of the cross-coupling capacitor must supply the base current for saturation. As a result, the collector voltage recovery rate must be slow in order to maintain saturation, and the voltage wave at the collector is far from a square wave.

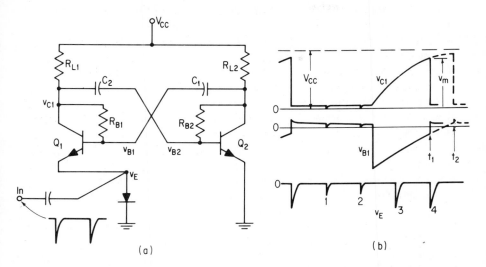

FIGURE 16-21   (a) Astable MV with synchronizing connection.
(b) Wave forms showing the effect of the synchronizing pulses.

Thus v_{C1} rises rather slowly (Fig. 16-21b) toward V_{CC}, and the transition occurs at a voltage v_m, which may be about 0.8 to 0.9 V_{CC}. In the absence of a synchronizing wave the timing of the transition is determined by the relaxation of v_{B1}, so that the period would end at instant t_2. This would be the free-running condition.

We digress to estimate the circuit requirement to keep Q_2 in saturation while v_{C1} is rising. Generally $R_{L1} < R_{B1}$, so that we may consider that the charging current of C_2 all comes via R_{L1} and that this current equals i_{b2}, the base current of Q_2. Therefore

$$i_{b2} \cong \frac{V_{CC} - v_{C1}}{R_{L1}} \tag{16-21}$$

To insure saturation, we prescribe that the *minimum* base current should be

$$i_{b2} = \frac{V_{CC}}{h_{FE}R_{L2}} \tag{16-22}$$

where h_{FE} is the minimum value expected at the edge of saturation. Combining (16-21) and (16-22) and assuming $R_{L1} = R_{L2}$, we calculate the maximum allowable v_{C1}, designated as v_m, and obtain

$$v_m = V_{CC}\left(1 - \frac{1}{h_{FE}}\right) \tag{16-23}$$

Thus if the minimum h_{FE} expected is 10, then v_m should not exceed 0.9 V_{CC}.
Now suppose that a train of negative pulses is applied to one emitter, such

that four times the pulse period is a little less that the free-running period of the *MV*, as shown in Fig. 16-21b. With pulses of a suitable height the *MV* will fall into step with, or *synchronize* with, the pulse train in such a way that every fourth pulse will start a transition in Q_1, thereby locking the *MV* to the pulse train. The magnitude of the trigger pulses reaching the emitter of Q_1 will depend on the pulse source impedance and on whether Q_1 is in conduction or not, so the pulse heights shown in Fig. 16-21b are only suggestive of typical test results. While Q_1 is in saturation the pulses tend to be smaller, as shown by pulses 1 and 2. At the instant that pulse 3 occurs the voltage v_{B1} is still too low to allow a transition. Pulse 4 is large enough to pull the emitter of Q_1 down below v_{B1}, thereby driving Q_1 into conduction and initiating the transition. This example provides a frequency division of four.

Sometimes a one-to-one correspondence is desired between the frequencies, and this can readily be accomplished by making the pulse repetition rate a little higher than the free-running *MV* frequency. Actually, the circuit will synchronize over a considerable frequency range in this case, but in the frequency division application the per-unit range of satisfactory synchonizing becomes smaller as the frequency division ratio increases.

When triggering pulses are applied only to one side of the *MV*, half of the wave maintains a constant duration, while the other varies in width to provide the synchronization. If desired, timing pulses may be fed to both sides, for example, by using the collector triggering scheme in Fig. 16-17. Frequency division up to a ratio of 10 to 1 is practical with this connection.

16-12
Monostable (one-shot) multivibrator

The monostable *MV* circuit may be regarded as a combination of half of a bistable *MV* with half of an astable *MV* (Fig. 16-22). One of the collector-to base paths is direct-coupled, and the other is ac coupled through C_2. The circuit will therefore have one preferred or normal stable state. When the circuit is triggered out of this state, it goes into the opposite, which is only temporarily stable. The circuit relaxes, as in the astable *MV*, and after a time delay it switches back to the stable state, where it will stay until another trigger pulse arrives. The output is a square pulse of prescribed duration. One application of the monostable *MV* is to convert an input consisting of a series of pulses of various shapes into a series of pulses of standardized width and amplitude. Another application is in timing circuits in which a fairly long pulse of moderate precision is required.

The monostable *MV* circuit in Fig. 16-22 includes a connection for triggering at the base of transistor Q_1. Transistor Q_2 is normally ON, owing to the base current supplied via R_{B2}, while Q_1 is held OFF by the connection

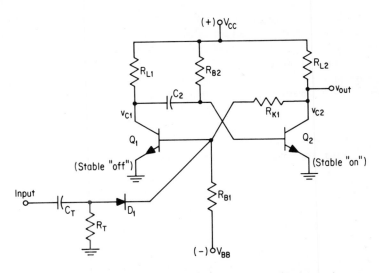

FIGURE 16-22   Monostable MV circuit showing base triggering.

through R_{B1} to the *negative* voltage V_{BB}. When a positive trigger pulse is applied to the base of Q_1, the circuit voltages vary as shown in Fig. 16-23. The first transition turns Q_1 ON and Q_2 OFF. The base of Q_2 is driven far negative, and the relaxation of the $C_2 R_{B2}$ circuit, as in the astable MV, provides the timing for the temporarily stable state. When v_{B2} rises to the point at which Q_2 conducts, the second transition, which returns the circuit to its original state, occurs.

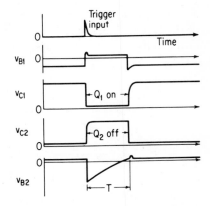

FIGURE 16-23   Wave forms in monostable MV circuit in Fig. 16-22.

The duration T of the output pulse corresponds to the half-period of the symmetrical astable MV, so we can use Eq. (16-19) to obtain

$$T \cong \tau \ln 2 = 0.69 R_{B2} C_2 \qquad (16\text{-}24)$$

The output may be taken at either collector, and v_{C1} will give a negative pulse or v_{C2} a positive pulse.

An example of the parameters in a monostable MV circuit† are the following: $R_{L1} = R_{L2} = 1.0$ k, $R_{B2} = 22$ k, $C_2 = 680$ pF, $R_{K1} = 10$ k,

†See Reference 16-9, p. 381.

$R_{B1} = 47$ k, $R_T = 1.0$ k, $C_T = 220$ pF, $V_{CC} = +10$ V and $V_{BB} = -10$ V. With medium-speed germanium alloy switching transistors having a minimum h_{FE} of 40, the pulse duration is about 10 μsec.

Additional applications of the monostable *MV* are to produce square pulses to be used as gating signals or to develop a trigger pulse, delayed a controllable time after an initial trigger.

16-13
The Schmitt trigger circuit

The Schmitt trigger circuit is a bistable circuit that responds to a dc voltage level or to the level of a varying voltage. The corresponding vacuum-tube circuit was originated by O.H. Schmitt in 1938. Applications of the Schmitt trigger include the conversion of a sine-wave input to a square-wave output and the discrimination between different signal levels or pulse amplitudes.

The Schmitt trigger circuit in Fig. 16-24a may be regarded as a two-stage amplifier with direct coupling between collector $C1$ and base $B2$ via resistor R_1 plus the emitter coupling due to resistor R_E common to the emitters. This emitter coupling will provide the feedback path. We inquire about the sign of the feedback assuming for the present that both transistors are operating in the active region. Also assume that $R_{L1} = R_{L2}$ and that R_E is about one-

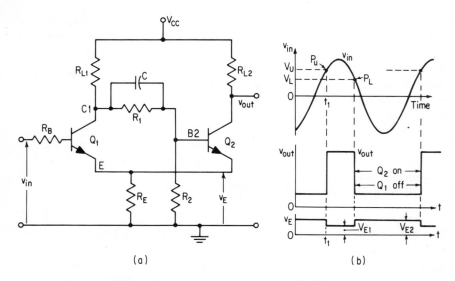

(a)   (b)

FIGURE 16-24   (a) Schmitt trigger circuit. (b) Wave forms for a sine wave input.

fifth of R_{L1}. To test for the sign of the feedback we imagine that a positive input signal Δv_{in} is impressed and trace the effects through the circuit. We expect that the first stage will invert the signal and amplify it. Thus the base $B2$ of Q_2 receives an amplified negative voltage signal, which acts to decrease the emitter current of Q_2. This current goes downward through R_E, and therefore the *change* in current produces a voltage *change* across R_E that is positive downward. This change is in the same sense around the emitter-to-base input loop of Q_1 as the original signal Δv_{in}, and therefore the circuit provides *positive* feedback .With the usual circuit parameters the initial changes are augmented, and the process of change will continue until the open-loop gain falls below unity. Thus we expect the same type of sudden transitions from one state to the other (and back again) as in the multivibrator circuits.

These transitions are illustrated by the wave forms in Fig. 16-24b, which show the circuit response to a sine-wave input. With a low, i.e., negative, input voltage, as at $t = 0$, the base-emitter diode of Q_1 is cut off, and therefore Q_1 is OFF and point $C1$ is nearly at the potential V_{CC}, because R_{L1} is small compared with R_1. The resistors R_1 and R_2 are chosen so that under this condition point $B2$ is positive to point E; thus Q_2 is ON. Now let us assume that R_{L2} is somewhat smaller than R_{L1}. If we neglect the collector-to-emitter saturation voltage of Q_2, we can calculate the value of V_{E2}, the value with Q_2 ON, to be

$$V_{E2} = \frac{R_E}{R_E + R_{L2}} V_{CC} \qquad (16\text{-}25)$$

since the current goes from V_{CC} to ground via R_{L2}, Q_2, and R_E.

Now when the instantaneous value of v_{in} rises above V_{E2} (by a small amount V_{BE1}, which we shall ignore) at point P_U in the wave form, the base current rises in Q_1. That is, Q_1 comes out of cutoff and moves into the active region. The sudden transition at t_1 ensues and v_{out} rises sharply. Point P_U is called the *upper trip* point and V_U is the corresponding input voltage level.

As v_{in} falls after the crest of the wave, there is a reverse transition at point P_L, at a lower input voltage V_L, called the *lower trip* point. We recall that $R_{L1} > R_{L2}$, and since $V_{E1} = R_E V_{CC}/(R_E + R_{L1})$, we see that $V_{E1} < V_{E2}$. For this reason† a lower value of v_{in} is needed to turn Q_1 off and start the transition on the descending portion of the v_{in} wave form. This produces a *hysteresis* effect. Typically, V_L may be 20 to 40 per cent below V_U.

The hysteresis effect is beneficial in a situation in which v_{in} contains a noise component. In this event, if V_L were equal to V_U, the circuit would trigger back and forth several times at the beginning of the main pulse in response to the noise. With $V_L < V_U$, such pulsations will only occur if the noise component exceeds $V_U - V_L$ in magnitude.

†In this account we have not considered the effects of the changes in the base currents needed to shift the circuit into the regenerative condition. These produce a hysteresis effect in addition to that due to differences in the collector resistances.

The capacitor C in Fig. 16-24a is a speed-up capacitor that facilitates the transitions. Resistor R_B is used to limit the base current of Q_1 for large positive excursions of v_{in}.

An example† of a circuit design is the following: $V_{CC} = 10$ V, $R_{L1} = 1.3$ k, $R_{L2} = 1.0$ k, $R_E = 240$ Ω, $R_2 = 8.2$ k, $R_1 = 6.8$ k, $C = 270$ pF, and $R_B = 1.3$ k. Using germanium alloy transistors having a minimum h_{FE} of 40, the trip levels are $V_U = 2.2$ V, and $V_L = 1.8$ V. The frequency limit for this circuit is about 100 kHz.

16-14
Time delays in a transistor switch

We have seen that in the multivibrator circuits the transistors are switched from OFF to ON and vice versa. When high switching rates are required, the time delays inherent in the transistor become important. The following is a qualitative account of these delays and their origin.

Often the transient response of a transistor is characterized by the results of a pulse test in a specified ciruict, such as that in Fig. 16-25. This common-emitter switch, or inverter, is normally held in the OFF state by the *negative* voltage V_{BB}. The input pulse is generally supplied from a source of low impedance through an input network similar to the one shown. We assume that the input pulse is an ideal square wave as shown by v_{in} in Fig. 16-26. The input pulse causes the base current i_b to rise from the small reverse leakage value to a nearly constant value I_{b1}, which is determined mainly by the resistance of the input network. However, the collector current does not rise

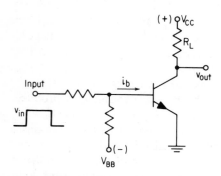

FIGURE 16-25   An inverter circuit for a test of transistor switching characteristic.

†See Reference 16-9, p. 382.

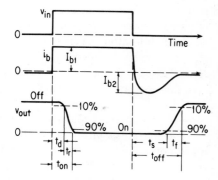

FIGURE 16-26   Pulse test of turn-on time, t_{on}, and turn-off time, t_{off}, in the inverter circuit.

instantly, as evidenced by the delay in the decay of v_{out}. The *turn*-ON *delay* time t_d is measured to the time at which v_{out} starts to fall. The *rise* time t_r refers to the time needed for the collector *current* to rise (or v_{out} to fall). The sum of t_d and t_r is the turn-on time t_{ON}. The points for 10 per cent and 90 per cent of the change of v_{out} are used to define the time delays.

After v_{in} drops back to zero at the end of the input pulse, there is a delay called the *storage* time t_s before v_{out} starts to rise appreciably. During this time the base current reverses, reaches the reverse maximum I_{b2}, and decays toward its leakage value. The time t_f, called the *fall* time, is needed for the collector *current* to fall (or v_{out} to rise). The *turn*-OFF time t_{OFF} is the sum of the storage time and the fall time. A medium-speed alloy transistor may have $t_{ON} = 0.25 \ \mu s$ and $t_{OFF} = 0.3 \ \mu s$, whereas a high-speed transistor may have time delays one or two orders of magnitude smaller.

We wish to discuss the whole sequence of the pulse test from the viewpoint of the concepts of internal transistor behavior developed in Secs. 3-11, 5-4, 5-5, and 7-12. At each junction there is a charge-depletion region which varies in width as the junction voltage varies. Thus the regions of space charge at the junctions vary in width and in magnitude of charge with the voltage and thereby create an effective capacitance at each junction. The turn-ON delay t_d, defined in Fig. 16-26, is mostly caused by these junction capacitances. Just before voltage v_{in} rises, the base-emitter junction is reverse-biased by V_{BB}, say, to a value V_B of a few volts. The collector-base junction is reverse-biased by $V_{CC} + V_B$, say, to about 10 V. Therefore C_e, the emitter junction capacitance, is charged approximately to V_B, and C_c, the collector capacitance, to $V_{CC} + V_B$. Before the transistor can enter the active region, the base-emitter junction must change from a reverse to a forward bias; therefore no collector current flows until V_{BE} rises through zero and reaches a small positive value. In this process the charges stored in C_e and C_c both change, and the total change is

$$\Delta Q = V_B(C_e + C_c) \tag{16-26}$$

Since C_e and C_c are both voltage-dependent, average values for the appropriate voltage ranges should be used in Eq. (16-26). The charge ΔQ must be supplied via the base, by the product of the base current I_{b1} times the time t_d; thus,

$$I_{b1}t_d \cong \Delta Q \tag{16-27}$$

This equation gives a basis for estimating the delay t_d

Consider next the action during the interval t_r. Here the transistor is operating in its *active* region, but we must examine the transient conditions in the base. Figure 16-27 and 16-28a will aid the discussion. The rise of the curve of total base minority charge Q_t shown in Fig. 16-27, coincides with the rise of collector current and with the fall of v_{out}. We consider an *npn* transistor with both junctions initially reverse-biased. Then the electron charge density

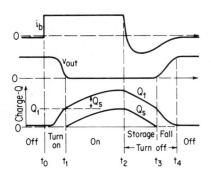

FIGURE 16-27 Variation of the total base minority charge, Q_t, and the excess charge, Q_s, in the pulse test of a transistor.

in the base is very low, as shown by the distribution curve 1 in Fig. 16-28a. As the base-emitter diode comes out of cutoff, the emitter begins to inject electrons into the base in increasing numbers, so that soon curve 2 results. Now we have nearly normal transistor action, with the electrons diffusing across the base and most of them reaching the collector junction to form the main component of collector current, except that the density distribution is rapidly changing. (We ignore the variation of effective base width with voltage in this discussion.) We assume that curve 3 in Fig. 16-28a corresponds to the edge of saturation. This condition is reached at instant t_1 in Fig. 16-27, at the end of the *turn*-ON interval.

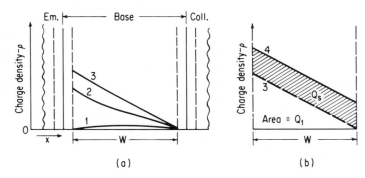

FIGURE 16-28 Distribution of the minority charge density, ρ, in the base; (a) up to saturation and (b) in saturation. Q_s is the excess stored charge.

We digress to interpret the meaning of the area under curve 1, 2, or 3 in Fig. 16-28a. If we think of an elementary transistor of constant cross section, we can see that the total minority charge stored in the base at any instant is proportional to the area under the appropriate charge density distribution curve.

At instant t_1 the stored charge has reached the value Q_1, which is represented by the area under curve 3. This gives the charge needed just to reach *saturation*. However, the base current continues to deliver charge after instant t_1 at a greater rate than demanded by recombination in the base. As a result the total stored charge rises further (see curve Q_t in Fig. 16-27). The value $Q_t - Q_1$ is called the *excess* stored charge and is labeled Q_s. At the end of the input pulse, at time t_2, the conditions in the base are as shown in Fig. 16-28b. Now the transistor is far into saturation and both junctions are forward-biased. As a result the electron density at the collector junction has increased, since electrons are also being injected from collector to base, though in smaller numbers than are being collected by the collector. The electron charge density takes the form of curve 4 in Fig. 16-28b. Thus the excess stored charge is represented by the area between curves 3 and 4, labeled Q_s.

At instant t_2 the input pulse terminates and the base current starts to reverse. The reverse base current starts to remove the stored minority charge; the excess charge being removed first. When Q_s reaches zero, at instant t_3, the operating point is again at the edge of saturation and the collector current starts to fall. Thus the storage delay time $t_3 - t_2$ depends on how great an excess charge was stored and on the magnitude of the reverse base current.

The behavior during the fall time is similar to that during the rise time, except for the detailed shapes of the curves of charge distribution while the charge is draining away. At instant t_4 both junctions are again reverse-biased and the transistor switch is again OFF.

Since in alloy transistors the diffusion process in the base is mainly responsible for the time delays t_r and t_f *and* for the loss of current gain at high frequencies, we might expect a relation between these phenomena. An approximate relation† has been developed on this basis for the quasi-exponential rise of the collector current during the rise time, as follows:

$$i_C \cong h_{FE} I_{b1} \left[1 - \exp\left(\frac{-\omega_T t}{h_{FE}}\right) \right] \qquad (16\text{-}28)$$

Here I_{b1} is the base current step and ω_T is the gain-bandwidth product defined in Sec. 7-13. The time constant of the exponential rise is h_{FE}/ω_T, which by use of Eq. (7-54) may be written $1/\omega_{\alpha e}$.

A limitation on Eq. (16-28) is that it applies only up to the saturation current $I_{CS} = V_{CC}/R_L$, beyond which $h_{FE} I_{b1}$ exceeds I_{CS}. In this event i_C rises on the exponential curve up to the level I_{CS} and thereafter remains constant. Thus the collector current can reach saturation in a time shorter than the time constant if $h_{FE} I_{b1} > I_{CS}$. We see that by providing excess base current, or *overdriving* the base, the rise time can be shortened.

When $h_{FE} I_{b1} > I_{CS}$, we can approximate the exponential by a straight line that has the slope of the right side of (16-28) taken at $t = 0$, namely, by

$$i_C \cong \omega_T I_{b1} t \qquad (16\text{-}29)$$

Using this linear approximation we can calculate the rise time t_r as the time for i_C to rise by the amount $0.8 I_{CS}$, with the result

$$t_r \cong \frac{0.8 I_{CS}}{I_{b1} \omega_T} \qquad (16\text{-}30)$$

which clearly shows that a higher drive current I_{b1} will shorten the rise time.

†See Reference 16-3, pp. 15-10.

Lindmayer and Wrigley† have presented an approximate formula for rise time which separates the effects of the minority charge stored in the base and the junction capacitances

$$t_r = 0.8 \frac{I_{CS}\tau_B + C_e V_E + V_{CC}C_c}{I_{b1} - \dfrac{I_{CS}}{h_{FE}}} \tag{16-31}$$

in which $\tau_B =$ the transit time, $I_{CS}\tau_B$ is the charge stored in the base, C_e and C_c are the junction capacitances, and V_E is the forward voltage across the emitter junction. Note that V_E equals $(kT/q)\ln(I_{CS}/I_{EO})$, where I_{EO} is the reverse leakage current across the emitter-base junction with the collector open-circuited. These authors also present a formula for the turn-ON time, as follows:

$$t_{\text{ON}} \cong \frac{V_B(C_e + C_c)}{I_{b1}} + \frac{9}{8}t_r \tag{16-32}$$

where t_r is given in (16-31). Formulas (16-31) and (16-32) confirm that the rise time and turn-ON time can be decreased by increasing I_{b1} above I_{CS}/h_{FE}. Further, a reduction in the transit time τ_B, as produced by the built-in field in the base of the drift-field transistor, also acts to speed up the transient response.

However, an excess value of base current has a serious drawback because it produces a greater excess stored charge and consequently a longer storage time. The use of a speed-up capacitor shunted by a fairly high resistor, as in the multivibrator circuits, will give a temporary overdrive without producing excessive charge storage. The resistor would be chosen to maintain saturation in the steady state. It is obvious that the speed-up capacitor should not be larger than needed to fulfil its purpose.

In conclusion we mention the technique of switching without driving the transistor into saturation. Circuits that use diodes to restrict the excursion of collector voltage to avoid saturation have been devised. These eliminate the storage delay and therefore exhibit improved switching times, but at the expense of added complication and cost. The modern high-speed transistor is so fast that saturated circuits may be used for most applications.

16-15
Further discussion and analysis
of multivibrator and trigger circuits

The foregoing treatment of multivibrator and trigger circuits was intended to emphasize the main phenomena, therefore a number of details that become

†J. Lindmayer and C. W. Wrigley, *Fundamentals of Semiconductor Devices*, D. Van Nostrand Company, Inc., Princeton, N.J., 1965, p. 287.

important in circuit design or in high-speed circuits have been omitted. We shall now examine some of these items, but for detailed circuit design procedures the reader should consult suitable references, such as References 16-1, 4, 5, 6, or 7.

a. Design of the bistable MV

We assume a symmetrical circuit (Fig. 16-15) and let $R_L = R_{L1} = R_{L2}$, $C = C_1 = C_2$, $R_K = R_{K1} = R_{K2}$ and $R_B = R_{B1} = R_{B2}$. The voltage levels V_E and V_{CC} are chosen first. Resistor R_L should be small for high switching speed, but it must be chosen so that the transistor dissipation capability is not exceeded. If an external load network is added, this will modify the choice of R_L. A tentative value of R_K is chosen, and then R_B is chosen to satisfy two requirements, namely, (1) R_B must be high enough to be sure that the ON transistor receives adequate base current to insure saturation, and (2) R_B must be small enough to insure that the OFF transistor is in the cutoff region. Requirement 1 must be met for the *minimum* expected h_{FE}. In careful calculations the leakage current I_{CBO}, and often I_{EBO}, and the values of $V_{BE\,ON}$ and of $V_{CE\,sat}$ must be considered, including temperature effects.

The choice of the coupling capacitors C_1 and C_2 depends on the requirements of their functions during the turn-ON of a particular transistor and during the turn-OFF. Consider first the turn-ON of Q_1 via coupling capacitor C_1. The sudden rise of v_{C2} (see Fig. 16-16) acts through C_1 to drive Q_1 into saturation. As was explained in the foregoing article, a definite quantity of charge must enter the base via the base terminal to drive Q_1 from cutoff to saturation. This charge passes through C_1 and as a result the voltage across C_1 changes by an amount equal to the charge divided by C_1. This voltage change tends to reduce the forward voltage on the base of Q_1. Thus a large value of C_1 tends to minimize the voltage change and to increase the base current drive; therefore to shorten the turn-ON time. However, an excessive value will cause an excess stored charge in the base, which may or may not dissipate before the end of the ON period.

Next consider the turn-OFF transient, during which the stored minority charge and the charge in the junction capacitances must be neutralized by the transient base current. The sudden fall of v_{C2} acting through C_1 causes a negative base current in Q_1 to turn Q_1 off. Reasoning similar to that in the previous paragraph shows that an increase in C_1 will, up to a point, reduce the turn-OFF time. C_1 should be big enough to give a large enough negative base current pulse to neutralize the stored minority charge and the junction capacitance charges.

If C_1 is too large, the time constant of the recovery transient of the collector voltage will be lengthened. Consider the wave of v_{C2} in Fig. 16-16 in the neighborhood of instant t_1. At instant t_1 the voltage of capacitor C_1 is the small value $(V_E + V_{CE\,\text{sat}})\, R_{K1}/(R_{K1} + R_{B1})$. After the transition the voltage of C_1 tends toward the large voltage $(V_{CC} - V_E)R_{K1}/(R_{K1} + R_{L2})$, since the left-hand terminal of C_1 is clamped at the base of the ON transistor Q_1. Here the small voltage V_{BE} of Q_1 and the leakage current of Q_2 are neglected. Because $R_{K1} > R_{L2}$, the rise of the voltage of C_1 and therefore of v_{C2} is mainly determined by the time constant $R_{L2}C_1$. Thus low values of load resistance and of speed-up capacitance favor a sharp rise of v_{C2} and a square-wave output.

b. Bistable MV with collector triggering

In this circuit (Fig. 16-17) the self-bias circuit should have a time constant long compared with the pulse period.

The trigger network capacitor C_T should be large enough to pass the pulses with little attenuation. The resistor R_T is needed to discharge C_T after each pulse. If R_T were absent, C_T would charge up and render the circuit inoperative. The time constant $R_T C_T$ should be small compared with the pulse period. An alternative circuit uses a diode to discharge C_T. In this circuit the diode replaces R_T, and its forward direction is toward V_{CC}. Various triggering circuits and their design are discussed by Hurley†.

c. Astable MV circuit

We shall assume that we have a symmetrical circuit (Fig. 16-19) and that $V_{BB} = V_{CC}$. Again let R_L, R_B, and C designate the circuit constants. The load resistor and transistor are chosen as for the bistable MV. The bias resistors are chosen to insure saturation as follows. We neglect the voltages V_{BE} and V_{CE} of the ON transistor, and so obtain the approximate value for R_B

$$R_B \leq h_{FE}R_L \tag{16-33}$$

where h_{FE} should be the minimum expected value of this parameter.

The base voltage wave forms in Fig. 16-20 show that the base is driven to a negative voltage nearly equal to V_{CC}, so the voltage stress on the base-emitter junction is nearly V_{CC} and on the base-collector junction is nearly $2V_{CC}$. Therefore the transistor should have a breakdown voltage BV_{EBO} greater than V_{CC} and a voltage BV_{CBO} of $2V_{CC}$ or higher. A diode can be inserted into the emitter lead to absorb most of the base-emitter reverse voltage and thereby reduce the requirement on BV_{EBO}.

A variable output frequency can be obtained by varying V_{BB} in Fig. 16-19. Alternatively, the values of V_{BB} and V_{CC} can be equal and the values of the capacitors or of the resistors R_B can be varied. An upper frequency limit is reached when the capacitors are too small to produce the transitions reliably

†R. B. Hurley, *Transistor Logic Circuits*, John Wiley & Sons, Inc., New York, 1961, pp. 299 ff.

or when delays due to stored base charge and junction capacitances become important.

d. *Monostable MV*

The transistors, load resistors, and bias circuit R_{K1}, R_{B1}, and V_{BB} (Fig. 16-22) are chosen as for the bistable *MV*. Bias resistor R_{B2} is chosen as outlined for the astable *MV*. Capacitor C_2 can be selected to give the desired output pulse duration by means of Eq. (16-24).

16-16
The blocking oscillator

The blocking oscillator is really a pulse generator which can be operated in the astable or monostable modes but not in the bistable mode. The elementary circuit in Fig. 16-29 shows that in this common-emitter version of the circuit the collector and base are tightly coupled through the two coils of a pulse transformer, which may have a ferrite or ferromagnetic core. The windings n_1 and n_2 are polarized so as to give regenerative feedback from collector to base. For example, if the transistor is assumed to be in the active region with collector current present, then the voltage across n_1 will induce a voltage in n_2 that tends to *increase* the base current. With the usual turn ratio of about 4 to 1, the forward voltage on the base is high enough to saturate the transistor during the pulse interval. The pulse is terminated by any circuit change that brings the transistor out of saturation and starts the regenerative transition in the opposite direction. The transistor

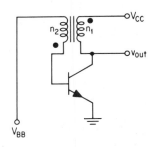

FIGURE 16-29 Elementary blocking oscillator circuit.

acts essentially as a switch, the pulse *timing* occurring during the ON state. The pulse current and power can be relatively high because the current is limited mainly by the small losses in the saturated transistor.

The pulse transformer must have special characteristics. It should have a low leakage inductance and a broad-band frequency characteristic. These characteristics, and also its magnetizing current requirement and tendency to saturate, have an effect on the circuit performance. Therefore blocking oscillator circuits are often designed for a particular transformer.

A blocking oscillator can be biased beyond cutoff and then triggered to give a single pulse. Alternatively, the circuit can be biased to operate in the astable mode so that the output consists of recurring pulses.

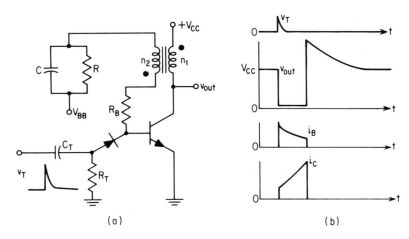

FIGURE 16-30   Monostable blocking oscillator.

A triggered monostable blocking oscillator is shown in Fig. 16-30a. The base circuit includes a series resistor R_B, the timing circuit RC, the bias voltage V_{BB}, and the triggering network comprising C_T, R_T, and the diode. We assume that V_{BB} cuts off the transistor in the absence of a trigger pulse. As the waves in Fig. 16-30b show, a positive trigger initiates the first transition. The trigger drives the base sufficiently positive to start the collector current, so that the regenerative action takes hold and a rapid transition into saturation ensues. Then winding n_1 sustains nearly the full source voltage V_{CC}, and therefore v_{out} drops nearly to zero. The voltage generated in coil n_2 by transformer action supplies a base current i_B that is more than adequate (at first) to saturate the transistor.

There are two main variations taking place during the pulse, and we consider these one at a time. First consider the variation of the collector current. At the first instant the collector current jumps up to a value $i_C(0)$ determined by the initial base current $i_B(0)$. We think of the transformer as ideal and assert that $i_B(0)n_2 = i_C(0)n_1$ according to the law of equal ampere-turns. But $i_B(0)$ is fixed by the voltages in the base circuit and by R_B (if we ignore the trigger); therefore $i_C(0)$ is also determined. Throughout the pulse the transformer winding n_1 must sustain a constant voltage, which we take to equal V_{CC}. To sustain this voltage, the magnetic flux in the core must be rising at a constant rate as demanded by the relation $V_{CC} = n_1 d\phi/dt$, where ϕ is the flux. Therefore an *increasing* value of i_C is needed to magnetize the core as the flux increases. If the core reaches magnetic saturation, the current i_C must increase at an accelerating rate to maintain a constant rate of rise of flux.

The other variation occurs in i_B. The voltage developed in coil n_2 stays constant during the pulse, but capacitor C begins to charge, and therefore the voltage across R_B and the current i_B begin to decrease.

These changes proceed until the point at which the rising instantaneous value of i_C is equal to the falling value of $h_{FE}i_B$. At this point the transistor comes out of saturation; the reverse transition takes place and the transistor returns to the cutoff state. However, the transformer core is left with a high magnetic flux that must decay after i_C goes to zero. This decay may produce a voltage peak on the wave of v_{out} with a subsequent relaxation as shown in Fig. 16-30b. Alternatively, the decaying transient may consist of a self-oscillation of the winding with its own capacitance, a phenomenon known as *ringing*. The excess voltage (which may break down the transistor) can be reduced by placing a diode across coil n_1, but the flux decays more slowly and the circuit recovery time is increased.

Blocking oscillators are used when a high-energy, low-impedance pulse generator of moderate precision is required. The output pulse is often taken from an added winding on the transformer, and the number of turns can be chosen to adapt to a range of load impedances. The circuit has a high energy efficiency. In multivibrators there is a power drain at all times, while in the blocking oscillator there is little power consumption between pulses. Another application is as a periodic switch, used for example to reset the output states of step counter circuits periodically. Furthermore, an astable blocking oscillator can be triggered to act as a frequency divider. Discussions of triggering and calculations relating to pulse length are presented by Littauer† and Strauss‡ respectively.

16-17
Pulse response of amplifiers

Amplifiers often must amplify pulses, sometimes—as in an oscilloscope amplifier—with as little distortion as possible and sometimes with simultaneous wave shaping—as in some amplifiers in nuclear radiation counters. Another example in which the amplifier transient response is important is in the video section of a television receiver, and pulse amplifiers are often called *video* amplifiers.

Suppose that a fairly long ideal voltage pulse (Fig. 16-31a) is applied to the input of a wideband amplifier. The amplified pulse will suffer a *time delay* and will be subject to a *rise time* at the pulse front, as shown to an expanded time scale in Fig. 16-31b. Furthermore, the top of the pulse may be distorted, as shown in Fig. 16-31c. The slanting top is said to have a *sag* or a *tilt*.

†See Reference 16-5, Chap. 15.
‡See Reference 16-8, Chap. 12.

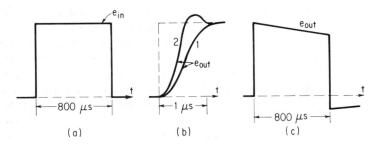

FIGURE 16-31   Pulse response of an amplifier.

We are mainly concerned with the amplifier transient response to a step function input, though the response to other pulse shapes may be of interest. The exact transient analysis of even a single stage of amplification leads to cumbersome expressions, and of multistage amplifiers becomes a formidable problem, and consequently our introduction to the subject must be largely qualitative.

a. The single pentode stage

We consider first the single pentode stage of Fig. 7-11 whose equivalent circuit, based on the assumption that $C_k \rightarrow \infty$, is given in Fig. 7-13. A wide-band frequency response is essential for good pulse response. Therefore the problem of the pulse response can be broken into two parts, first, the fast rise at the front of the pulse, and second, the longer time response that determines the sag. We can show that during the fast rise the voltage of the large coupling capacitor C in Fig. 7-13 will not change appreciably, so it has little effect on the transient. Therefore we can use the high-frequency equivalent circuit (Fig. 7-15) to calculate the rising transient. After a few microseconds or less the shunting capacitors are fully charged, and thereafter the coupling capaci-

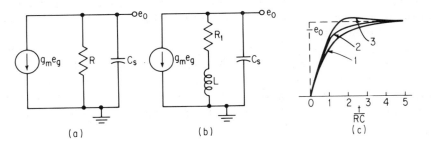

FIGURE 16-32   Consideration of amplifier rise time.

tor C begins to have an effect. Then the low-frequency equivalent circuit (Fig. 7-16) is applicable.

Let us analyze the rise time of the pentode stage by means of the high-frequency equivalent circuit in Fig. 16-32a. We recall that $R = r_p \| R_1 \| R_g$ and that $C_s = C_i + C_o$. In this circuit a step input voltage generates the current step $g_m e_g$. The output response is a rising exponential having a time constant RC_s, as shown by curve 1 in Fig. 16-32c. If we calculate the rise time T_R based on the 10 per cent and 90 per cent points, we find

$$T_R = 2.20 RC_s \qquad (16\text{-}34)$$

We recall from the discussion in Sec. 7-8 that the mid-band gain of the stage is

$$|A| = g_m R \qquad (7\text{-}31)$$

A comparison of Eqs. (16-34) and (7-31) shows that an attempt to increase the gain by increasing R will lead to a corresponding increase in the rise time. A better approach is to use a tube with a higher g_m, provided that the tube capacitances do not also rise proportionately. Pentodes having values of g_m of the order of 0.01 mho or higher have been developed. Such a tube may have a C_s of 15 pF in a typical circuit; therefore a value of load resistance yielding an R of 15 k would yield a rise time of 0.5 μs and a gain of 150. However, to attain a rise time of 0.1 μs the R would have to be 3 k and then the gain would drop to 30.

One method of improving the rise time is to place an inductor in series with the plate load resistor, as shown in the approximate equivalent circuit in Fig. 16-32b. When $L/R_1^2 C_s$ equals 0.25, the response follows curve 2 in Fig. 16-32c but if $L/R_1^2 C_s = 0.5$, there is an oscillatory overshoot as shown by curve 3. The degree of overshoot that can be tolerated depends on the application.

The shape of the top of the output pulse depends on the coupling network in the low-frequency equivalent circuit in Fig. 16-33a, which is derived from Fig. 7-16. Here $R_2 = r_p \| R_1$. The exponential decay shown in Fig. 16-33b has a time constant of $\tau = RC$. where $R = R_2 + R_g$. Comparison with the value of ω_1 in Eq. (7-34) shows that

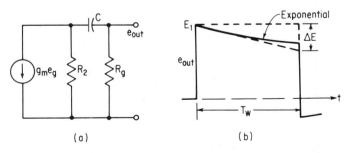

FIGURE 16-33   The tilt of an amplifier pulse response.

$$\tau = \frac{1}{\omega_1} \tag{16-35}$$

that is, the time constant is the inverse of the lower half-power radian frequency.

Generally the pulse duration T_w is small compared with τ. Then the linear approximation to the exponential shown by the dashed line in the figure is useful. The dashed line has the same slope at the origin as that of the exponential, i.e., a slope of $-E_1/\tau$. The geometry of Fig. 16-33b shows that $\Delta E/T_w$ is the magnitude of the slope, so $\Delta E/T_w = E_1/\tau$, and solving, we obtain

$$\frac{\Delta E}{E_1} = \frac{T_w}{\tau} \tag{16-36}$$

For example, if $\omega_1 = 200$ or $\tau = 0.005$ s, and if $T_w = 100 \ \mu s$, then $\Delta E/E_1 = 0.02$, or 2 per cent.

b. Multistage amplifiers

A cascade connection of amplifier stages will obviously have a greater over-all delay time and a longer rise time, but the quantitative effects are rather involved. This problem has been worked out mathematically for amplifiers whose individual stages do not have any overshoot. The results[†] of these calculations are of interest. The total delay time is the sum of the delay times of the individual stages. The rise time, however, is calculated as follows:

$$T_R = (T_1^2 + T_2^2 + \cdots + T_n^2)^{1/2} \tag{16-37}$$

where T_R is the over-all rise time and $T_1, T_2, \cdots, T_n$ are the rise times of the individual stages.

For example, if we have an oscilloscope whose main amplifier has a rise time of 20 ns (20×10^{-9} s) and whose preamplifier has a rise time of 40 ns, then the rise time of the combination would be $(20^2 + 40^2)^{1/2}$ or 44.7 ns. Equation (16-37) can also be used to estimate the rise time required in an oscilloscope to properly display a pulse of a known rise time. Suppose that the oscilloscope rise time is 0.04 μs and we want to observe a pulse that has a 0.2-μs rise time. The observed response will be 0.204 μs, a value in error by only 2 per cent.

No exact relation exists between the bandwidth of the general cascaded amplifier and its rise time. However, empirical studies[‡] give the following range of values:

---

†See, for example, J. M. Pettit and M. M. McWhorter, *Electronic Amplifier Circuits: Theory and Design*, McGraw-Hill Book Company, New York, 1961, pp. 107 ff.

‡Pettit and McWhorter, *ibid.*, p. 121.

$$\frac{0.35}{f_2} < T_R < \frac{0.45}{f_2} \tag{16-38}$$

The lower values fit best those amplifiers having no overshoot, whereas an amplifier with an overshoot of 5 per cent or more is likely to fall at the upper end of the range.

An analysis† of the response of cascaded stages, each of which can be represented by the model in Fig. 16-33a, with the resistor R_2 small compared with R_g, yields results relating to the *long-time* response of the amplifier. If the pulse duration is small compared with the time constant of the individual stages, then the slope of the over-all amplifier response at $t = 0$ is simply the sum of the slopes of the responses of the individual stages. For example, if one stage produces a $\Delta E/E_1$ of 1 per cent, then five identical stages will give $\Delta E/E_1 = 5$ per cent.

c. The transistor stage

The analysis of a transistor amplifier for pulse work could start with a consideration of the broad-band stage, as discussed in Sec. 7-12. A more complete analysis would consider the effect of the transient response of the transistor itself, as discussed in Sec. 16-14, on the transient response of the stage. Such calculations usually use a simplified version of a high-frequency transistor circuit model. For example,‡ the hybrid-pi circuit of Fig. 7-25b may be used, but with the simplification that $r_{ce} \to \infty$, $r_{b'c} \to \infty$, and that $C_{b'e}$ be increased to include the effect of $C_{b'c}$ by a line of reasoning like that used to give the enhanced input capacitance of a triode due to the Miller effect. In the pentode stage we found that the ratio of gain to rise time is *independent* of the load resistance. In contrast, in the transistor stage the ratio of gain to rise time is a function of the ratio of base resistance to load resistance.

16-18
Triggered linear sweep generator

The linear sweep generator (Fig. 16-34) combines several of the basic wave-shaping circuits. This system is often used to produce the *linear sweep* or *sawtooth* voltage wave needed to give the horizontal sweep of the trace on a cathode-ray oscilloscope tube (see Sec. 19-7). The object of the sweep voltage generator is to produce a wave that is an exact linear function of the

† G. E. Valley, Jr., and H. Wallman, eds., *Vacuum Tube Amplifiers*, M.I.T. Radiation Lab. Series, v. 18, McGraw-Hill Book Company, New York, 1948, pp. 85 ff.

‡ Pettit and McWhorter, *op. cit.*, p. 97 and references cited there.

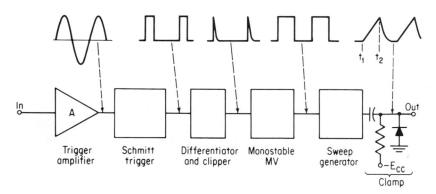

FIGURE 16-34   Block diagram of a triggered linear sweep generator for a *CR* oscilloscope.

time and that can be triggered by random test voltages or maintained in synchronism by a recurring test signal.

In the wave forms in Fig. 16-34 the test signal is assumed to be a sine wave. A portion of the signal is amplified, squared in a Schmitt trigger circuit, and then differentiated and the negative pulses clipped off. The positive pulses trigger the monostable *MV* and generate standard square pulses. These are shaped in the *sweep generator* circuit, which puts out a linear wave from instant t_1 to t_2. The sweep generator may consist of the Miller integrator or of a "bootstrap" circuit (Sec. 16-19). The dc restorer, or clamp, insures that the output wave returns to the same level each cycle.

We see that a linear voltage wave segment is generated every time that the signal rises above the level needed to trigger the Schmitt circuit. In actual oscilloscopes additional controls permit the inversion of the output of the trigger amplifier so that the sweep can be started on the opposite half-cycle of the signal wave if desired. There are also controls on the sweep generator that can alter the duration of the sweep.

16-19
The Miller integrator sweep circuit; bootstrap circuit

a. The Miller integrator sweep generator

The operational integrator circuit described in Chapter 14 serves as an excellent sweep (ramp) voltage generator. The basic circuit is reproduced in Fig. 16-35. It derives its name from the location and effect of the feedback

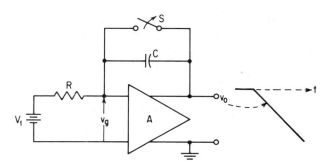

FIGURE 16-35   Miller integrator in principle.

capacitor C, which are the same as those of the capacitance which produces the Miller effect in amplifiers. The voltage gain A is assumed to be high, say 100 or over, and is negative real. Then, if the amplifier input current is negligible and its output impedance is zero, the output voltage v_0 at a time t after opening switch S will be, approximately,

$$v_o = -\frac{1}{RC}\int_0^t V_1\,dt = -\frac{V_1}{RC}t \qquad (16\text{-}39)$$

up until the time at which the amplifier saturates. According to this approximation the ramp function would have perfect linearity.

A closer examination of the Miller integrator circuit, including the error due to the finite gain A, will yield the solution for v_0 in the operational form

$$v_o = \frac{1}{1 + (1 - A)RCp}AV_1 \qquad (16\text{-}40)$$

If we compare Eq. (16-40) with the operational expression for the rising capacitor voltage in a series RC circuit with impressed voltage V_1, namely,

$$v_c = \frac{1}{1 + RCp}V_1 \qquad (16\text{-}41)$$

we see that the two differ in two respects. According to (16-40) the ultimate output voltage is AV_1 instead of V_1 and the time constant is $(1 - A)\,RC$ instead of RC. Thus in a Miller integrator in which $A = -100$ the ramp is an exponential rise, but the virtual final voltage is $-100\,V_1$ and the time constant is $101RC$. Of course, only the initial portion of the exponential curve is used, and therefore the linearity of the output is extremely good.

An elementary Miller integrator circuit is shown in Fig. 16-36. The capacitor C provides the feedback connection from the collector of the common-emitter stage back to its base. With switch S closed, the output voltage v_0 is near V_{cc}. When S is opened, the potential of point P starts to rise and v_0

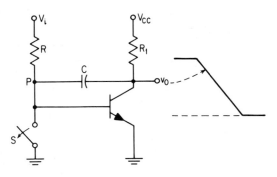

FIGURE 16-36   Elementary Miller integrator sweep circuit.

starts to fall. The Miller effect increases the time constant and the voltage gain increases the apparent ultimate change in output voltage. Of course, the actual output voltage change is limited to a little less than V_{cc}, since v_o varies from near V_{cc} to near zero.

In practical applications, as in *CRO* time base circuits, the function of switch S is replaced by a voltage gating signal plus a switching transistor. Vacuum tubes are also used in Miller integrators, for example, a single pentode stage will provide enough gain to give excellent linearity. Additional circuits are discussed by Littauer† and circuit design by Millman and Taub.‡

b. Bootstrap linear integrator

Suppose that we think of generating a ramp voltage by charging a capa-

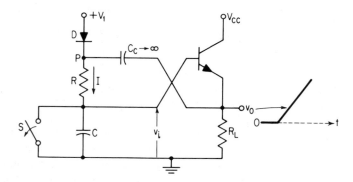

FIGURE 16-37   An elementary bootstrap circuit.

†Reference 16-5, pp. 468 ff.
‡Reference 16-6, Chap. 14.

citor in a series RC circuit from a fixed voltage source. In this situation the linearity suffers because the capacitor voltage rises exponentially. We have seen that the Miller integrator linearizes the response through use of the operational amplifier feedback technique. If a *constant current* is used to charge the capacitor, then a linear response results. The bootstrap circuit maintains a constant current in the series RC circuit by an appropriate variation of the source voltage in the series circuit.

The elementary circuit in Fig. 16-37 will show how this can be done. The transistor is in the emitter follower connection; therefore the voltage gain is approximately $+1$, and we shall assume that $v_o \cong v_i$. With switch S closed, the output is zero. When S is opened, C begins to charge, and v_i and v_o begin to rise. But v_o is coupled back through the large capacitor C_c to point P between the diode D and the resistor R. The potential at point P therefore starts to rise above V_1 (diode D becomes back-biased), and if $v_o = v_i$, the voltage across R will remain constant and the current I will remain constant, as desired. The action of the voltages has been compared to "lifting oneself by one's own bootstraps," hence the name applied to the circuit. We remark that the gain requirement on the amplifier is quite different from that in the Miller integrator circuit.

REFERENCES

16-1 J. F. Cleary, ed., *General Electric Transistor Manual*, 7th ed., General Electric Co., Syracuse, N.Y., 1964, Chaps. 3, 6, 7.

16-2 John M. Doyle, *Pulse Fundamentals*, Prentice-Hall, Inc., Englewood Cliffs, N.J., 1963.

16-3 L. P. Hunter, ed., *Handbook of Semiconductor Electronics*, 2d ed., McGraw-Hill Book Company, New York, 1962.

16-4 M. V. Joyce and K. K. Clarke, *Transistor Circuit Analysis*, Addison-Wesley Publishing Company, Inc., Reading, Mass., 1961, Chaps. 10–15.

16-5 Raphael Littauer, *Pulse Electronics*, McGraw-Hill Book Company, New York, 1965.

16-6 Jacob Millman and H. Taub, *Pulse, Digital and Switching Waveforms*, McGraw-Hill Book Company, New York, 1965.

16-7 W. D. Roehr and D. Thorpe, eds., *Switching Transistor Handbook*, 2d ed., Motorola, Inc., Phoenix, Ariz., 1963.

16-8 Leonard Strauss, *Wave Generation and Shaping*, McGraw-Hill Book Company, New York, 1960.

16-9 Engineering Staff of the Texas Instruments Co., *Transistor Circuit Design*, J. A. Walston and J. R. Miller, eds., McGraw-Hill Book Company, New York, 1963.

EXERCISES

16-1 Assume that a 10-V recurring pulse voltage of the form in Fig. 16-38 is impressed on the RC circuit in Fig. 16-1b. Let $R = 1$ MΩ and $C = 1$ μF. Sketch semi-quantitative output voltage wave forms over the time ranges in the figure for (a) the initial application of the pulse voltage, assuming that the initial charge in the capacitor is zero, and (b) for an interval long after the pulse wave is applied, i.e., in the steady state. Superimpose the output waves on the input waves in the format shown in the figure.

16-2 Assume that the input voltage wave in Fig. 16-38 is impressed on the RC circuit in Fig. 16-2a. Let $R = 1$ MΩ and $C = 2$ μF. Sketch the output voltage

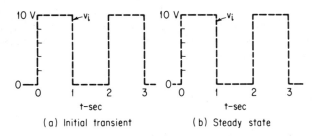

(a) Initial transient   (b) Steady state

FIGURE 16-38   Input pulse forms.

wave form over the time ranges in the figure for (a) the initial application of the pulse voltage, assuming $e_c(0) = 0$, and (b) the steady-state condition. (c) Repeat (a) and (b) except change C to 10 μF.

16-3 Verify Eq. (16-3). *Suggestion*: Establish a value of the capacitor voltage at the beginning of the positive pulse of e_i. Also make use of the requirement that e_o equals $-E_1$ just before the beginning and equals $+E_1$ at the end of the pulse.

16-4 The top of the output pulse in Fig. 16-1c for $\tau = T$ falls by the amount ΔE in time T. A measure of the *sag* or *tilt* of the output pulse is the ratio $\Delta E/E$. (a) Show that $\Delta E/E$ for this wave is equal to $[1 - \exp(-T/\tau)]$ (b) Show that if $\tau \gg T$, then $\Delta E/E \cong T/\tau$. *Suggestion*: Use the expansion $\exp x = 1 + x + x^2/2 + x^3/3!$ $+ \cdots$.

16-5 (a) Draw a circuit diagram of an RC integrator and label the input and output voltages. (b) Suppose that 5 pulses of the form in Fig. 16-38 are to be integrated, except that the pulses are each of 1-ms duration. Choose values of R and C for the integrator such that the error in the integration of the fifth pulse is approximately 2 per cent. (c) Discuss the possibility of error in this integrator due to capacitor leakage or dielectric absorption.

16-6 Let a single half-sine-shaped pulse (Fig. 16-4) of amplitude 100 V and duration T_1 be applied to an RC integrator circuit comprising $R = 0.1$ MΩ and $C = 1$ μF. (a) What is an approximate value of T_1 for which the capacitor voltage reaches a value of 2 V? (b) What change could be made in the integrator circuit to improve the accuracy of the integration, assuming that T_1 has the value calculated in (a)?

16-7 The voltage wave e_o on the right in Fig. 16-8 is impressed on a series circuit of $R = 10,000$ Ω and $C = 0.001$ μF. Let the sine wave portions of e_o be equal to $100 \sin 10^4 t$ V and let the constant portions be $+50$ and -50 V. Neglect the loading effect of the RC circuit. (a) Sketch the wave of voltage across R and indicate the approximate magnitude of the wave. (b) Use basic circuit theory to calculate the wave of voltage across R during the first (rising) sinusoidal portion of the impressed voltage wave. Assume that the initial charge in C is zero. Compare this result with the approximate result obtained by means of Eq. (16-6).

16-8 (a) Devise a circuit similar to that in Fig. 16-6 that will clip off both the tops and the bottom portions of a sine-wave input voltage. (b) Label the values of the components in your circuit to provide clipping levels of $+10$ V and -5 V.

16-9 The wave of v_i in Fig. 16-39 is impressed on the circuit shown. (a) Sketch the waveform of v_o for the steady-state condition if $\tau = RC = 8T_w$. (b) Repeat (a) but assume that the diode is reversed.

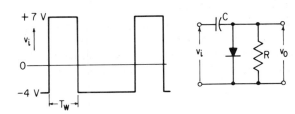

FIGURE 16-39

16-10 Consider the bistable MV circuit in Fig. 16-15 analyzed in Fig. 16-16. (a) Redraw the waves shown in Fig. 16-16 and add a wave showing voltage v_{B1}. (b) Why is the rise time of wave v_{C2} greater than its fall time?

16-11 (a) Consider the rising transient part of wave v_{C2} after Q_2 turns off in the bistable MV in Fig. 16-17. Show that, if transistor time delay effects are neglected and if V_E is taken to be constant and the base of Q_1 is assumed to be clamped at a small voltage above its emitter, the time constant of the rising transient equals $C_1 R_{K1} R_{L2}/(R_{K1} + R_{L2})$. (b) Calculate this time constant for a symmetrical circuit in which $C_1 = 220$ pF, $R_{K1} = 42$ k, and $R_{L2} = 2.2$ k. (c) What is the rise time under the conditions of (b)? (d) Explain why the fall time of the wave of v_{C2} is short compared with its rise time.

16-12 (a) Draw a circuit diagram of a collector-triggered MV and label the elements with the values given at the end of Sec. 16-9. (b) Estimate the values of V_E, $V_{C\ OFF}$, and $V_{C\ ON}$. Assume that the saturation value of V_{CE} is 0.2 V.

16-13 In the astable MV circuit in Fig. 16-19 let $C_1 = C_2 = C$, $R_{B1} = R_{B2} = R_B$ and $R_{L1} = R_{L2} = R_L$. Use the same simplifying assumptions as in Sec..16-10 to show that the free-running frequency is, approximately, $f = \{2R_BC \ln [1 + (V_{CC}/V_{BB})]\}^{-1}$. Discuss how the variation of V_{BB} can be used to control the frequency.

16-14 Choose the values of the resistances R_L, R_K, R_B, and R_E for a symmetrical, saturated bistable MV of the type in Fig. 16-17. Assume that $V_{CC} = 9$ V and let $V_E = 2$ V. Assume that the ambient temperature is 25°C and that cutoff currents may be neglected. The npn transistors to be used are characterized as follows: $V_{BE} = 0.3$ V for $I_C = 10$ mA dc and $I_B = 0.25$ mA dc, $V_{CE \, sat} = 0.2$ V for the same I_C and I_B values, $V_{CEO} = 25$ V max, $V_{EBO} = 25$ V max, transistor dissipation $= 150$ mW max, dc forward current transfer ratio $= h_{FE} = 20$ for $I_C = 10$ mA and $V_{CE} = 0.3$ V. Specify your calculated values of I_B of the ON transistor and of V_{BE} of the OFF transistor.

16-15 Choose values of R_L, R_{B1}, R_{B2}, R_{K1}, and C_2 in the monostable MV circuit in Fig. 16-22 to give a pulse width of 100 μs. Use the transistor data given in Exercise 16-14 and use $V_{CC} = 10$ V and $V_{BB} = -10$ V.

16-16 In the trigger circuit in Fig. 16-24a let $V_{CC} = 10$ V, $R_{L1} = 2.2$ k, $R_{L2} = 1.2$k, $R_E = 330$ Ω, $R_1 = 12$ k, $R_2 = 18$ k, $C = 220$ pF, and $R_B = 1.0$ k. The transistors are those described in Exercise 16-14. Find values of V_U and of V_L. Include estimated effects of voltages V_{BE} and of $V_{CE \, sat}$.

16-17 A pentode stage has a pulse response without overshoot that has a delay time of 10 ns and a rise time of 20 ns. A step input voltage is applied to an amplifier that consists of four identical cascaded stages of this type. Sketch the shape of the front of the output pulse and specify the delay time and the rise time.

17

Logic and Counting Circuits

17-1
Introduction

The multivibrator circuits considered in Chapter 16 were shown to exist in one or the other of two states. The multivibrators, and other related circuits, are employed in a class of systems in which the information passing through the system is in the *digital* rather than the *analog* form. As will be explained presently, this means that the information is contained in a group of states, which sometimes are represented by the digits of the binary number system. The electronic circuits that contain and transmit the information therefore need to exist in only one of two states, and minor variations in the amplitudes of the individual states do not introduce errors. By using an assemblage of electronic circuits, the information can be represented and processed with high speed and with a high degree of accuracy, though at the expense of having a complex system. In contrast, in an analog system the accuracy attainable is limited to that of the voltage level of the particular circuit.

Although digital computers, electronic counters, and digital instruments may contain a complex assemblage of circuits, there are relatively few basic circuits, and these are combined in a logical building block fashion to form the complete system. Thus the circuit interconnections rather than the internal circuit details are to be emphasized. Often a highly symbolic representation, similar to an assemblage of block diagrams, is used in the design and discussion of a complete system. Some of the basic circuits will be described, and

447

examples of their interconnection into simple systems will be presented. We begin with a review of the binary number system.

17-2
The binary number system

A review of the more familiar *decimal* digital number system will be helpful. In this system a number, such as 482, has the meaning shown by the following expression;

$$482 = 4 \times 10^2 + 8 \times 10^1 + 2 \times 10^0 \qquad (17\text{-}1)$$

The number 10 is called the *base* (or *radix*) of this system, and the digits of the system are 0, 1, 2, 3, ..., 9. If the number has a decimal fraction, an extension of the powers to negative exponents is needed. For example,

$$827.43 = 8 \times 10^2 + 2 \times 10^1 + 7 \times 10^0 + 4 \times 10^{-1} + 3 \times 10^{-2} \qquad (17\text{-}2)$$

These examples are special cases of the general expression for any digital number N, which may be written

$$N = d_n R^n + d_{n-1} R^{n-1} + \cdots d_1 R^1 + d_0 R^0 + d_{-1} R^{-1} + \cdots \qquad (17\text{-}3)$$

where the digits are the d's and R is the base. If the values of the digits are limited to integer values from 0 to $(R-1)$, then the representation is unique.

In the binary system the base is 2 and the digits are 0 or 1 (zero or unity). As an example consider the binary number 101 and express its value by means of (17-3)

$$N = 101(\text{binary}) = 1 \times 2^2 + 0 \times 2^1 + 1 \times 2^0 \qquad (17\text{-}4)$$

The decimal value of the number is therefore $4 + 0 + 1$, or 5.

A general form for the value of a binary number can be written, following Eq. (17-3), as follows:

$$N = (0 \text{ or } 1)2^n + (0 \text{ or } 1)2^{n-1} + \cdots (0 \text{ or } 1)2^0 + (0 \text{ or } 1)2^{-1} + \cdots \qquad (17\text{-}5)$$

The number may have a value with a fractional portion, for example,

$$1011.11 = 1 \times 2^3 + 0 \times 2^2 + 1 \times 2^1 + 1 \times 2^0 + 1 \times 2^{-1} + 1 \times 2^{-2} \qquad (17\text{-}6)$$

Thus the binary number 1011.11 has the value $8 + 0 + 2 + 1 + \frac{1}{2} + \frac{1}{4}$, or decimal number 11.75.

A comparison of some binary numbers with their decimal equivalents is shown in Table 17-1. The number of digits needed to express a particular value in the binary system is large compared with the number needed in the decimal system. Smaller numbers of digits are needed as the base is increased, such as in the ternary (base $= 3$) system, or the octonary (base $= 8$) system.

Simple rules apply to the arithmetical operations of addition, subtraction, multiplication, and division in the binary number system. Some examples are the following:

$$
\begin{array}{ccccc}
1 & 10 & 11 & 10 & 11 \\
\underline{+1} & \underline{+1} & \underline{-1} & \underline{-1} & \underline{+1} \\
10 & 11 & 10 & 1 & 100
\end{array}
$$

Short-cut rules† have been developed for the various arithmetical operations and for the conversion of numbers between the binary and the decimal systems. Particular attention has been paid to the arithmetical procedures that can be used advantageously in digital computers.

Table 17-1 Binary Numbers with Decimal Equivalents

Binary	Decimal	Binary	Decimal
0	0	1011	11
1	1	1100	12
10	2	1101	13
11	3	1110	14
100	4	1111	15
101	5	10000	16
110	6	10001	17
111	7	⋮	⋮
1000	8	100000	32
1001	9	⋮	⋮
1010	10	1100100	100

17-3
Elementary Boolean algebra

As was mentioned in Sec. 17-1, the number of types of digital circuits is relatively small and the main interest is in their interconnection to form a complete system. The design problem of making these interconnections can be eased by the use of formal logic, particularly symbolic logic. George Boole in 1847 presented a system of symbolic logic which included a set of rules for the manipulation of symbols to express logical propositions. This system, called Boolean algebra, is useful in the design of digital systems. We shall

†I. H. Gould and F. S. Ellis, *Digital Computer Technology*, Chapman and Hall, London, 1963, Chap. 2.

introduce the Boolean algebra by means of some elementary electrical switching circuits which illustrate logical propositions. Many electrical circuits have been devised that conform to the Boolean algebra, but the simplest circuits are those that use switches or relay contacts. These are used as examples in this section; others are presented in the following two sections.

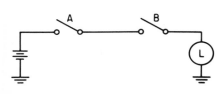

Consider the circuit in Fig. 17-1, which shows a source and a lamp connected by two switches (or relay contacts) A and B in series. We see that *two* conditions must be fulfilled in order to light the lamp. This logical proposition can be written symbolically as follows, if we let A represent switch A closed, B represent switch B closed, and R represent the results, i.e., lamp L lighted:

FIGURE 17-1   Illustrating the logical AND.

$$A \quad \text{AND} \quad B = R \qquad (17\text{-}7)$$

If only A is closed, we do not have R, or if only B is closed, we do not have R. Both A *and* B must be closed to obtain result R. This is an example of the logical AND. In a more general sense the states of A and B correspond to the truth or falsity of the premises in a logical proposition, and the state of R corresponds to that of the conclusion.

The symbolism can be augmented by using the digits of the binary number system to represent the *condition* or *input state* and the *result* or *output state*, as follows:

$$\begin{aligned}
&\text{condition present (or true)} = 1\\
&\text{condition absent (or false)} = 0\\
&\text{result present (or true)} \quad = 1\\
&\text{result absent (or false)} \quad = 0
\end{aligned}$$

These symbols are convenient for recording the different possible states of the quantities in proposition (17-7), as shown in Table 17-2, called a *truth table*. In terms of the switching circuit example, a 0 means that the particular switch is open, a 1 means that the switch is closed, and likewise a 0 in the R column means that the lamp is dark and a 1 means that the lamp is lighted.

Next we extend the idea of the logical AND to a situation in which three simultaneous conditions, namely, A, B, and C, are required to produce the result R. Then,

$$A \quad \text{AND} \quad B \quad \text{AND} \quad C = R \qquad (17\text{-}8)$$

For brevity, this is written in the form

$$A \cdot B \cdot C = R \qquad (17\text{-}9)$$

The truth table for (17-9) is shown in Table 17-3. Of all the possible combinations of input states, only one produces the result, or an output.

Next consider a situation in which the presence of *A or* of *B or* of *C* will produce the result. A situation in which this logic would apply is the following. Three persons, *A*, *B*, and *C* each have identical keys to a locked room. Therefore, if *A* or *B* or *C* appears, the room can be unlocked. Of course, if any two or if all three appear, the room can also be opened. The proposition may be written

$$A \quad \text{OR} \quad B \quad \text{OR} \quad C = R \qquad (17\text{-}10)$$

Table 17-2 Truth Table for $R = A$ AND B

A	B	$R = A$ AND B
0	0	0
1	0	0
0	1	0
1	1	1

Table 17-3 Truth Table for $R = A \cdot B \cdot C$

A	B	C	R
0	0	1	0
0	1	0	0
1	0	0	0
1	1	0	0
0	1	1	0
1	0	1	0
1	1	1	1

Table 17-4 Part of Truth Table for $A + B + C = R$

A	B	C	R
0	0	0	0
1	0	0	1
0	1	0	1
0	0	1	1
1	1	0	1
etc.			

But this is also written as follows:

$$A + B + C = R \qquad (17\text{-}11)$$

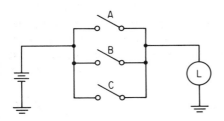

FIGURE 17-2 Switching circuit to illustrate the logical OR, i.e., $A + B + C = R$.

which is read "A or B or C produces R." The switching circuit that conforms to proposition (17-10) is shown in Fig. 17-2. If one or more of the parallel-connected switches is closed, the lamp will light. Part of the truth table for this circuit or for relation (17-11) appears in Table 17-4.

Another symbolic operation is that for the *negation* of a particular condition or result. Thus if we negate condition A we mean NOT A, which is written $\bar{A}$. Thus if $A = 0$, then $\bar{A} = 1$, or if $A = 1$, then $\bar{A} = 0$.

To summarize, we have symbols for AND, OR and NOT, as component operations of the Boolean algebra. Next we list some of the laws of Boolean algebra.

commutative laws	$A + B = B + A$	(17-12)
	$A \cdot B = B \cdot A$	(17-13)
associative laws	$(A + B) + C = A + (B + C)$	(17-14)
	$(A \cdot B) \cdot C = A \cdot (B \cdot C)$	(17-15)
distributive law	$A \cdot (B + C) = A \cdot B + A \cdot C$	(17-16)
special distributive law	$(A + B) \cdot (A + C) = A + B \cdot C$	(17-17)
DeMorgan's theorem	$\overline{(A + B)} = (\bar{A} \cdot \bar{B})$	(17-18)
	$\overline{(A \cdot B)} = \bar{A} + \bar{B}$	(17-19)

The following relations can be verified by constructing the corresponding truth tables;

$$A \cdot A = A$$
$$A + A = A$$
$$A + \bar{A} = 1$$
$$A \cdot \bar{A} = 0$$

(17-20)

The reader will notice that propositions (17-12) through (17-16) have the same forms as those for ordinary algebra, but relations (17-17) through (17-20) illustrate that Boolean algebra is essentially different. The validity of the Boolean relations can be established by straightforward substitution of 0's and 1's and verification of the identity of the two sides for all possible combinations. Representations of the two sides of (17-17) by means of switch-

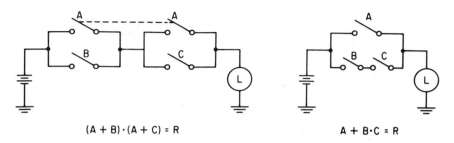

$$(A + B) \cdot (A + C) = R \qquad\qquad A + B \cdot C = R$$

FIGURE 17-3   Switching circuits to illustrate Eq. (17-17).

ing circuits, as in Fig. 17-3a and b will illustrate this procedure. If the result R for the two circuits is identical for every possible combination of the states of A, B, and C, then (17-17) is valid. In other words, the two sides of the relation should have identical truth tables.

17-4
Diode logic circuits: AND, OR

The performance of logical operations by means of switches or relays has a severely limited speed of response. These operations can also be performed by a variety of high-speed diode, transistor, or tube circuits. These circuits comprise some of the basic building blocks of a digital system.

An elementary diode logic circuit is shown in Fig. 17-4. The input switches A and B can be placed in either of two positions, 0 or 1. If either switch A or B is in position 0, or at ground, current flows via resistor R and one of the diodes to ground, and the voltage V_{out} will be zero, assuming that the diode forward drop is negligible. However, if *both A and B are in positions 1*, there will be an output voltage. Now diodes D_1 and D_2 carry current and clamp

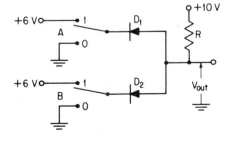

Switch A	Switch B	V_{out} volts
0	0	0
1	0	0
0	1	0
1	1	6

FIGURE 17-4   A diode logic circuit.

the output at $+6$ V. The table at the right in Fig. 17-4 shows the value of V_{out} for the various input combinations. If we *define* $+6$ V as the logical 1, and 0 V as the logical 0, then this table is the truth table for an output equal to A AND B. The foregoing definition gives what is known as *positive logic*. (When a negative pulse or voltage level represents the logical 1, the system is said to use *negative logic*.)

What is the output when the input voltages happen to be unequal? For example, what is V_{out} if the voltage at A in Fig. 17-4 is $+7$ V and at B is $+5$ V? With both switches on 1 we see that diode D_2 will conduct and clamp V_{out} at $+5$ V, while D_1 will be back-biased by 2 V. Thus the lower input voltage determines the output level.

The conventional diagram for a three-input AND circuit, also called a *gate*, is shown in Fig. 17-5a. Here we must understand that A, B, C, and V_{out} represent voltages to ground. The load resistance between V_{out} and ground is assumed to be very large, but in networks of logic circuits this assumption may not be valid.

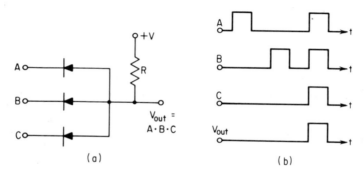

FIGURE 17-5   (a) A diode AND gate. (b) Example of input and output pulses.

In many digital systems the information is carried on pulses rather than by means of voltage levels. An example is shown in Fig. 17-5b, in which a positive pulse is considered to be the logical 1 and an absence of a pulse is the logical 0. When A and B and C are all 1's, then the output is 1. The output pulse height will approximate that of the smallest of the input pulses, provided that the source voltage V exceeds this magnitude.

The diode AND gate is also called a *coincidence circuit*, or *gate*. The circuit will have an output only when the pulses on the three inputs *coincide* in time. This property is useful in the analysis of pulses arising from nuclear radiation experiments.

Figure 17-6 shows a diode OR gate circuit in which the resistor returns to a negative voltage source. The circuit will, however, also function as an

OR gate if the resistor is terminated at ground. Suppose that input A has a positive potential and B and C have lower potentials. Then the output V_{out} will be slightly below the input A, since diode A is conducting and B and C are reverse-biased. In general, the output equals the highest of the input voltages if diode drop is neglected.

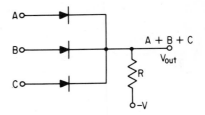

FIGURE 17-6   A diode OR gate.

Suppose that the inputs A, B, and C consist of equal amplitude positive pulses. Also let the output represent the logical 1 for an output pulse and logical 0 for the absence of a pulse. The output then gives the result $A + B + C$, expressed in Boolean terms. If the pulse height is 6 V and the diodes are assumed to be ideal, the voltage V_{out} has the values given in Table 17-5 for various inputs. The corresponding logical truth table is also shown.

Combinations of AND and OR gates can perform logical operations. Suppose that we want a circuit to give

$$(A + B) \cdot (A + C) = R \qquad (17\text{-}21)$$

Table 17-5   Characteristics of OR Gate

	Voltages, volts				Corresponding truth table		
A	B	C	V_{out}	A	B	C	V_{out}
0	0	0	0	0	0	0	0
6	0	0	6	1	0	0	1
0	6	0	6	0	1	0	1
0	0	6	6	0	0	1	1
6	6	0	6	1	1	0	1

Table 17-6   Truth Table for $(A + B) \cdot (A + C) = R$

A	B	C	R
0	0	0	0
0	0	1	0
0	1	0	0
0	1	1	1
1	0	0	1
1	0	1	1
1	1	0	1
1	1	1	1

We can connect two OR gates and an AND gate as in Fig. 17-7 and expect the output to be $(A + B) \cdot (A + C)$. However, in the basic AND gate in Fig. 17-5a the cathode sides of the diodes are either at zero volts or at signal potential, whereas in Fig. 17-7 the cathode side of each diode in the AND gate has a path via resistor R to $-V$. Further analysis is therefore needed to check to learn whether the circuit will function as expected.

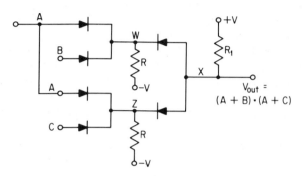

FIGURE 17-7   The diode logic circuit for $(A + B) \cdot (A + C)$.

The desired truth table is given in Table 17-6. Let us take a numerical example and check one of the conditions in the truth table to illustrate the technique. Let $R_1 = 2 \text{ k}$, $R = 1 \text{ k}$, $V = +20 \text{ V}$, $-V = -20 \text{ V}$, and let $+6 \text{ V}$ represent logical 1, and 0 V represent logical 0. As an example, let

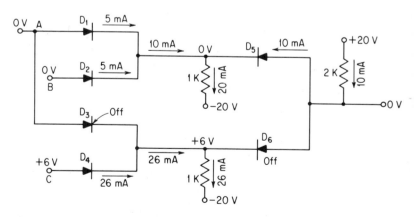

FIGURE 17-8   Electrical conditions in the circuit in Fig. 17-7 for $A = 0$, $B = 0$, $C = 1$, and $R = 0$.

$A = 0$, $B = 0$, and $C = 1$, so that R should be 0. If this network behaves in the desired fashion, the output is zero volts, with diodes D_1, D_2, D_4, and D_5 (in Fig. 17-8) conducting and D_3 and D_6 back-biased. The condition is verified by *assuming* that the diodes are acting as stated and then computing the currents in the conducting diodes and the voltages across the cut-off diodes. The latter must turn out to be reverse-bias voltages if the circuit is to function as assumed. The calculated currents and voltages (assuming ideal diodes) entered in Fig. 17-8 show that the circuit does indeed function properly for the assumed input conditions. The other input conditions in Table 17-6 can be analyzed in a similar way.

In a diagram of a complex system the circuit details of the logical elements are not essential, and graphical symbols that omit the details are used. Several different sets of symbols are in use, including the forms used in Fig. 17-9.

Often the application of Boolean algebra will simplify the network required for a particular relation. For example, the application of Eq. (17-17) leads to a simpler circuit with fewer components that will perform the function in Eq. (17-21). The details are left as an exercise for the reader.

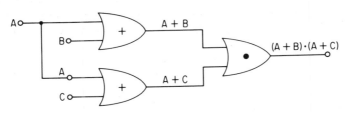

FIGURE 17-9 Symbolic representation of the circuit in Fig. 17-7.

17-5
Examples of transistor
logic circuits: NOT, NOR

The logical NOT can readily be obtained by means of an inverting amplifier as shown in Fig. 17-10. Here a logical input of 0 produces a 1 at the output, and an input of 0 gives an output of 1. If the logical variable A is applied at the input, we get NOT A or $\bar{A}$ at the output. Besides serving to negate the input, the inverting amplifier can also serve to restore the signal to a standard amplitude because it provides gain.

An OR gate followed by an inverter (Fig. 17-11a) is called a NOR (NOT-OR) gate. The output in the figure is $\overline{A + B + C}$.

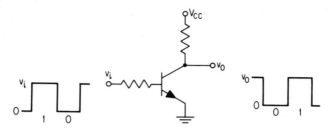

FIGURE 17-10   The saturating amplifier as an inverter, or NOT circuit.

A transistor NOR gate is shown in Fig.17-11b. The circuit performs both the OR and the NOT functions, as the following analysis will demonstrate. If both inputs are zero ($A = B = O$), then both transistors Q_1 and Q_2 are cut off and the output is nearly $+V$. If input A is positive and B still zero, Q_1 is conducting heavily and the output is nearly zero. Under this condition transistor Q_2 receives almost zero collector voltage, so that any input at B has no effect. The circuit is symmetrical, and therefore an input at B, while $A = 0$ will also give zero output. Thus the output represents $\overline{A + B}$.

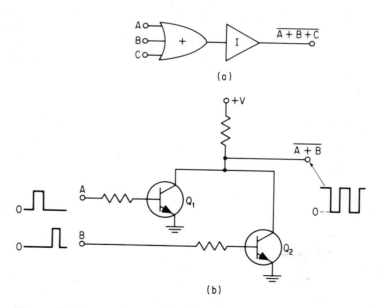

FIGURE 17-11   NOR (NOT-OR) gate: (a) Symbolic combination of OR gate and inverter. (b) *npn* transistor NOR gate.

In practice added circuit refinements may be needed in the NOR gate, such as bias circuits and speed-up capacitors to shunt the input resistors. The discussion of switching speed in Sec. 16-14 applies to the action of a transistor in a NOR gate or in an inverter.

17-6
Binary scalers

In Sec. 16-7 it was shown that *two* trigger pulses applied to a bistable multivibrator, or *binary*, will give *one* output pulse. Thus the circuit can be regarded as a *scale-of-two* counter. To extend these ideas we analyze the *scale-of-four* circuit shown in schematic form in Fig. 17-12. One possible detailed circuit for each binary is that shown in Fig. 16-16, but here we show only the trigger terminal T, the output terminals at the two collectors, A and $\bar{A}$, and the ground. Output A is called the *direct* output and $\bar{A}$ the *complementary* output. Differentiating networks connect binaries A and B and the output of binary B to the v_{out} terminal.

Negative input pulses will cause binary A to change state alternately, as shown in the wave form of v_A. Input pulse 2 causes the potential of terminal A to drop back to zero. This change sends a negative pulse to terminal T of binary B, thereby causing a change of state in B. Pulse 3 causes binary A to change state but does not affect B. Pulse 4 again causes binaries A and B to change state, and both binaries return to their original condition. Since we regard a *negative* pulse at v_{out} as an output, we see that there is *one* output pulse for every *four* input pulses. Thus the input pulse rate is scaled down by a factor of one-fourth.

Table 17-7 Sequence for Scale-of-Four Counter in Truth Table Form

After pulse	Before pulse	Binary B	Binary A	Count
0	1	0	0	0
1	2	0	1	1
2	3	1	0	2
3	4	1	1	3
4	5	0	0	

The sequence of states can be given in truth table form as in Table 17-7. A positive voltage at terminal A or B is regarded as the logical 1 and absence of voltage the logical 0. Then the states in binaries A and B represent the count in the binary number system, in the sequence 00, 01, 10, 11, and repeat. Here

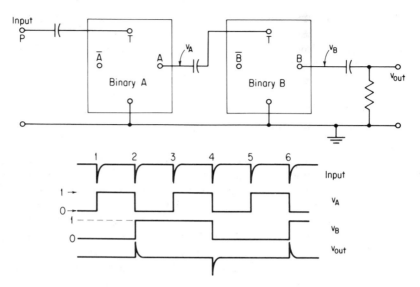

FIGURE 17-12   Two binaries in cascade produce a *scale-of-four* circuit.

the state of binary *A* represents the *least significant digit* and is placed on the right in the truth table. Then the states listed under the columns *BA* in the table give the binary count.

The scale-of-four circuit can be converted into an elementary counter by adding indicators (tungsten or neon lamps) to show the state of each binary and connecting an electromechanical register through an amplifier to v_{out} to total the negative output pulses. The total count would be four times the mechanical register reading plus the count stored in the two binaries. The counting rate would be limited by the maximum response rate of the register.

Each binary may be regarded as a memory device. For example, if the input pulses stop after pulse 3, the binaries will remain in the states $A = 1$ and $B = 1$, thereby illustrating a long-time memory capability.

There is also a short-time memory function within each binary during triggering (Sec. 16-7.). Consider the action during the collector triggering in the circuit of Fig. 16-17, which uses steering diodes. The two speed-up capacitors carry different charges just before the trigger pulse arrives, and they maintain this difference momentarily during the trigger. Thus the binary remembers its former state momentarily. This helps insure that the transition will go in the right direction.

In the *scale-of-sixteen* counter in Fig. 17-13 the same principles are applied as in the scale-of-four circuit, but the symbols for the binaries have been modified. The ground connection and the coupling capacitors are not shown. The symbols *L* have been added to indicate a readout device, such as a lamp.

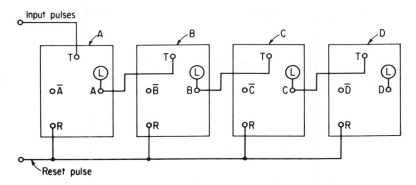

FIGURE 17-13 Scale-of-sixteen counter. T = trigger, R = reset, and L = readout.

These are needed only on the direct outputs A, B, C, and D, since the state of a complementary output can be deduced from the state of the direct output. A terminal labeled R has been added, which is used to *reset* the binary, i.e., to return the direct output terminal to the 0 state. This *resetting* operation is needed to obliterate the count remaining from a previous counting operation. A suitable pulse on the reset line will cause all the binaries that happen to be in the 1 state to return to the 0 state. The reset pulse is coupled to the binary by a network similar to that for the trigger, except that the pulse is conducted only to one side of the binary.

Table 17-8 Sequence for Scale-of-Sixteen Counter

After pulse	Before pulse	Binary D	Binary C	Binary B	Binary A	Decimal count
0	1	0	0	0	0	0
1	2	0	0	0	1	1
2	3	0	0	1	0	2
3	4	0	0	1	1	3
4	5	0	1	0	0	4
5	6	0	1	0	1	5
6	7	0	1	1	0	6
7	8	0	1	1	1	7
8	9	1	0	0	0	8
9	10	1	0	0	1	9
10	11	1	0	1	0	10
11	12	1	0	1	1	11
12	13	1	1	0	0	12
13	14	1	1	0	1	13
14	15	1	1	1	0	14
15	16	1	1	1	1	15
16	17	0	0	0	0	16

Table 17-9

| Binary | States of binaries for each decimal digit below | | | | | | | | | |
	0	1	2	3	4	5	6	7	8	9
8	0	0	0	0	0	0	0	0	1	1
4	0	0	0	0	1	1	1	1	0	0
2	0	0	1	1	0	0	1	1	0	0
1	0	1	0	1	0	1	0	1	0	1

The scale-of-sixteen circuit functions in much the same way as the scale-of-four circuit. As shown in Table 17-8, the counter goes to a count of fifteen and then repeats. Binary D gives a negative output pulse on every sixteenth count. As arranged in Table 17-8 with the state of binary A listed at the right and the others in order to the left, the tabular value of the states equals the binary number for the count. For example, after pulse number 11, the binaries indicate the number 1011, which equals the decimal number 11.

17-7
Diode matrix for decimal count readout

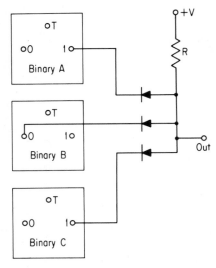

FIGURE 17-14 Sensing circuit for the count of five in a scale-of-eight counter.

The counters in the foregoing article give an output indication in the binary number system. For ease of interpretation a readout that gives each count by a single decimal readout indicator is preferable. A so-called *diode matrix* network will perform the desired decoding from the binary to a decimal count.

To illustrate the principle involved we consider a scale-of-eight counter comprising three binaries. Suppose that we want to sense the presence of the count of 5, which exists in the counter as binary number 101. The diode network shown in Fig. 17-14 will give an output only for a counter state of 101. We see that the sensing network is an AND circuit which responds to the output $A \cdot \bar{B} \cdot C$, that is, to the output 101.

To obtain a single output for each of the eight states of the scale-of-eight counter it is necessary to provide an AND circuit for each state. The resulting network is shown in Fig. 17-15. Each vertical wire with the associated diodes and resistor forms an AND circuit with the output terminal at the bottom of the diagram. For example, the AND circuit that senses the count of 5 corresponds to that in Fig. 17-14. Thus each count can be indicated by a readout device at a single terminal.

Suppose that another binary is added in Fig. 17-15 to give a scale-of-sixteen counter. A diode matrix for this counter can be developed from the matrix in Fig. 17-15 by adding two horizontal wires and eight vertical wires for the 16 (or 2^4) outputs. In general, for n binaries there would need to be 2^n vertical wires and 2^n outputs. In order to count and display large numbers in decimal form by this means, the system becomes unduly complex, so that other techniques are used.

One of these techniques involves counting directly in a decimal fashion, as will be described in the following article. Another is to use a so-called *binary-coded decimal* technique. The numerical information may be said to exist in a decimal form, but each separate decimal digit is expressed in a code of

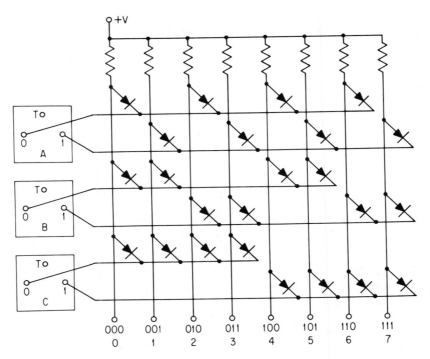

FIGURE 17-15 Diode matrix for decimal count readout.

four binary digits. In the most common code, called the 1-2-4-8 (or 8-4-2-1) code, there are four binaries whose outputs are assigned values of 8 or 0, 4 or 0, 2 or 0, and 1 or 0, Combinations of the binary outputs are weighted accordingly, for example, the digit 6 is obtained from the weights 0 + 4 + 2 + 0, or 6.

The binary-coded notation can be illustrated and compared with the decimal system by means of the hypothetical readout schemes shown in Fig. 17-16. Each numeral represents a lamp that can indicate the presence of that

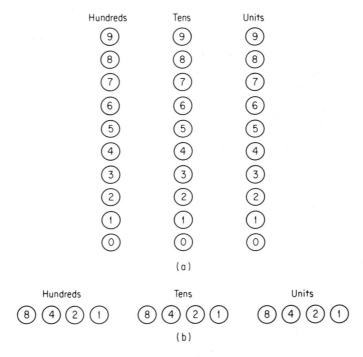

FIGURE 17-16 Comparison of (a) decimal readout and (b) binary-coded decimal readout.

digit. Thus both schemes can indicate decimal numbers from 1 to 999, but the decimal readout scheme requires thirty lamps, whereas the binary-coded decimal scheme requires only twelve lamps. Thus fewer elements are needed to store the number or to transmit it to other parts of the digital system.

The actual final readout is more convenient for the observer if it is converted from the binary-coded to the direct decimal form. This conversion can be accomplished by coupling the four binaries of one group to the outputs 0, 1, 2, ... 9 through a diode matrix. Table 17-9 shows the binary states for each digit, but the development of the matrix is left as an exercise for the reader.

17-8
Decimal counter

A number of decimal counting schemes have been developed. One scheme is based on the fact that the scale-of-sixteen counter circuit can be made to jump forward in its sequence of states so that it will return to the original state at the tenth input pulse. One method of causing this sequence is to add a feedback connection that conducts pulses from one output of binary D to the inputs of B and C, as shown in Fig. 17-17a. In this network the first seven input

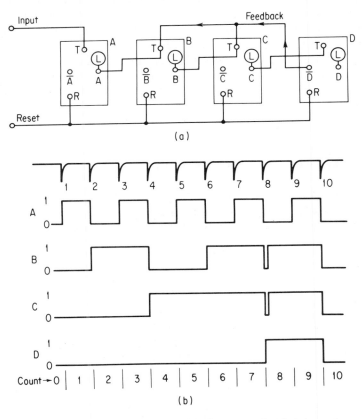

FIGURE 17-17   Decade counter based on a scale-of-sixteen circuit plus feedback. (a) Connection diagram and (b) wave forms.

pulses produce the same state changes as in the basic scale-of-sixteen circuit. The eighth pulse turns B and C OFF and D ON, as before, but the voltage change at $\bar{D}$ produces a negative feedback pulse that goes to B and C. The feedback pulse, which is slightly delayed in time after pulse eight, turns binaries B and C back ON. Then the binaries $DCBA$ are in the states 1110, that is to say, at a binary count that was equal to fourteen in the basic counter.

Then two more input pulses, numbers 9 and 10, return the circuit to the original state.

While the circuit is now a scale-of-ten circuit, the readout is in a modified binary system. To obtain a decimal readout, the binary outputs have to be decoded to give a decimal indication. Circuits have been devised to perform this function and to drive special indicator devices that display the numerals 0 to 9. The first commercial counters used neon tube indicators placed in a vertical column. Nowadays indicators are used that can show the numerals in one location, so that a horizontal row of indicators can present the number in the usual configuration. This is called an *in-line* readout. In one type of indicator the numerals are observed as a cathode glow discharge on thin wires formed into the numeral shape. In others the numerals are projected, one at a time, onto a translucent screen.

Several decimal counter stages can be connected in cascade, so that the tenth count of the first decade will register as unity in the second decade, and so on. Other features of commercial counters will be mentioned in Sec. 17-10.

17-9
Special counting devices

Several devices that can count directly in the decimal system in a manner analogous to the mechanical register are available. These obviate the necessity of a complex decoding network to convert binary counter states into a decimal readout.

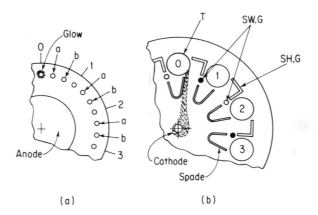

(a)   (b)

FIGURE 17-18   (a) Glow discharge transfer counter tube. (b) High-vacuum beam switching tube (Burroughs Corp.) $T =$ target output electrode and magnet. $SW.G$ = switching grids. $SH.G$ = shield grid.

In one of these devices (Fig. 17-18a) a glow discharge in a gas-filled tube is caused to take successive positions on a circular row of metal pins. The position of the negative glow on the pins indicates the count in the tube, so the tube acts as its own readout device. The tube behavior can be briefly described as follows. Assume that the glow is on pin 0 as shown in Fig. 17-18a, with the glow discharge circuit completed through the central anode. The glow can be made to transfer from pin 0 to pin 1 in a stepwise fashion via the guide pins *a* and *b*. A negative pulse is put on all electrodes labeled *a* to induce the glow to jump from 0 to *a*. A slightly delayed negative pulse on *b* makes the glow transfer from *a* to *b*. When the pulse on *b* dies out, the glow transfers to pin 1, since this pin has been held at a negative potential. All the *a* electrodes are connected together, and likewise all the *b* electrodes and all the numbered electrodes. Thus only two control connections, those to the two sets of guide pins, are needed to control the count.

A repetition of the sequence of pulses will move the glow from pin 1 to pin 2, and so on around the tube. When the glow moves from 9 to 0, an output pulse can be generated to control the next tube to indicate 1 in the next decade.

Pulse lengths of about 150 μsec are needed to effect a count, so the counting rate is limited to about 5000 per second, though somewhat higher rates are obtainable. The relatively low cost of the counters that use these tubes make them attractive for low-speed counting.

A much higher counting rate is achieved in the high-vacuum *beam-switching* tube shown in Fig. 17-18b. A centrally located hot cathode emits electrons radially into a space that has combined electric and magnetic fields. The electric field is provided by the potentials on the outer electrodes, which comprise a *spade* electrode, a *switching* grid, a *shield* grid, and a *target* electrode for each digit. The magnetic field is directed axially, or into the page, and is provided by rod magnets that double as the target electrodes.

The rather complex electron paths in the crossed electric and magnetic fields account for the characteristics of the tube. First suppose that all the outer electrodes are connected to act as an anode and the voltage on this anode is varied. At low voltages, assuming a constant magnetic field, the electrons emerge from the cathode at nearly zero velocity and start to accelerate radially outward in the direction of the electric field. But the magnetic field causes a sideways force so the electron paths form a curve in the plane of the page. With the low anode voltage the paths curve so much that the electron starts back toward the cathode. In this part of its path the electron velocity decreases and the electron returns near to the cathode with nearly zero velocity. This process repeats, so a whole swarm of electrons is moving about in curved paths without reaching any of the outer electrodes. If the accelerating voltage is increased, these paths enlarge, and eventually the spade electrodes will collect an electron current. In the normal operation of the tube the main electric field is low enough so that the electrons remain in paths near the cathode.

An electron beam is formed if one of the spade electrodes is lowered to near zero potential. With this low spade potential there is a potential trough that extends toward this spade. In the crossed electric and magnetic fields the electrons tend to spiral along the electric field lines, rather than to travel at right angles. As a result of the field line pattern the electrons form a beam somewhat as shown in Fig. 17-18b.

In operation each spade electrode is connected to a positive source through a resistor. When the beam hits a particular spade, the spade current is such as to reduce the spade potential to near zero and thereby *lock* the beam in this position. The beam geometry is such that the target receives a current larger than the spade current. The target is utilized as the output electrode, for example, the change of target potential can actuate a glow-type readout tube.

Beam switching is effected by putting pulses on the switching grids. These are connected in two groups of five that are alternated and are shown as open circles and filled circles in Fig. 17-18b. A negative pulse on a grid near the beam distorts the potential pattern sufficiently to cause some electrons to impinge on the next spade, such as the spade adjacent to target 1 in the figure. This rising spade current lowers the spade potential and the prior spade potential rises. As a result the beam switches very rapidly to the next position. The next grid is at a positive bias so the beam will remain locked until the second group of grids receives a negative pulse.

When the tube is applied as a decade counter the two sets of grids are driven by a bistable *MV*, and a readout device is connected to the targets. In effect the tube acts as a scale-of-five circuit driven by a scale-of-two binary but provides a full decade at the outputs. A counting rate of about 1 MHz is feasible.

17-10
Pulse rate meter (diode pump)

A simple and inexpensive method for measuring pulse repetition rate is the so-called *diode pump* circuit. This is used in some portable radiation monitors and tachometers and has other applications.

Basically, each pulse is made to charge a capacitor with a standardized charge Q, and then the capacitor is discharged through a dc microammeter. If the pulse period is T seconds, the average discharge current I will be

$$I = \frac{Q}{T} \qquad (17\text{-}22)$$

Thus I is a measure of the pulse repetition rate n, since $n = 1/T$.

Actually, two capacitors are used in the diode pump circuit (Fig. 17-19). The charge is temporarily stored in C_1, is delivered to C_2, and finally passes

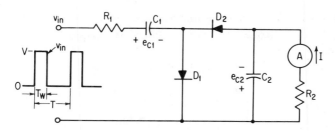

FIGURE 17-19   Circuit of pulse rate meter, or diode pump.

through the meter as current I. Proper circuit operation depends on the time constants $\tau_1 = R_1 C_1$ and $\tau_2 = R_2 C_2$; on the ratio of C_2 to C_1 and on the relation of τ_1 to the pulse width T_w and of τ_2 to the pulse period T.

Let us assume that C_1 and C_2 are initially discharged and then study the effect of starting an input pulse train. The input pulses are shaped to maintain a constant height of V volts. The first pulse will charge C_1 via the path R_1, C_1, and diode D_1. If the diode is ideal and if $\tau_1 \ll T_w$, capacitor C_1 will charge to the voltage V in a time less than T_w. The left-hand plate of C_1 will be positive. When the input pulse drops to zero, the charge on C_1 finds a discharge path around the loop comprising R_1, the source, C_2 and the diode D_2. Thus C_2 becomes charged, and the lower plate is positive.

Capacitor C_2 is chosen much larger than C_1. Suppose that $C_2 = 200C_1$. Then, if the effect of R_2 (and of C_2) is disregarded, we can say that the time constant of the discharging transient is approximately τ_1. Furthermore, the charge originally in C_1 is nearly all transferred to C_2, since voltage e_{c1} drops rapidly to about one two-hundredth of V. As an approximation we take the change in e_{c1} to be V. Then the increment in e_{c2}, designated Δe_{c2}, is given by

$$\Delta e_{c2} \cong \frac{C_1}{C_2} V \qquad (17\text{-}23)$$

Thus Δe_{c2} is small compared with V.

As C_2 becomes charged, voltage e_{c2} builds up and the current I starts, thereby tending to discharge C_2. The time constant $R_2 C_2$ is adjusted to be two or three times the pulse period T. Thus e_{c2} and I will partially decay from their initial values before the next pulse appears.

The second pulse will build up e_{c2} through the same mechanism by an increment nearly as large as the first. As a result I increases also. After several pulses an equilibrium is reached, the increment in e_{c2} due to the charge from C_1 being just equal to the decay in e_{c2} due to the discharge current I. The action of the diodes is much like that of the check valves in a water pump.

With the parameters chosen as outlined, the average level of e_{c2} will be at most only a few per cent of V, and Δe_{c2} can be calculated by Eq. (17-23) with little error. To calculate the average current, we observe that the charge Q delivered to ammeter A in time T is $C_2\Delta e_{c2}$. Using Eqs. (17-22), and (17-23), we write

$$I = \frac{Q}{T} \simeq \frac{C_2\Delta e_{c2}}{T} = \frac{C_2 C_1 V}{TC_2} = nC_1 V \qquad (17\text{-}24)$$

Thus I is a measure of the pulse rate n, if V is constant. Therefore the pulses must have a uniform height for accurate results.

A slight extension of the analysis will show that Eq. (17-24) gives the *average* pulse rate in case the input pulses are random in time.

17-11
Counters and their application

Counters are available commercially in a wide range of prices and capabilities, from the low-cost four- or five-digit cathode-glow-tube counter to the high-speed, solid-state instrument with an 8-digit display. The more sophisticated instruments can (1) count random events, (2) count events per unit time, and can measure (3) frequency, (4) frequency ratio, (5) phase angle, (6) period, and (7) time interval. By using an analog to frequency transducer ahead of the counter, one can measure most nonelectrical quantities such as force, strain, pressure, rotational speed, and temperature.

a. Frequency measurement

A simplified diagram of an instrument with its controls switched for the frequency measurement function is shown in Fig. 17-20. The wave to be measured is first sent through signal shaping circuits, for example, a chain consisting of an amplifier, Schmitt trigger, differentiator, and clipper. The resulting pulses go to an AND gate which is opened for a precisely measured

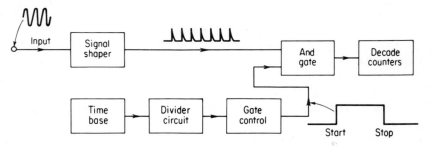

FIGURE 17-20   Counter arranged for frequency test.

time, often 0.1, 1.0, or 10 sec. The figure shows a typical timing control. The *time base* oscillator is the critical element here, and a precise crystal-controlled oscillator operating at 100 kHz, or 1 MHz, is used in the better counters. This frequency is divided down by frequency dividers and applied to the gate control circuit to give the *start-stop* signal to the AND gate.

The accuracy of the frequency measurement depends on the accuracy with which the time interval is known, which depends on the time base, and on an inherent ± 1 count ambiguity in the count. This arises because the period of the unknown frequency is unrelated to the test time interval. As a result, the last pulse to be counted may just be included in the count, or it may just be too late to be counted. For the lower frequencies this causes the major error. We consider three numerical examples to illustrate the accuracy of frequency measurements. For this purpose we assume that the time base (and gate time interval) is known to an accuracy of 2 parts per 10^6

Example 1: Test frequency $\cong 10^7$. Time base $= 0.1$ sec. Then the displayed count $\cong 10^6$. The accuracy then equals $\pm 2 \pm 1$, or ± 3, parts per 10^6

Example 2: Test frequency $\cong 10^7$, but time base $= 1.0$ sec. Then the displayed count $\cong 10^7$. The accuracy now equals $\pm 20 \pm 1$, or ± 21, parts per 10^7, or ± 2.1 parts per 10^6.

Example 3: Test frequency $\cong 10^2$. Time base $= 10$ s. Then the displayed count $\cong 10^3$. The accuracy then equals $\pm 0.002 \pm 1$, or ± 1.002 parts per 10^3. This example shows the importance of the ± 1 count ambiguity.

b. *Period measurement*

With low frequencies an improvement in accuracy is attained by the measurement of period instead of frequency. Figure 17-21 shows a block

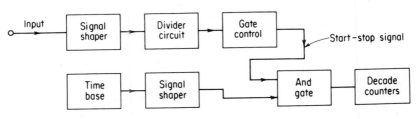

FIGURE 17-21   Counter arranged for average period measurement.

diagram for this test. For the measurement of a *single* period the divider circuit shown in the input chain is omitted. Thus the signal shaper and gate control provide a pair of start-stop signals exactly at successive positive-going zero points on the wave. Thus the counter counts the cycles of the time base frequency in one period of the unknown. Suppose that the unknown frequency is near 100 Hz, so its period is 0.01 sec. Assume also that the time base is at 1 MHz. Then the count in 0.01 sec will be near 10,000. The accuracy will be $\pm 0.02 \pm 1$, or ± 1.02 parts per 10^4, using the same assumption as before. This techniques gives a 10-fold improvement in the accuracy in this particular example.

c. Average period measurement

By using a frequency divider in the input chain (Fig. 17-21), the count for a selected number of periods may be obtained, and the average period may be calculated.

d. Time interval measurement

An arrangement similar to that in Fig. 17-21 can be used for time interval measurement. The first input pulse opens the gate and the second closes it, so the count measures the elapsed time. In some counters two separate input circuits are provided for the start and stop triggers so that trigger slopes and levels can be adjusted independently.

e. Errors due to noise

Care must be taken in frequency measurements that the noise voltage is low enough relative to the signal that false counts do not occur.

In period and time interval tests the noise on the signal introduces an additional error. Here the exact times of opening and closing the gate depend on the effect of the noise on the slope and level of the wave at the trigger points. This error is negligible with fast rise pulses.

f. Preset counters

In random counting it is sometimes desirable to have an output signal after a predetermined count has been reached. One example is in counting small parts coming off from a production line to indicate a lot for a package. Presetting requires that the preset number be stored in the counter and that a circuit be provided to respond when the count reaches the stored number. The output signal can operate a relay or sound an alarm.

g. Nuclear scalers

These are specialized counters whose input signal comes from a radiation transducer (Sec. 18-9). Often the input circuits include special features, such as a pulse height discriminator or a coincidence gate. The separation of the short, fast-rise pulses from the background noise may be a problem. Scaling and timing circuits are incorporated so that pulse-per-unit-time data can be displayed at the output.

h. Electrical output

In addition to the visual readout display there may be an electrical output intended to operate a digital data printer. The output is usually a binary-coded decimal voltage signal using the code 1-2-2-4 or 1-2-4-8, but may consist of a separate output for each digit of each counter decade.

REFERENCES

17-1   Davis Bartholomew, *Electrical Measurements and Instrumentation*, Allyn and Bacon, Inc., Boston, 1963, Chaps. 13, 14, 15.

17-2   E. J. Bukstein, *Digital Counters and Computers*, Holt, Rinehart and Winston, Inc., New York, 1960.

17-3   John M. Doyle, *Pulse Fundamentals*, Prentice-Hall, Inc., Englewood Cliffs, N. J., 1963, Chap. 18.

17-4   S. S. Hakim and R. Barrett, *Transistor Circuits in Electronics*, Hayden Publishing Company, New York, 1964, Chaps. 7, 8.

17-5   G. E. Hoerlies and M. E. Heilweil, *Introduction to Boolean Algebra and Logic Design*, McGraw-Hill Book Company, New York, 1964.

17-6   R. Littauer, *Pulse Electronics*, McGraw-Hill Book Company, New York, 1965, Chaps, 9, 17, 18.

17-7   Jacob Millman and H. Taub, *Pulse, Digital, and Switching Waveforms*, McGraw-Hill Book Company, New York, 1965, Chaps. 9,18.

17-8   Harold E. Soisson, *Electronic Measuring Instruments*, McGraw-Hill Book Company, New York, 1961, Chap. 11.

17-9   William A. Stanton, *Pulse Technology*, John Wiley & Sons, Inc., New York, 1964, Chaps. V, VI, VII.

17-10   *Transistor Manual*, 7th ed., General Electric Company, Syracuse, N.Y., 1964, Chaps 5, 7.

17-11   Technical Brochure BX535B: *Beam-X Applications Oriented Switch*, Burroughs Corp., Plainfield, N.J.

EXERCISES

17-1 Illustrate the two sides of expression (17-16) by means of switching circuits.

17-2 In switching circuits the negation of a particular input, say A, is accomplished by a switch or relay contact which opens (to represent $\bar{A}$) when switch A is closed. Devise a switching symbol to represent $\bar{A}$. Then devise switching circuits to represent the two sides of the logical relation: $A + B \cdot (\bar{A} + C) = A + B \cdot \bar{A} + B \cdot C$.

17-3 Use relation (17-17) to simplify (17-21). Then devise a diode logic circuit to perform the resulting logical operation and compare with Fig. 17-8. Use the same logic voltage levels as in Fig. 17-8. Specify the resistances used.

17-4 Assuming that the diodes are ideal, find the output voltages in Fig. 17-22 for each of the conditions: (a) $A = B = C = 0$ V, (b) $A = B = 0$ V, $C = 6$ V, and (c) $A = B = 6$ V, $C = 0$ V. (d) What is the Boolean expression for the output?

17-5 Assuming that the diodes are ideal, find the output voltages in Fig. 17-23 for the conditions: (a) $A = B = C = 0$ V, (b) $A = 6$ V, $B = C = 0$ V, and (c) $A = B = 6$ V, $C = 0$ V. (d) What is the Boolean expression for the output?

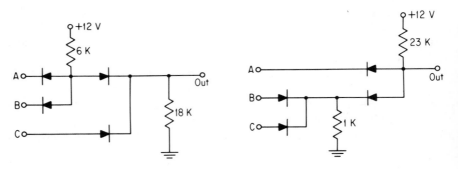

FIGURE 17-22   FIGURE 17-23

17-6 Devise an elementary diode and transistor logic circuit whose output will represent $\overline{A \cdot B + C \cdot D}$.

17-7 Consider a binary-coded-decimal output scheme in which four binaries carry the weights 8, 4, 2, and 1. Develop a diode matrix to connect between the four binaries and the readout lamps to indicate the decimal value of the binary states for each value from 0 to 9. *Suggestion*: see Table 17-9.

17-8 The frequency of an oscillator is measured by the following method. A 5.0-MHz standard frequency signal from the National Bureau of Standards station WWV is heterodyned with the output of the oscillator being tested. The intermediate frequency is measured on a counter using a 1-sec gate time (accurate to

2 parts per 10^6) and found to be 30,500 Hz. Additional tests show that the oscillator frequency is less than that of the standard signal. What is the frequency of the oscillator and what is the accuracy of the measured frequency? Assume that the standard frequency is known to ± 1 part in 5×10^7.

17-9 The diode pump circuit in Fig. 17-19 has the input wave shown there. Let $R_1 = 4000 \ \Omega$, $C_1 = 0.001 \ \mu\text{F}$, $R_2 = 800 \ \Omega$, $C_2 = 0.5 \ \mu\text{F}$, $V = 10 \ \text{V}$, $T_w = 20$ μsec, and $T = 200 \ \mu$sec. (a) What is the reading of the ammeter? (b) Sketch the wave form of e_{c2} for the steady state approximately to scale.

17-10 Suppose that both diodes in Fig. 17-19 are reversed but that the original input wave form is retained. Describe and explain the behavior of this modified circuit.

18

Transducers

18-1
Introduction

In a very broad sense a transducer is a device for converting one form of energy into another for the purposes of measurement or of obtaining signal information or developing a signal power output. Examples are the microphone (acoustic to electric), the loudspeaker (electric to acoustic), the thermocouple (thermal to electric), and the pitot-tube flow meter (velocity to pressure). Figure 18-1 shows in block diagram form a system for measuring

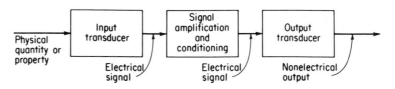

FIGURE 18-1   Measurement system with input and output transducers.

a physical quantity, such as temperature. For this purpose the input transducer might be a thermocouple that generates a few millivolts of signal voltage. After amplification this voltage could control a recorder which traces the time variation of the temperature. The recorder would incorporate

476

an output transducer which converts the electrical signal into a mechanical deflection. Often the system is called on *to control* the physical quantity being measured. For example, the output transducer might be an electrically operated valve in the steam supply that furnishes the heat to the region around the thermocouple, as in a steam-heated oven.

Owing to the vast extent of the field of transducers, we limit our discussion primarily to input, or sensing, transducers which have an electrical output. Only a few examples will be described, primarily to discuss such attributes as sensitivity, output impedance, and frequency range.

18-2
Classification of transducers

One basis for classification is that of the operating principle by which the physical phenomenon affects some electrical parameter in the transducer. These principles include effects on a resistance, reactance, a generated voltage, or a magnetic property. Additional principles used are the piezoelectric, photoelectric, and thermoelectric effects, the variation of an electron beam deflection, and effects of radioactivity.

a. Resistive transducers

Two broad classes of resistive transducers can be distinguished. In one, the resistance of the material used is itself changed, for example, by a magnetic field (Hall effect), or by temperature as in metallic wires and certain semiconductors (thermistors). In the second class the resistance is changed by a mechanical means such as the sliding of the arm of a potentiometer or the stretching of the wires of a strain gage.

b. Reactive transducers

A capacitive or inductive reactance change can be produced by any phenomenon which can change the spacing of two elements of a capacitor or the air gap of an inductor. The principles of these transducers are suggested in Fig. 18-2. In Fig. 18-2a the displacement x of the right-hand plate of a parallel-plate capacitor changes the capacitance. Alternatively, one plate may consist of a diaphragm which deflects under pressure and changes the capacitance. Figure 18-2b indicates a method of sensing the level of a dielectric liquid by means of the capacitance change. An inductive transducer (Fig. 18-2c) results if the air gap of an electromagnet is caused to change with a deflection to be measured and thereby changes its inductance and

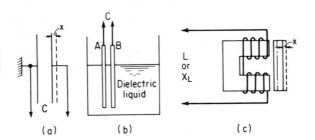

FIGURE 18-2   Reactive transducers (a) capacitive, for displacement x, (b) capacitive, for liquid level, and (c) inductive.

reactance. Each of these transducers has limitations as well as advantages. The capacitive transducers, for example, are sensitive to the capacitance of the lead wires from the transducer to the associated electronic circuits and so must be calibrated with the leads fixed in place. The simple inductive transducer suffers from a nonlinear relation between displacement and reactance change but readily provides good sensitivity.

c. Self-generating transducers

The small permanent-magnet dc tachometer generator used in servo applications is an example of this class. The ac tachometer generator is similar but generates an alternating voltage. In a piezoelectric transducer a mechanical force applied to a crystal develops a charge on electrodes on the crystal with an attendant output voltage.

A second basis for classification of transducers is the kind of phenomenon under observation. Some of the more important class headings are listed in Table 18-1, Several hundred commercial transducers are listed under the headings of Table 18-1 in an Instrument Society of America publication.†

Table 18-1   Physical Phenomena

Motion (displacement, velocity, acceleration)	Temperature
	Humidity
Dimension	Chemical composition analysis
Pressure	Time and frequency
Force and torque	Electric and magnetic quantities
Flow of materials	Nuclear and penetrating radiation
Sound	Electromagnetic radiation

†Reference 18-5.

A particular transducer may, however, be used to measure more than one aspect of a phenomenon. As an example, consider the relations among displacement, velocity, and acceleration for a linear motion in the direction x

$$a = \frac{dv}{dt} = \frac{d^2x}{dt^2} \tag{18-1}$$

If we have a transducer whose output voltage is proportional to the velocity v, we may use a differentiating circuit on the output to obtain a measure of the acceleration, or an integrating circuit to obtain the displacement.

18-3
Examples of displacement transducers

a. Wire resistance strain gage

When a wire is stretched, its length increases and the section decreases, so its resistance increases. If the strain is kept well within the elastic limit, the wire will have a reproducible strain-resistance relationship. The most common gage consists of a length of fine copper-nickel alloy wire (Fig. 18-3) which is mounted on thin paper with heavier lead wires attached. The gage unit is cemented to the surface of the member to be tested. When suitably cemented in place, the gage resistance will vary linearly with strain in both tension and compression.

A measure of the change in resistance to be expected with deformation is the

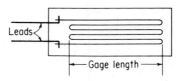

FIGURE 18-3   Resistance wire strain gage.

gage factor, defined as the ratio of the change in resistance per ohm to the change in length per unit length; thus

$$\text{gage factor} = \frac{\dfrac{\Delta R}{R}}{\dfrac{\Delta L}{L}} \tag{18-2}$$

For example, with an alloy gage having a gage factor of 2, the resistance change in a 120-Ω gage for a strain $\Delta L/L = 0.001$ will be $2 \times 0.001 \times 120$, or $0.24\ \Omega$. This strain is attained at about two-thirds of the tensile strength in mild steel.

In the foregoing example the change of resistance was only 0.2 per cent; therefore a rather sensitive and precise circuit is needed for strain-gage measurements. A simple Wheatstone bridge circuit is adequate for the measurement of static strains.

Electronic circuits are employed when dynamic tests are needed, as in tests on machines and airplane structures. Figure 18-4 shows a system for

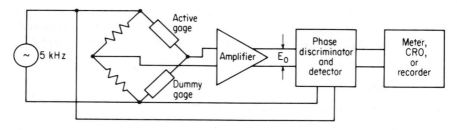

FIGURE 18-4   System for dynamic strain tests.

such tests. A dummy (unstrained) gage is used to provide compensation for strains due to thermal expansion. With a constant oscillator voltage the output of the amplifier E_o will vary linearly with the strain. However, the condition of zero strain, assuming a balanced bridge, gives zero output, and a certain strain in tension produces the same output magnitude as the same strain in compression. However, the phase of E_o reverses as tension changes to compression. Therefore a phase discriminator circuit is interposed between the amplifier and the indicating device. With a varying strain, voltage E_o has the nature of an amplitude modulated wave whose phase reverses as tension changes to compression. The output of the phase discriminator and detector follows the envelope of the modulated wave but changes from positive to negative when the phase changes.

b. Linear variable differential transformer

A transformer having a lightweight movable core (Fig. 18-5a) provides an excellent indicator of position or displacement. The magnetic path is mostly air, so that when the iron core is displaced, the magnetic field is strengthened on one side and weakened on the other. The two symmetrical secondary coils are wound opposing each other. If the core is exactly centered, the output voltage is zero. With the core displaced, one secondary voltage is dominant over the other and the output voltage varies linearly with displacement in a well-designed transducer.

The phase of E_{out} reverses on the two sides of the balanced position. Therefore a phase discriminator is generally used with the differential transformer so that the two directions of displacement may be distinguished.

The characteristics of a typical differential transformer transducer are

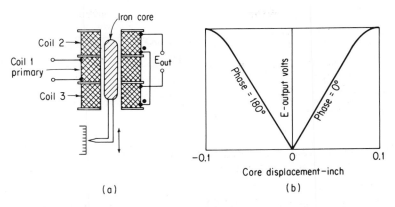

FIGURE 18-5   Linear variable differential transformer.

listed in Table 18-2. The sensitivity listed is on open-circuited output. Other designs cover displacement ranges from 0.005 to 1.0 in.

Table 18-2

Mass of core	14 g
Linear range of displacement	± 0.25 in.
Primary impedance at 2.4 kHz	$60 + j100$ Ω
Secondary impedance at 2.4 kHz	$320 + j830$ Ω
Maximum primary excitation	17 V
Sensitivity, volts per inch per volt of excitation	1.2

c. Piezoelectric transducers

A force applied to any crystal will deform the crystal lattice. In certain crystals, such as quartz, the internal ionic charges are placed in an asymmetric distribution, so the deformation leads to a surface charge. This is the piezoelectric effect.

Consider a slab of crystal cut in a particular direction relative to the crystallographic axes so as to enhance the piezoelectric effect (Fig. 18-6a) and fitted with foil electrodes. Such a slab will generate charges due to an applied force F which produces thickness compression, as shown, and also for other types of stress, such as transverse compression and thickness shear. Experiments show that the charge Q on one electrode is a direct function of the force

$$Q = dF \tag{18-3}$$

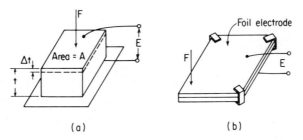

(a)   (b)

FIGURE 18-6   Piezoelectric transducers (a) slab in thickness compression and (b) bimorph twister.

where d is a constant. The developed voltage will be the charge divided by the capacitance $E = Q/C$, but $C = \epsilon A/t$; therefore

$$E = \frac{Qt}{\epsilon A} \qquad (18\text{-}4)$$

Replace Q in (18-4) by its value from Eq. (18-3) and find

$$E = \frac{dt}{\epsilon A} F \qquad (18\text{-}5)$$

For example, in an X-cut crystal of quartz the value of $d/\epsilon \cong 0.05$ V/m per N/m². If we assume $A = 4 \times 10^{-4}$ m², $t = 0.002$ m, and $F = 10$ N, we calculate a voltage E of 2.5 V.

A suddenly applied constant force would theoretically develop the voltage given by Eq. (18-5). We may inquire whether the leakage over the crystal edges and the supporting insulation would dissipate the generated charge and thereby cause the voltage to fall. This is indeed the most likely outcome. An equivalent circuit for the crystal will help us visualize this behavior and will aid us in analyzing the frequency dependence of the terminal voltage for harmonic forces. Such a circuit is shown in Fig. 18-7 together with the typical load impedance of the connecting cable and the input resistance of an amplifier. Order-of-magnitude values which we shall use for discussion are the following: $C_c = 10$ pF, $R_c = 10^{10}$ Ω, $C_L = 200$ pF, and $R_L = 10^6$ Ω.

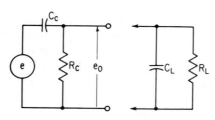

FIGURE 18-7   Equivalent circuit of a piezoelement. e = voltage generated by the deformation, C_c = capacitance of piezoelement, R_c = leakage resistance of element, and R_L, C_L = elements of load impedance.

If the voltage e were a step function due to a suddenly applied force, there would be a transient voltage e_o that would decay approximately according to the time constant $C_c R_L$, or $10 \times 10^{-12} \times 10^6$, or 10^{-5} s. With the load removed the time constant would be $C_c R_c$ or 0.1 s.

A harmonic voltage e will result from a force which varies harmonically about a constant value. At medium and high frequencies the reactances of C_c and C_L dominate the circuit. Then these reactances act as a voltage-divider, and the output voltage would bear the ratio $C_c/(C_L + C_c)$ (or in the example $1/21$) in relation to the generated voltage. At low frequencies the voltage e_o depends mainly on the reactance of C_c and the impedance of R_L and C_L in parallel. The low-frequency response can be improved by increasing C_c or R_L.

Several more complex types of piezoelements are in use. In one of these (Fig. 18-6b) two slabs are cemented together with their expanding diagonals at right angles. If voltage is applied, the resulting electrostriction produces a twisting effect, so this is called a *twister*. If clamped at three corners and loaded at the fourth, it is useful as a piezoelement.

Other piezoelectric crystals include Rochelle salt, ammonium dihydrogen phosphate, and the barium titanate ceramics. Some of these are subject to temperature and humidity limitations and may vary greatly in sensitivity.†

18-4
Measurement of velocity, acceleration, pressure

Linear velocities involving large displacements are usually not measured directly. A commonly used scheme is to measure the elapsed time for the object to travel a known distance. For example, the object can interrupt two light beams spaced a measured distance apart. Interrupting the first beam can start an electronic counter (timer), and interrupting the second can shut the counter off.

Rotational velocities are more readily measured. Small dc or ac permanent-magnet tachometer generators are convenient for this purpose. Another method is shown in Fig. 18-8. A many-toothed steel gear is placed on the rotating shaft. An induction pickup develops an induced voltage that operates a counter. By choosing the number of teeth and the gate time properly, the rpm or rps can be indicated directly on the counter.

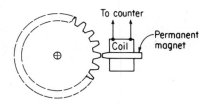

FIGURE 18-8 Measurement of angular speed.

A calibrated stroboscope will also measure rotational velocities. This

†For details, see Reference 18-2, pp. 74 ff.

device generates short-duration, high-intensity repetitive light flashes. The repetition rate is controlled by a multivibrator circuit and is indicated on a dial. The rate is adjusted until a mark on the shaft is illuminated once per revolution and appears to stand still. Then the flashing rate equals the revolution rate.

The mass-spring (or seismic) transducer (Fig. 18-9a) is used in measurements on moving vehicles, missiles, and the like where no fixed reference position is available. It consists of a rigid case a, a mass m, a spring k, and a damping means c. The motion of the mass relative to the case is detected by a transducer element, thus giving information on the deflection z. But the desired information is the motion x of the moving platform, such as a vibrating machine part. So we must deduce x from the observation on z.

Two examples of transducer elements for measuring z or dz/dt are shown. In Fig. 18-9b the piezoelectric crystal is assumed to be cemented securely

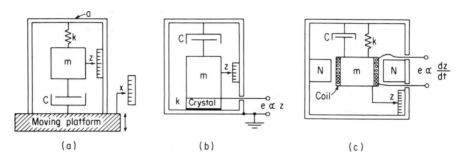

Figure 18-9 Mass-spring transducers. (a) In principle, (b) piezoelectric, and (c) moving coil, permanent magnet type.

to the mass m and to the case. Any vertical deflection then puts the crystal in compression or tension and develops a signal voltage output. (Practical devices may have a spring against the top of mass m). Under suitable conditions the voltage is proportional to the displacement z. In the electrodynamic pickup (Fig. 18-9c), the voltage developed is proportional to dz/dt, i.e., to the velocity of the coil relative to the case.

Usually the analysis of the relation between the variations of z and x is made for an impressed harmonic motion of the platform. A study of these relations as the frequency varies shows that over a certain frequency range the mass-spring transducer measures displacement or velocity and that over a different range it measures acceleration. As shown in the following section the range for a response proportional to *displacement* is at frequencies *high* compared with the natural resonant frequency of the mass-spring system. The useful frequency range for response to *acceleration* is *low* compared with the natural frequency of vibration. The system in Fig. 18-9b may have a natural frequency as high as 50 kHz owing to the high stiffness (spring constant) of the crystal and therefore is often used as an accelerometer.

Wire strain gages are also used as the sensing element. Transducers are made with unbonded wire gages which also act as the springs. These may have a natural frequency between 100 and 2,000 Hz.†

Pressure measuring devices are made by applying strain or displacement transducers to bourdon tubes, diaphragms, or pipes or pressure vessels. Sliding contact potential dividers, resistance strain gages, and piezoelements are among the transducers used in this application.

18-5
Analysis of the response of the mass-spring transducer to harmonic excitation

We have seen that the electrical signal is a function of the displacement z of the mass relative to the transducer case (Fig. 18-9a), but we are interested in the motion of the platform, i. e., in the variation in displacement x relative to a reference fixed in space. We shall assume a harmonic variation of x and find out the response at z.

Mass m has a displacement $x + z$ relative to the fixed reference. Therefore, the inertial force is $m[d^2(x + z)/dt^2]$. We assume a linear spring force on m of $-kz$ and a viscous friction force of $-c(dz/dt)$. By Newton's law

$$m \frac{d^2(x + z)}{dt^2} = -kz - c \frac{dz}{dt} \tag{18-6}$$

or

$$m \frac{d^2z}{dt^2} + c \frac{dz}{dt} + kz = -m \frac{d^2x}{dt^2} \tag{18-7}$$

Next assume

$$x = x_0 \cos \omega t \tag{18-8}$$

We disregard the transient response and assert that the steady-state response will be of the form

$$z = z_0 \cos (\omega t - \theta) \tag{18-9}$$

The solutions for z_0 and θ can be obtained by the same methods as for the analogous electrical circuit problem, with the results

$$\frac{z_0}{x_0} = \frac{\omega^2}{\left[\left(\frac{k}{m} - \omega^2 \right)^2 + \left(\frac{\omega c}{m} \right)^2 \right]^{1/2}} \tag{18-10}$$

†For further information on transducers and their application see Reference 18-1.

and

$$\theta = \tan^{-1} \frac{\dfrac{\omega c}{m}}{\dfrac{k}{m} - \omega^2} \tag{18-11}$$

The system has an *undamped natural radian frequency* ω_n given by

$$\omega_n = \sqrt{\frac{k}{m}} \tag{18-12}$$

Thus, a stiff spring or a light mass gives a high natural frequency. We also wish to express the damping as a fraction of the *critical* damping. Critical damping occurs for $c_c = 2\sqrt{km}$. Next define the normalized damping ζ as

$$\zeta = \frac{c}{c_c} = \frac{c}{2\sqrt{km}} \tag{18-13}$$

Now Eqs. (18-10) and (18-11) can be expressed in normalized form

$$\frac{z_o}{x_o} = \frac{\left(\dfrac{\omega}{\omega_n}\right)^2}{\left\{\left[1 - \left(\dfrac{\omega}{\omega_n}\right)^2\right]^2 + \left(\dfrac{2\zeta\omega}{\omega_n}\right)^2\right\}^{1/2}} \tag{18-14}$$

and

$$\theta = \tan^{-1} \frac{\dfrac{2\zeta\omega}{\omega_n}}{1 - \left(\dfrac{\omega}{\omega_n}\right)^2} \tag{18-15}$$

These relations show how the amplitude ratio and phase angle depend on ω/ω_n and ζ.

Since we are interested in the acceleration, we note that $\ddot{x}_o = d^2 x_o / dt^2 = -x_o\omega^2$ and replace x_o in Eq. (18-14) by its value $-\ddot{x}_o/\omega^2$ and obtain

$$\frac{z_o}{\ddot{x}_o} = -\frac{1}{\omega_n^2} \frac{1}{\left\{\left[1 - \left(\dfrac{\omega}{\omega_n}\right)^2\right]^2 + \left(\dfrac{2\zeta\omega}{\omega_n}\right)^2\right\}^{1/2}} \tag{18-16}$$

This will enable us to analyze the relation of the response z_o to the impressed acceleration $\ddot{x}_o$.

The family of curves in Fig. 18-10 shows how the relative displacement of the mass z_o/x_o varies with the frequency ratio ω/ω_n as given in Eq. (18-14). There is a region, at the higher frequencies and for the lowest damping ratios, where the response z_o is closely equal to x_o. For ζ between 0.6 and 0.7 we can say $z_o \cong x_o$ if $\omega > 3\omega_n$. This, then, is the region for the application of the seismic transducer to measurements of displacement and/or velocity. This instrument is designed to have a low value of ω_n relative to the

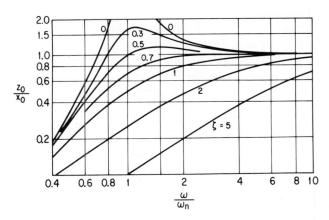

FIGURE 18-10   Amplitude ratio *vs.* frequency ratio, with damping ratio as parameter, for harmonic forcing function.

frequency range of interest, so it will have a weak spring or a high mass.
Thus, a maximum displacement limitation will arise. The device will have a
maximum frequency limitation owing to loss of sensitivity or to resonant
frequencies in the spring.

Can readings of z_0 be used to obtain the *acceleration* of the platform?
The curves of $z_0/\ddot{x}_0$ in Fig. 18-11, based on Eq. (18-16), help to answer this
question. When the forcing frequency is low compared with the natural
frequency, and for certain damping ratios, the amplitude of the response is
directly proportional to the peak acceleration of the platform. For $\zeta = 0.7$,
the frequency range is $\omega < 0.5\,\omega_n$ for a good approximation. An *acceler-*

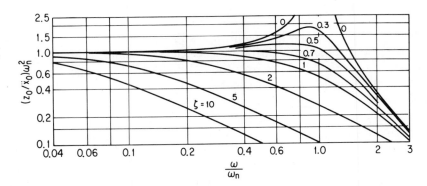

FIGURE 18-11   Ratio of amplitude of mass vibration to acceleration of the platform *vs.* frequency ratio, with damping ratio as
the parameter.

ometer, therefore, must have a high natural frequency and proper damping. However, ω_n cannot be made too high because the response z_o for a constant $\ddot{x}_o$ decreases according to the factor $1/\omega_n^2$, and the sensitivity would suffer.

If the *phase* of the response is of interest, then Eq. (18-15) can be used to obtain the needed information. In the accelerometer range, for example, the angle between the response and the acceleration may range up to about 30°.†

How does the seismic transducer respond to nonharmonic excitation? If the excitation is periodic, then the Fourier analysis can be used to predict the response, in a manner similar to that for the analogous problem in electric circuits. If the excitation is nonperiodic, say a single shock or pulse, it is again possible to deduce some measure of the expected response. The pulse is analysed by the Fourier integral into an infinite series. Then the response of the transducer to each component is computed and the results are summed. Thus, we see that a knowledge of the response to a harmonic excitation is basic to an understanding of the response to other excitations as well.

18-6
Transducers for temperature measurement

a. *Resistance thermometers*

The variation of the resistance of a metallic wire with its temperature provides a convenient and potentially accurate thermometer. The resistance is usually measured with a bridge, but a potentiometer may be used. Over small ranges of temperature the resistance varies according to the relation

$$R_T = R_o[1 + \alpha(T - T_o)] \qquad (18\text{-}17)$$

where R_T is the resistance at temperature T, R_o is the resistance at temperature T_o, and α is the temperature coefficient at temperature T_o. Typical values of α, referred to 25°C, are: for nickel 0.0067; for copper 0.0043, and for platinum 0.00392. Nickel can be used up to 300°C and platinum to 1000°C.

b. *Thermistors*

Thermistors are solid semiconductors, often made in the form of a small bead with attached wire leads. The material is usually a mixture of metallic oxides plus other metallic compounds which is formed into the desired shape, sintered at a high temperature, and sealed within a glass coating. Their tem-

†See Reference 18-1, p. 12-7.

perature coefficient of resistance is negative, and a typical value is -3.5 per cent per °C at room temperature, falling to -1.5 per cent per °C at 200°C. The resistivity variation follows the empirical relation

$$\rho_T = \rho_o \exp\left(\frac{B}{T} - \frac{B}{T_o}\right) \tag{18-18}$$

where ρ_T is the resistivity at T °K, ρ_o that at T_o °K, and B is a constant. The large temperature coefficient (8 or 9 times that of Cu or Pt at room temperature) means that a thermistor is a highly sensitive temperature-sensing device.

A thermistor can be used with a fixed resistor in a potential divider arrangement or as one arm of a Wheatstone bridge. The output voltage is a measure of the temperature. Typical room-temperature resistance values may range from 500 to 100,000 Ω. The measuring current must be kept small enough so that the thermistor is not heated too much above its environment.

Thermistors also find uses in temperature compensation, for example, of transistor bias circuits.

c. Thermocouples

Seebeck discovered that if the two junctions J_1 and J_2 (Fig. 18-12a) between two dissimilar metals A and B are at different temperatures T_1 and T_2, there will be an emf in the circuit and a current will flow. This is an example of the direct conversion of thermal energy into electrical energy. The emf is approximately a linear function of the temperature difference $\Delta T = T_2 - T_1$. A convenient way of measuring ΔT, therefore, should be to break the circuit and install a millivoltmeter V as in Fig. 18-12b. But this means that usually a third metal will be introduced, namely, C in the diagram. However, if junctions J_1 and J_3 are at the same temperature, then the emf will not be affected by the introduction of the third metal C.

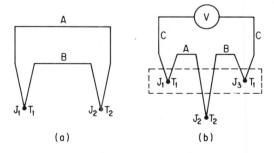

(a)   (b)

FIGURE 18-12   Thermocouple circuits.

The reading of the millivoltmeter will be affected by the resistance of the lead wires, and this resistance may change with temperature. For best accuracy, therefore, a null potentiometer is used to measure the emf. The emfs developed per degree Centigrade near 0°C for some common thermocouples are: for copper-constantan 42.4, for chromel-alumel 41, and for platinum-platinum + 10% rhodium 6.5, all in microvolts per degree. The maximum operating temperatures for these couples, in the same order, are about 300°C, 1200°C, and 1450°C. The emf is not exactly a linear function of temperature difference, so the calibration tables supplied by the thermocouple manufacturer should be used to convert emf to temperature difference.

What type of signal source does a thermocouple circuit present to the amplifier input on an electronic potentiometer? The source resistance will be low, of the order of 10 Ω or less. The emfs are low, for example, about 4.0 mV for 100°C temperature difference and are unidirectional but may fluctuate. The frequency of the fluctuation depends on the application but is usually less than a few cycles per second. To measure 4.0 mV to an accuracy of 1/4 per cent, the uncertainty must be less than 10 μV. Therefore, the noise voltage referred to the amplifier input must be correspondingly low. High-speed indicating and recording electronic potentiometers have been developed to satisfy these requirements.

18-7
Photosensitive transducers

A number of devices are able to detect radiations in the infrared, visible, or ultraviolet wavelength regions.

a. The phototube

A common form of the photoemissive type of device, or *phototube*, consists of a metallic cathode with a sensitive coating, and a wire anode, all enclosed in a glass envelope (Fig. 18-13a). The glass tube may be evacuated, as in the *vacuum phototube*, or filled with a rare gas at a pressure of about 1 or 2 mm Hg, as in the *gas-filled phototube*. Voltage-current curves typical of the two types of phototubes are shown in Fig. 18-13. The radiation is held constant for a particular curve. In the vacuum type the current is constant above 25 V. In the gas-filled type the current rises owing to gaseous ionization. This type has a higher sensitivity owing to the multiplication of the current by the ionization, but the maximum voltage is limited to about 90 V to avoid a glow discharge which may change the sensitive surface.

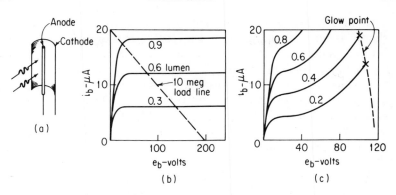

FIGURE 18-13 (a) Phototube structure, (b) vacuum phototube characteristics, and (c) gas-filled phototube characteristics.

b. Semiconductor types

Three photosensitive devices based on semiconductors are shown in principle in Fig. 18-14. Part a shows a *pn*-junction photodiode, which is sensitive to light striking at or very near the junction. The light photons must have enough energy, so that when a photon reacts with an electron in the valence energy band, the electron receives enough energy to move it to the conduction band. Thus, additional carriers, holes and electrons, are released by the radiation.

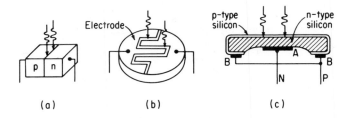

FIGURE 18-14 Semiconductor photodevices: (a) *pn*-junction photodiode, (b) photoconductive cell, and (c) solar cell.

Figure 18-14b shows a photoresistor or photoconductive cell. In this cell a thin strip of a semiconductor, such as cadmium sulfide, is deposited on a ceramic base. Electrode material that makes an ohmic contact with the semiconductor is applied; therefore the device is symmetrical. To obtain a desired value of resistance, a zigzag arrangement of the strip is often used, with the current flow across the short dimension of the strip. When light falls on the semiconductor the supply of carriers is increased and the resistance falls. However, when the light value is changed suddenly, the current change is not instantaneous, but a second or more may elapse before the current attains its final value. This delay is greater for weaker illumination.

Figure 18-14c shows one form of a special *pn*-junction device known as a *solar cell*. The sketch shows a cross-section view of a plate or wafer perhaps 1 by 2 cm in dimensions and 0.5 mm thick. The wafer is a single crystal of *n*-type silicon. An extremely thin (about 0.003 mm) *p*-type layer is formed on the wafer surfaces by the diffusion of boron, and after further processing and fitting with electrodes, the cell is complete. The radiation mostly goes through the thin *p*-type layer and is absorbed in the region of the *pn*-junction, with a resultant increase in the numbers of carriers.

Another type of photocell junction is formed between crystalline selenium and cadmium or cadmium oxide. Selenium cells have been available for many years and are common in photographic exposure meters.

The current-voltage characteristics of the *pn*-junction types can be explained with the aid of Fig. 18-15. In this diagram the voltage and current

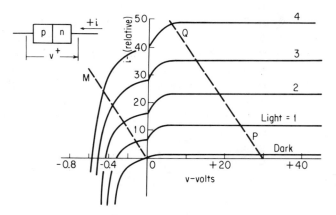

FIGURE 18-15   Characteristics of a photosensitive *pn*-junction. Note polarity conventions and change of scale for negative voltage.

have been taken as positive when the junction is biased in the *reverse* sense. Thus, the small current for positive voltages and a "dark" condition is the reverse saturation current of the junction. When light hits the junction, the current is increased, primarily by the increase in minority carriers near the junction.

In the second quadrant the current remains positive, but the voltage is negative. This combination would obtain if a resistor were placed across the device and thus the junction can act as a photovoltaic cell. Let us give a picture of the mechanism of the generation of the photovoltaic emf. For simplicity, consider the open-circuit condition. The light releases electron-hole pairs which are the primary cause of the terminal emf with the p-side positive. First consider the effect of the extra electrons. Those in the p-type material move by diffusion to the junction and then are swept across the junction by the electric field. Thus, the electron density tends to rise in the n-type material, partly owing to the motions of electrons just described and partly to the electrons liberated in the n-type material. We recall that the numbers of electrons crossing the junction in the two directions must be equal when the terminals are open. Consequently the extra flow toward the right must be balanced by an increased flow to the left. A similar flow and counterflow of holes is also occurring. The extra numbers of both carriers crossing the junction *with the field* must be counterbalanced by extra numbers overcoming the inner field. Therefore, the inner energy barrier must decrease, and this decrease appears as the open-circuit emf. Theory indicates that the photovoltaic emf expressed in volts can only approach the forbidden gap in electron volts as the incident radiation is increased. However, in silicon solar cells the practical limit is about 0.6 V, rather than the gap energy of 1.1 V.

c. *Photomultiplier tube*

A photodevice of great sensitivity is made by utilizing the phenomenon of secondary emission to amplify the photo current. The scheme is shown in Fig. 18-16a. By careful design, the photoelectrons are caused to hit electrode $D1$, called a *dynode*. Here they produce 2 to 8 secondary electrons. These are accelerated to dynode $D2$, where the process is repeated, and after several such stages the electrons are collected at an anode. Voltages of the order of 100 to 200 V are required between consecutive dynodes, so the total

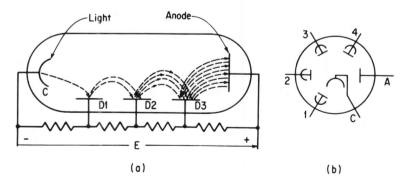

(a)   (b)

FIGURE 18-16   Photomultiplier tube (a) in principle, (b) circuit symbol.

voltage may be from 750 to over 2000 V, depending on the number of stages.

These tubes are available with different spectral sensitivity character-istics, including tubes sensitive in the ultraviolet. Because the secondary emission effect depends on the voltage, the sensitivity depends strongly on the voltage. The current magnification can be very great. Let there be n dynode stages and let the number of secondary electrons per incident elec-tron at each dynode be g; then the total amplification is

$$A = g^n \qquad (18\text{-}19)$$

For example, in a 9-dynode tube that has $g = 4$, the value of A is 4^9, or 2.62×10^5. A 9-stage multiplier (RCA 931A) has a typical current ampli-fication of 10^6 at its maximum rated voltage of 1250 V. This same tube has a luminous sensitivity of 3.3 A/lm (lumen) with an impressed voltage of 750 V.

Photomultiplier tubes are often used in scientific research for detecting weak radiation and in such instruments as spectrophotometers, colorimeters, and X-ray dosage instruments. Limitations of the tube for measuring weak radiation include dark current and noise. For a review of these limitations and for application information the reader is referred to Lion.†

18-8
Technical aspects of
photodevice applications

a. Circuits and symbols

A typical circuit for a photo tube is shown in Fig. 18-17a. The resistor R, which is of the order of megohms, develops a voltage often used to drive an amplifier. The analysis of this circuit is best done by the familiar graphical "load-line" method (see Fig. 18-13b).

In some applications the light is fluctuating, as in interrupted beam relays and in the detection of sound on film. Here the input capacitance of the amplifier may be important. The circuit can be analyzed by considering the phototube as a *current* generator, since terminal voltage variation has little effect on the current.

When a photodiode is used in series with a voltage source, as in Fig. 18-17b, the circuit analysis is the same as for the phototube (see load line PQ in Fig. 18-15).

When the photodiode is used as a photovoltaic cell, a different circuit symbol is used, as in Fig. 18-17d. The circuit response can be found by using a resistance line, such as OM in Fig. 18-15, and finding the intersection with the diode characteristic.

†Reference 18-2, pp. 245 ff.

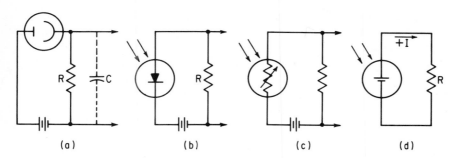

FIGURE 18-17   Circuits and symbols for photosensitive devices.
(a) Emission type phototube, (b) Photodiode (asymmetrical),
(c) photoconductive transducer, (d) photovoltaic cell (barrier
photocell), solar cell.

b. Spectral sensitivity curves

The device spectral sensitivity, that is, the variation of sensitivity with
the wavelength of the radiation, together with the spectral distribution of
the power in the incident radiation, determine the current response in a
particular situation. The sensitivity at or near a particular wavelength can be
measured by selecting a narrow band of wavelengths by means of a spectrom-
eter, shining this radiation on the device, and measuring the power in the
beam and the current response. The ratio of current to power is the sensitivity at that wavelength. However, data are often provided only in terms
of *relative* sensitivity at the different wavelengths.

Representative spectral sensitivity curves are shown in Fig. 18-18. Several

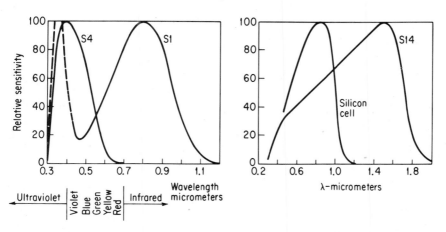

FIGURE 18-18   Representative spectral sensitivity curves.

phototubes have sensitive surfaces that give type $S1$ or $S4$ curves. A surface composed of cesium on oxidized silver gives curve $S1$. Curve $S4$ is obtained with a combination of antimony and an alkali metal. Representative curves are also shown for the silicon cell and for germanium ($S14$ response) pn-junction cells. The ultraviolet sensitivity is dependent on the absorption in the glass bulb, for example, ordinary glass absorbs completely below about 0.3 μm (micrometer).

Figure 18-18 shows that the photubes with $S1$ and $S4$ responses have a definite maximum wavelength beyond which the sensitivity is zero. This long-wave limit is readily explained by the relation between the energy of the incident photon hf and the work function E_w of the surface. The limit occurs when these energies are equal; thus,

$$hf = \frac{hc}{\lambda} = eE_w \tag{18-20}$$

Here h is Planck's constant, c the speed of light, e the electronic charge, and f and λ the frequency and wavelength of the radiation. Thus, a low work function surface is needed to have sensitivity at the longer wavelengths.

The long-wave limit for pn-junction photodiodes depends on the size of the forbidden gap. Thus, a germanium diode (curve $S14$) has a higher long wavelength limit than a silicon cell does. We recall that the forbidden gap for germanium is 0.67 eV, and for silicon 1.1 eV. Thus, a lower energy (longer wavelength) photon can excite an electron across the gap in the germanium device.

c. Light calculations; sources of radiation

One method for predicting the response of a photosensitive device is to have information on its response to a standard source of radiation. The source used for this purpose is a tungsten filament lamp operated at a color temperature of 2870°K, which radiates as shown in Fig. 18-19. The measurements and units are those customary in photometry and illumination studies, and these are based on the sensitivity of the human eye (Fig. 18-19). Though this approach has limited value in scientific work, where a response to a different range of wavelengths may be required, it is applicable where tungsten lamp sources are used. For these calculations we are concerned with:

1. The *luminous flux*, the rate of transmission of light through a given area, symbolized by F, and measured in *lumens*

2. The *illumination* falling on a suface, or flux per unit area, symbolized by E, and measured in *lumens per square foot*, or *footcandles*, and

3. The *intensity* of a source, or flux radiated per unit solid angle, symbolized by I, and measured in *candlepower*.

The illumination can be measured by a photoelectric footcandle-meter. If

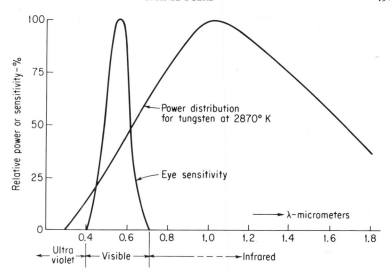

FIGURE 18-19 Power distribution for the tungsten lamp, and response of the human eye.

we measure the illumination falling normally on a surface of A square feet, then we can calculate the light flux

$$F = EA \qquad (18\text{-}21)$$

The intensity of a source in a particular direction is, from the definition,

$$I = \frac{dF}{d\omega} \qquad (18\text{-}22)$$

where $d\omega$ refers to a differential solid angle in steradians. For a point source, which radiates equally in all directions, we have $F = 4\pi I$, since the total solid angle around a point is 4π. Thus, the inverse-square law for illumination on an area placed perpendicularly to the light rays can be obtained as follows:

$$E = \frac{F}{A} = \frac{4\pi I}{4\pi r^2} = \frac{I}{r^2} \qquad (18\text{-}23)$$

where $4\pi r^2$ is the area of a sphere of radius r feet.

Example: A germanium pn-junction cell having an illumination sensitivity of 0.7 μA per footcandle is placed 8 in. from a 32-candlepower concentrated-filament tungsten lamp. What current is expected? The illumination will be, by (18-23), $32/(8/12)^2$ or 72 footcandles, and the current will be 0.7×72, or 50 μA.

Example:　A vacuum phototube has a sensitivity of 50 μA/lm. Its cathode has a projected area of 1.3 by 0.6 in. What is its sensitivity in microamperes per footcandle for uniform illumination? The area is 5.4×10^{-3} ft^2, so 1 lm requires $E = F/A = 1/5.4 \times 10^{-3} = 185$ fc. Therefore, the sensitivity is 50/185, or 0.27 μA/fc.

If desired, the spectral sensitivity curve can be altered to give a response over a narrower range of wavelengths by interposing a glass or gelatin filter between the source and the tube or cell. The response in this situation depends on the spectral characteristics of all three devices—the source, the filter, and the tube or cell. Systems of this type have been used in infrared-ray burglar alarms.

18-9
Transducers for ionizing radiations

Ionizing radiations include α and β particles and γ or X radiations. These cause ionization of gases and solids by several different mechanisms. Other radiations, such as the neutron flux in a nuclear reactor, can produce ionization by secondary processes. A complex array of transducers is available for the detection and measurement of ionizing radiations. The most important classes include *ionization chambers, proportional counters, Geiger-Müller counters, crystal counters,* and *scintillation counters.* We must be content with a brief account of the principles of an ionization chamber and of a Geiger-Müller (G-M) counter.

The individual ionizing particles or photons (γ or X rays) may arrive in the transducer at rates of a few per minute up to thousands per second. In one mode of operating a transducer no attempt is made to count the individual events but rather to obtain an average indication, or a *mean-level* measurement. In the other mode the individual events are resolved, and a system for counting the events is required. Often complex high-speed counting and analyzing instruments are employed.

a. Ionization chamber

This device has a pair of electrodes, shown as parallel plates in Fig. 18-20, between which the radiation passes. A dc source E applies enough voltage to sweep the ions formed by the radiation out of the gap. This is the saturation voltage and corresponds to the region AB on the curve in Fig. 10-1. Although the ionization chamber is used in both the pulse mode and the mean-level mode of operation, we shall discuss only the latter.

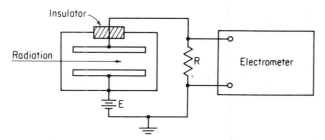

FIGURE 18-20   Ionization chamber.

In Fig. 18-20 the ionization current flows in resistor R and the resulting voltage is detected by an electrometer. The electrometer may be an electrostatic type, e.g., a Lindeman (quartz fiber) electrometer, or an electronic-type instrument. The ionization current may be extremely small, down to 10^{-15} A, therefore R may be as high as 10^{11} Ω. The speed of response of the circuit depends on the combined capacitance of the chamber and of the input to the electrometer C and the resistance R giving the time constant $\tau = CR$. Special techniques must be used when this time constant exceeds a few seconds.

b. Geiger-Müller (G-M) counter

The heart of the G-M counter system is the G-M tube. This is a gas-filled tube, usually consisting of a wire down the axis of a cylinder, as in Fig. 18-21. The tube is operated at a high voltage relative to that used on the ionization chamber, so that self-amplified ionization comes into play. As a result, a single α particle or γ ray can start a chain of events that will produce a relatively large pulse of current through the tube. The pulse may be amplified up to 10^8 times by the gaseous ionization.

This type of action occurs over a range of impressed voltages somewhat below the breakdown voltage. The incident radiation causes a group of primary electrons and ions, just as in the ionization chamber. The primary

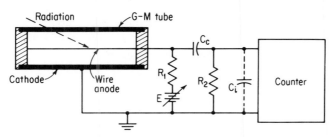

FIGURE 18-21   Geiger-Müller tube and circuit.

electrons are, however, able to start secondary ionizations in the gas leading to an *electron avalanche*, particularly in the strong field near the wire
anode. The few initial avalanches set off secondary avalanches at the surface
of the wire, mainly by the photoelectrons released by the ultraviolet rays
from the primary avalanches. The result is that a surface discharge spreads
rapidly (in the order of 1 μs) along the length of the wire. Thus, the current
pulse rises suddenly, in perhaps 1 μs. This part of the pulse is due mainly to
the motions of the fast-moving electrons, while the ions move more slowly.

Some means is provided in the G-M tube to stop or to *quench* the discharge. One commonly used means is an admixture of a polyatomic gas
like ethyl alcohol to the main gas, which may be argon. With this combination the ionization energy of the argon (15.7 eV) is greater than that of the
alcohol (11.3 eV). Therefore, the argon ions tend to rob electrons from the
alcohol molecules with concomitant emission of low-energy radiation. The
alcohol ions, upon striking the cathode, do not readily release secondary
electrons to keep the discharge going. Rather, the excess energy goes into
dissociating the alcohol molecules. Thus, there is a loss of the alcohol which
limits the life of the tube.

The output pulse requires 100 μs or more to decay while the discharge
is quenched and the heavy ions are swept out of the field. During this time
the tube will not respond to a new incoming ionizing particle. Furthermore,
a recovery time of the same order is needed before full-size pulses are again
produced. These effects limit the counting rate to about 3×10^4 pulses per
second.

The circuit speed of response for the arrangement in Fig. 18-21 depends
on the capacitance C_g of the G-M tube and on the circuit constants shown,
where C_i is the input capacitance to the counter. If we assume C_c to be large,
then the response time constant is $\tau = RC$, where $R = [R_1 \| R_2]$, and
$C = C_g + C_i$. The tube may be regarded as the source of a current pulse
(in parallel with C_g), on the assumption that τ is much larger than the time
required to collect the ions. This assumption is more likely to hold with
ionization chamber and proportional counters than with G-M counters.

Owing to the large current amplification in the G-M tube, the output
pulse is large, say from 1 to 10 V peak value, and the subsequent amplification and counting is simplified. The output pulses may, in practice, be
modified by pulse-shaping circuits or be selected as to amplitude by means
of level discriminator circuits before being counted.

REFERENCES

18-1 C. M. Harris and C. E. Crede, eds., *Shock and Vibration Handbook*, V. 1,
       Basic Theory and Measurements, McGraw-Hill Book Company, New York,
       1961, Chaps. 12–20.

18-2 K. S. Lion, *Instrumentation in Scientific Research: Electrical Input Transducers*, McGraw-Hill Book Company, New York, 1959.

18-3 G. R. Partridge, *Principles of Electronic Instruments*, Prentice-Hall, Inc., Englewood Cliffs, N.J., 1958, Chaps. 13-19.

18-4 W. J. Price, *Nuclear Radiation Detection*, McGraw-Hill Book Company, New York, 1958.

18-5 E. L. Minnar, ed., *ISA Transducer Compendium*, Inst. Soc. of America, Plenum Press, New York, 1963.

18-6 *RCA Tube Handbook HB*-3, Photosensitive Device Section, Radio Corp. of America, Harrison, N.J.

18-7 *RCA Photocells: Solid-state Photosensitive Devices*, Booklet 1CE-261A, Radio Corp. of America, Harrison, N.J., 1963.

EXERCISES

18-1 Suppose that the capacitive transducer in Fig. 18-2a consists of rigid, parallel plates, and that the fringing effect of the field can be neglected. Discuss the question of whether the relation between the capacitance C and the displacement x is linear.

18-2 A wire strain gage cemented on a structural member is connected into a Wheatstone bridge circuit. The gage resistance is 240 Ω, the gage length is 0.5 in., and the gage factor is 2.2. If the gage resistance change caused by tension in the member is 0.22 Ω, what is the strain in the member?

18-3 Suppose that the resistance of the active gage in a strain-gage bridge circuit has been increased from 100 to 100.3 Ω by a certain strain, while the other three arms remain at 100 Ω. Let the source voltage be 6 V and the source impedance be zero. The bridge output goes to an amplifier. (a) What is the input voltage to the amplifier if the amplifier input resistance is so high as to have no effect? (b) Suppose that R_{in} of the amplifier is 1000 Ω. What is the input voltage as a fraction of the value in (a)?

18-4 A linear variable differential transformer, which has the parameters in Table 18-2, is excited at 6 V rms at a frequency of 2.4 kHz. What is the rms transformer output voltage for a constant displacement of 0.01 in. for (a) open-circuited secondary, and (b) with a 1000-Ω input resistance transistor amplifier attached? Discuss any approximations made in the analysis.

18-5 A piezoelement-amplifier combination has the equivalent input circuit in Fig. 18-7. Let $C_c = 10$ pF, $R_c = 10^{10}$ Ω, and $C_L = 800$ pF. Assume that the applied vibration generates 1 V rms at a frequency of 2 Hz. (a) Calculate the rms voltage at the amplifier input if (a) $R_L = 10^6$ Ω and (b) $R_L = 20 \times 10^6$ Ω.

18-6 A seismic transducer has the form shown in Fig. 18-9c. Let the coil mass be 10 g and the spring constant be 10 N/m. (a) What is the undamped natural frequency f_n? (b) What value of damping constant is needed if the normalized damping required is 0.6? (c) When the transducer is calibrated by driving the transducer structure through a harmonic amplitude of 2-mm peak-to-peak (*p-p*) at a frequency of 20 Hz, the measured output voltage is 200 mV *p-p*. Then the transducer is applied to measure a harmonic vibration having a frequency of 8 Hz and the *p-p* output is 120 mV. What is the amplitude of this vibration? Include a correction for the nonideal response of the system. (d) What is the lowest frequency at which this transducer should be used if the correction due to nonideal response is to be ignored and if an amplitude error not to exceed 5 per cent is tolerated?

18-7 Consider a piezoelectric accelerometer constructed as in Fig. 18-9b. The accelerometer mass m exclusive of the mounting is 40 g. (a) What spring constant is required if the undamped natural frequency is to be 5 kHz? (b) With the spring constant as calculated in (a) the damping is adjusted to give a normalized damping factor of 0.5. To how high a frequency can the transducer be used if the normalized ratio of the amplitude of the vibration of mass m with respect to the transducer case to the acceleration of the case is not to exceed 1.05 of the low-frequency value?

18-8 The piezoelectric accelerometer described in Exercise 18-7 has a maximum rating expressed as 200 g's, i.e., 200 times standard gravity. If the vibration in question is harmonic, how large is the maximum allowable applied vibration amplitude at frequencies of (a) 40, (b) 100, (c) 400, and (d) 1000 Hz? Also calculate the peak crystal deflection corresponding to the maximum acceleration at these frequencies.

18-9 Use the *pn* photodiode characteristics in Fig. 18-15 on which to base a discussion of the problem of obtaining the maximum power output from a solar cell for a fixed value of illumination.

18-10 A 9-stage photomultiplier tube has a luminous sensitivity given by the empirical relation $S = 0.25 \, V^{4.2}$, where S is the sensitivity in microamperes per lumen and V is the voltage per stage. (a) What is the anode current for a light flux of 2 μlm when $V = 100$ V per stage? (b) Let the photocathode area of the multiplier tube be 0.3 in.² How far away would a 32-candlepower lamp need to be placed to give the light flux specified in (a) if no condensing lens is interposed? (c) If the sensitivity must be kept within ± 10 per cent of the value at $V = 100$ V, what variation is allowable in V?

18-11 A silicon solar cell has an area of 2 by 2 cm. When this cell is placed 1 ft from a 100-W tungsten lamp, it receives an illumination of 130 footcandles. When the load resistance across the cell is adjusted for maximum power the cell output is 6 mA at 0.4 V. What is the efficiency of power transfer if the lamp is assumed to radiate uniformly in all directions?

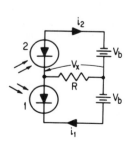

FIGURE 18-22

18-12 Two photodiodes are used in the circuit in Fig. 18-22 to detect the difference between the illumination values on the diodes. Assume that the diodes are operated in the linear region (see Fig. 18-15 in the range $v > +6$ V) so that the diode current can be expressed as $i = I_D + E(I_o + gv)$, where I_D is the dark current, E is the illumination, and I_o and g are constants. Find an analytical expression for v_x in terms of the two illuminations on the two photodiodes E_1 and E_2 and on the circuit and diode parameters when (a) R is infinite and (b) R is considered. Assume that I_D is negligible and that the diodes are identical. (c) What is the value of V_x if $E_1 = 101$, $E_2 = 99$ fc, $V_b = 40$ V, $R \to \infty$, $I_o = 1.0\ \mu A/fc$ and $g = 0.002\ \mu A/V \times$ ft cd (d) Repeat (c) if R is 0.1 MΩ.

19

Electronic Instruments

19-1
Introduction

Modern technology and science have made increasing demands for instruments that will measure and record data accurately and rapidly. Electronic instruments and data processing systems have played a large part in satisfying these demands.

In the foregoing chapters many circuits have been discussed that form the basis of laboratory instruments or portions of an instrument system. Examples are the *RC* oscillator, the counting and timing circuits, and the various transducers. In the present chapter electronic voltmeters, the cathode-ray oscilloscope, and a few examples of instruments that illustrate general principles are discussed.

19-2
Conventional test instruments

A short discussion of instrument terminology and of conventional indicating instruments will give a basis for comparison with the electronic types.

a. Definitions of some technical terms

The *accuracy* of an instrument is usually defined in terms of its *error*. At a particular indication I, the *error* E is defined to be

504

$$E = I - T \tag{19-1}$$

where T is the true value of the quantity. The *correction* is defined to be the negative of the error.

The *precision* of an instrument or of a measurement refers to its repeatability or consistency on successive trials.

An instrument's *resolution* is defined as the smallest increment of the measured quantity which can be detected with certainty.

The *random error* refers to the residual deviations which remain after all known errors have been corrected for.

Indicating instruments are rated in terms of their *limiting error*. For example, a voltmeter may be rated in the 0.5 per cent class. This means that the error at any major scale division should not exceed 0.5 per cent of *full scale* reading. Thus, at a reading of one-tenth of full scale a 0.5 per cent class instrument could be subject to an error of 5 per cent of the reading.

The *response time* of an instrument is defined to be the time after a step function is applied until the indication reaches a specified fraction, for example, 99 per cent, of the ultimate change.

b. dc Ammeters and voltmeters

These have as their moving element a coil galvanometer that moves in the field of a permanent magnet. The galvanometer coil is shunted by a low resistance in the ammeter, whereas in the voltmeter the coil is placed in series with a high resistance.

When an ammeter or a voltmeter is inserted into an electric circuit, the added resistance disturbs the circuit to a greater or lesser degree. A measure of the disturbing effect of the ammeter is the voltage drop across the instrument needed to give full-scale deflection. A typical value is 100 mV, so the disturbing effect would be considerable if the circuit voltage is a few volts.

The disturbing effect of inserting a voltmeter in a circuit depends on the current drawn by the voltmeter. For comparison purposes, this is judged by the total voltmeter resistance divided by the full-scale voltage, expressed in *ohms per volt*. The reciprocal of the ohms per volt is the full-scale current of the instrument. Thus, a multiscale voltmeter has the same ohms-per-volt rating on all the scales. In a rugged laboratory standard dc voltmeter the ohms per volt may be as low as 100, but in the less accurate voltmeters used in testing electronic circuits a value of 20,000 Ω/V is common. With the latter value the full-scale current is 50 μA, and a 100-V scale has 2 MΩ resistance. In some high-resistance circuits which may be encountered in electronic testing, even the 20,000-Ω/V voltmeter may draw too much current and a dc electronic voltmeter may be required.

c. The series-type ohmmeter

The indicating ohmmeter is commonly used for quick and convenient measurements of resistances when the accuracy required is not great. The

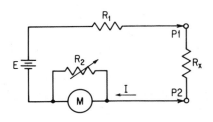

FIGURE 19-1   Ohmmeter circuit.

series ohmmeter circuit is shown in Fig. 19-1. The current I is a function of the unknown resistance R_x, so the meter scale of milliammeter M can be scaled in ohms. However, a *zero* adjustment is needed to compensate for changes in battery voltage. This is done by reducing R_x to zero (shorting probes $P1$ and $P2$ together) and adjusting R_2 until the ohms scale reading is zero, at full-scale current.

An elementary analysis will clarify two points about the ohmmeter scale. Let I_{fs} be the value of I when M reads full scale, after proper zero adjustment. Let the total series resistance of the circuit, except for R_x, be R_t. Then we write

$$I = \frac{E}{R_t + R_x} = \frac{\dfrac{E}{R_t}}{1 + \dfrac{R_x}{R_t}} = \frac{I_{fs}}{1 + \dfrac{R_x}{R_t}} \tag{19-2}$$

This equation shows that the meter deflection, which is proportional to I, is a nonlinear function of R_x. As a result, the ohms scale is nonlinear, especially as R_x becomes large compared with R_t.

To gain information concerning the ohmmeter resolution, we can calculate dI/dR_x from Eq. (19-2) and then form the following ratio, with the result

$$\frac{\dfrac{dI}{I_{fs}}}{\dfrac{dR_x}{R_x}} = \frac{-\dfrac{R_x}{R_t}}{\left(1 + \dfrac{R_x}{R_t}\right)^2} \tag{19-3}$$

This, then, is the change in current expressed as per unit of I_{fs} divided by the per unit change in R_x. The magnitude of the function in (19-3) is zero when $R_x = 0$ and approaches zero as $R_x \to \infty$ but goes through a maximum when $R_x = R_t$, or the point at which the meter reads one-half of full scale current. Therefore, the resolution in terms of percentage change in R_x is greatest at midscale, and readings on an ohmmeter should be taken in the neighborhood of midscale when possible.

d. The multimeter

A convenient test instrument, called a multimeter, or volt-ohm-milliammeter (VOM), contains a dc meter movement and switching arrangements to provide a wide range of scale ranges (Fig. 19-2). Often ac voltage ranges are provided on the same instrument. These use a full-wave rectifier bridge to drive the dc meter movement. Typical ohms-per-volt ratings are 20,000 on the dc ranges and 5000 on the ac ranges.

FIGURE 19-2   Multimeter, or volt-ohm-milliammeter. (Courtesy of the Simpson Electric Company.)

19-3
Electronic voltmeters

Electronic voltmeters employ tube or transistor amplifiers, usually stabilized by negative feedback, in combination with a step attenuator or range-change circuit, and a meter to indicate the output level. The modern cathode-ray oscilloscope with calibrated amplifiers serves as a voltmeter as well as a wave-form indicator. One of the prime advantages of electronic voltmeters is their high input impedance, and another is the wide frequency ranges available in the ac types.

a. dc Electronic voltmeters

The principle of one type of dc voltmeter is shown in Fig. 19-3. The circuit is essentially the same as that of the difference amplifier shown in Fig. 14-4 and has the freedom from drift of that circuit. The network may be viewed as a bridge circuit, with meter M across the balance points. This meter usually requires from $200 \mu A$ to 1 mA for full-scale deflection. The input potential divider is shown schematically, but in a commercial instrument the ratio would be adjustable in steps. Resistor R_2 may be as high as $10\ M\Omega$. On the lower scale ranges a typical value of total resistance is $10\ M\Omega$, and on higher ranges may be $100\ M\Omega$ or higher. Thus, the ohms-per-volt rating may range from 0.5 to $10\ M\Omega$ per volt.

When higher input resistances are required, the so-called electronic *electrometer* (Sec. 19-10) is used.

Another dc voltmeter circuit uses a twin-triode circuit similar to that in Fig. 19-3, except that the triodes act as cathode-followers, and the output meter is connected between the two cathodes. Partridge† discusses the design of the two types of voltmeters.

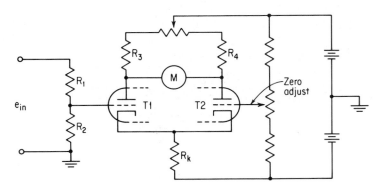

FIGURE 19-3   dc Electronic voltmeter.

The most sensitive range in a voltmeter having the circuit in Fig. 19-3 is on the order of 0.5 V full scale. Lower voltages down to a few millivolts are measured by instruments that include an internal voltage amplifier such as the modulator-type dc amplifier system in Fig. 14-12. The amplifier is

†Reference 19-6, pp. 38-49.

stabilized by the use of negative feedback. Voltages in the millivolt range are also measured by means of servo-controlled automatic potentiometers.

b. Peak-reading ac electronic voltmeters

We may be interested in different aspects of an unknown wave, such as its *peak, rectified average,* or *root-mean-square* value. Most ac electronic voltmeters respond to the peak or to the rectified average value of the wave. In the following article we shall refer to the errors that arise in an attempt to measure the rms value of a distorted wave with a peak-responsive or average-responsive instrument.

The simple diode peak-responsive voltmeter circuit in Fig. 19-4 is essentially a half-waver rectifier with a capacitor filter as discussed in Sec. 11-5. To use this circuit as a voltmeter we can either insert a microammeter in series with the resistor R, or we can read the direct voltage E_d with a dc electronic voltmeter. We recall that the current through the diode comes in pulses over the *peak* of the input voltage wave; therefore the concept of the voltmeter input

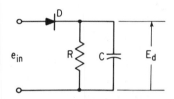

FIGURE 19-4   Principle of a diode voltmeter.

impedance is uncertain. One definition is based on the calculation of an equivalent resistance which, if placed directly across the input, would absorb the same power as the actual circuit. On this basis and assuming a sine voltage, the input resistance works out to be $R/2$.

The RC filter in Fig. 19-4 is usually designed with a time constant long enough so that the filter gives nearly ideal direct voltage with a 60-cycle sine impressed voltage. Then the voltmeter can be calibrated on 60-cycle voltage and used at higher frequencies up to the point at which errors due to inductance or diode capacitance are objectionable. The output meter may be scaled in rms values of a sine wave, but we should note that the deflection is actually proportional to the *positive peak* of the input wave. Test voltages in electronic circuits often have both dc and ac components superimposed, and usually the ac component (signal) is of major interest. Since the diode circuit under discussion would respond to the total wave, it is not commonly used for general testing.

The *shunt-fed RC diode voltmeter* circuit in Fig. 19-5 overcomes the objection just mentioned. Consider first the main circuit elements C, D, and R, and assume that R_1 and C_1 have no effect. Also assume that the RC time constant is very long compared with the period of the ac component of e_{in}. Then the capacitor C will, after several cycles, charge nearly to the positive

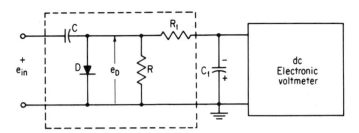

FIGURE 19-5   Shunt-fed RC diode voltmeter circuit.

peak value of e_{in}. The charge in C is maintained by current pulses at this positive peak but leaks off through R and the input circuit while the diode is nonconducting. Suppose that e_{in} comprises a dc plus an ac component. Then what is the wave form of e_D? The diode D prevents e_D from going positive, in fact, the dc voltage across C causes the wave of e_D to equal the ac component of e_{in} shifted downward so the positive peak is *clamped* at the zero level. As a result voltage e_D has a negative dc component equal to the positive peak of the ac component of e_{in}. This dc component is filtered out by the circuit R_1C_1 and is indicated on the dc electronic voltmeter.

In practical instruments range-changing networks are added. By enclosing the elements in the dotted rectangle in a small shielded probe at the end of a shielded cable, this voltmeter is adapted to RF voltage measurements up to frequencies of several hundreds of megacycles. Diode D may be a crystal rectifier or a small thermionic diode.

c. Average reading ac electronic voltmeters

A simple average reading voltmeter would be a series connection of a diode, a high resistance, and a microammeter. However, in order to use a high resistance, the microammeter would have to be very sensitive and delicate. Further, this voltmeter would be affected by the dc component of the test voltage.

Stable and precise instruments are available that depend basically on a stable feedback amplifier and an output rectifier. The principle of one commercial version of this voltmeter is shown in Fig. 19-6. The input circuit contains capacitor C to remove the dc component of the signal. A compensated input attenuator, which feeds the cathode follower CF and a high-gain amplifier, follows. The amplifier drives the dc meter M via the rectifier circuit, which in effect gives full-wave rectification. The amplifier is stabilized by the negative feedback voltage developed across R_f. According to Partridge[†] the gain without feedback of the amplifier in a particular commercial instrument is about 300,000. This is reduced to a net gain of about

†See Reference 19-6, p. 87.

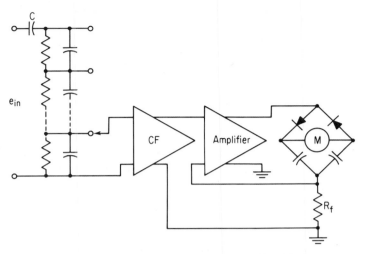

FIGURE 19-6   Average responsive ac vacuum-tube voltmeter.

260 with feedback. A 25 per cent drop in the g_m of the amplifier tubes would reduce the net gain by only 0.2 per cent.

This type of instrument has an effective input impedance in the order of 1.5-MΩ resistance shunted by 40 pF of capacitance. A typical rated accuracy is 3 per cent of full scale from 40 Hz to 1.5 MHz. Some models have full-scale ranges from 1 mV to 300 V. The scale is essentially linear in volts, therefore nonlinear in decibels.

An average-reading voltmeter made by Ballantine Laboratories, Inc. has an indication proportional to the logarithm of the voltage. The general arrangement (Fig. 19-7) is similar that of the instrument in Fig. 19-6 except in two respects. First, the rectifier output is proportional to the average value of the *positive half-cycle* of the ac component. Second, the output dc meter has a special design of the iron pole pieces such as to give a deflection proportional to the log of the voltage. A typical range has scale markings to cover a 10 to 1 range in voltage, for example, from 0.1 to 1.0 V, and the zero of the meter is suppressed below the 0.1-V mark. A logarithmic scale has a variation such that a certain increment in deflection, say 1°, corre-

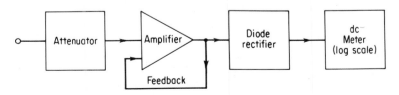

FIGURE 19-7   One-line diagram of a logarithmic ac voltmeter.

sponds to the same *percentage* change in the value at any point on the scale. The scale therefore provides the same inherent reading accuracy at any point on the scale. Furthermore, the decibel scales on the logarithmic voltmeter are linear scales.

d. *True rms ac electronic voltmeters*

In recent years several true rms electronic voltmeters have become available. These replace the high-frequency thermocouple instrument, which has a long response time, has a low impedance, and is easily burned out by overvoltage. One commercial true rms voltmeter uses thermocouples in its network, but the instrument has high input impedance and protective networks to reduce thermocouple burnout. The scheme is shown in Fig. 19-8.

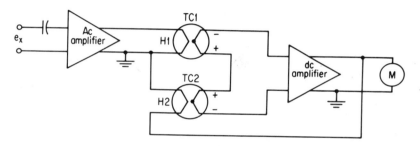

FIGURE 19-8   Showing the principle of a true rms voltmeter.

The voltage to be measured is amplified by a wide-band ac amplifier and applied to heater $H1$ of thermocouple $TC1$. A second thermocouple has its heater $H2$ driven by the output of the dc amplifier. The dc outputs of the two thermocouples are opposed, and the difference is applied to the dc amplifier input. This is therefore a type of error-controlled feedback system. When the error voltage has been reduced to zero, the two heaters, $H1$ and $H2$, are receiving the same true heating power. Therefore the indication on meter M gives a measure of the rms value of the ac part of the test voltage e_x.

19-4
Interpretation of electronic voltmeter readings

It is common practice to calibrate electronic voltmeters on a sine wave at power frequency and to mark the scale in rms values of the sine wave. However, when nonsinusoidal waves are tested on a peak-responsive or average-responsive meter, the reading may be far different from the true rms value of the wave, and therefore the question of the interpretation of the scale reading arises.

A *peak-responsive* meter scaled in rms values of a sine wave will indicate a value equal to $1/\sqrt{2}$, or 0.707, of the peak of the wave if the wave has no dc component. Parts b and c of Fig. 19-9 illustrate this point and also the

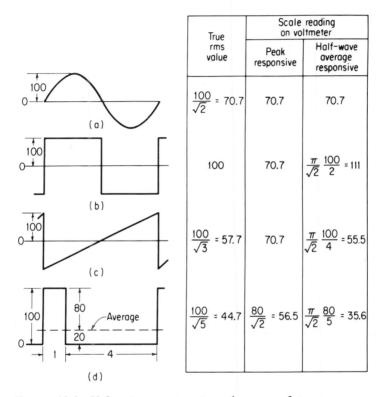

	True rms value	Scale reading on voltmeter	
		Peak responsive	Half-wave average responsive
(a)	$\dfrac{100}{\sqrt{2}} = 70.7$	70.7	70.7
(b)	100	70.7	$\dfrac{\pi}{\sqrt{2}}\dfrac{100}{2} = 111$
(c)	$\dfrac{100}{\sqrt{3}} = 57.7$	70.7	$\dfrac{\pi}{\sqrt{2}}\dfrac{100}{4} = 55.5$
(d)	$\dfrac{100}{\sqrt{5}} = 44.7$	$\dfrac{80}{\sqrt{2}} = 56.5$	$\dfrac{\pi}{\sqrt{2}}\dfrac{80}{5} = 35.6$

FIGURE 19-9　Voltmeter responses to various wave forms.

difference between the scale reading and the true rms value. When the wave has a dc component, as in Fig. 19-9d, the usual peak-responsive meter responds to the variations about the average value, or dc level. Thus, in Fig. 19-9d, the meter responds to a positive peak of 80 V, and the reading is $80/\sqrt{2}$ or 56.5 V. If the leads to the voltmeter were reversed, the reading would be only $20/\sqrt{2}$ or 14.1 V.

Consider a voltmeter scaled in rms values of a sine wave that responds to the *positive half-wave average* of the wave. On the sine calibrating wave the half-wave average equals $(1/\pi) \times$ (peak value), whereas the scale reading is $(1/\sqrt{2}) \times$ (peak value). Therefore, on other symmetrical waves the scale reading will be $(\pi/\sqrt{2}) \times$ (positive half-wave average of the wave). Examples are given Figs. 19-9b and c. Figure 19-9d illustrates the response to a wave that has a dc component, which the meter filters out. The meter responds to the variations about the average, in this case to the average value of the 80-V positive pulse.

An instrument that responds to the *full-wave average* will give the same readings as the half-wave average meter if the waves are symmetrical about the zero line. The response for waves that have a dc component can be calculated by an analysis similar to that in the foregoing paragraph.

When a distorted sine wave is tested, the reading depends not only on the magnitude of the harmonic components of the wave but also on their phase position. In general, the average-responsive meter gives a reading closer to the true rms value of the wave than the peak-responsive meter.

19-5
Electronic self-balancing
potentiometer; X-Y recorder

A potentiometer is an example of a comparison instrument in which an unknown voltage is compared to a known voltage. The difference, or error, is reduced to zero by adjustment of the known voltage. The system in Fig. 19-10 provides an automatic means of balancing the potentiometer. The error voltage e is the difference between the unknown e_x and the known voltage e_s. The error voltage acts as the input to amplifier A_1, which is usually a sensitive modulator-type dc amplifier whose output is at line frequency. The ac output of A_1 drives the power amplifier A_2, whose output goes to

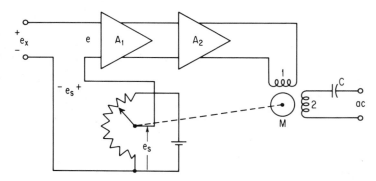

FIGURE 19-10   Simplified diagram of a servo-type self-balancing potentiometer.

phase 1 of the two-phase servo motor M. Phase 2 is supplied by a 90° phase-shifted voltage derived from the ac line. The motor drives the potential divider sliding contact, usually through gears and an endless cable, in such a direction as to reduce the error toward zero. If the sign of the error voltage reverses, the voltage output of amplifiers A_1 and A_2 also reverses, or its phase changes by 180°, so the motor will then reverse direction of rotation. This system is really a servomechanism, and its behavior can be analyzed by the methods discussed in Chapter 15.

A typical commercial instrument will have an indicator on a scale to indicate e_s (and therefore e_x) and usually has an ink pen that gives a record on a moving chart driven by a clock motor. Thus records of e_x as a function of the time are obtained. A means is provided for standardizing the voltage across the potential divider, as will be explained in Sec. 19-6.

The indicator in a typical potentiometer may have a full-scale travel of 25 cm, and multirange instruments may have full-scale ranges of, say, 2, 10, and 100 mV. The full-scale value is changed by changing the resistance network in the instrument. Higher voltage ranges are obtained by using precision voltage dividers, but these put a heavier load on the test voltage. The response time for response to within one per cent of final value

FIGURE 19-11 *X-Y* recorder. (Courtesy of Moseley Division of Hewlett-Packard, Inc.)

with a step input ranges from 0.5 to 10 sec or more. Usually a damping adjustment is provided. The amplifier input impedance may be important if the source of unknown emf has a sizable internal resistance. Potentiometers designed primarily for measuring thermocouple emfs may have an amplifier input impedance of 2000 to 8000 Ω, but higher values are available. Amplifier voltage gains of the order of 10^6 to 10^7 (120 to 140dB) are typical.

A useful instrument, known as an *X-Y recorder*, consists of two self-balancing potentiometers arranged so that one controls the x deflection and the other the y deflection of a recording pen. An example is shown in Fig. 19-11. In this device one servo controls the horizontal displacement of the vertical bar, which rides on a carriage, that carries the pen, and the other controls the vertical displacement of the pen along this bar. An *X-Y* recorder can plot a curve of any two physical quantities that can be converted by transducers into dc emfs. Thus, examples are light output versus temperature, magnetic flux density versus magnetizing current, and stress versus strain. Some models have a self-contained system for providing a linear deflection versus time, so that they can also be used as recorders.

19-6
Potentiometer circuits

Although we cannot devote much attention to the details of potentiometer circuits,† we want to consider one or two aspects that affect potentiometer application. Consider first the effect of the input resistance of the amplifier R_{in} in Fig. 19-12a, on the sensitivity of balance. In this diagram the unknown voltage e_x is derived from the hypothetical source circuit E, R_1, and R_2; whereas e_s is derived from the potential divider P that is a part of

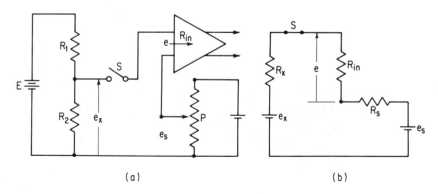

(a)   (b)

FIGURE 19-12   Potentiometer test circuit.

†See, for example, Reference 19-1, Chap. 10.

the potentiometer. We inquire about the value of e in the unbalanced condition when $e_s \neq e_x$. If we let e_x and e_s be the values when switch S is open, then we can use the Thévenin source equivalents for the test circuit and for the potential divider, as shown in Fig. 19-12b. We can calculate the current around this circuit as voltage $e_x - e_s$ divided by the total circuit resistance, and the error voltage e is R_{in} times the current; therefore,

$$e = \frac{R_{in}(e_x - e_s)}{R_{in} + R_x + R_s} \tag{19-4}$$

Thus, e is nearly equal to $e_x - e_s$ when $R_{in} \gg (R_x + R_s)$; otherwise the sensitivity to an off-balance condition is reduced.

In some applications, for example, in measuring thermocouple emfs, the value of R_x is low, perhaps a few ohms, and sensitivity would not be a problem. However, some measurements such as pH measurements in chemical work with glass electrodes are made in test circuits whose resistance may be in the megohm range. In such a situation the input resistance is very important, and special electrometer tubes may be required in the input stage to give the requisite input resistance.

A schematic diagram of a practical potentiometer circuit is shown in Fig. 19-13, though with some of the details omitted. The motor M drives

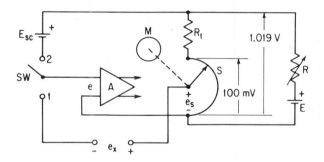

FIGURE 19-13 Elementary self-balancing potentiometer circuit.

the sliding contact on the precision slidewire S. When the current around the loop $E-R-R_1-S-E$ is correctly adjusted, there is a drop across S equal to the full-scale voltage of the potentiometer, taken to be 100 mV in this example, and 1.019 V across R_1 and S in series, as shown in the diagram. The "working" current is adjusted by moving switch SW to position 2 and adjusting rheostat R until the error voltage e is zero. Then the voltage across R_1 and S equals the standard cell voltage E_{sc}, assumed to be 1.019 V. In a commercial potentiometer this adjustment is made automatically by an auxiliary servo system that controls rheostat R. The resistors R_1 and S are proportioned so that the emf across S is exactly 100 mV after the working current has been standardized.

To use the instrument, switch SW is moved to position 1. Then the unknown voltage e_x opposes the known voltage e_s and the error voltage e acts to balance the potentiometer, as explained previously.

In a commercial multirange instrument provision is made for changing the resistances in the network, but using the same slidewire. For example, emfs of 2, 10, or 100 mV would appear across S on the different range settings, thereby giving corresponding full-scale readings.

In some measurement applications it may be desirable to suppress the zero of the scale. For example, in order to get more accurate temperature readings from a thermocouple over a limited high-temperature range it may be desirable to have the whole range of the slidewire correspond to e_x values only over the range from, say, 9 to 10 mV. Thus, the drop across the slidewire S, called the *span*, must be 1 mV. Therefore, we need to insert a precise voltage of 9 mV in series opposition to e_x, so that the potentiometer will balance only the excess voltage over 9 mV. The accurate opposing, or "bucking," voltage source can be devised in the laboratory that has an accurate dc reference voltage and a precise voltage divider. Circuits to perform the zero suppression function can be included in commercial instruments.

A few application circuits other than direct voltage-measuring circuits may be mentioned. Of course, many transducers permit measurement of nonelectrical quantities by means of a voltage. Current may be measured by sending the current through a precision resistor shunt and measuring the voltage across the shunt. Another scheme, which avoids the voltage drop entailed by the use of a shunt, consists in opposing the unknown current to a known current generated by the potentiometer voltage and a known resistance. The difference goes to the input of the error detector, and the voltage inserted in the test circuit is only the small error voltage. Other application circuits include those for the measurement of current ratio, resistance, and ac voltage, current, and power.

19-7
Cathode-ray oscilloscope

The modern *cathode-ray oscilloscope (or oscillograph)* is a precision instrument that not only permits observations of the forms of waves but also the measurement of their amplitudes and time duration. It is an indispensable tool in the electronics laboratory and in most research laboratories as well. The heart of the instrument is the cathode-ray tube itself.

a. Cathode-ray beam formation

The cathode-ray tube comprises (1) an electron "gun" to form the beam of electrons, (2) a deflecting system for deflecting the beam, and (3) a fluorescent screen on which the electron beam traces out the observed wave. A schematic diagram of a cathode-ray tube and associated power supply is shown in Fig. 19-14.

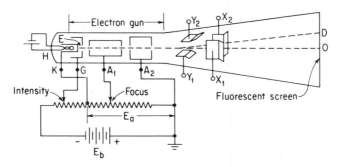

FIGURE 19-14　Schematic diagram of cathode-ray oscilloscope tube. K = cathode, E = electron emitting surface, G = grid, A_1 = first anode, and A_2 = second anode.

The electron gun must produce a fine pencil or beam of electrons that will converge to a focus at a small spot on the fluorescent screen, as at 0 in the undeflected position. The electrons originate at the oxide cathode emitter E, placed at the end of the separately heated cathode K. Next they pass through a hole in the electrode G, called the *modulator* or *grid* electrode. Then the beam passes through two cylindrical accelerating electrodes, anodes A_1 and A_2. When the electrons leave A_2, they have been accelerated to a speed corresponding to the total accelerating voltage from K to A_2, labeled E_a in the figure. Owing to the high vacuum in the tube the electrons do not lose energy owing to collisions with gas molecules. In many oscilloscopes the total accelerating voltage is about 2500 to 4000 V, though voltages of about 10,000 are found in high frequency instruments.

The grid electrode is charged negatively with respect to the cathode to a voltage of about 30 V. As this voltage is varied, the number of electrons in the beam also varies, thus giving a control over the beam current and the intensity of the fluorescent spot. In Fig. 19-14 this variation is provided by the potential divider labeled "*intensity*."

The natural tendency of a beam of electrons is to diverge on account of their mutual electrostatic repulsion. By arranging disk or cylindrical electrodes charged to successively higher positive potentials, as shown in Fig. 19-14, the beam is converted into a converging beam that can be made to focus at the screen. The focusing effect is a result of the action of the electric field on the electrons in the region between the grid and the first anode and in the region between the first and second anodes. These regions have an action on the electrons analogous to the action of a lens in a light beam, so they are called *electron lenses*. The focus is adjusted by varying the potential of the first anode. This potential is about one-fifth of the second anode potential.

The *"intensity"* and *"focus"* controls determine the beam current and the spot size on the screen. When the electrons hit the screen, part of their energy is converted into light and part into heat. The heat may damage the fluorescent material, so the spot should always be kept in motion to avoid "burning" the screen. After hitting the screen the electrons return to the power-supply circuit via the inside surface of the tube and the lead-in wire to A_2. The tube is sometimes coated with graphite over portions of the inner surface to facilitate return current and to act as an electrostatic shield.

b. Deflection of the beam

The beam can be deflected by setting up a transverse magnetic field through the neck of the tube. A more common method is to employ electrostatic forces on the electrons to deflect the beam. These forces are produced by the charges on pairs of small capacitor plates called *deflecting* plates between which the beam passes (Fig. 19-14). For example, if plate Y_2 is charged positively and plate Y_1 is charged negatively, the electrons will be forced upward while they pass between the plates and the beam will deflect upward to produce a "spot" at D. Thus plates Y_1 and Y_2 produce the *vertical* or *y-axis* deflection. Another pair of plates, X_1 and X_2, produce the *horizontal* or *x-axis* deflection. Thus, the spot can be deflected to any part of the screen by impressing one voltage across plates $Y_1 Y_2$ and another voltage across plates $X_1 X_2$. By combining suitably varying deflections, the spot will trace out wave forms, as will be explained presently.

The deflection is a linear function of the deflecting voltage for a constant accelerating voltage. Thus, the *deflection sensitivity* for a given accelerating voltage may be defined in terms of the deflection voltage needed for unit deflection. A typical deflection sensitivity is 25 V/cm for a 3000-V tube, consequently voltages of the order of 100 V are needed to give good-sized deflections. Oscilloscopes contain voltage amplifiers that extend the useful range to much lower values of input signals.

c. Recurrent linear sweep; triggered sweep

Cathode-ray oscilloscopes are often used for the observation of periodic wave forms of voltage or of current. For this purpose it is most convenient to cause the spot to trace out the wave repeatedly, so that successive waves fall on top of the preceding ones. Then if the repetition rate is over about 10 per second, the wave appears to the eye to be a stationary wave on the screen. A stationary wave will be traced out if a properly synchronized *linear sweep voltage* of the correct frequency is impressed on the *x*-axis plates, and the varying voltage is impressed on the *y*-axis plates.

A schematic representation of the scheme for producing stationary waves with a linear-time axis is shown in Fig. 19-15a. The wave to be observed is represented by e_y (Fig. 19-15b) and is connected to the y-axis plates. The

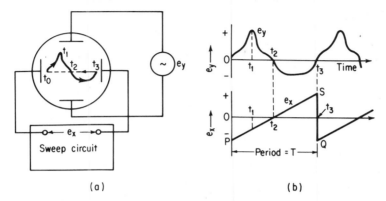

(a)   (b)

FIGURE 19-15   (a) Circuit diagram and (b) voltage wave forms, for linear sweep.

ideal sweep-voltage wave e_x rises linearly with time and then reverses suddenly as shown in the figure. This wave is often called a sawtooth wave from its peculiar shape. At the instant t_0 the voltage e_x drops to a negative maximum at P, so the spot deflects a maximum distance to the left. At instant t_1, taken at one-quarter of the period, or $T/4$, the value of e_x is half of the negative maximum, so the spot has moved half of the way to the origin. Similarly, the spot will continue to move to the right in direct proportion to the time because the voltage e_x is increasing at a constant rate. At instant t_3 the voltage suddenly reverses from S to Q, and the spot suddenly flies back to the starting point in Fig. 19-15a. While the x-axis plates have been producing the motion described above, the y-axis plates have produced a vertical deflection proportional to the instantaneous value of the voltage e_y. As a result, the wave of e_y is traced out in a rectangular coordinate graph on the screen. The direction of travel of the spot is indicated by the arrowheads in Fig. 19-15a.

The sawtooth sweep wave can be generated by the thyratron relaxation oscillator described in Sec. 12-2. To lock the sweep into synchronism with the signal at exactly the signal frequency (or a submultiple thereof) a small signal voltage is fed to the thyratron grid, as shown in Fig. 12-1a. Thyratron sweep circuits are severely limited at the upper frequencies, and therefore sweep circuits of the vacuum-tube or transistor *triggered-wave-form* type (Sec. 16-18) are commonly employed.

In the basic form of the triggered sweep the sweep voltage is held at a negative constant value until the sweep cycle is started by a trigger signal.

Further, the beam current is cut off, or the spot is *blanked out*, until the sweep is started. Figure 19-16 illustrates the application of the triggered sweep to the study of a short-time disturbance on the periodic signal wave e_y. The sweep voltage is initially at a negative level. We assume that the signal wave also is used to trigger the sweep, and that the sweep starts when the signal wave exceeds the level at point A. Thus the sweep voltage rises on the linear portion CD and then returns to the negative level at E. The duration of the sweep can be adjusted by means of controls on the sweep circuit to a desired value—in this case to the time from point A to point B on the test wave. As a result the portion AB of the wave is "stretched out" on the screen, as shown in Fig. 19-16b. The cycle repeats, starting at point F, so that the spot retraces its path on the screen once each period of the test wave. The spot is blanked out during the portions DEF of the sweep wave; thus the return trace or "*flyback*" does not appear on the screen.

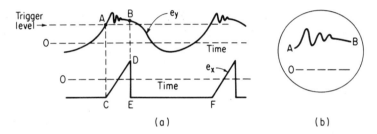

FIGURE 19-16   Illustrating a triggered sweep. (a) Wave forms and (b) scope presentation.

In commercial oscilloscopes a switching arrangement is provided so that the trigger signal can be derived from the test signal, from an internal trigger signal from the ac line, or from a separate external trigger. Adjustments are available for triggering at different levels and also for either positive or negative slopes of the trigger voltage. Automatic triggering circuits may also be provided which adjust the trigger level to give a stable sweep.

d. *Alternating sweep and Lissajous figures*

Sometimes an alternating voltage is impressed on the x-axis plates to provide the timing deflection. One of the most useful applications of this method is in the determination of the phase angle between two sinusoidally varying quantities, for example, between two voltage waves, or between a voltage wave and a current wave. When sinusoidal voltages of the same frequency are impressed both on the x-axis and on the y-axis plates, the resulting path of the spot is a straight line, a circle, or an ellipse, as illustrated for three special cases in Fig. 19-17. For simplicity the x and y deflections are shown as sine waves of equal amplitudes. This condition will exist if the two pairs of plates have equal deflection sensitivities and equal voltages are impressed on the two sets of plates. When the two waves are in phase as shown at (b), then the spot travels back and forth along the 45° line marked $\alpha = 0$ in Fig. 19-17a. When the y deflection lags behind the x deflection as in (c), the path of the spot is an ellipse. When the angle of lag is 90° as in (d), the spot travels around a circle.

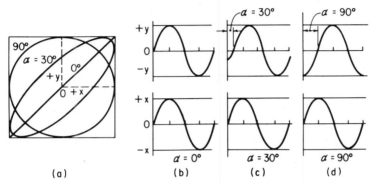

FIGURE 19-17   (a) Figures on screen produced by wave forms in (b), (c), and (d).

An analysis of the general case for deflections of the same frequency but of unequal amplitudes and displaced phase position will show how the phase angle can be determined from the diagram on the cathode-ray screen. Let the deflections be represented by

$$x = X_m \sin \theta \qquad (19\text{-}5)$$

and

$$y = Y_m \sin (\theta - \alpha) \qquad (19\text{-}6)$$

where X_m and Y_m are the maximum deflections in the x and y directions, respectively, and α is the angle by which the wave of y deflection lags the x deflection. The angle of lag α is illustrated in Fig. 19-17c and d. Equations (19-5) and (19-6) are the parametric equations of the ellipse illustrated in Fig. 19-18. One method of determining the angle α is to measure the distance X_1 to point P where the image cuts the x axis. Since y is zero

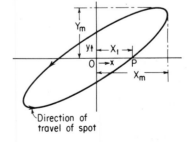

FIGURE 19-18 Elliptical image on oscilloscope screen, drawn for $\alpha = 30°$.

at point P, we find from Eq. (19-6) that $\theta = \alpha$ at this instant. Then we substitute X_1 for x and α for θ in Eq. (19-5) and find

$$\sin \alpha = \frac{X_1}{X_m} \qquad (19\text{-}7)$$

Thus the angle α is readily found in terms of X_1 and X_m. The accuracy obtainable falls off for small angles, say, below 10° and for angles greater than, say, 70°. This method can not distinguish an angle of *lead* from an equal angle of *lag* because the image appears the same in both cases. The only difference is that the spot travels around the path in opposite directions, but the eye cannot detect this difference at the usual frequencies.

A stationary pattern, called a Lissajous figure, is obtained when sine-wave deflections of different frequencies are produced simultaneously in the x and y directions and the two frequencies have an integral ratio, such as 2/1, 3/1, 5/4, etc. These figures are useful for the comparison of an unknown frequency with a known frequency as in the calibration of an oscillator against a standard frequency. The exact appearance of the figure depends on the phase displacement of the two waves as well as on their frequency ratio. Typical figures are shown in Fig. 19-19.

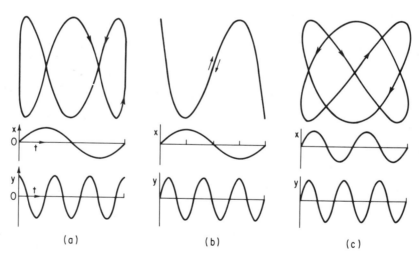

(a)   (b)   (c)

FIGURE 19-19 Typical Lissajous figures. (a) Frequency ratio 3/1, phase displacement 90°, (b) f ratio 3/1, phase angle 0°, and (c) f ratio 3/2, phase angle 0°. Arrows show direction of travel of spot on the screen.

e. *Deflection circuits and controls*

In a high-grade oscilloscope each pair of deflection plates is driven by an amplifier, usually of the direct-coupled type (Fig. 19-20). The amplifiers have calibrated gain controls, so that voltage measurements can be made. In a typical "low-frequency" oscilloscope the vertical amplifier has a bandwidth from dc to 400 or 500 kHz, whereas the "high-frequency" types have bandwidths of 5, 10, or 30 MHz or higher. Switches are provided to switch the amplifiers from "DC" to "AC" operation. In the "AC" connection the dc component of the signal will be filtered out.

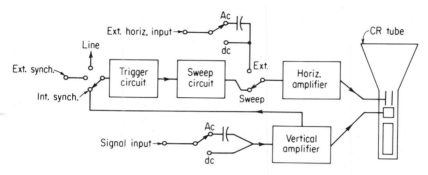

FIGURE 19-20   Block diagram of *CRO* deflection circuits.

As shown in Fig. 19-20, the trigger circuit can derive its input from one of three sources. If it is switched to INT SYNCH, the trigger signal comes from the test signal via the vertical amplifier. If switched to EXT SYNCH, a suitable voltage must be supplied to this terminal. If switched to LINE, a small voltage at the power-line frequency enters the trigger circuit. The sweep circuit has a multipoint switch that changes the spot sweep speed from perhaps 1 sec/cm to 1 μs/cm in the low-frequency oscilloscope or to 0.1 μs/cm or less in the high-frequency type.

f. *Oscilloscope application*

It is hardly possible to describe the many types of observations that can be made by means of an oscilloscope. Perhaps the most common application is to the study of recurrent wave forms. However, individual electrical transients can be recorded by photographic means with the aid of a *single sweep* circuit. The instrument can also be used as a high-speed *X-Y* indicator, and with suitable transducers can present graphs of pressure versus volume, stress versus strain, etc. One interesting application is to the repetitive tracing of a whole family of transistor characteristic curves.

Mention should be made of the *dual-beam* oscilloscope, in which there are two independent electron guns and deflection systems, so that two signals can be compared.

A related oscilloscope is the *dual-trace* instrument, in which there is a single gun and deflection system. The amplifier input is rapidly switched between two different input signals by an electronic switch circuit, which is similar to a free-running multivibrator. As a result, two test waves can be traced on the screen simultaneously, though the spot must jump back and forth between the two traces.

Occasionally the voltage of the modulator electrode is varied to vary the brightness of the beam. This technique can be used, for example, to put timing marks on the trace.

19-8
Phase meter

We have seen how the phase difference between two waves can be measured by means of a Lissajous figure (Sec. 19-7d). The phase discriminator in Sec. 13-9 can also be adapted to the measurement of phase.

The phase measuring system shown in Fig. 19-21 uses wave-shaping tech-

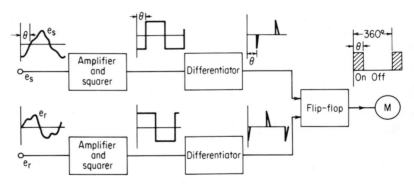

FIGURE 19-21   Block diagram of a phase meter.

niques and the properties of a flip-flop circuit to give a direct reading of phase on the dc meter M. As shown in the figure, there are two identical channels, one for the reference wave e_r and the other for the signal e_s. These voltages first go through amplifier and clipper stages that produce a square wave. The square wave must maintain the original phase θ. The square wave is passed through a differentiator to obtain the spike-shaped pulses needed to operate the flip-flop. However, only the negative pulses cause a change-of-state in the flip-flop. Thus, one side of the flip-flop stays ON during the interval θ between the two negative pulses and remains OFF the rest of the time. Meter M reads a value proportional to the average of the flip-flop output wave. If the ON current is I, then

$$I_{av} = \frac{on}{on + off} \times I = \frac{\theta}{360} \ I \qquad (19\text{-}8)$$

Thus, if M has a full-scale value of $I/2$, the phase angle scale on M is 0 to 180°. Other ranges can be obtained by changing the range of meter M.

We notice that this phase meter measures the angle between the positive-going zero crossings of the two waves. With distorted sine waves the harmonic components will shift the actual zero crossings with respect to the zero of the fundamental component of the wave. Therefore, this phase meter will not accurately indicate the phase between the fundamental-frequency components of distorted waves.

19-9

Instruments based on the Hall effect

***a.** The Hall effect*

The Hall effect refers to the transverse voltage generated in a current-carrying conductor which is subjected to a perpendicular magnetic field. The effect is very small in metallic conductors but is considerable in semiconductors.

Consider the rectangular block of p-type semiconductor in Fig. 19-22

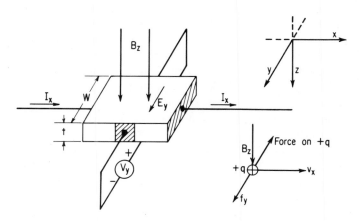

FIGURE 19-22   The Hall effect.

of width w and thickness t, which carries a steady current I_x in the $+ x$ direction. The steady magnetic field B_z points downward. We recall that if a positive charge q moves through this magnetic field with an x-directed velocity v_x, it will be subjected to a sideways-directed force given by

$$f_y = - qv_xB_z \qquad (19\text{-}9)$$

that is, the force is in the $-y$ direction. To apply this reasoning to the semi-conductor, we recall that the hole motion is equivalent to the motion of a positive charge. Thus, there is a force on the moving holes which tends to carry them to the edge of the block away from the observer and to charge this edge positively. As a result the voltmeter V_y will indicate the *Hall* emf across the two edges of the block.

The action just described proceeds until the force on the moving charge due to the magnetic field is just balanced by the electrostatic force of the internal electric field E_y due to the accumulated charges on the front and rear edges. A simple derivation will show that the field E_y is proportional to the current density in the block J_x and to B_z; thus,

$$E_y = RJ_xB_z \qquad (19\text{-}10)$$

where R is the *Hall coefficient*. But the average current density is given by $J_x = I_x/wt$, and the voltage is given by $V_y = E_yw$; therefore,

$$V_y = \frac{wRI_xB_z}{wt} = \frac{RI_xB_z}{t} \qquad (19\text{-}11)$$

We see from Eq. (19-11) that if we are concerned with a particular block of material, then

$$V_y = KI_xB_z \qquad (19\text{-}12)$$

where K is a constant. A closer examination of the Hall effect shows that R is a function of the carrier density, and this depends on the temperature. Therefore K depends on the temperature to some extent.

If we assume that the block is an n-type semiconductor but that I_x and B_z are the same as before, we conclude that V_y should have the opposite sign because the majority carriers are electrons. Experiments confirm these polarity effects and thereby provide a striking verification of the equivalence of hole motions to the motions of positive charges.

The foregoing discussion has assumed that either electrons or holes are predominant in the material. When they are present in nearly equal numbers their effects tend to cancel and the Hall effect is small.

Several practical devices are based on the Hall effect, including multipliers, function generators, modulators, wattmeters, and gaussmeters.

b. The gaussmeter

As Eq. (19-12) shows, the structure in Fig. 19-22 can be used as the probe of a gaussmeter. A constant current I_x is supplied (or in some cases a constant voltage), and the Hall voltage is a measure of the B field. The semiconductor may be indium arsenide or indium antimonide. A probe for transverse field measurement may have typical exterior dimensions of 4 by 10 by 0.5 mm, with an active area of 2 by 5 mm. Smaller probes are also made. A typical indium arsenide probe may have a sensitivity factor (K in Eq. 19-12) of 1 to 2 V/A-Wb/m^2 (0.1 to 0.2 V/A-kG). Thus, with a current of 100 mA a field of 200 G will typically generate a few millivolts.

Practical gaussmeters generally have two refinements of the basic circuit. One is an adjustment to neutralize the residual voltage that may be present when $B_z = 0$, due to inexact alignment of the connections for V_y or to thermal emf's. The other is some type of temperature compensation. In some gaussmeters the current is furnished by an oscillator at a frequency of, say, 1 kHz. Amplifiers and a phase-sensitive demodulator provide a meter indication. This system will respond to dc and also to ac magnetic fields at frequencies up to 2 or 3 hundred cycles per second.

19-10
Electrometer tubes and electrometer circuits

a. Electrometer tubes

The early electrometers consisted of refined models of the gold-leaf or the quartz-fiber electroscope. These have practically zero leakage current and may be regarded as instruments for the measurement of charge or of voltage. An electron tube can measure the voltage applied to its grid in terms of the change in the plate current. However, there is always some grid current, even when the grid is several volts negative. Special electrometer tubes have been developed which have very small negative grid currents in the range from 10^{-15} to 10^{-13} A. This current varies as shown in Fig. 4-10, except for the smaller values.

The principal causes of grid current when the grid is more than 2 V negative to the negative end of the filament are: (1) leakage over the insulation of the grid, (2) positive ion current to the grid due to ionization of the residual gas by electron impacts, and (3) electron release from the grid by light or other radiation (soft X rays). For more positive grid voltages an increasing number of electrons from the cathode have sufficient energy to reach the grid, so an electron current component is added to those listed above. At a grid voltage of around -1.0 V the electron current balances the other components, and the net grid current is zero.

In electrometer tubes the filament is operated at a low temperature so as to minimize the light given off. The control grid is highly insulated, and the plate voltage is kept low to reduce the ionization of the residual gas. The tube should be kept scrupulously clean and should be shielded from external light. Electrometer tubes are made in triode, tetrode, and pentode designs.

b. *Elementary electrometer circuit*

An elementary circuit that will illustrate some aspects of electrometer circuit operation is shown in Fig. 19-23. This shows an application to the measurement of an unknown current i_x which is assumed to come from a very high impedance source such as an ionization chamber. The idea is to pass i_x through the known resistance R_g to ground and thereby cause a change in grid voltage that is detected by the galvanometer (or microammeter) G in the plate circuit. But if the grid current i_c is an appreciable fraction of i_x, the basic assumption of the method is invalid and inaccuracy results.

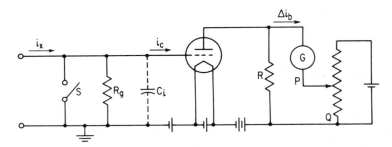

FIGURE 19-23   Electrometer circuit in principle.

Greater sensitivity can be attained if the galvanometer current is zero while quiescent plate current is flowing and changes in plate current cause a galvanometer reading. Figure 19-23 shows an elementary compensating network for applying this technique. The network is initially adjusted to cause G to read zero while switch S in the grid circuit is closed. If we assume that the resistance of the galvanometer branch is small compared with resistance R, then we can say as an approximation that the change in plate current Δi_b due to a change in grid potential Δe_c will all go through G. Then, assuming that r_p of the tube is large compared with the galvanometer branch resistance, Δi_b will have the value

$$\Delta i_b = g_m \, \Delta e_c \qquad (19\text{-}13)$$

But $\Delta e_c = R_g i_x$, assuming $i_c \ll i_x$, and therefore

$$\Delta i_b = g_m R_g i_x \qquad (19\text{-}14)$$

or

$$i_x = \frac{\Delta i_b}{g_m R_g} \qquad (19\text{-}15)$$

Typical values in (19-15) might be $\Delta i_b = 10^{-5}\,\text{A}$, $g_m = 50\,\mu\text{mhos}$, and $R_g = 2 \times 10^{11}\,\Omega$ (200,000 MΩ). Then $i_x = 10^{-5}/5 \times 10^{-5} \times 2 \times 10^{11} =$

10^{-12} A, and an electrometer tube grid current of 10^{-14} A would be tolerable.

When currents smaller than 10^{-12} or 10^{-13} A are to be measured, more complex circuits are used,† such as a balanced input circuit using two electrometer tubes so that the steady grid currents are balanced out. By taking extreme care currents as low as 5×10^{-18} A may be detected. Below about 10^{-13} A the circuit in Fig. 19-23 is no longer suitable owing to the extremely long time constants that develop in the grid circuit. For example, if $C_i = 8$ pF and R_g is raised to 10^{13} Ω (to develop $\Delta e_c = 200$ mV for $i_x = 2 \times 10^{-14}$ A), then $R_g C_i = 80$ sec. This is already an intolerably long time constant.

c. A feedback electrometer circuit

One might ask whether the circuit in Fig. 19-23 could be used to measure lower currents if a more sensitive meter G were used so that smaller voltage changes Δe_c could be measured. A limit is soon reached in this direction owing to the zero drift of G due to noise voltages such as the slight variations in the contact potential difference in the grid-cathode circuit.

The two-tube circuit‡ in Fig. 19-24 applies negative feedback to improve

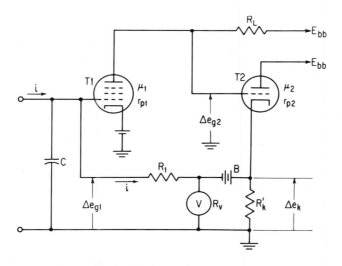

FIGURE 19-24   A feedback electrometer circuit.

the zero stability and to reduce the input resistance and thereby to lower the time constant of the input circuit. Tube $T1$ is the electrometer tube, and

†See Reference 19-6, pp. 112 ff.
‡N. F. Moody, "An Improved dc Amplifier for Portable Ionization Chamber Instruments," *Rev. Sci. Inst.* **22**, 236, 1951.

this stage develops the voltage gain. Tube $T2$ acts as a cathode follower, with a rugged voltmeter V as the output meter. A balancing battery B brings the reading of V to zero under quiescent conditions.

To derive expressions for the output voltage and the input resistance, we use the symbols defined in Fig. 19-24. We can write

$$\Delta e_{g2} = A_1 \, \Delta e_{g1} \tag{19-16}$$

where A_1 is the gain of the first stage, i.e.,

$$A_1 = \frac{-\mu_1 R_L}{r_{p1} + R_L} \tag{19-17}$$

We also express the output voltage as follows:

$$\Delta e_k = A_2 \, \Delta e_{g2} \tag{19-18}$$

where A_2 is the gain of the cathode follower stage, that is,

$$A_2 = \frac{\mu_2 R_k}{r_{p2} + R_k(\mu_2 + 1)} \tag{19-19}$$

where $R_k = [R'_k \,\|\, R_v]$. The increment in first tube grid voltage equals the drop across R_1 plus the output voltage; thus, assuming zero grid current,

$$\Delta e_{g1} = R_1 i + \Delta e_k \tag{19-20}$$

By algebraic manipulation of Eqs. (19-16), (19-18), and (19-20) we can obtain

$$\Delta e_k = \frac{A}{1 - A} R_1 i \tag{19-21}$$

where $A = A_1 A_2$. By using Eqs. (19-20) and (19-21), we can obtain

$$R_{\text{in}} = \frac{\Delta e_{g1}}{i} = \frac{R_1}{1 - A} \tag{19-22}$$

Equation (19-21) tells us that if A is about -20, then $|\Delta e_k|$ is about 95 per cent of $R_1 i$. The output voltage is developed across the voltmeter V of resistance R_v, which is small compared with R_1, so there is a large power gain.

Equation (19-22) shows that the input resistance is reduced by the factor $1/(1 - A)$, thereby lowering the time constant.

Example: Let $A_1 = -25$, $A_2 = 0.8$, $R_1 = 10^{13} \ \Omega$, and $i = 10^{-13}$ A. Then $A = -25 \times 0.8 = -20$, and $R_1 i = 1.0$ V. Equation (19-21) gives $\Delta e_K = (-20/21) \times 1.0 = -0.953$ V. Equation (19-22) gives $R_{\text{in}} = 10^{13}/21 = 4.75 \times 10^{11} \ \Omega$. If the input capacitance is taken as 10 pF, the time constant will be 4.75 sec. The feedback tends to reduce the grid signal. Thus, in this example we use Eq. (19-20) to calculate $\Delta e_{g1} = 1.00 - 0.953 = 0.047$ V. The small change in grid voltage is helpful in minimizing the effect of grid current of the electrometer tube.

d. *Other electrometer circuits*

A different electrometer uses a modulated input followed by an ac amplifier similar to the dc amplifiers described in Sec. 14-3. Electromechanical chopper switches may be used as the modulator, or an input capacitor with a vibrating plate.

REFERENCES

19-1 D. Bartholomew, *Electrical Measurements and Instrumentation*, Allyn and Bacon, Inc., Boston, 1963.

19-2 E. Bleuler and R. O. Haxby, eds., *Electronic Methods*, v. 2 of *Methods of Experimental Physics*, Academic Press Inc., New York, 1964.

19-3 R. H. Cerni and L. E. Foster, *Instrumentation for Engineering Measurement*, John Wiley & Sons, Inc., New York, 1962.

19-4 F. K. Harris, *Electrical Measurements*, John Wiley & Sons, Inc., New York, 1952.

19-5 H. V. Malmstadt, C. G. Enke, and E. C. Toren, Jr., *Electronics for Scientists*, W. A. Benjamin, Inc., New York, 1962, Chaps. 6–9.

19-6 Gordon R. Partridge, *Principles of Electronic Instruments*, Prentice-Hall, Inc., Englewood Cliffs, N. J., 1958.

19-7 S. D. Prensky, *Electronic Instrumentation*, Prentice-Hall, Inc., Englewood Cliffs, N. J., 1963.

19-8 F. E. Terman and J. M. Pettit, *Electronic Measurements*, 2d ed., McGraw-Hill Book Company, New York, 1952.

19-9 Harold E. Soisson, *Electronic Measuring Instruments*, McGraw-Hill Book Company, New York, 1961.

19-10 H. A. Strobel, *Chemical Instrumentation*, Addison-Wesley Publishing Company, Inc., Reading, Mass., 1960.

19-11 H. E. Thomas and C. A. Clarke, *Handbook of Electronic Instruments and Measurement Techniques*, Prentice-Hall, Inc., Englewood Cliffs, N. J., 1967.

EXERCISES

19-1 The meter M in the ohmmeter circuit in Fig. 19-1 has a full-scale current of 25 μA and a resistance of 1200 Ω. Find the values of R_1 and of R_2 needed so that when $R_x = 10,000\ \Omega$ the meter deflection is half scale.

19-2 Suppose that e_{in} in Fig. 19-5 has the value $4 + 2 \sin \omega t$ V. Assume that RC is about ten times the period of the ac component of e_{in}. Sketch wave forms of e_{in}, e_D, and e_C, the voltage across capacitor C, on the assumption that the effects of R_1 and C_1 are negligible. (b) What is the magnitude and wave form of the input voltage to the dc electronic voltmeter if R_1 and C_1 are properly chosen?

19-3 Draw a two-section compensated attenuator with sections like those in Fig. 19-6. Label the upper section R_1, C_1 and the lower section R_2, C_2. Assume that a voltage $\sqrt{2}\, E \sin \omega t$ is applied to the combination. Show that, if $R_1 C_1 = R_2 C_2$, the ratio of E_2 across the lower section to the total voltage E is independent of the frequency. (The compensated voltage divider will also attenuate a pulse without distortion. Imagine that a voltage pulse is expressed as an infinite series of harmonic voltages by means of the Fourier integral. Each term of the series will be attenuated by the same fraction, and therefore the attenuated terms will add to give the same shape of pulse, but of a lower magnitude.)

19-4 An average responsive ac electronic voltmeter has an equivalent input impedance of 1.5-MΩ resistance shunted by 40-pF capacitance. What is the *magnitude* of the input impedance at frequencies of (a) 5 kHz, (b) 100 kHz, and (c) 1.5 MHz?

19-5 An amplifier output voltage wave is expressible as $40 \cos 1000t + 10 \cos 2000t$ V. (a) What is the rms value of this wave? (b) What is the scale reading when this wave is applied to a voltmeter that responds to the positive peak of the wave but is scaled in rms values of a sine wave? (c) Repeat (b) for a voltmeter that responds to the positive half-wave average but is scaled in rms values of a sine wave.

19-6 A half-wave rectified sine wave has the value $100 \sin \omega t$ V for the first half-cycle and zero for the remainder of the cycle. This voltage wave is impressed on two electronic voltmeters, each of which has a capacitor in series with the input terminals. Both voltmeters are scaled in rms values of a sine calibrating wave. What is the reading on (a) the peak responsive voltmeter, and (b) the positive half-wave average responsive voltmeter?

19-7 Assume that in the circuit in Fig. 19-13 the value of E is 1.5 V, that slide-wire S comprises 200 Ω total, and that $e_s = 50$ mV when SW is open. Let the amplifier input resistance be 2000 Ω, and the Thévenin equivalent of the unknown voltage source consist of a 50.2 mV dc source in series with 500 Ω. What is the amplifier input voltage e when SW is switched to terminal 1?

19-8 In a cathode-ray tube electron gun the electrons gain kinetic energy at the expense of the potential energy due to the accelerating voltage V_a. By equating the energies, we find the electron velocity as it leaves the gun to be $(2q_e V_a/m)^{1/2}$, where q_e and m are the electronic charge and mass. In a particular CRO tube the electrostatic deflecting plates have a dimension of 2 cm along the axis of the tube and a spacing of 1 cm. If the accelerating voltage is 3000 V, what is the highest frequency signal that can be used on the deflecting plates if the time of flight of the electron past the plates is not to exceed 5 per cent of the period of the signal?

19-9 What general rule can be given for deducing the ratio of the two component frequencies from the Lissajous figure that they produce?

19-10 One pair of deflecting plates in a CRO and the associated wiring has a capacitance of 40 pF. This set of plates has a deflection sensitivity of 30 V/cm. (a) What rate of change of voltage is needed in a sawtooth linear sweep to produce a sweep rate of 0.5 μs/cm? (b) What current must be supplied to the deflecting plate system under this condition?

19-11 In the recording of single transients on a CRO screen by photographic means one limiting factor is the instantaneous linear velocity of the spot on the screen, called the *writing rate*. Suppose that in a particular situation the maximum writing rate that will record properly is 8×10^6 cm/sec. (a) Estimate the shortest rise time pulse that can be recorded if the pulse height is 3 cm and the horizontal deflection during the rise time is to be 2 cm. (b) Calculate the highest frequency of a single sine-wave transient that can be recorded if the wave is adjusted to have an 8-cm period and a *p-p* deflection of 6 cm.

19-12 It is desired to portray the pressure versus time variation in the cylinder of an air compressor on a *CR* oscilloscope. Assume that a pressure transducer is available which will generate a voltage adequate to apply to the amplifier in the oscilloscope. Show a block diagram similar to Fig. 19-20 for this test. Include a method of keeping the sweep in exact synchronism with the compressor shaft rotation. Note that the use of "internal" synchronization is not satisfactory.

19-13 Provide the derivation of Eq. (19-10) and show that $R = 1/nq$, where n is the number of carriers per unit volume and q is their charge. Recall that the force on a moving charge due to the magnetic field is $f_y = -B_z q v_x$; that $J_x = nqv_x$, and that the force due to the electric field is $f_y = qE_y$.

19-14 Show a diagram of a method by which a Hall effect device can be converted into a wattmeter to read time-average power and explain the theoretical basis of the method.

19-15 Suppose that a triode operating in the electrometer circuit in Fig. 19-23 has the parameters $g_m = 100$ μmhos and $r_p = 10^5$ Ω. Also let $R = 10,000$ Ω, the resistance of G be 200 Ω and the balancing battery equal 3.0 V. Assume that the value of i_b at the Q point is 0.25 mA. (a) Discuss the problem of operating the circuit and of the balancing network, if full-scale on G equals 20 μA. (b) What full-scale current sensitivity is required in G if a Δe_c of 0.4 V should produce full-scale deflection? (c) Use the circuit in this exercise as a basis for an explanation of why the Miller effect can be neglected when making estimates of the input capacitance C_i.

20

Electrical Noise

20-1
Introduction

An electrical noise voltage or current is any unwanted component that tends to interfere with the transmission or reception of information or signals. Some sources of electrical noise are inherent in the apparatus, for example, tube and transistor noise due to the "graininess" of the electric current and noise in conductors due to the thermal motion of the electrons. Other noise voltages arise due to atmospheric electricity or lightning, radio or TV stations, fluorescent lamps, the electric and magnetic fields of nearby power apparatus, mechanical vibration of tube elements or air capacitor plates, and the ripple voltage in dc power supplies.

20-2
Reduction of stray voltages

Some noise voltages can be reduced by obvious means, for example, by the use of cushioning or acoustic shielding against vibrations, or by the use of a voltage regulator on the dc supply.

The most effective way to mitigate the effects of external fields is to *shield* the circuit by placing it in a closed metal box. At low frequencies we may

536

separate the effects of electric and magnetic fields and discuss *electrostatic* coupling and shielding and *magnetic* coupling and shielding separately.

The coupling of an electrostatic field to a portion of a circuit may be simulated by a "stray" capacitance C_s in a circuit as shown in Fig. 20-1a.

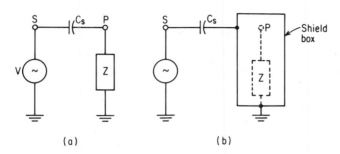

(a)   (b)

FIGURE 20-1   Electrostatic shielding.

Here S is an electrode that is charged by the voltage V and thus acts as a source of an electric field and P is a terminal on the apparatus such as the input terminal of an amplifier. Point P is connected to ground via an impedance Z. The stray voltage that develops at P thus depends on the relative values of Z and of C_s and on the frequency. If Z is a high impedance, the voltage developed on P is particularly likely to be troublesome. If electrode P and the wires connected thereto are completely surrounded by a conducting shield box (Fig. 20-1b), no field will penetrate the shield and no stray voltage will arise on P. The shield may consist of sheet metal or of fine wire mesh.

The input signal lead to an amplifier may be shielded by means of a flexible conducting sheath connected to the amplifier shield. An alternative arrangement is to use two inner conductors inside a grounded flexible conducting shield to carry the signal to the amplifier input. When high-frequency waves or fast pulses travel along such shielded cables, the details of the mode of transmission of the signals may become important. As outlined in Appendix E, the signals may be distorted and delayed, particularly if the cable is long.

When the signal level is low or the frequency is high, there is a risk that a stray voltage will be generated in so-called *ground loops* if a multiplicity of ground connections go from the amplifier circuit components to the shield. Furthermore, the currents in the ground connections may cause small voltages between the different "grounding" points on the shield. A preferred construction is shown in Fig. 20-2. Here an insulated ground bus wire (or plate) is used for the common connections of the low-level stage of an *RF* amplifier, and a single connection is made from the ground bus to the shield.

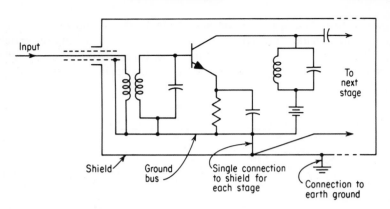

FIGURE 20-2   Preferred method of circuit grounding.

Usually a connection from the shield to earth ground (water pipe or ground rod) is desirable.

Often ac power must be conveyed to the inside of a shield box. Then the problem of avoiding disturbances (*RF* voltages, impulse voltages, etc.) that may enter the shield via the power wires arises. A similar situation is found when a shielded room is provided to shield sensitive electronic apparatus. A low-pass filter connected as in Fig. 20-3 will serve to reduce the stray voltages that enter via the power wires.

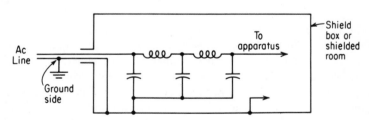

FIGURE 20-3   Showing filter for power supply to shield box or shielded room.

Magnetically induced voltages arise in transformer coils, in inductors, and even in loops of the connecting wires. The field surrounding a pair of wires carrying alternating current can be reduced by transposing the wires by twisting them together, or by the use of a coaxial line.

Electrostatic coupling occurs between the two windings of an ordinary iron-core transformer. This coupling may allow currents to flow via the secondary coil to ground through one of the impedances in the circuit and thereby produce an unwanted voltage. A grounded conducting shield placed between the two windings (Fig. 20-4) will remove this difficulty. The shield must, of course, have an insulating gap so as not to form a short-circuited turn around the core.

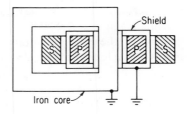

A box of high-permeability magnetic material placed around a coil will act to shield the surroundings from the field of the current-carrying coil. Conversely, such a shield will reduce the voltage induced in the coil from an external alternating magnetic field.

FIGURE 20-4 Principle of shield between transformer coils. P = primary coil and S = secondary coil.

When high frequencies are involved, the shielding around a coil is provided by a shield can of aluminum or copper. Then the eddy currents induced in the can act to prevent an appreciable fraction of the external field from penetrating the conducting shield. The effectiveness of such a shield can be judged by reference to the penetration of a plane electromagnetic wave, alternating in time, into the conductor. If the plane of the advancing wave is parallel to the plane of the conductor, then the current density in the conductor varies in time and falls off in magnitude as it penetrates the metal according to the relation

$$i = I_m \cos{(\omega t - \beta x)} \exp{(-\alpha x)} \qquad (20\text{-}1)$$

where I_m is the peak current density at the surface. Here β equals α and α is proportional to $\sqrt{\mu \sigma f}$, where μ is the permeability, σ is the conductivity of the metal, and f is the frequency. A similar expression holds for the variation of the magnetic intensity (field) with the depth. Hartshorn† calculates that a copper shield would have to be 4 cm thick to reduce the magnetic field to 0.2 per cent of the incident field when f is 100 Hz, but that if f is 10^6 Hz, then 1 mm of copper will reduce the field to less than 10^{-6} of its surface value. High-permeability ferromagnetic materials make useful shields at low and radio frequencies.

Additional information concerning shielding and circuit arrangement is presented by Terman and Pettit‡ and by Kelling.‖

20-3
Thermal noise

After the stray voltages from extraneous sources have been eliminated, there remain several sources of noise from within the electronic circuit itself.

†L. Hartshorn, *Radio-frequency Measurement by Bridge and Resonance Methods*, John Wiley & Sons, Inc., New York, 1941, Chap. 3.

‡F.E. Terman and J.M. Pettit, *Electronic Measurements*, 2d ed., McGraw-Hill Book Company, New York, 1952, pp. 676–683.

‖L. U. C. Kelling in *Industrial Electronics Handbook*, W. D. Cockrell, ed., McGraw-Hill Book Company, New York, 1958, Sec. 7a.

These seriously limit the maximum useful sensitivity and dynamic range of amplifiers and interfere with the amplification of weak signals.

One of these noise voltages arises because of the fluctuations in the energy (or velocity) of the electrons in a resistor. These fluctuations depend on the temperature and in classical terms are identified with the thermal agitation of the electrons. Consider first an open-circuited resistor. The random motions of the electrons would be expected to produce a varying potential difference between the ends of the resistor, since otherwise the electron motions would have to cancel each other's effect *exactly* at every instant of time. The resulting electrical noise is called *thermal noise, resistor noise,* or *Johnson noise* after J. B. Johnson, who reported on the effect in 1927.

Before attempting quantitative definitions of noise voltage, current, or power, we examine the phenomenon from the experimental viewpoint. Suppose that a resistor is connected from the input terminal to ground of a low-noise, high-gain amplifier and we record the output on an oscillograph. The output wave will give a clue, though indirect, about the wave form of the noise voltage at the terminals of the resistor at the input. The appearance of the wave form will depend on the bandwidth of the amplifier. With a wide-band amplifier the observed wave is an irregularly fluctuating wave with some slow variations, some high-frequency but jagged components, and occasional spikes of varying heights. With a narrow bandwidth amplifier the waves look somewhat like AM waves or beat phenomenon waves but with a continually varying composition. Suppose that a narrow bandwidth amplifier is used but that the center frequency of the passband is varied while the mean-square output voltage is observed. A remarkable result is found, namely, that the mean-square voltage is independent of the center frequency!

These experiments show that a quantitative expression of the noise power or voltage must deal with time-average values. Further, these average values can best be expressed as distribution functions of the frequency. One approach is to think of the noise voltage wave as sampled by a frequency-selective circuit and to use the time-average output to calculate the value of the distribution function at the center frequency.† The power distribution function for thermal noise is a constant independent of frequency. Nyquist showed that the open-circuit mean-squared thermal noise voltage developed in a resistance R is given by

$$E^2 = 4kTR\,\Delta f \tag{20-2}$$

where k is the Boltzmann constant, T is the absolute temperature of the

†See Reference 20-1, Chap. 2.

resistor, and Δf is the noise bandwidth of the measuring system to be defined presently.†

Consider a resistor of 50,000 Ω connected between the first grid and ground of a tube amplifier. What is the effective noise voltage within a bandwidth of 500 kHz? Assuming a temperature of 27°C (300°K) and inserting values in (20-2), we find $E^2 = 4.14 \times 10^{-10}$ or $E = 2.03 \times 10^{-5}$ V. We see that thermal noise seriously limits the maximum useful amplification, or, stated in another way, prevents the detection of small signal voltages.

The thermal-noise voltage in a resistor acts as if it were a voltage source in series with a noise-free resistor as shown in Fig. 20-5b. Alternatively, the Norton form of equivalent circuit comprising a noise current generator and shunting resistor (Fig. 20-5c) may be used. The mean-square noise current source has the value

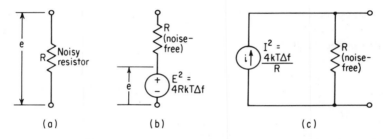

(a)   (b)   (c)

FIGURE 20-5   (a) A noisy resistor, (b) Thévenin equivalent noise generator, and (c) Norton equivalent noise generator.

$$I^2 = \frac{4kT\Delta f}{R} \tag{20-3}$$

It is of interest to calculate the *available noise power* that could be delivered by the noise source to a *matched* noise-free load resistor R connected across the noisy resistor thus,

$$P = \frac{E^2}{4R} = kT\Delta f \tag{20-4}$$

The fact that the noise power P is proportional to the bandwidth Δf implies that the distribution of noise power over the frequency spectrum is uniform. This conclusion has been tested experimentally and found to hold for resistors at room temperature over a frequency range up to the order of 10^{10} Hz. Thermal noise is called *white* noise in analogy with the distribution of wavelengths of white light over the optical spectrum.

†Symbols such as $\overline{e^2}$ and $\overline{E^2}$ have also been used for the noise voltage to emphasize its time-average nature. This nature must be kept in mind even though the averaging process is not explicitly indicated.

20-4
Circuit calculations
involving thermal noise

a. Noise bandwidth

It will be helpful to define the *noise bandwidth* of a transfer function $\mathbf{G}(f)$. Here $\mathbf{G}(f)$ is the ratio of the phasor output to the input quantity of a network and may be a voltage ratio, an impedance, etc. A mathematical definition of noise bandwidth is the following:

$$B = \frac{1}{G_o^2} \int_0^\infty |\mathbf{G}(f)|^2 \, df \qquad (20\text{-}5)$$

where G_o is the maximum absolute value of $\mathbf{G}(f)$. An example is shown in Fig. 20-6. We see that B has such a value that the rectangular area BG_o^2 equals the area under the curve $|\mathbf{G}(f)|^2$.

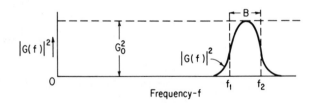

FIGURE 20-6   Noise bandwidth.

The noise bandwidth of a broad-band amplifier that has no peaks in its gain curve can be taken to be determined by its half-power frequencies as an approximation.

b. Parallel tuned circuit

A calculation of the average noise voltage across a parallel tuned circuit (Fig. 20-7) will show how this selective circuit affects the terminal voltage. The generator I represents the Norton generator noise source due to the resistance R. The coil and capacitor are regarded as loss free. The value of I^2 over a frequency range df at frequency f will be

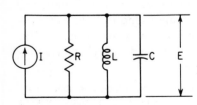

FIGURE 20-7   Parallel tuned circuit with Norton noise generator I.

$$I^2 = 4kT\frac{df}{R} \qquad (20\text{-}6)$$

To find the mean-square value of E we need to integrate the effect of I over all frequencies. First we recall (see Eq. (2-97)) the formula for the impedance of the parallel circuit

$$\mathbf{Z}(f) = \frac{\mathbf{E}}{\mathbf{I}} = \frac{1}{\frac{1}{R} + j\left(\omega C - \frac{1}{\omega L}\right)} \tag{20-7}$$

For convenience we define the resonance frequency f_o by the relation

$$4\pi^2 f_o^2 LC = 1 \tag{20-8}$$

and also the Q factor

$$Q = 2\pi f_o CR \tag{20-9}$$

Then we can combine (20-7), (20-8), and (20-9) to obtain

$$|\mathbf{Z}(f)|^2 = \frac{R^2}{\left[1 + Q^2\left(\frac{f}{f_o} - \frac{f_o}{f}\right)^2\right]} \tag{20-10}$$

If we multiply $|\mathbf{Z}(f)|^2$ by I^2 as given in (20-6), we obtain the contribution to E^2 from the noise in the frequency range df taken at frequency f. To obtain the total E^2, we need to integrate over all frequencies; thus,

$$E^2 = \int_0^\infty \frac{4kTR^2\,df}{R\left[1 + Q^2\left(\frac{f}{f_o} - \frac{f_o}{f}\right)^2\right]} \tag{20-11}$$

The integral of $df/\{1 + Q^2[(f/f_o) - (f_o/f)]^2\}$ from zero to infinity can be shown to have the value $\pi f_o/2Q$. Consequently,

$$E^2 = 4kTR\frac{\pi f_o}{2Q} = \frac{2\pi kTRf_o}{Q} \tag{20-12}$$

We note that the total noise voltage decreases as Q increases. This result is reasonable because the higher Q circuit is more selective.

An interpretation of the foregoing results in terms of noise bandwidth is readily made. We think of starting with Eq. (20-5) and replacing $\mathbf{G}(f)$ with $\mathbf{Z}(f)$ and G_o with R. Upon working out the value of B from (20-5), we obtain the same integral as before, that is,

$$B = \int_0^\infty \frac{df}{\left[1 - Q^2\left(\frac{f}{f_o} - \frac{f_o}{f}\right)^2\right]} = \frac{\pi f_o}{2Q} \tag{20-13}$$

Thus E^2 can be expressed as

$$E^2 = 4kTBR \tag{20-14}$$

This relation is the same as Eq. (20-2) except that here the more precisely defined bandwidth B replaces Δf.

For an example we let $f_o = 10^7$ Hz and $Q = 500$; then B works out to be 31.4 kHz. If we further let $T = 300°$K and $R = 10^4\ \Omega$, we find $E = 2.3\ \mu$V.

c. Two-terminal passive network

Consider a two-terminal passive network connected to an external impedance. In Fig. 20-8a the external impedance is the resistance R_1. An important theorem due to Nyquist facilitates the calculation of the noise power delivered *by the network* to the external impedance. Let the equivalent impedance of the network referred to its terminals be $\mathbf{Z}(f)$, where

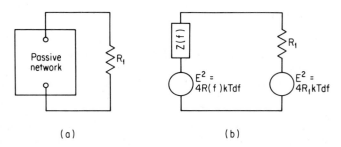

(a)   (b)

FIGURE 20-8   Nyquist's theorem.

$$\mathbf{Z}(f) = R(f) + jX(f) \tag{20-15}$$

at frequency f. The theorem states that the mean-square noise current delivered by the network to the external impedance is given by

$$I^2 = 4kT \int_0^\infty R(f)\,|\mathbf{G}(f)|^2 \; df \tag{20-16}$$

where $\mathbf{G}(f)$ is the complex transfer function relating current to driving voltage at the frequency f. The following example will clarify the meaning of the theorem.

Let the network consist of a fixed resistor R in series with an inductance L and let the external impedance be R_1. Then,

$$\mathbf{Z}(f) = R + j\omega L \tag{20-17}$$

Also,

$$\mathbf{G}(f) = \frac{\mathbf{I}}{\mathbf{E}} = \frac{1}{R + R_1 + j\omega L} \tag{20-18}$$

Thus the noise current I^2 *caused by the network* is, by (20-16),

$$I^2 = 4kT \int_0^\infty \frac{R\,df}{(R + R_1)^2 + 4\pi^2 f^2 L^2} \tag{20-19}$$

Of course in the circuit being considered (Fig. 20-8) the noise voltage due to resistor R_1 will also cause a current in the circuit. It will be left as an exercise for the reader to show that the exchange of power is equal when the temperature is the same throughout the system.

20-5
Definitions of noise temperature,
noise ratio, and noise figure

In an amplifier the thermal noise voltage at the input is due to the resistance component of the input network. If the amplifier contributed zero noise, then the noise voltage at the output would be equal to the input noise voltage within the noise bandwidth of the amplifier multiplied by the voltage gain. However, the amplifying devices (transistors or tubes) add noise voltages of their own. It should be emphasized that the contribution of the first stage is of primary importance since it is amplified to the greatest extent. Noise measurements or calculations are needed to study the various contributions to the total noise at the output, and quantitative definitions of the noise parameters are needed.

As a standard of reference the available thermal noise power at the reference temperature T_r, i.e., kT_rB (see Eq. (20-4)), at the input terminals is often used, since this is the irreducible minimum. It is customary to use $T_r = 290°K$.

a. Noise temperature

This term is applied to a two-terminal device, such as a resistor, or an antenna. Some resistors, such as metal-film and wire-wound types, develop only the basic thermal noise voltage. Other resistors, such as the carbon composition type, exhibit an excess noise above the thermal noise while carrying current. An equivalent *noise temperature* may be defined for a device that exhibits excess noise. It is that temperature at which the available *thermal* noise power per unit bandwidth would be equal to the *actual* available noise power per cycle at the two terminals. If we adopt the symbol P_n for the available power for $B = 1$ Hz, we see from Eq. (20-4) that the noise temperature T_n can be expressed as

$$T_n = \frac{P_n}{k} = 7.25 \times 10^{22}P_n \qquad (20\text{-}20)$$

If the noise is white noise, then P_n and T_n are independent of frequency, but in general they vary with frequency. For example, the excess noise in resistors often varies as $1/f$ over the low frequency range, say, below 1 or 2 kHz.

b. Noise ratio

The noise ratio of a two-terminal device is defined to be the ratio of the noise temperature T_n to the actual temperature T. Thus the noise ratio r_n can be expressed as

$$r_n = \frac{T_n}{T} = \frac{P_n}{kT} \tag{20-21}$$

Values of r_n greater than unity indicate that there is more noise present than if the noise were entirely thermal noise. The ratio r_n may also be expressed as $10 \log_{10} r_n$ dB.

c. Noise figure, noise factor

These terms are usefully applied to two-port devices like amplifiers, which may have internal noise sources. The *noise figure* of a two-port device may be defined by the ratio

$$F = \frac{N_{ao}}{N_{ar}} \tag{20-22}$$

where

N_{ao} = the total *available* noise power at the output per unit band-
     width

N_{ar} = that portion of N_{ao} due to the *available* thermal noise power
     of the input network at the standard reference temperature
     $T_r = 290°K$ $(17°C)$

Alternatively, the powers N_{ao} and N_{ar} are taken over the noise bandwidth of the device. If the device does not add any noise power to that introduced at the input, the noise figure will be unity.

An alternative definition of noise figure is phrased in terms of the ratio of available signal power to noise power both taken at the output to the same ratio taken at the input. This may be written

$$F = \frac{\dfrac{S_{ai}}{N_{ai}}}{\dfrac{S_{ao}}{N'_{ao}}} \tag{20-23}$$

where

S_{ai} = *available* signal power at the input within the noise band-
     width B

S_{ao} = the same quantity at the output

N_{ai} = *available* noise power at the input within bandwidth B due
     to the thermal noise in the signal generator at $290°K$, i.e.,
     $N_{ai} = k290B$

N'_{ao} = total *available* noise power at the output for a bandwidth B

When the two-port network introduces noise power from internal sources, then N'_{ao} is higher than it would otherwise be, and the noise figure is increased above unity. Thus a large noise figure means that the network has degraded the quality of the signal.

The terms in (20-23) can be illustrated by a calculation to verify that the noise figure of a *noise-free* amplifier is unity. The relevant quantities are shown in Fig. 20-9. Thus the input termination is the resistance R at tempera-

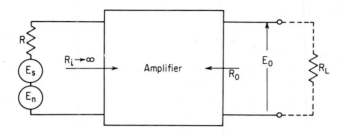

FIGURE 20-9   Network to illustrate the calculation of noise figure.

ture T_r (290°K), the amplifier input resistance is assumed to be infinite, and the output resistance is R_o. Also let the voltage gain be G_v in the passband. We shall calculate all quantities in Eq. (20-23) for the noise bandwidth B of the amplifier. Thus the mean-square thermal noise voltage at the input is $4kT_rBR$. Therefore

$$N_{ai} = \frac{E_n^2}{4R} = kT_rB \tag{20-24}$$

The available signal power at the input is

$$S_{ai} = \frac{E_s^2}{4R} \tag{20-25}$$

The available noise power at the output of the (noise-free) amplifier is

$$N'_{ao} = \frac{E_n^2 G_v^2}{4R_o} = \frac{kT_rRBG_v^2}{R_o} \tag{20-26}$$

Furthermore,

$$S_{ao} = \frac{E_s^2 G_v^2}{4R_o} \tag{20-27}$$

Upon inserting the quantities from (20-24) through (20-27) into (20-23), we obtain

$$F = \frac{E_s^2}{4R} \times \frac{1}{kT_rB} \times \frac{4R_o}{E_s^2 G_v^2} \times \frac{RkT_rBG_v^2}{R_o} = 1 \tag{20-28}$$

In most actual amplifiers the value of N_{ao} will be higher than given by (20-26) and F will exceed unity.

20-6
Device noise

a. Thermionic diode

We visualize the plate current of a diode as the net effect of the arrival of large numbers of electrons at the anode. Not only the discrete nature of the charge but also the random arrival times will tend to produce fluctuations in the current. These fluctuations about the mean or dc value produce the so-called *shot noise* associated with electron currents in tubes and transistors.

When a diode is operating under temperature-limited (saturated) conditions, the space charge is negligible and has no effect, and the random nature of the emission process causes the *full shot noise*. The diode is a constant current device under this condition; therefore the full shot noise within the bandwidth B is appropriately expressed as a Norton source of mean-square current of a value derived by W. Schottky

$$I^2 = 2q_e I_b B \tag{20-29}$$

where q_e is the electronic charge, and I_b is the dc plate current. This relation indicates that the shot noise is a white noise.

In a diode whose current is *space-charge limited* the shot noise is reduced considerably. This result is due to the potential minimum near the cathode which turns back the slower electrons. The fluctuations in the potential minimum caused by the noise current components may be regarded as producing a smoothing effect on the total current. The resulting *reduced shot noise* current is given by the same formula as (20-29) except for a reduction factor Γ^2; thus,

$$I^2 = 2\Gamma^2 q_e I_b B \tag{20-30}$$

Typical thoeretical values[†] of Γ^2 may range from 0.05 to 0.15.

b. Grid-controlled thermionic tubes

Triodes normally are operated with space-charge-limited current, and their shot noise is therefore reduced below that of an equivalent temperature-limited diode. The shot noise is usually expressed in terms of an equivalent resistance R_{eq} placed in the grid circuit. That is, an equivalent circuit is used assuming a noise-free tube and a grid resistor whose thermal noise at the standard temperature will produce the actual noise component in the plate current. An approximate value for R_{eq} for triodes that have amplification factors greater than 5 follows:

†See Reference 20-1, p. 73.

$$R_{eq} = \frac{2.5}{g_m} \qquad (20\text{-}31)$$

For example, if $g_m = 0.0025$ mhos, then $R_{eq} = 1000\ \Omega$.

In pentodes an additional noise component is present compared with triodes. This is caused by the random division of the space current between the screen grid and the plate and is called *partition* noise. An approximate expression for the equivalent grid resistance needed to represent the total noise in a pentode follows:

$$R_{eq} = R_{eqo}\left(1 + \frac{8I_c}{g_m}\right) \qquad (20\text{-}32)$$

Here R_{eqo} is the equivalent resistance for the tube connected as a triode (plate and screen joined), and I_c is the screen current. Although pentodes are basically noisier than triodes, a modern high-g_m pentode approaches the noise performance of a triode.

Additional types of noise in tubes include *induced grid noise* and *flicker effect*. The induced grid noise arises from the current induced in the grid circuit by an electron passing near the grid. The resulting noise has a rising frequency distribution and may become predominant at frequencies above 50 or 100 MHz. The noise due to the flicker effect seems to be associated with variations in the electron emission over patches of the oxide-coated cathode. This noise varies as $1/f$ and becomes negligible at frequencies above about 5 kHz.

c. Phototubes, ion counters

The currents through phototubes and ionization chambers and counters display a shot noise component of the Schottky type expressed by Eq. (20-29).

In a photomultiplier tube the first stage photo current also has the full shot noise component. In the electron multiplication process only a small increase in relative noise occurs, so the noise figure of the device is not far from unity, commonly being in the order of 1.15. Lion† discusses the noise in photomultipliers, including the effect of reducing the tube temperature in reducing the noise.

d. Transistor noise

Each of the basic processes that act on the charge carriers, i.e., diffusion, recombination, and thermal generation, are random processes that cause noise. In addition, noise is generated in the bulk resistance of the base and by surface imperfections that cause surface leakage. The latter effect is primarily

†K. S. Lion, *Instrumentation in Scientific Research*, McGraw-Hill Book Company, New York, 1959, pp. 252 ff.

responsible for the so-called $1/f$ noise, i.e., a component that varies inversely with the frequency.

The total noise inherent in the transistor can be expressed as a noise figure as defined in Eq. (20-22), or as an equivalent input noise resistance defined the same as R_{eq} for the triode. The noise figure is found to vary with frequency in a general way as shown in Fig. 20-10. The $1/f$ component generally becomes negligible above 0.5 or 1 kHz. At high frequencies the noise factor rises, owing to an added component that varies as f^2. This variation is accounted for by the reduction in signal gain at high frequencies whereas the noise associated with the dc collector current remains constant.

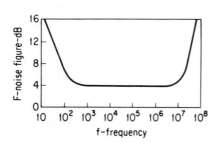

FIGURE 20-10   Narrow band noise figure *vs.* frequency for a transistor. Note: Noise figure in dB equals $10 \log F$.

Thornton *et al.*† consider the component currents in an idealized *pnp* transistor that contribute to the noise to include: (1) the main stream of holes moving from emitter to base and collected by the collector, (2) holes moving from emitter to base which recombine in the base, (3) holes thermally generated in the base which are injected into the emitter region, and (4) holes thermally generated in the base which move into the collector region (which cause leakage current I_{CBO}).

All these involve random processes, and the resulting noise due to each component can be expressed as a shot noise of the Schottky type. Therefore current generators can be used in the small-signal circuit model of the transistor to account for the different noise components. If we limit the discussion to conditions of transistor operation where I_C is large compared with I_{CBO}, we may neglect the effect of current component 4. Current component 1 produces a noise generator between emitter and collector. Components 2 and 3, which are independent sources of noise, can be combined to give a noise generator between base and emitter. The resulting hybrid-π equivalent circuit for the common-emitter connection is shown in Fig. 20-11. This diagram also includes the noise generator E_{bn}^2 due to the base resistance $r_{bb'}$.

Thornton *et al.*‡ present formulas for the values of the current generators over low-frequency and high-frequency ranges and also present techniques for minimizing the noise in transistor applications. A summary of their conclusions follows.

†R. D. Thornton, D. DeWitt, E. R. Chenette, and P. E. Gray, *Characteristics and Limitations of Transistors* (SEEC v. 1), John Wiley & Sons, Inc., New York, 1966, Chap. 5.
‡R. D. Thornton *et al.*, *loc. cit.*

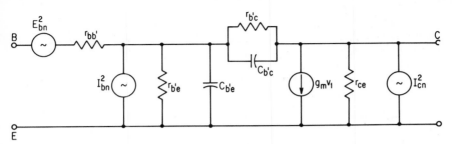

FIGURE 20-11   Hybrid- π transistor equivalent circuit including noise generators.

To achieve low noise in the middle frequency range it is necessary to operate with a low value of I_C, that is, with $|I_C| < 0.1\ kT/q_e r_{bb'}$. However, if I_C is made too low, other factors will cause the noise figure to rise again. The source resistance R_g should be chosen consistent with the relation $|I_B I_C|^{1/2} R_g q_e = kT$.

In the low-frequency range it is best to choose a low-noise type of transistor. Further advantage is gained by selecting an individual unit that exhibits a minimum $1/f$ noise. Operation at low values of I_C and V_{CE} generally will be helpful.

For high-frequency operation the transistor should have low values of $C_{b'c}$ and $r_{bb'}$ and high values of $|I_C/I_B|$ and of gain-bandwidth product ω_T.

In some situations the operation must be with low values of source resistance, e.g., $R_g < r_{bb'}$. Then choosing a transistor with a low $r_{bb'}$ is more important than using a high value of $|I_C/I_B|$.

20-7
Measurement of noise figure

Noise measurements require particular care in laboratory technique and in interpretation. The quantities to be measured are time averages of squared quantities. Theoretically the averaging should be done over an infinite time, but it is practical to use only a short averaging time. This time should be long enough so that increasing it does not change the results significantly.

Two common methods of measurement of the noise figure are (1) the so-called small-signal method, and (2) a method using a standard noise generator. We shall describe only the second method and assume that a temperature-limited diode is used as the standard noise source. The circuit arrangement for the test is given in Fig. 20-12. The variable component of output current or voltage should be observed by an rms-responsive instrument.

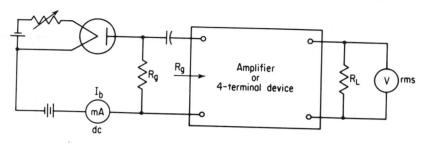

FIGURE 20-12   Arrangement for a test of amplifier noise figure.

The procedure may be outlined as follows. With the diode turned off a reading is taken of V_{rms} at the output and the output noise power P_1 is calculated. This power is the result of the thermal noise from R_g plus the effect of the noise developed in the amplifier or device (say, a radio receiver) to be tested. The different noise sources are independent and therefore their effects add directly. Then the diode is turned on and the current I_b is raised until the output noise power reaches a value P_2. Power P_2 includes the same noise components as P_1, but in addition includes the amplified shot noise added by the diode. This component is independent of the others, and their effects add directly. Since the diode noise power is known, the noise figure of the amplifier can be calculated, as shown by the following derivation.

Let G_p be the available power gain of the amplifier. Then the available output power P_1 with the diode inoperative is

$$P_1 = kT_rBG_p + N_E \tag{20-33}$$

where the first term is based on Eq. (20-4), and N_E is the available output noise power due to noise originating in the amplifier. When the noise diode is operating, we think of a Norton current source in shunt with R_g given by Eq. (20-29). Therefore the available output power P_2 becomes

$$P_2 = kT_rBG_p + \frac{2q_eI_bBR_gG_p}{4} + N_E \tag{20-34}$$

In the measurement P_1 and P_2 (or an indication proportional to P_1 and P_2)† are observed. We assume that I_b is adjusted until the power is doubled

$$P_2 = 2P_1 \tag{20-35}$$

The three relations (20-33), (20-34), and (20-35) allow N_E to be found, with the result

$$N_E = \frac{2q_eI_bBR_gG_p}{4} - kT_rBG_p \tag{20-36}$$

†Since a ratio of P_2 to P_1 will be used in the calculation which follows, it is only necessary to have an indication proportional to the available output power. Thus calibrations that would be required to obtain absolute values of P_1 and P_2 are avoided.

Next we apply the definition of F in Eq. (20-22); thus,

$$F = \frac{N_{ao}}{N_{ar}} = \frac{kT_r BG_p + N_E}{kT_r BG_p} \qquad (20\text{-}37)$$

Using the value of N_E from (20-36) and simplifying, we find

$$F = \frac{q_e}{2kT_r} I_b R_g \quad \text{for} \quad \frac{P_2}{P_1} = 2 \qquad (20\text{-}38)$$

Substituting for q_e and k and using $T_r = 290°\text{K}$ in (20-38) yields

$$F = 20 I_b R_g \qquad (20\text{-}39)$$

Because ratios of output power are used in the foregoing method the results will be independent of the value chosen for R_L.

The use of a calibrated noise diode is an accurate and convenient method of measuring noise figure. Other calibrated noise sources, such as a gaseous discharge tube, are also used, particularly at microwave frequencies.

REFERENCES

20-1 W. R. Bennett, *Electrical Noise*, McGraw-Hill Book Company, New York, 1960.

20-2 J. F. Cleary, ed., *General Electric Transistor Manual*, 7th ed., General Electric Company, Syracuse, N.Y., 1964, pp. 499 ff.

20-3 S. Goldman, *Frequency Analysis, Modulation and Noise*, McGraw-Hill Book Company, New York, 1948.

20-4 A. Van der Ziel, *Noise*, Prentice-Hall, Inc., Englewood Cliffs, N. J., 1954.

EXERCISES

20-1 In the equivalent circuit in Fig. 20-13 C_s represents the stray coupling capacitance from a 120-V, 60-cycle terminal V to an exposed lead wire MN. Assume

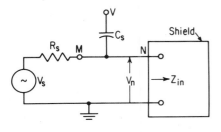

FIGURE 20-13

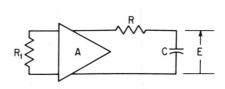

FIGURE 20-14

that Z_{in} of the shielded instrument (e.g., a CRO) consists of 1 MΩ shunted by 40 pF. Calculate the noise, or pickup, voltage V_n if $C_s = 0.5$ pF and (a) $R_s = 5000$ Ω (b) $R_s = 500$ kΩ.

20-2 In Fig. 20-14 amplifier A is an ideal, noise-free unity gain voltage amplifier and R_1 develops only the fundamental thermal noise. (a) Show that the mean square noise voltage E^2 at the terminals of the capacitor is kTR_1/RC and that the noise bandwidth is $1/4RC$. (b) Comment on the application of this RC filter for the reduction of the noise at the output of a measuring system which is measuring a slowly varying quantity. What are the limitations of this method?

20-3 Show that in the circuit in Fig. 20-8b the power delivered to $Z(f)$ by the right-hand noise generator is the same as that delivered to R_1 by the left-hand generator. Let $\mathbf{Z}(f) = R + j\omega L$.

20-4 A measurement of the noise voltage of a 10,000-Ω carbon resistor held at 300°K results in a value of E^2 of 2.21×10^{-15} V². The noise bandwidth of the measuring system is 10 Hz and the center frequency is 200 Hz. What is the noise temperature of the resistor?

20-5 Consider an amplifier that is terminated in matched resistors at both input and output, with $R_i = 3000$ and $R_L = 5000$ Ω. Assume that R_i develops only thermal noise and that its temperature is 290°K. The noise figure of the high-grade amplifier is 3.2 and its available power gain with the termination specified is 2000. (a) What is the available noise power added by the amplifier on a per cycle basis? *Suggestion*: Show that in general this quantity equals $kTG(F-1)$, where G is the available power gain of the amplifier. (b) What is the total noise power delivered to R_L if the amplifier noise bandwidth is 500 Hz? (c) Under the conditions of (b) what is the rms noise voltage at the output?

21

Data Acquisition, Transmission, Recording, and Processing; Telemetry

Introduction

The term *data processing* has evolved in recent years to describe the high-speed mathematical operations, generally performed by digital computers, that are carried out to analyze large masses of numerical data. Often these data consist of the numbers involved in business calculations, such as payroll figures, inventories, and the like. However, our interest is primarily in engineering and scientific data, that is, the numerical results of tests or experiments, and in the manner in which electronic techniques and devices are utilized in handling this data.

In the simplest experiment a single observer may observe a single instrument and record the slowly varying reading as a function of some other variable, say, of the time. He can record perhaps one reading every 5 sec.

If the measured quantity is varying more rapidly, a self-balancing potentiometer could be used to record the values on a strip chart, which could record the equivalent of two readings per second. If the variable is changing still more rapidly, a recording magnetic oscillograph with a high-speed galvanometer could be used. With a galvanometer that responds to frequencies up to 1200 Hz the equivalent "reading rate" might be 600/sec.

Thus far we have been concerned with the *analog* output of an instrument or transducer, but some elements will have an inherently digital output. One example is the Geiger counter. As we shall see presently, it is often

555

desirable to convert analog signals to the digital mode before further processing.

In practical tests the number of experimental variables is greater than one and may vary from a few to fifty or more. For example, in a gas turbine engine test readings may be needed of fuel rate, thrust, revolutions per second, temperature of inlet air, temperature of exhaust gases, temperature of selected rotor blades, etc. In a checkout test on a new design of aircraft extremely elaborate instrumentation is needed to measure and record the flight variables, the power plant variables, and the strains in the structural elements.

An added dimension of complexity may be added if the numerical data must be transmitted great distances without loss of accuracy. Historically, this need arose in such systems as waterworks and electric power systems, where a central control facility required data from outlying parts of the system. As a result *telemetering* systems were developed to meet this need. With the advent of satellites and space probes the transmission distances over which data had to be transmitted multiplied many times. The corollary problem of separating the signals from the noise became more onerous in these systems, which now are usually called *telemetry* systems.

Parallel developments in the communications industry greatly influenced the data processing field. Theoretical and practical developments from the telephone industry are of great value in instrumentation and data processing.

We shall next describe a few examples of electronic techniques applied to modern instrumentation and data transmission and processing.

21-2
Examples of data systems

A simple data recording system is shown in Fig. 21-1. In this system each sensor drives a separate *information channel* which terminates in a record on a strip-chart recorder. As will be explained later, the rate at which this

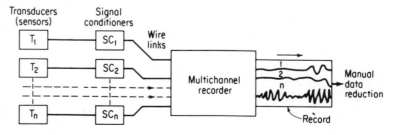

FIGURE 21-1 Elementary data acquisition system.

system can record information is limited by the frequency bandwidth response of the recorder. The system has an information-*storage* feature in the permanent chart record. When large amounts of data are handled by this system, the manual data reduction (reading points from the records, plotting subsidiary graphs, etc.) becomes a burdensome task. If the data must be recorded at a distance from the transducers, the wire links impose a limitation owing to their cost or to the added circuit resistance and noise.

Instrumentation systems for weather probes, satellites, missiles, and the like must include a *radio telemetry* link, as shown in elementary form in Fig. 21-2. Owing to the cost of the radio link in terms of money or power

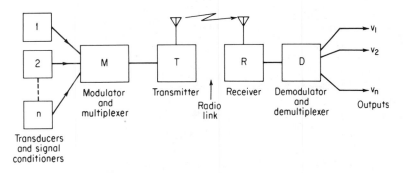

FIGURE 21-2   Elementary radio telemetry system.

(weight) requirement, there is generally only one radio link for transmitting the information from a number of sensors. This is accomplished by frequency-division or time-division multiplexing methods. In either system the type of modulation used on the radio link can be selected by the designer of the system.

As an example of a more complex instrumentation data system, consider the missile test-range data-acquisition system of Fig. 21-3. Here, the airborne sensors could include accelerometers to record pitch, yaw, and roll angle data; strain gages for structural analysis data; thermocouples for temperature data; photo cells for light intensity data; and, perhaps, Langmuir probes to test for plasma buildup on the missile's leading surfaces. All these sensor output wave forms may be *multiplexed* onto a single telemetry-transmitter antenna-terminal voltage wave form. At the telemetry receiver, the individual sensor wave forms are recovered by their time or frequency separation. An analog recorder may be used to provide visual test monitoring and as a backup to the storage of all data on a digital magnetic tape. The tape is written by the output of an *analog-digital* (A/D) *converter*. Meanwhile, a *radar* may be sensing the trajectory of the missile by recording the time

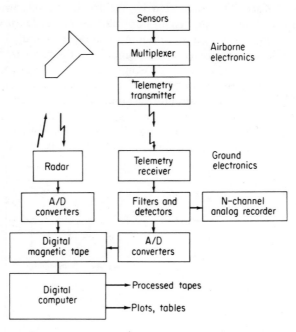

FIGURE 21-3   Missile data processing system.

of arrival of each reflected pulse for range information, and the antenna mount angles at maximum signal may be recorded for angular information.

Finally, all data may be calibrated, placed in time synchronism, and analyzed by post-flight operations in a general-purpose digital computer.

21-3
Some elements of data system theory

a. Noise and bandwidth

We recall from Sec. 20-3 that the mean-square voltage generated by the thermal noise in a resistance R is

$$N^2 = 4kTRB \tag{21-1}$$

where k is the Boltzmann constant, T is the temperature in degrees Kelvin, and B is the bandwidth (of the circuit at the resistor terminals) in cycles per second. The fact that N^2 is directly proportional to B implies that this voltage is a *white* noise.

Now consider the representative analog signal voltage v_s in Fig. 21-4a and its Fourier component spectrum in Fig. 21-4b. Since we are thinking of the signal as coming from a transducer and all transducers have a limited maximum frequency, it is safe to conclude that the Fourier spectrum will be bounded by a maximum frequency f_m. Suppose that this signal is passed through a channel which causes a noise voltage to be superimposed on the signal. To retain all components of the signal the channel bandwidth must extend up to and include frequency f_m, but to minimize the noise, the bandwidth should be no greater than this requirement dictates.

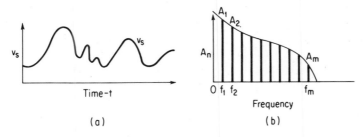

FIGURE 21-4   (a) Analog signal and (b) Fourier components.

The foregoing discussion concerns the original analog wave form. In most instrumentation systems the original wave form is modified before transmission by some kind of modulation, such as AM, FM, pulse amplitude, or pulse code modulation. For example, in time-division multiplexing, the wave must be sampled periodically, and this implies that some type of pulse modulation results. The type of modulation used has an important effect on the signal-to-noise ratio, on the rate of transmission of data, and on the errors at the receiving end of the channel.

b. Relation of sampling rate to maximum frequency component

The basic idea of sampling a continuous function, as in a time-division multiplex system, is shown in Fig. 21-5a. The function is shown as v_s in Fig. 21-5b. The commutator (sampler) selects segments of v_s and delivers these as the wave v_d (Fig. 21-5d) to the low-pass filter. The filter acts to smooth out the wave v_d so that after amplification the output is again a continuous function which is a good approximation of the original function v_s.

If the samples are taken too far apart on v_s, we can see that some of the faster fluctuations will not be sensed and will be lost. The question arises: How frequently must samples be taken so as to retain all the significant in-

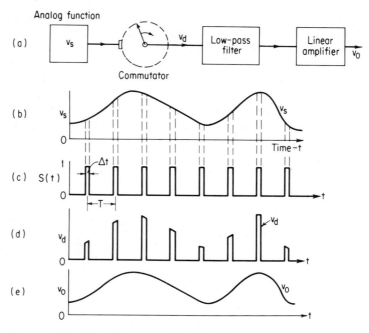

FIGURE 21-5   Sampling an analog signal.

formation in the signal? If we think of the Fourier series components of v_s, we can see that the components have frequencies that range only up to a maximum value, namely, f_m. Therefore, we can analyze the sampling of a single component of the form $A \cos 2\pi ft$ and know that f varies only up to a maximum value f_m.

The wave after sampling can be expressed as the product

$$s(t) A \cos 2\pi ft \tag{21-2}$$

where $s(t)$ is the *switching function* shown in Fig. 21-5c which has the period T, the frequency F, and passes the signal at its instantaneous amplitude for a time Δt at each sample. If we let $\alpha = T/\Delta t$ and express the function $s(t)$ by means of a Fourier series, we find

$$s(t) = \frac{1}{\alpha} + 2 \sum_{m=1}^{\infty} \frac{1}{m\pi} \sin \frac{m\pi}{\alpha} \cos 2m\pi Ft \tag{21-3}$$

where m takes the values $1, 2, 3, \cdots \infty$. Combining (21-2) and (21-3), we obtain

$$s(t) A \cos 2\pi ft = \frac{A}{\alpha} \cos 2\pi ft$$

$$+ \frac{2A}{\pi} \sum_{m=1}^{\infty} \frac{1}{m} \sin \frac{m\pi}{\alpha} \cos 2m\pi Ft \cos 2\pi ft \tag{21-4}$$

But if we apply the identity $\cos\theta\cos\beta = \frac{1}{2}[\cos(\theta+\beta)+\cos(\theta-\beta)]$ to the cosine product terms in (21-4), we obtain

$$s(t)A\cos 2\pi ft = \frac{A}{\alpha}\cos 2\pi ft$$

$$+\frac{A}{\pi}\sum_{m=1}^{\infty}\frac{1}{m}\sin\frac{m\pi}{\alpha}[\cos 2\pi(mF+f)t+\cos 2\pi(mF-f)t] \qquad (21\text{-}5)$$

This equation says that the sampled wave contains a term of the original frequency f (though reduced in amplitude) plus an infinite series of terms having frequencies that are f cycles per second above and below integral multiples of the sampling frequency F. These terms remind us of the side frequency terms in the AM-modulated wave.

Now we revert to the concept of the function v_s that contains a number of Fourier components having frequencies up to the maximum f_m. *Each component, after sampling, would be represented by Eq. (21-5)*, and the total sampled wave v_s would be obtained by summing over all the components. The result gives an infinite number of bands of discrete frequencies, several of which are depicted in Fig. 21-6. The first band goes from 0 to f_m, the next from $F-f_m$ to $F+f_m$, and so on.

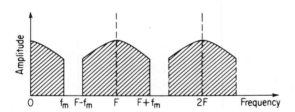

FIGURE 21-6   Sampled data frequency spectrum.

All the information needed to reconstruct the function v_s is contained in the first band from 0 to f_m. Therefore, an *ideal* low-pass filter, which cuts off just above f_m, will pass all the necessary components and will suppress all the higher frequencies. In this context the filter is called an *interpolation filter*, since in effect it smooths the function between the sampled points.

Consider what would happen if the sampling frequency F were made smaller but f_m remains the same. Then in Fig. 21-6 the components in the frequency range near $F-f_m$ would eventually overlap those just below f_m. The summation of components up to f_m would no longer reproduce the original function v_s, and errors would result. We see that, assuming the use of an ideal filter, *the sampling rate F must be greater than* $2f_m$. This rule is known as Shannon's sampling rate theorem, and it can be stated in more complete form as follows.

In order to recover a continuous variable from equally spaced samples, except for a time delay, the sampling repetition rate must be greater than twice the highest frequency (Fourier component) in the continuous variable.

The theorem recognizes the time delay that occurs in the ideal filter. In an actual filter the attenuation curve does not cut off sharply as in the ideal case. This means that F should be somewhat greater than $2f_m$ so that the filter curve can extend a little beyond f_m. Nichols and Rauch[†] state that sufficiently sharp cutoff filters can be constructed so that a sampling rate $F = 2.5f_m$ may be used without serious distortion. A discussion of the effect of different types of interpolation filters on the resulting errors and of the application of the sampling theorem has been presented by Gardenhire.[‡]

c. Digital methods; quantization of data

As the stability, precision, and flexibility requirements of a data system become more stringent, there is a greater advantage to the use of digital methods. Thus, data often are converted from the analog to the digital form (Sec. 21-7) and retained in this form for transmission and processing, and may be converted back to the analog form only at the final recording or display stage of the system. The potential advantages of the digital methods include (1) reduced error rate in transmission through noisy channels (though at a sacrifice of data rate), (2) improved stability of calibration, (3) higher precision, and (4) the availability of the general-purpose digital computer for direct processing of the digital data. Item 4 is perhaps the most important reason for using digital methods. For example, the storage methods, as on magnetic tapes, developed for the digital computer become available for data storage and are compatible with the computer for subsequent data processing.

Since digital representations imply discrete steps of values, it follows that an analog variable must be *quantized* before it can be converted to digital form. We now discuss some factors in the quantization of an analog function from the viewpoint of instrumentation system applications.[§]

It is safe to say that distortion-free values of a particular variable in a data system are constrained between a minimum and a maximum level. That is to say, the *dynamic range* is limited. At the low end the signal may be swamped by the noise on the channel. At the high end there is always a limitation due to saturation or to the limitations of the transducer. The situation can be viewed as in Fig. 21-7 in terms of the analog signal y that ranges between y_{min} and y_{max}. The *range* of the variable is

[†]Reference 21-12, p. 41.

[‡]L. W. Gardenhire, "Selecting Sampling Rates," *Instrument Soc. of Am. Tr.*, April, 1964, p. 59.

[§]Reference 21-10, Chap. 10.

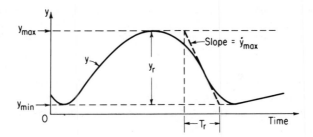

FIGURE 21-7   The dynamic range of a signal.

$$\text{range} = y_r = y_{\max} - y_{\min} \tag{21-6}$$

Although a mathematical function y would have an infinite number of values over the range y_r, any measurement is limited by the minimum increment in y that can be sensed owing to the limited *resolution* of the measuring device. Furthermore, every system has a limitation on its accuracy expressed as an allowable error. Now let

Δy = system resolution
ϵ = allowable error expressed as a per cent of y_r

Now we can calculate the number of discrete values n distinguishable in the range y_r; thus,

$$n = \frac{y_r}{\Delta y} + 1 \tag{21-7}$$

For example, if the range is 10 V and Δy is 0.5 V, then there are 21 meaningful values over the range (including both end values).

The system resolution can be expressed in terms of the allowable error; thus,

$$\Delta y = \frac{2\epsilon}{100} y_r \tag{21-8}$$

For example, if $\epsilon = 1$ per cent, then $\Delta y = 0.02\ y_r$.

Thus far the dynamic nature of the function has been ignored. To consider the time element we ask how frequently the function can be observed and still get a meaningful change. This depends on the resolution Δy and on the maximum rate of change of the variable, $\dot y_{\max}$. There is no point in observing the variable more often than needed to give readings separated by Δy. If we let ΔT be this minimum time, then

$$\Delta T = \frac{\Delta y}{\dot y_m} \tag{21-9}$$

This value can be expressed in another way if we introduce the concept of the minimum time T_r for the variable to change in a linear fashion over the range y_r. The requirement on T_r depends on $\dot{y}_{\max}$, as shown in Fig. 21-7, and is given by

$$T_r = \frac{y_r}{\dot{y}_{\max}} \tag{21-10}$$

The quantity T_r is taken to be the approximate *rise time* of the system. In most systems T_r varies inversely with the system bandwidth.

An expression for ΔT in terms of ϵ and T_r is obtained by combining (21-8), (21-9), and (21-10) with the result

$$\Delta T = \frac{2\epsilon T_r}{100} \tag{21-11}$$

Equation (21-11) gives the minimum time for the variable to change by the amount Δy if the system has the allowable error ϵ and rise time T_r.

d. Information content; information flow rate

The usual connotation of the word *information* refers to the *meaning* conveyed by groups of words (sentences) of a language. However, the term information has a different definition in the theory of communication that has been developed over the last two or three decades. This theory deals with such problems as the statistical analysis of the errors that occur during the transmission of coded messages through a transmission channel in the presence of noise. The messages may consist of groups of symbols, and each symbol may be represented, for example, by different voltage levels on a transmission line, or each symbol may be transmitted by a coded group of pulses. A single symbol group is defined to be a *word*. The maximum possible error-free rate of transmission of the symbol groups using optimum coding expressed as a function of the signal-to-noise power ratio was established by Shannon. In such studies all combinations of symbols are counted as words. If the symbols are the letters of the English alphabet, we see that the theory is not directly concerned with the transmission of meaningful messages, since many combinations will be meaningless (and unpronounceable).

We take a more limited approach and reconsider the quantization of an analog variable, which we assume to be a voltage. Suppose that we use the notation in Eq. (21-7), that is, we have n discrete levels of voltage, or n *states*. When each level is equally probable before message transmission, it is customary to define the information content H of *one sample* of voltage in terms of the logarithm of n; thus,

$$H = K \log n \tag{21-12}$$

where K is a constant that depends on the choice of the base of the logarithm.

The choice of a logarithmic function will appear reasonable if we think about the following situation. Assume that a transmission channel is transmitting F samples per second. Suppose, further, that each sample is taken from a quantity that is quantized into n levels. Then the number of different possible combinations that could be transmitted in 1 sec would be

$$\text{number of combinations per sec} = n^F \qquad (21\text{-}13)$$

Now if we double the number of samples per second (as by providing a parallel, identical transmission channel), we intuitively expect the information carried per second to be doubled, but expression (21-13) gives a squared value, or four times. By defining the information content as the logarithm of (21-13) ,as follows;

$$H_1 = \log n^F = F \log n \qquad (21\text{-}14)$$

the information H_1 transmitted per second becomes proportional to the number of samples per second, as seems reasonable. Further, insofar as F is proportional to the channel bandwidth, the information rate becomes proportional to the bandwidth. When the transmission channel transmits pulses that represent the 0's or 1's of the binary system, it is convenient to express the information content of a single pulse by taking $K = 1$ in Eq. (21-12) and use logarithms to the base 2; thus, since $n = 2$, we write

$$H = \log_2 n = \log_2 2 = 1 \qquad (21\text{-}15)$$

This unit of information is called the *bit,* a word obtained from a contraction of "binary digit."

Next we consider the idea of *channel capacity* but limit the discussion to binary pulse transmission. We refer back to Eq. (21-14) and assert that in T sec the information H would be

$$H = H_1 T = FT \log_2 2 = FT \quad \text{bits} \qquad (21\text{-}16)$$

We can relate the sampling rate F to the channel bandwidth B by using the Shannon sampling rate theorem (Sec. 21-3b). All the information transmitted in a bandwidth B is contained in equally spaced samples taken at the rate $F = 2B$. Thus the *rate* of transmission, called the *channel capacity,* can be expressed as

$$\text{channel capacity} = \frac{H}{T} = F = 2B \quad \text{bits/s} \qquad (21\text{-}17)$$

The foregoing analysis does not include any consideration of the effect of noise and therefore refers to binary pulse transmission on a noise-free channel.

As mentioned earlier, Shannon studied the effect of noise on the channel capacity (for the case of white noise having a Gaussian probability distribution) and obtained the result

$$\frac{H}{T} = B \log_2 \left[1 + \left(\frac{S}{N} \right)^2 \right] \quad \text{bits/s} \qquad (21\text{-}18)$$

where S is the rms signal voltage and N is the rms noise voltage. This formula gives the *ideal* rate of information transmission in the presence of noise. However, practical systems for error-free transmission fall far short of the ideal, even when complex techniques are used.

Equation (21-18) shows that theoretically it might be possible to increase the signal power (increase S/N) and thereby permit a reduction in the bandwidth B required for a given information rate. Actually, the opposite situation is more likely to prevail in practice. For instance, in radio telemetry it is preferable, or necessary, to work with low signal power, and therefore the bandwidth may have to be increased to maintain a required channel capacity. In FM radio there is a similar "trade-off" between bandwidth and S/N ratio. The transmitted frequency band is broadened to several times the width of the audiofrequency band, and a signal of equivalent quality (compared with the AM system) can be received with a lower S/N ratio.†

The listing of the transmission characteristics of some representative channels in Table 21-1 gives some idea of the ranges of bandwidth, S/N ratio, and channel capacity encountered in practice.

21-4
Data system requirements

Data system requirements for quantity and quality of data handling are usually expressed in terms of quantities defined in the foregoing article, namely, *bandwidth, dynamic range, channel capacity*, and *information storage capacity*.

Bandwidth effects are important in several portions of the missile data processing system of Fig. 21-3. These include the radar bandwidth which governs ranging accuracy; the antenna-pointing servomechanism bandwidth which affects angle accuracy; and the telemetry system bandwidth, which governs the number, sampling rate, and precision of the telemetry channels. Examples of analog recorder bandwidths are the following: strip chart recorder about 1 Hz; galvanometer recorder up to 5000 Hz; and magnetic tape recorder up to 10^6 Hz. To the extent that a system is wide in bandwidth, it is also fast in response time. This relationship was noted in the discussion of the pulse response of amplifiers in Sec. 16-16, and will appear again in relation to the response of a galvanometer (Sec. 21-6).

The dynamic range, discussed in Sec. 21-3c, is important in data processing systems. Typically, the input-output characteristic for a high-quality electronic amplifier is linear for a range of 40 dB. Dynamic range can be

---

†A quantitative study shows that this statement is true only for S/N values above a certain threshold. This effect and also the effect of the use of different kinds of modulation on channel capacity is discussed by Nichols and Rauch, Reference 21-12, pp. 48 ff.

extended in electronic amplifiers by predistortion, or by purposefully using a range-compression input-output function like a logarithmic shape. Logarithmic receivers have been built which permit the *RF* input to vary over a range of 100 dB.

In a system element which processes binary or other coded data, the word length and the quantization scheme determine the required dynamic range. For example, consider a 10-bit binary word with uniform quantization increments Δy in a voltage that can range from y_{min} to y_{max}. Since

Table 21-1 Transmission Characteristics of Representative Channels

Type of channel	Bandwidth B, Hz	Assumed $(S/N)^2$, dB	Theoretical channel capacity H/T, bits/s	Practical channel capacity H/T, bits/s
Audio	4,000	30	40,000	8,000
Video (television)	5,000,000	30	50,000,000	10,000,000
Telemetry system† of Explorer I	20	3	22	
Telemetry system† of Orbiting Geophysical Observatory	200,000	15	1,000,000	

†G. H. Ludwig, "Spacecraft Information Systems," in Proc. of the Int. School of Physics, "Enrico Fermi," Course XIX, B. Peters, ed., Academic Press, N. Y. & London, 1963, p. 377.

$2^{10} - 1 = 1023$, we see that

$$y_{max} = y_{min} + 1023 \, \Delta y \qquad (21\text{-}19)$$

Thus the dynamic range, expressed as a ratio, is

$$\text{dynamic range} = \frac{y_{max}}{y_{min}} = \frac{y_{min} + 1023\Delta y}{y_{min}} = 1 + \frac{1023\Delta y}{y_{min}} \qquad (21\text{-}20)$$

In the quantization process a maximum absolute error equal to $\Delta y/2$ may occur, owing to the difference between the actual function and the quantized level. Expressed as a *relative* error, the quantization error will vary over the range

$$\frac{\dfrac{\Delta y}{2}}{y_{min} + 1023\Delta y} \quad \text{to} \quad \frac{\dfrac{\Delta y}{2}}{y_{min}} \qquad (21\text{-}21)$$

Comparing (21-20) and (21-21), we see that

$$\text{dynamic range} = 1 + 1023 \times 2 \times (\text{largest relative error}) \qquad (21\text{-}22)$$

Thus the dynamic range can be "traded off" with the largest relative error.

On the other hand, if the quantization levels are made to increase logarithmi-
cally with the encoded voltage, a constant maximum relative error will result.
The dynamic range in dB will be proportional to the number of bits in the
word; for 1-dB quantization steps (maximum relative error of 0.06), the
10-bit word will give a dynamic range of 1024 dB, or expressed as a ratio,
$10^{51.2}$!

Dynamic range effects are important in the missile data processing system
of Fig. 21-3 in the telemetry channels for preserving the sensor-measurement
dynamic ranges, and in the radar receiver if missile echo areas are to be
measured over large ranges.

Requirements on channel *information flow rate* can be related to channel
capacity, as defined in Sec. 21-3d. Examples of representative practical
channel capacities are listed in Table 21-1.

Information can be stored in a variety of ways, including the output
records of the various analog recorders, the magnetic tape of the magnetic
tape recorder for both analog and digital data, and punched cards or paper
tape for digital data. The memories of the digital computer are used for
temporary storage of information.

21-5
Analog recording systems

Storage of electrical wave forms is commonly accomplished by graphic
recorders, magnetic tape recorders, and cathode-ray tube photography.

a. Graphic recorders

Graphic recording is performed at low frequencies by the dc strip-chart
recorders, in which the chart is driven continuously by a spring or electric
motor to give X-axis translation and the Y-axis position of an ink-pen or
hot-wire stylus is controlled by a d'Arsonval movement. In this movement,
the current to be recorded is passed through a moving coil suspended in the
field of a permanent magnet. Since the angular inertia of the recording
element is appreciable and since the required torque also depends upon the
angular acceleration of the element, the torque limitation of any movement
is reached at relatively low frequencies. Typically, a strip-chart recorder will
pass frequencies up to 1 Hz, 5 Hz, or 50 Hz, depending on its design. The
dynamic range is limited by friction in the bearings, which are heavier than in
indicator-type meters because of the mass of the recording element and the
moving coil. Considering a 2% of full-scale error quotation on these instruments, which is mainly due to friction effects, the dynamic range is 50:1 or 34
dB. The response of the d'Arsonval element recorder is analyzed in Sec. 21-6.

Graphic recording at higher frequencies is accomplished by galvanometer-type recorders, usually known as *magnetic oscillographs* (Fig. 21-8). Here the current wave form to be recorded is carried by a loop of fine wire, con-

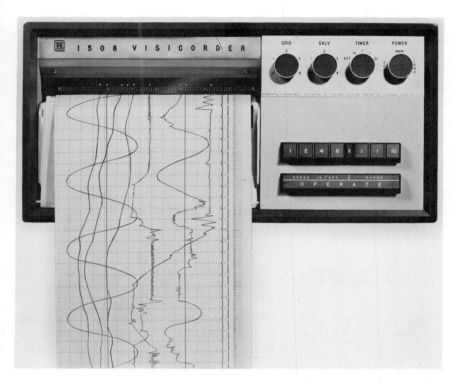

FIGURE 21-8   High-speed galvanometer recorder, or magnetic oscillograph. (Courtesy of Honeywell, Test Instruments Division.)

sisting of a few turns or a single-turn loop, suspended in the field of a permanent magnet. A thin (low-inertia) mirror, cemented to the wire, reflects a beam of light from a stationary light source. The X-axis translation is provided by pulling light-sensitive paper past the reflected beam; the Y-axis position of the recorded spot is proportional to the angular deflection of the coil. Different types of galvanometers can be obtained which have frequency passbands as low as 20 Hz to as high as 5000 Hz or higher. In the different designs sensitivity is "traded off" for passband, so that a high-sensitivity galvanometer will have a low passband. The galvanometer element is usually small, say, a cylinder having dimensions of 5 by 60mm. A number of galvanometers can be mounted in the same instrument so as to use the same light source and record on the same recording paper. These multichannel oscillographs are valuable when a large number of variables need to be recorded, as in check-out tests on aircraft. They are subject to errors due to misalignment and vibration; by proper calibration before each test, absolute accuracies to a few per cent of full scale can be achieved. Formerly the sensitive paper record had to be developed by wet-process photolaboratory techniques, but newer oscillographs use a sensitive paper that develops the latent image merely by the effect of ultraviolet light on the dry paper. Some oscillographs also contain a viewing mechanism that consists of a many-faceted rotating mirror and a translucent screen. The mirror throws the light beam from the galvanometer onto the screen and the rotation provides the time axis. With periodic waves a stationary pattern is observed, in analogy with that obtained with the recurring linear sweep on a cathode-ray oscilloscope.

b. Magnetic tape recorders

Electrical wave forms are stored on magnetic tape by producing a pattern of residual magnetic flux that depends on the input signal. The general scheme is shown in Fig. 21-9. During the recording process the tape first moves past a *demagnetizing* (or *erasing*) head and then past the *recording* (or *writing*) head. In order to reproduce the stored signals the tape is pulled past the heads again in the same direction, but the erasing head is retracted, the recording head is inactive, and the *reproducing* or *reading* head (or transducer) develops an output voltage. The process can be repeated many times.

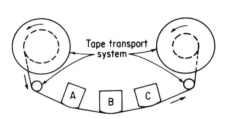

FIGURE 21-9 Schematic diagram of a general-purpose magnetic tape recorder. A = erasing head, B = recording head, and C = reproducing head.

Figure 21-10 shows a schematic diagram of a recording head that produces the flux variations along the length of the tape—a system called *longitudinal* recording. As the figure shows, the residual flux is developed in a thin layer of magnetic material (a mixture of iron oxides in a binder) applied to the plastic tape base. The recording process occurs in the fringing magnetic field near the narrow air gap. Ideally, the remanent longitudinal flux density in the tape will be a direct function of the recording coil current at the instant that the tape leaves the air gap. The actual residual flux patterns are, however, rather complex, and the remanent flux may depend on a number of factors.†

The wave form is reproduced by pulling the tape across an air gap in a

†C. D. Mee, *The Physics of Magnetic Recording*, North-Holland Pub. Co. and Interscience Publishers, John Wiley & Sons, Inc., New York, 1964.

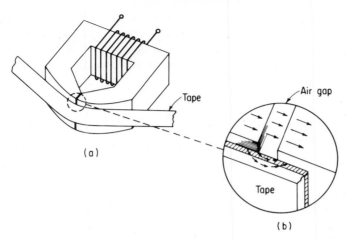

FIGURE 21-10   Elements of recording or reproducing head (after
C. D. Mee, *The Physics of Magnetic Recording*, John Wiley &
Sons, New York, 1964, p. 3).

head of the same form as the recording head. A fraction of the flux in a short
section of the tape is diverted to the core of the reproducing head and a
voltage is induced that is proportional to the rate of change of the flux.

The *direct* recording method described in the foregoing paragraphs has
a serious nonlinearity of amplitude response. This result is not surprising
in view of the nonlinear cyclical magnetization curve for ferromagnetic
materials. Several techniques have been developed to improve the response,
including the following;

1. Direct recording
   a. No bias field
   b. dc bias field
   c. Ultrasonic ac bias field
2. Frequency modulation (FM) recording

Direct recording without a bias field can be used for the recording of
pulses in digital systems, but for analog recording an ultrasonic ac bias
current is generally superimposed on the signal. The ac bias has a frequency
about 4 or 5 times the highest signal frequency, for example, 60 kHz for a
signal range to 12 kHz. The bias amplitude is made higher than the signal
amplitude; as a result the magnetic medium is carried around large hysteresis
loops offset by the signal component. When the medium leaves the recording
gap, the residual flux is closely proportional to the signal component.†
Furthermore, the ac bias improves the signal-to-noise ratio compared with
zero-bias recording.

†The detailed action of the ac bias is not completely understood. See *ibid.*, Chap. 2.

The following analysis will show that the magnitude of the reproducing head output voltage varies directly with the frequency. We assume that the remanent flux of the moving tape produces a cosine wave of flux in the reproducing head core that is proportional to the time function of the signal current

$$\phi_1(t) = k_1 \cos \omega t \tag{21-23}$$

The voltage induced in the reproducing head coil is proportional to the rate of change of the flux; thus,

$$e = -N\frac{d\phi_1}{dt} = Nk_1\omega \sin \omega t \tag{21-24}$$

We see that the voltage amplitude increases directly with the frequency or rises with frequency at the rate of 20 dB per decade, assuming constant flux amplitude.

There are two important consequences of this variation. First, to obtain the desired constant output amplitude independent of frequency, it is necessary to provide a conditioning amplifier that will integrate the voltage to compensate for the differentiation. In other words, the conditioning amplifier should have a gain that falls off at 20 dB per decade to compensate for the rising characteristics of the reproducer. Second, the signal-to-noise ratio falls as the frequency falls. At low frequencies the induced signal voltage drops, while the noise component inherent in the tape and amplifier remains nearly constant. Direct recording therefore is not suitable for frequencies below a certain value; 50 Hz is typical.

The upper frequency response is affected by both the recording and the reproducing process limitations, but we consider only those encountered in reproduction. That is, we assume that the tape carries a sinusoidal distribution of residual flux density along its length that is independent of frequency. Thus, there is a wave of flux distribution on the tape of wavelength λ related to the tape velocity v and the frequency f by the relation

$$f = \frac{v}{\lambda} \tag{21-25}$$

With a particular tape speed the wavelength becomes long compared with the reproducing head air gap d at low frequency. For example, if $v = 30$ in./sec and $f = 100$ Hz, we have $\lambda = 0.30$ in. An air gap width of, say, 0.25 mil will sample a small section of the wavelength on the tape. But as f increases and λ decreases, the air gap d becomes a greater and greater fraction of λ. Then the reproducer core flux depends on an average over a portion of the wavelength and the flux developed in the core falls off. Thus, at a frequency at which $\lambda = d$ the two edges of the gap span one wavelength, the average value is zero, the flux in the core drops to zero, and the output is zero. Using $v = 30$ in./sec and $d = 0.25$ mil, we calculate this frequency to be 30/0.25

$\times$ 10^{-3}, or 120,000 Hz. At a frequency of half this value the output will already be down about 4 dB below the ideal characteristic.

Direct recording has a limited accuracy owing to slight irrregularities in tape sensitivity but is useful for such applications as voice channels, which require a fairly wide bandwidth but no low-frequency response or absolute accuracy.

The general scheme of the FM (see Sec. 13-5) magnetic tape recording process is shown in Fig. 21-11. Here only the *frequency* obtained from the

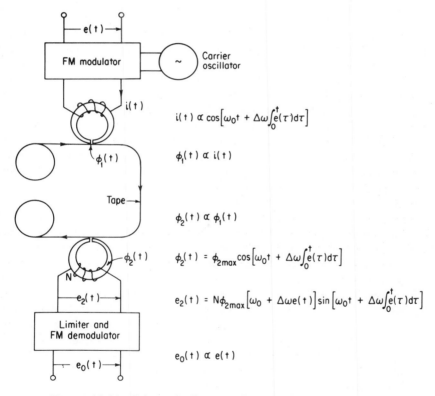

$$i(t) \propto \cos\left[\omega_0 t + \Delta\omega \int_0^t e(\tau)d\tau\right]$$

$$\phi_1(t) \propto i(t)$$

$$\phi_2(t) \propto \phi_1(t)$$

$$\phi_2(t) = \phi_{2max} \cos\left[\omega_0 t + \Delta\omega \int_0^t e(\tau)d\tau\right]$$

$$e_2(t) = N\phi_{2max}\left[\omega_0 + \Delta\omega e(t)\right]\sin\left[\omega_0 t + \Delta\omega \int_0^t e(\tau)d\tau\right]$$

$$e_0(t) \propto e(t)$$

FIGURE 21-11   Schematic diagram of FM magnetic tape recording, and related functions.

flux pattern on the tape is needed to convey the full information (amplitude and frequency) on the signal wave form. Hence, the flaws in the tape, such as oxide irregularities or worn spots, have less effect than with direct recording. Another advantage is that the system can record low frequencies, distortion-free, down to and including dc.

The upper signal frequency limit depends on the carrier frequency chosen, on the bandwidth needed to carry the information, and indirectly on the upper frequency limit set by the tape speed and reproducing head air gap. For example, let the unmodulated carrier frequency be 60 kHz, the bandwidth needed for the information be from 40 to 80 kHz, then the recorder would have to have a capability of at least 80 kHz. The signal frequency limit depends on the FM modulation process, that is, on the maximum frequency deviation, in this case ± 20 kHz, and on the degree to which the FM bandwidth is to be truncated by filtering. Based on 100 per cent modulation and retaining all sideband components above 1 per cent of the unmodulated carrier amplitude, the signal frequency limit in this example would be 9 kHz. We note that the bandwidth from 0 to 40 kHz is not used, but it can be employed in the FM multiplex system (Sec. 21-9).

Fluctuations in the tape speed during recording or playback are more serious in FM recording than in direct recording. The speed variations cause output variations called *wow* and *flutter*—terms that arose from the sound effects that result in audio systems. Flutter and wow are basically the same; the only difference is that variations which have a frequency above about 5 Hz are called flutter. In direct recording flutter produces a change in output amplitude and frequency that bears a direct relation to the signal values, and the changes are the same percentages as the speed changes. In FM recording the situation is quite different. Even if there is no signal, a change in speed produces an output. For example, if the FM system has a 100 per cent modulation frequency deviation of 20 per cent (of the carrier frequency), then a 1 per cent speed change will develop an output equal to 5 per cent of the fully modulated output whether a signal is present or not. Therefore, when the signal amplitude is small, the relative error due to speed change can become very large.

To summarize: FM systems have the advantage of recording down to zero frequency; they possess good signal-to-noise ratio, and they lend themselves readily to multiplexing, but they have the disadvantage of using a wider bandwidth for a given signal frequency and thus need a higher tape speed for a particular frequency limit, and they require more complex electric circuits and speed control and are more expensive than direct recording systems.

Several records can be recorded simultaneously by using a multiple recording head. For example, seven *tracks* can be placed side-by-side on a 1/2-in. tape.

c. Cathode-ray tube photography

A very common method of preserving electrical wave forms is to photograph them with an oscilloscope-mounted camera. This can be done in many ways, for example,

1. Periodic wave form. With the time sweep of the oscilloscope in synchronism, take an exposure for a single snapshot at the desired shutter speed.

2. Isolated pulselike wave form, or a piece of a continuous wave form. Leaving the camera shutter open, trigger the wave form across the oscilloscope face once.

3. Clocked, but nonsimilar wave form. For applications such as radar, sonar, or even electrocardiology, a record of each pulse can be obtained by synchronizing movie camera frames to the pulse rate. Also, a very compact display can be obtained on a single photograph by modulating the oscilloscope spot intensity with the signal amplitude, using an ordinary linear time sweep on the x axis and pulling the film upward across the face of the tube, giving as many pulses per inch as the spot size permits.

The ultimate bandwidth and dynamic range of direct photographic displays of single wave forms are usually limited by the amplifier and the spot size of the recording oscilloscope. Special tubes, for which is claimed 300 lines/inch resolution in both directions, on a 4-inch, tube, are available. Multiple exposures can be used to segment the signal's dynamic range and to shorten each time base in order to realize all the bandwidth and dynamic range of the oscilloscope. However, in the intensity-modulated display mentioned above in (3), the dynamic range is severely limited to about 35 dB since no more than about 60 gray levels are perceptible.

21-6
Response of the
galvanometer recorder

Ideally, the wave recorded by a d'Arsonval galvanometer recorder should be an accurate replica of the input voltage wave form. However, the moving system has inertia, and consequently the recorded wave cannot follow sudden changes in the voltage exactly. Moreover, analysis shows that the circuit resistance has an effect on the speed of response of the galvanometer. The recorder response is governed by the differential equation of the galvanometer. We now set up this equation and obtain the response to a step function input and the steady-state response to a sine wave input.

a. The differential equation of the galvanometer

Consider a rectangular coil of dimensions L by b (Fig. 21-12) which has N turns and is connected in a series circuit with a driving voltage $e(t)$ and an external resistance R_x. The coil resistance is R_c. Assume that the magnetic field is constant and radial in the air gap along the full length L. We wish to

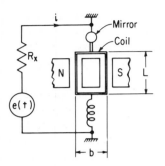

FIGURE 21-12 Galvano-
meter coil and external circuit.

calculate the variation of the angular deflection θ, so we must analyze the torques
operating on the coil.

To calculate the torque due to the magnetic force caused by the coil current i, we
first recall that the force on one conductor
of length L is BiL. The torque arm is $b/2$,
but there are 2 coil sides and there are N
turns, so the torque is

$$\text{magnetic torque} = BNLbi = Gi \quad (21\text{-}26)$$

where G replaces $BNLb$.

When the coil moves in the magnetic
field, there is a voltage induced in the coil
of value

$$\text{induced voltage} = -N\frac{d\phi}{dt} = -NBLb\frac{d\theta}{dt} = -G\dot{\theta} \quad (21\text{-}27)$$

Therefore the current depends on two voltages and the resistance (inductance
is neglected)

$$i = \frac{e(t) - G\dot{\theta}}{R_x + R_c} = \frac{1}{R}e(t) - \frac{G}{R}\dot{\theta} \quad (21\text{-}28)$$

where $R_x + R_c$ is replaced by R, the total circuit resistance.

Now the opposing, or mechanical, torque is made up of the inertial,
viscous friction and restoring torques. Upon equating the mechanical torque
to the magnetic torque Gi and using Eq. (21-28) for the current, we have

$$J\ddot{\theta} + D_1\dot{\theta} + S\theta = \frac{G}{R}e(t) - \frac{G^2}{R}\dot{\theta} \quad (21\text{-}29)$$

where J is the moment of inertia of the moving system (coil plus mirror or
stylus), D_1 is its viscous damping parameter, and S its stiffness coefficient.
Upon rearranging Eq. (21-29), we obtain

$$J\ddot{\theta} + \left(D_1 + \frac{G^2}{R}\right)\dot{\theta} + S\theta = \frac{G}{R}e(t) \quad (21\text{-}30)$$

We notice that the coefficient of $\dot{\theta}$ includes the quantity G^2/R, which comes
from the induced voltage in the coil and adds to the damping of the system.

Now we replace $(D_1 + G^2/R)$ by the symbol D and divide through by
S to obtain

$$\frac{J}{S}\ddot{\theta} + \frac{D}{S}\dot{\theta} + \theta = \frac{G}{RS}e(t) \quad (21\text{-}31)$$

This form of second-order differential equation with constant coefficients has received attention in Chapter 15; therefore, we can make use of the analysis presented there.

b. Response to step voltage; damping

First consider the response to a step voltage E. Then the right side of (21-31) becomes GE/RS and the equation becomes entirely analogous to Eq. (15-12). The solutions of (15-12) can, therefore, be used as solutions of (21-31) if we replace x by θ, X_i by GE/RS, and use the following forms:

$$\text{undamped radian frequency} = \omega_n = \sqrt{\frac{S}{J}} \qquad (21\text{-}32)$$

$$\text{damping ratio} = \zeta = \frac{D}{\sqrt{4JS}} \qquad (21\text{-}33)$$

The response curves in Fig. 15-7, therefore, give the response of the galvanometer to a step function. We see that a high natural frequency combined with a damping ratio of about 0.7 or 0.8 would give the closest approach to a step function response.

The damping coefficient D is a combination of the effect of the viscous damping through D_1 and of the electromagnetic damping through the term G^2/R. In low-frequency recorders the viscous damping is relatively small and the G^2/R term has considerable effect. Therefore, the external circuit resistance can be adjusted to provide the desired degree of damping. If the source resistance is inherently high, then a shunt resistor must be placed across the coil. With this connection the deflection sensitivity to source current is reduced, and the foregoing equations should be modified accordingly. Galvanometers intended for the higher frequency oscillographs usually have a higher value of viscous damping parameter D_1 (relative to the electromagnetic damping) provided by a liquid damping medium surrounding the coil. The viscosity of the liquid is chosen to give the desired damping at the normal operating temperature. Then the circuit resistance has little effect on the damping characteristic unless R_x becomes small.

c. Steady-state response to sine wave input

When the driving voltage is a sine wave, we expect the steady-state response to be a sine function of the same frequency but in general displaced in time phase. The response of the second-order system was discussed in Sec. 15-9, and again we shall make use of the results presented there; in particular of the curves of per-unit magnitude $G(\omega)$, and phase $\phi(\omega)$ versus ω/ω_n given in Fig. 15-13. Now $G(\omega)$ represents the amplitude of the wave of response θ relative to the response for a driving frequency ω of zero (dc response). These curves can be used to determine how high the frequency of the signal may rise before amplitude or phase errors become excessive. If we are interested only in the amplitudes, we see from Fig. 15-13a that with $\zeta = 0.6$ the amplitude stays within 0.3 dB (3.5 per cent) of the dc value for frequencies up to about $\omega = 0.8\ \omega_n$. However, Fig. 15-13b shows that the phase shift with $\zeta = 0.6$ and $\omega = 0.8\ \omega_n$ is 70°, so that if phase shift is important, it would be necessary to reduce the frequency limit. For example, at $\omega = 0.2\ \omega_n$ the phase error is about 15° with the same damping. The phase error could be reduced still more by using a lower damping ratio, but then the response to a step voltage would have a greater overshoot and a longer settling time. A compromise must be reached in the light of the requirements of the measurement problem in hand.

d. Response to complex periodic wave

A periodic wave can be represented by its Fourier harmonic components as discussed in Sec. 21-3 and Appendix D. Since we are dealing with a linear system, we are free to analyze the input wave into its Fourier components, calculate the response to each component, and obtain the total response by applying superposition. Owing to the computational labor involved, this is not an attractive method unless digital computer techniques are used. On the other hand, a qualitative understanding is gained by the concept of the Fourier components and their modification as they are reproduced by the recorder. For example, if a complex wave is known to have important components up to a maximum frequency ω_m, then components up to ω_m must be recorded without change in amplitude or phase. As the curves in Fig. 15-13 show, the requirement on the phase error is apt to restrict the frequency range rather severely.

e. Transient response

The discussion of the response to a step function given earlier illustrates one general method of obtaining the response to an arbitrary transient driving voltage, namely, (1) to use the classical method of solving the differential equation that includes the driving function on the right-hand side. This method is adequate for simple driving functions. For more complex functions two additional methods of analysis may be mentioned: (2) the use of the Fourier integral to represent the driving function as a *continuous* frequency spectrum of voltages and then to sum up the responses to this spectrum and (3) the use of operational methods, such as the Laplace transformation, or to find the response to the unit step function and then apply Duhamel's integral.

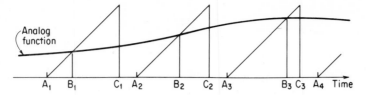

FIGURE 21-13   Time-base encoding.

21-7
Analog-digital converters

Continuous-valued electrical wave forms are converted to digital states in
a wide variety of ways. The simplest electromechanical relay, of course,
converts a continuous-valued dc current to one or the other of two binary
position states. Illustrative of electrical-to-electrical analog-to-digital converters are special-purpose logic circuits, time-base encoders, feedback
circuits which null the difference between the analog input and the digital
output converted back to analog form, and special beam tubes. Collectively
these circuits are called *analog-digital* (A/D) *converters*, or *digitizers*, or
coders.

The time-base encoder works as illustrated in Fig. 21-13. Periodically,
a sawtooth wave is generated. At the onset of each sawtooth, as at point
A_1 in the figure, a digital counter is started. When the sawtooth voltage
reaches the analog wave form, as at B_1, a comparator circuit senses the null
difference and stops the counting. Periodically, say at C_1, C_2, etc., the counter
register is read out and reset and the sawtooth returned to zero. This operation
requires that the register count through all encoding levels in each sampling
interval. Thus

$$(\text{counting frequency}) \ = \ (\text{sampling frequency}) \, (\text{number of encoding levels})$$
$$(21\text{-}34)$$

It is apparent from relation (21-34) that counting frequency limitations
preclude the use of time-base encoding when a combination of a high sampling rate and a small resolution is required.

A feedback type of A/D converter, using a "continuous balance" method,
is illustrated in Fig. 21-14. Periodically triggered by the clock pulses, the
counter increments up or down, depending upon the sign of the instantaneous
error. The counter is performing a digital integration, producing a single
time-constant feedback loop. If n bits are present in the output, $2^n - 1$ steps
are required to cover the entire range. Hence, the clock-pulse frequency must
be very high (many steps per second) when simultaneously a high resolution
(large n) is needed and a wide-bandwidth input is to be converted. None-
theless, this feedback configuration is used in commercial digital voltmeters.

579

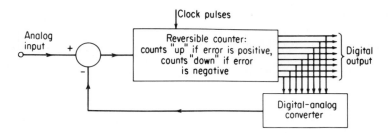

FIGURE 21-14   Continuous-balance encoding.

The counter can be made up from relay stepping switches and the digital-to-analog conversion performed by a potentiometer (see Sec. 21-9). The polarity sensing is accomplished by a chopper which samples alternately the input and the feedback signal. A phase comparison between the chopper driving signal and the sampled signal can obtain the polarity of the error very accurately. In this method, as in the time-base encoder method, the effective bandwidth of the encoder is limited by the counting frequency, but in a more complicated way.

This discussion has been confined to voltage-to-digital conversion. Techniques also exist for frequency-to-digital conversion. Time information (pulse duration or pulse position) can be simply converted to digital form by incrementing a digital counter during the appropriate periods.

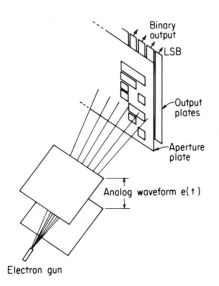

FIGURE 21-15   Beam encoding tube.

Mechanical shaft positions need to be converted to digital form in many systems. This conversion may be effected directly by brushes on code wheels mounted on the shaft. High-resolution (2^{19} positions of $360°$) conversion has been performed by sensing the capacitance change between a notched wheel on the shaft and a closely mounted stator disk. A potentiometer or a dc generator (synchro transmitter) and electrical analog-digital conversion is also common for shaft position encoding.

For very high encoding rates (20 MHz or more) and simultaneously high resolution, cathode-ray tubes can be used. Consider a tube in which a fan beam has been formed. The analog wave form to be encoded is used to modulate the beam angle, as in Fig. 21-15. An aperture plate passes only the binary pattern associated with each angle; a set of output plate circuits, with the least significant bit (LSB) on the right, will be conducting according to the instantaneous binary state.

21-8
Digital recording systems

Permanent storage of large quantities of digitized data is commonly accomplished by digital magnetic tape recorders, although several modern data-processing systems make effective use of punched-paper tape and also punched cards. Since the data representation is in a binary system or a binary-coded number system, it is sufficient to provide for a two-state or two-symbol storage. The symbols 1 and 0 can be, respectively, represented as a hole in paper tape or card or a region of positive-sense magnetization, or the absence of a hole in the paper tape or card or negative-sense magnetization. A sketch of such paper and magnetic tapes is shown on Fig. 21-16.

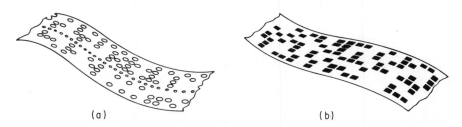

(a)   (b)

FIGURE 21-16   Digital recording media. (a) Punched paper tape with seven data channels plus a row of small sprocket holes. (b) Eight-channel digital magnetic tape, viewed with a layer of iron filings.

Paper-tape recording is limited in speed to 60 characters per second on 8 channels (480 bits/s), whereas magnetic recording is performed at well over 100,000 bits/s. Representative computer manufacturer's magnetic-tape formats have from 200 to 800 bits/in. on each of 7 or 8 channels, running at 60 in./s.

Digital magnetic tapes are written with direct (dc) recording magnetic heads (eight for the record in Fig. 21-16) spaced across the tape; the heads may record the binary symbols in several different ways. In the return-to-zero (RZ) method, the normally unmagnetized tape is magnetized for a fixed short distance with a positive-sense field for a binary 1, or negative-sense field for a binary 0. In the non-return-to-zero (NRZ) method, the tape is always saturated in one or the other direction. Each channel head reverses the magnetization upon encountering a change from 1 to 0 or 0 to 1. In the return-to-bias (RB) method, the normally magnetized tape is unchanged on a binary 0, but the magnetization is reversed for a fixed short distance on a binary 1.

Advantages of digital recording relative to analog recording include (1) high accuracy, (2) insensitivity to tape speed, (3) uncomplicated recording and reproducing circuits, and (4) tapes may be reproduced a number of times without loss of accuracy.

Errors in accurately aligned digital tapes can still occur owing to "drop-outs" or spotty magnetic oxide coatings. These errors become more frequent when the bit-packing density is high, so that smaller areas of oxide are depended upon for each bit. Redundant recording is frequently used to detect or correct these errors. This redundant recording often takes the form of parity bits, which indicate whether or not the number of binary 1's is even (or odd), counting across the tape or in a block along the tape.

Commercial units are available for analog to digital conversion, buffering, and so-called "formatting" of data into standard formats so that a remotely recorded tape may be later read directly into digital computers.

21-9
Digital-analog converters

The conversion from digital states to analog wave forms is accomplished in many different ways, depending upon the form (amplitudes, phases, or frequencies) and availability (parallel or series) of the digital states. For

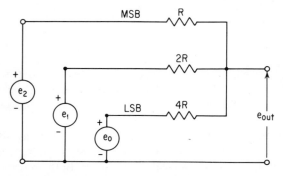

FIGURE 21-17   Binary-analog conversion.

illustration we describe the conversion from amplitude binary states as available in parallel from, say, a flip-flop register.

The conceptual and structural simplicity of this binary-analog conversion (also called decoding) is apparent when one considers that the only necessary mathematical operation is that of weighted addition of the binary places. For example, to obtain a least-increment of 1 V, the binary number 101 is converted to 5 V by attenuating 7-or-zero flip-flop voltage sources by the factors 4/7, 0/7, and 1/7 and adding the results. One commonly used circuit for accomplishing this is shown in Fig. 21-17.

In Fig. 21-17, the on-off voltage e_2 represents the most significant bit (MSB). The contribution of e_2 to the output e_{out} can be obtained from the voltage-divider ratio

$$\frac{\dfrac{(2R)(4R)}{2R+4R}}{R+\dfrac{(2R)(4R)}{2R+4R}}e_2 = \frac{4}{7}e_2 \tag{21-35}$$

The contribution from e_1 is similarly found to be $\frac{2}{7}e_1$, and the contribution from e_0 is $\frac{1}{7}e_0$. The necessary weighted sum at e_{out} is thus formed:

$$e_{out} = \tfrac{8}{14}e_2 + \tfrac{4}{14}e_1 + \tfrac{2}{14}e_0 \tag{21-36}$$

If the sources e_2, e_1, and e_0 were each flip-flops with 7-or-zero V levels, an output with 1-V least-increment would be obtained.

It is evident that expanding the simple circuit of Fig. 21-17 to give many-bit conversion could require impractical resistor sizes. A practical circuit for ten bits or more is shown in Fig. 21-18. There e_N represents the most

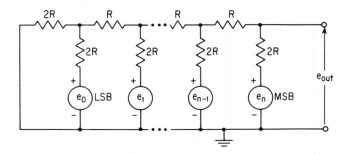

FIGURE 21-18   Ladder network for binary-analog conversion.

significant bit. The key to understanding this binary ladder realization is that the resistance looking left of each node on the top of the figure is exactly $2R\ \Omega$. Yet each node has a direct path to ground of resistance $2R\ \Omega$. Hence, the current from a fictitious voltage source across the output terminals would split at each node, half taking the direct path to ground and half continuing down the ladder. The branch containing e_N receives 2^{-1} of the total current; the branch containing e_{N-k} receives 2^{-1-k} of the total current. This 2^{-k} binary scaling is preserved in the reciprocal direction, so that the voltage contribution at the output node from source e_{N-k} is $2^{-1-k}e_{N-k}$ and the correct weighted sum is obtained by superposition. A current-source dual of the ladder of Fig. 21-18 is also used.† Decimal-analog conversion is frequently accomplished with the Kelvin-Varley potentiometer.‡

The percentage accuracy of the weighting networks tends to be better than the percentage accuracy of the component resistance values, since ratios are formed. In many-bit conversion, the largest contribution to absolute error is usually the reference voltage level,§ for the output is proportional to the reference voltage. Thus a 0.1% ripple in the analog output tends to destroy the information in the 10th binary place.

21-10
Multiplexing systems; telemetry

Often, many different wave forms need to be processed simultaneously through one channel. This latter "channel" could represent a single modulator in a telemetry system which monitors many observables aboard a spacecraft or could represent a single-track FM magnetic tape reel in a laboratory test where many measurements need be recorded simultaneously, or a single wide-band coaxial cable link carrying thousands of telephone messages simultaneously. In each case, the entire information content in a set of wave forms is carried in a single wave form which utilizes a wider frequency bandwidth. The sharing of the common channel is accomplished by either *frequency-division multiplexing* or *time-division multiplexing* or both.

Frequency-division multiplex can be used in telemetry as shown in Fig. 21-19. Here, the information contained in each channel is preserved by sharing the frequency band occupied by the transmitted signal. Frequency division multiplexing is used in the simultaneous recording on FM tape of several signals as illustrated in Fig. 21-20. The FM modulators provide a natural frequency division of the recorded signal, if their frequency deviations are held to, say, $\pm 7.5\%$ of each center frequency so that their frequency

†G. M. Grabbe, Simon Ramo, and Dean E. Woolridge, eds., *Handbook of Automation, Computation and Control,* **2**: *Computers and Data Processing,* John Wiley & Sons, Inc., New York, 1959.

‡Davis Bartholomew, *Electrical Measurements and Instrumentation,* Allyn and Bacon, Inc., Boston, 1963. A. F. Drum, "Calibration of a Kelvin-Varley Voltage Divider," *I. E. E. E. Trans. on Instrumentation and Measurement,* v. IM-3, No. 2, June–Sept., 1964. *Analog Digital Conversion Handbook,* Digital Equipment Corporation, Maynard, Massachusetts, 1964.

§*Analog Digital Conversion Handbook.*

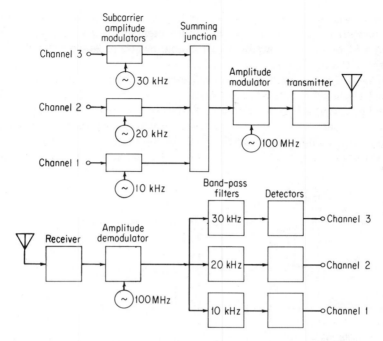

FIGURE 21-19   AM-AM telemetry system (frequency-division multiplex).

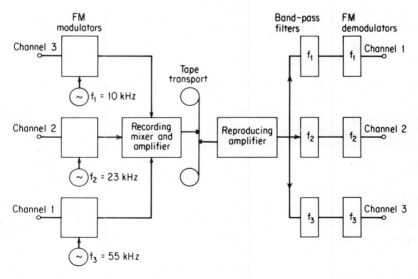

FIGURE 21-20   FM recording using frequency-division multiplex.

spectra will not overlap. For the frequencies of the figure, an octave of frequency separates the channels. Bandpass filters separate the signals once more, and FM demodulators tuned to the channel frequency centers f_1, f_2, and f_3 recover the original signals.

Time-division multiplex, or time sharing, of a channel is effected by successively switching the common channel to all separate signals. This switching can be accomplished in a number of ways. A mechanical, rotary commutator can in sequence apply short wave forms of voltage from a number of terminal pairs onto a single output terminal. Since the output voltage will be pulselike in nature, as suggested by Fig. 21-21, the signal is called pulse-amplitude

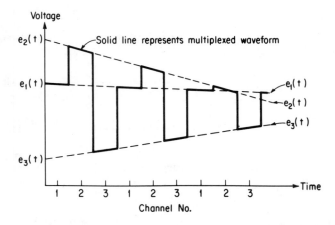

FIGURE 21-21   Pulse amplitude modulation (time-division multiplex.)

modulated (PAM). If this combined output is amplitude-modulated on a carrier for transmission, it can be called a PAM-AM telemetry system. At the receiving site, the signal is demodulated and synchronously decommutated to produce individual channel pulses. These channel pulses can be smoothed by low-pass filters to recover the original signal wave forms, provided the rate of sampling is sufficiently fast. Electronic switching by diode logic gates (Sec. 17-4) can, of course, be performed at much higher rates than by mechanical switching.

Similarly, the input terminals of an analog-digital converter may be successively switched to individual channel voltages, yielding a pulselike wave train which contains in sequence the channel voltages, each coded into serial digital form. Some of the wide variety of ways in which samples of channel voltages may be represented are:

PAM (Pulse amplitude modulation). Channel amplitude sample repre-sented as pulse height.

PDM (Pulse duration modulation). Channel amplitude sample repre-sented as pulse length.

PPM (Pulse position modulation). Channel amplitude sample repre-sented as interval between the pulse and a reference pulse.

PCM (Pulse code modulation). Channel amplitude sample represented as a sequence of pulses and blanks, as in a simple binary code.

When the common channel wave form is amplitude-modulated for transmission, the system is called PAM-AM, PDM-AM, etc.; if frequency-modulated, it is called PAM-FM, PDM-FM, etc.

21-11
Digital computers

A functional diagram of an electronic, stored-program general-purpose digital computer is shown on Fig. 21-22. Here, the "input" block represents the equipment used for inserting instructions and data into the machine;

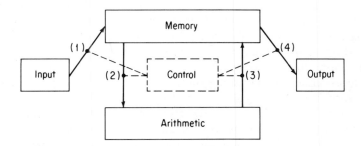

FIGURE 21-22   General-purpose digital computer.

it could be a card reader, magnetic tape reader, punched-paper tape reader, or a digital data-link terminal. The "memory" block represents the equip-ment used for storing the instructions (hence, the term "stored-program"), the data to be used, intermediate results, and the resulting computations; it could be a magnetic drum, a matrix of magnetic cores, or a magnetic disk. The "arithmetic" block represents the equipment used for adding two digital numbers together and for operations such as shifting the binary "place" or testing the sign of a number; it could consist mainly of three registers, con-nected together by an adder circuit. The "output" block represents the equipment used for observing the results of the computation; it may be a typewriter, a digital plotter, or a data-link terminal.

Operation of the computer in its simplest form is illustrated by the numbers on Fig. 21-22. The "control" function in a preset mode causes (1) the program together with the associated data to be read into the memory. Then (2) the program takes over the control function, shifting two binary numbers into "arithmetic" registers where they are added and the result placed in third register. The program then (3) shifts the result up into the memory where it awaits (4) the program output command.

Complicated programs could work with the same equipment and functions simply by repeating simple arithmetical and logical operations; multiplication by repeated addition, division by repeated subtraction, etc. However, most modern high-speed computers have wired logic to save programming and operation time by combining fundamental operations. Hundreds of these combined operations may be available; these may include multiplication, division, sequencing down the data in memory, and assigning memory locations (addresses) for the next data, depending upon the outcome of the last computation. Invariably, wired logic circuits perform error checking at each of the functions of input, memory fetch, arithmetic, memory store, and output.

General-purpose digital computers for scientific computation have been built which weighed many tons and occupied 10,000 ft² of floor space, but the trend is toward smaller units. By limiting input-output functions, memory size, program versatility, and speed, general-purpose digital computers for airborne weapon systems have been built which weigh less than 100 lbs and occupy no more than 1 ft³ of space.

The most important characteristics of general-purpose computers are their memory size, operating speed, versatility of input-output functions, and ease of programming. These characteristics are not independent because speed can be traded for memory size, for example, at the expense of programming time. Thus, a mathematical function whose computation time is lengthy may be stored as a table in a large memory for repeated fast application. Memory sizes range from a few thousand 32-bit words to millions; operating speed in modern digital computers as reckoned by average instruction rate (fetch, add, store, or fetch, multiply, store) ranges from thousands per second to a million instructions per second.

Special-purpose computers are often designed to take advantage of special forms of input-data or special computational circumstances. As a hypothetical example, consider the design of a pulsed-radar computer which is to detect the presence of stationary targets at essentially any range by summing the echo amplitude from pulse to pulse. Fig. 21-23 contains a simplified diagram of such a system. Here the echo amplitudes at each of N range locations are encoded periodically at a rate $1/T$ samples per second; each

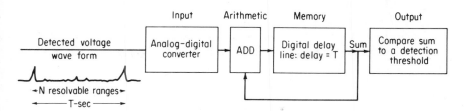

FIGURE 21-23   A hypothetical special-purpose digital computer.

sample is added at this rate to the sum of samples encoded at that range from the previous radar pulses, which has emerged from a digital delay mechanism. The delay can be accomplished for each binary place, by on-off compressive stressing of the end of a quartz or glass rod, or by torsional stressing of the end of a length of stiff wire; the on-off movement at the far end is sensed to recover the information T sec later. Since commercially-available digital delay lines can be pulsed at many megacycles per second, this example suggests that simpler special-purpose computers can well exceed the performance of general-purpose computers in specific applications.

21-12
Digital plotters

Whether in real-time control, data analysis, fault diagnosis, or scientific computing, results very often are more useful in graphical than in typewriter print-out form. Early means for graphical presentations have included oscilloscope-camera units and also galvanometer-recorders, which in turn were driven by the output of a digital-to-analog converter. The oscilloscope-camera method is severely limited in chart size and lacks versatility. The galvanometer recorder, although possessing a wide bandwidth (to 5000 Hz) lacks such useful features as printed axis legends and scales, curve labels, and accurate speed controls.

Compared with the above methods, modern digital plotting is performed with less speed (200 pen positions or a maximum of 2 in. of travel per second)† but with great precision and versatility. Economy is achieved by performing the plotting with peripheral computer-output equipment. This "off-line" mode permits the central computer to operate independently. Figure 21-24 outlines the plotter operation. A special plotter program sequences the data to be plotted and often carries instructions about plot size, scales, legends,

†IBM 1627 PLOTTER, File No. 162011710-03, IBM System Reference Library, IBM Product Publications Department, San Jose, California, no date.

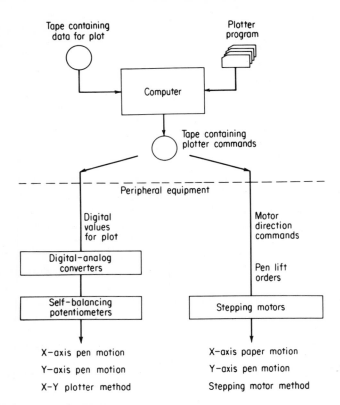

FIGURE 21-24   Two methods for digital plotting.

data-point symbols, and wild-point rules.

In the X-Y plotter method, the digital-number pulses may operate switch contacts on a potentiometer, producing an analog wave form which in turn is followed by a servo pen system.

In the stepping-motor method.† the digital data points are converted to binary commands for each of two incremental stepping motors‡ mounted at right angles. The Y motor moves the pen in the vertical direction as ordered; the X motor moves the paper in the horizontal direction as ordered. By an "increment" or "hold" bit and a "polarity" bit for each motor, one of eight compass directions may be ordered. In this incremental fashion, the pen point follows the line linearly connecting consecutive graph points and traces out letters or numerals.

†*Ibid.*
‡R. Bruce Kieburtz, "The Step Motor—The Next Advance in Control Systems", *I. E. E. E. Trans. on Automatic Control*, v. AC-9, pp. 98–104, Jan. 1964.

REFERENCES

21-1 D. Bartholomew, *Electrical Measurements and Instrumentation*, Allyn and Bacon, Inc., Boston, 1963.

21-2 D. A. Bell, *Information Theory and Its Engineering Applications*, 3d ed., Pitman Publishing Corporation, New York, 1962.

21-3 W. R. Bennett and J. R. Davey, *Data Transmission*, McGraw-Hill Book Company, New York, 1965.

21-4 B. B. Bycer, *Digital Magnetic Tape Recording: Principles and Computer Applications*, Hayden Publishing Company, New York, 1965.

21-5 R. H. Cerni and L. E. Foster, *Instrumentation for Engineering Measurement*, John Wiley & Sons, Inc., New York, 1962.

21-6 G. L. Davis, *Magnetic Tape Instrumentation*, McGraw-Hill Book Company, New York, 1961.

21-7 L. E. Foster, *Telemetry Systems*, John Wiley & Sons, New York, 1965.

21-8 S. Goldman, *Information Theory*, Prentice-Hall, Inc., Englewood Cliffs, N. J., 1953.

21-9 F. K. Harris, *Electrical Measurements*, John Wiley & Sons, Inc., New York, 1952.

21-10 M. L. Klein, H. C. Morgan, and M. H. Aronson, *Digital Techniques for Computation and Control*, Instruments Publishing Company, Pittsburgh, 1958.

21-11 G. A. Maley and E. J. Skiko, *Modern Digital Computers*, Prentice-Hall, Inc., Englewood Cliffs, N.J., 1964.

21-12 M. H. Nichols and L. L. Rauch, *Radio Telemetry*, 2d ed, John Wiley & Sons, Inc., New York, 1956.

21-13 H. G. M. Spratt, *Magnetic Tape Recording*, 2d ed., D. Van Nostrand Company, Inc., Princeton, N.J., 1964.

21-14 W. E. Stewart, *Magnetic Tape Recording Techniques*, McGraw-Hill Book Company, New York, 1958.

21-15 A. K. Susskind, ed., *Notes on Analog-Digital Conversion Techniques*, Technology Press, Cambridge, Mass., 1957.

21-16 D. M. Considine and S. D. Ross, eds., *Handbook of Applied Instrumentation*, McGraw-Hill Book Company, New York, 1964, Sec. 11.

EXERCISES

21-1 Assume that the sampling rate in the system in Fig. 21-5 is 30/sec. What is the highest sine-wave signal frequency that can be reproduced properly (a) if an ideal interpolation filter is used, and (b) if a practical filter is used?

21-2 Suppose that the signal voltage v_s in Fig. 21-5 has the sawtooth form shown in Fig. D-2, Appendix D, with a period of 0.01 sec. The sampling rate is to be chosen on the basis that Fourier components of the wave are to be transmitted that have amplitudes 0.1 or more of the amplitude of the fundamental frequency component. What sampling rate is required in a practical system?

21-3 A temperature measuring system has a rise time of 5 sec, a range of 300°C, and a system resolution of 0.6°C. Determine (a) the allowable error in per cent of the range and (b) the minimum time interval between successive meaningful observations of the temperature, if the temperature is changing at the rate of 24°C/sec.

21-4 A typical modern digital computer, in the single-precision mode, has a word length of 24 bits. Determine whether or not this word is sufficiently long to express the distance from the Earth to a Moon probe, using uniform quantization, with the least significant bit representing 5 feet.

21-5 An accelerometer has a sensitivity level of 0.5 g and a full-scale value of 50 g. How many bits are necessary to encode its output to a largest relative error of 1 per cent with uniform quantization over the 0.5 to 50 g interval?

21-6 In practical applications, the concept of a bandlimited signal is useful only after an "effective" bandwidth has been defined for the signals at hand. Consider the following signals and their bandwidth definitions:
(a) The output of a serial 6-bit analog-digital converter, which is triggered on the positive-going zero crossings of a 60 Hz sine wave. The maximum frequency contained in this signal is 5 times the bit rate.
(b) The analog video output of a radar with a two-target resolution of 150 ft in slant range. This distance resolution corresponds to 300 nanosec on the echo time axis. A "rule of thumb" for conversions to an effective bandwidth in Hz is to use the reciprocal of the time-axis resolution.
(c) A piezoelectric accelerometer is constructed as described in Exercise 18-7 with an undamped natural frequency of 5 kHz and a normalized damping factor of 0.5. A useful bandwidth of the output signal from this transducer could be determined from the transducer frequency response data in Fig. 18-11 and the highest frequency at which the response is equal to 1.05 times its low-frequency value.

Now, for the signals described in (a), (b), and (c), consider, respectively, the suitability of the following three channels: (1) A quality telephone line of 2500 Hz bandwidth, (2) A commercial television tape recorder of 4 MHz bandwidth, and (3) A telephone company digital data set, carrying 600 bits/sec.

21-7 Expand the discussion of Sec. 21-5b to derive an expression for the reproducer core flux amplitude when a magnetic tape carries a sinusoidal wave of wavelength λ. Assume that the reproducer core flux is exactly proportional to the integral of the flux density over a distance d along the tape. Using this expression show that an attenuation of 4 dB always occurs at a recorded frequency of $v/2d$, where v is the tape speed.

21-8 A test of the frequency response of an oscillograph galvanometer in a particular circuit gave the following data:

Frequency, Hz	0	200	400	600	850	1000	1200
Amplitude, per unit	1.0	1.01	1.12	1.24	1.36	1.23	0.90

Other tests show that the galvanometer natural frequency is 1000 Hz. (a) Estimate the galvanometer bandwidth based on the 3 dB point. (b) If the same galvanometer circuit were excited with a step function of voltage, would the galvanometer response give an overshoot? If so, what is the value of the overshoot and what is the time at which it occurs?

21-9 A recorder galvanometer has a natural frequency of 50 Hz and a resistance of 10 ohms. When the external circuit resistance is 190 ohms the normalized damping ratio is 0.4, and half of this damping is the effect of the induced voltage in the coil. What value of external circuit resistance is required to give a galvanometer damping ratio of 0.6?

21-10 An oscillograph galvanometer has a natural frequency of 2000 Hz and a damping ratio of 0.4. (a) What is its bandwidth based on the 3 dB point? (b) Over what range of frequencies can this galvanometer be used if the maximum allowable errors are 12 per cent for amplitude and 20° for phase?

21-11 Assume that the analog variable in the time-base encoding method shown in Fig. 21-13 varies from zero to the crest of the linear ramp. Let there be 1000 counts for the maximum amplitude. What is the maximum encoding error due only to the counting granularity in per cent of the maximum amplitude? Draw a sketch (see Fig. 21-13) illustrating the maximum error condition.

21-12 A time-base encoder is to provide uniformly-spaced encoding levels, spanning the range from 0 to 100 volts, with a maximum error of 0.05 per cent of full scale. How many encoding levels will be necessary? How many bits will be necessary to code the output in binary? What is the minimum counting frequency if the sampling frequency is to be 1000 Hz?

21-13 An information channel delivers a series of decimal numbers to be recorded in digital form, using direct RZ recording on binary magnetic tape. The numbers are in binary-coded decimal form using the code 8-4-2-1. How many 3-digit decimal numbers can be recorded per second on a single track if the tape speed is 30 in./sec, and 400 bits/in. are allowed? State what your assumptions are regarding spaces allowed between code groups and between numbers. Illustrate your answer with a sketch.

21-14 Determine the output impedance as a function of R for the encoding circuit of Fig. 21-17. Assume that there are N bits in the word, and that the resistance of the voltage source in each of the N branches is included in the indicated series resistance.

21-15 Verify the statement in Sec. 21-9 regarding the percentage accuracy of the weighting networks by calculating the largest percentage error in the output voltage of the circuit in Fig. 21-17 when e_2 alone is ON. Assume that the error arises only from the resistor values, and that the resistances are all within 0.1 per cent of their nominal values.

21-16 In a digital-analog voltage converter with a 0.25 per cent maximum error in the reference voltage, what are the binary places where information is likely to be destroyed?

21-17 Consider an FM multiplexing system similar to that in Fig. 21-20. Assume that the maximum carrier deviation is ± 5 per cent, the lowest center frequency is 2 kHz, the frequency limit of the magnetic tape is 55 kHz, and that the frequency $f_c - \Delta f_c$ of each higher band is twice the frequency $f_c + \Delta f_c$ of the adjacent lower band. (a) Specify the number of channels available and their center frequencies. (b) Assume that the lowest channel is assigned the frequency band from 1.2 to 2.8 kHz. What is the highest frequency of sine-wave signal that may be used in this channel if the criterion used in Fig. 13-10 is applied?

21-18 In the design of special purpose digital computers there is usually a tradeoff between instruction rate and memory size to produce a given computation rate. This tradeoff represents a balance between computation time and memory size required for storing tables of functions. To illustrate this tradeoff, consider that only the function $y = \sin \theta$ is to be computed, over a certain range in a time of 10 microsec. It is to be computed in the interval $-20°$ to $+20°$ with an absolute accuracy of 0.001 in 10 microsec. Assume that the operations of memory entry, addition, multiplication, and division all require the same length of time T and that the duration of all other operations may be neglected. Plot a rough curve of the required operation time T_x versus required memory size using the three points corresponding to the following schemes: (a) Having the function stored and simply look up the answer, (b) having the function and its first differences stored equally spaced at 11 places and linearly interpolate to obtain the answer, and (c) compute the function using the approximation $\sin \theta = \theta - (\theta^3/6)$.

21-19 In a certain radar, echo amplitudes from a satellite are encoded at a rate of 100 samples per second, in 512 levels, and recorded on a magnetic tape. These data are to be plotted against time by a digital plotter which uses stepping motors giving a speed of 200 pen positions per second, with 0.01 in. of travel each increment. (a) Could this plotter operate in real time? (b) For a 5 minute satellite pass, how many feet of graph (t-axis) will be required? (c) For a 5 minute satellite pass, what is the minimum required plotting time? The maximum?

A

Physical Constants, Abbreviations for Units, and Multiplying Factors

A-1
Physical constants

Symbol	Quantity	Magnitude
Å	angstrom unit	10^{-10} m
c	speed of light	2.998×10^8 m/s
e	charge of one electron	1.602×10^{-19} coul
eV	electron volt of energy	1.602×10^{-19} J
h	Planck's constant	6.626×10^{-34} J·s
k	Boltzmann's constant	1.380×10^{-23} J/deg
m	rest mass of the electron	9.109×10^{-31} kg
ϵ_0	permittivity of vacuum	8.855×10^{-12} F/m
μ_0	permeability of vacuum	$4\pi 10^{-7} = 1.257 \times 10^{-6}$ H/m

A-2
Abbreviations for units

Quantity	Abbreviation	Quantity	Abbreviation
Angstrom unit	Å	microfarad	μF
cycle per second	Hz	microsecond	μs
decibel	dB	microvolt	μV

degree	°	millivolt	mV
degree Kelvin	°K	milliampere	mA
electron volt	eV	millihenry	mH
farad	F	millijoule	mJ
gauss	G	newton	N
henry	H	ohm	Ω
joule	J	radian	rad
kilocycle per second	kHz	second	sec
lumen	lm	volt	V
megacycle per second	MHz	watt	W
microampere	μA	weber	Wb

A-3
Multiplying factors and prefixes

Symbol	Prefix	Factor		Example
T	tera	10^{12}	TΩ	teraohm
G	giga	10^{9}	GHz	gigahertz
M	mega	10^{6}	MΩ	megohm
k	kilo	10^{3}	kΩ	kilohm
m	milli	10^{-3}	mA	milliampere
μ	micro	10^{-6}	μA	microampere
n	nano	10^{-9}	ns	nanosecond
p	pico	10^{-12}	pF	picofarad

B

Selected Device Data
and Characteristics

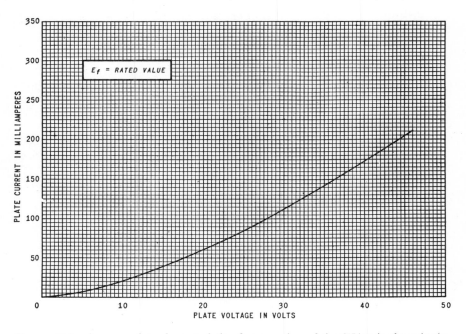

FIGURE B-1   Average plate characteristic of one section of the 6X4 twin thermionic diode. Cathode rating: 6.3 V, 0.6 A. Maximum ratings in rectifier service: Peak inverse voltage = 1250 V, recurring peak plate current per plate = 245 mA, and DC output current per plate with choke input filter = 35 mA. (Courtesy of the General Electric Company.)

597

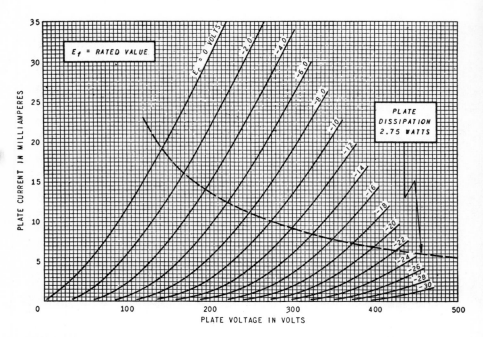

FIGURE B-2 Average plate characteristics of one section of type 12AU7A miniature medium-mu twin triode. The tube is suitable for use as a general-purpose
amplifier, phase inverter, oscillator, or multivibrator. Cathode ratings: 12.6 V,
0.15 A *or* 6.3 V, 0.3 A. Interelectrode capacitances, each section, with shield:
$C_{gp} = 1.5$ pF, $C_{in} = 2.0$ pF, and $C_{out} = 2.0$ pF.

Maximum ratings as class A_1 amplifier, each section: $E_b = 300$ V, DC cathode
current $= 20$ mA, and plate dissipation $= 2.75$ W; grid circuit resistance with fixed
bias $= 0.25$ MΩ, with cathode bias $= 1.0$ MΩ.

Parameters at $E_b = 250$ V, $E_c = -8.5$ V, $I_b = 10.5$ mA: $\mu = 17$, $r_p = 7700$ Ω,
$g_m = 2200$ μmho. (Courtesy of the General Electric Company.)

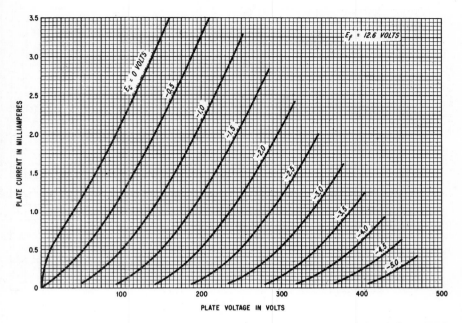

FIGURE B-3   Average plate characteristics of one section of type 12AX7A miniature high-mu twin triode. The tube is suitable for use in RC-coupled voltage amplifiers, phase inverters, multivibrators and industrial control circuits. Cathode ratings: 12.6 V, 0.15 A *or* 6.3 V, 0.3 A. Interelectrode capacitances, each section, with shield: $C_{gp} = 1.7$ pF, $C_{in} = 1.8$ pF, $C_{out} = 1.9$ pF.

     Maximum ratings: $E_b = 330$ V, plate dissipation $= 1.2$ W.

     Parameters at $E_b = 250$ V, $E_c = -2$ V, $I_b = 1.2$ mA: $\mu = 100, r_p = 62500\,\Omega$, $g_m = 1600\ \mu$mho. (Courtesy of the General Electric Company.)

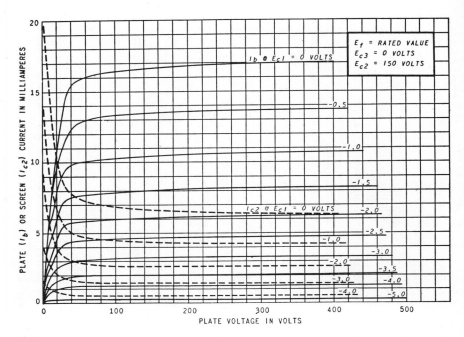

FIGURE B-4   Average plate characteristics of type 6AU6A miniature sharp-cutoff pentode. The tube is suitable for high-gain RF or IF amplifiers and for wide-band applications. Cathode rating: 6.3 V, 0.3 A. Interelectrode capacitances with shield: $C_{g1p} = 0.0035$ pF, $C_{in} = 5.5$ pF, $C_{out} = 5.0$ pF.

Maximum ratings: $E_b = 330$ V, $E_{c2} = 330$ V, plate dissipation $= 3.5$ W, screen dissipation $= 0.75$ W.

Typical operation as class A_1 amplifier: $E_b = 250$ V, $E_{c2} = 125$ V, $I_b = 7.6$ mA, $I_{c2} = 3.0$ mA, cathode bias resistor $= 100\ \Omega$, $r_p = 1.5$ MΩ (approx.), $g_m = 4500$ μmho. (Courtesy of the General Electric Company.)

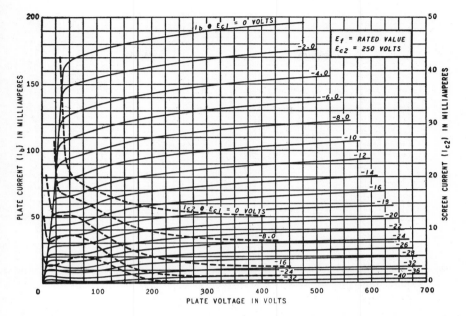

FIGURE B-5   Average plate characteristics of type 6L6GC beam-power tube primarily for use in AF power amplifier applications. Cathode rating: 6.3 V, 0.9 A. Inter-electrode capacitances, with shield: $C_{gp} = 0.6$ pF, $C_{in} = 10$ pF, $C_{out} = 6.5$ pF.

Maximum ratings: $E_b = 500$ V, $E_{c2} = 450$ V, plate dissipation = 30 W, screen dissipation = 5 W, grid 1 circuit resistance = 0.1 MΩ with fixed bias, = 0.5 MΩ with cathode bias.

Typical operation as class A_1 amplifier: $E_b = 300$ V, $E_{c2} = 200$ V, $E_{c1} = -12.5$ V, $I_b = 48$ mA, $r_p = 35000$ Ω, $g_m = 5300$ μmho. With peak AF signal of 12.5 V: $I_b = 55$ mA, $I_{c2} = 4.7$ mA, power output = 6.5 W, total harmonic distortion = 11 per cent. (Courtesy of the General Electric Company.)

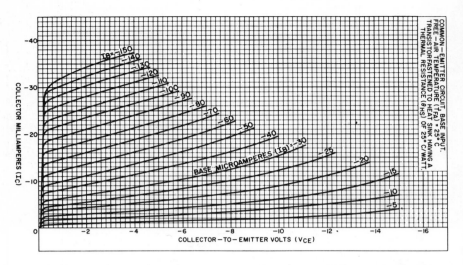

FIGURE B-6   Typical collector characteristics for type 2N2953 *pnp* alloy-junction germanium transistor at 25°C in a common-emitter circuit. This transistor is suitable for AF driver applications.

Maximum ratings: $V_{CBO} = -30$ V, $V_{EBO} = 25$ V, $I_C = -150$ mA, transistor dissipation in free air up to 55°C $= 120$ mW.

Electrical characteristics in free air at 25°C:

Collector cutoff current $I_{CBO} = -5$ μA max., at $V_{CB} = -20$ V.

Collector to base breakdown voltage $BV_{EBO} = -30$ V min., at $V_{EB} = -2$ V, $I_C = -0.05$ mA.

Emitter to base breakdown voltage $BV_{EBO} = -25$ V min., at $I_E = -0.05$ mA.

Small-signal common-emitter forward current transfer ratio $h_{fe} = 200$ min., 350 typ.; at $V_{CE} = -10$ V, $I_C = -10$ mA, $f = 1$ kHz.

Small-signal forward current transfer ratio cutoff frequency $f_{hfb} = 10$ MHz; at $V_{CB} = -12$ V, $I_C = -1$ mA. (Courtesy of Radio Corporation of America.)

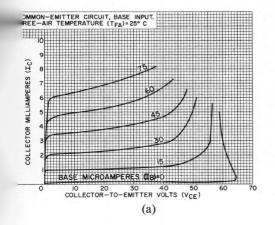

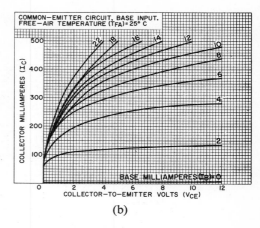

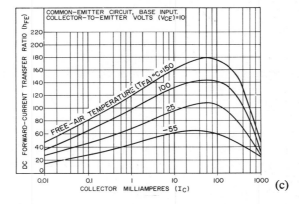

FIGURE B-7 Data for type 2N1613 *npn* planar silicon transistor at 25°C in a common-emitter circuit. (a) Typical collector characteristics at low currents. (b) Typical saturation characteristics. (c) h_{FE} vs. I_C with temperature as the parameter. This transistor is suitable for general-purpose small-signal and medium power switching applications.

Maximum ratings: $V_{CBO} = 75$ V, $V_{EBO} = 7$ V, $I_C = 1.0$ A; transistor dissipation (a) 0.8 W at free air temperature to 25°C, (b) 3.0 W at case temperature of 25°C.

Electrical characteristics at a case temperature of 25°C:
Collector cutoff current $I_{CBO} = 0.01$ μA max., at $V_{CB} = 60$ V.
Collector to base breakdown voltage $BV_{CBO} = 75$ V min., at $I_C = 0.1$ mA.
Emitter to base breakdown voltage $V_{EBO} = 7$ V min., at $I_E = 0.25$ mA.
Pulse test of saturation voltages: V_{BE}(sat) = 1.3 V max., V_{CE}(sat) = 1.5 V max., at $I_C = 150$ mA, $I_B = 15$ mA.
Small signal common-base parameters at $V_{CB} = 5$ V, $I_C = 1$ mA: $h_{ib} = 24$ Ω min., 34 Ω max.; $h_{ob} = 0.1$ μmho min., 0.5 μmho max.; $h_{rb} = 3 \times 10^{-4}$ max.
Small-signal common-emitter short-circuit current transfer ratio: (a) $h_{fe} = 30$ min., 150 max., at $V_{CE} = 5$ V, $I_c = 1$ mA, $f = 1$ kHz, (b) $h_{fe} = 3$ min., at $V_{CE} = 10$ V, $I_C = 50$ mA, $f = 20$ MHz. (Courtesy of Radio Corporation of America.)

603

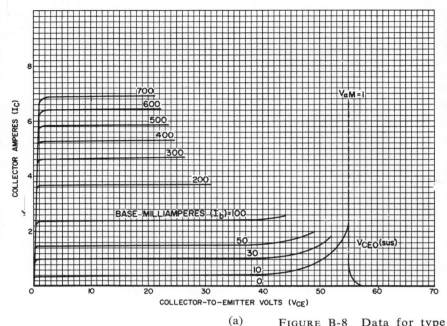

(a)

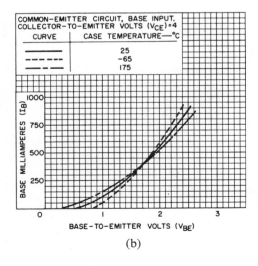

(b)

FIGURE B-8   Data for type 2N2338 *npn* diffused-junction silicon power transistor in a common-emitter circuit. (a) Typical collector characteristics at 25°C case temperature. (b) Typical input characteristics.

Maximum ratings: $V_{CBO} = 60$ V, $V_{EBO} = 40$ V, $I_C = 7.5$ A, $I_B = 5$ A, transistor dissipation $= 150$ W at 25°C case temperature, junction temperature range $-65°$ to $+200°$C.

Electrical characteristics at 25°C case temperature: Collector cutoff current $I_{CBO} = 0.2$ mA max. at V_{CB} of 30 V. Emitter cutoff current $I_{EBO} = 0.1$ mA max. at V_{EB} of 6 V. DC forward-current transfer ratio $h_{FE} = 15$ min. and $= 60$ max. at V_{CE} of 4 V and I_C of 3 A. DC collector to emitter saturation resistance $R_s = 0.5$ Ω at I_B of 0.3 A and I_C of 3 A. Small signal short-circuit forward-current transfer ratio cutoff frequency $f_{hfe} = 20$ kHz at V_{CE} of 4 V and I_C of 5 A. Collector to base capitance $C_{ob} = 400$ pF at V_{CB} of 40 V.

(Courtesy of Radio Corporation of America.)

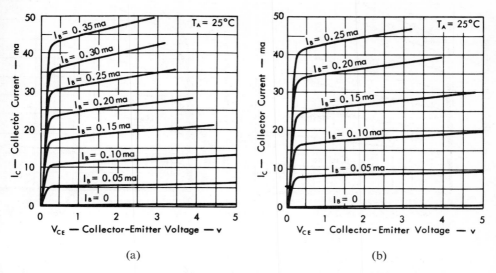

(a)   (b)

FIGURE B-9   Selected data on 2N1302, 2N1304, 2N1306 and 2N1308 alloy-junction *npn* germanium transistors suitable for medium-speed logic switching and general-purpose applications. (a) Typical common emitter collector characteristics for 2N1304. (b) Typical common emitter collector characteristics for 2N1308.

Maximum ratings at 25°C, all types: $V_{CB} = 25$ V, $V_{EB} = 25$ V, $I_C = 300$ mA, transistor dissipation = 150 mW at up to 25°C free-air temperature.

Electrical characteristics at 25°C free-air temperature:

	2N1302	2N1304	2N1306	2N1308
BV_{CBO}, volts min., at $I_C = 100$ μA	25	25	25	25
BV_{EBO}, volts min., at $I_E = 100$ μA	25	25	25	25
I_{CBO}, μA typ., at $V_{CB} = 25$ V	3	3	3	3
I_{EBO}, μA typ., at $V_{EB} = 25$ V	2	2	2	2
h_{FE}, min., at $V_{CE} = 1$ V, $I_C = 10$ mA	20	40	60	80
V_{CE}(sat), volts typ., at $I_C = 10$ mA and $I_B = 0.5$, 0.25, 0.17 and 0.13 mA respectively	.07	.07	.07	.07
h_{ib}, ohms typ., at $V_{CB} = 5$ V, $I_E = -1$ mA, $f = 1$ kHz	28	28	28	28
h_{rb}, typ., at $V_{CB} = 5$ V, $I_E = -1$ mA, $f = 1$ kHz	5×10^{-4}	5×10^{-4}	5×10^{-4}	5×10^{-4}
h_{ob}, μmho typ., at $V_{CB} = 5$ V, $I_E = -1$ mA, $f = 1$ kHz	0.34	0.34	0.34	0.34
h_{fe}, typ., at $V_{CE} = 5$ V, $I_C = 1$ mA, $f = 1$ kHz	105	120	135	170
f_{hfb}, MHz typ., at $V_{CB} = 5$ V, $I_E = 0$	12	14	16	20
C_{ob}, pF typ., at $V_{CB} = 5$ V, $I_E = 0$, $f = 1$ MHz	14	14	14	14
Switching characteristics at 25°C free-air temperature in a specified circuit, typical values:				
Delay time plus rise time, μsec	0.27	0.27	0.24	0.21
Storage time plus fall time, μsec	1.10	1.10	1.00	0.98

(Courtesy of Texas Instruments, Inc.)

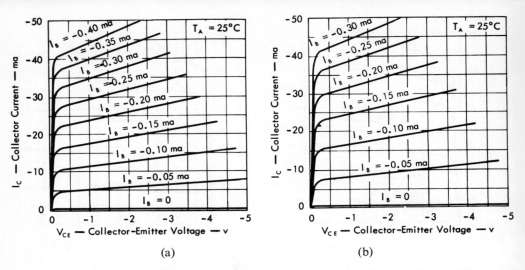

(a)   (b)

FIGURE B-10   Selected data on 2N1303, 2N1305, 2N1307 and 2N1309 alloy-junction *pnp* germanium transistors suitable for medium-speed logic switching and general-purpose applications. These types are complementary to types 2N1302, 2N1304, 2N1306 and 2N1308 respectively. (a) Typical common-emitter collector characteristics for 2N1305. (b) Typical common-emitter collector characteristics for 2N1309.

Maximum ratings at 25°C, all types: $V_{CB} = -30$ V, $V_{EB} = -25$ V, $I_c = -300$ mA, transistor dissipation = 150 mW at up to 25°C free-air temperature.

Electrical characteristics at 25°C free-air temperature:

	2N1303	2N1305	2N1307	2N1309
BV_{CBO}, volts min., at $I_C = -100$ μA	−30	−30	−30	−30
BV_{EBO}, volts min., at $I_E = -100$ μA	−25	−25	−25	−25
I_{CBO}, μA typ., at $V_{CB} = -25$ V	−2	−2	−2	−2
I_{EBO}, μA typ., at $V_{EB} = -25$ V	−1.5	−1.5	−1.5	−1.5
h_{FE}, typ., at $V_{CE} = -1$ V, $I_C = -10$ mA	100	115	130	160
V_{CE}(sat), typ., at $I_C = -10$ mA, and $I_B = -0.5$, -0.25, -0.17 and -0.13 mA respectively	−0.08	−0.08	−0.08	−0.08
h_{ib}, ohms typ., at $V_{CB} = -5$ V, $I_E = 1$ mA, $f = 1$ kHz	29	29	29	29
h_{rb}, typ., at $V_{CB} = -5$ V, $I_E = 1$ mA, $f = 1$ kHz	7×10^{-4}	7×10^{-4}	7×10^{-4}	7×10^{-4}
h_{ob}, μmho typ., at $V_{CB} = -5$ V, $I_E = 1$ mA, $f = 1$ kHz	0.40	0.40	0.40	0.40
h_{fe}, typ., at $V_{CE} = -5$ V, $I_C = -1$ mA, $f = 1$ kHz	115	130	150	190
f_{hfb}, MHz typ., at $V_{CB} = -5$ V, $I_E = 1$ mA	12	14	16	20
Switching characteristics at 25°C free-air temperature in a specified circuit, typical values:				
Delay time plus rise time, μsec	0.24	0.24	0.20	0.19
Storage time plus fall time, μsec	1.18	1.18	1.14	1.06

(Courtesy Texas Instruments, Inc.)

Data on type 2N708 silicon npn epitaxial high-speed switching transistor

This transistor is suitable for highspeed logic switching applications.

Maximum ratings: $V_{CB} = 40$ V, $V_{CE} = 15$ V, $V_{EB} = 5$ V, junction temperature 200°C; transistor dissipation (a) 1.2 W at 25°C case temperature (b) 0.68 W at 100°C case temperature (c) 0.36 W in free air at 25°C.

Approximate dimensions, without leads: 0.185 in. diam., 0.25 in. high.

Electrical characteristics at 25°C free-air temperature: Collector cutoff current I_{CBO}, 5 nA typ. and 25 nA max. at $V_{CB} = 20$ V. Emitter cutoff current I_{EBO}, 80 nA max. at $V_{EB} = 4$ V.

Collector to base breakdown voltage BV_{CBO}, 40 V min. at $I_C = 1$ μA.

Collector to emitter breakdown voltage BV_{CEO}, 15 V min. at $I_C = 30$ mA.

Emitter to base breakdown voltage BV_{EBO}, 5 V min. at $I_E = 10$ μA.

Collector saturation voltage V_{CE}(sat), 0.2 V typ. and 0.4 V max. at $I_C = 10$ mA, 10 mA, $I_B = 1$ mA.

Base-emitter saturation voltage V_{BE}(sat), 0.72 V min. and 0.80 V max. at $I_C = 10$ mA, $I_B = 1$ mA.

dc forward current transfer ratio h_{FE}, 15 min. at $I_C = 0.5$ mA and $V_{CE} = 1$ V.

Small-signal forward current transfer ratio h_{fe}, 3.0 min. and 4.5 typ. at $I_C = 10$ mA, $V_{CE} = 10$ V, $f = 100$ MHz.

Output capacitance C_{ob}, 3 pF typ. and 6 pF max. at $V_{CB} = 10$ V, $I_E = 0$.

(Courtesy of Motorola Semiconductor Products, Inc.)

C

Transformations among the Circuit Parameters

Relations among z, y, *and* h *parameters*

The basic network equations using the **z**, **y**, and **h** parameters are given in Eqs. (2-133) through (2-138). The determinants of these pairs of equations are given in Eqs. (2-143) and are rewritten here:

$$\Delta_z = \mathbf{z}_i\mathbf{z}_o - \mathbf{z}_r\mathbf{z}_f \qquad \Delta_y = \mathbf{y}_i\mathbf{y}_o - \mathbf{y}_r\mathbf{y}_f \qquad \Delta_h = \mathbf{h}_i\mathbf{h}_o - \mathbf{h}_r\mathbf{h}_f$$

The relations among the network parameters may be written in the following forms:

$$\mathbf{z}_i = \frac{\mathbf{y}_o}{\Delta_y} = \frac{\Delta_h}{\mathbf{h}_o} \qquad\qquad \mathbf{y}_i = \frac{\mathbf{z}_o}{\Delta_z} = \frac{1}{\mathbf{h}_i} \qquad\qquad \mathbf{h}_i = \frac{1}{\mathbf{y}_i} = \frac{\Delta_z}{\mathbf{z}_o}$$

$$\mathbf{z}_r = -\frac{\mathbf{y}_r}{\Delta_y} = \frac{\mathbf{h}_r}{\mathbf{h}_o} \qquad\qquad \mathbf{y}_r = -\frac{\mathbf{z}_r}{\Delta_z} = -\frac{\mathbf{h}_r}{\mathbf{h}_i} \qquad \mathbf{h}_r = -\frac{\mathbf{y}_r}{\mathbf{y}_i} = \frac{\mathbf{z}_r}{\mathbf{z}_o}$$

$$\mathbf{z}_f = -\frac{\mathbf{y}_f}{\Delta_y} = -\frac{\mathbf{h}_f}{\mathbf{h}_o} \qquad\quad \mathbf{y}_f = -\frac{\mathbf{z}_f}{\Delta_z} = \frac{\mathbf{h}_f}{\mathbf{h}_i} \qquad\quad \mathbf{h}_f = \frac{\mathbf{y}_f}{\mathbf{y}_i} = -\frac{\mathbf{z}_f}{\mathbf{z}_o}$$

$$\mathbf{z}_o = \frac{\mathbf{y}_i}{\Delta_y} = \frac{1}{\mathbf{h}_o} \qquad\qquad \mathbf{y}_o = \frac{\mathbf{z}_i}{\Delta_z} = \frac{\Delta_h}{\mathbf{h}_i} \qquad\qquad \mathbf{h}_o = \frac{\Delta_y}{\mathbf{y}_i} = \frac{1}{\mathbf{z}_o}$$

608

C-2
Approximate conversion relationships among the h parameters and the equivalent-T circuit parameters

Symbol	Common emitter	Common base	Common collector	Equivalent-T circuit
h_{ie}		$\dfrac{h_{ib}}{1+h_{fb}}$	h_{ic}	$r_b + \dfrac{r_e}{1-a}$
h_{re}		$\dfrac{h_{ib}h_{ob}}{1+h_{fb}} - h_{rb}$	$1 - h_{rc}$	$\dfrac{r_e}{(1-a)r_c}$
h_{fe}		$-\dfrac{h_{fb}}{1+h_{fb}}$	$-(1+h_{fc})$	$\dfrac{a}{(1-a)}$
h_{oe}		$\dfrac{h_{ob}}{1+h_{fb}}$	h_{oc}	$\dfrac{1}{(1-a)r_c}$
h_{ib}	$\dfrac{h_{ie}}{1+h_{fe}}$		$-\dfrac{h_{ic}}{h_{fc}}$	$r_e + (1-a)r_b$
h_{rb}	$\dfrac{h_{ie}h_{oe}}{1+h_{fe}} - h_{re}$		$h_{rc} - 1 - \dfrac{h_{ic}h_{oc}}{h_{fc}}$	$\dfrac{r_b}{r_c}$
h_{fb}	$-\dfrac{h_{fe}}{1+h_{fe}}$		$-\left(1+\dfrac{1}{h_{fc}}\right)$	$-a$
h_{ob}	$\dfrac{h_{oe}}{1+h_{fe}}$		$-\dfrac{h_{oc}}{h_{fc}}$	$\dfrac{1}{r_c}$
h_{ic}	h_{ie}	$\dfrac{h_{ib}}{1+h_{fb}}$		$r_b + \dfrac{r_e}{1-a}$
h_{rc}	$1 - h_{re}$	1		$1 - \dfrac{r_e}{(1-a)r_c}$
h_{fc}	$-(1+h_{fe})$	$-\dfrac{1}{1+h_{fb}}$		$-\dfrac{1}{1-a}$
h_{oc}	h_{oe}	$\dfrac{h_{ob}}{1+h_{fb}}$		$\dfrac{1}{(1-a)r_c}$
a	$\dfrac{h_{fe}}{1+h_{fe}}$	$-h_{fb}$	$\dfrac{1+h_{fc}}{h_{fc}}$	
r_c	$\dfrac{1+h_{fe}}{h_{oe}}$	$\dfrac{1}{h_{ob}}$	$-\dfrac{h_{fc}}{h_{oc}}$	
r_e	$\dfrac{h_{re}}{h_{oe}}$	$h_{ib} - \dfrac{h_{rb}}{h_{ob}}(1+h_{fb})$	$\dfrac{1-h_{rc}}{h_{oc}}$	
r_b	$h_{ie} - \dfrac{h_{re}}{h_{oe}}(1+h_{fe})$	$\dfrac{h_{rb}}{h_{ob}}$	$h_{ic} + \dfrac{h_{fc}}{h_{oc}}(1-h_{rc})$	

Auxiliary formulas:

$$r_m = ar_c \qquad r_d = r_c - r_m = r_c(1-a)$$

D

Outline of the Fourier Analysis of Periodic Functions, with an Application to Electric Circuit Calculations

Many of the wave forms in electronic work are periodic. Examples are equally spaced pulses, sawtooth waves, and half and full rectified waves. In practical systems these non-sine waves can be expressed by the sum of a constant term plus an infinite series of cosine and sine terms. In linear circuit calculations it is sometimes useful to express non-sine voltage or current sources by their equivalent Fourier series, and then to calculate the circuit output by considering each term of the series separately and superposing the effects. Even when these calculations become too time consuming (unless aided by a digital computer), the insights obtained from the Fourier series concept are often of great value. Fourier series are also applied to relate pulse shape to bandwidth requirements in information transmission analysis.

Let us think of a known periodic function $f(t)$, which is to be expressed by the sum of a constant term plus an infinite series of cosine terms plus a similar series of sine terms; thus,

$$f(t) = \frac{a_o}{2} + \sum_{n=1}^{\infty} a_n \cos\left(n\frac{2\pi t}{T}\right) + \sum_{n=1}^{\infty} b_n \sin\left(n\frac{2\pi t}{T}\right) \tag{D-1}$$

where $f(t)$ has the period T. The constant term is seen to be the average value of the function, as follows:

$$\frac{a_o}{2} = [f(t)]_{av} = \frac{1}{T}\int_0^T f(t)\, dt \tag{D-2}$$

To find the values of the coefficients a_n or b_n, we multiply both sides of Eq.

610

(D-1) by $\cos n(2\pi t/T)$ or $\sin n(2\pi t/T)$. The only term that does not vanish on the right side of Eq. (D-1) after multiplication and integration over a complete period is

$$\int_{-T/2}^{+T/2} a_n \cos^2 \left(n\frac{2\pi t}{T}\right) dt \quad \text{or} \quad \int_{-T/2}^{+T/2} b_n \sin^2 \left(n\frac{2\pi t}{T}\right) dt \qquad (D\text{-}3)$$

These terms evaluate to $\frac{1}{2}a_n T$ or $\frac{1}{2}b_n T$. Thus it follows that

$$a_n = \frac{2}{T}\int_{-T/2}^{+T/2} f(t) \cos\left(n\frac{2\pi t}{T}\right) dt$$
$$b_n = \frac{2}{T}\int_{-T/2}^{+T/2} f(t) \sin\left(n\frac{2\pi t}{T}\right) dt \qquad (D\text{-}4)$$

We see that the unknown coefficients on the right side of Eq. (D-1) can be evaluated through Eqs. (D-2) and (D-4).

The series can also be expressed in terms of ω by replacing $2\pi/T$ by ω in Eqs. (D-1) and (D-4), with the result

$$f(t) = \frac{a_o}{2} + \sum_{n=1}^{\infty} (a_n \cos n\omega t + b_n \sin n\omega t) \qquad (D\text{-}5)$$

where

$$a_n = \frac{\omega}{\pi}\int_{-\pi/\omega}^{+\pi/\omega} f(t) \cos n\omega t\, dt$$
$$b_n = \frac{\omega}{\pi}\int_{-\pi/\omega}^{+\pi/\omega} f(t) \sin n\omega t\, dt$$

A compact form of the Fourier series is obtained by the use of the complex exponential functions. We recall that $\cos x = (e^{jx} + e^{-jx})/2$ and $\sin x = (e^{jx} - e^{-jx})/2j$. If these forms are introduced into Eq. (D-1) and the result is manipulated, it can be shown that the Fourier series can be expressed in the form

$$f(t) = \sum_{n=-\infty}^{+\infty} c_n e^{jn(2\pi t/T)} \qquad (D\text{-}6)$$

where

$$c_o = \frac{a_o}{2} = \frac{1}{T}\int_d^{d+T} f(t)\, dt$$
$$c_n = \frac{1}{T}\int_d^{d+T} f(t)e^{-jn(2\pi t/T)}dt$$

Here d is the time at some convenient starting point for the integration, usually 0 or $-T/2$. We remark that the coefficients c_n are generally complex numbers. Equation (D-6) gives the Fourier series in the so-called *complex exponential form*.

Example 1: We first find the Fourier series for the square wave shown in Fig. D-1. We use the series in Eq. (D-6), choose $d = 0$, and calculate

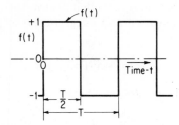

FIGURE D-1   Square wave.

$$c_o = \frac{1}{T}\left[\int_0^{T/2} dt + \int_{T/2}^T (-1)\, dt\right] = 0$$

and

$$c_n = \frac{1}{T}\left[\int_0^{T/2} e^{-jn(2\pi t/T)}dt + \int_{T/2}^T (-1)e^{-jn(2\pi t/T)}dt\right] = \frac{(e^{-jn\pi} - 1)^2}{jn2\pi}$$

But $e^{-jn\pi} = \cos n\pi - j\sin n\pi = \cos n\pi = (-1)^n$ for n an integer. Then $(e^{-jn\pi} - 1)^2 = (-2)^2$ for n odd and equals zero for n even. Therefore

$$c_n = \frac{(-2)^2}{jn2\pi} = \frac{2}{jn\pi} \quad \text{for} \quad n = 1, 3, 5, \ldots$$

$$c_n = 0 \qquad\qquad\quad \text{for} \quad n = 2, 4, 6, \ldots$$

Using these results in Eq. (D-6), we find

$$\begin{aligned}
f(t) &= \frac{2e^{j(2\pi t/T)}}{j\pi} + \frac{2e^{j3(2\pi t/T)}}{j3\pi} + \cdots \frac{2e^{jn(2\pi t/T)}}{jn\pi} && \text{to } n \to \infty \\
&+ \frac{2e^{-j(2\pi t/T)}}{-j\pi} + \frac{2e^{-j3(2\pi t/T)}}{-j3\pi} + \cdots \frac{2e^{jn(2\pi t/T)}}{+jn\pi} && \text{to } n \to -\infty
\end{aligned}$$

(D-7)

Combining similar terms in (D-7) leads to the series

$$f(t) = \frac{4}{\pi}\sin\frac{2\pi t}{T} + \frac{4}{3\pi}\sin\frac{6\pi t}{T} + \cdots \tag{D-8}$$

Example 2:   A similar analysis of the sawtooth wave in Fig. D-2 will show that the Fourier series for this wave is given by

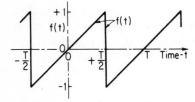

FIGURE D-2   A sawtooth wave.

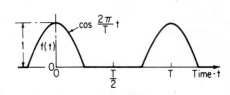

FIGURE. D-3   Half-wave rectified wave.

$$f(t) = \frac{2}{\pi}(\sin \omega t - \tfrac{1}{2} \sin 2\omega t + \tfrac{1}{3} \sin 3\omega t + \cdots) \qquad \text{(D-9)}$$

Example 3: The Fourier series for the half-wave rectified wave shown in Fig. D-3 is the following:

$$f(t) = \frac{1}{\pi} + \frac{1}{2} \cos \frac{2\pi t}{T} + \frac{2}{3\pi} \cos 2 \cdot \frac{2\pi t}{T} - \frac{2}{15\pi} \cos 4 \cdot \frac{2\pi t}{T} + \cdots \qquad \text{(D-10)}$$

It is instructive to sketch the first few terms of this series and, by adding the ordinates graphically, show how the sum of the series begins to approach the original function.

Now we turn to an application of the Fourier series technique to a circuit problem. Suppose that an ideal voltage source has the sawtooth wave form in Fig. D-2 so that Eq. (D-9) gives the series of voltage terms that represents the wave. Let this source be impressed on a series circuit comprising a resistance R and an inductance L. What is the resulting current? We apply superposition and calculate the current that each voltage term would produce if it were acting alone and then add the terms. For example, the second voltage term has the radian frequency 2ω and the amplitude $-1/\pi$ V. The impedance of the RL circuit to this frequency is $R + j2\omega L$, so the resulting current term is

$$-\frac{1}{\pi(R^2 + 4\omega^2 L^2)^{1/2}} \sin(2\omega t - \phi_2) \qquad \text{(D-11)}$$

where

$$\phi_2 = \tan^{-1}\frac{2\omega L}{R}$$

Each voltage term produces a current term, and the total current becomes

$$i(t) = \frac{2 \sin(\omega t - \phi_1)}{\pi(R^2 + \omega^2 L^2)^{1/2}} - \frac{\sin(2\omega t - \phi_2)}{\pi(R^2 + 4\omega^2 L^2)^{1/2}}$$
$$+ \frac{2 \sin(3\omega t - \phi_3)}{3\pi(R^2 + 9\omega^2 L^2)^{1/2}} + \cdots \qquad \text{(D-12)}$$

where the phase angles are given by $\phi_n = \tan^{-1}(n\omega L/R)$. We notice that when $\omega L \gg R$, the higher frequency terms in (D-12) rapidly diminish, thus the 3ω term is approximately one-ninth of the first term.

In the foregoing examples the waves had such types of symmetry that only a cosine or a sine series was needed, but in general both series are required. Questions relating to the effect of symmetry and concerning the limitations of the Fourier series technique are beyond the scope of this outline.†

†See, for example, H. H. Skilling, *Electrical Engineering Circuits*, 2d ed., John Wiley & Sons, Inc., New York, 1965, Chaps. 14, 15; or C. R. Wylie, Jr., *Advanced Engineering Mathematics*, 3rd ed., McGraw-Hill Book Company, New York, 1966, Chap. 6.

E

Transmission Lines; Delay Lines

E-1
Introduction

We have assumed that the voltage and current are, at a particular instant, the same at every point along the wires that connect different pieces of apparatus. However, if the wires are long or if the signals involve high frequencies or fast pulses, the assumption of uniform voltage and current is no longer valid. In fact, the waves or pulses travel along the conductors with a finite speed, and they may become distorted and attenuated as they advance. Furthermore, waves may be reflected from the end of the line and then combine with the forward traveling wave.

The time delay involved in the passage of the signal down the line may be a troublesome feature, or it may be adapted to serve practically useful ends. For example, in high-speed CR oscilloscopes the signal for the vertical deflection may go through an artificial *delay line* installed within the oscilloscope, whereas the trigger voltage for the horizontal sweep is not delayed. As a result, the sweep can start before the deflection begins, and the start of the wave is more clearly portrayed. Other applications of delay lines are in precise pulse generation circuits, in computer circuits, in pulse shaping, and in radar and TV systems.

Our treatment of this complex subject will be limited to a brief study of the loss-free transmission line to introduce the concepts of the velocity of

614

propagation, forward and reverse waves, and characteristic impedance of the line. Then we shall discuss reflections at the terminating impedances, and practical delay lines.

E-2
Waves on transmission lines;
speed of propagation;
characteristic impedance

Figure E-1 illustrates two common forms of transmission lines. Part (a) shows the familiar two-wire line similar to an overhead open-wire telephone line. Part (b) shows a coaxial cable, which has an inner conductor and a con-

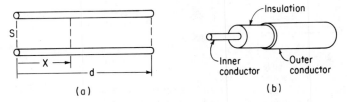

FIGURE E-1   (a) Two-wire line and (b) coaxial cable.

centric outer conductor separated by a solid dielectric. Sometimes the solid dielectric is replaced by insulating discs or an edge-wound insulating ribbon so that the insulation between the conductors is mostly air.

To review some fundamantals of wave motion we imagine that a sinusoidal voltage is switched on to the sending end s of the two-wire line. At a time t_1 sec later the voltage distribution along the length of the line will take the form of the solid curve in Fig. E-2. This distribution will be moving to

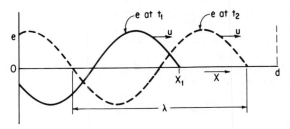

FIGURE E-2   Voltage waves on a transmission line at times t_1 and t_2, where $t_2 > t_1$.

the right with a speed u that depends on the physical characteristics of the line, but for an open-wire line this speed is very close to the speed of light, or 3×10^8 m/s. The figure also shows the displaced distribution at the later time t_2. If we recall the relation between wavelength λ, frequency f, and velocity u, i.e., $u = \lambda f$, or $\lambda = u/f$, we can calculate the wavelength of a particular wave. Thus a 10-MHz signal has a wavelength of 30 m on an open-wire line. Therefore any line longer than 2 or 3 m would have to be considered a "long transmission line" rather than a lumped resistance and inductance for a 10-MHz signal.

Next we shall outline the theory of the loss-free line using the symbols shown in Fig. E-3a. Actual lines have resistance and inductance that depend

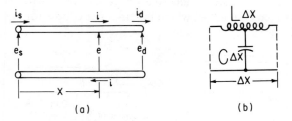

FIGURE E-3   (a) Voltage and current symbols defined. e_s = sending end voltage. e_d = load end voltage. (b) Representation of length Δx of loss-free line.

on the conductors and have insulation losses and capacitance that depend on the geometry and the insulation. For high-frequency signals or for pulses the resistance losses and leakage losses may be ignored in order to obtain an approximate theory that is often sufficiently accurate. A section of the loss-free line of length Δx can be represented by an inductance $L\Delta x$ and a capacitance $C\Delta x$ connected as in Fig. E-3b, where L is the line inductance per unit length and C is the capacitance per unit length. Temporarily we shall use the symbols $e(x, t)$ and $i(x, t)$ for the line voltage and current to emphasize that they are functions of both distance and time. The voltage drop over the element Δx is due to the inductance and may be written

$$e(x + \Delta x, t) - e(x, t) = \Delta e(x, t) = -L\Delta x \frac{\partial i(x, t)}{\partial t} \qquad \text{(E-1)}$$

We divide by Δx, let Δx approach zero, and change the notation to e and i for the line voltage and current, and find

$$\frac{\partial e}{\partial x} = -L \frac{\partial i}{\partial t} \qquad \text{(E-2)}$$

The change in line current in the length Δx is caused by the current drained through $C\Delta x$, thus the change in current is expressed by

$$i(x + \Delta x, t) - i(x, t) = \Delta i(x, t) = -C\Delta x \frac{\partial e(x, t)}{\partial t} \qquad \text{(E-3)}$$

Using the same techniques as for the voltage, we find

$$\frac{\partial i}{\partial x} = -C\frac{\partial e}{\partial t} \qquad \text{(E-4)}$$

We can get an equation involving only the voltage by differentiating (E-2) with respect to x, and (E-4) with respect to t, and eliminating $\partial^2 i/\partial t\, \partial x$ to find

$$\frac{\partial^2 e}{\partial x^2} = LC\frac{\partial^2 e}{\partial t^2} \qquad \text{(E-5)}$$

By a similar method we can obtain

$$\frac{\partial^2 i}{\partial x^2} = LC\frac{\partial^2 i}{\partial t^2} \qquad \text{(E-6)}$$

We note that (E-5) and (E-6) are identical in form; therefore the same form of solutions will be obtained for the current and for the voltage.

Next we define the symbol u, as follows:

$$u^2 = \frac{1}{LC} \quad \text{or} \quad u = \frac{1}{\sqrt{LC}} \qquad \text{(E-7)}$$

Then trial by substitution will show that terms of the forms

$$f(x - ut) \quad \text{and} \quad g(x + ut) \qquad \text{(E-8)}$$

will satisfy the basic partial differential equation (E-5). The terms in (E-8) represent arbitrary functions, which are assumed to have second derivatives. In any particular situation the functions must be chosen to fit the initial conditions. Now the voltage may be expressed as

$$e = f(x - ut) + g(x + ut) \qquad \text{(E-9)}$$

The terms on the right represent two waves; the *forward* traveling wave $f(x - ut)$ and the *reverse* wave $g(x + ut)$. Consider only the forward wave at successive times t_1 and t_2, where $t_2 > t_1$. Then we have the arguments $(x - ut_1)$ and $(x - ut_2)$. The functions $f(x - ut_1)$ and $f(x - ut_2)$ are distributions of the *same form*, but the second is displaced in the $+x$ direction from the first.

An example of the behavior of the forward wave of voltage is shown in Fig. E-4a. In the loss-free line the square pulse at t_1 would be displaced a distance $u(t_2 - t_1)$ to the right at instant t_2 but would retain its original form. In an actual line the line losses may cause distortion similar to that shown.

Next we investigate the relation of i to e. Let us assume that

$$e = Z_0 i \qquad \text{(E-10)}$$

where Z_0 is a constant. We use this relation in Eqs. (E-2) and (E-4) to eliminate e and obtain

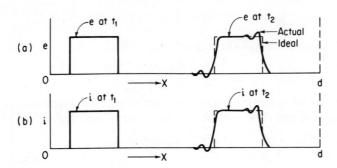

FIGURE E-4   Propagation of a pulse along a line.

$$Z_o \frac{\partial i}{\partial x} = -L \frac{\partial i}{\partial t} \qquad \text{(E-11)}$$

and

$$\frac{\partial i}{\partial x} = -C Z_o \frac{\partial i}{\partial t} \qquad \text{(E-12)}$$

Now divide (E-11) by (E-12) and find

$$Z_o = \frac{L}{C Z_o} \quad \text{or} \quad Z_o^2 = \frac{L}{C} \quad \text{or} \quad Z_o = \pm \sqrt{\frac{L}{C}} \qquad \text{(E-13)}$$

Therefore

$$e = \pm \sqrt{\frac{L}{C}} \, i \qquad \text{(E-14)}$$

Thus e and i are directly proportional to one another. The proportionality constant Z_0 is called the *characteristic impedance* or the *surge impedance* of the line. For loss-free lines the characteristic impedance has the nature of a resistance, but with lossy lines the mathematical treatment is such that Z_0 is a complex number. The plus sign in (E-14) is used with the forward wave and the minus sign with the reverse wave. For example, a *positive* forward voltage wave is accompanied by a *positive* current wave (positive charge must move to the right to advance the voltage distribution). However, a *positive* reverse voltage wave requires a *negative* current wave, if the current sign convention is kept the same.

Formulas for Z_0 may be obtained by inserting the well-known expressions for the inductance and capacitance for a particular line geometry into (E-13). For the two-wire line in air remote from the earth the result is

$$Z_o \cong 120 \ln \frac{D}{r} \qquad \text{(E-15)}$$

where r is the radius of the nonmagnetic wire and D is the center-to-center wire spacing. A pair of 1-mm-radius wires spaced 30 cm has a value of Z_0 of 409 Ω. The common forms of TV twin-conductor lead-in lines have a Z_0 of about 300 Ω.

For the single conductor coaxial line

$$Z_o \cong \frac{60}{\sqrt{\epsilon_r}} \ln \frac{r_2}{r_1} \tag{E-16}$$

where ϵ_r is the relative permittivity of the dielectric, r_1 is the inner conductor radius, and r_2 is the radius over the insulation. A typical coaxial cable has polyethylene insulation with $\epsilon_r = 2.3$ and has a value of r_2/r_1 equal to 3.5. Then Z_0 is about 50 Ω. Another common standard cable has a Z_0 of 75 Ω.

E-3
Reflections of waves on
transmission lines

Suppose that a step voltage wave is launched on a transmission line as by switching a voltage source on to the sending end. After a time $t = x_1/u$ the forward voltage wave will have the form shown in Fig. E-5a.

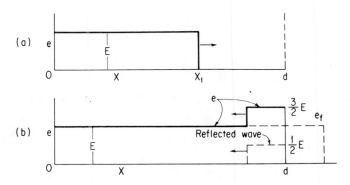

FIGURE E-5   (a) Step voltage approaching end of line. (b) Component waves and resultant voltage after reflection.

If the line is infinitely long, then the voltage wave will advance forever and there will be no reflected wave.

Now consider a step voltage wave on a line of length d, as in Fig. E-5a, but which is terminated in a resistance R_0 equal to the characteristic impedance. Then the ratio e/i at the end of the line must equal R_0 by Ohm's law. According to Eq. (E-10) the ratio of e to i of the wave itself equals Z_0, or in this case R_0. Therefore the boundary condition at the end does not disturb the voltage-current relation of the wave. As a result, the energy in the wave is dissipated in R_0 and there is *no reflected wave*.

Next consider a step-voltage wave on a line terminated in a resistor R not equal to Z_0. Then reflected waves of voltage and current develop of such magnitudes that the ratio of the instantaneous actual voltage to current at the end of the line equals R. In general, the voltages at any boundary obey superposition, expressed as follows:

forward wave + reverse wave + voltage already present
$$= \text{resultant voltage at the boundary} \quad \text{(E-17)}$$

In the situation at hand this relation reduces to

forward wave + reverse wave = resultant voltage at the boundary (E-18)

To reduce these ideas to mathematical form we need the symbols

e_d, i_d actual voltage and current at $x = d$
e_f, i_f voltage and current of forward wave
e_r, i_r voltage and current of reverse wave

The voltage and current at the end of the line, after the forward wave reaches this point, may be expressed as

$$e_d = e_f + e_r \quad \text{(E-19)}$$

and

$$i_d = i_f + i_r \quad \text{(E-20)}$$

We know from Eq. (E-14) that

$$i_f = \frac{e_f}{R_0} \quad \text{and} \quad i_r = -\frac{e_r}{R_0} \quad \text{(E-21)}$$

At the end of the line we require that $e_d/i_d = R$. Therefore, in view of (E-19) and (E-20),

$$\frac{e_d}{i_d} = \frac{e_f + e_r}{i_f + i_r} = R \quad \text{(E-22)}$$

Combining (E-21) and (E-22) to eliminate the currents yields

$$e_r = \frac{R - R_0}{R + R_0} e_f \quad \text{(E-23)}$$

The *reflection coefficient* ρ is defined so that $e_r = \rho e_f$; then

$$\rho = \frac{R - R_0}{R + R_0} \quad \text{(E-24)}$$

We note from (E-19) that

$$e_d = (1 + \rho)e_f \quad \text{(E-25)}$$

A little analysis will show that

$$i_r = -\rho i_f \quad \text{(E-26)}$$

and that

$$i_d = (1 - \rho)i_f \qquad \text{(E-27)}$$

For example, if $R = 3R_0$; then $\rho = 1/2$, and the reflected waves have half of the amplitudes of the original waves. The voltage distribution shortly after reflection occurs is shown schematically in Fig. E-5b. The solid line represents the actual (resultant) voltage, and the dashed lines represent the component forward and reflected waves. Of course, there is no voltage to the right of $x = d$, and the forward voltage is shown here only to indicate how far it would have traveled had the line extended beyond $x = d$.

When the reflected waves reach the sending end they will produce new reflections if the terminating resistance is different from R_0, or no reflection if the terminating resistance equals R_0.

E-4
Electromagnetic delay lines

Delay lines are used to provide a delayed signal and in various pulse-forming circuits. Two main types exist: (1) the distributed parameter lines similar to those discussed in the foregoing paragraphs, and (2) lumped parameter lines constructed of a number of inductors and capacitors.

The wave velocity in the open-wire line is near the speed of light, $c = 3 \times 10^8$ m/s. The speed of progapation in the coaxial cable constructed as in Fig. E-1b is somewhat lower and is given closely by $c/\sqrt{\epsilon_r}$. A calculation of the length of polyethylene-insulated coaxial cable needed to give a delay of 1 μs gives $10^{-6} \times 3 \times 10^8/\sqrt{2.3}$, or nearly 200 m. Such cables are not practical for microsecond delays but can be used for nanosecond delays.

Much greater delays for a given length are obtained with the helical delay line (Fig. E-6). In this line the inductance is increased by winding the inner conductor in the form of a solenoid on an insulating core. In some designs the inductance is increased still more by using a ferrite core within the fine-wire helix. The capacitance is also increased by using thinner insulation. The outer conductor consists of a braid of *insulated* copper wires, which are joined at the ends of the cable. This

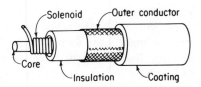

FIGURE E-6   Helical delay line.

construction reduces the eddy current losses. Helical delay lines are available in designs that have delays of from about 0.14 to 3.4 μs/m.

We recall that $|Z_0| = \sqrt{L/C}$. In the helical delay line the inductance is enhanced more than the capacitance compared with a conventional line;

therefore Z_0 is greater. Furthermore, the capacitance and inductance can be adjusted in the design to provide a desired value of Z_0. Thus values of Z_0 in the range from 900 to 4000 Ω can readily be obtained.

Lumped parameter delay lines are built up of recurring π or T low-pass LC filter sections, and their design is based on filter theory. These lines are characterized by a characteristic impedance and a delay time just as for the smooth lines. When square pulses are sent over these lines the pulses tend to become distorted. The front of the pulse acquires a slope so that the rise time is lengthened. The top of the pulse is likely to have oscillations owing to *ringing* between the inductive and capacitive elements of the line.

E-5
Examples of delay line application

An example of a circuit that uses a delay line to generate a pulse of precise time duration is shown in Fig. E-7a. Here the delay line is represented by the standard symbol, and it could be either of the smooth line or the lumped

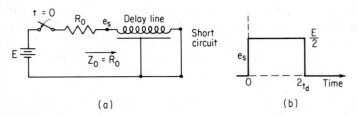

(a)   (b)

FIGURE E-7   (a) Step voltage impressed through R_0 on a delay line short-circuited at the far end. (b) Voltage pulse at input.

parameter type. The voltage E is impressed at $t = 0$ and thereby causes a step-voltage forward wave to start down the line. The input impedance of the line met by the forward wave is Z_0. The resistor R_0 (made equal to Z_0) and the line impedance act to give a voltage divider effect; therefore the forward wave has a magnitude of $E/2$. When this wave reaches the short circuit at the far end, a reflected voltage wave of magnitude $-E/2$ starts back toward the sending end, since $\rho = -1$ according to (E-24). The reverse voltage wipes out the voltage on the line, and at a time $2t_d$, where t_d is the one-way delay time, the voltage at the sending end drops to zero. Thus a time diagram of the voltage e_s gives a pulse of duration $2t_d$ (Fig. E-7b).

A second example is illustrated in Fig. E-8. The line is assumed to be initially uniformly charged to the voltage E along its entire length by means

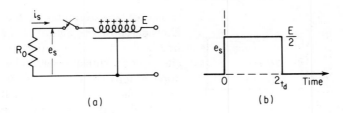

FIGURE E-8   (a) Delay line charged to E volts, then discharged through R_0. (b) Voltage pulse at e_s.

not shown in the diagram. Then the line is discharged through a resistance R_0 at the left end, where the actual voltage is designated as e_s. We see that initially there will be a forward voltage wave but no reverse wave. Applying relation (E-17), we write

$$e_f + 0 + E = e_s \qquad (\text{E-28})$$

By Ohm's law we have $e_s = -R_0 i_s$. In the absence of a reverse wave we assert that $i_s = i_f$; therefore

$$e_s = -R_0 i_f \qquad (\text{E-29})$$

But $e_f = R_0 i_f$, or $i_f = e_f/R_0$. Using this in (E-29), we find

$$e_s = -e_f \qquad (\text{E-30})$$

Combining (E-30) with (E-28) to eliminate e_f, we obtain

$$e_s = \frac{E}{2} \qquad (\text{E-31})$$

Furthermore, the forward voltage wave is a negative step wave of amplitude $e_f = -E/2$, which serves to lower the voltage on the line to $+E/2$. This wave reaches the open end of the line in t_d sec, and since $\rho = +1$, is reflected at the a value of $-E/2$ V. As a result, line voltage falls to zero progressively as the reflected wave returns, and the line is entirely discharged after $2t_d$ sec. The voltage pulse at the left end is a square pulse of duration $2t_d$ (Fig. E-8b). The stability of the pulse duration is excellent, because it depends only on the stability of the constants of the line and not on the parameters of a transistor or tube.

Figure E-9 shows a blocking oscillator circuit which embodies a short-circuited delay line. The delay line acts to fix the pulse width, provided that the normal blocking oscillator action (Sec. 16-16) would give a greater pulse width. We recall that in the normal action of the blocking oscillator a trigger pulse inserted (for example) in the base circuit puts the transistor into conduction, so that the collector voltage v_C falls and the transistor saturates. The rising collector current eventually brings the transistor out of saturation and the reverse regenerative transition occurs, thereby cutting off the

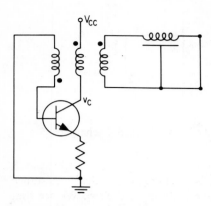

FIGURE E-9   Pulse width of a blocking oscillator is controlled by a delay line.

transistor and terminating the pulse. Consider now the action of the delay line in Fig. E-9. The initial transition energizes the transformer, and voltages appear across all three windings. A positive step voltage wave is thereby launched on the delay line. The right-hand transformer winding is now, in effect, loaded with the characteristic impedance of the line. As explained in connection with Fig. E-7, the short-circuit at the end of the line causes a negative reflected wave, and the line voltage is progressively wiped out by this wave. After the reflected wave returns to the transformer winding, the winding is in effect short-circuited. This lowers the voltage across all the transformer windings. The voltage across the transistor is raised, thereby bringing the transistor out of saturation and starting the reverse transition. Thus the pulse width equals twice the delay time of the line.

REFERENCES

E-1 J. Millman and H. Taub, *Pulse, Digital, and Switching Waveforms*, McGraw-Hill Book Company, New York, 1965, pp. 798–808.

E-2 R. Littauer, *Pulse Electronics*, McGraw-Hill Book Company, New York, 1965, pp. 60–72, 80–85.

E-3 A. T. Starr, *Electronics*, 2d ed., Sir Isaac Pitman & Sons, Ltd., London, 1959, pp. 169–189, 217–222.

E-4 E. M. Williams and J. B. Woodford, *Transmission Circuits*, The Macmillan Company, New York, 1957.

Index

A

Abbreviations for units, 595
Accelerometer, 484–488
Acceptor atoms, 65
Accuracy of an instrument, definition of, 504
Admittance, complex, 34
Admittance parameters for two-terminal-pair
    network, 50
Alternating wave, features, 28
Ammeter, moving coil dc, 505
Amplification factor of a triode, 97
Amplifier:
    balanced, class B, 207
        power and efficiency, 209
    calculation of noise figure for, 546
    class A, class AB, class B, class C, definitions
        of, 162
    dc, chopper modulated, 347
    dc, chopper-stabilized wideband, 349
        Bode diagram for, 351
    dc, modulator type, 347
    dc and direct-coupled, 337 ff
        drift in, 338–340, 349
        transistor, 339, 346
    difference, 340 ff
        analysis of single stage, 341
        balanced input, 342
        common-mode:
            gain, definition of, 343
            input, 342
            noise voltage in, 343
            rejection factor, 344
    differential; see Amplifier, difference
    discrimination factor, 344
    direct-coupled, elementary, 337
    distortion in, 93, 205, 208
    drift in, 338–340, 349
    feedback; see Feedback amplifier
    general features of, 161
    harmonic distortion in, 205
    magnetic, 218
        self-saturating type, 220
    as a network element, 162
    noise figure, calculation, 546
    operational; see Operational amplifier
    power, 200 ff
        class A common-emitter transistor, 203
        class A with output transformer, 201
        class C, 210
        controlled rectifier as, 216

Amplifier (*cont.*):
    distortion and harmonics in output wave,
        205
    features, 200
    pulse response, 435–439
        of multistage, 438
        of pentode stage, 436
        of transistor stage, 439
    Q point and current waves for class B and
        class C, 200
    transistor:
        approximate calculations using h param-
            eters, 155
        bias circuits for, 178–182
        bias stability, analysis, 182
        calculations using h parameters, 153
        cascade connection of common emitter,
            190
        common base, 142
        common collector (emitter follower), 144
        common emitter, 138–142, 187, 190
            current gain at midband, 191
            effect of frequency on current gain,
                191–194
            elementary, 121
        comparison of basic types, 146, 149
        dc and direct-coupled, 339, 346
    triode:
        capacitor output filter, ideal, 94
        cathode follower, analysis, 100
        common cathode, small signal, analysis,
            99
        common grid, analysis, 102
        design by graphical method, 92
        dynamic transfer characteristic, 90
        effect of choice of Q point on distortion,
            93
        graphical analysis, 88
        with output transformer, 95
        quiescent point, 89
        voltage amplification, definition of, 91
    vacuum tube:
        effect of cathode bias circuit on voltage
            gain, 166
        effect of interelectrode capacitances, 171
        grounded cathode, determination of Q
            point in, 164
        output filter, effect on voltage gain, 168
        RC-coupled pentode, 173–178
            frequency response of, 174 ff
    wideband, 174 ff, 187, 190 ff, 349

625